Cassell's Dictionary of
Foreign Words and Phrases

CASSELL'S DICTIONARY OF

Foreign Words and Phrases

Adrian Room

CASSELL

Cassell, an imprint of Weidenfeld & Nicolson
Wellington House
125 Strand
London
WC2R 0BB

First published 2000
by Cassell & Co.

This edition 2002
Reprinted 2003

Distributed in the United States by Sterling Publishing Co. Inc.
387 Park Avenue South, New York, NY 10016–8810

British Library Cataloguing in Publication Data
A catalogue entry for this book is available from the British Library

ISBN 0–304–35766–9

Printed and bound in Great Britain by
Bookmarque Ltd, Croydon, Surrey

Contents

Acknowledgements

Editor	Adrian Room
Publisher	Richard Milbank
Phonetics Consultant	Professor J.C. Wells
Database Editor	Rebecca Skipwith
Proof-readers	Michael Janes
	Patricia Moore
Database Technology	Librios
Typesetting	Gem Graphics

Introduction

This new dictionary aims to provide a full background to some 5000 words and phrases that, although used by English speakers and writers, are perceived to be foreign and not fully assimilated into the language.

The impact of the classics

Many Latin words became established in English from medieval times onwards, such as *abacus*, *basilica*, *census*, *delirium*, *fulcrum*, *lyceum*, *militia*, *modicum*, *proviso* and *virago*. Some of these, such as *lyceum*, *museum* and *psyche*, were in turn borrowed from Greek, which itself has contributed such words as *acme*, *bathos*, *epos*, *hoplite*, *melisma*, *strophe* and *upsilon*. It will be noticed that such borrowings in the main relate to the arts and sciences, and this academic characteristic is even more perceptible in the many Latin phrases adopted in legal or scholarly language, such as *ad hominem*, *bona vacantia*, *casus belli*, *de jure*, *habeas corpus*, *ipso facto*, *jus sanguinis* and *persona non grata*.

The contribution of modern languages

In modern times there is hardly a language in the world that has not contributed elements of its vocabulary to the English language. England's geographical and historical links with France have not surprisingly resulted in the adoption of a large number of French words and phrases. Some, like their Latin forebears, are learned, such as *abattu*, *à huis clos*, *brevet d'invention*, *corps diplomatique*, *droit de seigneur*, *idée fixe*, *mésalliance*, *ordonnance*, *soutache* and *tâtonnement*. Others are more homely, such as *baton*, *café*, *gaga*, *gauche*, *lingerie* and *matelot*. Mention of *café* and *lingerie* is a reminder that many French imports are to do with food, drink and fashion, such as *absinthe*, *aigre-doux*, *aperitif*, *baguette*, *bavaroise*, *boudoir*, *brassière*, *champignon*, *Chardonnay*, *cognac*, *courgette*, *duvet*, *flambé*, *maillot*, *marinade*, *petit pain*, *petit point*, *peignoir*, *rotisserie*, *tournedos* and *vin ordinaire*. The impact of French on the English-speaking world has been considerable, as exemplified *par excellence* by *Dieu et mon droit*, the motto of the English (and later British) sovereigns, and *honi soit qui mal y pense*, the motto of the Order of the Garter.

Where French is the language of the dinner and dressing tables, Italian is that of the music room and concert hall. Terms such as *allegro*, *andante*, *opera*, *pizzicato* and *sonata* are familiar to many, and some of the words have passed from a specific definition to a general sense, such as *crescendo* and *staccato*. Italian is also the language of art and architecture, as seen in *cupola*, *dado*, *graffiti*, *ovolo*, *pavonazzo*, *pergola*, *piazza*, *relievo* and *sfumato*. Literature has similarly adopted *canto*, *novella*, *scenario* and *stanza*, among others.

Some words of Spanish origin, such as *armada*, smack of the sea and date from the time when *hidalgos* encountered English sea dogs in the 16th century. Others are more recent, such as *guerrilla*, *matador*, *pueblo* and *rodeo*, these last two coming from Latin America, first to North America, then to Britain.

Several German borrowings are technical, political, military or literary, such as *ablaut*, *bebung*, *blitz*, *diktat*, *Festschrift*, *führer*, *gauleiter*, *Gestapo*, *hinterland*, *junker*, *kriegspiel* and *panzer*.

Many Arabic adoptions came through European Spanish, such as the words beginning *al-*, Arabic for 'the', such as *alcalde*, *alcayde*, *alfalfa*, *alguazil* and *Alhambra*. (Some have been fully assimilated, such as *algebra*, *alkali* and *almanac*, so do not appear in this dictionary.)

Hebrew words, especially those relating to the Bible or religion, often found their way into English via Latin and Greek, such as *alleluia*, *amen*, *manna*, *Messiah* and *rabbi*.

Special mention should be made of the large number of Sanskrit, Urdu or Hindi words that came into English through British contacts in India. Typical of them are *dungaree*, *gymkhana*, *khaki*, *maharaja*, *mantra*, *nawab*, *pukka*, *pundit*, *shampoo* and *thug*.

For the rest, one can merely give a sampling of the many languages that have donated words, either directly or through the medium of another (usually European) language, such as Afrikaans *trek*, Algonquian *wampum*, Australian Aboriginal *corroboree*, Basque *jai alai*, Breton *menhir*, Chinese *sampan*, Czech *robot*, Dutch *keeshond*, Eskimo *kayak*, Finnish *sauna*, Gaelic *pibroch*, Hawaiian *ukelele*, Hungarian *paprika*, Icelandic *saga*, Irish *mavourneen*, Japanese *kimono*, Javanese *batik*, Kiswahili *bwana*, Malay *sarong*, Malayalam *copra*, Maori *whare*, Nahuatl *chilli*, Norwegian *ski*, Persian *bazaar*, Polish *mazurka*, Portuguese *veranda*, Provençal *troubadour*, Quechua *pampas*, Russian *vodka*, Swedish *ombudsman*, Taino *cacique*, Tamil *mulligatawny*, Thai *wat*, Tibetan *yeti*, Tongan *taboo*, Tungus *shaman*, Tupi-Guarani *tapioca*, Turkish *kiosk*, Welsh *eisteddfod*, Yiddish *schmooze*.

Principles of inclusion in the dictionary

Conspicuous by their absence in the dictionary are names of plants and animals, unless familiar in the form of food or fabrics or acquiring some derivative sense. This is because almost all names of non-indigenous flora and fauna remain foreign, and it is often hard to tell to what degree they have become fully assimilated into English. Clearly African *chimpanzee*, Arabic *giraffe* and Australian

Aboriginal *kangaroo* have. But has Malay *orang-utan* or Afrikaans *aardvaark*? Probably not. This particular linguistic area is therefore best left aside. The same applies to plants. Greek *aspidistra* is hardly thought of now as foreign, but Modern Latin *convolvulus* still has an un-English look. On the other hand the clearly foreign Sinhalese *bo* tree has a Buddhist association, so is included, as is the alien Tupi-Guarani *ipecacuanha*, whose root is used in medicine. One further sample of the situation is seen in the *tomato*, clearly now a regular English word, and the *avocado*, still foreign-looking. Both are of Nahuatl origin. The latter, however, is included, not as a plant but as a particular type of fruit.

The degree of assimilation of many learned Latin and (especially) Greek terms is also hard to establish. These are also strictly limited in their representation, so that few medical or scientific terms will be found. Greek *aphasia* and *paranoia* are thus absent, as are Latin *fibula* and *tibia*. On the other hand a number of relatively esoteric or even rare words and phrases are unashamedly included, since they are or have been current in English. Examples are Arabic *abaya*, the word for a particular type of garment, and Latin *sartor resartus*, a phrase for a particular type of human being.

A special feature of the dictionary is the inclusion of a number of familiar phrases or even sentences that rarely appear in other dictionaries of this type. Examples are Latin *dulce et decorum est pro patria mori*, French *l'état, c'est moi*, German *Kirche, Küche, Kinder* and Welsh *pleidiol wyf i'm gwlad*, this last familiar as the inscription on the edge of a £1 coin. Proper names will also be found, such as the names of the ancient Hebrew months (such as *Abib*) and the months in the French Revolutionary calendar (such as *Fructidor*), together with personal names that have gained a figurative sense, such as *Mata Hari*. Abbreviations also figure, from the everyday *a.m.* and *p.m.* to the more recondite *AMDG* and *SPQR*.

Spelling and pronunciation

An observation should finally be made regarding spelling and pronunciation. Many foreign words and phrases are notoriously difficult to spell and pronounce correctly. For some there are alternative spellings. For others there are alternative plurals. Others again have variant pronunciations. Thus *abatis* can also be spelt *abattis*, *colossus* can have a Latin plural, *colossi*, or an English one, *colossuses*, *nougat* can be said French fashion, 'noogah', or closer to English 'nugget', and *escalope* can be stressed on the first syllable, 'escalope', or the second, 'escalope'. In the latter case the initial 'e', moreover, sounds more like 'i'. All these variables are catered for in the dictionary. The recommendations, however, may not accord with those in other dictionaries or even with the speaker's individual preference. We give *abaci* as the plural of *abacus*, while *The New Oxford*

Dictionary of English gives *abacuses*. The spelling, in particular, can often cause problems. Does one write *guerrilla* or *guerilla*? (We suggest both are acceptable.) And how about the legal *habeas corpus*, which even *Osborn's Law Dictionary* (8th edition, 1993), to its shame, enters as *habeus corpus*?

The usual English method of dealing with the spoken form of a foreign word or phrase is the typical British compromise. Anything close to the original language can sound affected, while a complete anglicization can seem coarse. French *protégé* thus wavers between the 'uvular' *r* and tight *é* of the native original and an English approximate 'protegy' (leading some to confuse the word itself with 'prodigy' or even 'progeny'). Because foreign words and phrases are by definition not assimilated into the language, therefore, their 'correct' or educated pronunciation remains variable, and the dictionary here can only indicate what is normally regarded as the best or at any rate standard. But at least it does give *some* guidance for an area of language that is on the whole more often encountered in written form than spoken. There are, after all, some terms that many of us hesitate to say at all, such as *chautauqua*, *katharevusa*, *Oireachtas* and *schiavone*, and there are certainly those who happily persist in pronouncing *macho* as 'macko'.

Adrian Room
March 2000

How to use the Dictionary

The structure of the entries

Each entry has two and sometimes three component parts. The first part is the definition, which includes pronunciation, variant forms and inflections of the word or phrase, its part of speech and any appropriate labels. The second part is the etymology, which gives the period when the word or phrase entered English, its language(s) of origin and, if appropriate, the literal sense of the headword. A third part, distinguished by a bullet point, is frequently added to provide a further note or comment on the history of the word or phrase. All three sections can be seen in the entry featured below.

> **Abendland** (ah´bəntland) *n.* the West, esp. Western
> civilization regarded as in decline.
> **Early 20C. German**, lit. evening land.
> ● The word became familiar from the title of
> Oswald Spengler's book *Der Untergang des*
> *Abendlandes* 'The Decline of the West' (1918–22)
> in which he argues that civilizations undergo a
> thousand-year cycle of growth and decline.

Labels

Descriptive labels in brackets have been added where appropriate. They fall into three main categories – stylistic labels, e.g. (*coll.*), (*poet.*), (*offensive*), geographical labels, e.g. (*N Am.*), (*Sc.*), and field or subject labels, e.g. (*Law*), (*Biol.*). A list of abbreviations used appears on pp. xii–xiii.

Cross-references

The word cross-referred to appears with small capitals for usual lower case, e.g. See ACHARNEMENT; Abbr. of **Latin** ANNO DOMINI.

Symbols

Obsolete and archaic words and phrases are preceded by a dagger sign †.

Uncertain or speculative word histories are preceded by a query ?, which may be interpreted as 'perhaps'.

Hypothetical word forms are preceded by an asterisk *.

Proprietary terms

This book includes some words which are or are asserted to be proprietary names. The presence or absence of such assertions should not be regarded as affecting the legal status of any proprietary name or trademark.

Chief Abbreviations

*denotes a book of the Bible
†denotes a book of the Apocrypha

a.	adjective
aa.	adjectives
abbr.	abbreviation
abl.	ablative
acc.	accusative
*Acts	Acts of the Apostles
adapt.	adaptation
adv.	adverb
Afr.	African
alt.	altered, alteration; alternative
Anat.	Anatomy
Ang.-Ind.	Anglo-Indian
appar.	apparently
Archit.	Architecture
assim.	assimilated, assimilation
assoc.	associated, association
Astrol.	Astrology
Astron.	Astronomy
at. no.	atomic number
attrib.	attributive, attribute
augm.	augmentative
Austral.	Australia, Australian
AV	Authorized Version (of the Bible)
b.	born
Biol.	Biology
Bot.	Botany
c.	circa, about
Can.	Canada, Canadian
cent.	century
cents.	centuries
Chem.	Chemistry
coll.	colloquial
comb.	combination
Comput.	Computing
conj.	conjunction; conjugation
constr.	construction, constructed; construed

contr.	contraction
corr.	corresponding
cp.	compare
d.	died
*Dan.	Daniel
dat.	dative
def.	definition
deriv.	derivation, derivative
derog.	derogatory
*Deut.	Deuteronomy
dial.	dialect, dialectal
dim.	diminutive
E	East, eastern
†Ecclus.	Ecclesiasticus
esp.	especially
etym.	etymology
euphem.	euphemistic
exc.	except
*Exod.	Exodus
*Ezek.	Ezekiel
facet.	facetious
fem.	feminine
fig.	figurative
fl.	floruit, flourished
freq.	frequentative
fut.	future
gen.	genitive
*Gen.	Genesis
Geol.	Geology
Geom.	Geometry
ger.	gerund, gerundive
Gram.	Grammar
Her.	Heraldry
Hist.	History
imit.	imitative
imper.	imperative
incept.	inceptive
ind.	indicative

influ.	influenced	p.p.	past participle
int.	interjection	pred.	predicative
Ir.	Irish	pref.	prefix
iron.	ironic	prep.	preposition
*Isa.	Isaiah	pres.	present
		pres.p.	present participle
*Jer.	Jeremiah	Print.	Printing
*John	Gospel according to St John	priv.	privative
*Judg.	Judges	prob.	probably
		pron.	pronoun
lit.	literally	pronun.	pronunciation
*Luke	Gospel according to St Luke	*Ps.	Psalms
		Psych.	Psychology
m.	masculine		
Math.	Mathematics	ref.	reference, referring
*Matt.	Gospel according to St Matthew	rel.	related
Med.	Medicine	*Rev.	Revelation
Mil.	Military		
Mineral.	Mineralogy	S	South, southern
Mus.	Music	S Afr.	South Africa, South African
		Sc.	Scottish
N	North, northern	Shak.	Shakespeare
n.	noun	sing.	singular
N Am.	North America, North American	sl.	slang
Naut.	Nautical	subj.	subjunctive
neg.	negative	suf.	suffix
neut.	neuter	superl.	superlative
New Zeal.	New Zealand		
nn.	nouns	Theol.	Theology
nom.	nominative	trans.	translation
*Num.	Numbers		
		ult.	ultimately
*Obad.	Obadiah	US	United States of America
obs.	obsolete	usu.	usually
orig.	originally, origin		
		v.	verb
part.	participle	var.	variant
pass.	passive	verb.a.	verbal adjective
perf.	perfect	verb.n.	verbal noun
perh.	perhaps	v.i.	verb intransitive
pers.	person; personal	voc.	vocative
*Phil.	Epistle to the Philippians	v.phr.	verb phrase
Philos.	Philosophy	v.t.	verb transitive
phr.	phrase	vv.	verbs
pl.	plural		
poet.	poetical	W	West, western
pop.	popular, popularly	W Ind.	West Indian
poss.	possibly		
		Zool.	Zoology

Guide to Pronunciation

Introduction

The respelling scheme used for pronunciation is designed to provide a compromise between accuracy and understanding by the majority of users. The number of specialized phonetic symbols and additional accents or marks on letters is kept to a minimum in order to fulfil this aim. A full list of symbols/letters and their equivalents follows below, with transcriptions given alongside the words used as examples.

Pronunciations are given in round brackets.

The particular variety of pronunciation aimed for is that of the 'ordinary educated English speaker', which some users will recognize under the label of 'Received Pronunciation'.

Where variant spellings differ in pronunciation (and this includes stress) from the main headword, partial or full pronunciations are also given for these. Where partial pronunciations appear, it should be assumed that the remaining (untranscribed) part of the word concerned is pronounced as before, or with only predictable (and often unconscious) slight vowel modifications associated with the new pronunciation pattern.

Stress

Stress (´) is shown in pronunciations immediately after the syllable which is stressed, as in compère (kom´peə). Stress is not given on words of one syllable and is usually given only once on compounds composed of two or more words.

Symbols

Vowel sounds:

ah	far	(fah)		o	not	(not)
a	fat	(fat)		ō	note	(nōt)
ā	fate	(fāt)		oi	boy	(boi)
aw	fall	(fawl)		oo	blue	(bloo)
e	bell	(bel)		ow	bout	(bowt)
ē	beef	(bēf)		ŭ	sun	(sŭn)
œ	her	(hœ)		u	foot	(fut)
i	bit	(bit)		ū	muse	(mūz)
	happy	(hap´i)		ə	again	(əgen´)
ī	bite	(bīt)				

Note: the natural sound of many unstressed vowels is represented, as shown above, by the symbol ə; others are (more accurately) transcribed as (-i-), as in *kebab* (kibab´)

Centring diphthongs (incorporating an historical 'r' sound):

eə	fair	(feə)
iə	fear	(fiə)
īə	fire	(fīə)
ūə	pure	(pūə)
uə	poor	(puə)

Foreign vowels not dealt with by the main system:

(i) Nasalized:

ã	(bon) vivant	(vēvã´)
ĩ	vin	(vĩ)
õ	bon (vivant)	(bõ)

(ii) Front rounded:

ü	(déjà) vu	(vü)
	Übermensch	(ü´bəmensh)

Consonants

b	bit	(bit)		n	nut	(nŭt)
ch	church	(chœch)		ng	sing	(sing)
d	dance	(dahns)		p	pit	(pit)
dh	this	(dhis)		r	run	(rŭn)
f	fit	(fit)		s	sit	(sit)
g	get	(get)		th	thin	(thin)
h	hit	(hit)		v	van	(van)
j	just	(jŭst)		w	win	(win)
k	kit	(kit)		y	yet	(yet)
kh	loch	(lokh)		z	maze	(māz)
l	lid	(lid)		zh	measure	(mezh´ə)
m	man	(man)				

Note: where a sound represented by a two symbols, e.g. (-ow-) occurs within a pronunciation and confusion could arise regarding syllable division, a centred dot is inserted to show where the syllable break occurs, as in *Weltanschauung* (velt´anshow·ung)

DICTIONARY OF FOREIGN WORDS AND PHRASES

aba (ab´ə), **abba** *n.* a sleeveless outer garment worn by Arabs.
19C. **Arabic** *'abā'*.

abaca (ab´əkə) *n.* **1** Manila hemp. **2** the plant from which this is obtained, *Musa textilis*.
18C. **Spanish** *abacá*, from Tagalog *abaká*.

abacus (ab´əkəs) *n.* (*pl.* **abaci** (-sī)) **1** a counting-frame; an apparatus of beads sliding on wires for facilitating arithmetical calculations. **2** (*Archit.*) a flat stone crowning the capital of a column and supporting the architrave.
14–15C. **Latin**, from Greek *abax* counting table, ? from Hebrew *'ābāq* dust.
• The abacus was originally a board sprinkled with fine sand for marking on.

à bas (a ba´) *int.* down with.
18C. **French**, from *à* to + *bas* bottom, base.

abatis (ab´atis, -tē), **abattis** *n.* (*pl.* **abatis**, **abatises**, **abattis**, **abattises**) a defence work made of felled trees with their boughs directed outwards.
18C. **French**, from Old French *abatre* to beat down.

abatjour (abazhooə´) *n.* a skylight.
19C. **French** *abat-jour*, from Old French *abatre* to beat down + *jour* day, light.

abattoir (ab´ətwah) *n.* a slaughterhouse.
19C. **French**, from *abattre* to fell.

abat-voix (abavwah´) *n.* a sounding-board, as over a pulpit.
19C. **French**, from Old French *abatre* to beat down + *voix* voice. Cp. ABATJOUR.

abattu (abatü´) *a.* cast down; dejected.
19C. **French**, p.p. of *abattre* to beat down, from Old French *abatre*, ult. from Latin *battere* to beat.

abaya (əbā´yə) *n.* an outer garment without sleeves, as worn by Arabs.
19C. **Arabic** *'abāya*.

abba (ab´ə) *n.* **1** father (in the invocation *Abba, father*). **2** an episcopal title in the Syriac and Coptic churches.
14–15C. **Ecclesiastical Latin**, from Ecclesiastical Greek, from Aramaic *'abbā* father, ult. of imit. orig.

abbé (ab´ā) *n.* **1** a French abbot. **2** in France, a title used in addressing any cleric; any man entitled to wear clerical dress.
16C. **French**, from Ecclesiastical Latin *abbas*, *abbatis* abbot.

Abendland (ah´bəntland) *n.* the West, esp. Western civilization regarded as in decline.
early 20C. **German**, lit. evening land.
• The word became familiar from the

title of Oswald Spengler's book *Der Untergang des Abendlandes* 'The Decline of the West' (1918–22) in which he argues that civilizations undergo a thousand-year cycle of growth and decline.

Abib (āʹbib) *n.* the first month of the ancient Hebrew calendar, corresponding to Nisan.
16C. Hebrew *'āḇīḇ* ear of corn.

à bientôt (a byītōʹ) *int.* goodbye for now, see you soon.
early 20C. French, lit. to soon, from *à* to + *bientôt* soon, from *bien* well + *tôt* early.

ab imo pectore (ab imō pektawʹrā) *adv.* sincerely, enthusiastically.
17C. Latin from the bottom of the breast, from *ab* from + abl. sing. of *imum pectus*, lit. deepest breast.
• For the Romans the breast was the seat of both reason and emotion. Cp. English 'from the bottom of one's heart'.

ab initio (ab inishʹiō) *adv.* from the beginning.
17C. Latin *ab* from + *initio*, abl. sing. of *initium* beginning.

Abitur (abituəʹ) *n.* (in Germany) a set of examinations taken in the final year of secondary school.
mid-20C. German, abbr. of *Abiturientenexamen* leavers' examination, from ABITURIENT + *Examen* examination.

Abiturient (abituərientʹ) *n.* (*pl.* **Abiturienten** (-enʹtən)) (in Germany) a candidate for the Abitur.
19C. German leaver, from Modern Latin *abiturire* to wish to leave. Cp. ABITUR.

ablaut (abʹlowt) *n.* a vowel change in the middle of a word indicating

modification in meaning, as in *sit, set, rise, raise, ring, rang, rung.*
19C. German, from *ab* off + *Laut* sound.

à bon chat, bon rat (a bō sha bō raʹ) *adv.* used to express the idea that it takes cunning to outwit cunning.
19C French, lit. to a good cat, a good rat.
• The phrase has an approximate equivalent in the English 'set a thief to catch a thief'.

abonnement (abonmãʹ) *n.* (*pl.* **abonnements** (-mã)) **1** a subscription, esp. for a newspaper etc. **2** a season ticket.
19C. French, from *abonner* to subscribe, from obs. *bonne* (now *borne*) limit.

ab origine (ab orijʹini) *adv.* from the beginning, from the creation of the world.
16C. Latin, from *ab* from + abl. of *origo* beginning, source. Cp. English *aborigine.*

ab ovo (ab ōʹvō) *adv.* from the beginning.
16C. Latin from the egg, from *ab* from + abl. sing. of *ovum* egg.

ab ovo usque ad mala (ab ōvō uskwi ad mahʹlə) *adv.* from beginning to end.
16C. Latin from the beginning to the end, lit. from the egg to the apples, from *ab* from + abl. sing. of *ovum* egg + *usque* all the way + *ad* to + acc. pl. of *malum* apple.
• The allusion is to a Roman meal, in which egg was a common appetizer or 'starter' and an apple the dessert.

abracadabra (abrəkədabʹrə) *int.* used as a magic word by conjurors when performing tricks. ~*n.* **1** a word used as a charm, a jingle or nonsensical phrase. **2** nonsense, gibberish.
16C. Latin, cabbalistic word first found 2C, ult. from Greek, of unknown orig. ? Rel. to Greek ABRAXAS.

abraxas (əbrak´səs) *n.* **1** a word used as a charm, denoting a power which presides over 365 others, and used by some Gnostics to denote their supreme god. **2** a gem with this word, or the corresponding mystical image engraved on it.
18C. Late Greek, of unknown orig. Cp. ABRACADABRA.
• The word is said to have been coined in the 2C by the Egyptian Gnostic Basilides to express 365, each Greek letter having a numerical value.

abrazo (abrath´o, abras´o, əbraz´ō) *n.* (*pl.* **abrazos** (abrath´os, abras´os, əbraz´ōz)) an embrace, a hug, esp. as a form of greeting.
early 20C. Spanish embrace.

abscissa (əbsis´ə) *n.* (*pl.* **abscissas, abscissae** (-ē)) (*Math.*) the x co-ordinate that shows the distance of a point from a vertical axis along a horizontal line.
17C. Modern Latin *abscissa* (*linea*) cut (line), from fem. p.p. of *abscindere* to cut off, from *ab* from + *scindere* to cut.

abseil (ab´sāl) *v.i.* to descend a vertical or steeply sloping surface, such as a rock face, using a rope attached at the top and wound round the body. ~*n.* a descent involving abseiling.
mid-20C. German *abseilen*, from *ab* down + *Seil* rope.
• The word is not related to English *sail*, despite the association with sailing down. Cp. RAPPEL.

absinthe (ab´sinth, absīt´), **absinth** *n.*
1 wormwood. **2** a liqueur flavoured with wormwood.
14–15C. French, from Latin *apsinthium*, from Greek *absinthion* wormwood, ult. of non-Indo-European orig.

absit omen (absit ō´men) *int.* may the threatened evil not take place; God forbid.

16C. Latin may this omen be absent, from *absit*, 3rd pers. pres. subj. of *abesse* to be absent + *omen* omen.

a cappella (a kəpel´ə, ah kəpel´ə), **alla cappella** (ala) *a., adv.* (*Mus.*) (of choral music) without instrumental accompaniment.
19C. Italian in chapel style.

accablé (akablā´) *a.* crushed, overwhelmed.
19C. French, p.p. of *accabler* to overwhelm, from Latin *ad* to, + French dial. *aachabler* to fell, from Popular Latin *catabola*, ult. from Greek *katabolē* throwing down.

accelerando (əcheləran´dō, əks-) *a., adv.* (*Mus.*) with increasing speed. ~*n.* (*pl.* **accelerandos, accelerandi** (-dē)) a passage to be performed in this way.
19C. Italian, pres.p. of *accelerare* to accelerate.

acciaccatura (əchakətuə´rə) *n.* (*pl.* **acciaccaturas, acciaccature** (-rā)) (*Mus.*) a short grace note played rapidly.
19C. Italian, from *acciaccare* to crush, ? from Spanish *achacar* to accuse falsely.

accidie (ak´sidi), **acedia** (əsē´diə) *n.* an abnormal mental condition characterized by extreme apathy and listlessness.
19C. Old French *accide*, from Medieval Latin *accidia*, alt. of Late Latin *acedia*, from Greek *akēdia*, from *a-* without + *kēdos* care, concern.

accouchement (akooshmā´) *n.* childbirth, delivery.
18C. French, from *accoucher*, from *a-* to + *coucher* to lie. Cp. archaic English 'lying-in'.

accoucheur (akooshœ´) *n.* a person who assists women at childbirth.
18C. French. Cp. ACCOUCHEMENT.

Aceldama (əkelˊdəmə, əselˊ-), **aceldama** *n.* a scene of bloodshed or slaughter. 17C. Greek *Akeldama*, from Aramaic *ḥăqel děmā* field of blood.

• The field of blood was a field near Jerusalem purchased by the chief priests with the 30 pieces of silver returned by Judas, and used as a burial-place (Acts i.19).

acetabulum (asətabˊūləm) *n.* (*pl.* **acetabula** (-lə)) **1** an ancient Roman vessel for holding vinegar. **2** (*Anat.*) a cavity in any bone designed to receive the protuberant head of another bone, e.g. the socket of the hip-joint in man. **3** the socket in which the leg of an insect is inserted. **4** any one of the suckers on the arms of a cuttlefish. **5** the cup-shaped fructification of many lichens. **6** the receptacle of certain fungi. 14–15C. Latin *acetum* vinegar + -*abulum* vessel, container.

acharné (ashahˊnā) *a.* bloodthirsty, ferocious, enthusiastic. 19C. French, p.p. of *acharner*. See ACHARNEMENT.

acharnement (ashahˊnəmā) *n.* **1** bloodthirsty fury, ferocity. **2** gusto. 18C. French, from *acharner* to give a taste of flesh (to dogs), from *a*- to + Old French *char* (Modern French *chair*), from Latin *caro, carnis* flesh, meat.

à cheval (a shəvalˊ) *adv.* **1** astride. **2** in command of two communication lines. **3** with a stake on two equal chances. 19C. French on horseback, from *à* on + *cheval* horse.

Achtung (ahkhtungˊ) *int.* look out! mid-20C. German attention!, lit. respect, from *achten* to respect.

• The German military command became familiar in World War II.

acme (akˊmi) *n.* **1** the top or highest point, perfection (of achievement, excellence etc.). **2** the maturity of life. **3** the crisis or turning-point of a disease. 16C. Greek *akmē* highest point, rel. to *akē* point.

• The word was long written in Greek letters in English usage.

à coup sûr (a koo süəˊ) *adv.* certainly, definitely. 19C. French, lit. with sure stroke, from *à* to, at + *coup* blow, stroke + *sûr* sure.

acropolis (əkropˊəlis) *n.* the citadel or elevated part of a Greek town, esp. that of Athens. 17C. Greek *akropolis*, from *akros* top + *polis* city.

acroter (əkrōˊtə, akˊrətə), **acroterium** (akrətēˊriəm), **acroterion** (-tēˊrion) *n.* (*pl.* **acroters, acroteria**) **1** a pedestal on a pediment, for the reception of a figure. **2** (*usu. pl.*) a pinnacle. 17C. Greek *akrōtērion* extremity.

actualités (aktūalitāˊ) *n.pl.* news, current affairs, events from real life. mid-20C. French news, pl. of *actualité* topicality, reality, from *actuel* real, actual.

acumen (akˊūmən) *n.* acuteness of mind, shrewdness. 16C. Latin, from *acuere* to sharpen, from *acus* needle.

acushla (əkushˊlə) *n.* (*Ir.*) darling. 19C. Irish, short for *a cuisle mo* (*chroidhe*) O vein of my (heart), from voc. int. *a* + *chuisle*, voc. of *cuisle* vein + *mo* (of) my (+ *chroidhe*, gen. of *croidhe* heart).

AD *adv.* in the year of our Lord Abbr. of **Latin** ANNO DOMINI.

adagio (ədahˊjiō, -zhiō) *adv.* (*Mus.*) slowly, gracefully. ~*a.* slow, graceful. ~*n.* (*pl.* **adagios**) a slow movement or

passage of a soft, tender, elegiac character.
17C. Italian, from *ad agio* at ease. Rel. to AGIO.

Adar (ā´dah) *n.* the sixth civil month, or twelfth ecclesiastical month of the Jewish year (corresponding to part of February and March).
14–15C. Hebrew *'ădār*.

addendum (əden´dəm) *n.* (*pl.* **addenda** (-də)) **1** a thing to be added, an addition. **2** an appendix.
17C. Latin, neut. ger. of *addere* to add.

ad eundem gradum (ad ā·undem grad´əm) *adv.* used of the admission of a student to a university at a stage of learning equivalent to that reached at a previous university
18C. Latin to the same degree, from *ad* to + acc. sing. of *idem gradus* same degree.

à deux (a dœ´) *a., adv.* of or between two (people).
19C. French *à* to + *deux* two.

ad hoc (ad hok´, hōk´) *a., adv.* for a particular purpose only, specially.
17C. Latin to this, from *ad* to + neut. acc. sing. of *hic* this.

ad hominem (ad hom´inem) *a., adv.* **1** directed to or against the person, not disinterested. **2** (of an argument) based on or appealing to emotion rather than reason.
16C. Latin to the person, from *ad* to + acc. sing. of *homo, hominis* person, man.

adieu (ədū´, ədyœ´) *int.* (*pl.* **adieux** (-z)) goodbye, farewell. ~*n.* a farewell.
14–15C. Anglo-French *adeu*, from Old French *adieu*, from *a* to + *Dieu* god. Cp. ADIOS.
• The full original phrase was *a Dieu* (*vous*) *commant* I commend (you) to God.

ad infinitum (ad infinī´təm) *adv.* to infinity, without end.
17C. Latin to infinity, from *ad* to + acc. of *infinitus* boundless (space).

ad interim (ad in´tərim) *a., adv.* for the meantime.
18C. Latin, from *ad* to + *interim* meanwhile. See INTERIM.

adios (adios´) *int.* goodbye.
19C. Spanish *adiós*, from *a* to + *Dios* god. Cp. ADIEU.
• The full original phrase was *a Dios vos acomiendo* I commend you to God.

Adivasi (ahdivah´si) *n.* (*pl.* **Adivasis**) a member of any of the aboriginal tribes of India.
mid-20C. Modern Sanskrit *ādivāsī*, from *ādi* the beginning + *vāsin* inhabitant.

ad kalendas graecas (ad kalen´dahs grī´kahs) *adv.* never.
17C. Latin, lit. to the Greek calends, from *ad* to + acc. of *kalendae graecae* Greek calends.
• The Greeks had no calends in their calendar. In the Roman calendar the calends were the first day of any month. Cp. English 'not in a month of Sundays' etc.

ad lib (ad lib´), **ad libitum** (lib´itum, lībē´təm) *adv.* **1** at pleasure, to any extent. **2** (*Mus.*) at the performer's discretion to change time or omit passages.
17C. Latin according to pleasure, from *ad* to + acc. sing. of *libitum* pleasure.
• The abbreviation dates from the 19C.

ad litem (ad lī´təm) *a.* (of a guardian) appointed for a lawsuit.
18C. Latin according to the lawsuit, from *ad* to + acc. sing. of *lis, litis* lawsuit.

ad nauseam (ad naw´ziam, -si-) *adv.* to the point of producing disgust or nausea.
17C. Latin to sickness, from *ad* to + acc. sing. of *nausea* (sea)sickness.

Adonai (ədō´nī, adənī´) *n.* the Lord; a name for God in the Old Testament.
14–15C. Hebrew *'ăḏōnāy* my lord.
● The name was originally a substitute for Jehovah.

ad personam (ad pœsō´nam) *adv.* to the person. ~*a.* personal.
mid-20C. Latin to the person, from *ad* to + acc. sing. of *persona* person.

ad rem (ad rem´) *a., adv.* to the point, to the purpose.
16C. Latin to the matter, from *ad* to + acc. sing. of *res* thing, matter.

adsum (ad´səm) *int.* I am present; here (used, esp. in the older public schools, as a response to a roll call).
16C. Latin, 1st pers. sing. pres. ind. of *adesse* to be present.

ad valorem (ad vəlaw´rem) *a., adv.* (of a tax) in proportion to the value of the goods.
17C. Latin according to the value, from *ad* to + acc. sing. of Late Latin *valor* value.

advocaat (ad´vəkah) *n.* a sweet thick liqueur containing raw egg and brandy.
mid-20C. Dutch advocate.
● The liqueur was used by advocates to clear the throat.

advocatus diaboli (advəkahtəs dēab´əlē, -kā- dīab´əlī) *n.* **1** a person who puts the opposing view in a discussion without necessarily supporting it, a devil's advocate. **2** an official in the Roman Catholic Church responsible for contesting a person's suitability for beatification or canonization.
19C. Modern Latin, lit. devil's advocate, from *advocatus* advocate + gen. sing. of *diabolus* devil.
● The official who presents the evidence in support of a person's canonization is called *advocatus Dei* God's advocate.

adytum (ad´itəm) *n.* (*pl.* **adyta** (-tə)) the innermost and most sacred part of a temple.
17C. Latin, from Greek *aduton,* neut. sing. (used as n.) of *adutos* impenetrable.

aegis (ē´jis) *n.* **1** in Greek myth, a shield belonging to Zeus or Athene. **2** protection, a protective influence, usu. in set phrase 'under the aegis of'.
17C. Latin, from Greek *aigis.*
● The shield is said to have been made of goatskin, and the word is popularly derived from Greek *aix, aigos* goat.

aegrotat (ī´grətat) *n.* **1** a note certifying that a student is sick. **2** a degree awarded to a student unable to sit the relevant examinations because of illness.
18C. Latin he is sick, 3rd pers. sing. pres. ind. of *aegrotare* to be ill, from *aeger, aegris* sick, ill.

aetatis (ītah´tis) *prep.* at the age of (on portraits to indicate the age of the sitter).
19C. Latin of the age, gen. sing. of *aetas* life, age.
● The word is often abbreviated as *aet.*

affaire (afeə´) *n.* a love affair.
19C. French affair (of the heart). Cp. AFFAIRE DU COEUR.

affairé (afeə´rā) *a.* busy.
early 20C. French, p.p. of (*s'*)*affairer* to be busy, from *affaire* affair.

affaire d'honneur (afeə donœ´) *n.* (*pl.* **affaires d'honneur** (afeə)) **1** a duel.

2 a matter of honour, any figurative moral challenge.
19C. French affair of honour, from *affaire* affair, matter + *d'* of + *honneur* honour.

affaire du coeur (afeə dü kœ´), **affaire de coeur** (də kœ´) *n.* a love affair.
19C. French affair of (the) heart, from *affaire* affair + *du* of the or *de* of + *cœur* heart.

affettuoso (afetuō´sō) *adv.* (*Mus.*) with feeling.
18C. Italian, from Late Latin *affectuosus*.

affiche (əfēsh´) *n.* a poster, placard.
19C. French, from *afficher,* from Old French *aficher*, from Late Latin *affigicare*, from Latin *ad* to + *figere* to fix.

affidavit (afidā´vit) *n.* a voluntary affirmation sworn before a person qualified to administer an oath.
16C. Medieval Latin he declared on oath, 3rd pers. sing. perf. ind. of Latin *affidare*, from *ad* to + *fidare* to trust.

aficionado (əfishənah´dō) *n.* (*pl.* **aficionados**) a keen follower or fan.
19C. Spanish amateur, p.p. (used as n.) of *aficionar* to inspire a liking for, from *afición* fondness, from Latin *affectio* favourable disposition.

a fortiori (ā fawtiaw´ri, ah) *adv.* with still more reason, much more, still more conclusively.
17C. Latin *a fortiori* (*argumento*) from stronger (evidence).

afreet (af´rēt, əfrēt´), **affrite**, **afrit** *n.* a demon or monster of Muslim mythology.
18C. Arabic *'ifrīt*, prob. from Persian *āfrīda* created being.

aga (ah´gə), **agha** *n.* a Turkish civil or military officer of high rank.

16C. Turkish *ağa* master, lord, from Mongolian *aqa*.

agaçant (agasā´) *a.* irritating, annoying.
early 20C. French annoying, pres.p. of *agacer* to irritate, to aggravate, from Popular Latin *adaciare*, from Latin *acies* sharpness, blending with *agacer* to call shrilly, from dial. French *agace* magpie, from Old High German *agaza*.

agal (agahl´) *n.* a band worn by Bedouin Arabs that keeps the keffiyeh in place.
19C. Bedouin pronun. of **Arabic** *'iķāl* bond, rope for hobbling a camel.

agape (ag´əpē) *n.* (*pl.* **agapes, agapae** (-pē)) **1** a 'love-feast', a kind of feast of fellowship held by the early Christians in connection with the Lord's Supper. **2** (*Theol.*) Christian love.
17C. Greek *agapē* brotherly love.

agapemone (agəpem´əni) *n.* an abode of love.
19C. Greek, from *agapē* love + *monē* abode.
● The term was originally the name of a religious community where free love was practised, founded in 1849 in Spaxton, Somerset, by Henry James Prince, curate of Charlynch, near Bridgwater, and his rector, Samuel Starky.

agar-agar (āgahr ā´gah), **agar** *n.* a gelatinous substance obtained from seaweeds and used for the artificial cultivation of bacteria.
19C. Malay.

agenda (əjen´də) *n.* **1** (*pl.* **agendas**) a list of the business to be transacted. **2** (*pl.*) things to be done, engagements to be kept.
17C. Latin, pl. of *agendum*, neut. ger. (used as n.) of *agere* to do, to be about.

agent provocateur (azhã provokatœ´)
n. (*pl.* **agents provocateurs** (azhã
provokatœ´)) a person employed to
detect suspected political offenders by
leading them on to some overt action.
19C. French provocative agent.

agger (aj´ə) *n.* **1** a mound. **2** the rampart
of a Roman camp.
14–15C. Latin, from *aggere*, from *ad* to
+ *gerere* to carry.

aggiornamento (adjawnamen´to,
əjawnəmen´tō) *n.* a bringing up to
date.
mid-20C. Italian, lit. adjournment.
• The term specifically referred to the
modernization of Roman Catholic policy
resulting from the second Vatican
Council (1962–65).

agio (aj´iō) *n.* (*pl.* **agios**) **1** the difference
in value between one kind of currency
and another. **2** money-changing. **3** the
charge for changing notes for cash, or
one kind of money for another.
17C. Italian *agio* ease, convenience.
Rel. to English *ease*.

agiotage (aj´iōtij) *n.* **1** money-changing.
2 speculation in stocks. **3** stock-jobbing.
18C. French, from *agioter* to speculate,
from Italian AGIO.

agitato (ajitah´tō) *adv., a.* (*Mus.*) in an
agitated manner.
19C. Italian agitated.

agitprop (aj´itprop) *n.* the dissemination,
usu. through the arts, of political, esp.
pro-Communist, propaganda.
early 20C. Russian *agit(atsiya)* agitation
+ *prop(aganda)* PROPAGANDA.

agma (ag´mə) *n.* **1** the symbol (ŋ) used to
represent the speech sound ng as in
sing. **2** this speech sound.
mid-20C. Late Greek, from Greek
fragment.

agnolotti (anyəlot´i) *n.* small pieces of
pasta stuffed with meat etc.
mid-20C. Italian, a dim. pl. of *agnolo*
lamb.

agnomen (agnō´mən) *n.* (*pl.* **agnomina**
(agnom´inə)) a fourth name sometimes
appended to the cognomen by the
ancient Romans, usu. in honour of a
great exploit.
17C. Latin, from *ad* to + *nomen* name.

Agnus Dei (agnŭs dā´ē) *n.* **1** a figure of a
lamb bearing a flag or cross, the emblem
of St John the Baptist in art. **2** a part of
the Mass beginning with the words
Agnus Dei. **3** a musical setting of this
part of the Mass. **4** a cake of wax
stamped with such a figure of a lamb
and blessed by the Pope.
14–15C. Latin Lamb of God, from *agnus*
lamb + gen. sing. of *deus* god.

à gogo (ə gō´gō) *adv.* in abundance,
galore.
mid-20C. French, from *à* + *gogo*, redupl.
of base of *gogue* merriment.

agraffe (əgraf´), (*N Am. also*) **agrafe** *n.*
1 a sort of hook, formerly used as a
clasp or fastening. **2** a cramp used by
builders to hold stones together.
17C. French *agrafe*, from *agrafer* to hook.

agrément (agremã´) *n.* (*pl.* **agréments**
(-mã´)) official approval given to the
diplomatic representative of another
country.
early 20C. French agreement.
• In the plural, *agréments* was used
in the 18C to mean agreeable qualities
or circumstances. A specialized sense
soon after was that of grace notes or
embellishments in a musical piece.

ahimsa (əhim´sə) *n.* the Hindu and
Buddhist doctrine of non-violence
towards all living things.
19C. Sanskrit, from *a-* non- + *hiṃsā*
violence.

à huis clos (a wē klō´) *adv.* behind closed doors, in private; in camera.
19C. Obsolete French *à* to, *huis* door, *clos* m. sing. p.p. of *clore* to close, from Latin *claudere*. Cp. IN CAMERA.
• The obsolete French *huis* has now been replaced by *porte*, and *clore* by *fermer*.

aide (ād) *n.* an assistant, a help.
18C. Abbr. of **French** AIDE-DE-CAMP.

aide-de-camp (ād·dəkamp´, -kā´, ed-) *n.* (*pl.* **aides-de-camp** (-kamp´, -kā´)) an officer who receives and transmits the orders of a general or other senior officer.
17C. French camp adjutant, lit. help of (the) camp, from *aide* help + *de* of + *camp* camp.
• The expression is often abbreviated to ADC in English.

aide-mémoire (ādmemwah´) *n.* (*pl.* **aides-mémoire**, **aides-mémoires** (ādmemwah´)) an aid to memory, a memorandum, a memorandum-book.
19C. French, lit. aid-memory, from *aide* aid, help + *mémoire* memory.

aigre-doux (egrədoo´), (*fem.*) **aigre-douce** (-doos´) *a.* bitter-sweet.
14–15C. French, from *aigre* bitter + *doux* sweet.

aigrette (ā´grit, āgret´) *n.* **1** an ornamental feather or plume, esp. from the egret.
2 a spray of gems worn on the head.
3 any light feathery tuft or spray.
18C. French egret.

aiguille (āgwēl´, ā´-) *n.* **1** a slender, needle-shaped peak of rock. **2** an instrument used in boring holes for blasting.
18C. French needle, from Popular Latin *acucula*, dim. of Latin *acus* needle.

aikido (īkē´dō) *n.* a Japanese martial art using throws, locks and twisting techniques to turn an opponent's own momentum against them.
mid-20C. Japanese *aikidō*, from *ai* together + *ki* spirit + *dō* way.

aileron (ā´ləron) *n.* the hinged portion on the rear edge of the wing-tip of an aeroplane that controls lateral balance.
early 20C. French, dim. of *aile* wing.

aîné (ā´nā) *a.* elder.
19C. French, lit. born before, from Old French *ains* before + Modern French *né* born. Cp. CADET.

aioli (īō´li), **aïoli** *n.* mayonnaise flavoured with garlic.
early 20C. French, from Provençal *ai* garlic + *oli* oil.

à la (a´ la) *prep.* in the manner of.
16C. French, from À LA MODE¹.
• The phrase is commonly found in descriptions of dishes, e.g. *à la broche* (cooked) on a spit, *à la meunière* (see MEUNIÈRE). See also entries below.

à la carte (a la kaht´) *a., adv.* **1** (of a menu) having each dish priced separately. **2** (of a dish) priced separately, not part of a set menu. **3** with the freedom to select what you want.
19C. French according to the menu.
• The converse is TABLE D'HÔTE.

à la fourchette (a la fawshet´) *adv.*
1 with a fork. **2** (of a meal) requiring the use of a fork only.
19C. French, from *à* with + *la* the + *fourchette* fork.

à la mode (a la mōd´) *adv., a.*
1 fashionable. **2** (of meat) braised in wine. **3** (*N Am.*) served with ice cream.
16C. French according to the manner.

albata (albā´tə) *n.* an alloy like silver; a variety of German silver.
19C. Latin, fem. of *albatus* clothed in white, from *albus* white.

albedo (albē´dō) *n.* (*pl.* **albedos**) the fraction of incident light reflected by a planet or other body or surface.
19C. Ecclesiastical Latin whiteness, from Latin *albus* white.

albino (albē´nō) *n.* (*pl.* **albinos**) **1** a human being, or animal, having the colour pigment absent from the skin, the hair and the eyes, so as to be abnormally light in colour. **2** a plant in which little or no chlorophyll is developed.
18C. Spanish and Portuguese, from *albo* white.
● The term was originally applied by the Portuguese to albinos among African blacks.

album (al´bəm) *n.* **1** a blank book for the insertion of photographs, poetry, drawings or the like. **2** (*N Am.*) a visitors' book. **3** a collection of pieces of recorded music issued on one or more long-playing records, cassettes, CDs etc.
17C. Latin blank tablet, use as n. of neut. of *albus* white.
● The word was first current in English from the German use of the Latin phrase *album amicorum* album of friends, meaning an autograph book.

alcalde (alkal´dā) *n.* the judge or mayor of a Spanish, Portuguese or Latin American town.
16C. Spanish, from Arabic *al-ḳāḍī* the judge. Cp. CADI.

alcayde (alkād´), **alcade**, **alcaide** *n.*
1 the governor of a fortress in Spain, Portugal etc. **2** the warder of a prison, a gaoler.
16C. Spanish, from Arabic *al-ḳā'id* the leader.

alcheringa (alchəring´gə), **alchera** (al´chərə) *n.* the golden age or dreamtime in the mythology of Australian Aboriginals.
19C. Australian Aboriginal (Aranda) in the dreamtime, from *aljerre* dream + -*nge*, abl. suf. form.

al dente (al den´ti, -tā) *a.* (esp. of cooked pasta) firm when bitten.
mid-20C. Italian to the tooth, from *al* to the + *dente* tooth.

alea jacta est (ahliə yak´tə est) *int.* the die is cast, irrevocable action has been taken.
19C. Latin, from *alea* die, dice + 3rd pers. perf. pass. of *iacere* to throw.
● The words are said to have been spoken by Julius Caesar at the crossing of the Rubicon (49 BC), the stream that marked the boundary between Italy and Cisalpine Gaul. In leading his army across it, Caesar broke the law forbidding a general to lead an army out of his province. The crossing committed Caesar to war against the Senate and Pompey.

aleph (al´ef) *n.* the first letter of the Hebrew alphabet.
12–14C. Hebrew *'ālep* ox. Cp. ALPHA.
● The Hebrew letter evolved from the hieroglyph of an ox's head.

alfalfa (alfal´fə) *n.* a plant, *Medicago sativa*, with flowers and leaves similar to those of clover, that is widely cultivated as forage, a salad vegetable and a commercial source of chlorophyll.
19C. Spanish, from Arabic *al-faṣfaṣa* the best (kind of) fodder.

alfresco (alfres´kō) *a., adv.* in the open air, open-air.
18C. Italian *al fresco* in the fresh. See FRESCO.

alguazil (algwəzil´) *n.* **1** a mounted official at a bullfight. **2** in Spain or other Spanish-speaking countries, an inferior officer of justice, a constable.
16C. Spanish, from Arabic *al-wazīr*, from *al* the + *wazīr* vizier.

Alhambra (alham´brə) *n.* the Moorish palace and citadel at Granada in Spain.
16C. Spanish, from Arabic *al-ḥamrā'* the red (house).

alias (ā´liəs) *adv.* otherwise (named or called). ~*n.* (*pl.* **aliases**) an assumed name.
14–15C. Latin at another time, from *alius* other.

alibi (al´ibī) *n.* (*pl.* **alibis**) **1** the plea (of a person accused) of having been elsewhere when the offence was committed; the evidence to support such a plea. **2** (*coll.*) an excuse (for failing to do something). ~*v.t.* (*ṁrd pers. sing. pres.* **alibis**, *pres.p.* **alibiing**, *past*, *p.p.* **alibied**) to provide with an alibi. ~*v.i.* to provide an alibi.
17C. Latin elsewhere, loc. adv. of *alius* other.
• The original sense was legal only.

aliquot (al´ikwot) *a.* (*Math.*) of or relating to a number that is contained an integral number of times by a given number. ~*n.* an integral factor, an aliquot part.
16C. French *aliquote*, from Latin *aliquot* some, several, from *alius* one of two + *quot* how many.

alla breve (alə brā´vi) *n.* (*Mus.*) a time signature including two or four minims to the bar.
18C. Italian according to the breve, from *alla* to the + *breve* breve.

Allah (al´ə) *n.* the name of God among Arabs and Muslims.
16C. Arabic *'allāh*, prob. contraction of *al-'ilāh* the god, from *al* the + *'ilāh* god.
• The name implies Allah's uniqueness as *the* god.

allargando (alahgan´dō) *adv.* (*Mus.*) getting slower and fuller in tone.

19C. Italian broadening, pres.p. of *allargare* to widen, to broaden.

allée (al´ā) *n.* (*pl.* **allées** (al´ā)) a walk or passage in a garden or park.
19C. French, from *aller* to go, rel. to English *alley*.

allegretto (aləgret´ō) *a.*, *adv.* (*Mus.*) a little slower than allegro. ~*n.* (*pl.* **allegrettos**) a movement or passage to be performed allegretto.
18C. Italian, dim. of ALLEGRO.

allegro (əleg´rō) *a.* (*Mus.*) brisk, lively. ~*adv.* briskly, quickly. ~*n.* (*pl.* **allegros**) a movement or passage in allegro time or manner.
17C. Italian lively.

alleluia (aliloo´yə), **alleluya**, **hallelujah** (hal-) *int.* praise be to God. ~*n.* **1** an utterance of 'alleluia', an offering of praise to God. **2** a song of praise to God. **3** the part of a Mass containing this.
pre-1200. Ecclesiastical Latin, from Greek *allēlouia*, from Hebrew *hallĕlūyāh* praise Jah (God), from imper. pl. of *hallēl* to praise.

allemande (al´imand, al´mand, almād´) *n.* **1** any of various German dances of the 17th and 18th cents. **2** the music for or suitable for this (occurring as a movement in a suite).
17C. French, fem. of *allemand* German.

allodium (əlō´diəm), **alodium**, **allod** (al´od) *n.* (*pl.* **allodia, alodia, allods**) landed property held in absolute ownership.
17C. Medieval Latin, from Frankish *all* all + *ōd* estate, wealth.

alluvion (əloo´viən) *n.* **1** the wash of the sea against the land. **2** (*Law*) the formation of new land by the action of flowing water.
16C. French, from Latin *alluvio*, *alluvionis*, from *alluvium* ALLUVIUM.

alluvium (əloo´viəm) *n.* (*pl.* **alluvia**) (a fine-grained fertile soil derived from) transported matter which has been washed away and later deposited by rivers, floods or similar causes.
17C. Latin, neut. of *alluvius* washed against, from *alluere*, from *ad* to + *-luere*, comb. form of *lavare* to wash.

alma (al´mə), **almah** *n.* an Egyptian dancing girl.
18C. Arabic *'ālima* singer, orig. (as fem. a.) learned, from *'alima* to know.

alma mater (almə mā´tə, mah´-), **Alma Mater** *n.* the university, college or school that a person attended.
17C. Latin bounteous mother.
• This was originally the title given to certain Roman goddesses, such as Ceres and Cybele.

aloha (əlō´hə) *int.* **1** hello, welcome. **2** goodbye, farewell.
19C. Hawaiian love, affection, pity.

alpargata (alpahgah´tə) *n.* a light, rope-soled canvas shoe, an espadrille.
19C. Spanish. Cp. ESPADRILLE.

Alpenhorn (alp´ənhawn), **alphorn** (alp´-) *n.* a very long wooden horn used by herdsmen in the Swiss Alps.
19C. German, from *Alpen* Alps + *Horn* horn.

alpenstock (alp´ənstok) *n.* a long stick shod with iron, used in mountaineering.
19C. German, from *Alpen* Alps + *Stock* stick.

alpha (al´fə) *n.* **1** the first letter of the Greek alphabet (A, α). **2** a first-class mark for a piece of work, in an examination etc.
11–12C. Latin, from Greek, from Semitic. Cp. ALEPH.
• In sense 1 the word is common in the phrase 'alpha and omega', meaning the beginning and the end. The allusion is biblical (Rev. i.8). See OMEGA.

alt (alt) *n.* (*Mus.*) high tone; the higher register of sounds.
16C. Provençal, from Italian *alto* ALTO.

alter ego (awltə ē´gō, al-, eg´-) *n.* (*pl.* **alter egos**) **1** a second self. **2** a trusted friend. **3** a plenipotentiary.
16C. Latin other self, from *alter* other + EGO.

althorn (alt´hawn) *n.* an instrument of the saxhorn family, esp. the E flat alto or tenor saxhorn.
19C. German, alt ALTO + *Horn* horn.

altissimo (altis´imō) *adv.* (*Mus.*) in the second octave above the treble stave.
18C. Italian, superl. of *alto* ALTO.

alto (al´tō) *n.* (*pl.* **altos**) **1** the lowest female voice, contralto. **2** the highest adult male voice, countertenor. **3** a singer possessing such a voice. **4** the part of the music sung by persons possessing the alto voice. **5** an alto instrument, esp. an alto saxophone. ~*a.* **1** to be sung by altos. **2** being the second- or third-highest in pitch of a family of instruments.
16C. Italian, from Latin *altus* high.

alto-relievo (altōrəlyā´vō) *n.* (*pl.* **alto-relievos**) **1** high relief, standing out from the background by more than half the true proportions of the figures carved. **2** a sculpture of this type.
17C. Italian *alto-rilievo*, from *alto* high + *rilievo* RELIEVO.

alumnus (əlŭm´nəs) *n.* (*pl.* **alumni** (-nī)) **1** a former pupil or student (of a particular place of education). **2** (*N Am.*) a graduate.
17C. Latin nursling, from *alere* to nourish. Cp. ALMA MATER.

a.m. *adv.* in the morning, before noon.
17C. Abbr. of **Latin** *ante meridiem* before
noon, from *ante* before + acc. of
meridies noon, midday. Cp. P.M.
• The abbreviation is sometimes
misunderstood as deriving from *ante
meridian*, by association with the fact
that the sun crosses the meridian at
noon. English *meridian* is also
ultimately from Latin *meridies*. The full
Latin phrase dates from the 16C.

amabile (amah´bili) *adv.* (*Mus.*) amiably,
tenderly, sweetly.
17C. Italian amiable.

amadou (am´ədoo) *n.* a tinder prepared
from a dried fungus steeped in saltpetre,
used as a match and a styptic.
18C. French, of uncertain orig.
• The word is said to derive from
Provençal *amadou* amorous, from the
readiness of the tinder to ignite.

amah (ah´mə) *n.* (in the Far East and
India) a maidservant or nanny.
19C. Portuguese *ama* nurse.

amanuensis (əmanūen´sis) *n.* (*pl.*
amanuenses (-sēz)) a person employed
to write what another dictates or to copy
manuscripts.
17C. Latin, from *a manu*, in phr. *servus a
manu* slave at hand + *-ensis* belonging
to.

amaretto (aməret´ō) *n.* (*pl.* **amaretti**
(-et´i)) an almond-flavoured liqueur
from Italy.
early 20C. Italian, dim. of *amaro* bitter,
with ref. to the bitter almonds.

amateur (am´ətə, -chə) *n.* **1** a person who
practises anything as a pastime, as
distinguished from one who does so
professionally. **2** a person who competes
in a sport for enjoyment rather than
payment. **3** a person who is fond of an
art, pastime etc., a devotee. **4** (*derog.*) a
person who dabbles or is unskilled in a
subject. ~*a.* **1** engaging in something for
enjoyment; not professional, not
receiving payment. **2** involving or for
amateurs. **3** amateurish.
18C. French, from Italian *amatore*, from
Latin *amator* lover.

ambiance (ābiās´), **ambience**
(am´biəns) *n.* a surrounding atmosphere
or influence, an environment.
mid-20C. French, from *ambiant*, from
Latin *ambire* to go round.

ambo (am´bō) *n.* (*pl.* **ambos, ambones**
(-bō´nēz)) a pulpit or reading desk in
early medieval churches.
17C. Medieval Latin *ambo, ambonis*,
from Greek *ambōn* rim, edge of cup.

ambrosia (ambrō´ziə) *n.* **1** the fabled
food of the gods. **2** anything very
pleasant to the taste or the smell. **3** bee-
bread. **4** a composite plant of the genus
Ambrosia, allied to wormwood.
16C. Latin, from Greek immortality,
from *ambrotos* immortal, from *a-*
without + *brotos*, from *mbrotos mortal.

AMDG *adv.* to the greater glory of God.
Abbr. of **Latin** *ad maiorem Dei gloriam*,
from *ad* to + acc. of *maior gloria* greater
glory + gen. of *Deus* God.
• The Latin phrase dates from the 17C.

amen (ahmen´, ā´men) *int.* so be it, may
it be as it has been asked, said or
promised (said esp. at the end of a
prayer or hymn). ~*n.* **1** an utterance of
the word 'Amen', an expression of
assent. **2** a concluding word.
pre-1200. Ecclesiastical Latin, from
Greek *amēn*, from Hebrew *'āmēn*
certain, from base *'mn* to be certain.

amende honorable (əmānd
onorah´blə) *n.* (*pl.* **amendes
honorables** (əmānd´ onorah´blə)) an
open or public apology, often
accompanied by some form of amends.
17C. French honourable reparation.

âme perdue (ahm peədü´) *n.* (*pl.* **âmes perdues** (ahm peədü´)) a desperate person.
19C. French, lit. lost soul, from *âme* soul + fem. p.p. of *perdre* to lose.

amicus curiae (əmēkəs kū´riē) *n.* (*pl.* **amici curiae** (əmēsī)) (*Law*) a disinterested adviser in a court of law.
17C. Modern Latin friend of the court, from *amicus* friend + gen. sing. of CURIA.

amigo (əmē´gō) *n.* (*pl.* **amigos**) (*N Am., coll.*) a friend (also often used as a form of address).
19C. Spanish, from Latin *amicus* friend.

amir (əmiə´), **ameer** *n.* the title of several Muslim rulers, esp. formerly in India and Afghanistan.
16C. Persian and Urdu, from Arabic *'amīr* commander, from *amara* to command. Cp. EMIR.

amontillado (əmontilah´dō) *n.* (*pl.* **amontillados**) a kind of medium dry sherry.
19C. Spanish, from *Montilla*, a town in S Spain.
• The sherry-type wine *Montilla* takes its name from the same town.

amoretto (aməret´ō) *n.* (*pl.* **amoretti** (-ti)) a cupid.
16C. Italian, dim. of *amore* love.

amoroso[1] (əmərō´zō) *adv., a.* (*Mus.*) to be performed lovingly.
17C. Spanish and Italian, from Medieval Latin *amorosus* amorous.

amoroso[2] (əmərō´zō, -sō) *n.* (*pl.* **amorosos**) a full rich type of sherry.
17C. Spanish amorous. Cp. AMOROSO[1].
• The wine is so named from its sweetness.

amour (əmuə´) *n.* a love affair, esp. a secret one; an amorous intrigue.
12–14C. Old French, from Latin *amor* love.
• The original meaning was love itself. Cp. AMOUR COURTOIS, AMOUR PROPRE. The current sense prevailed from the 16C.

amour courtois (amuə kuətwah´) *n.* courtly love, the medieval social and literary conventions concerning love and etiquette developed by the troubadours in S France.
19C. French, from *amour* love + *courtois* courtly.

amour propre (amuə propr´, prop´rə) *n.* self-esteem.
18C. French self-love, from *amour* love + *propre* own.

amphora (am´fərə) *n.* (*pl.* **amphoras**, **amphorae** (-ē)) an ancient two-handled vessel for holding wine, oil etc.
12–14C. Latin, from Greek *amphoreus*, from *amphi* around + *phoreus* bearer. Cp. AMPULLA.

ampoule (am´pool), (*N Am.*) **ampule** (-pūl) *n.* a sealed phial containing one dose of a drug.
17C. French, from Latin AMPULLA.

ampulla (ampul´ə) *n.* (*pl.* **ampullae** (-ē)) **1** a nearly globular flask with two handles, used by the ancient Romans. **2** a vessel for holding consecrated oil, wine etc. **3** (*Biol.*) the dilated end of any vessel. **4** a spongiole of a root.
14–15C. Latin, dim. of *ampora* AMPHORA.

amrita (amrē´tə) *n.* the ambrosia of the gods in Hindu mythology.
18C. Sanskrit *amṛta* an immortal, nectar. Cp. AMBROSIA.

amuse-gueule (amüzgœl´) *n.* a snack, an appetizer, an hors d'oeuvre.
late 20C. French, lit. amusement for the mouth, from *amuser* to amuse + *gueule* mouth.
• The snack is intended to serve as a

foretaste of the main meal to come.
French *gueule* is normally used of an
animal's mouth, the regular word for
mouth being *bouche*. Cp. BONNE
BOUCHE.

anabasis (ənab´əsis) *n.* (*pl.* **anabases**
(-sēz)) **1** a military advance up-country.
2 the expedition of Cyrus the Younger
into Asia (401 BC), narrated by
Xenophon.
18C. Greek going up, from *anabainein*
to go up, to mount, from *ana* up +
bainein to go. Cp. KATABASIS.

anacoluthon (anəkəloo´thon) *n.*
(*pl.* **anacolutha** (-thə)) **1** lack of
grammatical sequence in a sentence.
2 a change of structure in a sentence
that renders it ungrammatical.
18C. Late Latin, from Greek
anakolouthon, neut. sing. of a.
anakolouthos lacking sequence, from
an- not + *akolouthos* following.

anagnorisis (anəgnor´isis) *n.* (*pl.*
anagnorises (-sēz)) in Greek tragedy,
a recognition that leads to the
denouement.
18C. Greek *anagnōrisis*, from *ana* up +
gnōrizein to recognise.

analgesia (anəljē´ziə) *n.* loss of
sensibility to pain.
18C. Greek *analgēsia* painlessness, from
a without + *algeein* to feel pain.

ananas (ənah´nəs, an´ənas), **anana** *n.*
the pineapple plant or its fruit.
16C. French and Spanish, from
Portuguese *ananás*, from Guarani
naná.

anaphora (ənaf´ərə) *n.* **1** (*Gram.*) **a** the
commencement of successive sentences
or clauses with the same word or words.
b the use of a word, such as a pronoun,
to refer to a preceding word or phrase
without repetition. **2** the consecration

and offering of the elements at the
Eucharist.
16C. Latin, from Greek repetition, from
ana back, again + *pherein* to carry.

anaptyxis (anəptik´sis) *n.* the insertion
of a short vowel between two
consonants to facilitate pronunciation.
19C. Modern Latin, from Greek
anaptuxis unfolding, from *ana* up +
ptuxis folding.

anastrophe (ənas´trəfi) *n.* inversion of
the natural order of the words in a
sentence or clause.
16C. Greek *anastrophē* turning back,
from *ana* back + *strephein* to turn. Cp.
STROPHE.

anathema (ənath´əmə) *n.* (*pl.*
anathemas, **anathemata**
(anəthem´ətə)) **1** an object of loathing.
2 the formal act by which a person or
thing is cursed, excommunication.
3 the person or thing cursed. **4** a curse,
denunciation.
16C. Ecclesiastical Latin, from Greek
var. of *anathēma* votive offering, from
anatithenai to set up, from *ana* up +
tithenai to put, to place.

ancien régime (āsyā räzhēm´) *n.* (*pl.*
anciens régimes (āsyā räzhēm´)) **1** the
political and social system of France
before the French Revolution. **2** any
superseded order.
18C. French former regime, from *ancien*
ancient + *régime* REGIME.

andante (andan´ti) *a., adv.* (*Mus.*)
moderately slow. ~*n.* a moderately slow
movement, piece or passage.
18C. Italian, pres.p. of *andare* to go.

andantino (andantē´nō) *a., adv.* (*Mus.*)
rather quicker than andante. ~*n.* (*pl.*
andantinos) a movement or piece of
this character.
19C. Italian, dim. of ANDANTE.

andouille (ādoo´ē) *n.* (*pl.* **andouilles**
(-ē)) a kind of pork sausage eaten as an
hors d'oeuvre.
17C. French, of unknown orig.
● According to some, the French word
derives from Popular Latin *inductile*,
from Latin *inducere* to introduce, since
the sausage is made by 'introducing' or
stuffing the pork into the skin.

angelus (an´jələs) *n.* (*pl.* **angeluses**)
1 a short devotional exercise in the
Roman Catholic Church in honour of
the Incarnation. **2** the angelus bell.
17C. Latin, from the opening words,
Angelus domini nuntiavit Mariae The
angel of the Lord announced to Mary.

angina pectoris (anjīnə pek´təris)
n. a heart condition marked by
paroxysms of intense pain due to over-
exertion when the heart is weak or
diseased.
18C. Latin quinsy of the chest, from
angina quinsy + gen. sing. of *pectus*
breast, chest.

anglice (ang´glisē, -si) *adv.* in English.
17C. Medieval Latin, from Latin *Anglus*
English.

angostura (ang·gəstū´rə) *n.* a febrifugal
bark, used also in the preparation of
bitters.
18C. *Angostura* (now Ciudad Bolívar),
a town in Venezuela.

angst (angst) *n.* a nonspecific feeling of
anxiety and guilt produced esp. by
considering the imperfect human
condition.
early 20C. German *Angst* fear.

anima (an´imə) *n.* **1** (*Psych.*) a person's
true inner self, as opposed to the
persona. **2** the feminine aspect of the
male personality.
early 20C. Latin air, breath, mind.

animateur (animətœ´) *n.* a person who
is the animating force behind
something; a promoter, a sponsor.
mid-20C. French animator.

animé (an´imā) *n.* **1** a West Indian resin,
used for varnish. **2** any of various
similar resins.
16C. French, from Tupi *wana'ni.*

animoso (animō´sō) *adv.* (*Mus.*) with
spirit.
18C. Italian. See ANIMUS.

animus (an´iməs) *n.* **1** animosity. **2** a
motive, intention or spirit actuating
feeling, usu. of a hostile character.
3 (*Psych.*) the masculine part of the
female personality.
19C. Latin spirit, mind.

ankh (angk) *n.* a cross with a loop above
the crosspiece, that was in ancient Egypt
the emblem of life, or male symbol of
generation.
19C. Egyptian life, soul.

ankus (ang´kəs) *n.* an elephant goad.
19C. Hindi *ăkus*, from Sanskrit *aṅkuśa.*

anna (an´ə) *n.* a former monetary unit
and coin of India, Burma and Pakistan,
equal to one sixteenth of a rupee.
17C. Hindi *ānā.*

annatto (ənat´ō), **anatta** (ənat´ə),
anatto (-ō) *n.* **1** an orange-red dye used
to colour food, fabric etc. **2** the tropical
American tree, *Bixa orellana*, from
whose pulpy seeds this dye is obtained.
17C. Carib.

Anno Domini (anō dom´inī) *adv.* in the
year of Our Lord (indicating a date
reckoned from the beginning of the
Christian era). ~*n.* (*coll.*) old age.
16C. Latin in the year of the Lord,
from abl. of *annus* year + gen. of
dominus lord.

annus horribilis (anəs, anus hori´bilis)
n. a year of personal or general
misfortune and calamity.
late 20C. Modern Latin horrible year,
based on ANNUS MIRABILIS.
● The phrase came into popular use
following the Queen's use of it in her
speech at the Guildhall, London, in
1992, after a year of troubles including
a fire at Windsor Castle, the divorce of
Princess Anne and Captain Mark
Phillips and the separation of the Duke
and Duchess of York.

annus mirabilis (anəs, anus
mirah´bilis) *n.* (*pl.* **anni mirabiles** (anē
mirah´bilēz)) a remarkable year (usu.
applied in English history to 1666, year
of the Great Fire of London etc.).
17C. Modern Latin wonderful year.

anomie (an´omi), **anomy** *n.* the
breakdown or absence of moral and
social standards in an individual or
society.
mid-20C. French, from Greek *anomia*,
from *anomos* lawless, from *a-* without
+ *nomos* law.
● The word was introduced in its
current sense by the French sociologist
Émile Durkheim in *Suicide* (1897).

Anschauung (an´showung) *n.* (*pl.*
Anschauungen (-ung·ən)) an outlook,
an attitude, a point of view.
early 20C. German a looking at, from
anschauen to look at.
● The term arose from Kantian
philosophy in the 19C in which it was
used for an intuition or immediate
apprehension by sense.

Anschluss (an´shlus) *n.* the forced union
of Austria with Germany in 1938.
early 20C. German, from *anschliessen*
to join, to annex.

ante (an´ti) *n.* **1** the stake which a poker
player puts down after being dealt a
hand, but before drawing. **2** (*coll.*)
amount paid, price. ~*v.t.* (*third pers. sing.
pres.* **antes,** *pres.p.* **anteing,** *past, p.p.*
anted) **1** to stake. **2** to pay.
19C. Latin before.
● The word is common in the phrase 'to
up the ante' meaning to raise the stakes.

ante-bellum (antibel´əm) *a.* existing
before the war, esp. the American Civil
War.
19C. Latin *ante bellum* before the war,
from *ante* before + acc. sing. of *bellum*
war.

antependium (antipen´diəm) *n.* (*pl.*
antependia (-iə)) a covering for the
front of an altar, a frontal.
16C. Medieval Latin, from *ante* before
+ Latin *pendere* to hang.

anthemion (anthē´miən) *n.* (*pl.*
anthemia (-ə)) a palmette, honeysuckle
or conventional leaf or floral design.
19C. Greek flower.

anti (an´ti) *prep.* opposed to. ~*n.* (*pl.*
antis) an opponent of a policy, political
party etc.
18C. Greek opposite.

antipasto (antipas´tō) *n.* (*pl.* **antipastos,
antipasti** (-tē)) an hors d'oeuvre.
17C. Italian before food, from Latin *ante*
before + *pasto*, from Latin *pastus* food.
● The word was not generally current
until the mid-20C.

antipodes (antip´ədēz) *n.pl.* **1** a place on
the surface of the globe diametrically
opposite to another. **2** a pair of places
diametrically opposite. **3** the direct
opposite of some other person or thing.
4 people who live directly opposite to
each other on the globe. **5** (**the
Antipodes**) Australia and New Zealand.
12–14C. French, or from Late Latin,
from Greek, pl. of *antipous* with feet
opposite, from *anti* opposite + *pous,
podos* foot.
● The Antipodes are virtually opposite

Britain geographically. The word originally applied to the inhabitants of the antipodes, rather than the place itself. The current sense prevailed from the 16C.

antistrophe (antis´trəfi) n. **1** the return movement from left to right of a Greek chorus, answering the movement of a strophe. **2** the poem or choral song recited during this movement. **3** any choral response.
16C. Late Latin, from Greek *antistrophē*, from *antistrephein* to turn against.

antithesis (antith´əsis) n. (*pl.* **antitheses** (-sēz)) **1** the direct opposite. **2** opposition, contrast. **3** sharp opposition or contrast between words, clauses, sentences or ideas. **4** a counter proposition.
14–15C. Late Latin, from Greek, from *antitithenai*, from *anti* opposite + *tithenai* to set, to place. Cp. THESIS.

à outrance (a ootrãs´) adv. **1** to the end. **2** to the death.
17C. French, from *à* to + *outrance* going beyond bounds, from Old French *outrer* to pass beyond, from *outre* beyond. Cp. OUTRÉ.

apartheid (əpah´tāt, -tīt, -thīt) n. (a policy of) racial segregation.
mid-20C. Afrikaans separateness, from Dutch *apart* apart + *-heid* -hood.

aperçu (apœsoo´, -sü´) n. **1** a concise exposition, an outline, a brief summary. **2** an insight.
19C. French, p.p. of *apercevoir* to perceive.

aperitif (əperitēf´) n. a short drink, usu. alcoholic, taken as an appetizer.
19C. French *apéritif*, from Medieval Latin *aperitivus*, var. of Late Latin *apertivus*, from *apertus*, p.p. of *aperire* to open.

● An aperitif is regarded as opening the digestive processes.

à perte de vue (a peət də vü´) adv. as far as the eye can see.
18C. French, lit. to loss of sight, from *à* to + *perte* loss + *de* of + *vue* sight.

apex (ā´peks) n. (*pl.* **apexes, apices** (ā´pisēz)) **1** the top or summit of anything. **2** the culmination, climax.
17C. Latin tip, top.

apfelstrudel (ap´fəlstroodəl, -stroo´-) n. a dessert of Austrian origin consisting of flaky pastry filled with a spiced apple mixture.
mid-20C. German, from *Apfel* apple + STRUDEL.

● The partly anglicized form *apple strudel* is sometimes found.

apocope (əpok´əpi) n. a cutting off or dropping of the last letter or syllable of a word.
16C. Late Latin, from Greek *apokopē*, from *apokoptein* to cut off, from *apo* from, away + *koptein* to cut.

apocrypha (əpok´rifə) n.pl. **1** writings or statements of doubtful authority. **2** (**the Apocrypha**) a collection of 14 books in the Old Testament, included in the Septuagint and the Vulgate (not written in Hebrew originally and not recognized by the Jews or inserted in the Authorized Version of the Bible).
14–15C. Ecclesiastical Latin, neut. pl. of *apocryphus*, from Greek *apokruphos* hidden, from *apokruptein* to hide.

● The term was originally applied to any works of uncertain authorship. Its application to non-canonical Old Testament books dates from the 16C.

apodyterium (apəditiə´riəm) n. (*pl.* **apodyteria** (-riə)) the apartment in ancient baths or palaestras where clothes were taken off.

17C. Latin, from Greek *apodutērion*, from *apoduein* to strip, from *apo* from, away + *-duein* to put, to dress.

à point (a pwï) *adv.* **1** at or to exactly the right point. **2** in cookery, cooked exactly the right amount, not overdone or underdone.
early 20C. French to (the) point.

apologia (apəlō´jiə) *n.* a vindication or formal defence of one's conduct, views etc.
18C. Latin defence, apology.
• The currency of the word is largely due to Cardinal Newman's *Apologia pro Vita Sua* (1864).

apologue (ap´əlog) *n.* a fable designed to impress some moral truth upon the mind, esp. a beast-fable or a fable of inanimate things.
16C. French, or from Late Latin *apologus*, from Greek *apologos* story, from *apo* from, away + *logos* discourse. See also LOGOS.

aporia (əpaw´riə, əpor´iə) *n.* **1** in rhetoric, a real or affected doubt about what to do. **2** a difficulty, a puzzling thing.
16C. Late Latin, from Greek, from *aporos* impassable, from *a* without + *poros* passage.

a posteriori (a postiəriaw´ri, ah) *a., adv.* reasoning from consequences, effects, things observed to causes; inductive, as opposed to *a priori* or *deductive*.
17C. Latin from what comes after. Cp. A PRIORI.

apotheosis (əpothiō´sis) *n.* (*pl.* **apotheoses** (-sēz)) **1** deification, transformation into a god. **2** a sublime example of something. **3** a deified ideal. **4** enrolment among the saints.
16C. Ecclesiastical Latin, from Greek *apotheōsis*, from *apotheoun* to deify, from *apo* from, away + *theos* god.

apparat (apərat´, ap´-) *n.* (*Hist.*) the party organization of the Communist party in the Soviet Union and similar states.
mid-20C. Russian, from German *Apparat* apparatus, from Latin *apparatus*, from *apparare* to make ready.

apparatchik (apərat´chik, ap´-) *n.* **1** a member of an apparat. **2** a bureaucrat or official in any political party or other organization, esp. a zealous one. **3** a Communist agent.
mid-20C. Russian, from APPARAT + agent ending *-chik*.

apparatus criticus (apərātəs, -rah-krit´ikəs) *n.* the annotations, notes, variant readings etc. used in literary criticism and investigation.
19C. Modern Latin critical apparatus.

appellation contrôlée (apəlasyō kōtrō´lā), **appellation d'origine contrôlée** (dorēzhēn) *n.* a guarantee, in the labelling of some French wines and foodstuffs, that the product conforms to statutory regulations in respect of its origin, quality, strength etc.
mid-20C. French controlled appellation.
• The phrase is often abbreviated to *AC*.

appliqué (ap´likā) *n.* ornamental work laid on some other material.
18C. French, use as n. of p.p. of *appliquer* to apply.

appoggiatura (əpojətoo´rə, -tū´-) *n.* (*Mus.*) a grace note before a significant note.
18C. Italian, from *appoggiare* to lean on, to rest.

appui (apwē´) *n.* **1** the stay (of a horse) upon the bridle-hand of its rider. **2** (*Mil.*) defensive support.
16C. French, from *appuyer* to support, to rest on, from Late Latin *appodiare* to lean on, from *ad* to + *podium* support. Cp. PODIUM.

après-goût (aprāgoo´) *n.* (*pl.* **après-goûts** (-goo´)) an aftertaste.
19C. French, from *après* after + *goût* taste.

après moi le déluge (aprā mwah lə delūzh´) *int.* used to express the idea that the existing order of things is not likely to last beyond one's own lifetime or period of influence.
19C. French, lit. after me the flood.
• A variant but less common form *après nous le déluge* after us the flood has been attributed to Madame de Pompadour (1721–64), mistress of Louis XV, following the French defeat by the Prussians at Rossbach (1757).

après-ski (apreskē´) *n., a.* (of or intended for) the social time following a day's skiing.
mid-20C. French after skiing, from *après* after + SKI.

a priori (ā priaw´ri, -rī, ah) *adv.* from the cause to the effect; from abstract ideas to consequences; deductively. ~*a.* **1** deductive; derived by reasoning from cause to effect. **2** prior to experience. **3** abstract and unsupported by actual evidence.
16C. Latin from what is before.
• The opposite is A POSTERIORI.

apropos (aprəpō´) *adv.* **1** opportunely, seasonably. **2** by the way. ~*a.* **1** bearing on the matter in hand; to the point. **2** appropriate. **3** opportune, seasonable.
17C. French *à propos*, from *à* to + *propos* purpose.

aqua (ak´wə) *n.* **1** water, liquid, solution. **2** the colour aquamarine. ~*a.* aquamarine.
mid-20C. Latin water.

aqua fortis (akwəfaw´tis), **aquafortis** *n.* (*Chem.*) nitric acid.
15C. Latin strong water. See AQUA. Cp. FORTE².

Aqua Libra® (akwə lē´brə) *n.* a drink made from mineral water and fruit juices.
late 20C. Latin *aqua* water + *libra* balance.
• The name perhaps puns on EQUILIBRIUM.

aqua pura (akwə pūə´rə) *n.* pure water.
18C. Latin, from *aqua* water + fem. of *purus* pure.
• The term arose in pharmacy for pure or distilled water but later gained a semi-facetious use with regard to a non-alcoholic drink (or to water as an additive to an alcoholic one).

aqua regia (akwə rē´jə) *n.* (*Chem.*) a mixture of nitric and hydrochloric acids, capable of dissolving gold and platinum.
17C. Latin royal water.
• The mixture is so called because it can dissolve the 'noble' metals (gold and platinum).

aquarelle (akwərel´) *n.* **1** a kind of painting in Chinese ink and very thin transparent watercolours. **2** the design so produced.
19C. French, from Italian *acquarella* watercolour, from *acqua*, from Latin AQUA.

aquarium (əkweə´riəm) *n.* (*pl.* **aquariums, aquaria** (-riə)) **1** an artificial tank, pond or vessel in which aquatic animals and plants are kept alive. **2** a place in which such tanks are exhibited.
19C. Neut. sing. (used as *n.*) of **Latin** *aquarius* pertaining to water, from *aqua* water.
• The word is based on VIVARIUM.

aquavit (ak´wəvēt, -vit), **akvavit** (ak´və-) *n.* an alcoholic spirit flavoured with caraway seeds.
19C. Norwegian, Swedish and Danish *akvavit* AQUA VITAE.

aqua vitae (akwə vē´tī) *n.* strong spirits, brandy etc.
15C. **Latin** water of life. Cp. *eau de vie.*
● The phrase was originally an alchemists' term for unrectified alcohol.

à quoi bon? (a kwah bō´) *int.* what is the use?, what is the good of it?
early 20C. **French**, lit. to what good?

araba (ərah´bə) *n.* an Oriental wheeled carriage.
19C. **Turkish**, from Arabic 'ā*ba* gun carriage.

arabesque (arəbesk´) *a.* **1** Arabian in design. **2** in the style of arabesque.
~*n.* **1** surface decoration composed of flowing lines fancifully intermingled, usu. representing foliage in a conventional manner, without animal forms. **2** a posture in ballet dancing with one leg raised behind and the arms extended.
17C. **French**, from Italian *arabesco*, from *arabo* Arabic.
● Moorish architecture uses intricate ornamentation as Islam forbids the representation of living creatures.

arabica (ərab´ikə) *n.* **1** coffee or coffee beans from the tree *Coffea arabica*, widely grown in South America. **2** this tree.
early 20C. **Latin**, fem. of *arabicus*, from Greek *arabikos* Arabian.

arak (ar´ək), **arrack** *n.* a distilled spirit from the East, esp. one distilled from coconut or rice.
17C. **Arabic** '*araḳ* sweat, sweet juice, from '*araḳ at-tamr* juice of dates.

Arbeit macht frei (ahbīt mahkht frī´) *int.* work will make you free.
mid-20C. **German**, lit. work makes free.
● The phrase, of anonymous origin, was inscribed on the gates of Dachau concentration camp in 1933 and subsequently on those of Auschwitz, as

a grotesque distortion of the Protestant work ethic.

arboretum (ahbərē´təm) *n.* (*pl.* **arboretums, arboreta** (-tə)) a botanical garden for the rearing and exhibition of rare trees.
19C. **Latin** place with trees, from *arbor* tree.

arbor vitae (ahbaw vē´tī) *n.* **1** the tree of life. **2** any of several Asian and North American evergreens of the genus *Thuja*. **3** a dendriform appearance in a vertical section of the cerebellum.
17C. **Latin** tree of life, from *arbor* tree + gen. sing. of *vita* life.

Arcades ambo (ahkādēz am´bō) *n.* (*often derog.*) two people of the same character or tastes, esp. in literature, art or music.
19C. **Latin**, lit. both Arcadians.
● The phrase is from Virgil's *Eclogues* (1C BC), meaning both poet-musicians. The English application implies an interest in 'idle' pursuits.

arcana (ahkah´nə, -kā´-) *n.* either of the two divisions, major or minor, of the Tarot pack.
16C. **Latin**, pl. of ARCANUM.

arcanum (ahkā´nəm) *n.* (*pl.* **arcana** (-nə)) **1** anything hidden. **2** a mystery, a secret, esp. one of the supposed secrets of the alchemists.
16C. **Latin**, neut. sing. (used as n.) of *arcanus* secret.

archon (ah´kon) *n.* any one of the nine chief magistrates of ancient Athens after the time of Solon.
16C. **Greek** *arkhōn* ruler, from *arkhein* to rule.

arcus senilis (ahkəs senē´lis) *n.* a bow- or ring-shaped opaque area around the cornea of the eye, often seen in elderly people.
18C. **Latin** senile bow.

ardente (ahden´ti) *a.* (*Mus.*) ardent, fiery.
18C. **Italian**, from Latin *ardens*, *ardentis*, pres.p. of *ardere* to burn.

à rebours (a rəbuə´) *adv.* in the wrong way, against the grain.
early 20C. **French**, from *à* from + Old French *rebors* (Modern French *rebours*) rough, perverse, the wrong side, from Popular Latin *rebursus*, from Latin *reburrus* rough-haired, bristly.
● *À rebours* (1884) was the title of a book about a 19C decadent by the French novelist Joris-Karl Huysmans (1848–1907).

arête (əret´) *n.* a sharp ascending ridge of a mountain.
19C. **French**, from Latin *arista* ear of corn, fishbone.

argent (ah´jənt) *n.* **1** (*Her.*) the white colour representing silver. **2** †silver. ~*a.* **1** (*poet.*) silver. **2** silvery-white.
16C. **French**, from Latin *argentum* silver.

argot (ah´gō) *n.* **1** the phraseology or jargon of a class or group. **2** thieves' slang. **3** slang generally.
19C. **French**, of unknown orig.
● The word is perhaps related to Old French *hargoter* to quarrel, a variant of *harigoter* to tear. It is not related to English *jargon*.

aria (ah´riə) *n.* (*Mus.*) a song, esp. in an opera or oratorio, for one voice supported by instruments.
18C. **Italian**, from Latin *aera*, acc. of *aer* air.

arietta (ariet´ə) *n.* (*Mus.*) a short lively air, tune or song.
18C. **Italian**, dim. of ARIA.

ariette (ariet´) *n.* (*Mus.*) an arietta.
19C. **French**, from Italian ARIETTA.

arioso (ahriō´zō, -sō) *a., adv.* (*Mus.*) in a songlike style, melodious(ly). ~*n.* (*pl.* **ariosos**) a piece or passage played arioso.
18C. **Italian**, from ARIA.

ariston metron (ariston met´ron) *n.* the golden mean.
18C. **Greek** (the) best measure, from neut. of *aristos* best + *metron* measure.
● The Greek sense uses 'best' to mean showing no excess in either direction, i.e. 'best' as perfectly balanced.

armada (ahmah´də) *n.* **1** an armed fleet, esp. the fleet sent by Philip II of Spain against England in 1588. **2** any large (armed) force.
16C. **Spanish**, fem. of *armado* armed, p.p. of *armar*, from Latin *armare*, from *arma* weapons.

armamentarium (ahməmenteə´riəm) *n.* (*pl.* **armamentariums**, **armamentaria** (-iə)) the equipment, medicines etc. collectively, that are available to a doctor or other medical practitioner.
19C. **Latin** arsenal, armoury, from *armamentum*, from *arma* weapons.

arma virumque cano (ah´mə virum´kwi kanō´) *int.* I sing of arms and the man.
19C. **Latin**.
● The words are the opening to Virgil's *Aeneid* (1C BC). Their use in English is usually high-flown, with regard to some great or heroic person or deed.

armes parlantes (ahm pahlãt´) *n.pl.* (*Her.*) coats of arms which show devices that directly illustrate the name of the bearer, e.g. that represent the name Churchill by a church and a hill.
18C. **French** speaking arms, from *armes* weapons + *parlantes*, pl. pres.p. of *parler* to speak.

armiger (ah´mijə) *n.* **1** an esquire. **2** a person entitled to heraldic bearings.
16C. Latin bearing arms, from *arma* arms + *gerere* to bear.

armoire (ahmwah´) *n.* a chest, a cupboard.
16C. French cupboard.

arpeggio (ahpej´iō) *n.* (*pl.* **arpeggios**) (*Mus.*) **1** a chord played on a keyed instrument by striking the notes in rapid succession instead of simultaneously. **2** the notes of a chord played or sung in ascending or descending progression, esp. as an exercise.
18C. Italian, from *arpeggiare* to play on the harp, from *arpa* harp.

arrêt (arā´, əret´) *n.* (*pl.* **arrêts** (arā´, ərets´)) an authoritative sentence or decision, a decree.
17C. French judgement, decision, ruling, lit. arrest, from *arrêter* to arrest, to halt.
• The French application is either (historically) to the monarch or to parliament.

arrière-ban (arieəbā´) *n.* **1** in French history, a summons to the king's vassals to do military service. **2** an army mobilized by this means.
16C. French, from Old French *ariereban*, alt. of *arban*, from Germanic *hari* army + *ban* proclamation.
• The term has been influenced by Old French *arere* (Modern French *arrière*) behind.

arrière-garde (arieəgahd´) *n.* (*pl.* **arrière-gardes** (-gahd´)) rearguard.
19C. French, from *arrière* rear + *garde* guard. Cp. AVANT-GARDE.
• The semi-anglicized form *arrière-guard* has been current since the 14–15C.

arrière-pensée (arieəpā´sā) *n.* **1** a mental reservation. **2** an unrevealed intention.
19C. French, lit. behind-thought, from *arrière* behind + PENSÉE.

arrivé (arēvā´), (*fem.*) **arrivée** *a.* successful, having made one's way.
early 20C. French, p.p. of *arriver* to arrive. Cp. English *to arrive* in coll. sense to achieve success, to gain recognition.

arrivederci (ərēvədœ´chi, -deə´-) *int.* goodbye, to our next meeting.
19C. Italian until we see each other again, from *a* until + *rivedere* to see again + *ci* us. Cp. AUF WIEDERSEHEN, AU REVOIR.

arriviste (arēvēst´) *n.* **1** a social climber, a parvenu. **2** a self-seeker, esp. in politics.
early 20C. French, from *arriver* to arrive.

arroba (arō´bə) *n.* **1** a unit of weight used in some Spanish-speaking countries equivalent to 25 pounds (11.35 kilograms). **2** a unit of weight used in some Portuguese-speaking countries equivalent to 33 pounds (15 kilograms).
16C. Spanish, from Arabic *ar-rub'*, from *ar*, form of *al* the + *rub* quarter.
• The weight was originally a quarter of a quintal.

arrondissement (arõdēs´mä) *n.* **1** a territorial division of a French department. **2** an administrative district of some large French cities, esp. Paris.
19C. French from *arrondir*, *arrondiss-* to make round.

arroyo (ərō´yō) *n.* (*pl.* **arroyos**) (*N Am.*) a dried-up watercourse, a rocky ravine.
19C. Spanish.

ars gratia artis (ahz grāshə ah´tis) *int.* art for art's sake.
19C. Latin, lit. art for the sake of art, from *ars* art + abl. sing of *gratia* favour, sake + gen. sing. of *ars*.
• The phrase was adopted by the 'aesthetic' or 'pure art' movement that

flourished in France and England in the late 19C. The French Symbolists expressed similar sentiments in French *l'art pour l'art*. The words were generally popularized as the motto of the MGM film studios.

arsis (ah´sis) *n.* (*pl.* **arses** (-sēz)) the stressed syllable in metre, esp. in Greek or Latin verse.
14–15C. Late Latin, from Greek lifting, raising, from *airein* to raise.

artel (ahtel´) *n.* a cooperative organization of peasants, craftsmen etc. in the former Soviet Union or pre-revolutionary Russia.
19C. Russian *artel'*, from Italian *artiere* artisan, craftsman.

artiste (ahtēst´) *n.* **1** a public performer, an actor, dancer, musician, acrobat etc. **2** a highly proficient cook, hairdresser etc.
19C. French artist.

Art Nouveau (aht noovō´, ah) *n.* a style of decorative art of the late 19th and early 20th cents., characterized by sinuous curving forms.
early 20C. French new art.
• The style took its name from a Paris gallery called *L'Art Nouveau* opened in 1895 by the art dealer Siegfried Bing, a leading propagandist for modern design.

as (as) *n.* (*pl.* **asses**) a Roman copper coin, orig. of twelve ounces (340 grams) but frequently reduced.
16C. Latin.

asana (ah´sənə) *n.* any of the positions taught in yoga.
mid-20C. Sanskrit *āsana*, from *āste* he sits.

ascesis (əsē´sis) *n.* (*pl.* **asceses** (-sēz)) the practice of self-discipline.
19C. Greek *askēsis* exercise, from *askein* to exercise.

ashram (ash´rəm) *n.* **1** (in India) a hermitage for a holy man or place of retreat for a religious community. **2** any place of religious or communal life modelled on an Indian ashram.
early 20C. Sanskrit *āśrama* hermitage.

askari (askah´ri) *n.* (*pl.* **askari, askaris**) an indigenous E African soldier.
19C. Arabic *'askarī* soldier.

asper (as´pə) *n.* (*Hist.*) a small Turkish silver coin, later only a monetary unit.
14–15C. French *aspre*, from Late Greek *aspron*, from Latin *asper* (*nummus*) newly minted (coin).
• Latin *asper* literally means rough and was applied to coins which would not yet have worn smooth.

assai (əsī´) *adv.* (*Mus.*) very, as in *largo assai*, very slow.
18C. Italian enough, from Popular Latin *adsatis*, from *satis* enough.

assegai (as´əgī), **assagai** *n.* (*pl.* **assegais, assagais**) a slender lance of hard wood, esp. that of the southern African tribes.
17C. Obsolete French *azagaie* (now *zagaie, sagaie*), or from Portuguese *azagaia*, or from Spanish *azagaya*, from Arabic (coll.) *az-zaġāya*, from *az*, form of *al* the + Berber *zaġāya* spear.

assignat (as´ignat, asinyah´) *n.* paper money issued by the Revolutionary Government of France (1790–96) on the security of state lands.
18C. French, from Latin *assignatum*, neut. p.p. of *assignare* to distribute.

assumpsit (əsŭmp´sit) *n.* (*Law, Hist.*) **1** an oral or unsealed contract, founded on a consideration. **2** an action to enforce such a contract.
16C. Latin he has taken upon himself, 3rd pers. sing. perf. ind. of *assumere* to assume.

Asti (as´ti) *n.* (*pl.* **Astis**) an Italian white wine.
19C. *Asti*, a province in NW Italy.

astrakhan (astrəkan´, -kahn´) *n.* **1** the tightly curled, usu. black or grey fleece obtained from lambs orig. from Astrakhan. **2** a fabric with a pile in imitation of this.
18C. *Astrakhan*, a city in central Asia (now in SW Russia).

ataman (at´əmən) *n.* (*pl.* **atamans**) an elected leader or general of the Cossacks.
19C. **Russian** HETMAN.

à tâtons (a tatō´) *adv.* gropingly, feeling one's way.
early 20C. French, from *tâter* to touch, to feel, to try, rel. to English *taste*. Cp. TÂTONNEMENT.

atelier (ətel´yā, at´-) *n.* a workshop, an artist's studio.
17C. **French**, from Old French *astelier*, from *astelle* splinter of wood.

a tempo (a tem´pō) *adv., a.* (*Mus.*) in the original tempo or time.
18C. **Italian** in time. Cp. TEMPO.

athenaeum (athənē´əm), (*N Am.*)
atheneum *n.* **1** a literary or scientific club or institution. **2** a literary club-room, a public reading-room or library.
18C. **Latin** *Athenaeum*, from Greek *Athēnaion* temple of Athene in ancient Athens, where teachers taught and speakers and writers declaimed.

atman (aht´mən) *n.* in Hinduism, the innermost self, the soul or the Universal Soul, the supreme spiritual principle.
18C. **Sanskrit** *ātman* breath, soul.

à travers (a traveə´) *prep.* across, through, athwart.
19C. **French**, lit. by traverse.
• The phrase to some extent replaces obsolete English *a-travers* (14–15C).

atrium (at´riəm, ā´-) *n.* (*pl.* **atria, atriums**) **1** the central court in an ancient Roman house. **2** a central hall rising the whole height of a large building and usu. with a glass roof and galleries on the upper floors. **3** a central hall or glazed court with rooms opening off it. **4** a forecourt or vestibule in front of a church. **5** (*Anat.*) a body cavity esp. either of the two upper chambers of the heart into which the veins pour the blood.
16C. **Latin**, of unknown orig.

à trois (a trwah´) *adv.* in a group of three, shared by three.
19C. **French**, from *à* to, by + *trois* three. Cp. À DEUX, MÉNAGE À TROIS.

attaché (ətash´ā) *n.* **1** a junior member of an ambassador's staff. **2** a specialist attached to an ambassador's staff.
3 (*N Am.*) an attaché case.
19C. **French**, p.p. of *attacher* to attach.

attar (at´ə), **otto** (ot´ō) *n.* a fragrant essence, or essential oil, esp. of roses.
17C. **Persian** ʿitr, or from Arabic ʿiṭr, coll. Arabic ʿaṭar perfume, essence.

attentat (atāta´) *n.* an attack, an attempted assassination.
17C. **French**, from Medieval Latin *attentatum*, neut. p.p. (used as n.) of *attentare*, var. of Latin *attemptare* to attempt. Cp. English *attempt* (on the life of).

aubade (ōbahd´) *n.* **1** a poem or musical piece announcing or greeting dawn. **2** music performed at daybreak.
17C. **French**, from Spanish *albada*, from *alba* dawn.

auberge (ōbœzh´, -beəzh´) *n.* an inn in France.
16C. **French**, from Provençal *alberga* lodging, rel. to German *Herberge* inn, from Old High German *heriberga* army shelter.

aubergine (ō´bəzhēn) *n*. **1** the eggplant, *Solanum melongena*. **2** its ovoid, characteristically dark purple fruit used as a vegetable and in stews. **3** a dark purple colour.
18C. French, from Catalan *alberginia*, from Arabic *al-bāḍinjān*, from *al* the + Persian *bādingān*, from Sanskrit *vātiṃgaṇa*.

AUC *abbr*. (in Roman dates) from the foundation of the city.
Latin *ab urbe condita*, lit. from the founded city, with ref. to Rome.
• The dates were calculated from 753 BC, a year arbitrarily fixed by Varro.

au contraire (ō kontreə´) *adv*. on the contrary.
18C. French, from *au* on the + *contraire* contrary.

au courant (ō koorā´) *a*. fully informed, up to date with the situation.
18C. French in the current.

au fait (ō fā´) *a*. **1** having up-to-date knowledge, fully informed. **2** familiar, well acquainted (with).
18C. French to the fact.

Aufklärung (owf´kleərung) *n*. the Enlightenment, an 18th-cent. philosophical movement which stressed the importance of rationality and questioned tradition.
19C. German, lit. clearing up, from *auf* up + *klar* clear.

au fond (ō fõ´) *adv*. basically.
18C. French at the bottom.

auf Wiedersehen (owf vē´dəzān) *int*. farewell, goodbye.
19C. German to the seeing again, from *auf* to + *wieder* again + *sehen* to see.
Cp. ARRIVEDERCI, AU REVOIR.

au grand sérieux (ō grã seriœ´) *adv*. in all seriousness (in reference to a matter that one would not normally take seriously).
19C. French, lit. to the great serious.

au gratin (ō grat´i) *a*. (of a dish) with a light crust, usu. made by browning breadcrumbs and cheese.
19C. French with the GRATIN.

auguste (owgoost´), **august** *n*. a type of circus clown who plays the role of the clumsy bungler.
early 20C. French, from German *August* the forename, from Latin *augustus* revered.
• The German forename came to mean fool, clown, presumably as an ironic use of the 'noble' original.

au naturel (ō natūərel´) *a., adv*. **1** in the natural state. **2** uncooked or plainly cooked. **3** (*coll., euphem.*) naked.
19C. French in the natural state.

au pair (ō peə´) *n*. a person, esp. a girl, from a foreign country who performs domestic tasks in exchange for board and lodging. ~*v.i*. to work as an au pair.
19C. French on equal terms.

au pied de la lettre (ō pye də la letr´, let´rə) *adv*. absolutely literally, down to the last detail.
18C. French, lit. to the foot of the letter.

aura (aw´rə) *n*. (*pl*. **auras, aurae** (-rē))
1 a distinctive atmosphere or quality.
2 a subtle emanation from any body, esp. a mystic light produced by and surrounding the body of a living creature which is said to be visible to people of supernormal sensitivity.
3 (*Med*.) a sensation (as of a current of cold air rising to the head) that precedes an attack in epilepsy, hysteria etc.
14–15C. Latin, from Greek breath, breeze.

aureole (aw´riōl), **aureola** (-rē´ələ) *n*.
1 the gold disc surrounding the head or

body in early pictures of religious figures, and denoting glory, a nimbus. **2** a glorifying halo, glory. **3** the halo round the moon in total eclipses of the sun, a corona. **4** a halo of radiating light round the sun or moon.

15C. French *auréole*, from Latin *aureola*, fem. of *aureolus*, dim. of *aureus* golden, from *aurum* gold.

au revoir (ō rəvwah´) *int.* farewell, goodbye.

17C. French to the seeing again, from *au* to the + *revoir* to see again. Cp. ARRIVEDERCI, AUF WIEDERSEHEN, HASTA LA VISTA, Russian *do svidaniya*, English *see you* (*later*).

aurora (awraw´rə) *n.* (*pl.* **auroras, aurorae** (-rē)) **1** a peculiar illumination of the night sky common within the polar circles, consisting of streams of light ascending towards the zenith. **2** (*poet.*) morning twilight, dawn.

14–15C. Latin *Aurora*, a goddess of the dawn in Roman mythology, from an Indo-European source that also gave English *east*.

aurora australis (awrawrə ostrah´lis) *n.* the aurora seen in the S hemisphere.

18C. Latin southern dawn.

● The term was based on AURORA BOREALIS.

aurora borealis (awrawrə bawriah´lis) *n.* the aurora seen in the N hemisphere.

18C. Latin northern dawn.

● The term was coined for the phenomenon in 1621 by the French physicist Pierre Gassendi (1592–1655).

au secours! (ō səkuə´) *int.* help!

19C. French, lit. to the aid, from *au* to the + *secours* aid, assistance, rel. to English *succour*.

Ausgleich (ows´glīkh) *n.* a settlement, an agreement, esp. that concluded between Austria and Hungary in 1867.

19C. German, lit. balancing out, from *aus* out + *gleich* same, equal.

Auslese (ows´lāzə) *n.* a usu. sweetish white wine from Germany or Austria made from selected ripe grapes.

19C. German, from *aus* out + *Lese* picking, vintage.

auspex (aws´peks) *n.* in ancient Rome, a person who took the auspices; an augur.

16C. Latin, from *avispex*, from *avis* bird + *-spex* observer, from *specere* to look.

aut Caesar, aut nihil (owt sē´zə owt nī´hil, ni-) *int.* all or nothing, either complete success or utter failure.

17C. Latin, lit. either Caesar or nothing.

● The expression is attributed to the emperor Caligula (AD 12–41): *aut frugi hominem esse oportere dictitans, aut Caesarem* 'he was always saying that one must either be thrifty, or Caesar' (Suetonius *Caligula* xxxvii). The implications of these words are quite different, however.

auteur (ōtœ´, aw-) *n.* a film director who is thought of as having a more than usually dominant role in the creation of their films and a unique personal style.

mid-20C. French author.

autobahn (aw´təbahn) *n.* a motorway in Germany, Austria or Switzerland.

mid-20C. German, from *Auto* automobile + *Bahn* road.

auto-da-fé (awtōdafā´) *n.* (*pl.* **autos-da-fé** (awtō-)) **1** a sentence pronounced by the Inquisition. **2** the execution of this judgement. **3** the burning of a heretic.

18C. Portuguese act of faith, from *auto* act + *da* of + *fé* faith.

automat (aw´təmat) *n.* **1** a vending machine. **2** (*N Am.*) a restaurant or room equipped with automatic machines for supplying food etc.

17C. German, from French *automate*, from Latin AUTOMATON.

automaton (awtom´ətən) *n.* (*pl.* **automatons, automata** (-tə)) **1** a machine that is activated by a concealed mechanism and power source within itself, a robot. **2** a machine of this kind that simulates human or animal actions. **3** a person who acts mechanically or leads a life of monotonous routine.
17C. Latin, from Greek, from neut. (used as n.) of *automatos* acting of itself, from *autos* self + -*matos* thinking, animated.

autopista (awtōpēs´tə) *n.* a motorway in Spain.
mid-20C. Spanish, from *auto* automobile + *pista* track, PISTE.

autoroute (aw´tōroot) *n.* a motorway in France.
mid-20C. French, from *auto* automobile + *route* road.

autostrada (aw´tōstrahdə) *n.* a motorway in Italy.
early 20C. Italian, from *auto* automobile + *strada* road.

autres temps, autres moeurs (ōtrə tã´, ōtrə mœ´) *int.* other days, other ways, one should adapt one's behaviour according to the circumstances.
early 20C. French, lit. other times, other customs. Cp. MOEURS.
● The French expression corresponds to English 'when in Rome, do as the Romans do'.

Av (av), **Ab** (ab) *n.* the fifth ecclesiastical month, or eleventh civil month of the Jewish year (corresponding roughly with August).
18C. Hebrew *'āb*.

avalanche (av´əlahnsh) *n.* **1** a mass of snow, ice and debris falling or sliding from the upper parts of a mountain.

2 a sudden overwhelming arrival or build-up. **3** the cumulative production of charged particles resulting from the collisions of a single charged particle with matter to produce further particles which in turn collide etc. ~*v.i.* to descend or arrive like an avalanche. ~*v.t.* to overwhelm as or like an avalanche.
18C. French, from Romansh, alt. of dial. *lavanche* (of unknown orig.) blended with *avaler* to descend.

avant (avã´) *adv., a.* before, in front.
French before, ult. from Latin *ab* from + *ante* before.

avant-garde (avãgahd´) *a.* **1** in advance of contemporary artistic tastes or trends; experimental, progressive. **2** radical, daring. ~*n.* the people who create or take up avant-garde or experimental ideas, esp. in the arts.
14–15C. French AVANT + *garde* guard.

avanti! (avan´ti) *int.* forward!, carry on!, go ahead!, keep going!
early 20C. Italian in front, before, ahead. Cp. EN AVANT.
● The word became familiar from the watchword of Mussolini (1883–1945), *Avanti popoli* forward with the people.

avant la lettre (avã la letr´, let´rə) *adv.* before the idea was thought of, in advance of one's time.
mid-20C. French, lit. before the letter.

avant-propos (avãprəpō´) *n.* preface, preliminary matter.
early 20C. French, lit. before-talk, from *avant* before + *propos* talk, discourse. Cp. English 'foreword'.

avatar (av´ətah) *n.* **1** in Hinduism, the descent of a god or released soul to earth. **2** the incarnation of a Hindu god; incarnation. **3** a manifestation, a phase. **4** an archetypal example of a concept or principle.

18C. Sanskrit *avatāra* descent, from *ava* down, away + *tār-* to pass over.

ave atque vale (ahvā atkwi vah´lā) *int.*
1 hail and farewell, hello and goodbye.
2 (*facet.*) a greeting to someone seen only briefly.
19C. Latin, from *ave* hail + *atque* and + *vale* farewell.
• The words conclude Catullus' poem addressed to his dead brother, *Atque in perpetuum, frater, ave atque vale* 'And for all time, brother, hail and farewell' (*Carmina* CI) (1C BC).

Ave Maria (ahvā məri´ə) *n.* **1** the Hail Mary; the angelical salutation (Luke i.28) with that of St Elisabeth (i.42), to which a prayer is added, the whole being used as a form of devotion. **2** the ave-bell.
12–14C. Latin hail, Mary.

Avesta (əves´tə) *n.* the sacred scriptures of Zoroastrianism.
19C. Persian, from Pahlavi *âvistâk* lore. Cp. ZEND.

avgolemono (avgəlem´ənō) *n.* Greek chicken soup made with egg yolks and lemon.
mid-20C. Modern Greek *augo* egg + *lemono* lemon.

avizandum (avizan´dəm) *n.* (*Sc. Law*)
1 private consideration by a judge or court before passing judgement. **2** a period of time given to this.
17C. Medieval Latin, neut. ger. of *avizare* to consider, to advise.

avocado (avəkah´dō) *n.* (*pl.* **avocados**)
1 (*also* **avocado pear**) the pear-shaped fruit of a Central American tree, *Persea americana*. **2** this tree. **3** a green colour, either a dull green resembling the skin or a light green resembling the flesh of the fruit. ~*a.* of the colour avocado.
17C. Spanish, alt. (influ. by *avocado*

lawyer, advocate) of *aguacate*, from Nahuatl *ahuacatl*.

avoirdupois (avwahdoopwah´, -dū-, avədəpoiz´) *n.* **1** a system of weights based on the unit of a pound of 16 ounces, equal to 7000 grains (0.4536 kilograms). **2** (*esp. N Am.*) weight, heaviness.
12–14C. Old French *aveir de peis* goods of weight, from *aveir* (Modern French *avoir*), use as n. of *avoir* to have (from Latin *habere* to have) + *de* of + *peis*, *pois* (Modern French *poids*) weight.

à votre santé! (a votrə sātā´) *int.* your health!, cheers!
early 20C. French to your health, from *à* to + *votre* your + *santé* health.
• A similar drinking toast exists in other languages, e.g. Italian *a vostra salute*, Russian *za vashe zdorov'ye*. Cp. SLAINTE.

awheto (əwā´tō), **aweto** *n.* (*pl.* **awhetos**, **awetos**) (*New Zeal.*) a caterpillar affected with a parasitic fungus, from the dried body of which a tattoo dye is obtained.
19C. Maori.

ayah (ī´ə) *n.* a nurse for European children or a maidservant in a European household in the Indian subcontinent or in other former British territories.
18C. Portuguese *aia*, fem. of *aio* tutor.

ayatollah (īətol´ə) *n.* a leader of the Shiite Muslims in Iran.
mid-20C. Persian, from Arabic *'āyatu-llāh* sign of God, from *āya* sign, model + ALLAH.

ayurveda (ahyəvā´də, -vē´də) *n.* an ancient Hindu system of medicine, health and healing.
early 20C. Sanskrit *āyur-veda* science of life. See VEDA.

B

baas (bahs) *n.* (*S Afr.*) boss, overseer.
17C. **Dutch** master.

baba (bah´bah) *n.* (**rum baba**) a small
cake soaked in rum.
19C. **French**, from Polish (married)
peasant woman.

babiche (babēsh´) *n.* (*Can.*) laces or
thongs made of rawhide.
19C. **Canadian French**, from Micmac
a:papi:č.

babouche (bəboosh´), **babuche** *n.* a
Turkish heel-less slipper.
17C. **French**, from Arabic *bābūj*, from
Persian *pāpūš*, from *pa* foot + *pūš*
covering.

babu (bah´boo), **baboo** *n.* (*pl.* **babus,
baboos**) 1 in the Indian subcontinent,
Hindu gentleman, a respectful title
corresponding to English Mr. 2 (*Ang.-
Ind., offensive*) an Indian clerk who
writes English; a Bengali with a
superficial English education.
18C. **Hindi** *bābū* father, ult. of imit. orig.
Cp. ABBA.

babushka (bəboosh´kə) *n.* 1 a
grandmother, an old woman. 2 a
Russian triangular headscarf.
mid-20C. **Russian** grandmother, dim. of
baba old woman. Cp. BABA.

baccarat (bak´ərah), **baccara** *n.* a
gambling card game between banker and
punters.
19C. **French** *baccara*, of unknown orig.

bach (bahkh) *n.* a dear, a little one, a
friend (usu. as a term of address).
19C. **Welsh** (dial.), lit. little.

Backfisch (bak´fish) *n.* (*pl.* **Backfische**
(-fish·ə)) a teenage girl.
19C. **German**, lit. fish for frying, from
backen to bake, to fry + *Fisch* fish. Cp.
English 'small fry'.

badinage (bad´inahzh, -nij) *n.* light
good-humoured, playful talk, banter.
17C. **French**, from *badiner* to joke, from
badin fool, from Late Latin *badare* to
gape.

bagarre (bagah´) *n.* a tumult, a scuffle, a
brawl.
19C. **French**, from Provençal *bagarro*.

bagasse (bəgas´) *n.* 1 the refuse products
in sugar-making. 2 cane-trash.
19C. **French**, from Spanish *bagazo*
residue.

bagatelle (bagətel´) *n.* 1 a game played
on a nine-holed board with pins
obstructing the holes, with nine balls
to be struck into them. 2 a trifle, a
negligible amount. 3 (*Mus.*) a light piece
of music.

17C. French, from Italian *bagatella*, prob. dim. of Latin *baca* berry, or Italian *baga* baggage.

bagel (bā´gəl) *n.* a ring-shaped bread roll.
early 20C. Yiddish *beygel*, from Germanic.

bagnio (ban´yō) *n.* (*pl.* **bagnios**) **1** a brothel. **2** an oriental prison for slaves. **3** a bathing-house, a bath.
16C. Italian *bagno*, from Latin *balneum* bath.
• Sense 2 is said to derive from a former Roman bath at Constantinople, converted into a prison.

baguette (baget´), **baguet** *n.* **1** a narrow stick of French bread. **2** a precious stone cut into a rectangular shape. **3** (*Archit.*) a small semicircular moulding.
18C. French, from Italian *bacchetto*, dim. of *bacchio*, from Latin *baculum* staff.

bahadur (bəhah´duə) *n.* a ceremonious title formerly given in India to officers and distinguished officials.
18C. Urdu and Persian *bahādur*, from Mongolian *baatar* brave, hero.
• The English soldier Lord Roberts, 1832–1914, was nicknamed Bobs Bahadur.

baht (baht) *n.* (*pl.* **baht**) the standard unit of currency in Thailand.
18C. Thai *bāt.*

baignoire (bānwah´) *n.* a box at the theatre on the lowest tier.
19C. French bath tub. Cp. BAGNIO.
• The French *baignoire* was originally a dressing room at a public bath.

bain-marie (bīmərē´) *n.* (*pl.* **bains-marie** (bī-)) a vessel of boiling water into which saucepans are put for slow heating; a double saucepan.
18C. French, translating Medieval Latin *balneum Mariae*, translating Medieval

Greek *kaminos Marias* Maria's furnace, from Maria the Jewess, legendary alchemist.

Bairam (bīram´) *n.* either of two Muslim festivals following the Ramadan, the *Lesser* lasting three days, the *Greater*, which falls seventy days later, lasting four days.
16C. Obsolete Turkish *baïrām* (now *bayram*), ult. from Persian *baẓrām*.

bajada (bəhah´də), **bahada** *n.* a broad slope of alluvial deposit at the foot of an escarpment.
19C. Spanish descent, slope, from *bajar* to lower, to go down.

bajra (bahj´rə) *n.* a type of Indian millet.
19C. Hindi *bājrā.*

baklava (bəklah´və), **baclava** *n.* a cake made from layered pastry strips with nuts and honey.
17C. Turkish.

baksheesh (bak´shēsh) *n.* a gratuity, a tip (used without the article).
18C. Persian *bakšīš*, from *bakšīdan* to give.

balalaika (baləlī´kə) *n.* a three-stringed triangular-shaped musical instrument resembling a guitar.
18C. Russian, prob. imit. of sound.

balboa (balbō´ə) *n.* the unit of currency in Panama.
early 20C. Vasco Núñez de *Balboa*, *c.*1475–1519, Spanish explorer and discoverer of the Pacific Ocean.

bal costumé (bal kostümā´) *n.* (*pl.* **bals costumés** (bal kostümā´)) a fancy-dress ball.
19C. French, lit. costumed ball.

ballade (bəlahd´) *n.* **1** a poem consisting of three eight-lined stanzas rhyming *a b a b b c b c,* each having the same line

as a refrain, and with an envoy of four lines, an old form revived in the 19th cent. **2** (*Mus.*) a short lyrical piano piece or similar composition.
14–15C. French, from Provençal *balada* dance, song to dance to, from *balar* to dance.

ballerina (baləre´nə) *n.* (*pl.* **ballerinas**, **ballerine** (-nā)) a female ballet dancer; a female dancer taking a leading part in a ballet.
18C. Italian, fem. of *ballerino* dancing master, from *ballare* to dance.

ballet (bal´ā, -li) *n.* **1** a form of dramatic representation consisting of dancing and mime to set steps. **2** an example of this. **3** a piece or suite of music for this. **4** a company performing this.
17C. French, from Italian *balletto*, dim. of *ballo* ball.

ballista (bəlis´tə) *n.* (*pl.* **ballistae** (-ē), **ballistas**) a military engine used in ancient times for hurling stones, darts and other missiles.
16C. Latin, ult. from Greek *ballein* to throw.

ballon d'essai (balō desā´) *n.* (*pl.* **ballons d'essai** (balō)) a trial balloon, an initial experiment used to ascertain public opinion before implementation of a new policy, procedure etc.
19C. French trial balloon.
● The original sense was a small balloon sent up to determine the direction of the wind before a passenger balloon ascended.

bal masqué (bal maskā´) *n.* (*pl.* **bals masqués** (bal maskā´)) a masked ball.
18C. French, from *bal* ball + p.p. of *masquer* to mask.

balsa (bawl´sə) *n.* **1** an American tropical tree, *Ochroma lagopus*. **2** balsa wood.
17C. Spanish raft.

balti (bal´ti) *n.* a type of curry composed of meat and vegetables cooked in an iron pot.
late 20C. Hindi *bāltī* bucket, scoop, from shape of dish in which cooked.

bambino (bambē´nō) *n.* (*pl.* **bambinos**, **bambini** (-ni)) **1** a child, a baby. **2** an image of the infant Jesus in the crib, exhibited at Christmas in Roman Catholic churches.
18C. Italian, dim. of *bambo* silly. Cp. BIMBO.

banc (bangk), **banco** (-ō) *n.* (*Law*) the judicial bench.
18C. Latin *in banco* on the bench.

banco (bang´kō) *n.* bank money of account, as distinguished from ordinary currency.
18C. Italian bank.

bandeau (ban´dō) *n.* (*pl.* **bandeaux** (-dōz)) **1** a narrow band or fillet for the head. **2** a bandage.
18C. French, from Old French *bandel*, dim. of *bande* band.

banderilla (bandərē´yə, -rēl´-) *n.* a little dart ornamented with ribbons, which bullfighters stick in the neck of the bull.
18C. Spanish, dim. of *bandera* banner.

banderole (ban´dərōl), **banderol** *n.* **1** a long narrow flag with a cleft end flying at a masthead. **2** any small ornamental streamer. **3** the small square of silk hanging from a trumpet. **4** a flat band with an inscription, used in the decoration of buildings of the Renaissance period.
16C. French *banerole*, later *banderole*, from Italian *banderuola*, dim. of *bandiera* banner.

banket (bang´kit, -ket´) *n.* a gold-bearing conglomerate.
19C. Afrikaans almond toffee.
● The rock is so named from its colour.

banlieue (bãˊlyœ) *n.* **1** the territory outside the walls but within the jurisdiction of a town or city. **2** suburbs, precincts.
19C. French, from Latin *banleuca*, from *bannus* ban + *leuca* league.

bannerol (banˊərōl) *n.* a banner about a yard or metre square, borne at the funeral of eminent personages and placed over the tomb.
16C. French, earlier form of BANDEROLE.

banquette (bāketˊ) *n.* **1** a built-in cushioned seat along a wall. **2** a bank behind a parapet on which soldiers mount to fire. **3** the long seat behind the driver in a French diligence.
17C. French, from Italian *banchetta*, dim. of *banca* bench, shelf.

banshee (banˊshē) *n.* a supernatural being, supposed in Ireland and the Scottish Highlands to wail round a house when one of the inmates is about to die.
17C. Irish *bean sídhe*, from Old Irish *ben síde*, from *ben* woman + *síde* of the fairies.

banyan (banˊyan), **banian** (-yən) *n.*
1 a Hindu merchant or shop-keeper, a Bengali broker or hawker. **2** a loose morning-gown or jacket. **3** the banyan tree.
16C. Portuguese, from Gujarati *vāṇiyo* man of the trading caste, from Sanskrit *vāṇija* merchant.
• The banyan tree came to be so called by Europeans from a particular tree under which traders had built a pagoda.

banzai (banzīˊ, banˊ-) *int.* a Japanese battle-cry, patriotic salute or cheer. ~*a.* reckless.
19C. Japanese ten thousand years (of life to you). Cp. Chinese *wàn* ten thousand, *suì* year.

barbette (bahbetˊ) *n.* **1** a mound of earth in a fortification on which guns are mounted to be fired over the parapet. **2** a platform for a similar purpose on a warship.
18C. French, from *barbe* beard + dim. suf. *-ette*.

barcarole (bahkərōlˊ), **barcarolle** *n.*
1 a song sung by Venetian gondoliers. **2** a composition of a similar kind.
18C. French *barcarolle*, from Italian (Venetian) *barcarola* gondolier, from *barca* boat.

barchan (bahˊkən) *n.* a shifting sand dune in the shape of a crescent.
19C. Turkic *barkhan*.

barège (barezhˊ) *n.* a light gauzy dress fabric.
19C. French, from *Barèges*, a village in SW France, where orig. made.

bargan (bahgˊən), **barragan** (barˊə-) *n.* a boomerang.
19C. Australian Aboriginal.

bar mitzvah (bah mitsˊvə) *n.* **1** a Jewish boy who has reached the age of religious responsibility, usu. on his 13th birthday. **2** the ceremony and celebration marking this event.
19C. Hebrew *bar miṣwāh* son of commandment. Cp. BAT MITZVAH.

barouche (bərooshˊ) *n.* a double-seated four-wheeled horse-drawn carriage, with a movable top, and a seat outside for the driver.
19C. German (dial.) *Barutsche*, from Italian *baroccio* two-wheeled, ult. from Latin *birotus*, from *bi-* two + *rota* wheel. Cp. French *brouette* wheelbarrow.

barracan (barˊəkən), **baracan** *n.*
1 (*Hist.*) a coarse cloth resembling camlet. **2** a thin silky material.
17C. French *barracan*, *bouracan*, from Arabic *burrukān*, from Persian *barak* cloak made of camel's hair.

barranca (bərang´kə) n. (pl. **barrancas**) (NAm.) a deep gorge, with steep sides.
17C. Spanish.

barre (bah) n. a wall-mounted horizontal rail used for ballet exercises.
early 20C. French bar.

barré (bar´ā) n. (Mus.) the laying of a finger across a particular fret of a guitar etc., to raise the pitch for the chord being played.
19C. French, p.p. of barrer to bar.

barrette (bəret´) n. (NAm.) a hair-clasp.
early 20C. French, dim. of BARRE.

barrico (bərē´kō) n. (pl. **barricoes**) a small cask, a keg.
16C. Spanish barrica cask.

barrio (bar´iō) n. (pl. **barrios**) a Spanish-speaking community or district, usu. sited in the poorer areas of cities in the SW US.
19C. Spanish, ? from Arabic.

bas-bleu (bahblœ´) a. **1** wearing blue worsted stockings, applied (contemptuously) to a literary society that met at Montagu House, London, in the latter part of the 18th cent. **2** (of women) affecting learning or literary tastes. ~n. a woman affecting learning or literary tastes.
18C. French blue stocking.
• The French phrase is a translation of English blue stocking.

bascule (bas´kūl) n. **1** an apparatus on the principle of the lever, in which the depression of one end raises the other. **2** a bascule bridge.
17C. French see-saw, from stem of battre to beat + cul buttocks.

bashibazouk (bashibəzook´) n. (Hist.) a Turkish irregular soldier, noted for lawlessness and atrocious brutality.
19C. Turkic baş´bozuk wrong-headed, from baş head + bozuk out of order.

basho (bash´ō) n. (pl. **basho, bashos**) a tournament in sumo wrestling.
late 20C. Japanese place.

basilica (bəsil´ikə, -zil´-) n. (pl. **basilicas**) **1** a large oblong building with double colonnades and an apse, used as a court of justice and an exchange. **2** such a building used as a Christian church. **3** a church built on the same plan. **4** any one of the seven principal churches of Rome founded by Constantine the Great (4th cent.). **5** a church having special privileges granted by the Pope.
16C. Latin royal palace, from Greek basilikē, fem. (used as n.) of basilikos royal, from basileus king.

basmati (basmah´ti) n. a type of rice with a slender grain, delicate fragrance and nutty flavour.
19C. Hindi bāsmatī fragrant.

bas-relief (bahrəlēf´, bas-) n. **1** low relief, a kind of sculpture in which the figures project less than one half of their true proportions above the plane forming the background. **2** a carving in low relief.
17C. French, from Italian BASSO-RELIEVO.

bassinet (basinet´) n. **1** an oblong wicker basket with a hood at the end, used as a cradle. **2** a pram of similar shape.
16C. French, dim. of bassin basin.

basso (bas´ō) n. (pl. **bassos, bassi** (-si)) a bass singer.
18C. Italian, from Latin bassus low.

basso profundo (basō profun´dō) n. (pl. **basso profundos, bassi profundi** (basi profun´di)) **1** the lowest bass voice. **2** a singer with such a voice.
19C. Italian deep bass, from basso bass + profundo deep.

basso-relievo (basōrəlyä´vō) *n.* (*pl.*
basso-relievos) **1** low relief, bas-relief.
2 a sculpture in low relief.
17C. Italian *basso-rilievo*, from *basso*
low (see BASSO) + *rilievo* RELIEVO.

basta! (bas´ta) *int.* enough!; stop!; it
doesn't matter!
16C. Italian, from *bastare* to be enough,
to suffice, from Popular Latin to bear,
to support, from Greek *bastazein* to bear,
to carry.

bastide (bastēd´) *n.* a country house in
S France.
18C. French, from Provençal *bastida*,
fem. p.p. (used as n.) of *bastir* to build.
● An early 16C sense in English was
fortified town.

bastille (bastēl´) *n.* (*Hist.*) **1** a fortified
tower. **2** (*Mil.*) a small wooden fort.
3 any one of a series of huts defended
by entrenchments. **4** a prison, a
workhouse.
14–15C. Old French, from *bastide*, from
Provençal *bastida*, fem. p.p. (used as n.)
of *bastir* to build.
● The word is familiar from the Bastille,
Paris, a 14C fortress used as a state
prison in the 17C and 18C. Its storming
by the mob on 14 July 1789 marked the
start of the French Revolution.

bastinado (bastinä´dō) *n.* (*pl.*
bastinadoes) **1** a method of corporal
punishment or torture inflicted with a
stick on the soles of the feet. **2** a rod, a
stick, a cudgel. ~*v.t.* (*ṁrd pers. sing. pres.*
bastinadoes, *pres.p.* **bastinadoing**,
past, p.p. **bastinadoed**) to beat with a
stick, esp. on the soles of the feet.
16C. Spanish *bastinada*, from *bastón*
stick, cudgel. See BATON.

basuco (bəsoo´kō) *n.* an impure form of
cocaine which is highly addictive.
late 20C. Colombian Spanish, ? rel. to
Spanish *bazucar* to shake vigorously.

batata (bətah´tə) *n.* the sweet potato.
16C. Spanish, from Taino.

bateau (bat´ō) *n.* (*pl.* **bateaux** (-z)) a
long, light, flat-bottomed river-boat,
tapering at both ends, used in Canada.
18C. French boat, from Old English, or
from Scandinavian.

bateau-mouche (batōmoosh´) *n.* (*pl.*
bateaux-mouches (batōmoosh´)) a
riverboat for sightseers on the Seine in
Paris.
early 20C. French, lit. fly-boat, from
bateau boat + *mouche* fly.
● The name alludes to the small size of
the landing stages.

bateleur (batəlœ´), **bateleur eagle** *n.* an
African eagle, *Terathopius ecaudatus*,
having a short tail and a crest.
19C. French juggler, mountebank.
● The bird is so named for its tilting
motion in flight.

bath (bath) *n.* a liquid measure among
the ancient Hebrews, containing about
6½ gallons.
14–15C. Hebrew *baṭ*.

bathos (bā´thos) *n.* **1** ridiculous descent
from the sublime to the commonplace
in writing or speech. **2** anticlimax.
17C. Greek depth.
● Sense 1 was introduced by Pope in
the treatise *Peri Bathous, or the Art of
Sinking in Poetry* (1727), the title being
a parody on Longinus' *Peri Huphous*
('On the Sublime') (1C AD).

batik (bat´ik, bətēk´) *n.* **1** a method of
printing designs on fabric by masking
areas to be left undyed with wax.
2 fabric or a piece of cloth produced by
this method.
19C. Javanese painted.

batiste (bətēst´) *n.* a fine cotton or linen
fabric. ~*a.* made of batiste.

19C. **French**, earlier *batiche*, ? from base of *battre* to beat.
• According to some, the word is from *Baptiste* of Cambray, the original maker (13C).

bat mitzvah (baht mits´və) *n.* **1** a Jewish girl who has reached the age (usu. twelve years) of religious responsibility. **2** the celebrations marking this event.
mid-20C. **Hebrew** *baṭ miṣwāh* daughter of commandment, based on BAR MITZVAH.

baton (bat´on, bat´ən) *n.* **1** the wand used by a conductor of an orchestra etc. in beating time. **2** a short stick transferred between successive team-mates in a relay-race. **3** a knobbed staff carried and swung into the air at the head of a parade or twirled by majorettes etc. **4** a truncheon used as a weapon. **5** a staff or club. **6** a bar marking divisions on the face of a clock etc. **7** (*Her.*) a diminutive of the bend sinister, used in English coats of arms as a badge of bastardy.
~*v.t.* to strike with a policeman's baton or truncheon.
16C. **French** *bâton*, earlier *baston*, from Late Latin *bastum* stick.

battement (bat´mā) *n.* (*pl.* **battements** (bat´mā)) a beating leg movement in dancing.
19C. **French** beating. Cp. BATTERIE.

batterie (batrē´) *n.* (*pl.* **batteries** (batrē´)) a movement in which the feet are beaten together in a leap in dancing.
19C. **French** beating, from *battre* to beat.

battue (batoo´) *n.* **1** driving game from cover by beating the bushes. **2** a shoot on this plan. **3** a wholesale slaughter.
18C. **French**, fem. p.p. (used as n.) of *battre* to beat.

battuta (batoo´tə) *n.* (*pl.* **battute** (-tā)) (*Mus.*) **1** a bar. **2** the beating of time.
18C. **Italian**, from *battere* to beat.

Bauhaus (bow´hows) *n.* (the principles of) a radical German school of architecture and the arts founded in 1919 and dedicated to achieving a functional synthesis of art design and technology.
early 20C. **German** house of building, from *Bau* building + *Haus* house, inversion of *Hausbau* building of a house.

bavaroise (bavəwahz´, bavarwahz´), **bavarois** (bavəwah´, bavarwah´) *n.* a cold dessert containing cream and set custard.
19C. **French**, fem. (used as n.) of a. *bavarois* Bavarian.
• The dish is said to have been brought to France by a French chef who had been working in Bavaria.

bayadère (bayadeə´) *n.* a Hindu dancing girl.
16C. **French**, from Portuguese *bailadeira*, from *bailar* to dance. Cp. BALLET.

bayou (bī´yoo) *n.* (*N Am.*) **1** the outlet of a lake or river. **2** a sluggish watercourse.
18C. **American French**, from Choctaw *bayuk*.

bazaar (bəzah´) *n.* **1** an Eastern market place, where goods of all descriptions are offered for sale. **2** a sale of useful or ornamental articles, often handmade or second-hand, in aid of charity. **3** a shop where a variety of (ornamental) goods are sold.
16C. **Italian** *bazarro*, from Turkish, from Persian *bāzār* market.

Béarnaise (bāənāz´) *n.* a rich sauce made with egg yolks, lemon juice or wine vinegar, herbs and shallots.
19C. **French**, fem. of *béarnais* of Béarn, a region of SW France.

beau (bō) *n.* (*pl.* **beaus** (bōz), **beaux** (bō, bōz)) **1** a woman's lover. **2** a man unduly

attentive to dress and social fashions.
~*v.t.* **1** to act as beau to. **2** to escort.
17C. French, a. used as n., ult. from
Latin *bellus* fine, beautiful. Cp. BELLE.

beau geste (bō zhest) *n.* (*pl.* **beaux
gestes** (bō zhest)) a display of
magnanimity, a generous act.
early 20C. French fine gesture.
● Beau Geste is the nickname of
Michael Geste, the fictional young
Englishman who joins the French
foreign legion and has gruelling
adventures in the desert in P.C. Wren's
best-selling romantic novel *Beau Geste*
(1924).

beau idéal (bō idäahl´) *n.* an ideal of
excellence or beauty, a perfect model.
19C. French, lit. ideal beauty.
● The phrase is sometimes
misinterpreted as meaning 'beautiful
ideal', but French *beau* is a noun and
idéal the adjective describing it.

Beaujolais (bō´zhəlā) *n.* a usu. red, light
Burgundy wine from the Beaujolais
district.
19C. French *Beaujolais*, a district of
SE France.

beau monde (bō mond´, mōd´) *n.*
fashionable society.
17C. French, lit. fine world.

Beaune (bōn) *n.* a usu. red Burgundy
wine.
19C. French *Beaune*, a town in E France.

beau sabreur (bō sabrœ´) *n.* (*pl.* **beaux
sabreurs** (bō sabrœ´)) a dashing
adventurer.
19C. French, lit. handsome swordsman.
● *Le Beau Sabreur* was the nickname of
Joachim Murat (1767–1815), renowned
French cavalry officer and king of
Naples (1808–15). *Beau Sabreur* (1926)
was subsequently the title of a P.C. Wren
novel, the sequel to *Beau Geste*,
concerning Beau's brother John.

beaux arts (bōz ah´) *n.pl.* fine arts.
19C. French *beaux-arts* fine arts,
beautiful arts.
● The current sense was promoted by
Charles Batteux' *Les Beaux-Arts réduits à
un même principe* (1746), in which he
divided the arts into the useful, the
beautiful (sculpture, painting, music,
poetry) and those which combined the
useful and the beautiful (architecture,
eloquence).

beaux yeux (bōz yœ´) *n.pl.* beautiful
eyes, admiring glances, favourable
regard.
19C. French beautiful eyes.

bebung (bā´bung) *n.* (*Mus.*) a technique
in clavichord playing whereby the pitch
of a sustained note is varied by altering
the pressure of the fingertip.
19C. German trembling, from *beben* to
shake, to tremble.

beccafico (bekəfē´kō) *n.* (*pl.* **beccaficos**)
a small migratory songbird, of the genus
Sylvia, eaten as a delicacy in continental
Europe.
17C. Italian, from *beccare* to peck + *fico*
fig.
● The bird is regarded as a delicacy
when fattened on figs and grapes.

béchamel (bā´shəmel) *n.* a white sauce
made with cream or milk and flavoured
with onions and herbs.
18C. French, from Louis, Marquis de
Béchamel, 1630–1703, steward of Louis
XIV of France, its inventor.

bêche-de-mer (beshdəmeə´) *n.* (*pl.*
bêche-de-mer, bêches-de-mer (besh-))
1 the sea-slug or trepang, *Holothuria
edulis*, an echinoderm eaten by the
Chinese. **2** a creole spoken in the
W Pacific, Beach-la-mar.
18C. Pseudo-French, from Portuguese
bicho do mar worm of the sea.
● Trade in trepang with the Chinese

was conducted in bêche-de-mer, also known as Beach-la-mar or Bislama.

Bedouin (bed′uin), **Beduin** *n.* (*pl.* **Bedouin, Beduin**) **1** a nomadic Arab, as distinguished from one living in a town. **2** a gypsy, a wanderer. ~*a.* **1** of or relating to the nomadic Arabs. **2** nomad. **14–15C. Old French** *beduin* (Modern French *bédouin*), from Arabic *badawī*, pl. *badawīn*, from *badw* desert.

beguine (bigēn′) *n.* music or dance in bolero rhythm, of South American or West Indian origin.
early 20C. American French, from French *béguin* flirtation, fancy, from Old French *beguine* BEGUINE.
• The original sense of French *béguin* was Beguine headdress, worn by members of the lay sisterhood of this name in the Low Countries, where their order was founded in the 12C.

begum (bā′gəm) *n.* **1** a queen, princess or lady of high rank in the Indian subcontinent. **2** (**Begum**) the title of a married Muslim woman.
17C. Urdu *begam*, from Early Turkic *begim*, from source of BEY + 1st pers. sing. poss. suf. *-im*.

beige (bāzh) *n.* **1** a light brownish yellow colour. **2** a fabric made of undyed and unbleached wool. ~*a.* **1** of a light brownish yellow. **2** †grey.
19C. French of unknown orig.
• The original French sense was the colour of natural wool. The word is unlikely to be related to Italian *bambagia* cotton wool.

bekah (bē′kah) *n.* an ancient Hebrew weight and coin, equivalent to half a shekel (Exod. xxxviii.26).
17C. Hebrew *beqa'*.

bel canto (bel kan′tō) *n.* a style of operatic singing characterized by purity of tone and exact phrasing.

19C. Italian fine song. Cp. BELLE, CANTO.

bel esprit (bel esprē′) *n.* (*pl.* **beaux esprits** (bōz esprē′)) **1** a person of genius. **2** a wit.
17C. French fine mind. Cp. BELLE, ESPRIT.

bel étage (bel etahzh′) *n.* the most splendid storey of a house, usu. the first floor.
19C. French fine floor.

belga (bel′gə) *n.* a former Belgian unit of exchange, equivalent to five francs.
mid-20C. Latin *Belga* a Belgian.

belle (bel) *n.* **1** a beautiful woman. **2** a reigning beauty.
17C. French, fem. of *bel* BEAU, from Latin *bella*, fem. of *bellus* beautiful, pretty, orig. dim. of *bonus* good.

belle âme (bel ahm′) *n.* a high-minded person, a lofty soul.
19C. French, lit. fine soul.

belle époque (bel āpok′) *n.* a period of comfortable living and prosperity.
mid-20C. French fine period.
• The expression originally applied in France to the years between *c.*1890 and the outbreak of World War I, corresponding to the Edwardian period in England.

belle laide (bel lād′) *n.* (*pl.* **belles laides** (bel lād′)) a woman who is attractive in spite of being ugly.
early 20C. French, from fem. of *beau* beautiful + *laid* ugly. Cp. JOLIE LAIDE.

belles-lettres (belletr′, -let′rə) *n.pl.* (*also constr. as sing.*) polite literature, the humanities, pure literature.
17C. French fine letters. Cp. BEAUX ARTS.

Bel Paese® (bel paā′zi) *n.* a mild Italian cream cheese.

early 20C. **Italian** beautiful country. Cp.
BELLE, PAYSAGE.

● The name was adopted from the title
of Antonio Stoppani's book *Il bel paese*
(1875), describing the Italian
countryside.

bema (bē´mə) *n.* **1** the sanctuary,
presbytery or chancel of a church. **2** the
platform from which Athenian orators
spoke.
17C. **Greek** *bēma* step, raised place.

ben (ben) *n.* a mountain peak in Scotland
etc.
18C. **Gaelic and Irish** *beann*
prominence, peak, height.

benedicite (benidī´siti) *int.* bless you,
good gracious. ~*n.* **1** the invocation of a
blessing. **2** grace before meat. **3** the Song
of the Three Holy Children, one of the
canticles in the Prayer Book. **4** (*Mus.*) a
setting of this.
14–15C. **Latin**, 2nd pers. pl. imper. of
benedicere to wish well to, to bless,
from *bene* well + *dicere* to say.
● The earliest sense was blessing,
deliverance.

bene esse (ben´i esi) *n.* well-being,
welfare.
17C. **Modern Latin**, from Latin *bene*
well + use as n. of *esse* to be.

bénéficiaire (benefisyeə´) *n.* a
beneficiary, one who profits by
something.
19C. **French**.

ben trovato (ben trōvah´tō) *a.* **1**
characteristic or appropriate, if not true.
2 well made up or invented.
19C. **Italian** well found.
● The phrase is familiar from the 16C
Italian saying *se non è vero, è molto ben
trovato* 'if it is not true, it is a happy
invention'.

ben venuto (ben venoo´tō) *int.* welcome.
19C. **Italian**, lit. well come, from *bene*
well + p.p. of *venire* to come. Cp French
bienvenu, English *welcome*.

berceuse (beəsœz´) *n.* (*pl.* **berceuses**
(beəsœz´)) **1** a lullaby, a cradle song. **2** a
piece of lulling instrumental music.
19C. **French**, from *bercer* to rock + fem.
suf. *-euse*.

beret (ber´ā) *n.* a round, brimless flat cap
fitting the head fairly closely.
19C. **French** *béret*, from dial. and Old
Provençal *berret*. See BIRETTA.

berg (bœg) *n.* (*S Afr.*) a mountain or hill
(often used in place names).
19C. **Afrikaans**, from Dutch mountain.

bergère (beəzheə´) *n.* (*pl.* **bergères**
(-zheə´)) a type of well-padded,
cushioned armchair.
18C. **French** shepherdess.
● The suggestion is of a soft seat
selected by a shepherdess when
guarding her sheep, the chair's
decorative colouring matching her dress.
Such chairs were popular in the 18C,
when there was a vogue for things
pastoral.

bergschrund (beəg´shrůnd) *n.* a
crevasse or fissure between the base of
a steep slope and a glacier or névé.
19C. **German**, from *Berg* mountain +
Schrund cleft, crevice.

beriberi (beriber´i, ber´-) *n.* a
degenerative disease due to a deficiency
of vitamin B1.
18C. **Sinhalese**, from *beri* weakness.

bersagliere (beəsalyeə´rā) *n.* (*pl.*
bersaglieri (-rē)) **1** a sharpshooter. **2** a
member of a crack corps in the Italian
army.
19C. **Italian**, from *bersaglio* target.

beta (bē´tə) *n.* **1** the second letter of the Greek alphabet (Β, β). **2** a second-class mark given to a student's work. **3** (*Astron.*) (**Beta**) the second star (in brightness or position) in a constellation. **4** the second of a series of numerous compounds and other enumerations.
12–14C. Latin, from Greek.

bête noire (bet nwah´) *n.* (*pl.* **bêtes noires** (bet nwah´)) a pet aversion.
19C. French black beast.

beth (beth) *n.* the second letter of the Hebrew alphabet.
12–14C. Hebrew *bēṯ* house, from orig. shape of letter.

bethel (beth´əl) *n.* **1** a Nonconformist chapel. **2** a mission room. **3** a seamen's church, esp. afloat.
17C. Hebrew *bēṯ-'el*, from *bēṯ* house (of) + *'el* god.
● The Hebrew word is translated as 'house of God' in Gen. xii.17–19.

bethesda (bithez´də) *n.* a Nonconformist chapel.
19C. *Bethesda*, name of pool in John v.2–4, from Aramaic *bēṯ* house (of) + *hesdā* grace, favour.

bêtise (betēz´) *n.* **1** a foolish act or remark. **2** folly.
19C. French stupidity, from *bête* foolish, from Old French *beste* beast.

beurre manié (bœ mahnyā´) *n.* a mixture of butter and flour added to a sauce to thicken it.
mid-20C. French handled butter.

bey (bā), **beg** (beg) *n.* (*Hist.*) a governor of a Turkish town, province or district.
16C. Turkish *beg*. Cp. BEGUM.

bezique (bizēk´) *n.* **1** a game of cards for two players, using a double pack. **2** the combination of the jack of diamonds and queen of spades in this game.
19C. French *bésigue*, ? from Persian *bāzīgar* acrobat, from *bāzī* game.

bhaji (bah´ji) *n.* (*pl.* **bhajis**) **1** an Indian vegetable dish. **2** a small cake or ball of vegetables mixed with gram flour and deep-fried.
mid-20C. Hindi *bhājī* fried vegetables.

bhakti (bŭk´ti) *n.* religious devotion as a means of salvation in Hinduism.
19C. Sanskrit.

bhang (bang), **bang** *n.* **1** the dried leaves of hemp, *Cannabis sativa.* **2** an intoxicating or stupefying liquor or drug made from these.
16C. Portuguese *bangue*, from Persian and Urdu *bang*, assim. to Hindi *bhāṅ*, from Sanskrit *bhaṅg*.

bhangra (bang´grə) *n.* music based on a fusion of Asian and contemporary pop music.
mid-20C. Punjabi *bhāngrā*, name of a traditional harvest dance.

bheesti (bēs´ti), **bheesty, bhistee, bhisti** *n.* (*pl.* **bheesties, bhistees, bhistis**) in the Indian subcontinent, a servant who supplies water to a house.
18C. Urdu *bhīstī*, from Persian *bihištī* person of paradise, prob. of facet. orig.

bibelot (bib´əlō) *n.* a small article of virtu, a knick-knack.
19C. French, from redupl. of *bel* beautiful. Cp. BON-BON.

bibliotheca (bibliōthē´kə) *n.* (*pl.* **bibliothecas, bibliothecae** (-kē)) **1** a library. **2** a bibliography.
19C. Latin, from Greek *bibliothēkē* library, from *biblion* book + *thēkē* repository. Cp. DISCOTHEQUE.
● Old English *bibliothēce* was the original name of the Bible in English.

bidet (bē´dā) *n.* a low basin for bathing the genital and anal area.
 17C. **French** pony, ass, from *bider* to trot, of unknown orig.
 • The basin is so called from the position of the user.

bidon (bidō´) *n.* (*pl.* **bidons** (-dō´)) a container for liquids, a petrol can, an oil drum.
 19C. **French**, from Scandinavian *bisa* jar.

bidonville (bē´dənvil, bidŏvēl´) *n.* a shanty town built of flattened oil drums, esp. a slum settlement on the outskirts of a N African city.
 mid-20C. **French**, from BIDON + *ville* town.

Biedermeier (bē´dəmīə) *a.* **1** (of a style of furniture) common in Germany in the first half of the 19th cent. **2** (*derog.*) (of German painting) conventional, bourgeois.
 early 20C. Gottlieb *Biedermeier*, a fictitious German poet created by Ludwig Eichrodt in 1855.
 • Biedermeier was presented as a naive and unintentionally comic poet and his name came to be associated, at first contemptuously, with the art styles of the period, 1815–48.

bien-aimé (byīnemā´) *n.* beloved, a dear person.
 19C. **French**, lit. well loved, from *bien* well + p.p. of *aimer* to love.

bien élevé (byīn elevā´) *a.* well-educated, properly brought up.
 early 20C. **French** well raised, from *bien* well + p.p. of *élever* to raise, to educate.

bien entendu (byīn ātādü´) *adv.* of course, that goes without saying.
 19C. **French**, lit. well understood, from *bien* well + p.p. of *entendre* to hear, to understand.

bien-être (byīnetr´, -et´rə) *n.* a state of well-being.
 19C. **French**, from *bien* well + use as n. of *être* to be.

biennale (bienah´lā) *n.* **1** a biennial art or music festival. **2** (**Biennale**) an international art festival held in Venice every other year since 1895.
 mid-20C. **Italian**, from Latin *biennis* of two years.

bien pensant (byī pāsā´) *n.* (*pl.* **bien pensants** (pāsā´)) **1** a right-thinking person. **2** (*derog.*) a person who complies mindlessly with current moral trends.
 early 20C. **French**, from *bien* well + pres.p. of *penser* to think.

bienséance (byīsāās´) *n.* decorum.
 17C. **French**, lit. well-befitting, from *bien* well + *séant*, pres.p. of *seoir* to befit. Cp. SEANCE.

bierwurst (biə´vœst) *n.* a kind of coarse pork and beef German sausage flavoured with garlic.
 mid-20C. **German**, lit. beer sausage.

biga (bē´gə, bī´-) *n.* (*pl.* **bigae** (-gē)) a two-horse chariot.
 17C. **Latin**.

bigarreau (big´ərō) *n.* (*pl.* **bigarreaux** (-ərō), **bigarreaus**) a type of sweet cherry, usually heart-shaped and with firm flesh.
 17C. **French**, from *bigarré* variegated, from Old French *garre* bicoloured, prob. from Germanic.

bijou (bē´zhoo) *n.* (*pl.* **bijoux** (bē´zhoo)) **1** a jewel, a trinket. **2** anything that is small, pretty or valuable. ~*a.* small, pretty or valuable.
 17C. **French**, from Breton *bizou* finger ring, from *biz* finger.

bijouterie (bēzhoo´təri) *n.* jewellery, trinkets.
19C. **French**, from *bijou* jewel, from Breton *bizou* ring, from *biz* finger.

bikini (bikē´ni) *n.* (*pl.* **bikinis**) a brief, two-piece swimming costume.
mid-20C. *Bikini*, an atoll in the Marshall Islands, N Pacific, where the atom bomb was tested, 1946.
● The costume was apparently named from its 'explosive' effect when first seen.

+**bilbo** (bil´bō) *n.* (*pl.* **bilbos, bilboes**)
1 a rapier, a sword. 2 (*fig.*) a bully, a swashbuckler.
16C. *Bilbao*, a city in N Spain, famous for its weapon manufacture.

Bildungsroman (bil´dungzrōmahn) *n.* a novel dealing with the emotional and spiritual education of its central figure.
early 20C. **German**, from *Bildung* education + *Roman* novel.

billabong (bil´əbong) *n.* 1 a stream flowing from a river to a dead end. 2 a creek that fills seasonally.
19C. **Australian Aboriginal** (Wiradhuri) *bila* river + *bang* channel dry except after rain.
● The word is popularly associated with the name of the *Bell* River, New South Wales.

billet-doux (bilādoo´) *n.* (*pl.* **billets-doux** (bilādooz´)) (*often facet.*) a love letter.
17C. **French** sweet note.

biltong (bil´tong) *n.* (*S Afr.*) strips of lean meat dried in the sun.
19C. **Afrikaans**, from Dutch *bil* buttock, ox rump + *tong* tongue.

bimbo (bim´bō) *n.* (*pl.* **bimbos**) (*sl., usu. derog.*) 1 an attractive person, esp. a woman, who is naive or of limited

intelligence. 2 a foolish or stupid person. 3 a whore.
early 20C. **Italian** little child, baby. Cp. BAMBINO.

bint (bint) *n.* (*sl., offensive*) a girl or woman.
19C. **Arabic** daughter, girl.
● The word gained popular currency in English from its use by servicemen in Egypt in World Wars I and II.

biretta (biret´ə), **berretta** *n.* a square cap worn by clerics of the Roman Catholic and Anglican Churches.
16C. **Italian** *berretta* or from Spanish *birreta*, fem. dims. corr. to Old Provençal *berret* BERET, based on Late Latin *birrus* hooded cape, ? of Celtic orig.
● According to some, the word is from Greek *purros* flame-coloured, red.

biriani (biriah´ni), **biryani** *n.* an Indian dish of spiced rice mixed with meat or fish.
mid-20C. **Urdu**, from Persian *biryānī*, from *biriyān* fried, grilled.

bis (bis) *adv.* (*Mus.*) encore, again (a direction that a passage is to be repeated).
17C. **French**, from Latin twice.
● In French *bis* corresponds to English ENCORE as a call for a repeat performance.

bise (bēz) *n.* a keen, dry, northerly wind prevalent in Switzerland and adjacent countries.
12–14C. **French**, of unknown orig.
● The word is not likely to derive from Popular Latin *aura bisia* grey wind, as sometimes proposed.

bismillah (bismil´ə) *int.* in the name of Allah (spoken by Muslims at the beginning of any undertaking).
18C. **Arabic** *bi-smi-llāh* in the name of God, the first word of the Koran.

bisque¹ (bisk), **bisk** *n.* a rich soup made by boiling down fish, birds or the like.
17C. French crayfish soup. ? From *Biscaye* (Vizcaya), a province of N Spain (on the Bay of *Biscay*).

bisque² (bisk) *n.* in tennis, golf etc., a stroke allowed at any time to the weaker party to equalize the players.
17C. French, of unknown orig.
• The word is said on tenuous grounds to come from the province of *Biscay* (BISQUE¹), whose inhabitants are experts at pelota, a game resembling tennis.

bisque³ (bisk) *n.* a kind of unglazed white porcelain used for statuettes.
17C. French, from Old French *besquit*, ult. from Latin *bis* twice + *coctus* cooked.
• English *biscuit* is of identical origin.

bistre (bis´tə), (*esp. N Am.*) **bister** *n.* a transparent brownish yellow pigment prepared from soot. ~*a.* coloured like this pigment.
18C. French, of unknown orig.

bistro (bēs´trō) *n.* (*pl.* **bistros**) a small bar or restaurant.
early 20C. French, of uncertain orig.
• The word is perhaps from earlier *bistingo*, apparently a variant of colloquial *bistouille* drink of coffee mixed with brandy. It is probably not from Russian *bystro!* quick!, a supposed call of Russian soldiers for service in a bar.

bizarre (bizah´) *a.* **1** odd, strange. **2** of mixed or discordant style. **3** irregular, in bad taste.
17C. French, from Italian *bizzarro* angry, of unknown orig.
• The word is related to Spanish and Portuguese *bizarro* handsome, brave, from Basque *bizar* beard (a symbol of strength).

blague (blahg) *n.* pretentiousness, humbug.
19C. French, ? from Dutch *blagen* to swell.

blagueur (blahgœ´) *n.* a pretentious person, a teller of tall stories.
19C. French, from BLAGUE.

blanc de blanc (blã də blã´) *n.* a white wine made from white grapes only.
mid-20C. French, lit. white of white.

blancmange (bləmonzh´) *n.* milk (usu. sweetened) thickened with cornflour or gelatine to form a jelly-like dessert.
14–15C. Old French *blanc mangier* (Modern French *blanc-manger*), from *blanc* white + *mangier* food.
• Blancmange was originally a dish of white meat or fish. The current sense emerged in the 16C. The final -*r* of the French word was dropped in English only in the 18C.

blanquette (blãket´) *n.* a stew of white meat, esp. veal, in a white sauce.
18C. French, from Old French *blanchet*, from *blanc* white.

blasé (blah´zā) *a.* **1** dulled in sense or emotion. **2** worn out through over-indulgence, used up.
19C. French, p.p. of *blaser* to cloy, from Dutch *blasen* to blow.

blin (blin) *n.* (*pl.* **blini** (blin´i), **bliny**, **blinis** (blin´iz)) a kind of pancake, usually with a filling.
19C. Russian, prob. from a Slavonic source ult. rel. to English *mill*.

blintz (blints), **blintze** *n.* a thin, stuffed pancake.
early 20C. Yiddish *blintse*, from Russian *blinets*, dim. of BLIN.

blitz (blits) *n.* (*coll.*) **1** intense enemy onslaught, esp. an air raid. **2** an intensive campaign. **3** intensive activity.

4 (the Blitz) the German air raids on London in 1940. ~*v.t.* **1** to make an enemy onslaught on. **2** to mount an intensive campaign against. **3** to subject to intensive activity.
mid-20C. German, abbr. of *Blitzkrieg*, from *Blitz* lightning + *Krieg* war.

bloc (blok) *n.* a combination of parties, or of nations.
early 20C. French block, from Germanic.

blond (blond) *a.* **1** fair or light in colour. **2** having light hair and a fair complexion. ~*n.* a person who has light hair and a fair complexion.
15C. Old French, from Medieval Latin *blundus*, *blondus* yellow, ? from Germanic.

blouson (bloo´zon) *n.* a short, loose jacket fitted or belted in at the waist.
early 20C. French, from *blouse* shirt.

blucher (bloo´khə, -chə) *n.* (*usu. in pl., Hist.*) a strong leather half-boot.
19C. Gebhard von *Blücher*, 1742–1819, Prussian general, who wore such boots in battle.

blutwurst (bloot´vœst) *n.* a black pudding.
19C. German, from *Blut* blood + WURST.

bo (bō), **bodhi** (bō´di) *n.* the peepul or pipla tree, a fig tree, *Ficus religiosa*, held sacred by the Buddhists and planted beside their temples.
19C. Sinhalese *bōgaha*, from *bō*, from Pali and Sanskrit *bodhi* perfect knowledge (see BUDDHA) + *gaha* tree.

bocage (bəkahzh´) *n.* woodland scenery represented in ceramics.
16C. French, from Old French *boscage*, from Latin *boscum* bush.

Boche (bosh) *n.* **1** (*derog.*) a German, esp. a soldier. **2 (the Boche)** Germans, esp.

German soldiers, collectively. ~*a.* German.
early 20C. French sl., from *Alboche*, var. of *Allemoche*, argot form of *Allemand* German.
• The inserted *b* is apparently by association with slang *caboche* head, or *tête de boche* wooden head.

bock (bok) *n.* **1** a strong German beer. **2** a large beer glass. **3** a large glass of beer.
19C. French, from abbr. of German *Eimbockbier*, from *Einbecker Bier* Einbeck beer, from *Einbeck*, a town in central Germany.

bockwurst (bok´vœst) *n.* a type of large frankfurter.
mid-20C. German, from BOCK + WURST.

bodega (bədē´gə) *n.* a shop selling wine, esp. in a Spanish-speaking country.
19C. Spanish, from Latin *apotheca*. See BOUTIQUE.

Bodhisattva (bodisaht´və) *n.* in Mahayana Buddhism, a person who postpones entry into nirvana in order to help suffering beings.
19C. Sanskrit one whose essence is enlightenment, from *bodhi* perfect knowledge (see BUDDHA) + *sattva* essence, being. Cp. BO.

Boer (buə, bō´ə, baw) *n.* a South African of Dutch birth or extraction. ~*a.* of or relating to the Boers.
19C. Dutch *boer* farmer.

boeuf bourguignon (bœf buəgēnyō´) *n.* a casserole of beef cooked in red wine.
early 20C. French beef of Burgundy, from *bœuf* beef + *bourguignon*, from *Bourgogne* Burgundy.

boîte (bwŭt) *n.* (*pl.* **boîtes** (bwŭt)) a small French restaurant or nightclub.
early 20C. French box.

boîte de nuit (bwŭt də nwē´) n. (pl.
boîtes de nuit (bwŭt)) a small French
nightclub.
early 20C. French, lit. box of (the) night.
Cp. BOÎTE.

bolas (bō´ləs) n. a missile, used by South
American Indians, formed of balls or
stones strung together and flung round
the legs of the animal aimed at.
19C. Spanish and Portuguese, pl. of
bola ball.

bolero n. (pl. **boleros**) **1** (bəleə´rō) **a** a
lively Spanish dance. **b** (*Mus.*) music for
or in the time of this dance. **2** (bol´ərō)
a short jacket worn over a bodice.
18C. Spanish, from *bola* ball.

bolivar (bol´ivah) n. (pl. **bolivars,
bolivares** (-ah´res)) the standard unit of
currency in Venezuela.
19C. Simón *Bolívar*, 1783–1830, South
American soldier and statesman.

boliviano (bəliviah´nō) n. (pl.
bolivianos) the standard unit of
currency in Bolivia, equal to 100
centavos.
19C. Spanish. From Simón *Bolívar*. See
BOLIVAR.

bologna (bəlō´nyə, bəlon´yə), **Bologna
sausage** n. a large smoked sausage of
mixed meats, also called a *polony*.
19C. *Bologna*, a city in N Italy.

Bolshevik (bol´shəvik), **Bolshevist**
(bol´shəvist) n. **1** (*Hist.*) a member of the
Russian majority Socialist party which
came to power under Lenin in 1917. **2** a
political revolutionary. **3** (*often derog.*) a
political agitator. ~a. that is a Bolshevik;
of or relating to Bolsheviks.
early 20C. Russian *bol'shevik* majority
member, from *bol'she* greater, comp. of
bol'shoǐ big. Cp. MENSHEVIK.

bolus (bō´ləs) n. (pl. **boluses**) **1** medicine
in a round mass larger than a pill. **2** a
round lump of anything. **3** anything
mentally unpalatable.
16C. Late Latin, from Greek *bōlos* clod,
lump of earth.

bombe (bomb, bōb) n. an ice cream
dessert moulded into a rounded, bomb
shape.
19C. French bomb.

bombé (bom´bā, bō´-) a. protruding or
round-fronted, as of furniture.
early 20C. French, p.p. of *bomber* to
swell out, from *bombe* bomb.

bombora (bombaw´rə) n. (*Austral.*)
dangerous broken water, usu. at the base
of a cliff.
mid-20C. Australian Aboriginal.

bon (bō) a. good.
16C. French, from Latin *bonus*.
• The word is found in various phrases
that have entered English, such as those
below.

bon accueil (bon akœy´) n. good
reception, due honour.
19C. French, from *bon* good + *accueil*
welcome, reception, from Popular Latin
accolligere to welcome, to receive.

bona fide (bōnə fī´di) adv. in good faith.
~a. genuine.
16C. Latin with good faith, abl. of *bona
fides*, from *bonus* good + *fides* faith.

bonanza (bənan´zə) n. **1** a rich mine.
2 a successful enterprise. **3** a run of
luck. ~a. **1** very successful. **2** highly
profitable.
19C. Spanish fair weather, prosperity,
from Latin *bonus* good.

bon appétit (bon apetē´) int. good
appetite!, enjoy your meal!
19C. French, from *bon* good + *appétit*
appetite.
• The expression is used as a 'toast' to
someone about to start a meal. English

rarely uses 'good appetite' in this sense, unlike other languages. Apart from French, cp. Italian *buon appetito*, Russian *priyatnogo appetita* etc.

bona vacantia (bōnə vəkan´tiə) *n.pl.* (*Law*) unclaimed goods.
18C. Latin ownerless goods, from *bona* goods (from *bonus* good) + neut. pl. of *vacans, vacantis*, pres.p. of *vacare* to be empty, to be ownerless.

bon-bon (bon´bon, bõ´bõ) *n.* **1** a sweet, esp. of fondant. **2** a Christmas cracker.
18C. French, redupl. of *bon* good.

bonbonnière (bõbonyeə´) *n.* a fancy box for sweets etc.
19C. French, from BON-BON.

bon chic, bon genre (bõ shēk bõ zhã´rə) *a.* well-bred and elegant, smart and stylish, 'preppy'.
late 20C. French, lit. good style, good form. Cp. CHIC, GENRE.
• The expression arose among the French 'smart set' in the 1980s and is colloquially abbreviated to BCBG. To be described thus is to be the equivalent of a British 'Sloane Ranger'.

bon enfant (bon ãfã´) *n.* an agreeable companion.
19C. French, lit. good child, from *bon* good + *enfant* child.
• English 'good kid' is used somewhat similarly.

bongo (bong´gō) *n.* (*pl.* **bongos, bongoes**) a small hand drum of a type often played in pairs.
early 20C. American Spanish *bongó*, from W African.

bon gré, mal gré (bõ´ grã mal´ grã) *adv.* willy-nilly, whether one wants it or not.
19C. French, lit. good will, bad will, from *bon* good or *mal* bad + *gré* will. Cp. MALGRÉ.

bonhomie (bonəmē´) *n.* good nature, geniality.
18C. French, from *bonhomme* good man, from Medieval Latin *bonus homo*.

bonjour (bõzhuə´) *int.* good day.
16C. French good day, from *bon* good + *jour* day.

bon marché (bõ mahshā´) *a.* cheap.
19C. French, lit. good market, from *bon* good + *marché* market.
• The name is familiar as that of the Bon Marché, a cut-price department store opened in the rue de Sèvres, Paris, in 1852.

bon mot (bõ mō´) *n.* (*pl.* **bons mots** (bõ mō´, bõ mōz´)) a witticism.
18C. French good word, from *bon* good + *mot* word.

bonne (bon) *n.* **1** a nursemaid. **2** a maid (of French nationality).
18C. French, fem. of *bon* good, implying woman.
• French children formerly addressed female domestics as *ma bonne* my good (woman) or *ma chère bonne* my dear good (woman).

bonne bouche (bon boosh´) *n.* (*pl.* **bonne bouches** (boosh´), **bonnes bouches** (bon)) a tasty titbit.
16C. French good mouth, meaning good taste in the mouth.

bonne chance (bon shãs´) *n.* good luck!
early 20C. French, from fem. of *bon* good + *chance* luck, chance.

bonne femme (bon fam´) *a.* (*following n.*) cooked simply and garnished with fresh vegetables and herbs.
19C. French, lit. (in the manner of a) good housewife, from fem. of *bon* good + *femme* wife, woman.

bonsai (bon´sī) *n.* (*pl.* **bonsai**) **1** (*also* **bonsai tree**) a potted tree or shrub

cultivated into a dwarf variety by skilful pruning of its roots. **2** the art or practice of cultivating trees or shrubs in this manner.
early 20C. Japanese, from *bon* tray + *sai* planting.

bonsella (bonsel´ə) *n.* (*S Afr.*) a tip, a present.
late 20C. Zulu *ibhanselo* gift and Xhosa *ukubasele* to give a present. Cp. BAKSHEESH.

bon ton (bõ tõ´) *n.* fashion, good style.
18C. French good tone, from *bon* good + *ton* tone.

bon vivant (bõ vēvã´) *n.* (*pl.* **bon vivants** (bõ vēvã´), **bons vivants**) a person fond of good living.
17C. French good living (person). Cp. BON VIVEUR.

bon viveur (bõ vēvœ´) *n.* (*pl.* **bon viveurs** (bõ vēvœ´), **bons viveurs**) a bon vivant.
19C. Pseudo-French good liver.
• The term was based on BON VIVANT.

bon voyage (bon voiahzh´, bõ vwayahzh´) *n., int.* a pleasant journey, farewell.
17C. French good journey, from *bon* good + *voyage* journey.
• English lacks a corresponding two-word wish. Cp. Italian *buon viaggio*, Spanish *buen viajo*, German *gute Reise*, Russian *schastlivogo puti*, Finnish *hyvä matkaa* etc.

bonze (bonz) *n.* a Buddhist religious teacher in Japan, China and adjacent regions.
16C. French *bonze* or from Portuguese *bonzo*, prob. from Japanese *bonzō* priest.

bora (baw´rə) *n.* a keen, dry NE wind in the upper Adriatic.
19C. Italian (dial. var of) *borea*, from Latin, from Greek *boreas* N wind.

borak (baw´rak) *n.* (*Austral., New Zeal., sl.*) chaff, banter.
19C. Australian Aboriginal (Wathawurung) *burag*.

Bordeaux (bawdō´) *n.* (*pl.* **Bordeaux** (-dōz)) a red, white or rosé wine from Bordeaux.
16C. French *Bordeaux*, a city in SW France.

bordello (bawdel´ō) *n.* (*pl.* **bordellos**) a brothel.
16C. Italian, from Old French *bordel*, dim. of *borde* small farm.

borné (baw´nā) *a.* narrow-minded, limited.
18C. French, p.p. of *borner* to limit, from Popular Latin *bodina* limit, ? from Gaulish.

borsch (bawsh), **borscht, bortsch** (bawch) *n.* Russian beetroot soup.
19C. Russian *borshch*.
• The original sense of the Russian word was hogweed (now *borshchevik*), *Heracleum sphondylium*, from which the soup was at one time made. The term was retained for the soup when beetroot was substituted for hogweed.

bosquet (bos´kit), **bosket** *n.* **1** a grove. **2** a plantation of small trees and underwood in a garden or park.
18C. French *bosquet*, from Italian *boschetto*, dim. of *bosco* wood. Cp. BOUQUET.

bossa nova (bosə nō´və) *n.* **1** a Brazilian dance resembling the samba. **2** the music for such a dance.
mid-20C. Portuguese new tendency, from *bossa* tendency + *nova*, fem. sing. of *novo* new.

botargo (bətah´gō) *n.* (*pl.* **botargos, botargoes**) a relish made of the roes of the mullet and tuna.

16C. Italian, from Medieval Greek
arghotarakho, ? from Coptic
outarakhon, from *ou* the + Greek
tarikhion pickle.

bottega (botā´gə) *n.* a café, a wine shop.
19C. Italian. Cp. BODEGA, BOUTIQUE.

bottine (botēn´) *n.* **1** a buskin. **2** a light
kind of boot for women and children.
16C. French, dim. of *botte* boot.

bouchée (booshā´) *n.* (*pl.* **bouchées**
(-shā´)) a small baked confection, such
as a patty or pastry.
19C. French, lit. mouthful, from *bouche*
mouth.

bouclé (boo´klā) *n.* **1** a looped yarn.
2 the thick, curly material woven from
such yarn. ~*a.* woven from looped
yarn.
19C. French, p.p. of *boucler* to buckle,
to curl.

boudoir (boo´dwah) *n.* a small, elegantly
furnished room, used as a lady's private
apartment.
18C. French *bouder* to sulk, to pout,
based on *dortoir* dormitory (from *dormir*
to sleep), *parloir* parlour (from *parler* to
talk) etc.
• French *bouder* is itself of imitative
origin.

bouffant (boo´fā) *a.* full, puffed out, as a
hairstyle.
19C. French, pres.p. of *bouffer* to swell,
prob. ult. of imit. orig.

bougie (boo´zhi) *n.* **1** a wax candle.
2 (*Med.*) a smooth, flexible, slender
cylinder used for exploring or dilating
passages in the human body.
18C. French, from *Bougie* (Arabic
Bijāya), a town in N Algeria with a
former trade in wax candles.
• French *bougie* replaced *chandelle*
candle in the 19C.

bouillabaisse (booyəbes´) *n.* a rich fish
stew or chowder, popular in S France.
19C. French, from Provençal
bouiabaisso, from imper. *bous* boil +
abaisse lower, i.e. bring quickly to the
boil then let simmer down.

bouilli (booyē´) *n.* meat gently simmered.
17C. French, p.p. (used as n.) of *bouillir*
to boil.
• The French word is also the source of
English *bully beef*.

bouillon (booyŏ´) *n.* **1** broth, soup. **2** a
fleshy excrescence on a horse's foot.
3 a puffed flounce.
17C. French, from *bouillir* to boil. Cp.
COURT BOUILLON.

boule[1] (bool), **boules** *n.pl.* a French game
resembling bowls, played with metal
balls.
early 20C. French bowl.

boule[2] (boo´li) *n.* a Greek legislative body.
19C. Greek *boulē* senate, council.

boulevard (boo´ləvahd) *n.* **1** a public
walk on the rampart of a demolished
fortification. **2** a broad street planted
with trees. **3** (*esp. N Am.*) an arterial
road, trunk road.
18C. French, from Middle Dutch
bolwerc, from Germanic source also of
English *bulwark*.

bouleversé (boolveəsā´) *a.* amazed,
upset, shocked.
19C. French, p.p. of *bouleverser*, lit. to
turn as a bowl, from *bouler* to bowl (cp.
BOULE[1]) + *verser* to turn. Cp. English
bowled over.

bouquet (bukā´, buk´ā, bō-) *n.* **1** a bunch
of flowers. **2** the perfume exhaled by
wine. **3** a compliment.
18C. French, orig. clump of trees, from
dial. var. of Old French *bos*, *bois* wood.

bourdon (buə´dən) *n.* (*Mus.*) **1** a bass
stop on an organ. **2** a bass reed in a

harmonium. **3** the lowest bell in a peal
of bells. **4** a low undersong or
accompaniment. **5** the drone of a
bagpipe.
12–14C. Old French drone, of imit.
orig.

bourg (buəg) *n.* **1** a town built under the
shadow of a castle. **2** a market town.
14–15C. Old French, from Medieval
Latin *burgus* borough.

bourgeois (buə´zhwah) *n.* (*pl.*
bourgeois) **1** (*sometimes derog.*) a
person of the mercantile, shopkeeping
or middle class. **2** a French citizen.
~*a.* **1** of or relating to the middle class
or capitalist classes. **2** commonplace,
unintellectual. **3** middle-class in
outlook.
16C. French, from Late Latin *burgus*
castle, ult. from Germanic.

bourree (boo´rā), **bourrée** *n.* **1** a folk
dance from the Auvergne and Basque
provinces. **2** a musical composition in
this rhythm.
17C. French *bourrée*, fem. p.p. (used as
n.) of *bourrer* to hit, to knock.
● French *bourrée* originally meant a
bundle of sticks, firewood. The current
sense came from a dance around a fire
of such sticks.

bourse (buəs) *n.* **1** a (French) foreign
exchange for the transaction of
commercial business. **2** (**the Bourse**)
the Paris equivalent of the Stock Market.
16C. French, from Medieval Latin *bursa*
purse.

boustrophedon (boostrəfē´dən, bow-)
a., adv. written alternately from left to
right and from right to left.
17C. Greek as the ox turns in ploughing,
from *bous* ox + -*strophos* turning +
adverbial suf. -*don*.

boutique (bootēk´) *n.* **1** a fashionable
clothes shop. **2** any small specialist

shop. **3** a shop within a department
store, hotel, airport lounge etc.
18C. French, from Old Provençal *botica*,
from Latin *apotheca*, from Greek
apothēkē storehouse. Cp. BODEGA.

bouton (boo´tō) *n.* **1** a pimple, pustule,
boil. **2** the hollow at the end of the
tongue of the honey bee.
19C. French button, from *bouter* to
grow.

boutonnière (bootonyeə´) *n.* a flower or
flowers worn in the buttonhole.
19C. French buttonhole. Cp. BOUTON.

bouts rimés (boo rē´mā) *n.pl.* a game in
which a list of rhymed endings is
handed to each player to fill in and
complete the verse.
18C. French rhymed endings.

bouzouki (buzoo´ki) *n.* a Greek stringed
instrument similar to the mandolin.
mid-20C. Modern Greek *mpouzouki*.
Cp. Turkish *bozuk* spoilt, referring to
roughly made instruments.

boyar (boi´ah, boyah´), **boiar, boyard**
(boi´əd) *n.* (*Hist.*) a member of the old
Russian nobility.
16C. Russian *boyarin*, pl. *boyare*. ? Rel.
to BEY.

boyla (boi´lə) *n.* a sorcerer.
19C. Australian Aboriginal.

braggadocio (bragədō´chiō) *n.* **1** an
empty boaster. **2** empty boasting.
16C. Pseudo-Italian pers. name
Braggadochio, boastful character in
Spenser's *Faerie Queene* (1590, 1596).
● The name itself is based on *brag* or
braggart + the Italian augmentative
suffix -*occio*.

brahma (brah´mə), **brahmaputra**
(-poo´trə) *n.* **1** any bird of an Asian breed
of domestic fowl. **2** this breed.
19C. *Brahmaputra*, a river in India.

Brahmin (brah´min), **Brahman** (-mən) *n*. **1** a member of the highest Hindu caste, the priestly order. **2** (*N Am.*) a person of superior intellectual or social status, a highbrow. **3** a breed of Indian cattle.
12–14C. **Sanskrit** *brāhmaṇa* one of Brahmin caste, from *brahman* prayer.

brancard (brang´kəd) *n*. a horse litter.
16C. **French** litter, from *branche* branch.

bras d'honneur (brah donœ´) *n*. a rebuke, an insult, the French equivalent of a 'V-sign' or 'finger': a combination of an upward thrusted fist and a slapped upper arm, implying 'up you'.
19C. **French**, lit. arm of honour.

brasserie (bras´əri) *n*. a (usu. small) restaurant, orig. one serving beer as well as wine etc. with the food.
19C. **French**, orig. brewery, from *brasser* to brew, from Latin *braces* spelt.

brassière (braz´iə, bras´-) *n*. a women's undergarment for supporting the breasts.
early 20C. **French** child's reins, camisole, from *bras* arm.

bratwurst (brat´vœst) *n*. a kind of German sausage.
early 20C. **German**, from *Brat* spit + WURST.

bravado (brəvah´dō) *n*. (*pl.* **bravadoes**) **1** ostentatious defiance. **2** swaggering behaviour. **3** an insolent menace.
16C. **Spanish** *bravada*, from *bravo* BRAVO².

bravo¹ (brahvō´, brah´vō), (*fem.*) **brava** (brah´və) *int*. (*superl.* **bravissimo** (-vis´imō), **bravissima** (-mə)) capital!, well done! ~*n*. (*pl.* **bravoes, bravos**) **1** a cry of approval. **2** a cheer.
18C. **French**, from Italian bold, good.

bravo² (brah´vō) *n*. (*pl.* **bravoes, bravos**) **1** a hired assassin. **2** a bandit, a desperado.
16C. **Italian** bold, good.

bravura (brəvūə´rə) *n*. **1** (*Mus.*) brilliance of execution. **2** a display of daring and skill in artistic execution. **3** a piece of music that calls out all the powers of an executant. ~*a*. requiring or showing bravura.
18C. **Italian**, from *bravo* bold, good.

breccia (brech´iə) *n*. a rock composed of angular, as distinguished from rounded, fragments cemented together in a matrix.
18C. **Italian** gravel, rubble, rel. to French *brèche* breach, German *brechen* to break, from Germanic base of English *break*.

brehon (brē´hən) *n*. an ancient hereditary Irish judge.
16C. **Irish** *breitheamhan*, gen. pl. of *breitheamh*, from *breith* judgement.

breloque (brəlōk´) *n*. an ornament attached to a watch-chain.
19C. **French** drumbeat, prob. of imit. orig.

bremsstrahlung (bremz´shtrahlung) *n*. (*Physics*) the electromagnetic radiation caused by an electron colliding with or slowed down by the electric field of a positively charged nucleus.
mid-20C. **German**, from *bremsen* to brake + *Strahlung* radiation.

brevet d'invention (brevā dīvāsyō´) *n*. certificate of invention, patent.
19C. **French**, from *brevet*, dim. of *bref* brief + *d'* of + *invention* invention.
● The term is the equivalent of English 'letters patent'.

breveté (brevtā´) *a*. patented.
19C. **French**, p.p. of *breveter* to patent.

bric-a-brac (brik´əbrak), **bric-à-brac**, **bricabrac** *n*. fancy ware, curiosities.
19C. **French**, from obs. *à bric et à brac* at random, prob. of imit. orig.

bricolage (brikəlahzh´, brēko-) *n.* a rough-and-ready construction or assemblage, a piece of DIY.
mid-20C. French, from *bricoler* to do odd jobs, to tinker, from *bricole* a type of ballista, from Italian *briccola*, of unknown orig.

bricole (brik´əl, -kōl´) *n.* **1** in billiards, the rebound of a ball from a wall or cushion. **2** in tennis or billiards, an indirect stroke.
16C. Old French, from Provençal *bricola* or Italian *briccola*, of unknown orig.

Brie (brē) *n.* a soft white cheese orig. produced in France.
19C. French *Brie*, an agricultural region in NE France.

brigue (brēg) *n.* strife, intrigue. ~*v.i.* (*ṁrd pers. sing. pres.* **brigues**, *pres.p.* **briguing**, *past, p.p.* **brigued**) to intrigue.
14–15C. Old French, from Italian *briga* strife.

brinjal (brin´jəl), **brinjall** *n.* esp. in the Indian subcontinent, an aubergine.
17C. Portuguese *berinjela* AUBERGINE.

brio (brē´ō) *n.* spirit, liveliness.
18C. Italian liveliness, of Gaulish orig.

brioche (briosh´, brē´-) *n.* **1** a kind of light sweet bread. **2** a sponge cake.
19C. French, from *brier*, alt. of *broyer* to grind small.

briquette (briket´), **briquet** *n.* **1** a block of compressed coal dust. **2** a slab of artificial stone. ~*v.t.* (*pres.p.* **briquetting**, **briqueting**, *past, p.p.* **briquetted**, **briqueted**) to compress (mineral matter etc.) into bricks by heat.
19C. French, dim. of *brique* brick.

brise-bise (brēzbēz´) *n.* a net curtain over the lower part of a window.
early-20C. French, lit. break-wind (i.e. windbreak). Cp. BRISE-SOLEIL, BISE.

brise-soleil (brēzsolā´) *n.* a screen etc. for shutting out direct or excessive sunlight.
mid-20C. French, lit. break-sun.

britzka (brits´kə), **britska** *n.* an open carriage with a calash top.
19C. Polish *bryczka*, dim. of *bryka* wagon.

brocard (brō´kəd) *n.* **1** an elementary principle of law. **2** a sarcastic jest.
16C. French, or from Medieval Latin *brocardus*, from *Brocard* or *Burchart*, *c*.965–1025, bishop of Worms, compiler of *Decretum*, a collection of canon law.

broccoli (brok´əli) *n.* **1** a variety of cabbage which has greenish flower heads. **2** the stalk and head of this eaten as a vegetable.
17C. Italian, pl. of *broccolo* cabbage sprout, dim. of *brocco* shoot.

brochette (broshet´) *n.* **1** a skewer. **2** small pieces of food grilled together on a skewer (like a kebab).
15C. French, dim. of *broche* spit.

brochure (brō´shə) *n.* a small pamphlet.
18C. French stitched work, from *brocher* to stitch.
● A pamphlet was originally made by stitching a few pages together.

broderie anglaise (brōdəri äglez´) *n.* open embroidery on cambric or linen.
19C. French English embroidery.

bronco (brong´kō) *n.* (*pl.* **broncos**) a wild or half-tamed horse of California or New Mexico.
19C. Spanish rough, rude.

brouhaha (broo´hah·hah) *n.* a tumult, a row.
19C. French, of imit. orig.

bruit (broot) v.t. to rumour, to noise abroad. ~n. **1** an abnormal sound from the internal organs of the body heard through a stethoscope. **2** †noise, tumult, rumour, report.
15C. Old French, p.p. (used as n.) of *bruire* to roar, from alt. of Latin *rugire* to roar, by assoc. with source of English *bray*.

brûlé (broo´lā) a. cooked with caramelized brown sugar.
early 20C. French burnt, p.p. of *brûler* to burn.

brume (broom) n. mist, fog, vapour.
18C. French fog, from Latin *bruma* winter.

brunette (brunet´), (*N Am.*) **brunet** n. a girl or woman with dark hair and a dark complexion. ~a. **1** brown-haired. **2** of dark complexion.
16C. French *brunet* (m.), *brunette* (fem.), dim. of *brun* brown.

bruscamente (brooskəmen´ti) adv. (*Mus.*) **1** strongly accented. **2** roughly.
19C. Italian roughly, abruptly, from *brusco* rough, abrupt. Cp. BRUSQUE.

bruschetta (brusket´ə) n. (pl. **bruschettas, bruschette** (-tā)) a type of Italian open toasted sandwich, eaten as an appetizer or snack.
late 20C. Italian, from *brusco* sharp, tart. Cp. BRUSQUE.
● The toasted bread is properly drenched in olive oil, served with garlic and dipped in coarse salt to taste. Hence 'sharp'.

brusque (brŭsk, broosk) a. rough or blunt in manner.
17C. French lively, fierce, harsh, from Italian *brusco* sharp, tart.

brut (broot) a. (of wine) dry, unsweetened.
19C. French rough, raw, from Latin *brutus* heavy, stupid.

brutum fulmen (brootəm fŭl´men) n. (pl. **bruta fulmina** (brootə fŭl´minə)) an empty threat.
17C. Latin, lit. unfeeling thunderbolt.
● The phrase is from Pliny's *Natural History* II, xliii (AD 77): *bruta fulmina et vana* 'insensitive and harmless thunderbolts'.

Buddha (bud´ə) n. **1** the title given to Gautama, the founder of Buddhism, by his disciples. **2** a statue or picture of the Buddha.
17C. Sanskrit enlightened, p.p. of *budh-* to awake, to know.

budgeree (bŭj´əri), **budgery** a. (*Austral., coll.*) good, excellent.
18C. Australian Aboriginal (Dharuk) *bujiri.*

buffet (buf´ā) n. **1** a cupboard or sideboard for the display of plate, china etc. **2** (*dial.*) a low stool, footstool or hassock. **3** a refreshment bar. **4** dishes of food set out on a table from which diners help themselves.
18C. French, from Old French *bufet, buffet*, of unknown orig.
● A connection with Scots *buffet* low stool, also from Old French *bufet*, has been proposed.

buffo (buf´ō) n. (pl. **buffi** (-ē), **buffos**) a singer in a comic opera. ~a. burlesque, comic.
18C. Italian puff of wind, buffoon.

buhl (bool), **boule, boulle** n. **1** brass, tortoiseshell etc. cut into ornamental patterns for inlaying. **2** work so inlaid. ~a. (*attrib.*) inlaid with buhl.
19C. German *Buhl* and French *boule*, from André Charles *Boule*, 1642–1732, French cabinetmaker.

bulgar (bŭl´gə), **bulgur** n. wheat that has been boiled and then dried.
early 20C. Turkish, from Persian *bulğūr* bruised grain.

bulla (bul'ə) *n.* (*pl.* **bullae** (-ē)) **1** (*Hist.*) a round pendant worn by Roman children. **2** a seal appended to a papal document. **3** a watery vesicle, a blister. **19C. Latin** bubble.

bumiputra (boomipoot'rə) *n.* (*pl.* **bumiputra, bumiputras**) a Malaysian of indigenous Malay origin. ~*a.* of or relating to the bumiputra. **mid-20C. Malay**, from Sanskrit son of the soil.

bund (bŭnd) *n.* an embankment, a dam or causeway. **19C. Urdu** *band*, from Persian.

Bundesrat (bun'dəzraht) *n.* **1** the Upper House of Parliament in Germany or Austria. **2** the federal council of Switzerland. **19C. German**, from gen. of *Bund* confederation + *Rat* council.

Bundestag (bun'dəztahg) *n.* the Lower House of Parliament in Germany. **19C. German**, from gen. of *Bund* confederation + *tagen* to confer.

Bundeswehr (bun'dəzv> vea) *n.* the Federal German Armed Forces. **mid-20C. German**, from gen. of *Bund* confederation + *Wehr* defence. Cp. WEHRMACHT.
● The Bundeswehr was established by the Treaty of Paris (1954–55) under Supreme Allied Command.

bundook (bŭn'duk) *n.* a musket or rifle, a gun. **19C. Urdu** *bandūk*, from Persian *bundūk* firearm.

bundu (bun'doo) *n.* (*S Afr.*) the back of beyond, the far interior. **mid-20C. Shona** *bundo* grasslands.

bunyip (bŭn'yip) *n.* (*Austral.*) **1** the fabulous rainbow serpent that lives in pools. **2** an impostor.
19C. Australian Aboriginal (Wemba-Wemba) *banib*.

bureau (bū'rō) *n.* (*pl.* **bureaux** (-rōz), **bureaus**) **1** a writing table with drawers for papers. **2** (*N Am.*) a chest of drawers. **3** an office. **4** a public office. **5** a government department. **17C. French** (Old French *burel*), orig. woollen stuff, baize (used for covering writing desks), prob. from *bure*, var. of *buire* dark brown, from Latin *burrus* fiery red, from Greek *purros* red.
● Sense 3 evolved in the 19C.

bureau de change (būrō də shäzh') *n.* (*pl.* **bureaux de change** (būrō)) an office or kiosk (e.g. in an airport, railway station) for exchanging currencies. **early 20C. French**, lit. office of exchange.

burette (būret'), (*N Am.*) **buret** *n.* a graduated glass tube for measuring small quantities of liquid. **19C. French**, from *buire* ewer, from Frankish *būk* belly.

burgoo (bœgoo') *n.* (*pl.* **burgoos**) **1** a kind of oatmeal porridge or thick gruel eaten by sailors. **2** (*N Am.*) a thick soup or stew. **17C. Arabic** *burḡul*. See BULGAR.

burin (būə'rin) *n.* **1** the cutting tool of an engraver on copper. **2** a triangular steel tool used by marble-workers. **3** an early Stone Age flint tool. **17C. French**, from Italian *burino* (now *bulino*), from Germanic base of English *bore*.

burka (bœ'kə) *n.* the long veil or veiled, loose overgarment worn by Muslim women. **19C. Urdu and Persian** *burḳa'*, from Arabic *burḳu'*.

burlesque (bœlesk') *a.* **1** drolly or absurdly imitative. **2** mock-serious or mock-heroic. ~*n.* **1** mockery, grotesque imitation. **2** literary or dramatic representation caricaturing other work. **3** (*N Am.*) a form of theatrical variety show characterized by lewd humour, singing and dancing and striptease. ~*v.t.* (*pres.p.* **burlesquing**, *past, p.p.* **burlesqued**) **1** to produce a grotesque imitation of. **2** to travesty. **17C. French**, from Italian *burlesco*, from *burla* ridicule, joke, fun, of unknown orig.

burletta (bœlet´ə) *n.* **1** a comic opera. **2** a musical farce. **18C. Italian**, dim. of *burla*. See BURLESQUE.

burnous (bənoos´), **burnouse** (-ooz´) *n.* a mantle or cloak with a hood, worn by Arabs. **16C. French**, from Arabic *burnus*.

burrito (bərē´tō) *n.* (*pl.* **burritos**) a tortilla with a filling of beef, cheese, chicken or beans. **mid-20C. American Spanish**, dim. of BURRO.

burro (bŭr´ō) *n.* (*pl.* **burros**) (*esp. N Am.*) a donkey. **19C. Spanish** donkey.

Bursch (buəsh) *n.* (*pl.* **Burschen** (buə´shən)) lad, youth, student, esp. a senior student at a German university. **19C. German**, from Medieval Latin *bursa* bag, purse. Cp. English *bursary*.

bushido (bushē´dō) *n.* the code of honour of the Japanese samurai. **19C. Japanese** military knight's way, from *bushi* samurai + *dō* way.

bustee (bŭs´tē) *n.* in the Indian subcontinent, a settlement or a collection of huts. **19C. Hindi** *bastī* dwelling, settlement.

bustier (bŭs´tiā, bus´-) *n.* a strapless bodice. **late 20C. French**, from *buste* bust.

butte (būt) *n.* (*N Am.*) an abrupt, isolated hill or peak. **19C. French** hill with a target, from *but* target.

bwana (bwah´nə) *n.* (in Africa) sir, master. **19C. Kiswahili**, from Arabic *abūna* our father. ● The word was familiar in colonial times as a respectful form of address by a black person to a white man.

C

caballero (kabəlyeə´rō) *n.* (*pl.* **caballeros**) a Spanish gentleman.
19C. Spanish cavalier. Cp. CHEVALIER.

cabana (kəbah´nə) *n.* (*esp. N Am.*) a small hut, cabin or tent on the beach or at a swimming-pool, used for changing by bathers.
19C. Spanish *cabaña*, from Late Latin *capanna*, *cavana* cabin.

cabaret (kab´ərā) *n.* **1** an entertainment or floor show consisting of singing, dancing etc. **2** a restaurant or nightclub where such entertainment is provided.
17C. Old French, from var. of Middle Dutch *camaret*, *cambret*, from Old Picard *camberet* little room.
• The word is not from Latin *caput arietis* ram's head, as sometimes proposed, in supposed allusion to a tavern sign.

cabbala (kəbah´lə), **cabala, kabala, kabbala** *n.* **1** a traditional exposition of the Pentateuch attributed to Moses. **2** mystic or esoteric doctrine.
16C. Medieval Latin *cabbala*, from Hebrew (rabbinical) *qabbālāh* tradition, from *qibbēl* to receive, to accept.

Cabernet (kab´ənā) *n.* **1** a variety of black grape used to make a dry red wine, Cabernet Franc. **2** wine made from these grapes.
19C. French, name of grape variety orig. from Bordeaux, France.
• The word was originally recorded in English as *Carbenet* or *Carbonet*, suggesting a connection with the French *charbon* coal, in reference to the colour of the grape.

cabochon (kab´əshon) *n.* a precious stone polished, and having the rough parts removed, but without facets.
16C. Old French, dim. of *caboche* head.

cabotage (kab´ətij) *n.* **1** (*Naut.*) **a** coastal navigation or shipping. **b** trade between the ports of the same country. **2** the restriction of a country's internal air traffic to carriers belonging to that country.
19C. French, from *caboter* to coast along, ? ult. from Spanish *cabo* cape, headland.

cabotin (kabotī´), (*fem.*) **cabotine** (-tēn´) *n.* (*pl.* **cabotins** (-tī´), **cabotines** (-tēn´)) a third-rate actor, a seeker after publicity.
early 20C. French strolling player, ? from source of CABOTAGE.

cabretta (kəbret´ə) *n.* a type of soft leather made from the skin of a South American sheep.
19C. Spanish, dim. of *cabra* nanny goat.

cabriole (kab´riōl) *a.* (of table and chair legs) shaped in a reflex curve. ~*n.* in

ballet, a leap in which one leg is stretched out and the other is struck against it.
18C. French, from *cabrioler*, earlier *caprioler*, from Italian *capriolare* to leap. See CAPRIOLE.

cabriolet (kabriōlā´, kab´-) *n.* **1** a covered, horse-drawn carriage with two wheels. **2** a type of motor-car with a folding top.
18C. French, dim. of *cabriole* leap. See CAPRIOLE.
• The carriage is so named for its springy, bouncing motion.

cacciatore (kachətaw´ri), **cacciatora** (-rə) *a.* (of meat dishes, esp. chicken) cooked with tomatoes, onions, mushrooms, herbs etc.
mid-20C. Italian hunter.
• The term refers to a dish such as huntsmen would eat. Cp. CHASSEUR.

cache (kash) *n.* **1** a place in which provisions, arms etc. are hidden. **2** the hidden provisions, arms etc. **3** a temporary auxiliary memory allowing high-speed retrieval of frequently used data. ~*v.t.* to hide or conceal in a cache.
18C. French, from *cacher* to hide.

cache-peigne (kashpen´, kash´-) *n.* a bow or trimming for a hat, usually worn at the back.
19C. French, from *cacher* to hide + *peigne* comb.

cache-pot (kash´pō) *n.* an ornamental holder for a plant pot.
19C. French, from *cacher* to hide + *pot* pot.

cache-sexe (kashseks´, kash´-) *n.* a covering for the genitals.
early 20C. French, from *cacher* to hide + *sexe* sex.

cachet (kash´ā) *n.* **1** a seal. **2** a stamp, a characteristic mark. **3** a sign of authenticity. **4** a mark of excellence.

5 prestige. **6** (*Med.*) a flat capsule in which unpleasant-tasting drugs can be administered.
17C. French, from *cacher* to hide, to press, from alt. of Latin *coactare* to constrain.

cachou (kash´oo, -shoo´) *n.* **1** a small pill-like sweet for perfuming the breath. **2** catechu.
16C. French, from Portuguese *cachu*, from Malay *kacu*. Cp. CATECHU.

cachucha (kəchoo´chə) *n.* a lively Spanish dance in triple time.
19C. Spanish small boat, cup, prob. from *cacho* shard, piece, prob. from Popular Latin *cacculus* pot, from alt. of Latin *caccabus*, from Greek *kakkabos*, of Semitic orig.

cacique (kəsēk´), **cazique** *n.* **1** a chief of the indigenous inhabitants of the West Indies or the neighbouring parts of America. **2** a local political leader in this area.
16C. Spanish or French, from Taino lord, chief.

cacodemon (kakədē´mən), **cacodaemon** *n.* **1** an evil spirit. **2** a nightmare. **3** an evil person.
16C. Greek *kakodaimōn* evil genius, from *kakos* bad + *daimōn* divinity, genius.

cacoethes (kakōē´thēz) *n.* **1** a bad habit. **2** an irresistible urge.
16C. Latin, from Greek *kakoēthes*, use as n. of a. *kakoēthes* ill-disposed, from *kakos* bad + ETHOS.

cadastre (kədas´tə) *n.* an official register of the ownership of land as a basis of taxation.
18C. French, from Provençal *cadastro*, from Italian *catastro*, earlier *catastico*, from Late Greek *katastikhon* list, register, from *kata stikhon* line by line.

cadenza (kəden´zə) *n.* (*pl.* **cadenzas**) (*Mus.*) a vocal or instrumental flourish of indefinite form at the close of a movement.
18C. **Italian** cadence.

cadet (kədet´) *n.* **1** a young trainee in the army, navy, air force or police. **2** a young volunteer who receives military training while at school. **3** a younger son. **4** the younger branch of a family. **5** (*Hist.*) a young man, esp. a younger son, who served in the army as a volunteer in the hope of gaining a commission. **6** (*New Zeal.*) a sheep-farming apprentice or trainee.
17C. **French**, earlier *capdet*, from Gascon dial., from dim. of Latin *caput*, *capitis* head.
• The original meaning, younger son or brother, arose because Gascon officers in the French army were usually younger sons or lesser heads of noble families.

cadi (kah´di, kā´-), **kadi, qadi** *n.* (*pl.* **cadis, kadis, qadis**) the judge of a Muslim town or village.
16C. **Arabic** *ḳāḍī* judge. Cp. ALCALDE.

cadre (kah´də, kah´dri) *n.* **1** the permanent establishment or nucleus of a regiment; the skeleton of a regiment. **2** any similar nucleus or basic structure, esp. of key personnel. **3** a group of revolutionary activists. **4** a member of such a group.
19C. **French**, from Italian *quadro*, from Latin *quadrus* square.

caduceus (kədū´siəs) *n.* (*pl.* **caducei** (-siī)) the winged staff of Mercury, borne by him as messenger of the gods.
16C. **Latin**, from Greek (Doric) *karukeion*, rel. to Attic Greek *kērukeion*; neut. a. (used as n.) from *kērux*, *kērukos* herald.

caesura (sizūə´rə), (*NAm.*) **cesura** *n.* (*pl.* **caesuras, caesurae** (-rē), (*NAm.*)

cesuras, cesurae) **1** in classical prosody, the division of a metrical foot between two words, esp. in the middle of a line. **2** in modern prosody, a pause about the middle of a line.
16C. **Latin**, from *caesus*, p.p. of *caedere* to cut.

cafard (kafah´, kaf´ah) *n.* depression, low spirits.
16C. **French** cockroach, hypocrite, ? from Late Latin *caphardum* university gown.
• According to some, the word is from Arabic *kāfir* unbeliever. Cp. KAFFIR.

café (kaf´ā) *n.* **1** a small restaurant serving coffee, tea etc. and light inexpensive meals or snacks. **2** a coffee house or coffee bar. **3** coffee.
19C. **French** coffee, coffee house.

café au lait (kafā ō lā´) *n.* coffee with milk, white coffee.
18C. **French**, from *café* coffee + *au* with + *lait* milk. Cp. CAFÉ NOIR.

café chantant (kafā shātā´) *n.* (*pl.* **cafés chantants** (kafā shātā´)) a café with live musical entertainment.
19C. **French**, lit. singing café, from CAFÉ + pres.p. of *chanter* to sing.

café noir (kafā nwah´) *n.* black coffee.
19C. **French**, from *café* coffee + *noir* black.

cafeteria (kafitiə´riə) *n.* (*pl.* **cafeterias**) a restaurant in which customers fetch their own food and drinks from the counter.
19C. **American Spanish** *cafetería*, from *café* coffee. See CAFÉ.

cafetière (kafətyeə´, -tiə´), **cafetiere** *n.* a type of coffee-pot fitted with a plunger that forces the grounds to the bottom and holds them there while the coffee is poured.
19C. **French**, from *café* coffee. See CAFÉ.

cagoule (kəgool´), **kagoule** *n.* a lightweight weatherproof jacket, usu. hooded.
mid-20C. French cowl, from Latin *cucullus* hooded cape.

cahier (ka´yā) *n.* **1** a notebook. **2** the report of a committee, esp. concerning policy.
19C. French, from Popular Latin *quaternus*, from Latin *quaterni* set of four. Cp. CARNET.
• The simplest form of notebook is a page folded in four.

caïque (kīēk´, kā-), **caique** *n.* **1** a light rowing boat used on the Bosporus. **2** a small sailing vessel of the E Mediterranean.
17C. French, from Italian *caicco*, from Turkish *kayˆk*.

ça ira (sa iəra´) *int.* all will be well, things will work out.
18C. French, lit. that will go, from *ça* that + 3rd pers. sing. fut. of *aller* to go.
• The phrase was popularized in France by a revolutionary song of *c.*1790. It is said to have originated with Benjamin Franklin, who may have uttered it in 1776 when asked for news of the American Revolution.

caisson (kā´sən, kəsoon´) *n.* **1** a large, watertight case or chamber used in laying foundations under water. **2** a similar apparatus used for raising sunken vessels. **3** a floating vessel used as a dock gate. **4** an ammunition chest or wagon. **5** a sunken panel in ceilings etc.
17C. French large chest, from Italian *cassone*, assim. to French *caisse* case.

calabrese (kaləbrā´zi) *n.* a type of green broccoli.
mid-20C. Italian Calabrian, from *Calabria*, a region of S Italy.

calamanco (kaləmang´kō) *n.* (*pl.* **calamancoes**) **1** a Flemish woollen cloth with a fine gloss, and chequered on one side, much in use in the 18th cent. **2** (*usu. pl.*) a garment of this cloth.
16C. Orig. unknown. Cp. Dutch *kalmink*, German *Kalmank*, French *calmande*.

calando (kəlan´dō) *a., adv.* (*Mus.*) gradually becoming softer and slower.
19C. Italian slackening, from *calare* to lower, to drop.

calandria (kəlan´driə) *n.* (*pl.* **calandrias**) a sealed cylindrical vessel with tubes passing through it, used as a heat exchanger, e.g. in nuclear reactors.
early 20C. Spanish, from Greek *kulindros* cylinder.

caldarium (kaldeə´riəm) *n.* (*pl.* **caldaria** (-riə)) a Roman hot bath or room where such baths were taken.
18C. Latin, from *calidus* hot.

caldera (kaldeə´rə) *n.* (*pl.* **calderas**) a large, deep volcanic crater.
19C. Spanish, from Late Latin *caldaria* pot for boiling.

calembour (kaləbuə´) *n.* (*pl.* **calembours** (-buə´)) a pun.
19C. French, of unknown orig.

caliche (kalē´chi) *n.* **1** a deposit of sand, gravel or clay containing minerals (esp. Chile saltpetre), found in very dry regions. **2** a crust of sand cemented with calcium carbonate on the surface of soil in very dry regions.
19C. American Spanish, from Spanish pebble in a brick, from *cal* lime.

calliope (kəlī´əpi) *n.* (*N Am.*) a series of steam-whistles that produce musical notes when played by a keyboard.
19C. Greek *Kalliopē* Calliope, the Muse of epic poetry, whose name means beautiful-voiced, from *kallos, kalli-* beauty + *ōps, opos* voice.

calotte (kəlot´) *n.* **1** a small skullcap worn by Roman Catholic ecclesiastics. **2** a caplike crest on a bird's head. **3** anything cap-shaped. **4** a recess hollowed out in the upper part of a room, chapel etc. to reduce the apparent height.
17C. French, ? rel. to *cale* caul.

caloyer (kal´əyə) *n.* a Greek Orthodox monk, esp. of the order of St Basil.
16C. French, from Italian *caloiero*, from Ecclesiastical Greek *kalogēros*, from *kalos* beautiful + *gērōs* old age.

calpac (kal´pak), **calpack, kalpack** *n.* a high, triangular felt cap worn in the East.
16C. Turkish *kalpak*.

calque (kalk) *n.* a loan translation, a literal translation of a foreign expression.
mid-20C. French copy, tracing, from Italian *calcare* to trample, to press, from Latin *calcare*.

calumet (kal´ūmet) *n.* the tobacco-pipe of the North American Indians, used as a symbol of peace and friendship; the peace pipe.
17C. French, dial. var. of *chalumeau*, from Late Latin *calamellus*, dim. of *calamus* reed. Cp. CHALUMEAU.

calvados (kal´vədos) *n.* apple brandy made in Normandy.
early 20C. French *Calvados*, a department in Normandy, France.

calzone (kaltsō´nā) *n.* (*pl.* **calzones, calzoni** (-ni)) a folded pizza containing a filling.
mid-20C. Italian trouser leg.
● The pizza is so called from its shape.

camaraderie (kamərah´dəri) *n.*
1 comradeship. **2** good fellowship and loyalty among intimate friends.
19C. French, from *camarade* comrade.

camarilla (kaməril´ə) *n.* (*pl.* **camarillas**) a cabal.
19C. Spanish, dim. of *camara* chamber.

cambré (kā´brā) *a.* curved, arched.
early 20C. French, p.p. of *cambrer* to camber, ult. from Latin *camur* curved inwards.
● In ballet the term is used of the body when bent from the waist sideways or backwards.

Camembert (kam´əmbeə) *n.* a soft rich cheese from Normandy.
19C. French *Camembert*, a village in Normandy, France.

camera obscura (kamərə əbskū´rə, obs-) *n.* (*pl.* **camera obscuras**) a dark box, or small room, admitting light through a small pinhole or double-convex lens which projects an image of external objects on an internal screen.
18C. Latin dark chamber.
● The camera obscura was known to Euclid (3C BC) but was popularized by Giovanni Battista della Porta in 1569 and first used for photographic purposes by Thomas Wedgwood in 1794.

camerlengo (kaməleng´gō), **camerlingo** (-ling´-) *n.* (*pl.* **camerlengos, camerlingos**) a papal treasurer.
17C. Italian, from Frankish, ult. from Latin *camera* chamber.

ça m'est égal (sa met egahl´) *int.* it's all the same to me, I don't mind.
19C. French, lit. that is equal to me.

camino real (kamēnō rāahl´) *n.* the best or most successful way of achieving an end.
early 20C. Spanish *camino real* royal road.
● The original *Camino Real* was the main road that in the 16C connected the cities of Gijón, León and Madrid in Spain. In California a coastal road called *El Camino Real* was built during the

Spanish period (1542–1821). The phrase is sometimes misunderstood in English by false association with the James Bond film *Casino Royale* (1967) (or the Ian Fleming novel on which it is based).

camion (kam´iō) *n.* **1** a heavy lorry. **2** a dray.
19C. **French**, of unknown orig.

camisole (kam´isōl) *n.* an underbodice.
19C. **French**, from Italian *camiciola* or Spanish *camisola*, dim. of (respectively) *camicia*, *camisa*, from Late Latin *camisia*. See CHEMISE.

Camorra (kəmor´ə) *n.* **1** a lawless secret society in S Italy, dating from the old kingdom of Naples. **2** any similar group.
19C. **Italian**, ? from Spanish *camorra* dispute, quarrel.

camouflage (kam´əflahzh) *n.* **1** disguise, esp. the concealment of guns, vehicles etc., from the enemy by means of deceptive painting and covering. **2** the natural colouring or markings of some animals, which resemble their surroundings and thus conceal them from predators. **3** concealment of one's actions. ~*v.t.* to disguise.
early 20C. **French**, from thieves' slang *camoufler*, from Italian *camuffare* to disguise, to deceive, with *l* by assoc. with French *camouflet* snub, whiff of smoke in the face.

campagna (kampahn´yə) *n.* open country.
16C. **Italian**, from Late Latin *campania*. Cp. English *champagne*.
• The word is now usually associated with the *Campagna di Roma*, the lowland plain surrounding the city of Rome.

campesino (kampesin´o, kampəsē´nō) *n.* (*pl.* **campesinos** (kampesin´os, kampəsē´nōz)) a peasant farmer in Spain or a Spanish-speaking country.
mid-20C. **Spanish**, from *campo* field.

campo (kam´pō) *n.* (*pl.* **campos**) an area of level or undulating grassland, esp. in Brazil.
19C. **American Spanish or Portuguese** field, open country, from Latin *campus* field.

campus (kam´pəs) *n.* (*pl.* **campuses**) **1** the buildings and grounds of a university or college. **2** a geographically separate part of a university or college. **3** the academic world in general.
18C. **Latin** field.
• The word was first used of the grounds at Princeton University, New Jersey, USA.

canaille (kanī´) *n.* the rabble, the mob.
16C. **French**, from Italian *canaglia* pack of dogs, from *cane* dog.

canapé (kan´əpā), **canape** *n.* **1** a small thin piece of bread or toast topped with cheese, fish etc. **2** a sofa.
19C. **French** bed curtain, from Latin *conopeum* net over a bed.
• The topping 'sits' on bread or toast as if on a sofa. The French word is directly linked to English *canopy*.

canard (kanahd´) *n.* **1** an absurd story, a hoax, a false report. **2** an aircraft having a tailplane mounted in front of the wings.
19C. **French** duck.
• Sense 1 comes from the French phrase *vendre un canard à moitié* to half-sell a duck, i.e. not to sell it at all, so to deceive, to make a fool of.

canasta (kənas´tə) *n.* a card game similar to rummy, played by two to six players, using two packs of playing cards.
mid-20C. **Spanish** basket, from Latin *canistrum*.

cancan (kan´kan) *n.* a stage dance of French origin performed by female dancers, involving high kicking of the legs.

19C. **French**, said to be redupl. of
canard duck. Cp. CANARD.
● According to some, the word is from
French *cancan* gossip, scandal, from
Latin *quamquam* although, and yet, a
word typical of scholarly discussion in
medieval times.

candela (kandel´ə, -dē´-) *n.* a unit of
luminous intensity.
mid-20C. **Latin** candle.

candelabrum (kandəlah´brəm),
candelabra (-brə) *n.* (*pl.*
**candelabrums, candelabra,
candelabras**) a high, ornamental
candlestick or lampstand, usually
branched.
19C. **Latin**, from *candela* candle.

ça ne fait rien (san fã riī´) *int.* **1** it
doesn't matter. **2** you're welcome.
early 20C. **French**, lit. it makes nothing.
● The phrase is mostly used in
response to an expression of thanks.

canephora (kənē´fərə) *n.* (*pl.*
canephorae (-rē)) a sculptured figure
of a young woman carrying a basket on
her head.
17C. **Latin**, from Greek *kanēphoros*,
from *kaneon* basket + *-phoros* carrying.

cangue (kang), **cang** *n.* a heavy wooden
collar or yoke, formerly fixed round the
neck of criminals in China.
17C. **French**, from Portuguese *canga*
yoke, from Annamese *gong*.

cannelloni (kanəlō´ni) *n.pl.* rolls of
sheet pasta filled with meat etc. and
baked.
mid-20C. **Italian**, augm. pl. of *cannello*
stalk.

cannelure (kan´əlūə) *n.* **1** (*Archit.*) a
flute, a channel. **2** a groove round a
projectile.
18C. **French**, from *canneler* to groove, to
flute, from *canne* reed.

Canopus (kənō´pəs) *n.* **1** the bright star
in the constellation Argo. **2** a Canopic
vase.
16C. **Latin**, from Greek *Kanōpus* name
of an ancient Egyptian city.

Cantab (kan´tab) *a.* of Cambridge
(University).
18C. **Abbr.** of **Modern Latin**
Cantabrigiensis, from *Cantabrigia*
Cambridge.

cantabile (kantah´bilā) *a., adv.* (*Mus.*) in
an easy, flowing style. *~n.* a piece or
passage in cantabile style.
18C. **Italian** that can be sung, from
cantare to sing.

cantaloupe (kan´təloop), **cantaloup** *n.*
a small, round, ribbed musk-melon.
18C. **French**, from *Cantaluppi*, a papal
estate near Rome, where it was first
grown on being introduced from
Armenia.

cantata (kantah´tə) *n.* (*pl.* **cantatas**)
(*Mus.*) a poem, a short lyrical drama or
(usu.) a biblical text, set to music, with
solos and choruses.
18C. **Italian** *aria cantata* sung air, with
fem. p.p. of *cantare* to sing.

cantatore (kantətaw´ri) *n.* a male
professional singer.
19C. **Italian** singer, from Latin *cantator*,
from *cantare* to sing.

cantatrice (kantətrē´chā, kātatrēs´) *n.* a
female professional singer.
19C. **French or Italian**, from Latin
cantatrix.

cantilena (kantilā´nə) *n.* (*pl.* **cantilenas**)
(*Mus.*) **1** a ballad. **2** plainsong. **3** a
simple flowing melody or style.
18C. **Italian**, from Latin *cantilena* song,
from *cantillare* to sing low, to hum,
from *cantare* to sing.

cantina (kantē´nə) *n.* (*pl.* **cantinas**) a bar
or wine shop, esp. in Spanish-speaking
countries.
19C. Spanish and Italian cellar, from
Italian *canto* corner, reserved area.

canto (kan´tō) *n.* (*pl.* **cantos**) **1** any one
of the principal divisions of a poem.
2 the upper voice part in choral music.
3 †a song.
16C. Italian song, from Latin CANTUS.

canton *n.* **1** (kan´ton, -ton´) **a** a division
of a country, a small district. **b** a
political division of Switzerland.
2 (kan´tən) (*Her.*) a small division in
the corner of a shield.
16C. Old French, from Provençal,
oblique case of var. of Latin *canthus*.

Cantuar (kan´tūah) *a.* of Canterbury. ~*n.*
Canterbury (the official signature of the
Archbishop of Canterbury).
18C. Abbr. of **Modern Latin**
Cantuariensis, from *Cantuaria*
Canterbury.

cantus (kan´təs) *n.* (*pl.* **cantus**) **1** a chant
or style of singing used in the medieval
church. **2** the upper voice part in choral
music; canto.
16C. Latin song. Cp. CANTO.

canyon (kan´yən), **cañon** *n.* a deep gorge
or ravine with precipitous sides, esp.
of the type formed by erosion in the
western plateaus of the US.
19C. Spanish *cañón* tube, pipe, augm. of
caña, from Latin *canna* reed.

canzona (kantsō´nə) *n.* (*pl.* **canzone**
(-nā)) a musical setting of the words of a
canzone.
19C. Italian, var. of CANZONE.

canzone (kantsō´nā) *n.* (*pl.* **canzoni**
(-ni)) **1** a Provençal or Italian song. **2** a
song resembling a madrigal. **3** a type of
instrumental music.
16C. Italian song. Cp. CANZONA,
CHANSON.

caoutchouc (kow´chook) *n.* raw rubber,
the coagulated juice of certain tropical
trees, which is elastic and waterproof.
18C. French, from obs. Spanish
cauchuc, from Quechua *kauchuk*.

cap-à-pie (kapəpē´) *adv.* (*poet. or facet.*)
from head to foot (armed or dressed).
16C. Old French *cap a pie* (Modern
French *de pied en cap*) head to foot,
from Latin *caput* head + *ad* to + *pes,
pedis* foot.

capias (kā´pias, kap´-) *n.* (*Law*) a judicial
writ ordering an officer to arrest the
person named.
14–15C. Latin you are to seize, 2nd pers.
sing. pres. subj. of *capere* to take.

capo (kap´ō) *n.* (*pl.* **capos**) **1** the head of
a branch of the Mafia. **2** (*Mus.*) a capo
tasto.
mid-20C. Italian, from Latin *caput*
head.

caponier (kapəniə´), **caponiere** *n.* a
covered passage across the ditch of a
fortified place.
17C. Spanish *caponera* capon pen.
● A caponier was originally a place for
keeping capons.

caporal (kapərahl´) *n.* a coarse kind of
French tobacco.
19C. French corporal.
● The tobacco is so called from its
superiority to the *tabac du soldat*
soldier's tobacco.

capot (kəpot´) *n.* the winning of all the
tricks at piquet by one player. ~*v.t.*
(*pres. p.* **capotting**, *past, p.p.* **capotted**)
to win all the tricks from.
17C. French, ? from *capoter*, dial. var. of
chapoter to castrate. Cp. KAPUT.

capo tasto (kapō tas′tō) *n.* (*pl.* **capo tastos**) (*Mus.*) a bar fitted across the fingerboard of a guitar or similar instrument, to alter the pitch of all the strings simultaneously.
19C. Italian head stop.

capote (kəpōt′) *n.* a long cloak or overcoat, usu. with a hood.
19C. French, dim. of *cape* cape.

cappuccino (kapuchē′nō) *n.* (*pl.* **cappuccinos**) **1** white coffee, esp. from an espresso machine, often topped with whipped cream or powdered chocolate. **2** a drink of this.
mid-20C. Italian Capuchin.
• The coffee is so called from its colour, that of the habit worn by certain Capuchin monks.

capriccio (kəprē′chō, -chiō) *n.* (*pl.* **capriccios, capricci** (-chē)) **1** (*Mus.*) a lively composition, more or less free in form. **2** a fanciful work of art.
17C. Italian CAPRICE.

caprice (kəprēs′) *n.* **1** a sudden impulsive change of opinion, mood or behaviour. **2** a whim, a fancy. **3** a disposition to this kind of behaviour. **4** a capriccio.
17C. French, from Italian *capriccio* head with hair standing on end, horror, from *capo* head + *riccio* hedgehog.
• The current sense evolved by association with Italian *capra* goat.

capriole (kap′riōl) *n.* **1** a leap made by a horse without advancing. **2** in ballet, a leap made from bent knees. ~*v.i.* to perform a capriole.
16C. French (now *cabriole*), from Italian *capriola*, from *capriolare* to leap, from *capriolo* roebuck, from Latin *capreolus*, dim. of *caper, capri* goat.

capuche (kəpoosh′) *n.* a hood, esp. the long pointed hood of the Capuchins.
16C. French (now *capuce*), from Italian *cappuccio* hood, cowl. Cp. CAPPUCCINO.

caput (kap′ət) *n.* (*pl.* **capita** (-itə)) the head, the top part.
18C. Latin head.

carabiniere (karəbinyeə′rā) *n.* (*pl.* **carabinieri** (-ri)) a member of the national police force in Italy.
19C. Italian carabineer.

caracol (kar′əkol), **caracole** (-kōl) *n.* **1** a half turn or wheel made by a horse or its rider. **2** a winding staircase. ~*v.i.* (*pres.p.* **caracoling**, *past, p.p.* **caracoled**) **1** to perform a caracol. **2** to caper. ~*v.t.* to make (a horse) caracol.
17C. French snail's shell, spiral. Rel. to ESCARGOT.

carafe (kəraf′, -rahf′, kar′əf) *n.* **1** a wide-mouthed glass container for wine or water at table. **2** as much wine or water as a carafe will hold.
18C. French, from Italian *caraffa*, prob. from Arabic *ġarafa* to draw water.

caramba (kəram′bə, karam′ba) *int.* an exclamation of surprise or dismay.
19C. Spanish, of unknown orig.

carambola (karəmbō′lə) *n.* (*pl.* **carambolas**) **1** the star fruit. **2** the SE Asian tree, *Averrhoa carambola*, that bears this fruit.
16C. Portuguese, prob. from Marathi *karambal.*

carambole (kar′əmbōl) *n.* in billiards, a cannon. ~*v.i.* to make a cannon.
18C. French red ball in billiards, from Spanish *carambola*, appar. from *bola* ball. Prob. not rel. to CARAMBOLA.

caravanserai (karəvan′sərī), **caravansary** (-ri), **caravansera** (-rə) *n.* (*pl.* **caravanserais, caravansaries, caravanseras**) an Oriental inn with a large courtyard for the accommodation of caravans of merchants or pilgrims.
16C. Persian *kārwānsarāy*, from *kārwān* caravan + *sarāy* palace (cp. SERAGLIO).

carbonade (kahbənād´, -nahd´),
carbonnade n. a beef stew made with
beer.
17C. **French**, from Spanish *carbón* coal.

carbonado (kahbənā´dō, -nah´-) n. (*pl.*
carbonados, carbonadoes) a black,
opaque diamond of poor quality, used
industrially in drills etc.
16C. **Portuguese** carbonated.

Carbonari (kahbənah´ri) n.pl. **1** members
of a secret republican society in Italy
and France in the early part of the 19th
cent. **2** any republican revolutionists.
19C. **Italian**, pl. of *carbonaro* collier,
charcoal burner, from *carbone* coal, ult.
from Latin *carbo, carbonis* carbon.
• The Carbonari were reputed to have
evolved from a secret medieval society
whose members were originally
charcoal burners.

caret (kar´ət) n. in writing or printing, a
mark (^) used to show that something,
which may be read above or in the
margin, is to be inserted.
17C. **Latin** it lacks, 3rd pers. sing. pres.
ind. of *carere* to be without, to lack.

caries (keə´riēz) n. (*pl.* **caries**) **1** decay of
the bones or teeth. **2** decay of vegetable
tissue.
16C. **Latin** decay.

carillon (kəril´yən, kar´ilən) n. **1** a set
of bells played by the hand or by
machinery. **2** a tune played on such
bells. **3** a musical instrument (or part of
one) imitating such bells. ~v.i. (*pres.p.*
carillonning, *past, p.p.* **carillonned**)
to play a carillon.
18C. **French**, from alt. of Old French
carignon, quarregnon, from Popular
Latin *quatrinio, quatrinionis*, from Latin
quaternio group of four bells.

carioca (kariō´kə) n. **1** a South American
dance like the samba. **2** music for this
dance. **3** (*coll.* **Carioca**) a native or
inhabitant of Rio de Janeiro.

19C. **Portuguese**, from Tupi *cari* white
+ *oca* house.

carmagnole (kahmənyōl´) n. a lively
song and dance popular during the
French Revolution.
18C. **French** style of jacket popular in
French Revolution, from *Carmagnola*,
a town in Piedmont, NW Italy.

carnet (kah´nā) n. **1** a document allowing
the transport of vehicles or goods across
a frontier. **2** a book of vouchers, tickets
etc.
19C. **French** notebook, from Old French
quaer (Modern French CAHIER), from
Popular Latin *quaternus*, from Latin
quaterni set of four, from *quattuor* four.
• The original sense was a page folded
into four.

carousel (karəsel´), (*esp. N Am.*)
carrousel n. **1** (*N Am.*) a merry-go-
round. **2** a rotating conveyor belt for
luggage at an airport. **3** a rotating
container which delivers slides to a
projector.
17C. **French** *carrousel*, from Italian
carosello tourney, either from Italian
dial. *carusello* ball of clay (which the
contestants threw at each other), or from
Arabic *kurraj* child's toy of model
harnessed horses.
• The word is not related to English
carousal.

carpaccio (kahpach´iō) n. an Italian hors
d'oeuvre comprising thin slices of raw
meat or fish, sometimes served with a
dressing.
early 20C. **Italian**, augm. of *carpa* carp.

carpe diem (kahpā dē´em) *int.* make the
most of the present.
19C. **Latin** seize the day.
• The words come from Horace: *carpe
diem, quam minimum credula postero*
'seize the day, put no trust in the future'
(*Odes* I, xi) (1C BC).

carriole (kar´iōl), **cariole** *n*. **1** a small open carriage. **2** a light covered cart. **3** (*Can.*) an ornamental sledge.
18C. **French**, from Italian *carriuola*, dim. of *carro* carriage.

carte (kaht) *n*. **1** a card. **2** a menu.
14–15C. **French**, from Latin *carta* paper.

carte blanche (kaht blāsh´) *n*. (*pl.* **cartes blanches** (kaht blāsh´)) unlimited power to act.
17C. **French** blank paper, from *carte* card, paper + fem. of *blanc* white.
• The phrase refers to a paper with only the signature written on it, on which the recipient may write his own terms.

carte de visite (kaht də vizēt´) *n*. (*pl.* **cartes de visite** (kaht)) a small photographic portrait mounted on a card.
19C. **French** visiting card, from *carte* card + *de* of + *visite* visit.
• The portraits were originally introduced in 1858 as visiting cards.

carte du jour (kaht dü zhooə´) *n*. (*pl.* **cartes du jour** (kaht)) the menu for a particular day.
19C. **French**, lit. card of the day, from *carte* card + *du* of the + *jour* day.

cartel (kahtel´) *n*. **1** an agreement (often international) among manufacturers to keep prices high, to control production etc. **2** in politics, an alliance between two parties to further common policies.
16C. **French**, from Italian *cartello* placard, challenge, dim. of *carta*, from Latin *charta*.

cartouche (kahtoosh´), **cartouch** *n*. **1** (*Archit.*) a scroll on the cornice of a column. **2** an ornamental tablet in the form of a scroll, for inscriptions etc. **3** an elliptical figure containing the hieroglyphics of Egyptian royal or divine names or titles.
17C. **French**, from Italian *cartoccio*, from *carta* paper.

cascara (kaskah´rə) *n*. **1** (*also* **cascara sagrada** (səgrah´də)) the bark of a North American buckthorn, *Rhamnus purshiana*, used as a laxative. **2** (*also* **cascara buckthorn**) this shrub or tree.
19C. **Spanish** *cáscara* (*sagrada*) (sacred) bark.

†cascarilla (kaskəril´ə) *n*. **1** the aromatic bark of the West Indian shrub *Croton eluteria*. **2** this shrub.
17C. **Spanish**, dim. of *cáscara* bark.

casino (kəsē´nō) *n*. (*pl.* **casinos**) a public establishment, or part of one, used for gambling.
18C. **Italian**, dim. of *casa* house, from Latin *casa* cottage.

casque (kask) *n*. **1** (*poet.*) a helmet. **2** (*Zool.*) a horny cap or protuberance on the head or beak of some birds.
17C. **French**, from Spanish *casco* helmet.

cassata (kəsah´tə) *n*. a type of ice cream containing nuts and candied fruit.
early 20C. **Italian** little case.

casserole (kas´ərōl) *n*. **1** an earthenware, glass etc. cooking pot with a lid. **2** the food cooked in such a pot, esp. a meat dish cooked slowly in the oven. ~*v.t.* to cook in such a pot.
18C. **French**, from *cassole*, dim. of *casse*, from Provençal *casa*, from Late Latin *cattia* ladle, pan, from Greek *kuathion*, dim. of *kuathos* cup.

cassette (kəset´) *n*. **1** a small plastic case containing a length of audiotape, to be inserted into a cassette deck or cassette recorder; an audio cassette. **2** a similar container of videotape; a video cassette. **3** a similar container of photographic film, to be inserted into a camera.
18C. **French**, dim. of *casse*, *caisse* case.

cassino (kas´ēnō) *n.* a card game for two to four players.
18C. **Italian**, var. of CASINO.

cassis (kas´ēs) *n.* a usu. alcoholic cordial made from blackcurrants.
19C. **French** blackcurrant, from Latin *cassia* tree with aromatic bark.

cassolette (kasəlet´), **cassolet** *n.* a small casserole dish.
19C. **French**, from Provençal *casoleta*, dim. of *casola*, from *casa*. See CASSEROLE.
• An earlier 17C sense was a vessel for burning perfumes.

cassoulet (kas´əlā) *n.* a dish consisting of haricot beans stewed with bacon, pork etc.
mid-20C. **French**, dim. of dial. *cassolo* stewpan, tureen.

castrato (kastrah´tō) *n.* (*pl.* **castrati** (-tē)) (*Hist.*) a male soprano castrated before puberty to retain the pitch of his voice.
18C. **Italian**, p.p. (used as n.) of *castrare* to castrate.

casus belli (kahsus bel´ē, kāsəs bel´ī) *n.* (*pl.* **casus belli**) an act that provokes or justifies war.
19C. **Latin**, from *casus* chance + *belli*, gen. of *bellum* war.

catafalque (kat´əfalk) *n.* a temporary stage or tomblike structure for the coffin during a state funeral service.
17C. **French**, from Italian *catafalco*, of unknown orig.
• The French word is related to French *échafaud* scaffold and so to English *scaffold*.

catalogue raisonné (katəlog rāzon´ā) *n.* (*pl.* **catalogues raisonnés** (katəlog rāzon´ā)) a catalogue in which a description of the items is given.
18C. **French**, lit. reasoned catalogue.

catamaran (kat´əməran) *n.* **1** a double-hulled boat. **2** a raft made by lashing two boats together. **3** a raft made by lashing logs together. **4** (*coll.*) a vixenish woman.
17C. **Tamil** *kaṭṭu-maram*, lit. tied wood.

catechu (kat´əchoo) *n.* a brown astringent gum, obtained chiefly from the Asian tree *Acacia catechu*, used in tanning.
17C. **Modern Latin**, from Malay *kacu*. Cp. CACHOU.

catechumen (katikū´mən) *n.* a person who is under Christian instruction preparatory to receiving baptism.
14–15C. **Ecclesiastical Latin** *catechumenus*, from Greek *katēkhoumenos*, pres.p. pass. of *katēkhein* to instruct orally.

catena (kətē´nə) *n.* (*pl.* **catenas**, **catenae** (-nē)) **1** a chain. **2** a connected series.
17C. **Latin**, as in Ecclesiastical Latin *catena patrum* chain of the Fathers (of the Church).

cathedra (kəthē´drə) *n.* **1** the bishop's throne in a cathedral. **2** a professorial chair.
14–15C. **Latin**, from Greek *kathedra* chair.

catholicon (kəthol´ikon) *n.* a universal medicine; a panacea.
14–15C. **French**, from Modern Latin *catholicum* (*remedium*) universal (remedy).

caudillo (kowdē´lyō, kaw-) *n.* (*pl.* **caudillos**) in Spanish-speaking countries, a military leader or head of state.
19C. **Spanish**, from Late Latin *capitellum*, dim. of *caput*, *capitis* head.

cause célèbre (kōz sālebr´, -leb´rə) *n.*
(*pl.* **causes célèbres** (kōz sālebr´,
-leb´rə)) a famous or notorious lawsuit
or controversy.
18C. French famous case, from *cause*
case + *célèbre* famous, celebrated.

causerie (kōzərē´, kō´-) *n.* **1** an essay or
article in a conversational style. **2** an
informal talk.
19C. French, from *causer* to talk, from
Latin *causari* to bring a lawsuit.

ça va (sa va´) *int.* (*also interrog.*) all right,
fine, OK.
19C. French, lit. it is going. Cp. WIE
GEHT'S?

cavalcade (kavəlkād´) *n.* **1** a company
or procession of riders on horseback.
2 a procession of motor vehicles. **3** any
procession.
16C. French, from Italian *cavalcata*,
from *cavalcare* to ride, from Latin
caballus horse.

ça va sans dire (sa va sã diə´) *int.* that
goes without saying.
19C. French.
● The English expression is a direct
translation of the French.

cavatina (kàvətē´nə) *n.* (*pl.* **cavatinas**)
1 a short, simple song. **2** a similar
instrumental composition.
19C. Italian, from *cavata* production of
sound, from *cavare* to extract, to dig out.

cave (kā´vi) *int.* look out!
14–15C. Latin beware!, imper. sing. of
cavere to beware. Cp. CAVEAT.

caveat (kav´iat) *n.* **1** a warning, a caution.
2 (*Law*) a process to stop or suspend
proceedings.
16C. Latin let him beware, 3rd pers.
sing. pres. subj. of *cavere* to beware.

caveat emptor (kaviat emp´taw) *int.* let
the buyer beware; the purchaser is
responsible for the quality of the
purchase.
16C. Latin, from CAVEAT + *emptor*
purchaser.
● The expression has a defined
application in English law. Under
Roman law *caveat venditor* let the seller
beware had a similar force.

cavo-relievo (kahvōrəlyā´vō) *n.* (*pl.*
cavo-relievos) a sculpture made by
hollowing out a flat surface and leaving
the figures standing out to the original
surface level.
19C. Italian *cavo-rilievo* hollow relief,
from *cavo* hollow + *rilievo* RELIEVO.

cedi (sē´di, sā´-) *n.* (*pl.* **cedi, cedis**) the
standard unit of currency in Ghana.
mid-20C. Ghanaian, ? alt. of English
shilling.

cedilla (sədil´ə) *n.* **1** a mark (¸) placed
under a *c* in French, Portuguese etc., to
show that it has the sound of *s*. **2** a
similar mark used in other languages,
such as Turkish, to denote other sounds.
16C. Spanish (now also *zedilla*), dim. of
zeda (letter) Z. Cp. ZETA.
● The mark was formerly used in
Spanish.

ceilidh (kā´li) *n.* an informal gathering,
esp. in Scotland or Ireland, for music,
dancing etc.
19C. Irish *céilidhe* (now *céili*), from
Old Irish *céilide* visit, from *céile*
companion.

celesta (səles´tə) *n.* (*pl.* **celestas**) a
keyboard instrument in which steel
plates are struck by hammers.
19C. Pseudo-Latin, appar. based on
French *céleste* heavenly. See CELESTE.

celeste (səlest´) *n.* **1** a celesta. **2** a voix
céleste.
19C. French *céleste* celestial, from Latin
caelestis, from *caelum* heaven.

census (sen´səs) *n.* (*pl.* **censuses**) **1** an official enumeration of the inhabitants of a country. **2** the statistical result of such an enumeration. **3** any similar enumeration.
17C. **Latin**, from *censere* to assess.

centavo (sentah´vō) *n.* (*pl.* **centavos**) **1** a hundredth part of the basic unit of currency of Portugal and some Latin American countries. **2** a coin of this value.
19C. **Spanish and Portuguese**, from Latin *centum* hundred.

centesimo (sentes´imō, chentez´-) *n.* (*pl.* **centesimos**) **1** a hundredth part of the basic unit of currency of Italy, Panama, Uruguay etc. **2** a coin of this value.
19C. **Italian** *centesimo* and **Spanish** *centésimo*, from Latin *centesimus* hundredth part.

centime (sã´tēm) *n.* **1** a hundredth part of the basic unit of many currencies, e.g. the French franc. **2** a coin of this value.
19C. **French**, from Old French *centiesme, centisme* (Modern French *centième*), from Latin *centesimus* hundredth part.

centimo (sen´timō, then´-) *n.* (*pl.* **centimos**) **1** a hundredth part of the basic unit of currency in Spain, Paraguay, Venezuela etc. **2** a coin of this value.
19C. **Spanish** *céntimo*, from Latin *centesimus* hundredth part.

cento (sen´tō) *n.* (*pl.* **centos**) **1** a composition of verses from different authors. **2** a string of quotations etc.
17C. **Latin** patchwork garment.

cerise (sərēs´, -rēz´) *n.* a red colour, cherry red. ~*a.* of this colour.
19C. **French** cherry.

certiorari (sœtiəreə´rī, -rah´rē) *n.* (*Law*) a writ issuing from a superior court calling for the records of or removing a case from a court below.
14–15C. **Late Latin**, pass. of Latin *certiorare* to inform, from *certior*, comp. of *certus* certain.

cervelat (sœ´vəlat, -lah) *n.* a kind of smoked sausage made from pork or beef.
17C. **French** (now *cervelas*), from Italian *cervellata* Milanese sausage made of meat and pig's brain (Italian *cervello* brain).

c'est la vie (se la vē´) *int.* that's life!
early 20C. **French**.

ceteris paribus (kātəris par´ibus) *adv.* other things being equal.
17C. **Modern Latin**, abl. pl. of *ceterus* remaining over + *par* equal.

cf. *int.* compare.
Abbr. of **Latin** *confer*, 2nd pers. sing. imper. of *conferre* to compare.
● The Latin word dates from the 19C. Cp. the similar abbreviation *cp.*, which can represent either English *compare* or Latin *compara*, 2nd pers. sing. imper. of *comparare* to compare.

Chablis (shab´lē) *n.* a dry white wine made at Chablis.
17C. **French** *Chablis*, central France.

cha-cha (chah´chah), **cha-cha-cha** (chahchahchah´) *n.* (*pl.* **cha-chas, cha-cha-chas**) **1** a ballroom dance of Latin American origin. **2** music for this dance. ~*v.i.* (*pres.p.* **cha-chaing**, *past, p.p.* **cha-chaed, cha-cha'd**) to dance the cha-cha.
mid-20C. **American Spanish**, of imit. orig. Cp. CHACONNE.

chaconne (shəkon´) *n.* **1** (*Mus.*) a set of variations over a continuously repeated ground bass. **2** (*Hist.*) a Spanish dance in triple time; music for this dance.
17C. **French**, from Spanish *chacona*, prob. of imit. orig., from sound of castanets used in dance. Cp. CHA-CHA.

chacun à son goût (shakī a sŏ goo´) *int.*
everyone to their taste, to each his own.
19C. French, from *chacun* each one + *à*
to + *son* his, her + *goût* taste.
• The expression is sometimes wrongly
thought to derive from French *chacun a
son goût* everyone has their taste. The
French themselves usually say *chacun
son goût.*

chador (chŭd´ə), **chadar, chuddar** *n.* a
large veil, worn over the head and body
by Muslim women.
17C. Urdu *chādar*, from Persian *čādar*
sheet, veil.

chagrin (shəgrin´, shag´-) *n.* vexation,
disappointment, mortification. ~*v.t.*
(*pres.p.* **chagrining**, *past, p.p.*
chagrined) to vex, to disappoint, to
mortify.
17C. French rough skin, from Turkish
*sağr^* rump, influ. by French *grain* grain.
• The French word also gave English
shagreen sharkskin used for decoration,
rough untanned leather.

chaise (shāz) *n.* **1** a light horse-drawn
carriage for travelling or pleasure. **2** a
post-chaise. **3** a chaise longue.
17C. French, var. of *chaire* chair.

chaise longue (shāz lŏg´) *n.* (*pl.*
chaises longues (shāz lŏg´)) **1** a type of
sofa for reclining on, with a back and
armrest at one end only. **2** a chair with
support for the legs.
19C. French long chair.

chakra (chŭk´rə, chak´-) *n.* (*pl.* **chakras**)
in yoga, a centre of spiritual power in
the human body.
18C. Sanskrit *cakra* circle, rel. to
English *wheel*. Cp. CHARKA.

chalet (shal´ā) *n.* **1** a small house or hut
on a mountainside, esp. in Switzerland.
2 a small low house with projecting
eaves. **3** a small dwelling, usu. of wood,
used esp. for holiday accommodation.

19C. Swiss French, dim. of Old French
chasel farmstead, from deriv. of Latin
casa hut, cottage.

challah (khahlah´, hah´lə), **hallah** *n.*
(*pl.* **challahs, challoth** (-lot´), **hallahs,
halloth**) a loaf of white bread, usu.
plaited, eaten by Jews on the Sabbath.
19C. Hebrew *ḥallāh*, prob. from *ḥll* to
hollow, to pierce.

chalumeau (shal´ümō) *n.* (*pl.*
chalumeaux (-mō)) **1** a musical
instrument with a reed mouthpiece,
the precursor of the modern clarinet.
2 (**chalumeau register**) the lowest
register of the clarinet.
18C. French, from Late Latin
calamellus, dim. of *calamus* reed.

chalutz (hahluts´, khah-), **halutz** *n.*
(*pl.* **chalutzim** (-lootsēm´, -loot´sim),
halutzim) a member of a group of
immigrants to Israel who established
the first agricultural settlements
(kibbutzim).
early 20C. Hebrew *ḥălūs* pioneer.

chamade (shəmahd´) *n.* (*Mil., Hist.*) the
beat of a drum or sound of a trumpet
demanding or announcing a surrender
or parley.
17C. French, from Portuguese *chamada*,
from *chamar*, from Latin *clamare* to
shout.

Chambertin (shā´bətī) *n.* a dry red
Burgundy wine.
18C. French *Chambertin*, the vineyard
of origin, in the Côte de Nuits, E France.

chambré (shom´brā) *a.* (of wine) warmed
to room temperature.
mid-20C. French, p.p of *chambrer* to
keep in a room, from *chambre* room.

chamois *n.* (*pl.* **chamois** (-wah, -wahz))
1 (sham´wah) a goatlike European
antelope, *Rupicapra rupicapra*.
2 (sham´i) chamois leather.

16C. Old French, prob. from a pre-Roman Alpine word rel. to German *Gemse* chamois.

champignon (shā´pinyō, cham´pinyən) *n.* an edible mushroom, esp. the fairy-ring champignon, *Marasmius oreades*.
16C. French, dim. of *champagne* plain.

champlevé (shā´ləvā) *n.* **1** enamelling by the process of inlaying vitreous powders into channels cut in the metal base. **2** an object so enamelled. ~*a.* of or relating to this process.
19C. French, from *champ* field + *levé* raised.

chandelier (shandəliə´) *n.* a hanging branched frame for a number of lights.
17C. French, from *chandelle* candle.

chandelle (shandel´) *n.* an abrupt upward turn of an aircraft, using its momentum to increase the rate of climb. ~*v.i.* to carry out this manoeuvre.
early 20C. French candle.

chanson (shā´sō) *n.* a song.
15C. French, from Latin *cantio*, *cantionis*. See CANZONE.

chanson de geste (shāsō də zhest´)) *n.* (*pl.* **chansons de geste** (shāsō də zhest´)) an Old French epic poem of the 11th–15th cents., usu. celebrating heroic exploits.
19C. French song of heroic deeds.
● The earliest and most famous example of the genre was the *Chanson de Roland* (*c.*1100).

chantage (shātahzh´, chahn´tij) *n.* extortion of money by blackmail.
19C. French, from *chanter* to sing.
● The implication is that if the extortioner does not get his money he will 'sing' by broadcasting real or imaginary scandalous revelations.

chanterelle (shahntərel´) *n.* an edible fungus, *Cantharellus cibarius*.
18C. French, from Modern Latin *cantharellus*, dim. of *cantharus*, from Greek *kantharos* drinking vessel.
● The fungus is so called because of its funnel shape.

chanteuse (shātœz´) *n.* a female nightclub singer.
19C. French, fem. of *chanteur* singer, from *chanter* to sing.

Chantilly (shantil´i, shan´tili) *n.* **1** (*also* **Chantilly lace**) a delicate type of lace. **2** (*also* **Chantilly cream**) whipped cream, usu. sweetened or flavoured.
18C. French *Chantilly*, a town near Paris, France.

chaparajos (chaparā´khōs, sha-), **chaparejos**, **chaps** (chaps) *n.pl.* leather leggings worn by cowboys.
19C. Mexican Spanish *chaparreras*, from *chaparra*, *chaparro*. See CHAPARRAL.
● The spelling with -*ajo*, -*ejo* has perhaps been influenced by Spanish *aparejo* equipment. The leggings were worn by cowboys to protect their trousers against the thorns of the chaparral.

chaparral (shapəral´) *n.* (*N Am.*) a thicket of low evergreen oaks, or of thick undergrowth and thorny shrubs.
19C. Spanish, from *chaparra*, *chaparro* dwarf evergreen oak.

chapati (chəpat´i), **chapatti**, **chupatty** *n.* (*pl.* **chapatis**, **chapattis**, **chupatties**) in Indian cookery, a round, thin loaf of unleavened bread.
19C. Hindi *capātī*, from *capānā* to flatten, to roll out, ult. from Dravidian.

chapeau (shap´ō) *n.* (*pl.* **chapeaux** (-ōz)) a hat.
15C. French, from Old French *chapel*, from Latin *capellum*, dim. of *cappa* cap.

chapelle ardente (shapel ahdăt´) n. (pl.
chapelles ardentes (shapel ahdăt´)) a
chamber for the lying-in-state of a
distinguished person.
19C. **French**, lit. burning chapel.
• The allusion is to the candles and
torches that illumine the chamber.

chaperone (shap´ərōn), **chaperon** n.
1 a married or elderly woman who
accompanies a young unmarried woman
on social occasions or in public places.
2 any person who accompanies or
supervises young people in public
places. ~v.t. to act as chaperone to.
14–15C. **Old French** headdress, from
chape cape, hood.
• A chaperone was originally a hood or
cap. The current sense arose in the 18C
to denote an older woman who
'sheltered' a younger as a hood shelters
the face.

chappal (chap´əl, chŭp´-) n. a leather
sandal worn in India.
19C. **Hindi** *cappal*.

charabanc (shar´əbang) n. (dated) a
coach for day trippers.
19C. **French** *char-à-bancs* carriage with
seats.
• The charabanc was originally a horse-
drawn vehicle, and was superseded by
the motor coach.

charade (shərahd´) n. **1** (pl., usu. constr.
as sing.) a game in which a word or
phrase is guessed from actions or
utterances representing each syllable
and the whole word or phrase. **2** any of
the clues in this game. **3** a ridiculous
pretence. **4** a type of riddle.
18C. **French**, from Provençal *charrado*
conversation, from *charra* chatter, prob.
of imit. orig.

charas (chah´rəs) n. hashish, cannabis
resin.
19C. **Hindi** *caras*.

charcuterie (shahkoo´təri) n. **1** a shop
selling cold cooked meats and similar
products. **2** these products.
19C. **French**, from obs. *char* (Modern
French *chair*) *cuite* cooked flesh.

Chardonnay (shah´dənā) n. **1** a white
grape grown in the Burgundy region of
France and elsewhere, used to make
wine. **2** a white wine made from these
grapes.
early 20C. **French** *Chardonnay*, a village
in E central France.

chargé d'affaires (shahzhā dafeə´),
chargé (shah´zhā) n. (pl. **chargés
d'affaires** (shah´zhā), **chargés**) **1** a
diplomatic agent acting as deputy to
an ambassador. **2** an ambassador to a
country of minor importance.
18C. **French** (one) charged with affairs.

charisma (kəriz´mə), **charism** (kar´izm)
n. (pl. **charismata** (-mətə), **charisms**)
1 personal magnetism or charm enabling
one to inspire or influence other people.
2 a quality which inspires admiration or
devotion. **3** a divinely given power or
talent.
17C. **Ecclesiastical Latin**, from Greek
kharisma, from *kharis* favour, grace.

charivari (shahrivah´ri), (esp. N Am.)
shivaree (shivərē´) n. (pl. **charivaris,
shivarees**) **1** a mock serenade of
discordant music. **2** a confusion of
sounds, a hubbub.
17C. **French**, ? from Popular Latin
caribaria, from Greek *karebaria*
headache, or ult. of imit. orig.

charka (chah´kə), **charkha** n. (pl.
charkas, charkhas) an Indian
spinning wheel, used esp. for spinning
cotton.
19C. **Urdu** *charka* spinning wheel, from
Persian *čarka*, rel. to Sanskrit *cakra*
wheel. Cp. CHAKRA, CHUKKA.

charlatan (shah´lətən) *n.* a person who pretends to have skill or knowledge; a quack; an impostor.
17C. French, from Italian *ciarlatano*, from *ciarlare* to babble, to patter, of imit. orig.
• The word is said by some to derive from Italian *cerretano* inhabitant of *Cerreto*, a town in central Italy.

charlotte (shah´lət) *n.* a kind of pudding made with fruit and thin slices of bread or layers of breadcrumbs etc.
18C. French, ? from female forename *Charlotte*.
• The pudding is popularly said to be named for Queen *Charlotte*, 1744–1818, wife of George III, a patron of apple growers. Attempts to derive the word from the obsolete English *charlet* 14–15C, a type of custard containing milk, eggs, pork etc. boiled to a curd, cannot be sustained.

Charmeuse (shahmœz´) *n.* a soft silky fabric with a smooth finish.
early 20C. French, fem. of *charmeur* charmer.

charqui (chah´ki) *n.* beef cut into strips and dried in the sun, jerked beef.
17C. American Spanish, from Quechua *cc'arki* dried flesh in long strips.

chartreuse (shahtrœz´) *n.* **1** a pale green or yellow liqueur made with aromatic herbs. **2** the colour of this. **3** a dish of fruit in jelly. ~*a.* of the colour of chartreuse.
19C. French, fem. of *Chartreux* Carthusian.
• The liqueur was originally made by the Carthusian monks of La Grande Chartreuse, near Grenoble, France. The place name probably derives from the *Caturiges*, the Alpine people who settled in the region in pre-Roman times. Their own name in turn apparently derives from Gaulish *catu*

battle + *riges*, pl. of *rix* king. They were thus the 'kings of battle'.

chasse (shas) *n.* a liqueur drunk after coffee.
18C. French, abbr. of *chasse-café*, lit. chase-coffee. See CAFÉ.

chassé (shas´ā) *n.* a gliding step in dancing. ~*v.i.* (*pres.p.* **chasséing**, *past*, *p.p.* **chasséd**) to perform this step.
19C. French, p.p. of *chasser* to chase.
• The step is so called because one foot displaces the other as if chasing it. The French word also gave English *sashay* to walk ostentatiously.

chassepot (shas´pō) *n.* a breech-loading rifle used in France, 1866–74.
19C. French, from Antoine A. *Chassepot*, 1833–1905, its French designer.

chasseur (shasœ´) *n.* **1** a huntsman. **2** a light-armed French soldier. **3** a uniformed attendant. ~*a.* (esp. of chicken) cooked in a sauce of white wine and mushrooms.
18C. French hunter, from *chasser* to hunt, to chase. Cp. CACCIATORE.

chassis (shas´i) *n.* (*pl.* **chassis** (-iz)) **1** the framework of a motor vehicle, aeroplane etc. **2** a framework supporting a piece of electronic equipment. **3** the base-frame of a cannon or gun carriage.
17C. French *châssis*, from Latin *capsa* box.

chateau (shat´ō), **château** *n.* (*pl.* **chateaux** (-tōz), **châteaux**) a castle or country house in French-speaking countries.
18C. French *château* castle, from Latin *castellum*, dim. of *castrum* camp, fortified post.

chateaubriand (shatōbrē´ā) *n.* a thick steak of beef cut from the fillet.
19C. French, from François René,

Vicomte de *Chateaubriand*, 1768–1848, French writer and statesman.
• The steak is said to be so called because it was specially prepared (grilled and served with Béarnaise sauce) for Chateaubriand by his chef, Montmirel, when he was French ambassador in London in 1822.

chatelain (shat´əlān) *n.* the lord of a castle.
14–15C. Old French *chastelain* (Modern French *châtelain*), from Latin *castellanus* one living in a fortress.
• A *chatelaine* was originally a female castellan who wore a special belt for carrying keys etc.

chatoyant (shətoi´ənt, shatwayā´) *a.* having a changeable lustre or colour, like that of a cat's eye in the dark. ~*n.* a stone with changing lustre, such as the cat's-eye.
18C. French, pres.p. of *chatoyer* to glisten, to shimmer, from *chat* cat.

chatty (chat´i) *n.* an Indian earthen pitcher or water-pot.
18C. Hindi *cāṭī*, from Tamil *caṭṭi*.

chaud-froid (shōfrwah´) *n.* a dish of cold meat in an aspic sauce.
19C. French, lit. hot-cold.
• The dish is so called because the hot cooked meat is allowed to grow cold before being eaten.

chauffeur (shō´fə, -fœ´) *n.* a person employed to drive a motor car. ~*v.t.* to drive (a car or a person) as a chauffeur. ~*v.i.* to act as a chauffeur.
19C. French stoker, fireman, from *chauffer* to heat.

chaussée (shosā´) *n.* (*pl.* **chausées** (shosā´)) a causeway, a high road, especially in France or Belgium.
19C. French, ult. from the same source as English *causeway*, from Latin *calx* limestone.

chautauqua (chawtawk´wə, shə-) *n.* (*Hist.*, *N Am.*) an institution providing adult education, entertainment etc., esp. at outdoor meetings in the summer.
19C. *Chautauqua*, a county and lake in New York State, USA.

chef (shef) *n.* a professional cook, esp. the head cook of a restaurant etc.
19C. French head, chief, from Latin *caput* head.

chef d'équipe (shef dekēp´) *n.* (*pl.* **chefs d'équipe** (shef)) the manager of a sports team, especially as responsible for travelling arrangments.
late 20C. French head of team. See CHEF, ÉQUIPE.

chef-d'oeuvre (shādœvr´, -dœv´rə) *n.* (*pl.* **chefs-d'oeuvre** (shādœvr´, -dœv´rə)) a masterpiece.
17C. French chief (piece) of work. Cp. CHEF, OEUVRE.

Cheka (chek´ə) *n.* (*Hist.*) the secret police in Russia (1917–22).
early 20C. Russian *che, ka*, pronunciation of initials of *Chrezvychaïnaya komissiya* Extraordinary Commission.
• The full Russian title was *Chrezvychaïnaya komissiya po bor'be s kontrrevolyutsieĭ i sabotazhem* Extraordinary Commission for Combating Counterrevolution and Sabotage.

chela (chā´lə) *n.* (*pl.* **chelas**) a student or novice in esoteric Buddhism.
19C. Hindi *celā*.

chemin de fer (shəmī də feə´) *n.* a variety of baccarat.
19C. French railway (lit. road of iron).
• The game is said to be so named because of the speed at which it is played. French *chemin de fer* is a direct rendering of English *railway*.

chemise (shəmēz´) *n*. **1** an undergarment of linen or cotton worn by women. **2** a straight, loose-fitting dress.
12–14C. **Old French**, from Late Latin *camisia* shirt, nightgown. Cp. CAMISOLE.

chemisette (shemizet´) *n*. **1** a woman's light bodice. **2** a piece of lace worn in the opening of a dress below the throat.
19C. **French**, dim. of CHEMISE.

chenille (shənēl´) *n*. **1** a round tufted or fluffy cord of silk or worsted. **2** a pile fabric made with similar yarn.
18C. **French** hairy caterpillar, from Latin *canicula*, dim. of *canis* dog.
• The material is so named from its furry appearance.

cheongsam (chongsam´, chiong-) *n*. a Chinese woman's long, tight-fitting dress with slit sides.
mid-20C. **Chinese** (Mandarin) *chángshān*, from *cháng* long + *shān* unlined upper garment.

cherchez la femme (sheəshā la fam´) *int*. look for the woman (expressing the suspicion that an otherwise or otherwise unexplained event has probably been directly or indirectly caused by a woman).
19C. **French**.
• The phrase was popularized from its occurrence in Alexandre Dumas *père*'s novel *Les Mohicans de Paris* (1864).

chéri (sherē´), (*fem*.) **chérie** *n*. darling, dear one.
19C. **French**, p.p. of *chérir* to cherish, from *cher* dear, from Latin *carus*.
• French *chérie* gave the English female first name Cherie.

chernozem (chœ´nəzem), **tschernosem** *n*. a dark-coloured, very fertile soil found in temperate climates.
19C. **Russian**, from *chërnyǐ* black + Slavonic base of *zemlya* earth.

che sarà sarà (kā sərah sərah´) *int*. what will be, will be.
16C. **Italian**, from *che* what + 3rd pers. sing. fut. of *essere* to be.
• The expression was popularized by the song *Que será será*, sung by Doris Day in 1956, these words being the Spanish equivalent.

chetnik (chet´nik) *n*. (*Hist*.) a member of a Serbian nationalist guerrilla force active before and during the two World Wars.
early 20C. **Serbo-Croat** *četnik*, from *četa* band, troop.

cheval (shəval´) *n*. horse, frame.
15C. **French**, from Latin *caballus* horse.
• The word is not used independently in English but only in combination, as for *cheval glass* (19C) a large swinging mirror mounted on a frame, so called from its resemblance to a rider in the saddle.

cheval de bataille (shəval də batī´) *n*. (*pl*. **chevaux de bataille** (shəvō)) an obsession, a pet subject.
19C. **French**, lit. battle horse, warhorse. Cp. English 'hobbyhorse'.

cheval-de-frise (shəvaldəfrēz´) *n*. (*pl*. **chevaux-de-frise** (-vō-)) a portable fence, consisting of a bar armed with two rows of long spikes, for checking attacks by cavalry etc.
17C. **French** horse of Friesland.
• The fences were named ironically from their use by the Friesians, who had no cavalry.

chevalier (shevəliə) *n*. **1** a member of some foreign orders of knighthood or of the French Legion of Honour. **2** †a knight. **3** a chivalrous man.
14–15C. **Old French**, from Medieval Latin *caballarius*, from Latin *caballus* horse.

chevalier d'industrie (shəvaliā dīdüstrē´) *n.* (*pl.* **chevaliers d'industrie** (shəvaliā)) an adventurer, a swindler.
18C. French, lit. knight of industry, from CHEVALIER + *d'* of + *industrie* industry.
● 'Industry' here has its obsolete sense (in both French and English) of 'resourcefulness', 'ingenuity'. A *chevalier d'industrie* lives by his wits.

chevelure (shəvlūə´) *n.* (*pl.* **chevelures** (-lūə´)) a head of hair.
14-15C. Old French *cheveléure* (Modern French *chevelure*), from Latin *capillatura*, from *capillatus* hairy, from *capillus* hair.

chevet (shəvā´) *n.* an apse.
19C. French pillow, from Latin *capitellum* top opening in a tunic, from *caput, capitis* head.
● The eastern extremity of a French Gothic church, considered externally, resembles the top of a bed, where one rests one's head.

chèvre (shev´rə) *n.* a type of cheese made from goats' milk.
mid-20C. French goat, from Latin *capra*.

chevrette (shəvret´) *n.* a thin goatskin leather used for gloves.
19C. French, dim. of CHÈVRE.

chevron (shev´rən) *n.* **1** a V-shaped badge on the sleeve of a uniform, esp. of a non-commissioned officer in the armed forces. **2** one of a series of horizontal V-shaped marks on a road sign, usu. indicating a bend. **3** (*Her.*) an inverted V shape, an honourable ordinary representing two rafters meeting at the top. **4** (*Archit.*) a zigzag moulding. **5** any V-shaped stripe or pattern.
14-15C. Old French, from Latin *caper* goat.
● The badge is perhaps so called from the angular shape of a goat's hind legs.

chez (shā) *prep.* at the house of.
18C. French, from Old French *chiese*, from Latin *casa* cottage.

chez nous (shā noo´) *adv.* at our house, in our family.
19C. French, from CHEZ + *nous* us.
● The phrase was at one time a popular suburban house name.

chi (kī) *n.* the 22nd letter of the Greek alphabet (X, χ).
14-15C. Greek *khi*.

Chianti (kian´ti) *n.* (*pl.* **Chiantis**) a dry red wine from Tuscany.
19C. Italian *Chianti* Mountains, Tuscany.

chiaroscuro (kiahrəskoo´rō, -skuə´-) *n.* (*pl.* **chiaroscuros**) **1** the treatment or effects of light and shade in drawing, painting etc. **2** a drawing in black and white. **3** variety or contrast in a literary work etc. ~*a.* **1** obscure. **2** half-revealed.
17C. Italian *chiaro* clear, bright + *oscuro* dark, obscure.

chiasmus (kīaz´məs) *n.* (*pl.* **chiasmi** (-mī)) the inversion of order in parallel phrases, as in *you came late, to go early would be unreasonable.*
17C. Modern Latin, from Greek *khiasmos*, from *khiazein* to mark with a chi, from *khi* CHI.

chibouk (chibook´), **chibouque** *n.* a long Turkish pipe for smoking.
19C. French *chibouque*, from Turkish *çubuk*, earlier *çˆbˆk*, tube, pipe.

chic (shēk) *n.* **1** smartness, style. **2** the best fashion or taste. ~*a.* (*comp.* **chic-er**, *superl.* **chic-est**) stylish, elegant.
19C. French, ? from German *Schick* skill, rather than Spanish *chico* little.

chicane (shikān´) *n.* **1** an artificial obstacle on a motor-racing track. **2** in bridge or whist, a hand of cards

containing no trumps. **3** chicanery. ~*v.i.*
†to use chicanery. ~*v.t.* †to cheat, to
deceive.
17C. French *chicaner* to pursue at law,
to quibble, of unknown orig.
• The original sense was sense 3. Sense
2 evolved in the 19C, and sense 1 in the
mid-20C.

Chicano (chikah´nō, -kā´nō) *n.* (*pl.*
Chicanos) a person of Mexican origin
living in the US.
mid-20C. Spanish, alt. of *mejicano*
Mexican, from *Méjico* Mexico.

chicharron (chēchərōn´, chicharon´)
n. (*pl.* **chicharrones** (chēchərō´niz,
chicharon´es)) a piece of crackling
served as a delicacy.
19C. American Spanish *chicharrón*.

chichi (shē´shē) *a.* **1** showy, affectedly
pretty or fashionable. **2** (of a person)
fussy; pretentious; affected. ~*n.* **1** the
quality of being chichi. **2** something that
is chichi.
early 20C. French, prob. imit., but
suggestive of CHIC.
• The word is not related to *chi-chi*
half-caste girl, Eurasian woman, which
is imitative of the speech of some
Eurasians in India.

chiffon (shif´on) *n.* **1** a gauzy semi-
transparent fabric. **2** (*pl.*) trimmings,
esp. of dresses. ~*a.* **1** made of chiffon.
2 (of puddings) having a fine, light
consistency.
18C. French, from *chiffe* rag, from
Germanic. Rel. to English *chip*.

chignon (shēn´yō) *n.* a coil or knot of
long hair at the back of the head.
18C. French nape of the neck, from var.
of Latin *catena* chain.

chilli (chil´i), **chili, chile** *n.* (*pl.* **chillies,
chilies, chiles**) the hot-tasting ripe pod
of a species of capsicum, esp. *Capsicum*
annuum, used to flavour, sauces, pickles
etc.
17C. Spanish *chile*, from Nahuatl *chilli*.

chilli con carne (chili kon kah´ni) *n.* a
Mexican dish of minced meat with
beans in a chilli sauce.
19C. Spanish CHILLI with meat.

chimera (kimiə´rə, kī-), **chimaera** *n.*
1 a fabulous fire-eating monster, with
a lion's head, a serpent's tail, and the
body of a goat. **2** any incongruous
conception of the imagination. **3** an
imaginary terror. **4** any cartilaginous fish
of the family Chimaeridae. **5** (*Biol.*) a
hybrid of genetically dissimilar tissues.
14–15C. Latin *chimaera*, from Greek
khimaira she-goat, monster, from
khimaros he-goat.
• The original chimera was said to be a
monster personifying snow or winter
(Greek *khiōn* snow, *kheimōn* winter).

chimichanga (chimichang´gə) *n.* a
deep-fried rolled tortilla with a savoury
filling.
mid-20C. Mexican Spanish trinket.

chiné (shēnā´, shē´-) *a.* (of fabric) having
a mottled pattern.
19C. French, p.p. of *chiner* to dye the
warp of, from *Chine* China.
• The warp or weft threads of the fabric
were dyed to give it a mottled pattern in
a supposed Chinese style.

chino (chē´nō) *n.* (*pl.* **chinos**) **1** a tough,
twilled cotton fabric. **2** (*pl.*) trousers,
often off-white, made of this fabric.
mid-20C. American Spanish toasted.
• The original sense was a Spanish
American of mixed blood, with skin of a
light brown ('toasted') colour. The word
was then applied to military trousers of
this colour.

chinoiserie (shinwah´zəri, shē-, -rē´) *n.*
1 a style of Western art and architecture

using Chinese motifs. **2** an object or objects in this style.
19C. French, from *chinois* Chinese.

chipolata (chipəlah´tə) *n.* (*pl.* **chipolatas**) a small sausage.
19C. French, from Italian *cipollata* dish of onions, from *cipolla* onion.
● The sausage was originally flavoured with onion. The word is unrelated to English *chip*.

chi-rho (kīrō´) *n.* (*pl.* **chi-rhos**) a Christian monogram of the Greek letters chi (X) and rho (P).
19C. Greek CHI + *rho*, the first two letters of *Khristos* Christ.
● The emperor Constantine used the monogram on his standards following a vision in AD 312, in which he was told 'By this sign thou shalt conquer'. It was subsequently taken up in Christian art. Cp. IHS.

chiton (kī´tən, -ton) *n.* **1** an ancient Greek tunic. **2** a woman's dress in this style. **3** a mollusc of the genus *Chiton,* having a shell made up of overlapping plates.
19C. Greek *khitōn* tunic.

chocho (chō´chō) *n.* (*pl.* **chochos**) (*W Ind.*) a choko.
18C. Spanish, of American Indian orig.

choko (chō´kō) *n.* (*pl.* **chokos**) (*Austral., New Zeal.*) a succulent vegetable like a cucumber.
18C. Spanish, of American Indian orig.

choli (chō´li) *n.* (*pl.* **cholis**) an Indian woman's garment, a short tight-fitting bodice worn under a sari.
early 20C. Hindi *colī.*

chop suey (chop soo´i) *n.* (*pl.* **chop sueys**) a Chinese dish of shredded meat and vegetables served with rice.
19C. Chinese (Cantonese dial.) *zá suì* mixed bits, miscellaneous scraps.

chorizo (chərē´zō, chaw-) *n.* (*pl.* **chorizos**) a highly seasoned pork sausage made in Spain or Mexico.
19C. Spanish.

chou (shoo) *n.* (*pl.* **choux** (shoo)) **1** a small ball of pastry filled with cream. **2** a rosette or ornamental knot on a woman's hat or dress.
18C. French cabbage, from Latin *caulis.*
● The *chou* is named from its appearance.

chouette (shooet´) *n.* a player in a two-handed game such as backgammon or piquet who plays against a number of others as a means of enabling three players to compete with one other.
19C. French, lit. barn owl, dim. of Old French *chou,* from Frankish *kāwa,* ult. of imit. orig.
● The player is a 'lone hand', just as the barn owl is a 'lone hunter'.

choux (shoo) *n.* a rich light pastry made with eggs.
18C. French pl. of *chou* cabbage, from Latin *caulis.*
● The pastry is so called because it is used for making cabbage-shaped buns.

chowkidar (chō´kidah) *n.* (*Ang.-Ind.*) a watchman.
17C. Urdu *chaukīdār,* from Hindi *caukī* prison + Urdu and Persian *-dār* keeper. Cp. dated English *chokey* prison.

chow mein (chow mān´) *n.* a Chinese dish of meat and vegetables served with fried noodles.
19C. Chinese *chăo miàn* fried noodles.

chukka (chŭk´ə), **chukker** *n.* any of the periods into which a polo game is divided.
19C. Hindi *cakar,* from Sanskrit *cakra* circle, wheel.

churidars (choo´ridahz) *n.pl.* tight-fitting trousers worn by Indian men and women.
19C. Hindi *churi* + *dar* tight-fitting.

churinga (chəring´gə) *n.* (*pl.* **churinga, churingas**) (*Austral.*) a sacred amulet.
19C. Australian Aboriginal (Aranda) *tywerrenge.*

churrasco (churas´kō) *n.* a meat dish of South America, consisting of steak barbecued over wood or charcoal.
early 20C. American Spanish, prob. from dial. *churrascar* to burn.

chutzpah (khuts´pə, huts´-) *n.* (*sl.*) barefaced audacity.
19C. Yiddish, from Aramaic *ḥuṣpā.*

chypre (shēpr, shē´prə) *n.* a strong sandalwood perfume.
19C. French Cyprus, where prob. orig. made.

ciabatta (chəbat´ə, -bah´tə) *n.* (*pl.* **ciabattas**) **1** a moist type of Italian bread made with olive oil. **2** a loaf of this bread.
late 20C. Italian slipper, ref. to shape of loaf.

ciao (chow) *int.* (*coll.*) used to express greeting or leave-taking.
early 20C. Italian, dial. alt. of *schiavo* (I am your) slave, from Medieval Latin *sclavus* slave.

ciborium (sibaw´riəm) *n.* (*pl.* **ciboria** (-riə)) **1** a vessel with an arched cover for the Eucharist. **2** a shrine or tabernacle to receive this. **3** (*Archit.*) a baldachin canopy or shrine.
16C. Medieval Latin, from Greek *kibōrion* cup-shaped seed vessel of the Egyptian water-lily.
● In sense 1 the word has probably been influenced by Latin *cibus* food.

cicerone (chichərō´ni, sisə-) *n.* (*pl.* **cicerones, ciceroni** (-rō´ni)) a guide who explains the curiosities and interesting features of a place to strangers.
18C. Italian, from Latin *Cicero, Ciceronis.*
● Cicero (106–43 BC) was a noted Roman orator and the word was originally applied by English tourists to the guides in Rome, famous for their verbosity.

cicisbeo (chichizbā´ō) *n.* (*pl.* **cicisbei** (-bā´ē)) the recognized lover of a married woman.
18C. Italian, of unknown orig.
● The word is said by some to be an inversion of Italian *bel cece* beautiful chickpea.

ci-devant (sēdəvā´) *a.* former, of a past time. ~*adv.* formerly. ~*n.* a French aristocrat during the Revolution.
18C. French formerly, from phr. *ci-devant noble* formerly a noble (formula used of an aristocrat who lost his title in the Revolution), from *ci* here + *devant* before.

ci-gît (sēzhē´) here lies (inscribed on gravestones).
early 20C. French here lies, from *ci* here + 3rd pers. sing. pres. indic. of *gésir* to lie, from Latin *iacere* to lie. Cp. GÎTE.

cimbalom (sim´bələm) *n.* a Hungarian type of dulcimer.
19C. Hungarian, from Italian *cembalo, cimbalo* CYMBALO.

cineaste (sin´iast), **cineast** *n.* **1** a cinema enthusiast. **2** a person who makes films.
early 20C. French *cinéaste*, from *ciné*, abbr. of *cinéma* cinema + *-aste*, from *enthousiaste* enthusiast.

cinéma-vérité (sēnāmə vā´rētā), **ciné-vérité** (sēnā-) *n.* cinema which approaches a documentary style by using realistic settings, characters etc.
mid-20C. French, lit. cinema verity.

cinque (singk), **cinq** *n.* five, esp. the five at cards or dice.
14–15C. Old French *cinc*, *cink* (Modern French *cinq*), from Latin *quinque* five.

cinquecento (chingkwichen´tō) *n.* the revived classical style of art and literature that characterized the 16th cent., esp. in Italy.
18C. Italian five hundred. Cp. QUATTROCENTO.
● Italian regards the 16C as the 1500s.

circa (sœ´kə) *prep.* about, around (often used with dates). ~*adv.* about, nearly.
19C. Latin about, around.

ciré (sē´rā) *n.* satin or other fabric with a waxed surface. ~*a.* having such a surface.
early 20C. French, p.p. of *cirer* to wax.

cire perdue (siə pœdū´) *n.* a method of casting bronze, using wax which is subsequently melted and replaced by the metal.
19C. French lost wax, from *cire* wax + fem. p.p. of *perdre* to lose.

cirque (sœk) *n.* **1** (*Geol.*) a semicircular basin in a hillside or valley, caused by erosion. **2** (*poet.*) a circus or arena. **3** (*poet.*) a ring.
17C. French, from Latin *circus* circle, circus.

cithara (sith´ərə) *n.* (*pl.* **citharas**) an instrument resembling a lyre.
18C. Latin, from Greek *kithara* stringed musical instrument.

citius, altius, fortius (kit´iəs, al´tiəs, faw´tiəs) *int.* faster, higher, stronger (the motto of the Olympic Games).
early 20C. Latin, comp. of adv. of *citus* swift, *altus* high, *fortis* strong.
● The phrase was devised as the motto of the modern Olympic Games in 1918 and incorporated in the Olympic emblem in 1920.

citole (sit´ōl, -ōl´) *n.* (*Hist.*) a stringed musical instrument.
14–15C. Old French, from Latin CITHARA.

clachan (klakh´ən) *n.* a small village or hamlet in the Highlands of Scotland.
14–15C. Gaelic and Irish *clachán*, prob. from *clach* stone.

clair-de-lune (kleədəloon´) *n.* a soft white or pale blue-grey colour.
19C. French, lit. moonlight.

clairvoyance (kleəvoi´əns) *n.* **1** the (supposed) power of perceiving future events or objects not present to the senses. **2** unusual sensitivity or insight.
19C. French, from *clair* clear + *voyant*, pres.p. of *voir* to see.

claque (klak) *n.* **1** a body of hired applauders. **2** the system of engaging applauders.
19C. French, from *claquer* to clap, of imit. orig.

clarabella (klarəbel´ə) *n.* (*pl.* **clarabellas**) an organ stop giving a powerful fluty tone.
19C. Latin *clarus* (fem. *clara*) clear + *bellus* (fem. *bella*) beautiful.

clavicembalo (klavichem´bəlō) *n.* (*pl.* **clavicembalos**) a harpsichord.
18C. Italian, from Medieval Latin *clavicymbalum*, from *clavis* key + *cymbalum* cymbal.

clef (klef) *n.* (*Mus.*) a symbol at the beginning of a stave denoting the pitch and determining the names of the notes according to their position on the stave.
16C. French, from Latin *clavis* key.

clepsydra (klep´sidrə) *n.* (*pl.* **clepsydras, clepsydrae** (-drē)) an ancient instrument used to measure time by the dropping of water from a graduated vessel through a small opening.
14–15C. Latin, from Greek *klepsudra*, from *kleps-*, comb. form of *kleptein* to steal + *hudōr* water.

cliché (klē´shā), **cliche** *n.* **1** a hackneyed phrase. **2** anything hackneyed or overused. **3** (*Print.*) a stereotype, esp. a stereotype or electrotype from a block. **4** a photographic negative.
19C. French, p.p. (used as *n.*) of *clicher* to stereotype, prob. of imit. orig.
● French *clicher* is said to represent the sound of a die striking molten metal. Sense 1 dates from the late 19C.

clientele (klēontel´) *n.* **1** clients collectively. **2** customers, patients, the patrons of a theatre or restaurant. **3** followers or adherents. **4** clientship.
16C. French *clientèle*, from Latin *clientela* clientship.
● Sense 4 was taken direct from Latin. Sense 1 dates from the 19C and was borrowed from French.

clique (klēk) *n.* **1** an exclusive set. **2** a coterie of snobs.
18C. Old French, from *cliquer* to make a noise, from Middle Dutch *klikken* to click.

clochard (kloshah´) *n.* (*pl.* **clochards** (-ah)) a French beggar or vagrant.
mid-20C. French, from *clocher* to limp, from Popular Latin *cloppicare*, from Latin *cloppus*.

cloche (klosh) *n.* **1** a glass cover, orig. bell-shaped, put over young or tender plants to preserve them from frost. **2** a close-fitting bell-shaped hat.
19C. French bell.

cloisonné (klwazənā´, klwah´-, klwahzon´-) *a.* partitioned, divided into compartments. ~*n.* cloisonné enamel.

19C. French, p.p. of *cloisonner*, from *cloison* partition, from Popular Latin *clausio, clausionis*, from *clausus* closed.

cloqué (klō´kā, klok´-) *n.* a type of fabric with an embossed surface.
early 20C. French blistered, from *cloque* blister, rel. to *cloche* bell.

cloture (klō´chə) *n.* (*N Am.*) closure of debate in a legislative body. ~*v.t.* to closure.
19C. French *clôture*, from Old French *closure* closure.

clou (kloo) *n.* **1** the centre of interest or attraction. **2** the principal idea.
19C. French nail, stud.

coco-de-mer (kōkōdəmeə´) *n.* **1** a palm tree of the Seychelles, *Lodoicea maldivica*. **2** the fruit of this tree, a double coconut.
19C. French coco from the sea.
● The tree is so called as it was first known from its nuts, which were found floating in the sea.

cocotte[1] (kəkot´) *n.* a small dish in which food is cooked and served.
early 20C. French, from *cocasse*, from Latin *cucuma* cooking vessel.

cocotte[2] (kəkot´) *n.* (*dated*) a prostitute, a woman from the demi-monde.
19C. French child's nickname for a hen. Cp. French *poule* hen, promiscuous young woman.

coda (kō´də) *n.* (*pl.* **codas**) **1** (*Mus.*) an adjunct to the close of a composition to enforce the final character of the movement. **2** in ballet, the concluding part of a dance. **3** any concluding part, event etc.
18C. Italian, from Latin *cauda* tail.

codex (kō´deks) *n.* (*pl.* **codexes, codices** (kō´disēz, kod´-)) **1** a manuscript volume, esp. of the Bible or of texts of classics. **2** (*Med.*) a list of prescriptions.

16C. Latin *codex, codicis* block of wood, block split into leaves, book.

cogito (kō´gitō, -jitō) *n.* (*Philos.*) the principle that a being exists because it thinks or has awareness.
19C. Latin I think, 1st pers. sing. pres. indic. of *cogitare*.
• The concept comes from the formula COGITO ERGO SUM.

cogito ergo sum (kō´gitō œgō sum´, -jitō) I think, therefore I am.
19C. Latin.
• The philosophical tenet *cogito, ergo sum* appears in the 1641 Latin edition of René Descartes' *Le Discours de la méthode* (1637) as a translation of the French original formula *Je pense, donc je suis*. Cp. COGITO.

cognac (kon´yak) *n.* French brandy of fine quality, esp. that distilled in the neighbourhood of Cognac.
16C. French *Cognac*, a town and region in W France.

cognomen (kognō´mən) *n.* (*pl.* **cognomens, cognomina** (-nom´inə))
1 a surname. **2** the last of the three names of an ancient Roman citizen.
3 a title, a name. **4** a nickname.
17C. Latin, from *co-*, assim. form of *cum* with + *gnomen* name.

cognoscente (konyəshen´ti) *n.* (*pl.* **cognoscenti** (-ti)) a connoisseur.
18C. Italian one who knows (now *conoscente*), Latinized form of *conoscente*, from Latin *cognoscens, cognoscentis*, pres.p. of *cognoscere* to know.

coifféur (kwafœ´) *n.* a hairdresser.
19C. French, from *coiffer* to dress the hair, from Old French *coife* headdress, from Late Latin *cofia* helmet.

coiffure (kwafūə´) *n.* **1** a method of dressing the hair, a hairstyle. **2** †a headdress.

19C. French, from *coiffe*, from Old French *coife* headdress, from Late Latin *cofia* helmet, and the source of English *coif*.

collage (kolahzh´) *n.* **1** a picture made of pieces of paper, fabric etc., glued on to a surface. **2** the art form in which such pictures are made. **3** any collection of diverse things or ideas.
early 20C. French gluing, from *colle*, from Greek *kolla* glue.

collectanea (kolektā´niə) *n.pl.* a collection of passages from various authors, a miscellany or anthology.
17C. Latin, neut. pl. of *collectaneus*, from *collectus*, p.p. of *colligere* to collect.
• The word is used as an adjective in Caesar's *Dicta collectanea* (1C BC) and as a noun in Solinus' *Collectanea rerum memorabilium* (3C AD).

collegium (kəlē´jiəm) *n.* (*pl.* **collegiums, collegia** (-jiə)) **1** a college of cardinals. **2** an administrative board.
19C. Latin association, from *collega* colleague.

cologne (kəlōn´) *n.* eau-de-Cologne.
19C. French, abbr. of EAU-DE-COLOGNE.

colonnade (kolənād´) *n.* a series or range of columns at regular intervals.
18C. French, earlier *colonnate*, from *colonne* column, based on Italian *colonnato*.

colophon (kol´əfon) *n.* **1** a publisher's identifying symbol. **2** a device or inscription formerly at the end of a book, giving the printer's name, place, date of publication etc.
17C. Late Latin, from Greek *kolophōn* summit, finishing touch, prob. rel. to Latin *collis* hill.
• Sense 1 evolved in the mid-20C.

coloratura (kolərətoo´rə) *n.* (*Mus.*) **1** the ornamental use of variation, trills etc. in vocal music. **2** a singer, esp. a soprano, capable of singing such ornamented music.
18C. **Italian**, from Late Latin *coloratus* coloured.

colossus (kəlos´əs) *n.* (*pl.* **colossuses, colossi** (-sī)) **1** a statue of gigantic size. **2** any gigantic person, animal or thing. **3** a person of great power or genius.
14–15C. **Latin**, from Greek *kolossos*, name given by Herodotus to statues of ancient Egyptian temples, appar. from an Aegean language.
● The name became widely familiar from the Colossus of Rhodes, a gigantic statue said to have straddled the harbour entrance on the island of Rhodes in ancient Greece in the 3C BC.

colporteur (kōl´pawtə, -paw´-) *n.* a person who travels about selling religious books, tracts etc.
18C. **French**, from *colporter*, prob. alt. of *comporter*, from Latin *comportare* to transport, from *com-* with + *portare* to carry.

columbarium (koləmbeə´riəm) *n.* (*pl.* **columbaria** (-riə)) **1** a pigeon house; a dovecote. **2** a place of interment, esp. among the ancient Romans, fitted with niches like pigeon-holes to receive the cinerary urns. **3** a hole left in a wall to receive the end of a timber.
18C. **Latin**, from *columba* dove.

coma[1] (kō´mə) *n.* (*pl.* **comas**) a state of absolute unconsciousness, characterized by the absence of any response to external stimuli or inner need.
17C. **Modern Latin**, from Greek *kōma, kōmatos*, rel. to *koitē* bed, *keisthai* to lie down.

coma[2] (kō´mə) *n.* (*pl.* **comae** (-mē)) **1** (*Astron.*) the nebulous covering of the nucleus of a comet. **2** (*Bot.*) the assemblage of branches constituting the head of a forest tree. **3** (*Bot.*) the tuft of hairs terminating certain seeds.
17C. **Latin**, from Greek *komē* hair of the head.

comédie humaine (komedē ümen´) *n.* (*pl.* **comédie humaines** (ümen´)) the sum of human activities or a literary representation of this.
19C. **French**, lit human comedy.
● The phrase became familiar as the collective title of 91 interconnected novels and stories by Honoré de Balzac (1799–1850).

comédie larmoyante (komedē lahmwahyāt´) *n.* (*pl.* **comédie larmoyantes** (lahmwahyāt´)) a sentimental or moralizing comedy.
19C. **French**, lit. weeping comedy.
● The term was originally applied to the plays of Pierre-Claude Nivelle de La Chaussée (1701–85), author of such comedies as *La Fausse Antipathie* (1733) and *L'Homme de fortune* (1751).

comedienne (kəmēdien´) *n.* a female comedian.
19C. **French** *comédienne*, fem. of *comédien* comedian.

comédie noire (komedē nwah´) *n.* (*pl.* **comédie noires** (nwah´)) a humorous treatment of unpleasant or upsetting themes.
mid-20C. **French**, lit. black comedy.
● The English equivalent, 'black comedy', is now more widely used.

Comintern (kom´intœn) *n.* the Third Communist International, founded in Moscow in 1919, dissolved in June 1943.
early 20C. **Russian** *komintern*, abbr. of *Kom*munisticheskiĭ *Intern*atsional Communist International.

comitadji (komitajˊi), **komitadji, komitaji** *n.* a member of a band of Balkan guerrillas.
early 20C. Turkish *komitacī* member of a (revolutionary) committee, from *komite* committee.

commando (kəmahnˊdō) *n.* (*pl.* **commandos**) (*Mil.*) **1** a body of men called out for military service; a body of troops. **2** a body of troops selected and trained to undertake a specially hazardous raid on or behind the enemy lines. **3** a member of such a body. **4** a mobile amphibious force. **5** (*Hist.*) an armed force of Boers in South Africa. ~*a.* of or relating to a commando.
18C. Portuguese (now *comando*), from *commandar* to command.
● Senses 2 and 3 date from World War II.

comme ci comme ça (kom sē kom saˊ) *a.* middling, indifferent, so-so. ~*adv.* indifferently.
mid-20C. French like this like that, from *comme* like, as + *ci* this, *ça* that.

commedia dell'arte (kəmādiə delahˊti) *n.* Italian comedy of the 16th–18th cents., using improvisation and stock characters.
19C. Italian comedy of art.

comme il faut (kom ēl fōˊ) *a.* as it should be, correct, genteel.
18C. French as it is necessary, from *comme* like, as + *il* it + *faut*, 3rd pers. sing. pres. of *falloir* to be necessary.

commendam (kəmenˊdam) *n.* **1** (*Hist.*) the holding of a vacant ecclesiastical benefice in trust until an incumbent was appointed. **2** the holding of a benefice in the absence of the regular incumbent. **3** a benefice so held.
16C. Ecclesiastical Latin, acc. sing of *commenda*, from phr. *dare in commendam* to give (a benefice) in charge, from *commendare* to entrust.

commère (komˊeə), **commere** *n.* a female compère.
early 20C. French, fem. of COMPÈRE.

commis (komˊi) *n.* (*pl.* **commis** (komˊi, komˊiz)) **1** an agent. **2** an apprentice or assistant waiter or chef.
16C. French, p.p. (used as n.) of *commettre* to entrust.

communiqué (kəmūˊnikā) *n.* an official announcement.
19C. French, p.p. (used as n.) of *communiquer* to communicate.

compadre (kompahˊdri) *n.* (*NAm., coll.*) a friend.
19C. Spanish godfather, benefactor.

compagnon de voyage (kompanyō də vwahyahzhˊ) *n.* (*pl.* **compagnons de voyage** (kompanyō)) a travelling companion, a fellow traveller.
18C. French, lit. companion of (the) voyage.

compendium (kəmpenˊdiəm) *n.* (*pl.* **compendiums, compendia** (-diə)) **1** a handbook or reference book. **2** an abridgement. **3** an epitome, a summary. **4** a brief compilation. **5** a collection of board or card games in one box. **6** any similar collection or package.
16C. Latin profit, saving, from *com-*, alt. of *cum* with + *pendere* to weigh.

compère (komˊpeə), **compere** *n.* a person who introduces the items in a stage or broadcast entertainment. ~*v.t.* to act as compère of. ~*v.i.* to act as compère.
18C. French godfather, from Medieval Latin *compater*, from *com-*, alt. of *cum* with + *pater* father.
● The current sense dates from the early 20C.

complaisant (kəmplāˊzənt) *a.* **1** courteous, deferential. **2** acquiescent, obliging.

17C. French obliging, pres.p. of *complaire* to acquiesce in order to please, from Latin *complacere* to be very pleasing.

compos mentis (kompos men'tis), (*coll.*) **compos** (kom'pos) *a.* in one's right mind.
17C. Latin, lit. master of the mind, from *compos* (*com-*, alt. of *cum* with + *potis* powerful) + gen. sing. of *mens*, *mentis* mind. Cp. NON COMPOS MENTIS.

compote (kom'pōt) *n.* fruit stewed or preserved in syrup.
17C. French, from Old French *composte*, from Latin *composita*, fem. p.p. (used as n.) of *componere* to compound, to place together.

comprador (kom'prədaw), **compradore** *n.* 1 (*Hist.*) in China and Japan, a Chinese or Japanese person employed by a European business house as an agent or intermediary. 2 an agent of a foreign power.
17C. Portuguese buyer, from Latin *comparator*, from *comparare* to purchase, from *com-*, alt. of *cum* with + *parare* to furnish.

compte rendu (kõt rãdü') *n.* (*pl.* **comptes rendus** (kõt rãdü')) a statement, report or review.
19C. French account rendered, from *compte* account, from Latin *computare* to reckon + p.p. of *rendre* to give back.

con amore (kon amaw'rā) *adv.* 1 with devotion. 2 (*Mus.*) lovingly, tenderly.
18C. Italian with love, from *con*, from Latin *cum* with + *amore*, from Latin *amor* love.

con brio (kon brē'ō) *adv.* (*Mus.*) with vigour or spirit.
19C. Italian with vigour, from *con*, from Latin *cum* with + BRIO.

concertante (konchətan'ti) *n.* (*pl.* **concertanti** (konchətan'ti)) (*Mus.*) 1 a piece of music containing a number of solo passages. 2 (*Hist.*) instrumental parts that are present throughout a musical composition.
18C. Italian, part. n. of *concertare* to arrange, to bring into agreement.

concertino (konchətē'nō) *n.* (*pl.* **concertinos**) (*Mus.*) 1 a short concerto. 2 the soloist or soloists playing in a concert.
18C. Italian, dim. of CONCERTO.

concerto (kənshœ'tō, -chiə'-) *n.* (*pl.* **concertos, concerti** (-ti)) a composition for a solo instrument or solo instruments with orchestral accompaniment.
18C. Italian, from *concertare* to arrange, to bring into agreement.

concerto grosso (kənshœtō gros'ō, -chiə'-) *n.* (*pl.* **concerti grossi** (kənshœti gros'i, -chiə'-)) a composition for an orchestra and a group of soloists playing together.
18C. Italian, lit. big concerto.
● The style was popularized by the *concerti grossi* of Arcangelo Corelli (1653–1713), published posthumously in 1714, and especially by Bach's *Brandenburg Concertos* (1720–21).

conchiglie (kongkē'li, -liā) *n.* pasta formed into small shell shapes.
early 20C. Italian, lit. little shells, ult. from Latin *concha* shell, the source of English *conch*.

concierge (konsieəzh') *n.* 1 a doorkeeper, a porter, a janitor. 2 a hotel employee who assists guests by booking tours etc.
16C. French, from Old French *cumcerges*, ? from Popular Latin *conservius*, from Latin *con-*, alt. of *cum* with + *servus* slave.

concours (kŏkuə´, kŏ´-) n. (pl. **concours** (kŏkuə´, kŏ´kuəz)) **1** a competition. **2** a concours d'élégance.
mid-20C. French contest.

concours d'élégance (kŏkuə dālāgās´) n. a competition for the best car etc. judged on appearance rather than performance.
mid-20C. French contest of elegance.

condottiere (kondotyeə´ri) n. (pl. **condottieri** (kondotyeə´ri)) (Hist.) **1** a leader of a troop of mercenaries, esp. in Italy. **2** a member of such a troop.
18C. Italian, from condotta contract, from fem. p.p. of condurre to conduct.

conférencier (kŏferāsyā´) n. (pl. **conférenciers** (-syā´)) a lecturer, a public speaker, a compère.
19C. French, from conférence conference.

confetti (kənfet´i) n. **1** bits of coloured paper thrown at weddings etc. **2** sweets thrown at carnivals in Italy.
19C. Italian, pl. of confetto sweet, bon-bon.
• Sense 2 was the original sense.

confiteor (kənfit´iaw), **Confiteor** n. a Roman Catholic formula of confession.
12–14C. Latin I confess, first word of the formula Confiteor Deo Omnipotenti I confess to Almighty God, etc.

confrère (kŏ´freə, kon´-) n. a fellow-member of a profession, religion, association etc.
14–15C. Old French, from Medieval Latin confrater, from con-, alt. of cum with + frater brother.

con fuoco (kon fwok´ō) adv. (Mus.) with fire and spirit.
19C. Italian with fire. Cp. CON BRIO, CON SPIRITO.

conga (kong´gə) n. **1** a Latin American dance performed by several people in single file. **2** the music for this dance. **3** a conga drum. ~v.i. (ṁrd. pers. sing. pres. **congas**, pres.p. **congaing**, past, p.p. **congaed** (-gəd)) to perform this dance.
mid-20C. American Spanish, from Spanish, fem. of congo of the Congo.

congé (kŏ´zhā) n. **1** leave-taking, departure, farewell. **2** dismissal. **3** permission to depart; leave. **4** (Archit.) a type of concave moulding.
14–15C. Old French congié (Modern French congé), from Latin commeatus passage, leave to pass, from commeare to go and come, from com-, alt. of cum with + meare to go.

congé d'élire (kŏzhā deliə´) n. **1** formal permission to elect a nominated candidate. **2** permission given to a dean and chapter to elect a bishop nominated by the Crown.
16C. French leave to elect, from CONGÉ + d' to + élire to elect.

congeries (kənjiə´rēz, -jer´iēz) n. (pl. **congeries**) a collection or heap of particles, things, ideas etc.
16C. Latin heap, pile, from congerere to heap up.

congou (kong´goo), **congo** (-gō) n. a kind of Chinese black tea.
18C. Abbr. of **Chinese** gōngfu chá tea for the discerning, from gōngfu effort + chá tea.

con moto (kon mō´tō) adv. (Mus.) briskly, with movement.
19C. Italian with movement, from con, from Latin cum with + moto movement.

connoisseur (konəsœ´) n. **1** a person skilled in judging, esp. in the fine arts. **2** a critic, a person of taste. **3** a person with expert knowledge or appreciation (of).

18C. Old French (Modern French *connaisseur*), from *conoistre, conoiss-* (Modern French *connaître*) to know.

conquistador (konkwis´tədaw, -kēstədaw´) *n*. (*pl*. **conquistadors, conquistadores** (-daw´rāz)) any of the Spanish conquerors of America in the 16th cent.
19C. Spanish, from *conquistar* to conquer, from *conquista* conquest.

conservatoire (kənsœ´vətwah) *n*. a public school of music or other fine art.
18C. French, from Italian *conservatorio* conservatory.
• Italian *conservatorio* was originally the term for a hospital or school for orphans and foundlings where a musical education was given.

consommé (kənsom´ā) *n*. a clear soup made by boiling meat and vegetables to form a concentrated stock.
19C. French, p.p. (used as n.) of *consommer*, from Latin *consummare* to bring together, to finish up. Not rel. to English *consume*.

con sordino (kon sawdē´nō) *adv*. (*Mus.*) with a mute.
19C. Italian with (a) mute, from *con*, from Latin *cum* with + SORDINO.

consortium (kənsaw´tiəm) *n*. (*pl*. **consortia** (-tiə), **consortiums**) **1** an association of companies, financial interests etc. **2** fellowship, coalition, union. **3** (*Law*) the right of a husband or wife to association with the other.
19C. Latin, from *consors, consortis* partner.

conspectus (kənspek´təs) *n*. (*pl*. **conspectuses**) **1** a general sketch or survey. **2** a synopsis.
19C. Latin, p.p. (used as n.) of *conspicere* to observe.

con spirito (kon spir´itō) *adv*. (*Mus.*) in a lively manner, with spirit.
18C. Italian with spirit, from *con*, from Latin *cum* with + *spirito* spirit.

consul (kon´səl) *n*. **1** an official appointed by a state to reside in a foreign country to protect its mercantile interests and citizens there. **2** (*Hist.*) either of the two supreme magistrates of ancient Rome, invested with regal authority for one year. **3** (*Hist.*) each of the three supreme magistrates of the French Republic, 1799–1804.
14–15C. Latin, rel. to *consulere* to take counsel.
• The original sense was sense 2. The title then passed to sense 3, with sense 1 emerging in the 16C.

contadina (kontədē´na, kontədē´nə) *n*. (*pl*. **contadine** (-tədē´nā), **contadinas** (-tədē´nəz)) an Italian peasant girl or woman.
19C. Italian, fem. of CONTADINO.

contadino (kontədē´no, kontədē´nō) *n*. (*pl*. **contadini** (-tədē´ni), **contadinos** (-tədē´nōz)) an Italian peasant or countryman.
17C. Italian, from *contado* county, agricultural area round a city.

conte (kōt) *n*. a tale, esp. a short story in prose.
19C. French tale.

Conté (kon´tā), **conté** *a*. (*attrib.*) denoting a type of hard crayon or pencil used by artists etc.
19C. French, from Nicolas Jacques *Conté*, 1755–1805, French inventor.

contessa (kontes´ə) *n*. (*pl*. **contessas**) an Italian countess.
19C. Italian, from Medieval Latin *comitissa*.

continuo (kəntin´ūō) *n*. (*pl*. **continuos**) (*Mus.*) a bass part with harmony

indicated by shorthand marks; thorough bass.
18C. Italian, from Latin *continuus* continuous.

continuum (kəntinˊūəm) *n.* (*pl.* **continua** (-ūə), **continuums**) **1** an unbroken mass, series or course of events. **2** a continuous series of component parts that pass into each other.
17C. Latin, neut. sing. (used as n.) of *continuus* continuous.

conto (konˊtō) *n.* (*pl.* **contos**) a Portuguese or Brazilian monetary unit, equal to 1000 escudos or cruzeiros.
17C. Portuguese, from Latin *comptus* count.

contra (konˊtrə) *n.* (*pl.* **contras**) a counter-revolutionary guerrilla fighter in Nicaragua.
late 20C. Abbr. of **Spanish** *contrarrevolucionario* counter-revolutionary.

contralto (kəntralˊtō) *n.* (*pl.* **contraltos, contralti** (-tē)) **1** the lowest of the three principal varieties of the female voice, the part next above the alto in choral music. **2** a person who sings this part. **3** music written for this part. ~*a.* singing or arranged for contralto.
18C. Italian, from *contra* against + ALTO.

contrecoup (kōˊtrəkoo) *n.* a repercussion, an adverse consequence.
18C. French, from *contre* against + *coup* blow.

contredanse (konˊtrədahns), **contradance** *n.* a French version of the English country dance.
19C. French, alt. of English *country dance* by assoc. with *contre* against, opposite.

contretemps (kōˊtrətã) *n.* (*pl.* **contretemps** (-tãz)) **1** an unexpected event which throws everything into confusion. **2** an awkward or embarrassing occurrence or situation. **3** a disagreement, a confrontation.
17C. French, orig. motion out of time, from *contre* against + *temps* time.

convenance (konˊvənahns, kŏvnãsˊ) *n.* (*usu. pl.*) conventional usage or propriety.
15C. French, from *convenir* to suit, from Latin *convenire* to come together.

conversazione (konvəsatsiōˊni) *n.* (*pl.* **conversaziones, conversazioni** (-ni)) a social meeting devoted to literary, artistic or scientific subjects.
18C. Italian conversation.

copeck (kōˊpek, kopˊ-), **kopeck, kopek** *n.* a Russian monetary unit and coin, one hundredth of a rouble.
17C. Russian *kopeĭka*, dim. of *kopˊë* lance.
● The coin originally bore the figure of a tsar (Ivan IV) carrying a lance.

copita (kəpēˊtə) *n.* (*pl.* **copitas**) a tulip-shaped sherry glass.
19C. Spanish, dim. of *copa*, from Popular Latin *cuppa* cup.

copra (kopˊrə) *n.* the dried kernel of the coconut, yielding coconut oil.
16C. Portuguese and Spanish, from Malayalam *koppara* coconut.

coq au vin (kok ō vīˊ) *n.* a stew of chicken in red wine.
mid-20C. French cock in wine.

coquelicot (kokˊlikō) *n.* **1** a name for any of the species of red-flowered field poppies. **2** a reddish-orange colour, the colour of the poppy flowers.
18C. French red poppy, var. of *coquerico* cock-a-doodle-do.
● The colour of the poppy flowers is compared with that of a cock's comb.

coquette (kəket´) n. **1** a female flirt; a jilt. **2** a hummingbird of the genus *Laphornis*. ~v.i. to coquet.
17C. French, fem. of *coquet*, dim. of *coq* cock.

coquille (kokē´) n. a scallop shell.
19C. French, from Medieval Greek *kokhulia*, pl. of *kokhulion*, from Greek *kogkhē* conch.

coquina (kōkē´nə) n. a type of soft, whitish limestone formed from broken shells and coral.
19C. Spanish shellfish, cockle, from Old Spanish *coca*, from Medieval Latin, from Latin *concha* shell.

cor (kaw) n. (*Mus.*) a horn.
19C. French horn, from Latin *cornu*.

coram populo (kawram pop´ūlō) adv. in public.
16C. Latin before the public, from *coram* in the presence of + abl. sing. of *populus* people.

cor anglais (kawr ong´glā) n. (*pl.* **cors anglais** (kawz ong´glā, kawr)) **1** the English horn, a woodwind instrument of the oboe family, slightly lower in pitch than the oboe. **2** a person who plays the cor anglais in an orchestra. **3** an organ stop producing the sound of a cor anglais.
19C. French, lit. English horn.
• A derivation from French *cor anglé*, literally angled horn, has also been proposed with reference to the instrument's former curved shape.

coranto (kəran´tō) n. (*pl.* **corantos**) a rapid kind of dance.
16C. Alt., by addition of Italian ending *-o*, of COURANT.

cordillera (kawdilyeə´rə) n. a ridge or chain of mountains, esp. used (*in pl.*) of the Andes, and the continuation of these in Central America and Mexico.

18C. Spanish, from *cordilla*, dim. of *cuerda*, from Latin *chorda* cord.

cordoba (kaw´dəbə) n. **1** the basic monetary unit of Nicaragua, equal to 100 centavos. **2** a coin of this value.
early 20C. Spanish, from Fernando Fernández de *Córdoba*, c.1475–c.1525, Spanish governor of Nicaragua.

cordon bleu (kawdō blœ´) a. (of food or cookery) of the highest standard. ~n. (*pl.* **cordons bleus** (kawdō blœz´)) a cook or chef of the highest calibre.
18C. French blue ribbon, from *cordon* cord + *bleu* blue.
• The original *cordon bleu* was the sky-blue ribbon worn by the Knights Grand Cross of the French order of the Holy Ghost, the highest order of chivalry under the Bourbon kings. The term was then extended to other orders of excellence.

cordon sanitaire (kawdō saniteə´) n. (*pl.* **cordons sanitaires** (kawdō saniteə´)) **1** a line of guards surrounding a disease-infected area, to cut off communication and so prevent the spread of the disease. **2** any similar preventative measure or set-up designed to isolate or protect.
19C. French sanitary cordon, from *cordon* cord + *sanitaire* sanitary.

cornetto (kawnet´ō), **cornett** (kaw´nit) n. (*pl.* **cornetti** (-tē), **cornetts**) an old woodwind instrument with finger holes and a cup-shaped mouthpiece.
19C. Italian, dim. of CORNO.

corniche (kawnēsh´) n. a coast road, esp. one along the face of a cliff.
19C. French, from Italian *cornice*, prob. from Latin *cornu* horn, influ. by Greek *kornis* coping-stone. Cp. English *cornice*.

corno (kaw´nō) n. (*pl.* **corni** (-nē)) (*Mus.*) a horn.
19C. Italian, from Latin *cornu* horn.

corps (kaw) *n.* (*pl.* **corps** (kawz)) **1** (*Mil.*) **a** a body of troops having a specific function. **b** a grouping of two or more divisions of an army, forming a tactical unit in the field. **2** a group of people employed in the same job, working together or in the same place.
16C. French, from Latin *corpus* body.

corps de ballet (kaw də bal´ā) *n.* a body of supporting dancers in a ballet.
19C. French, lit. body of (the) ballet.

corps d'élite (kaw dālēt´) *n.* an elite body selected from a larger group.
19C. French body of (the) elect.

corps diplomatique (kaw diplōmatēk´) *n.* the body of ambassadors and their staff attached to a seat of government, the diplomatic corps.
18C. French diplomatic body.
● The term gave CD as an abbreviation frequently displayed on the rear of cars belonging to embassies.

corpus (kaw´pəs) *n.* (*pl.* **corpora** (-pərə), **corpuses**) **1** a body. **2** the mass of anything. **3** a collection of writings or of literature. **4** a body of spoken or written material used for linguistic analysis. **5** (*Anat.*) the main part of an organ or any part of an organism.
14–15C. Latin body.
● The original sense was literal. Sense 3 dates from the 18C, and sense 4 from the mid-20C.

Corpus Christi (kawpəs kris´ti) *n.* the festival of the body of Christ, first celebrated in 1311, held in honour of the real presence in the Eucharist on the Thursday after Trinity Sunday.
12–14C. Latin body of Christ.

corpus delicti (kawpəs dilik´tī) *n.* (*Law*) the aggregation of facts which constitute a breach of the law.
19C. Latin, lit. body of the offence.
● In a murder trial the expression is sometimes wrongly used of the dead body, by association with Latin *corpus* and English *corpse*.

corral (kərahl´) *n.* **1** an enclosure (orig. of emigrants' wagons in American Indian territory) for cattle, horses etc. or for defence. **2** an enclosure for capturing elephants and other animals. ~*v.t.* (*pres.p.* **corralling**, *past, p.p.* **corralled**) **1** to pen up. **2** to form into a corral. **3** (*N Am., sl.*) to get, to acquire, to lay hold of.
16C. Spanish and Portuguese *curral*. Cp. KRAAL.

corregidor (kəreg´idaw) *n.* the chief magistrate of a Spanish town.
16C. Spanish, from *corregir*, from Latin *corrigere* to correct.

corrida (kərē´də) *n.* **1** a bullfight. **2** bullfighting.
19C. Spanish *corrida* (*de toros*) course (of bulls). See TOREADOR.

corrigendum (korijen´dəm) *n.* (*pl.* **corrigenda** (-ə)) an error needing correction, esp. in a book.
19C. Latin, neut. ger. of *corrigere* to correct.

corroboree (kərob´ərē) *n.* **1** a festive or warlike dance of the Australian Aborigines. **2** any noisy party.
18C. Australian Aboriginal (Dharuk) *garabari*.

cortege (kawtezh´), **cortège** *n.* **1** a procession, esp. at a funeral. **2** a train of attendants.
17C. French *cortège*, from Italian *corteggio*, from *corteggiare* to attend court, from *corte* court.

Cortes (kaw´tes) *n.* the legislative assemblies of Spain and (formerly) Portugal.
17C. Spanish and Portuguese, pl. of *corte* court.

cortex (kaw´teks) *n.* (*pl.* **cortices** (-tisēz))
1 (*Bot.*) **a** the layer of plant tissue
between the vascular bundles and the
epidermis. **b** bark. 2 (*Anat.*) the outer
layer of an organ, such as the kidney or
brain.
14–15C. Latin bark.

corvee (kawvā´, kaw´-) *n.* 1 (*Hist.*) an
obligation to perform a day's unpaid
labour for a feudal lord, as the repair
of roads etc. 2 work done in lieu of
paying taxes. 3 forced labour. 4 any
burdensome task imposed on one.
12–14C. Old French *corvée*, from
Provençal *corroada*, from Latin
corrogata (*opera*) requisitioned (work),
from neut. pl. p.p. of *corrogare* to
summon, from *cum* with + *rogare* to
ask.

corvette (kawvet´) *n.* (*Naut.*) 1 a small,
fast escort vessel armed with anti-
submarine devices. 2 (*Hist.*) a flush-
decked, full-rigged ship of war, with one
tier of guns.
17C. French, ult. dim. of Middle Dutch
korf basket, kind of ship.
• Sense 1 dates from World War II.

coryphaeus (korifē´əs) *n.* (*pl.* **coryphaei**
(-fē´ī)) 1 the leader of a chorus in a
classical play. 2 a chief, a leader.
17C. Latin, from Greek *koruphaios* chief,
chorus leader, from *koruphē* head, top.

coryphée (korifā´) *n.* a chief dancer in a
corps de ballet.
19C. French CORYPHAEUS.

Cosa Nostra (kōzə nos´trə) *n.* the branch
of the Mafia operating in the US.
mid-20C. Italian our thing, from *cosa*
thing + *nostra*, fem. of *nostro* our.

così così (kozē´ kozē´) *adv.* so-so, not too
bad, fair to middling.
mid-20C. Italian. Cp. COMME CI
COMME ÇA.

costa (kos´tə) *n.* (*pl.* **costas**) a strip of
coastline, esp. in Spain, developed as a
resort.
19C. Spanish coast.
• Areas such as the *Costa del Sol*
('sunny coast') in S Spain and the *Costa
Brava* ('wild coast') in NE Spain gave
rise to facetious pseudo-Spanish names
such as *Costa Geriatrica* for a resort
mainly populated by elderly people or
Costa del Crime for an area favoured by
criminals.

costumier (kostū´miə) *n.* a maker of or
dealer in costumes.
19C. French, from *costumer* to costume.

coterie (kō´təri) *n.* 1 a set of people
associated together for friendly
conversation. 2 an exclusive circle of
people in society; a clique.
18C. Old French, ult. from Middle Low
German *kote* cottage.
• The original sense of the Old French
word was a group of tenants holding
land together.

cothurnus (kəthœ´nəs) *n.* (*pl.* **cothurni**
(-nī)) 1 the buskin worn by actors in
ancient Greek and Roman tragedy.
2 tragedy. 3 the tragic style.
18C. Latin, from Greek *kothornos*.

cotillion (kətil´yən), **cotillon** (kotēyō´)
n. 1 an 18th-cent. French ballroom
dance for four or eight people. 2 the
music for this. 3 (*N Am.*) a ball (for
dancing). 4 (*N Am.*) a dance somewhat
like a quadrille.
18C. French *cotillon* petticoat, dance,
dim. of *cotte* coat. Cp. COTTA.
• The dance is presumably so named
from the costumes worn by women in
the original peasant dance on which it
is said to be based.

cotta (kot´ə) *n.* a short surplice.
19C. Italian, from Frankish, of
unknown orig.

couchant (kow´chənt) *a.* (*Her.*) (of an animal) lying down with the head raised.
14–15C. Old French, pres.p. of *coucher* to lie down.

couchette (kooshet´) *n.* **1** a seat in a continental train which converts into a sleeping berth. **2** a carriage with such seats. **3** a similar seat on a cross-channel ferry.
early 20C. French, dim. of *couche* couch, bed.

coudé (koodā´) *a.* (*Astron.*) (of a reflecting telescope) in which light rays are bent by mirrors to a point of focus, e.g. on a photographic plate, off the axis of the telescope. ~*n.* such a telescope.
19C. French, p.p. of *couder* to bend at right angles, from *coude* elbow, from Latin *cubitum* cubit.

coulee (koo´li, -lā), **coulée** (koolā´) *n.*
1 (*Geol.*) a molten or solidified lava flow. **2** (*N Am. dial.*) a ravine or gully.
19C. French *coulée* flow, from *couler* to flow, from Latin *colare* to filter, to strain, from *colum* strainer.

couleur de rose (koolœ də roz´) *a.*
1 rose-coloured. **2** (*fig.*) cheerful, optimistic.
14–15C. French rose colour.
● Sense 2 evolved in the 18C.

coulis (koo´lē) *n.* (*pl.* **coulis** (koo´lēz)) a thin purée.
19C. French, from Old French *coleiz*, from Latin *colare* to strain, to filter.
● The word was formerly current in English as *cullis* (14–15C), but was then used for a type of broth or gravy made from meat or fish, not a sieved sauce made of vegetables or fruit, as now.

coulisse (koolēs´) *n.* **1** a grooved timber in which a sluice-gate or a partition slides. **2** a side-scene in a theatre. **3** (*pl.*) the space between the side-scenes.

4 a place for informal or unofficial discussion or dealing.
19C. French, use as n. of fem. of *coulis* sliding, from *coulisser* to slide. Cp. English *portcullis*, lit. sliding door.

couloir (kool´wah) *n.* a steep gully or long, narrow gorge on a precipitous mountainside.
19C. French channel, from *couler* to flow, from Latin *colare* to filter.

coup (koo) *n.* **1** a stroke, a telling or decisive blow. **2** a victory. **3** a successful move, piece of strategy or revolution.
4 a coup d'état. **5** in billiards, a stroke putting a ball into a pocket without its touching another.
14–15C. Old French, from Medieval Latin *colpus*, from Latin *colaphus*, from Greek *kolaphos* blow with the fist.
● The original sense (to the 16C) was a blow in combat. The current sense dates from the 18C.

coup de foudre (koo də foodr´, foo´drə) *n.* (*pl.* **coups de foudre** (koo)) **1** a sudden and overwhelming event.
2 love at first sight.
18C. French stroke of lightning, from COUP + *de* of + *foudre* lightning, thunderbolt, from Latin *fulgur*, from *fulgere* to shine.

coup de grâce (koo də grahs´) *n.* (*pl.* **coups de grâce** (koo)) **1** a finishing stroke; an action that puts an end to something. **2** a death blow administered to put an end to suffering.
17C. French stroke of grace, from COUP + *de* of + *grâce* grace. Cp. English 'mercy killing'.

coup de main (koo də mī´) *n.* (*pl.* **coups de main** (koo)) a sudden and energetic attack.
18C. French stroke of the hand, from COUP + *de* of + *main*, from Latin *manus* hand.

coup de maître (koo də met´rə) n. (pl.
coups de maître (koo)) a master stroke.
18C. French stroke of master, from COUP
+ *de* of + *maître* master, from Latin
magister.

coup de soleil (koo də solā´) n. (pl.
coups de soleil (koo)) sunburn.
18C. French stroke of the sun, from
COUP + *de* of + *soleil*, from Latin *sol*
sun. Cp. English *sunstroke*.

coup d'état (koo dātah´) n. (pl. **coups
d'état** (koo)) a sudden and violent
change of government, esp. of an illegal
and revolutionary nature.
17C. French stroke of state, from COUP
+ *d'* of + *état* state.

coup de théâtre (koo də tāahtr´,
tāah´trə) n. (pl. **coups de théâtre** (koo))
1 a dramatic turn of events in a play.
2 a sensational dramatic effect or device.
3 a notable theatrical success.
18C. French stroke of theatre, from COUP
+ *de* of + *théâtre* theatre.

coup d'oeil (koo dœy´) n. (pl. **coups
d'oeil** (koo)) **1** a quick comprehensive
glance. **2** a general view.
18C. French stroke of eye, from COUP
+ *d'* of + *œil*, from Latin *oculus* eye.

coupe (koop) n. **1** a dessert made of fruit
or ice cream. **2** the shallow glass dish in
which such desserts are served.
19C. French goblet, from Medieval Latin
cuppa.

coupé (koo´pā), (*NAm.*) **coupe** (koop) n.
1 (*usu., NAm.* **coupe**) a two-doored car
with an enclosed body. **2** (*Hist.*) (**coupé**)
a four-wheeled closed carriage. **3** (*Hist.*)
(**coupé**) a half compartment with glazed
front at the end of a railway carriage.
18C. French, p.p. of *couper* to cut. See
COUP.
● In senses 1 and 2, the word is short
for *carrosse coupé* cut carriage, meaning
one that has been shortened.

coupon (koo´pon) n. **1** a form that may
be detached or cut out e.g. from an
advertisement, and used as an order
form, entry form for a competition etc.
2 a football pools entry form. **3** a piece
of paper which can be exchanged for
goods in a shop. **4** a voucher. **5** a
detachable ticket or certificate entitling
to food ration etc. **6** a detachable
certificate for the payment of interest on
bonds.
19C. French piece cut off, from *couper*
to cut.

coupure (koopūə´) n. in fortifications, a
passage, esp. one cut through the glacis
to facilitate sallies by the besieged.
18C. French, from *couper* to cut.

courant (kurant´) a. (*Her.*) in a running
attitude. ~n. (*Mus.*) **1** (*also* **courante**)
a an old dance with a running or gliding
step. **b** the music for this.
17C. French, pres.p. of *courir*, from
Latin *currere* to run.

courgette (kuəzhet´) n. a small kind of
vegetable marrow.
mid-20C. French, dim. of *courge* gourd.

court bouillon (kawt boo´yon, kuə
booyō̃´) n. a stock made with vegetables,
water and wine or vinegar, used
especially for cooking fish in.
17C. French, from *court* short +
BOUILLON.

couscous (koos´koos) n. **1** a N African
dish of pounded wheat steamed over
meat or broth. **2** the wheat used in this
dish.
17C. French, from Arabic *kuskus* millet
grain, prob. of Berber orig.

coûte que coûte (koot kə koot´) int.
cost what it may, no matter what it takes.
18C. French, lit. (let it) cost what (it)
costs.
● The phrase is sometimes altered in
English to *coûte qui coûte*.

couture (kətūə´, koo-, -tuə´) n.
1 dressmaking. 2 dress-designing.
early 20C. **French**, from Old French
cousture sewing, from Late Latin
consutura, from Latin *consutus*, p.p. of
consuere to sew together, from *con-*, alt.
of *cum* with + *suere* to sew.

couturier (kətūə´riā, koo-) n. a dress-
designer or dress-maker.
19C. **French**, from COUTURE.

couvade (koovahd´) n. a custom among
certain peoples, by which a father
during the birth of his child performs
certain acts and abstains from certain
foods etc.
19C. **French**, from *couver* to hatch, from
Latin *cubare* to lie.
● The French word was adopted in this
sense from a misunderstanding of the
expression *faire la couvade* to sit doing
nothing.

couvert (koovee´) n. a place setting in a
restaurant.
18C. **French** covering. Cp. English *cover*
in the same sense.

couverture (koo´vətjuə) n. chocolate for
coating cakes, sweets etc.
mid-20C. **French** covering.

cracovienne (krəkōvien´) n. a lively
Polish dance, a ballet dance in a Polish
style.
19C. **French**, fem. of *cracovien*, a. from
Cracovie Kraków, a city in S Poland.
● The dance originated in the Kraków
region. It is also known by its Polish
name of *krakoviak* or *krakowiak*.

crannog (kran´əg) n. an ancient lake-
dwelling, common in Scotland and
Ireland, built up from the lake bottom
on brushwood and piles, and often
surrounded by palisades.
17C. **Irish** *crannóg* or Gaelic *crannag*
timber structure, from *crann* tree, beam.

craquelure (krak´lūə, -lūə) n. a maze of
small cracks in the varnish on the
surface of a painting.
early 20C. **French**, from *craquer* to crack.

crayon (krā´ən, -on) n. 1 a stick or pencil
of coloured chalk or similar material.
2 a drawing made with crayons. 3 the
carbon pencil of an electric arc lamp.
~v.t. 1 to draw with crayons. 2 to sketch.
17C. **French**, from *craie*, from Latin
creta chalk, clay.

crèche (kresh, krāsh) n. 1 a day nursery
in which young children are taken care
of. 2 a model of the scene of the birth of
Jesus.
18C. **French** manger, from Germanic
base of English *crib*.

credenza (kriden´zə) n. (pl. **credenzas**)
1 a credence table. 2 a sideboard or
cupboard.
19C. **Italian**, from Medieval Latin
credentia, from Latin *credens*, *credentis*,
pres.p. of *credere* to believe.
● The reference is probably to a side
table on which food was placed for
tasting or 'assaying'.

credo (krā´dō, krē´-) n. (pl. **credos**)
1 (**Credo**) the Apostles' Creed or the
Nicene Creed. 2 (**Credo**) a musical
setting of either of the creeds, esp. of
the Nicene Creed. 3 the statement of a
belief.
12–14C. **Latin** I believe, 1st pers. sing.
pres. indic. of *credere* to believe.
● The word is from the opening phrase
of the Apostles' Creed and Nicene
Creed, *Credo in unum Deum* I believe in
one God.

credo quia absurdum (krā´dō kwēə
əbsœ´dəm, krē´dō) int. I believe because
it is absurd.
18C. **Latin**, from CREDO + *quia* because
+ *absurdum* absurd.
● The phrase is a variant of Tertullian's

words *Certum est quia impossibile est* 'It is certain because it is impossible' in *De Carne Christi* (3C AD).

crème (krem) *n.* cream.
19C. French cream.

crème brûlée (krem broolā´) *n.* (*pl.* **crèmes brûlées** (krem broolā´), **crème brûlées** (broolāz´)) **1** a dessert consisting of cream or custard covered with caramelized sugar. **2** a portion of this dessert.
19C. French burnt cream, from CRÈME + fem. p.p. of *brûler* to burn. Cp. BRÛLÉ.
● The dessert was earlier known (from 18C) by its English name, *burnt cream*. Cp. CRÈME CARAMEL.

crème caramel (krem karəmel´, kar´-) *n.* (*pl.* **crèmes caramel** (krem), **crème caramels** (-melz)) **1** a dessert consisting of a set custard coated with liquid caramel. **2** a portion of this dessert.
19C. French, from earlier *crème au caramel* caramel cream.
● It is the caramel that is 'burnt' in this dish and in CRÈME BRÛLÉE. *Crème au caramel* is now a different dessert, with caramel-flavoured cream, not a coating of caramel.

crème de cacao (krem də kəkah´ō, kəkā´ō) *n.* (*pl.* **crèmes de cacao** (krem), **crème de cacaos** (kəkah´ōz, kəkā´ōz)) **1** a chocolate-flavoured liqueur. **2** a glass of this liqueur.
mid-20C. French chocolate cream, from CRÈME + *de* of + *cacao* cacao.
● French *crème* in the name of liqueurs denotes a creamlike smoothness.
Cp. CRÈME DE CASSIS, CRÈME DE MENTHE.

crème de cassis (krem də kasēs´) *n.* (*pl.* **crèmes de cassis** (krem)) **1** a blackcurrant-flavoured liqueur. **2** a glass of this liqueur.

mid-20C. French blackcurrant cream, from CRÈME + *de* of + CASSIS.

crème de la crème (krem də la krem´) *n.* the pick, best, most select, elite.
19C. French cream of the cream, from CRÈME + *de la* of the.
● English *cream* in the sense the best dates from the 16C.

crème de menthe (krem də month´, mŏth, menth´) *n.* (*pl.* **crèmes de menthe** (krem), **crème de menthes** (months´, mŏth, menths´)) **1** a peppermint-flavoured liqueur. **2** a glass of this liqueur.
early 20C. French (pepper)mint cream, from CRÈME + *de* of + *menthe* mint.

crème fraîche (krem fresh´) *n.* a type of thick, slightly soured cream.
mid-20C. French fresh cream, from CRÈME + fem. of *frais* fresh. Cp. FROMAGE FRAIS.

Creole (krē´ōl) *n.* **1** a person of European parentage in the West Indies or Spanish America. **2** in Louisiana, a person descended from French or Spanish ancestors. **3** a person of mixed European and black parentage. **4** (**creole**) the native language of a region, formed from prolonged contact between the original native language(s) and that of European settlers. ~*a.* relating to the Creoles or a creole language.
17C. French *créole*, earlier *criole*, from Spanish *criollo*, prob. from Portuguese *crioulo* black person born in Brazil, home-born slave, from *criar* to nurse, to breed, from Latin *creare* to create.

crêpe (krăp, krep), **crepe** *n.* **1** crape. **2** a crapy fabric other than mourning crape. **3** a thin pancake. **4** crêpe paper. **5** crêpe rubber.
18C. French, earlier *crespe*, use as n. of Old French *crespe* curled, frizzled, from Latin *crispus* curled.

crêpe de Chine (krăp, krep də shēn´) *n.* crape manufactured from raw silk.
19C. French CRÊPE of China.

crêpe Suzette (krep soozet´, krăp), **crêpe suzette** *n.* (*pl.* **crêpes Suzette** (krep, krăp), **crêpes suzettes** (krep soozets´, krăp)) a thin pancake in a hot orange or lemon sauce, served flambéed as a dessert.
early 20C. French Suzette pancake.
• The phrase is popularly but improbably linked with that of a companion of the Prince of Wales at Monte Carlo in 1896, for whom the French chef Henri Carpentier is said to have invented the dish.

crescendo (krishen´dō) *n.* (*pl.* **crescendos, crescendi** (-di)) **1** (*Mus.*) (a musical passage performed with) a gradual increase in the force of sound. **2** a gradual increase in force or effect. **3** a climax, high point. ~*adv., a.* with an increasing volume of sound. ~*v.i.* (*ṁrd pers. sing. pres.* **crescendoes,** *pres.p.* **crescendoing,** *past, p.p.* **crescendoed**) to increase in loudness or intensity.
18C. Italian, pres.p. of *crescere* to increase, from Latin *crescere* to grow.

cretin (kret´in) *n.* **1** a person mentally and physically disabled because of a (congenital) thyroid malfunction. **2** (*coll.*) a very stupid person.
18C. French *crétin*, from Swiss French *creitin, crestin*, from Latin *Christianus* Christian.
• The Swiss French name was originally applied to dwarfed or deformed persons in Alpine valleys. They were called 'Christian' as a recognition that they were human beings, at a time when the disabled were often considered closer to animals.

cretonne (kreton´, kret´on) *n.* a cotton fabric with pictorial patterns, used for upholstering, frocks etc.

19C. French, of uncertain orig.
• According to some, the word is from *Creton*, a village in N France, where the fabric is said to have been originally made.

crevasse (krəvas´) *n.* **1** a deep fissure in a glacier. **2** (*N Am.*) a break in an embankment or levee of a river.
19C. French, from Old French *crevace*.

crève-coeur (krevkœ´) *n.* heartbreak, bitter disappointment.
early 20C. French, lit. break-heart, from *crever* to break, to burst + *cœur* heart.

crevette (krəvet´) *n.* (esp. in cookery) a shrimp, a prawn.
early 20C. French, Norman dial. form of *chevrette*, dim. of *chèvre* goat, alluding to the creature's leaping movement.

criant (kriã´), (*fem.*) **criante** (kriãt´), **criard** (kriah´), (fem.) **criarde** (kriahd´) *a.* (of a colour) garish, clashing.
19C. French, pres.p. of *crier* to shout, to cry or deriv. of *crier*.

cri de coeur (krē də kœ´) *n.* (*pl.* **cris de coeur** (krē)) a heartfelt appeal or protest.
early 20C. French cry of the heart, from *cri* cry + *de* of + *cœur*, from Latin *cor* heart.

crime passionnel (krēm pasyonel´) *n.* (*pl.* **crimes passionnels** (krēm pasyonel´)) a crime, esp. murder, committed because of, usu. sexual, passion and jealousy.
early 20C. French crime of passion, from *crime* crime + *passionnel*, a. from *passion* passion.

crinoline (krin´əlin, -lēn) *n.* **1** a stiff fabric of horsehair formerly used for petticoats, etc. **2** a petticoat of this material. **3** any stiff petticoat used to expand the skirts of a dress. **4** a large hooped skirt, orig. worn in the mid-19th cent. **5** the whalebone hoops for such a

skirt. **6** a series of nets extended round a warship to keep off torpedoes.
19C. French, from Latin *crinis* hair + *linum* thread.

crise (krēz) *n.* (*pl.* **crises** (krēz)) a crisis.
14–15C. French.
● The word now only occurs in phrases such as those below.

crise de conscience (krēz də kõsyãs´) *n.* a crisis of conscience.
mid-20C. French, from CRISE + *de* of + *conscience* conscience.

crise de foi (krēz də fwah´) *n.* an attack of doubt or disillusionment.
19C. French, lit. crisis of faith, from CRISE + *de* of + *foi* faith.
● The expression originally had a religious application.

critique (kritēk´) *n.* **1** a critical essay or judgement. **2** the art of criticism. **3** the analysis of the basis of knowledge.
~*v.t.* to make a critique of.
17C. French, from Greek *kritikē* (*tekhnē*), the critical (art), criticism.

crochet (krō´shā, -shi) *n.* a kind of knitting done with a hooked needle.
~*v.t.* to knit or make in crochet. ~*v.i.* to knit in this manner.
19C. French, dim. of *croc* hook, with -*ch*- from *crochié* hooked.

croissant (krwas´ã) *n.* a crescent-shaped roll of rich flaky pastry.
16C. French.
● The word was originally a variant of English *crescent*. The current sense dates from the 19C.

cromlech (krom´lekh, -lek) *n.* **1** a circle of standing stones. **2** a prehistoric structure in which a large flat stone rests horizontally on upright ones, a dolmen.
17C. Welsh, from *crom*, fem. of *crwm* bowed, arched + *llech* flat stone.

croque-monsieur (krokməsyœ´) *n.* a toasted ham and cheese sandwich.
mid-20C. French, lit. munch-sir.
● The dish is said to have first appeared in a café in the Boulevard des Capucines in Paris. The origin of the term is uncertain, but it may have a kind of equivalent in English 'Gentleman's Relish'.

croquette (krəket´, krō-) *n.* a savoury ball made with meat, potato etc. fried in breadcrumbs.
18C. French, from *croquer* to crunch.

croquis (krokē, krōkē´) *n.* (*pl.* **croquis** (krokē, krōkēz´)) a rough draft or sketch.
19C. French, from *croquer* to sketch, from *croc* hook.

crostini (krostē´nē) *n.pl.* small pieces of toasted or fried bread covered with a topping.
mid-20C. Italian, pl. of *crostino* little crust. Cp. CROUTON.

croupier (kroo´piā) *n.* **1** a person who superintends a gaming table and collects the money won by the bank. **2** a vice-chairman or -chairwoman at a public dinner.
18C. French.
● A French *croupier* was originally a person who rode behind on the croup of a horse. From this the sense passed to a person who stood behind a gambler to give advice, and finally gave the current sense.

croûte (kroot), **croute** *n.* (*pl.* **croûtes** (kroot), **croutes**) a small piece of toasted or fried bread.
early 20C. French crust. Cp. CROUTON.

crouton (kroo´ton) *n.* a small cube of fried or toasted bread, served with soup or salads.
19C. French, from CROÛTE.

cru (kroo, krü) *n*. **1** a French vineyard or group of vineyards producing wine of a particular quality. **2** a quality of wine.
19C. French, from *crû*, p.p. of *croître* to grow.

crudités (kroodētā´) *n.pl.* raw vegetables served as an hors d'oeuvre, often with a dip or sauce.
mid-20C. French, pl. of *crudité* rawness.

cruller (krŭl´ə) *n*. (*N Am*.) a light, sweet, often ring-shaped cake, deep-fried in fat.
19C. Dutch *kruller*, from *krullen* to curl.

crux (krŭks) *n*. (*pl.* **cruxes, cruces** (kroo´sēz)) **1** the real essential. **2** anything exceedingly puzzling.
17C. Latin cross.

cruzado (kroozah´dō) *n*. (*pl.* **cruzados**) a former coin and monetary unit of Brazil, replaced by the cruzeiro.
16C. Portuguese bearing a cross.

cruzeiro (kroozeə´rō) *n*. (*pl.* **cruzeiros**) a coin and monetary unit of Brazil, equal to 100 centavos.
early 20C. Portuguese large cross.

csardas (chah´dash), **czardas** *n*. (*pl.* **csardas, czardas**) a Hungarian national dance, moving from a slow to a quick tempo.
19C. Hungarian *csárdás*, from *csárda* inn.

cuesta (kwes´tə) *n*. a hill ridge with a gentle slope ending in a steep scarp slope.
19C. Spanish slope, from Latin *costa* rib, side.

cui bono? (kwē bō´nō, bon´ō) *adv., int.* for whose benefit?, who stands to gain?
17C. Latin to whom (is it) a benefit?, from *cui*, dat. sing. of *qui* who, which + abl. sing. of *bonum* good thing.
● The full form of the phrase is *cui bono est?* to whom is it a benefit?,
attributed by Cicero to one Lucius Cassius.

cuisine (kwizēn´) *n*. **1** a style of cooking. **2** cookery.
18C. French kitchen, from Latin *coquina, cocina*, from *coquere* to cook.

cul-de-sac (kŭl´disak) *n*. (*pl.* **culs-de-sac** (kŭl-), **cul-de-sacs**) **1** a street or lane open only at one end. **2** a route or course of activity that leads nowhere. **3** (*Anat*.) a vessel, tube or gut open only at one end.
18C. French bottom of the sack, from *cul* bottom + *de* of + *sac* sack.
● The phrase was first used in sense 3.

culottes (kūlots´) *n.pl.* women's flared trousers cut to resemble a skirt.
19C. French, pl. of *culotte* knee breeches, from *cul* bottom, backside. Cp. SANS-CULOTTE.

cum (kŭm) *prep*. combined with, together with.
14–15C. Latin with.

cumbia (kŭm´biə) *n*. **1** a type of dance music similar to salsa, orig. from Colombia. **2** a dance using this music.
mid-20C. Colombian Spanish, ? from Spanish *cumbé*.

cum grano salis (kŭm grahnō sah´lis) *adv*. with a pinch of salt, not too seriously.
17C. Latin with a grain of salt, from *cum* with + abl. sing. of *granum* grain + gen. sing. of *sal* salt.

cumshaw (kŭm´shaw) *n*. in China etc., a present, a tip. ~*v.t.* to give a present to, to tip.
19C. Chinese (dial.) *gămsiâ*, (Mandarin) *gănxiè*, from *găn* to be grateful + *xiè* to thank.
● The word was originally a phrase used by Chinese beggars.

cupola (kū´pələ) *n.* **1** a little dome. **2** a lantern etc. on the summit of a dome. **3** a spherical covering to a building, or any part of it. **4** a cupola furnace. **5** a revolving dome or turret on a warship. **6** (*Biol.*) a domelike organ or part, esp. the extremity of the canal of the cochlea.
16C. Italian, from Late Latin *cupula* little cask, small vault, dim. of *cupa* cask.

curaçao (kūrəsah´ō, koo-), **curaçoa** (-sō´ə) *n.* (*pl.* **curaçaos, curaçoas**) a liqueur flavoured with bitter orange peel, sugar and cinnamon, orig. from Curaçao.
19C. *Curaçao*, a Caribbean island of the lesser Antilles, producing oranges used in the liqueur's flavouring.

curare (kūrah´ri) *n.* the dried extract of plants from the genera *Strychnos* and *Chondodendron*, used by the Indians of South America for poisoning arrows, and formerly employed in physiological investigations as a muscle relaxant.
18C. Spanish and Portuguese, from Carib *kurari*.

curé (kū´rā) *n.* a parish priest in France etc., a French rector or vicar.
17C. French, from Medieval Latin *curatus* person having cure (charge) of a parish.
● French *curé* corresponds in sense to English *vicar*, while English *curate* corresponds to French *vicaire*.

curette (kūret´) *n.* (*Med.*) a surgeon's instrument used for scraping a body cavity. ~*v.t., v.i.* to scrape or clean with a curette.
18C. French, from *curer* to take care of, to clean, from Latin *curare* to care for.

Curia (kū´riə), **curia** *n.* (*pl.* **Curiae** (-ē), **curiae**) **1** the papal court. **2** the temporal administration of the Vatican. **3** (*Hist.*) **a** any of the ten subdivisions of the three Roman tribes, as instituted by Romulus. **b** the building in which they met, the Roman senate house.
17C. Latin, ? from Old Latin *co-viria coalition of men.

curiosa (kūriō´sə) *n.pl.* **1** unusual (collectable) objects. **2** erotic or pornographic books.
19C. Latin, neut. pl. of *curiosus* curious.

currach (kŭr´ə, -əkh), **curragh** *n.* a skiff made of wickerwork and hides, a coracle.
14–15C. Irish and Gaelic *curach* small boat.

curriculum (kərik´ūləm) *n.* (*pl.* **curricula** (-lə)) **1** a fixed course of study at a school etc. **2** a programme of activities.
19C. Latin running, course, race chariot, from *currere* to run.

curriculum vitae (kərik´ūləm vē´tī) *n.* (*pl.* **curricula vitae** (-lə), **curricula vitarum** (-tah´rəm)) a brief outline of one's education, previous employment, and other achievements.
early 20C. Latin, lit. course of life, from *curriculum* + gen. of *vita* life.
● In job applications and the like the term is usually abbreviated to CV.

cursillo (kœsil´ō) *n.* (*pl.* **cursillos**) an informal spiritual retreat of members of the Roman Catholic Church, esp. in Latin America.
mid-20C. Spanish little course.

cush-cush (kush´kush) *n.* a variety of yam, *Dioscorea trifida* of South America.
19C. ? Ult. of African orig.

cuspidor (kŭs´pidaw) *n.* a spittoon.
18C. Portuguese spitter, from *cuspir* to spit, from Latin *conspuere* to spit on.

custos (kŭs´təs) *n.* (*pl.* **custodes**
(-tō´dēz)) a keeper, a custodian.
14–15C. Latin.

cutch (kŭch) *n.* catechu.
18C. Malay *kachu*. Cp. CATECHU,
CACHOU.

cuvée (koovā´) *n.* a batch or blend of
wine.
19C. French vatful, from *cuve*, from
Latin *cupa* cask, vat.

cuvette (kūvet´) *n.* a shallow dish for
holding liquids in a laboratory.
17C. French dim. of *cuve*. See CUVÉE.

cwm (kum) *n.* **1** a valley in Wales.
2 (*Geol.*) a cirque, a corrie.
19C. Welsh valley, rel. to English *coomb*.

cyma (sī´mə) *n.* (*pl.* **cymas, cymae** (-mē))
1 (*Archit.*) a convex and a concave curve
forming the topmost member of a
cornice. **2** (*Bot.*) a cyme.
16C. Modern Latin, from Greek *kuma*
billow, wave, from *kuein* to become
pregnant.

cymatium (sīmā´tiəm, -shəm) *n.* (*pl.*
cymatia (-tiə, -shə)) a cyma.
16C. Latin ogee, Ionic volute, from
Greek *kumation*, dim. of *kuma* CYMA.

cymbalo (sim´bəlō) *n.* (*pl.* **cymbalos**)
(*Mus.*) the dulcimer, a stringed
instrument played by means of small
hammers held in the hands.
19C. Italian *cembalo*, *cimbalo*, from
Latin *cymbalum* cymbal. Cp. CIMBALOM.

cynocephalus (sīnōsef´ələs) *n.* **1** a
dog-headed man in ancient mythology.
2 a flying lemur.
12–14C. Latin, from Greek
kunokephalos dog-headed, from *kuōn*,
kunos dog + *kephalē* head.

cy près (sē prā´) *a., adv.* (*Law*) as near as
practicable (referring to the principle
of applying a bequest as nearly as
possible to the testator's aim when that
aim is impracticable). ~*n.* an
approximation.
19C. Anglo-French as near as (French
ci-près).

D

da capo (da kah´pō) *adv.* (*Mus.*) (repeat) from the beginning.
18C. Italian from the beginning, from *da* from + CAPO.

d'accord (dakaw´) *int.* agreed, all right, OK.
early 20C. French, lit. of accord.
● The French themselves use the phrase freely in conversation to express agreement or simply to denote active participation.

dacha (dach´ə), **datcha** *n.* (*pl.* **dachas, datchas**) a country house or cottage in Russia.
19C. Russian grant of land, from *dat'* to give.

dacoit (dəkoit´), **dakoit** *n.* in the Indian subcontinent or Burma (Myanmar), a member of a band of armed robbers.
18C. Hindi *ḍakait*, from *ḍākā* gang robbery.

dado (dā´dō) *n.* (*pl.* **dados, dadoes**) **1** an arrangement of wainscoting or decoration round the lower part of the walls of a room. **2** the cube of a pedestal between the base and the cornice.
17C. Italian die, cube, from Latin *datum* die.
● A dado was originally the cube of a pedestal, to which the lower part of a room wall corresponds.

dagga (dag´ə, dakh´ə) *n.* (*S Afr.*) **1** a type of hemp used as a narcotic. **2** any plant of the genus *Leonotis* also so used.
17C. Afrikaans, from Nama.

dagoba (dah´gəbə) *n.* (*pl.* **dagobas**) a dome-shaped Buddhist shrine containing relics.
19C. Sinhalese *dāgaba*, from Pali *dhātu-gabbha* receptacle for relics.

dahabeeyah (dah·həbē´yə) *n.* a type of sailing-boat on the Nile.
19C. Arabic *ḍahabīya* golden.
● The word was originally used for the gilded state barge of the Muslim rulers of Egypt.

Dáil (doil) *n.* the lower house of the parliament of the Republic of Ireland.
early 20C. Irish *Dáil* (*Éireann*) Assembly (of Ireland). Cp. SEANAD.
● The Dáil was first established in 1919, when Irish republicans proclaimed an Irish state.

daimio (dī´myō) *n.* (*pl.* **daimio, daimios**) the official title of a former class of feudal lords in Japan.
18C. Japanese, from *dai* great + *myō* name.

daimon (dī´mōn) *n.* a genius or attendant spirit.
19C. Greek *daimōn*.

daiquiri (dak´əri, dī´-) *n.* (*pl.* **daiquiris**) a cocktail made of rum and lime-juice.
early 20C. *Daiquiri*, a rum-producing district of SE Cuba.

dak (dahk), **dawk** (dawk) *n.* (*Hist.*) the Indian post or transport by relays of runners, horses etc.
18C. Hindi *ḍāk*.

Dalai Lama (dalī lah´mə) *n.* the spiritual leader of Tibetan Buddhism, previously also the temporal ruler of Tibet.
17C. Mongolian *dalai* ocean + LAMA.
● The sense of ocean is presumably meant to suggest breadth and depth of wisdom or range of power.

dalasi (dəlah´si) *n.* (*pl.* **dalasi, dalasis**) the standard monetary unit of the Gambia.
late 20C. Local Gambian name of former coin.

dal segno (dal sen´yō) *adv.* (*Mus.*) (repeat) from point indicated.
19C. Italian from the sign, from *dal* from the + *segno* sign.

dan (dan) *n.* **1** in martial arts, any of the black-belt grades of proficiency. **2** a person who has reached such a level.
mid-20C. Japanese step, grade.

dancette (dahnset´) *n.* **1** (*Archit.*) the chevron or zigzag moulding in Norman work. **2** (*Her.*) a fesse with three indentations.
19C. French *dancetté*, from *danché*, earlier obs. *dansié*, from Latin *dens*, *dentis* tooth.

danse macabre (dās məkah´brə) *n.* in medieval art, literature and music, a representation of a dance in which Death leads people to their graves.
19C. French, lit. macabre dance.
● French (and English) *macabre* are possibly derived from French *Macabé* a Maccabee, referring to a miracle play depicting the slaughter of the Maccabees, as told in the apocryphal books named after them.

danseur (dāsœ´) *n.* a male ballet dancer.
19C. French dancer, from *danser* to dance.

dariole (dar´iōl) *n.* a dish cooked in a usu. flowerpot-shaped mould.
14–15C. Old French, var. of *doriole* gilded.
● The Old French word was originally used for a type of bun with a golden brown exterior.

dashiki (dah´shiki) *n.* (*pl.* **dashikis**) a type of loose shirt worn esp. by blacks in America.
mid-20C. Prob. from **Yoruba**, from Hausa.

data (dā´tə) *n.pl.* (*often sing. in constr.*) **1** facts or information from which other things may be deduced. **2** the information operated on by a computer program.
17C. Latin, pl. of DATUM.

dataria (dəteə´riə) *n.* the papal chancery at Rome from which all bulls are issued.
16C. Medieval Latin, from *datum*, p.p. of *dare* to give.

datum (dā´təm) *n.* (*pl.* **data**) a quantity, condition, fact or other premise, given or admitted, from which other things or results may be found.
18C. Latin, neut p.p. of *dare* to give. Cp. DATA.

daube (dawb) *n.* a stew of meat braised with wine etc.
18C. French, from Italian *addobbo* adornment, influ. by French *adouber* to dub (a knight).

dauphin (dō´fĭ, daw´fin) *n.* (*Hist.*) the heir apparent to the French throne

(from the fact that the principality of Dauphiné was an apanage of his).
14–15C. French, from Old French *daulphin* dolphin.

• *Dauphin* was the family name of the lords of Viennois or *Dauphiné*.

deasil (dē´zəl), **deiseal** (dē´shəl) *n.* (*Sc.*) motion towards the right, in the direction of the hands of a clock or of the apparent motion of the sun.
18C. Gaelic *deiseil*. Rel. to Latin DEXTER.

debacle (dābah´kəl, di-), **débâcle** (dā-) *n.* **1** a complete failure. **2** a stampede. **3** a breaking up of ice in a river. **4** breaking up and transport of rocks and gravel by a sudden outburst of water.
19C. French *débâcle*, from *débâcler* to unbar, from priv. pref. *dé-* + *bâcler* to bar.

debris (deb´rē, dā´brē) *n.* **1** broken rubbish, fragments. **2** (*Geol.*) fragmentary matter detached by a rush of water.
18C. French *débris*, from obs. *débriser* to break down, to break up, from priv. pref. *dé-* + *briser* to break.

debut (dā´bū, deb´ū) *n.* **1** a first appearance before the public, esp. of a performer. **2** the presentation of a debutante at court. ~*v.i.* (*pres.p.* **debuting**, *past, p.p.* **debuted**) to make a debut.
18C. French *début*, from *débuter* to lead off.

debutante (deb´ūtahnt, dā´-), **débutante** *n.* **1** a young woman making her social debut. **2** a female performer making her debut.
19C. French, fem. of *débutant*, pres.p. of *débuter* to lead off. Cp. DEBUT.

• Sense 1 is popularly abbreviated as deb. Cp. English 'deb's delight' as a colloquial term for an eligible young man at a social function at which young women make their debut.

decemvir (disem´və) *n.* (*pl.* **decemviri** (-rī)) **1** any one of the various bodies of ten magistrates appointed by the Romans to legislate or rule, esp. the body appointed in 451 BC to codify the laws. **2** a member of any governing council of ten.
14–15C. Latin, sing. of *decemviri*, orig. *decem viri* ten men. Cp. DUUMVIR.

déclassé (dāklasā´, -klas´-), (*fem.*) **déclassée** *a.* having lost social position or estimation.
19C. French, p.p. of *déclasser*, from priv. pref. *dé-* + *classe* class.

décolleté (dākol´tā), (*fem.*) **décolletée** *a.* **1** (of a dress) low-necked. **2** wearing a low-necked dress. ~*n.* a low-cut neckline.
19C. French, p.p. of *décolleter* to expose the neck, from priv. pref. *dé-* + *collet* collar of a dress.

decor (dā´kaw), **décor** *n.* the setting, arrangement and decoration of a room or of a scene on the stage.
19C. French *décor*, from *décorer* to decorate.

decorum (dikaw´rəm) *n.* (*pl.* **decorums**) **1** decency and propriety of words and conduct. **2** etiquette, polite usage. **3** a requirement of decency or etiquette.
16C. Latin, use as n. of neut. sing. of *decorus* seemly.

découpage (dākoopahzh´) *n.* the art of decorating furniture etc. with cut-out patterns.
mid-20C. French, from *découper* to cut up, to cut out, from priv. pref. *dé-* + *couper* to cut.

decrescendo (dēkrishen´dō) *adv., a.* (*Mus.*) diminuendo. ~*n.* (*pl.* **decrescendos**) a diminuendo.

19C. Italian, pres.p. of *decrescere* to decrease. Cp. DIMINUENDO.

decus et tutamen (dek´əs et tūtah´men) *n.* an ornament and a protection.
late 20C. Latin.
• The words were inscribed on the milled edge of a one-pound coin from 1983. They were earlier used on the edges of silver crown pieces from 1662 and on gold five-guinea pieces from 1668. The motto itself is said to have been devised by John Evelyn (1620–1706). The words describe the purpose served by edge inscriptions, the 'protection' being against 'clipping'.

dedans (dədã´) *n.* **1** an open gallery at the end of a real-tennis court. **2** the spectators in this gallery.
18C. French inside, interior.

de facto (dā fak´tō) *adv.* (*formal*) in fact. ~*a.* existing in fact.
17C. Latin of fact, from *de* of + abl. sing. of *factum* fact.

dégagé (dāgah´jā), (*fem.*) **dégagée** *a.* relaxed, casual, detached.
17C. French, p.p. of *dégager* to set free, from *dé-* de- + *-gager*, from *engager* to engage. Cp. English *disengage*.

dégringolade (degrīgolahd´) *n.* a rapid descent or deterioration, a decline into decadence.
19C. French, from *dégringoler* to descend rapidly, from *dé-* down, away + Old French *gringole* hill, from Middle Dutch *crinc* curve, bend, rel. to English *crinkle*, *cringe*.

de gustibus non est disputandum (dā gustibus nōn est dispūtan´dəm) *int.* there is no accounting for tastes.
17C. Latin, lit. about tastes there is no disputing. Cp. CHACUN À SON GOÛT.

de haut en bas (də ōt ā bah´) *adv.* condescendingly, in a manner assuming superiority.

17C. French from above to below, from *de* from + *haut* high (cp. HAUTEUR) + *en* in, to + *bas* low.

Dei gratia (dāē grah´shiə) *adv.* (*formal*) by the grace of God.
17C. Latin by the grace of God, from *Dei*, gen. sing. of *Deus* God + *gratia*, abl. sing. of *gratia* grace.

déjà vu (dāzhah vü´), **deja vu** *n.*
1 (*Psych.*) an illusion of already having experienced something one is experiencing for the first time. **2** lack of originality, familiarity through repetition.
early 20C. French already seen, from *déjà* already + p.p. of *voir* to see.

déjeuner (dā´zhənā) *n.* breakfast, luncheon.
18C. French, use as n. of *déjeuner* to break one's fast, from Old French *desjeüner*, from priv. pref. *des-* + *jeün*, from Latin *ieiunus* fasting.

de jure (dē joo´ri, dā, yoo´-) *adv.* (*formal*) by right, legally. ~*a.* rightful.
16C. Latin of law, from *de* of, from + abl. sing. of *ius*, *iuris* law.

dekko (dek´ō) *n.* (*pl.* **dekkos**) (*coll.*) a quick look. ~*v.i.* (3rd pers. sing. pres. **dekkos**, *pres.p.* **dekkoing**, *past, p.p.* **dekkoed**) to look.
19C. Hindi *dekho*, polite imper. of *dekhnā* to look.

delaine (dilān´) *n.* **1** a kind of untwilled wool muslin. **2** a fabric of wool and cotton.
19C. French, shortening of *mousseline de laine*. See MOUSSELINE.

del credere (del krā´dərā) *adv., n.* (subject to) a guarantee, esp. the guarantee of a selling agent that the buyer is solvent.
18C. Italian of belief, of trust.

dele (dē´li) *v.t.* (*pres.p.* **deleing**, *past, p.p.*
deled) (*Print.*) to take out, omit,
expunge; to mark for deletion. ~*n.* a
mark indicating deletion; a deletion.
18C. Latin, 2nd pers. sing. imper. of
delere to delete.

delicatessen (delikətes´ən) *n.* **1** a shop
or part of a shop selling cold meats and
cheeses and specialist prepared foods.
2 such products.
19C. German *Delikatessen* (pl.) or Dutch
delicatessen (pl.), from French
délicatesse, from *délicat* delicate.
• In sense 1 the word is now often
colloquially abbreviated to *deli*.

delirium (dilir´iəm) *n.* **1** a wandering
of the mind, perversion of the mental
processes, the results of cerebral activity
bearing no true relation to reality,
characterized by delusions, illusions
or hallucinations, caused by fever etc.
2 frantic excitement or enthusiasm,
rapture, ecstasy.
16C. Latin, from *delirare* to deviate, to
be deranged, from *de* from + *lira* ridge
between furrows, i.e. lit. to leave the
furrow. Cp. English 'off one's trolley'.

delirium tremens (dilir´iəm trem´enz)
n. an acute phase in chronic alcoholism,
in which hallucinations and trembling
are experienced.
19C. Modern Latin trembling DELIRIUM.
• The term was coined in 1813 by
Dr Thomas Sutton (*c.*1767–1835) in his
Tracts on Delirium Tremens. Its current
meaning did not emerge until later. The
name is popularly abbreviated as DTs.

delta (del´tə) *n.* (*pl.* **deltas**) **1** the fourth
letter of the Greek alphabet (Δ, δ).
2 a delta-shaped alluvial deposit at the
mouth of a river. **3** a fourth-class mark
given to a student's work. **4** (*Astron.*)
(**Delta**) the fourth star (in brightness
or position etc.) in a constellation.
5 (*Math.*) an increment in a variable.
12–14C. Latin, from Greek.

de luxe (di lŭks´) *a.* luxurious, of
superior quality.
19C. French of luxury, from *de* of +
LUXE.

démarche (dā´mahsh) *n.* **1** a diplomatic
approach. **2** a method of procedure.
3 an announcement of policy.
17C. French, from *démarcher* to take
steps, from priv. pref. *dé-* + *marcher* to
walk.

démenti (dāmā´tē) *n.* (*pl.* **démentis**) an
official contradiction of a rumour etc.
16C. French, from *démentir* to
contradict, from priv. pref. *dé-* + *mentir*
to lie.

dementia (dimen´shə) *n.* (*Med.*) serious
deterioration of the mental faculties,
with memory loss, mood swings etc.
18C. Latin, from *demens*, *dementis* mad,
from *de* from + *mens*, *mentis* mind. Cp.
English 'out of one's mind'.

demi-mondaine (dem´imondān) *n.* a
prostitute.
19C. French, from *demi-monde*, lit. half
world.
• The French word implies a world half
in and half out of society, as described
in Alexandre Dumas' play *Le Demi-
monde* (1855), about the threat to the
institution of marriage posed by
prostitutes.

demi-pension (demipōs´yŏn) *n.*
(French) hotel accommodation with half
board.
mid-20C. French half board, from *demi-*
half + PENSION.

demitasse (dem´itas) *n.* **1** a small coffee
cup. **2** a small cup of coffee.
19C. French half-cup, from *demi-* half +
tasse cup.

demi-vierge (demivyeəzh´) *n.* (*pl.* **demi-
vierges** (-vyeəzh´)) a woman who takes
part in sexual actvity while retaining
her virginity.

early 20C. **French** half virgin.

• The phrase comes from the title of Marcel Prévost's novel *Les Demi-vierges* (1874).

demivolte (dem´ivolt) *n.* an artificial motion of a horse in which it raises its legs in a particular manner.
17C. **French**, from *demi-* half + *volte* (VOLT).

démodé (dāmō´dā) *a.* out of fashion.
19C. **French**, p.p. of *démoder* to go out of fashion, from priv. pref. *dé-* + *mode* fashion.

de mortuis nil nisi bonum (dā maw´tūēs nil nisi bon´əm) *int.* do not speak ill of the dead.
18C. **Latin**, lit. of the dead nothing but good.

• The phrase is traditionally attributed to Chilon of Sparta (6C BC).

demos (dē´mos) *n.* the people, as distinguished from the upper classes; the mob.
18C. **Greek** *dēmos* people.

denarius (dinah´riəs) *n.* (*pl.* **denarii** (-riī)) a Roman silver coin, worth ten asses; a penny.
14–15C. **Latin** *denarius nummus* coin containing ten (asses), from *deni* by tens.

dengue (deng´gi) *n.* an acute fever common in the tropics, characterized by severe pains, a rash and swellings.
19C. **West Indian Spanish**, from Kiswahili *denga*, *dinga*, in turn from Spanish *dengue* affectation.

• The reference is to the stiffness of the neck and shoulders that the disease causes, giving the sufferer an affected or fastidious air.

de nos jours (də nō juə´) *a.* (*postpositive*) of this period, of our time.

early 20C. **French** of our days, from *de* of + *nos*, pl. of *notre* our + *jours*, pl. of *jour* day.

denouement (dānoo´mā), **dénouement** *n.* **1** the unravelling of a plot or story. **2** the catastrophe or final solution of a plot. **3** an outcome.
18C. **French** *dénouement*, from *dénouer* to untie, from priv. pref. *dé-* + *nouer* to knot.

de novo (dā nō´vō) *adv.* anew.
17C. **Latin** from new, from *de* from + *novo*, abl. sing. of *novus* new.

deoch an doris (dokh an dor´is), **doch an dorris** *n.* (*Sc., Ir.*) a drink taken just before leaving.
17C. **Gaelic** *deoch an doruis*, Irish *deoch an dorais* drink at the door, from *deoch* drink + *an* the + *dorus* door, gen. sing. *doruis* (Gaelic) or *doras*, gen. sing. *dorais* (Irish).

Deo gratias (dāō grah´shiəs) *int.* thanks be to God.
16C. **Latin** (we give) thanks to God, from *Deo*, dat. of *Deus* God + *gratias*, acc. pl. of *gratia*.

dépaysé (dāpā´zā), (*fem.*) **dépaysée** *a.* that is away from home or familiar surroundings.
early 20C. **French** removed from one's country, from priv. pref. *dé-* + *pays* country.

dépêche (dāpesh´) *n.* a message; a dispatch.
19C. **French**, from *dépêcher* to send, to dispatch, from priv. pref. *dé-* + *-pêcher*, from Late Latin *pedicare*, from *pedica* fetter. Not rel. to English *dispatch*.

depot (dep´ō) *n.* **1** a place of deposit, a storehouse. **2** a building for the storage and servicing of buses, trains or goods vehicles. **3** (*N Am.*) a railway or bus station. **4** (*Mil.*) **a** a storehouse for equipment. **b** a station for recruits. **c** the headquarters of a regiment. **d** that portion of the battalion at headquarters while the rest are abroad.

18C. French *dépôt*, from Old French *depost*, from Latin *depositum*, p.p. of *deponere* to put aside.

de profundis (dā prəfun´dis) *adv.* from the depths of penitence or affliction. ~*n.* a cry from the depths of penitence or affliction.

14–15C. Latin from the depths, from *de* from + *profundis*, abl. pl. (used as n.) of *profundus* deep.

• The phrase represents the opening Latin words of Ps. cxxx: *De profundis clamavi ad te, Domine* Out of the depths have I cried unto thee, O Lord. Modern use of the phrase sometimes contains an implicit allusion to Oscar Wilde's apologia *De Profundis* (1905), written after being sentenced to a term of imprisonment in Reading Gaol.

déraciné (dāras´ēnā), (*fem.*) **déracinée** *a.* uprooted from one's environment, displaced geographically or socially.

early 20C. French uprooted, p.p. of *déraciner*, from *dé* up, out + *racine* root.

derailleur (dirā´lə) *n.* a bicycle gear in which the chain is moved between different sprockets.

mid-20C. French *dérailleur*, from *dérailler*, from priv. pref. *dé-* + *rail* rail.

de règle (də regl´, reg´lə) *a.* (*pred.*) customary, correct.

19C. French from the rule, from *de* of, from + *règle* rule.

de rigueur (də rigœ´) *a.* required by fashion.

19C. French from strictness, from *de* of, from + *rigueur* strictness, rigour.

dernier (dœ´niā) *a.* last.

17C. French last, from Old French *derrenier*, from *derrein*, from Popular

Latin *deretranus*, from *de-retro*, from *retro* behind. Cp. DERRIÈRE.

dernier cri (dœ´niā krē) *n.* the last word, the latest fashion.

19C. French, lit. last cry.

derrière (derieə´) *n.* (*coll., euphem.*) the buttocks, the behind.

18C. French behind, from Popular Latin *de-retro*. See DERNIER.

derris (der´is) *n.* an extract of the root of tropical trees of the genus *Derris,* which forms an effective insecticide.

19C. Modern Latin, from Greek leather covering.

• The reference is to the leather covering of the pod.

dervish (dœ´vish) *n.* a member of one of the various Muslim ascetic orders, whose devotional exercises include meditation and often frenzied physical exercises.

16C. Turkish *derviş*, from Persian *darvīš* poor, religious mendicant. Cp. FAKIR.

desaparecidos, los (los desaparesē´dos) *n.pl.* those lost or separated from their families.

late 20C. Spanish the disappeared ones.

• The term originally applied to those persons who disappeared in Argentina during the so-called 'Dirty War' under the military government of 1976–83. Such people were assumed to have been murdered by state forces.

deshabille (dāzabē´), **déshabillé** (dezab´ēā), **dishabille** (disabē´) *n.* state of undress, state of being partly or carelessly attired.

17C. French *déshabillé*, use as n. of p.p. of *déshabiller* to undress, from priv. pref. *des-* + *habiller* to dress.

desideratum (dizidərah´təm) *n.* (*pl.* **desiderata** (-tə)) anything desired, esp. anything to fill a gap.

17C. Latin, neut. sing. (used as n.) of p.p. of *desiderare* to desire.

désorienté (dāzawriātā´), (*fem.*)
désorientée *a.* bewildered, at a loss, having lost one's bearings.
early 20C. French disorientated, p.p. of *désorienter*.

détente (dātăt´) *n.* relaxation of tension between nations or other warring forces.
early 20C. French slackening, relaxation.

détenu (dātənü´) *n.* a person kept in custody, a prisoner.
19C. French, use as n. of p.p. of *détenir* to detain.

detour (dē´tuə) *n.* **1** a roundabout way. **2** a deviation, a digression. **3** (*N Am.*) a road diversion. ~*v.t.* to send by an indirect route. ~*v.i.* to make a deviation from a direct route.
18C. French *détour* change of direction, from *détourner* to turn away.

détraqué (dātrakā´), (fem.) **détraquée** *a.* deranged, psychologically disturbed.
early 20C. French, p.p. of *détraquer* to derange, to put out of order, from *dé* out + *trac* trace, track.

detritus (ditrī´təs) *n.* **1** (*Geol.*) accumulated matter produced by the disintegration of rock. **2** debris, rubbish.
18C. Latin, p.p. of *deterere* to rub away.

de trop (də trō´) *a.* superfluous, in the way.
18C. French excessive, from *de* of + *trop* too much.

deus (dā´us) *n.* god.
12–14C. Latin god.

deus ex machina (dā´us eks mak´inə) *n.* **1** in Greek and Roman drama, a god brought on to resolve a seemingly

irresolvable plot. **2** a contrived denouement.
17C. Modern Latin, lit. god from the machine, trans. Greek *theos ek mēkhanēs*.
● In classical drama, actors playing gods were suspended over the stage by such a machine.

Deutschmark (doich´mahk), **Deutsche Mark** (doich´ə) *n.* the standard unit of currency of Germany.
mid-20C. German *deutsche Mark* German mark, from *deutsch* German + *Mark* mark.

Devanagari (dāvənah´gəri) *n.* the formal alphabet in which Sanskrit and certain vernaculars are usually written.
18C. Sanskrit, from *deva* god + NAGARI, an earlier form of the script.

†devoir (dəvwah´) *n.* **1** a duty. **2** (*usu. pl.*) politeness, courtesy.
12–14C. Old French *deveir* (Modern French *devoir*), from Latin *debere* to owe.

devore (dəvaw´rā), **dévoré** *a.* (of a fabric, esp. velvet) having a design etched with acid.
early 20C. French *dévoré*, p.p. of *dévorer* to eat up, to devour.

dévot (dāvō´) *n.* a devotee.
18C. French, use as n. of a. devout.

dewan (diwahn´) *n.* **1** chief financial minister of an Indian state. **2** prime minister of an Indian state.
17C. Urdu, from Persian *dīwān* DIVAN (in sense fiscal register). Cp. DOUANE.

dexter (deks´tə) *a.* **1** (*Her.*) situated on the right of a shield (to the spectator's left) etc. **2** †of, relating to or situated on the right-hand side.
16C. Latin right, from base represented also by Greek *dexios*.

dey (dā) *n.* the title of the old sovereigns of Algiers, Tripoli and Tunis.
17C. French, from Turkish *day^* maternal uncle (used also as a courtesy title).

dhal (dahl), **dal, dahl** *n.* **1** a split grain, pulse. **2** an Asian soup or purée made from this.
17C. Hindi *dāl.*

dharma (dah´mə) *n.* in Hinduism and Buddhism, the fundamental concept of both natural and moral law, by which everything in the universe acts according to its essential nature or proper station.
18C. Sanskrit established thing, decree, custom.

dhobi (dō´bi) *n.* (*pl.* **dhobis**) in the Indian subcontinent, a washerman.
19C. Hindi *dhobī*, from *dhob* washing.

dhoti (dō´ti) *n.* (*pl.* **dhotis**) a loincloth worn by male Hindus.
17C. Hindi *dhotī.*

dhow (dow) *n.* a ship with one mast, a very long yard, and a lateen sail, used on the Arabian Sea.
18C. Arabic *dāwa*, prob. rel. to Marathi *ḍāw.*

diable au corps (diahbl ō kaw´, diahblə) *n.* restless energy, a spirit of devilry.
19C. French, lit. devil in the body, from *diable* devil + *au* in the + CORPS.

diablerie (diah´bləri) *n.* **1** dealings with the devil. **2** diabolism, magic or sorcery. **3** rascality, devilry.
18C. French devilry, from *diable* devil.

diabolo (diab´əlō, dī-) *n.* (*pl.* **diabolos**) a game with a double cone spun in the air by a cord on two sticks, an adaptation of the old game of the devil on two sticks.
early 20C. Italian, from Ecclesiastical Latin *diabolus* devil.

diaeresis (dīer´əsis), (*N Am.*) **dieresis** *n.* (*pl.* **diaereses** (-sēz), (*N Am.*) **diereses**)
1 a mark placed over the second of two vowels to show that it must be pronounced separately, as in *naïve*. **2** in prosody, a pause where the end of a foot coincides with the end of the word.
16C. Latin, from Greek *diairesis*, from *diairein* to take apart, from *dia-* apart + *hairein* to take.

diamanté (dēəmon´tā) *n.* material covered with glittering particles, such as sequins. ~*a.* decorated with glittering particles.
early 20C. French, p.p. of *diamanter* to set with diamonds, from *diamant* diamond.

Diaspora (dīas´porə) *n.* **1** (*Hist.*) the dispersion of the Jews after the Babylonian captivity. **2** Jews living outside Palestine, or now, outside Israel. **3** a dispersion or migration of any people.
19C. Greek, from *diaspeirein* to disperse, from *dia-* apart + *speirein* to sow, to scatter.
• The term itself originated in the Septuagint (Greek version of the Old Testament): *hesē diaspora hen pasais basileiais tēs gēs* shalt be a dispersion in all kingdoms of the earth (AV shalt be removed into all the kingdoms of the earth) (Deut. xxviii.25).

diatessaron (dīətes´əron) *n.* (*pl.* **diatessarons**) **1** a harmony of the four Gospels. **2** (*Mus.*) †the interval of a fourth, composed of a greater and lesser tone and a greater semitone.
14–15C. Late Latin, from Greek *dia tessarōn* composed of four.
• The term comes from the title given by Tatian (2C BC) to his *Evaggelion dia tessarōn* Gospel made of four, an account of the Gospels in a single narrative.

dicast (dik´ast), **dikast** *n.* in Greek history, one of 6000 Athenians chosen each year to act as judges.
19C. Greek *dikastēs* judge, from *dikazein* to judge, from *dikē* judgement.

dictum (dik´təm) *n.* (*pl.* **dicta** (-tə), **dictums**) 1 a positive or dogmatic assertion. 2 (*Law*) OBITER DICTUM. 3 a maxim, a saying.
16C. Latin, neut. p.p. (used as n.) of *dicere* to say.

didicoi (did´ikoi), **didakai** (-də-), **diddicoy** *n.* (*sl.*) an itinerant traveller or tinker, who is not a true Romany.
19C. Appar. alt. of **Romany** *dik akei* look here.

dies (dē´āz) *n.* (*pl.* **dies**) a day.
17C. Latin day.

diesis (dī´əsis) *n.* (*pl.* **dieses** (-sēz)) 1 the double dagger (‡); a reference mark. 2 (*Mus.*) the difference between three true major thirds and one octave.
14–15C. Latin, from Greek quarter-tone, from *diienai* to send through, from *dia* through + *ienai* to send.

dies non (dīēz non´, dēāz) *n.* 1 a day on which business cannot be transacted. 2 a day that does not count.
19C. Latin, lit. a non day.
• In sense 1 the term is an abbreviation of *dies non juridicus* 'day not judicial'.

Dieu et mon droit (dyœ ā mō drwah´) *int.* God and my right (the motto of the English sovereigns).
12–14C. French.
• The phrase originated in 1198, when Richard I routed Philip Augustus of France at the battle of Gisors. He had led his men into action with the words as a battle cry and after his victory wrote: 'It is not we who have done it, but God and our right through us'. Edward III declared himself king of France in 1340 and adopted the words as his motto.

differentia (difərən´shiə) *n.* (*pl.* **differentiae** (-shiē)) something which distinguishes one species from another of the same genus.
17C. Latin, neut. pl. pres.p. (used as n.) of *differe* to differ.

difficile (difisēl´) *a.* stubborn, intransigent.
16C. French difficult.

digamma (dīgam´ə) *n.* (*pl.* **digammas**) (*F*) a letter in the oldest Greek alphabet, which had the sound of *w*.
17C. Latin, from Greek, from *di-* two + GAMMA.
• The letter is so named from its resemblance to two gammas placed one above the other.

digitalis (dijitā´lis) *n.* 1 the dried leaves of the foxglove, which act as a cardiac sedative. 2 any member of a genus of scrophulariaceous plants, *Digitalis*, containing the foxglove.
17C. Modern Latin, use as n. of Latin *digitalis* pertaining to the finger, based on German *Fingerhut* thimble, foxglove.

diktat (dik´tat) *n.* 1 a settlement imposed, after a war, on the defeated. 2 an order or statement allowing no opposition.
mid-20C. German, from Latin *dictatum*, neut. p.p. (used as n.) of *dictare* to dictate.

dilemma (dilem´ə, dī-) *n.* 1 an argument in which a choice of alternatives is presented, each of which is unfavourable. 2 a position in which a person is forced to choose between equally unfavourable alternatives. 3 inability to decide between two alternatives. 4 a difficult situation.
16C. Latin, from Greek *dilēmma*, from *di-* two + *lēmma* assumption, premiss.

dilettante (dilətan´ti) *n.* (*pl.* **dilettanti** (-ti), **dilettantes**) 1 a lover or admirer of the fine arts. **2** a superficial amateur, a would-be connoisseur, a dabbler. ~*a.* **1** amateurish, superficial. **2** art-loving. **18C. Italian**, verbal a. (used as n.) from *dilettare*, from Latin *delectare* to delight. Cp. AMATEUR.

• The English use of the word is associated with the 18C Grand Tour, on which wealthy young British aristocrats travelled to Italy to study the remains of classical antiquity.

diligence (dil´ijəns) *n.* a public stagecoach, formerly used in France and adjoining countries.
17C. French, abbr. of *carrosse de diligence* coach of speed.

diminuendo (diminūen´dō) *a., adv.* (*Mus.*) gradually decreasing in loudness. ~*n.* (*pl.* **diminuendos, diminuendi** (-di)) **1** a gradual decrease in loudness. **2** a passage characterized by this. ~*v.i.* (*3rd pers. sing. pres.* **diminuendoes**, *pres.p.* **diminuendoing**, *past, p.p.* **diminuendoed**) to decrease gradually in loudness.
18C. Italian diminishing, pres.p. of *diminuire*, from Latin *deminuere* to diminish.

dim sum (dim sŭm´), **dim sim** (sim´) *n.* a Chinese dish of small steamed dumplings with various fillings.
mid-20C. Chinese *tím sam*, from *tím* dot + *sam* heart.

• The name refers to the small centre filling.

DIN (din) *n.* a method of classifying the speed of photographic film by sensitivity to light (the greater the light sensitivity the higher the speed).
mid-20C. Abbr. of **German** *Deutsche Industrie-Norm* German Industrial Standard.

dinar (dē´nah) *n.* **1** the standard unit of currency in the countries which formerly made up Yugoslavia. **2** the

standard unit of currency of various N African and Middle Eastern countries.
17C. Arabic and Persian *dīnār* or Turkish and Serbo-Croat *dinar*, from Late Greek *dēnarion*, from Latin DENARIUS.

dinero (dineə´rō) *n.* (*N Am., sl.*) money.
17C. Spanish coin, money, from Latin DENARIUS.

Ding an sich (ding an zikh´) *n.* (*Philos.*) a thing in itself.
19C. German thing in itself, from *Ding* thing + *an* in + *sich* self.

dinges (ding´əs) *n.* (*S Afr., coll.*) a name for any person or thing whose name is forgotten or unknown; a thingummy.
19C. Dutch *ding* thing.

Dioscuri (dīoskū´rē) *n.pl.* the twins Castor and Pollux.
16C. Greek *Dioskouroi*, from *Dios*, gen. of *Zeus* + *kouros* boy, son.

diploma (diplō´mə) *n.* (*pl.* **diplomas**) **1** a certificate of a degree, licence etc. **2** a document conveying some authority, privilege or honour. **3** a charter, a state paper.
18C. Latin, from Greek folded paper, from *diploun* to make double, to fold, from *diploos* double.

• The original sense was that of a folded document conveying a privilege.

Directoire (direk´twah) *a.* of or relating to the costume and furniture of the Directory period in France, 1795–99.
18C. French directory.

• The French revolutionary government known as the *Directoire* was so named for its five *directeurs* (directors) or ministers.

dirham (diə´rəm), **dirhem** *n.* **1** the standard unit of currency of several N African and Middle Eastern countries. **2** an Eastern measure of weight.
18C. Arabic, from Greek *drakhmē* an Attic weight and coin.

dirigisme (dir´izhizm) *n.* state control of economic and social affairs.
mid-20C. French, from *diriger*, from Latin *dirigere* to direct.

dirndl (dœn´dəl) *n.* **1** an Alpine peasant woman's dress with tight-fitting bodice and full gathered skirt. **2** any full skirt like this.
mid-20C. German, dial. dim. of *Dirne* girl.

discobolus (diskob´ələs) *n.* (*pl.* **discobuli** (-lī)) in ancient Greece, a discus-thrower.
18C. Latin, from Greek *diskobolos*, from *diskos* DISCUS + *bolos* throwing, from *ballein* to throw.

discotheque (dis´kətek) *n.* **1** a club or public place where people dance to recorded pop music. **2** mobile apparatus for playing records at a discotheque. **3** a party.
mid-20C. French *discothèque* (orig.) record library, based on *bibliothèque* library. See BIBLIOTHECA.
• The word is now almost always abbreviated to *disco*.

discus (dis´kəs) *n.* (*pl.* **discuses**) **1** in ancient Greece, a metal disc thrown in athletic sports, a quoit. **2** a similar disc, with a thick, heavy middle, thrown in modern field events.
17C. Latin, from Greek *diskos*.

diseur (dēzœ´) *n.* a reciter.
19C. French talker, from *dire* to say.

disjecta membra (disjektə mem´brə) *n.pl.* scattered fragments of a written work.
18C. Alt. of **Latin** *disiecti membra poetae* limbs of a dismembered poet.
• The Latin phrase is from Horace's *Satires* (I,iv) (1C BC).

distingué (dēstang·gā´), (*fem.*)
distinguée *a.* having an air of nobility or dignity.

19C. French, p.p. of *distinguer* to distinguish.

distrait (distrā´), (*fem.*) **distraite** (-trāt´) *a.* absent-minded, abstracted, inattentive.
14–15C. French, from Old French *destrait*, p.p. of *destraire*, from Latin *distrahere* to distract.
• The original sense was distracted in mind. The current sense dates from the 18C.

dit (dē) *a.* **1** named. **2** reputed.
19C. French, p.p. of *dire* to say.

dithyramb (dith´iram, -ramb) *n.* **1** in ancient Greece, a choric hymn in honour of Bacchus, full of frantic enthusiasm. **2** any wild, impetuous poem or song.
17C. Latin *dithyrambus*, from Greek *dithurambos*, prob. of non-Indo-European orig.

ditto (dit´ō) *n.* (*pl.* **dittos**) **1** what has been said before. **2** the same thing. **3** a similar thing. ~*a.* similar. ~*v.t.* (*3rd pers. sing. pres.* **dittoes**, *pres.p.* **dittoing**, *past, p.p.* **dittoed**) to repeat (what someone else has said or done).
17C. Italian, dial. var. of *detto* said, from Latin *dictus*, p.p. of *dire* to say.

diva (dē´və) *n.* (*pl.* **divas**) a famous female singer, a prima donna.
19C. Italian, from Latin goddess.

divan (divan´) *n.* **1** in oriental countries, a court of justice, the highest council of state. **2** (*poet.*) a council, a council chamber. **3** a cigar shop. **4** a smoking saloon. **5** a thickly-cushioned backless seat or sofa against the wall of a room. **6** †a collection of poems by one author. **7** a restaurant.
16C. French, or from Italian *divano*, from Turkish *dīvān*, from Persian brochure, anthology, register, court, bench. Cp. DEWAN, DOUANE.
• A divan was originally an oriental council of state, held in a room with a cushioned seat. Sense 5 arose in the 18C.

divertimento (divœtiment´ō) *n.* (*pl.* **divertimenti** (-tē), **divertimentos**) a piece of entertaining music, esp. a suite for a small group of instruments.
19C. Italian diversion. Cp. DIVERTISSEMENT.

divertissement (dēvœtēs´mä) *n.* **1** an interlude, a light entertainment. **2** (in ballet) a short dance, esp. showcasing a dancer's skills. **3** (*Mus.*) a divertimento.
18C. French diversion, from *divertir*, *divertiss-* to divert.

Dives (dī´vēz) *n.* a wealthy man.
14–15C. Late Latin rich man, use as n. of Latin *dives* rich (after the parable of Lazarus and the rich man, Luke xvi.19–31).
● The word is not a personal name, despite the capital initial.

divide et impera (divē´dä et im´perah) *int.* divide and rule.
17C. Latin.
● The maxim is attributed to Louis XI of France by Prosper Mérimée in his novel *La Chronique du règne de Charles IX* (1829).

Diwali (diwah´li) *n.* a Hindu festival honouring Lakshmi, the goddess of wealth, celebrated from October to November and marked by the lighting of lamps.
17C. Hindi *diwālī*, from Sanskrit *dīpāvalī*, *dīpalī* row of lights, from *dīpa* light, lamp.

dixie (dik´si) *n.* a pot for cooking over an outdoor fire.
early 20C. Hindi *degcī* cooking pot, from Persian *degča*, dim. of *deg* iron pot.

djellaba (jel´əbə), **djellabah**, **jellaba** *n.* a cloak with wide sleeves and a hood, worn by men in N Africa and the Middle East.
19C. Moroccan Arabic *jellāb*.

dobra (dō´brə) *n.* (*pl.* **dobras**) the standard monetary unit of São Tomé e Príncipe.
late 20C. Portuguese fold, from Latin *dupla*, fem. of *duplus* double.

Docetae (dōsē´tē) *n.pl.* a sect in the early Church who maintained that Christ had not a natural but only a phantasmal or celestial body.
18C. Medieval Latin, from Patristic Greek *Dokētai*, from Greek *dokein* to seem, to appear.

doctrinaire (doktrineə´) *a.* visionary, theoretical, impractical. ~*n.* a person who theorizes in politics without regard to practical considerations; a theorizer, an ideologist.
19C. French, from *doctrine* doctrine.
● The word was originally used by French political extremists of those who supported a 'doctrine' of compromise.

doek (duk) *n.* (*S Afr.*) a head-cloth, worn by married women.
18C. Afrikaans cloth.

doge (dōj) *n.* (*Hist.*) the title of the chief magistrate of the republics of Venice and Genoa.
16C. French, from Italian, from Venetian Italian *doze*, ult. from Latin *dux*, *ducis* leader.

dogma (dog´mə) *n.* (*pl.* **dogmas**) **1** an established principle, tenet or system of doctrines put forward to be received on authority, esp. that of a Church, as opposed to one deduced from experience or reasoning. **2** a positive, magisterial or arrogant expression of opinion.
16C. Late Latin, from Greek *dogma*, *dogmatos* opinion, decree, from *dokein* to seem good, to think.

†doit (doit) *n.* **1** a small Dutch copper coin worth about half a farthing. **2** any small piece of money, a trifle.
16C. Middle Dutch *duit*.

dojo (dō´jō) *n.* (*pl.* **dojos**) **1** a room where martial arts are practised. **2** a mat on which martial arts are practised.
mid-20C. Japanese, from *dō* way, pursuit + *-jō* place.

dolce (dol´chā) *adv.* (*Mus.*) sweetly, softly. ~*a.* (of music) sweet, soft.
19C. Italian, from Latin *dulcis* sweet.

dolce far niente (dol´chā fah nien´ti) *n.* sweet idleness.
19C. Italian, lit. sweet doing nothing.

Dolcelatte (dolchālat´i) *n.* a kind of soft, blue-veined, Italian cheese.
mid-20C. Italian *dolce latte* sweet milk, from DOLCE + *latte*, from Latin *lac*, *lactis* milk.

dolce vita (dolchā vē´tə) *n.* a life of luxury and self-indulgence.
mid-20C. Italian sweet life.

doli capax (doli kap´aks) *a.* (*Law*) capable of having the wrongful intention to commit a crime (the status of a child over the age of 14).
17C. Latin capable of crime, from gen. sing. of *dolus* guile, fraud + *capax* capable.
• A child under this age is legally *doli incapax* incapable of crime, although exceptional circumstances can lead to the prosecution of a child between ten and 14.

dolina (dolē´nə), **doline** (dolēn´) *n.* (*Geol.*) a funnel-shaped depression in the earth.
19C. Slovene valley.

dolma (dol´mə) *n.* (*pl.* **dolmas**, **dolmades** (-mah´dhez)) a vine leaf stuffed with rice and meat.
17C. Modern Greek *ntolmas*, from Turkish *dolma*, from *dolmak* to fill, to be filled.

dolman (dol´mən) *n.* (*pl.* **dolmans**) **1** a long Turkish robe, open in front, and with narrow sleeves. **2** a woman's loose mantle with dolman sleeves. **3** a hussar's jacket or cape with the sleeves hanging loose.
16C. French *doliman*, from Turkish *dolama*, lit. act of winding, from *dolamak* to wind.

dolmen (dol´men) *n.* a cromlech; the megalithic framework of a chambered cairn, consisting usually of three or more upright stones supporting a roof-stone.
19C. French, ? from Cornish *tolmen* hole of a stone, via Breton *tol* table + *men* stone. Cp. MENHIR.

doloroso (dolərō´sō, -zō) *a.*, *adv.* (*Mus.*) (to be performed) in a soft, dolorous manner.
19C. Italian, from Latin *dolorosus* dolorous.

DOM *abbr.* to God the best and greatest.
Abbr. of **Latin** *Deo Optimo Maximo* to God, the best, the greatest, from dat. of *Deus Optimus Maximus*.

domaine (dəmān´) *n.* a vineyard.
mid-20C. French domain.

Domine dirige nos (dominā dirij´ā nōs) *int.* Lord, direct us (the motto of the City of London).
19C. Latin.
• The phrase is based on the Latin version of Ps. xxxi.3.

dominee (doo´mini) *n.* a minister in any of the Afrikaner Churches in South Africa.
mid-20C. Afrikaans and Dutch, from Latin *domine*, voc. of *dominus* lord, master.

domino (dom´inō) *n.* (*pl.* **dominoes**) **1** any of 28 oblong dotted pieces, orig. of bone or ivory, used in playing

dominoes. **2** a masquerade dress worn for disguise by both sexes, consisting of a loose black cloak or mantle with a small mask. **3** a kind of half mask.
17C. French hood worn by priests in winter, ? ult. from Latin *dominus* lord, master.
• Sense 2 is the earliest sense. Sense 1 is said to derive from the black colour of the backs of the pieces, like that of the masquerade garment.

Dominus illuminatio mea (dominəs iloominahtiō mā´ə) *int.* the Lord is my light (the motto of Oxford University).
19C. Latin.
• The phrase comes from the Latin version of Ps. xxvii.1.

Don (don) *n.* **1** a title formerly restricted to Spanish noblemen and gentlemen, now common to all men in Spain, Sir, Mr. **2** a Spanish gentleman. **3** a Spaniard. **4** (*N Am., sl.*) an important member of the Mafia.
16C. Spanish, from Latin *dominus* lord, master.

dona (dō´nə) *n.* (*sl.*) **1** a woman. **2** a sweetheart.
17C. Portuguese or Spanish *doña*, from Latin *domina*, fem. of *dominus*. See DON. Cp. DONNA.

doner kebab (donə kibab´) *n.* spit-roasted lamb served in pitta bread, usually with salad.
mid-20C. Turkish *döner kebap*, from *döner* rotating + *kebap* KEBAB.

dong (dong) *n.* the standard unit of currency of Vietnam.
19C. Vietnamese coin, piastre.

donga (dong´gə) *n.* (*S Afr., Austral.*) a gully, a watercourse with steep sides.
19C. Nguni.

donjon (dŭn´jən) *n.* the grand central tower or keep of a castle, esp. a medieval Norman one, the lower storey generally used as a prison.
12–14C. Old French dungeon.

donna (don´ə) *n.* **1** an Italian lady. **2** (**Donna**) an Italian title for, or form of address to, a lady, Madame, madam.
17C. Italian lady, from Latin *domina*. See DONA.

donnée (don´ā), **donné** *n.* **1** a subject, a theme. **2** an assumption, a fact.
19C. French, fem. p.p. (used as n.) of *donner* to give. Cp. English 'given' in the sense of assumption.

doolally (doolal´i) *a.* (*sl.*) insane, eccentric.
early 20C. *Deolali*, a town near Bombay (Mumbai), India, location of a military sanatorium.

doolie (doo´li) *n.* a covered litter of bamboo.
17C. Hindi *ḍolī*, dim. of *ḍolā* cradle, swing, litter, from Sanskrit *ḍolā* to swing.

dop (dop) *n.* (*S Afr.*) **1** a kind of cheap brandy. **2** a measure of any spirit.
19C. Afrikaans, of uncertain orig.
• The word is perhaps from *doppe* husks of grapes or *dop* cup.

doppelgänger (dop´əlgengə, -gangə) *n.* the apparition of a living person; a wraith.
19C. German, lit. double-goer, from *Doppel* double + *Gänger* goer.

Dopper (dop´ə) *n.* a member of the Reformed Church of South Africa, characterized by extreme simplicity of manners and dress.
19C. Afrikaans of uncertain orig.
• The word is perhaps from *doper* Baptist, although *dompen* to suppress and *dorper* townsman have also been suggested.

dorp (dawp) *n.* (*S Afr.*) a small town.
15C. Dutch village.

dos-à-dos (dōzədō´) *a.* (of two books) bound together but facing in opposite directions. ~*n.* (*pl.* **dos-à-dos**) a seat designed for sitting back-to-back.
19C. French back to back, from *dos* back, from Popular Latin *dossum*, from Latin *dorsum* + *à* to.

dossier (dos´iā, -iə) *n.* a collection of papers and other documents relating to a person, a thing or an event.
19C. French bundle of papers in a wrapper with a label on the back, from *dos* back, from Popular Latin *dossum*, from Latin DORSUM.

dot (dot) *n.* a dowry.
19C. French, from Latin *dos*, *dotis* dowry.

douane (dooahn´) *n.* a Continental custom house.
17C. French, from Italian *duana*, from Arabic *dīwān* office, from Old Persian *dīwān* DIVAN. Cp. DEWAN.

double entendre (dooblātā´drə) *n.* **1** a word or phrase with two interpretations, one of which is usually indelicate. **2** a humour which relies on double entendres.
17C. Obsolete French double understanding (now *double entente*), from *double* double + *entendre* to understand.

doubloon (dəbloon´) *n.* **1** (*Hist.*) a Spanish and South American gold coin (orig. the double of a pistole). **2** (*pl., sl.*) money.
17C. French *doublon* or Spanish *doblón*, from *doble* double.

doublure (dooblūə´) *n.* an ornamental lining for a book cover.
19C. French lining, from *doubler* to line.

douceur (doosœ´) *n.* a small present; a gift, a bribe.
14–15C. French, from var. of Latin *dulcor* sweetness.

douche (doosh) *n.* **1** a jet of water or vapour directed upon some part of the body. **2** an instrument for applying this. ~*v.t.* to apply a douche to, esp. to flush out (the vagina or other cavity). ~*v.i.* to take a douche.
18C. French, from Italian *doccia* conduit pipe, from *docciare* to pour by drops, from Latin *ductus* duct.

doyen (doi´en, dwah´yā) *n.* the senior member of a body of people.
14–15C. French dean, from Old French *dien*, from Late Latin *decanus* chief of a group of ten, from Latin *decem* ten.
● The word is directly related to English *dean*.

dragée (drazh´ā) *n.* **1** a sweetmeat consisting of a nut, fruit etc. with a hard sugar coating. **2** a small silver-coloured sugar ball for decorating cakes. **3** a chocolate-covered sweet. **4** a pill with a hard sugar coating.
17C. French, from Medieval Latin *drageia*, ? from Latin *tragemata* sweetmeats, from Greek.

dragoman (drag´əmən) *n.* (*pl.* **dragomans, dragomen**) a person who acts as guide, interpreter and agent for travellers in the Middle East.
14–15C. Obsolete French (now *drogman*), from Italian *dragomanno*, from Medieval Greek *dragoumanos*, from Arabic *tarjumān*, from *tarjama* to interpret, with last element assim. to English *man*. Cp. TARGUM.

dragonnade (dragənād´) *n.* **1** (*usu. pl.*) the persecutions of Protestants in France during the reign of Louis XIV by means of dragoons who were quartered upon them. **2** a persecution by means of

troops. ~*v.t.* to persecute by this means.
18C. French.

dramatis personae (dramətis pəsō´nī)
n.pl. **1** the set of characters in a play.
2 a list of these.
18C. Latin persons of the drama, from
Late Latin *dramatis*, gen. sing. of *drama*
drama + nom. pl. of *persona* person.

dramaturge (dram´ətœj) *n.* a dramatist,
a playwright.
19C. French, from German *Dramaturg*,
from Greek *dramatourgos*, from *drama*,
dramatos drama + -*ergos* worker.

Drambuie® (dramboo´i, -bū´-) *n.* a
liqueur with a Scotch whisky base.
19C. Gaelic *dram buidheach* satisfying
drink or *dram buidhe* yellow drink (or
both).

Drang nach Osten (drang nahkh ost´ən)
n. the traditional German tendency
towards expansion into the East.
early 20C. German, lit. drive to (the)
East.
• The reference is to the gradual
migration of the Germanic peoples of
N Europe eastwards, penetrating Slavic-
speaking regions. This 'drive', from the
9C on, set the precedent for Hitler's
more forceful push eastwards (and
westwards) in the 1930s.

dressage (dres´ahzh) *n.* the training of
a horse in deportment, obedience and
response to signals given by the rider's
body.
mid-20C. French, lit. training, from
dresser to train, to drill.

droguet (drōgā´) *n.* a ribbed woollen
fabric, a kind of rep.
19C. French drugget.

droit (droit) *n.* (*Law*) **1** a right, a due.
2 a legal right.
14–15C. Old French, from use as n. of
var. of Latin *directum*, neut. of *directus*
direct.

droit de seigneur (drwah də senyœ´) *n.*
(*Hist.*) the supposed right of a feudal
lord in many countries of medieval
Europe to have sexual intercourse with
a tenant's bride on her wedding night.
19C. French, lit. right of (the) lord.
Cp. JUS PRIMAE NOCTIS.

droshky (drosh´ki) *n.* (*pl.* **droshkies**)
1 a Russian open four-wheeled vehicle
in which the passengers ride astride a
bench, their feet resting on bars near the
ground. **2** a public cab in Germany.
19C. Russian *drozhki* (pl.), dim. of *drogi*
wagon, hearse, pl. of *droga* centre pole
of a carriage.

drum (drŭm), **drumlin** (-lin) *n.* (*Geol.*)
a long, narrow ridge of drift or alluvial
formation.
18C. Gaelic and Irish *druim* back,
ridge.

Druse (drooz), **Druze, Druz** *n.* a member
of a politico-religious sect of Islamic
origin, inhabiting the region of Mt
Lebanon in Syria.
18C. French, from Arabic *Durūz*, pl. of
Durzī, var. of *Darazī*, from name of
Muḥammad ibn *Ismā´īl ad-Darazī*,
d.1019, one of the founders.
• Darazī's own name means tailor.
Hence the name of *Darzee*, the tailor
bird in Rudyard Kipling's *Jungle Book*
(1894). Cp. DURZI.

druse (drooz) *n.* **1** a cavity in a rock
lined or studded with crystals. **2** the
crystalline lining of this.
19C. French, from German, from Old
High German *druos* gland, bump.

duan (doo´ahn) *n.* a canto.
18C. Gaelic and Irish.

ducat (dŭk´ət) *n.* **1** (*Hist.*) a coin, of gold
or silver, formerly current in several
European countries. **2** any coin.
3 (*pl., sl.*) money, cash.

14–15C. Italian *ducato* or Medieval Latin *ducatus* duchy, territory of a duke, from Latin *dux, ducis* leader.

• A ducat was originally a silver coin minted in 1140 by Robert II of Sicily as Duke of Apulia.

Duce (doo´chi) *n.* the official title of Benito Mussolini, 1883–1945, when head of the Fascist state in Italy.
early 20C. Italian leader. Cp. FÜHRER.

duchesse (dooshes´, dŭch´is) *n.* **1** a heavy satin. **2** a dressing table with a tilting mirror. **3** a table cover or centrepiece.
18C. French duchess.

dudeen (doodēn´) *n.* (*Ir.*) a short clay tobacco pipe.
19C. Irish *duídín,* dim. of *dúd* pipe.

duello (dūel´ō) *n.* (*pl.* **duellos**) **1** a duel. **2** the rules of duelling.
16C. Italian duel.

duende (dooen´dā) *n.* **1** a demon, an evil spirit. **2** inspiration, magnetism.
early 20C. Spanish.

duenna (dūen´ə) *n.* (*pl.* **duennas**) an elderly woman employed as companion and governess to young women, a chaperone.
17C. Spanish *duenna* (now *dueña*), from Latin *domina* lady, mistress. Cp. DONA, DONNA.

duiker (dī´kə) *n.* **1** any of several small African antelopes of the genus *Cephalophus.* **2** a southern African cormorant, *Phalacrocorax africanus.*
18C. Dutch diver, from Middle Dutch *dūker,* from *dūken* to dive.

• The antelope is so called from its habit of plunging through bushes when alarmed.

Dukhobor (doo´kəbaw), **Doukhobor** *n.* a member of a Russian mystical sect

of the 18th and 19th cents. who were oppressed for their passive resistance to state control and militarism, and migrated in large numbers from their homes in the Caucasus to Canada.
19C. Russian, from *dukh* spirit + *borets* wrestler.

dulce domum (dŭlsi dō´məm) *n.* home, sweet home.
19C. Latin sweet 'home', from neut. of *dulcis* sweet + *domum* to the house, homeward.

• The phrase comes from the refrain of a 17C Latin song popular at Winchester College. The words properly mean 'sweet (sound of the word) home'.

dulce et decorum est pro patria mori (dul´chā et dikaw´rəm est prō pat´riə mor´ē) it is pleasant and proper to die for one's country.
18C. Latin.

• The words come from Horace's *Odes* (III,ii) (1C BC).

dulia (dū´liə), **douleia** (doolī´ə) *n.* the lowest of the three degrees of adoration recognized in the Roman Catholic Church, the reverence paid to angels, saints etc.
14–15C. Medieval Latin, from Greek *douleia* servitude, from *doulos* slave.

Duma (doo´mə) *n.* **1** a legislative body in Russia and some other republics in the former Soviet Union. **2** (*Hist.*) the old Russian parliament or chamber of representatives, a legislative and revising body whose authority was limited by the veto of the Tsar, first summoned in 1906.
19C. Russian, from base of *dumat'* to think, ult. rel. to English *doom.*

dumdum (dŭm´dŭm) *n.* a soft-nosed expanding bullet that lacerates the flesh.
early 20C. *Dum Dum,* a town and

arsenal near Calcutta, India, where first produced.

• The town's name comes from Hindi *damdamā* mound.

dumka (dum´kə) *n.* (*Mus.*) a type of Slavic folk ballad, combining slow, melancholy sections with livelier passages.
19C. Czech, from Slavic base rel. to Russian DUMA.

Dummkopf (dum´kopf) *n.* a stupid person, a fool, a blockhead.
19C. German, from *dumm* stupid + *Kopf* head.
• The term originated in the US.

dum·spiro spero (dum spiərō sper´ō) *int.* while there's life, there's hope.
17C. Latin, lit. while I breathe, I hope.
• The words are the motto of South Carolina and of many British families.

dun (dŭn) *n.* a hill, a mound, an earthwork (largely used in place names).
18C. Irish *dún*, from Gaelic *dùn* hill, hill fort, rel. to obs. Welsh *din*.

Dunelm (dŭn´elm) *a.* of Durham (University). ~*n.* Durham (the official signature of the Bishop of Durham).
18C. Abbr. of Modern Latin *Dunelmensis*, from *Dunelmum* Durham.

dungaree (dŭng·gərē´) *n.* **1** a coarse kind of calico used for overalls. **2** (*pl.*) trousers with a bib.
17C. Hindi *duṅgrī*.

duniwassal (doo´niwahsəl) *n.* a Highland gentleman of inferior rank, a yeoman.
16C. Gaelic *duine* man + *uasal* noble, of gentle birth.

Dunker (dŭng´kə) *n.* a member of a sect of German-American Baptists.
18C. Pennsylvania German dipper.
• Members of the sect are so called

because of their practice of total immersion during baptism.

duo (dū´ō) *n.* (*pl.* **duos**) **1** a pair of performers who work together. **2** (*Mus.*) a duet.
16C. Italian, from Latin two.

duomo (dwō´mō) *n.* (*pl.* **duomos**) an Italian cathedral.
16C. Italian, lit. dome.

dupondius (dūpon´diəs) *n.* (*pl.* **dupondii** (-diī)) a coin in ancient Rome, worth two asses.
17C. Latin, from *duo* two + *-pondius*, from *pondus* weight.

durbar (dœ´bah) *n.* (*Hist.*) **1** an Indian ruler's court. **2** a state reception by an Indian ruler or by a British governor. **3** a hall of audience.
17C. Urdu, from Persian *darbār* court.

durchkomponiert (duəkhkom´poniət, duəkh´-) *a.* (*Mus.*) having different music for each stanza.
19C. German, from *durch* through + *komponiert* composed.

durra (dur´ə) *n.* a kind of sorghum, *Sorghum bicolor,* cultivated for grain and fodder.
18C. Arabic *ḍura.*

durrie (dŭr´i), **dhurrie** *n.* a coarse cotton fabric, made in squares, and used in the Indian subcontinent for carpets, curtains, coverings for furniture etc.
19C. Hindi *darī.*

durum (dūə´rəm) *n.* a variety of spring wheat, *Triticum durum,* with a high gluten content, used mainly for the manufacture of pasta.
early 20C. Latin *durum,* neut. of *durus* hard.

durzi (dœ´zi) *n.* (*pl.* **durzis**) an Indian tailor.
19C. Urdu, from Persian *darzī.*
Cp. DRUSE.

duumvir (dūŭm´və) *n.* (*pl.* **duumvirs**) either of two officers or magistrates in ancient Rome appointed to carry out jointly the duties of any public office. **17C. Latin**, sing. of *duum virum*, gen. of *duo viri* two men.

duvet (doo´vā, dū´-) *n.* a quilt stuffed with down or man-made fibres, used as a bed covering instead of blankets and a sheet. **18C. French** down, var. of *dumet*, dim. of *dum*, *dun*, from Scandinavian source of English *down*.

dux (dŭks) *n.* (*Sc., Austral., New Zeal.*) the top pupil of a school. **18C. Latin** leader.

DV *int.* God willing, if nothing prevents it.
Abbr. of **Latin** *Deo volente*, abl. of *Deus volens* God willing.
● The Latin phrase dates from the 18C.

dwaal (dwahl) *n.* (*S Afr.*) a state of bewilderment. **mid-20C. Afrikaans** to wander, to roam.

dybbuk (dib´uk) *n.* (*pl.* **dybukkim** (-kim), **dybbuks**) in Jewish folklore, the soul of a dead sinner which enters the body of a living person and takes control of their actions. **early 20C. Yiddish** *dibek*, from Hebrew *dibbūq*, from *dāḫaq* to cling, to cleave.

E

eau-de-Cologne (ōdəkəlōnˊ) n. a scent consisting of a solution of volatile oils in alcohol.
19C. French water of Cologne.
● The scent was originally produced at Cologne and came to England through France. The French name has been popularly enhanced by its spoken suggestion of 'odour Cologne'.

eau-de-Javelle (ōdəzhavelˊ) n. a solution of sodium or potassium hypochlorite, used as a bleach or disinfectant.
19C. French water of Javelle.
● Javelle (properly Javel) was a village outside (now a suburb of) Paris, where the solution was first produced.

eau-de-Nil (ōdənēlˊ) n., a. (of) a pale greenish colour.
19C. French water of (the) Nile.
● The colour is supposed to resemble that of the waters of the Nile.

eau-de-vie (ōdəvēˊ) n. brandy.
18C. French water of life. Cp. English *whisky*, from Gaelic *uisce beatha* water of life.

Ebor (ēˊbaw) a. of York. ~n. York (the official signature of the Archbishop of York).
18C. Abbr. of **Modern Latin** *Eboracensis*, from *Eboracum* York.
● The Ebor Handicap is an annual flat race run at York.

écarté (ākahˊtā) n. **1** a game of cards played by two people with 32 cards. **2** a ballet position in which one arm and leg are extended.
19C. French, p.p. of *écarter* to discard from *é-* out of + *carte* card.
● The game is so called because each player can discard certain cards.

Ecce Homo (eki hōˊmō) n. a painting or sculpture representing Christ crowned with thorns, as before Pilate.
14–15C. Latin behold the Man, from *ecce* lo! + *homo* man.
● The phrase comes from the words of Pilate in the Vulgate (the Latin version of the Bible), AV 'Behold the man!' (John xix.5).

echelon (eshˊəlon) n. **1** (a group of persons in) a level, stage or grade of an organization etc. **2** (*Mil.*) the arrangement of troops, ships, aircraft etc. as in the form of steps, with parallel divisions one in advance of another. ~*v.t.* to form in echelon.
18C. French *échelon*, from *échelle* ladder, from Latin *scalae*, flight of stairs.

echt (ekht) a. genuine, authentic.
early 20C. German genuine, from Middle Dutch.

eclair (iklerˊ, ā-) n. an iced, finger-shaped cream-filled pastry.

19C. French *éclair* lightning, from *é-* out of + *clair*, from Latin *clarus* bright, clear.
● The word is popularly said to refer either to the pastry's gleaming coating of fondant icing or to the 'streak' of cream through its centre.

†**éclaircissement** (ikleəsēs´mã, ā-) *n.* an explanation or clearing up of a subject of dispute or misunderstanding.
17C. French, from *éclaircir*, *éclairciss-* to clear up. See ECLAIR.

éclat (āklah´) *n.* **1** brilliant success. **2** acclamation, applause. **3** splendour, striking effect.
17C. French, from *éclater* to burst out, from Popular Latin *exclapitare*, from *ex* out of + v. of imit. orig. rel. to English *clap*.

écorché (ākawshā´) *n.* an anatomical figure with the muscular system exposed for the purpose of study.
19C. French, p.p. of *écorcher* to flay, from Popular Latin *excorticare*, from *ex* out of + Latin CORTEX.

écossaise (ekosāz´) *n.* **1** a Scottish dance in duple time. **2** the music to it.
19C. French, fem. of *écossais* Scottish. Cp. SCHOTTISCHE.

écraseur (ākrazœ´) *n.* an instrument for removing tumours etc. without effusion of blood.
19C. French crusher, from *écraser* to crush, from *é-* out of + *-craser*, rel. to English *craze*.

ecru (ek´roo, ākrü´) *a.* of the colour of unbleached linen. *~n.* this colour.
19C. French *écru* raw, unbleached, from *é-* out of + *cru*, from Latin *crudus* raw.

écu (ākū´, ākü´) *n.* (*Hist.*) **1** a French silver coin of varying value, usu. considered as equivalent to the English crown. **2** a French five-franc piece.
16C. French, from Latin *scutum* shield.

eddo (ed´ō) *n.* (*pl.* **eddoes**) a tropical plant of the arum family, esp. *Colocasia esculenta* and *C. macrorhiza*, the roots of which are used as food, taro.
17C. Of W African orig. Cp. Fante *edwó* yam, *ndwo* root.

edelweiss (ā´dəlvīs) *n.* a small white composite plant, *Gnaphalium alpinum*, growing in rocky places in the Alps.
19C. German, from *edel* noble + *weiss* white.
● The word is popularly said to have been coined to attract 19C tourists to the Alps, but it is more likely to be a folk name referring to the white starlike bracts.

édition de luxe (ādēsiō də lüks´) *n.* (*pl.* **éditions de luxe** (ādēsiō)) a handsomely printed and bound edition of a book.
19C. French luxury edition.

editio princeps (idish´io prin´seps) *n.* (*pl.* **editiones principes** (-ō´nēz, -sipēz)) the first printed edition of a book.
19C. Modern Latin, lit. first publication.

effendi (ifen´di) *n.* (*pl.* **effendis**) **1** a learned man or a man of social standing in the E Mediterranean. **2** (*Hist.*) master, as a title of respect in Turkey.
17C. Turkish *efendˆ*, from Modern Greek *aphentē*, voc. of *aphentēs*, from Greek *authentēs* lord, master.

effleurage (eflərahzh´) *n.* in massage, a stroking movement of the hand. *~v.i.* to use such a movement. *~v.t.* to massage (a person) using such a movement.
19C. French, from *effleurer* to stroke lightly, lit. to remove the flower, from *é-* out of + *fleur* flower.

effluvium (ifloo´viəm) *n.* (*pl.* **effluvia** (-viə)) an emanation affecting the sense of smell, esp. a disagreeable smell and vapour as from putrefying substances etc.

17C. Latin, from *effluere*, from *ex* out of + *fluere* to flow.

e.g. *abbr.* for example.
Abbr. of **Latin** *exempli gratia* for the sake of an example, from gen. sing. of EXEMPLUM + abl. sing. of *gratia* goodwill, grace.

égarement (āgah´mã) *n.* confusion, bewilderment.
early 20C. French, from *égarer* to lead astray, to confuse, from *é-* away, out + Frankish *waron* to take care, to guard, rel. to English *ward*.
● The adjective *égaré* is also used in English.

ego (ē´gō, eg´ō) *n.* (*pl.* **egos**) **1** individuality, personality. **2** the self-conscious subject, as contrasted with the non-ego, or object. **3** (*Psych.*) the conscious self, which resists on the one hand the threats of the super-ego, and on the other the impulses of the id. **4** (*coll.*) self-confidence or self-conceit.
19C. Latin I.

eheu, fugaces (āhū foogah´sēz) *int.* used to express regret for the speed at which time passes.
19C. Latin, in full *eheu fugaces … / labuntur anni* alas, the fleeting years slip away, from the opening lines of Horace's *Odes* II, xiv (1C BC).

Eid (ēd), **Id** *n.* a Muslim festival.
17C. Arabic *'īd* festival, from Aramaic.

eidolon (īdō´lon) *n.* (*pl.* **eidolons, eidola** (-lə)) **1** an image, likeness or representation. **2** an apparition, a spectre.
17C. Greek *eidōlon* image.

einkorn (īn´kawn) *n.* a variety of wheat, *Triticum monococcum*, used for feeding animals.

early 20C. German, from *ein* one + *Korn* corn, seed.

ein Volk, ein Reich, ein Führer (īn folk īn rīkh īn für´ə) *int.* one people, one realm, one leader.
mid-20C. German. Cp. FÜHRER, REICH, VOLK.
● The Nazi slogan also appears in the form *ein Reich, ein Volk, ein Führer*.

eirenicon (īrē´nikon), **irenicon** *n.* a measure or proposal intended to make or restore peace.
17C. Greek *eirēnikon*, neut. sing. of *eirēnikos* peaceful.

eisteddfod (īstedh´vod, -ted´fod) *n.* (*pl.* **eisteddfods, eisteddfodau** (-vodī)) a competitive congress of Welsh bards and musicians held annually to encourage native poetry and music.
19C. Welsh session, from *eistedd* to sit.

Eiswein (īs´vīn) *n.* wine made from grapes picked when covered in frost.
mid-20C. German, from *Eis* ice + *Wein* wine.

eiusdem generis (āūsdem jen´əris) *a.* (*Law*) of the same kind.
17C. Latin of the same kind, from gen. sing. of IDEM + GENUS.

ekka (ek´ə) *n.* (*Ang.-Ind.*) a small one-horse carriage.
19C. Hindi *ikkā*, lit. single, from Sanskrit *eka* one.

élan (ilan´, ālā´), **elan** *n.* energy and confidence.
19C. French, from *élancer*, from *é-* out of + *lancer* to throw.

élan vital (ilan, ālā vētal´) *n.* an intuitively perceived life-force, any hidden creative principle.
early 20C. French vital energy.
● The concept was introduced by the French philosopher Henri Bergson in

L'Évolution créatrice (1907), in which he opposed the *élan vital* to inert matter.

El Dorado (el dərah´dō), **eldorado, Eldorado** *n.* **1** any place where money or profit is easily obtained. **2** an inexhaustible mine. **3** an imaginary land of gold in South America, between the Orinoco and Amazon.
19C. **Spanish** the gilded, from *el* the + *dorado* gilded.
● Sense 3 was the original sense.

electrum (ilek´trəm) *n.* **1** an alloy of gold and silver in use among the ancients. **2** native gold containing silver. **3** an alloy of copper, zinc and nickel, also called *German silver*.
14–15C. **Latin**, from Greek *ēlektron* amber, electrum.

elemi (el´əmi) *n.* a gum resin obtained from the Philippine tree, *Canarium luzanicum,* used in pharmacy.
16C. **Modern Latin**, from Arabic *al-lāmī*.

elenchus (ileng´kəs) *n.* (*pl.* **elenchi** (-kī)) (*Logic*) a refutation.
17C. **Latin**, from Greek *elegkhos* argument of refutation.

elite (ālēt´), **élite** *n.* **1** the best part, the most powerful. **2** a type size for typewriters of twelve characters per inch (2.54 centimetres).
18C. **French** *élite,* fem. of obs. p.p. (used as n.) of *élire,* from var. of Latin *eligere* to choose.

El Niño (el nē´nyō) *n.* a warm ocean current in the S Pacific, arising every few years, which affects the South American coast directly and causes climatic disturbance over a much larger area.
19C. **Spanish** *El Niño* (*de Navidad*) the (Christmas) Child, Baby Jesus.
● The name refers to the time when the current occurs, between Christmas and March.

eloge (ālōzh´) *n.* an encomium, a panegyric, esp. a discourse in honour of a deceased person.
16C. **French** *éloge,* from Latin *elogium* short epitaph, from alt. of Greek *elegeia* elegy.
● The Latin altered form probably arose by confusion with *eulogium* eulogy.

Elohim (ilō´him) *n.* the ordinary name of God in the Hebrew Scriptures.
16C. **Hebrew** *'ĕlōhīm* lit. gods.
● The Hebrew plural word to describe the one God is usually explained as a 'plural of majesty' although the word is also used in the Old Testament in reference to polytheistic cultures.

eloi, eloi, lama sabachthani? (ēloi ēloi lahmə sabakhthah´ni) *int.* my God, my God, why hast thou forsaken me? (the last recorded utterance of Jesus on the cross).
19C. **Aramaic**.
● The Aramaic words are quoted in the New Testament (Matt. xxvii.46, Mark xv.34).

Elul (ē´lul) *n.* the sixth month of the Jewish ecclesiastical, and the twelfth of the civil year, beginning with the new moon of September.
16C. **Hebrew** *'ĕlūl*.

Elysium (iliz´iəm) *n.* **1** in Greek mythology, the abode of the souls of heroes after death. **2** a place or state of perfect happiness.
16C. **Latin**, from Greek *Elusion* (*pedion*) (plain of the) blessed.
● The Greek name is of non-Greek origin.

embargo (imbah´gō) *n.* (*pl.* **embargoes**) **1** a prohibition by authority upon the departure of vessels from ports under its jurisdiction. **2** a complete suspension of foreign commerce or of a particular branch of foreign trade. **3** a hindrance, check, impediment. **4** a prohibition or

restraint, as on publication. ~*v.t.* (*3rd pers. sing. pres.* **embargoes,** *pres.p.* **embargoing,** *past, p.p.* **embargoed**) **1** to lay an embargo upon. **2** to seize for purposes of state. **3** to requisition, to seize, to confiscate. **4** to prohibit, to forbid.
17C. Spanish, from *embargar* to arrest, to impede, from Latin *in* in + *barra* bar.

embarras de choix (ābara də shwaˊ) *n.* a perplexing number of things to choose from.
17C. French embarrassment of choice, from *embarras* embarrassment + *de* of + *choix* choice.

embarras de richesse (ābara də rēshesˊ), **embarras de richesses** (rēshesˊ) *n.* a perplexing abundance of wealth, more than one needs or can manage.
18C. French, lit. embarrassment of riches. Cp. EMBARRAS DE CHOIX.
• The words are from the title of a comedy *L'Embarras des richesses* (1726) by the Abbé d'Allainval.

embonpoint (ābõpwāˊ) *n.* plumpness of person or figure. ~*a.* **1** plump, well-nourished. **2** stout. **3** (*euphem.*) fat.
17C. French phr. *en bon point* in good condition, from *en* in + *bon* good + *point* condition.

embouchure (ābooshuəˊ, om-) *n.* **1** (*Mus.*) **a** the shaping of the lips to the mouthpiece of a brass or wind instrument. **b** the mouthpiece of such an instrument. **2** the mouth of a river etc.
18C. French, from *s'emboucher* to discharge itself by a mouth, from *emboucher* to put in the mouth, from *en* in + *bouche* mouth.

embourgeoisement (ābuəzhwahzmāˊ, -buəˊ-) *n.* the gradual admission of primitive peoples to citizenship of a civilized state.

mid-20C. French, from *embourgeoiser* to make BOURGEOIS.

emeritus (imerˊitəs) *a.* **1** (*placed after the noun*) having served one's term of office and retired with an honorary title. **2** in ancient Rome, retired from public service. ~*n.* (*pl.* **emeriti** (-tī)) a person who has served their term and retired from an office.
18C. Latin, p.p. of *emereri* to earn (one's discharge) by service, from *ex* out of + *mereri* to deserve.

émeute (imūtˊ) *n.* **1** a seditious or revolutionary outbreak. **2** a riot or popular disturbance.
18C. French, from Old French *esmote*, from *esmeu* (Modern French *ému*), p.p. of *esmovoir* (Modern French *émouvoir*), based on *meute* crowd, uprising.

émigré (emˊigrā), **emigre** *n.* an emigrant, esp. one of the royalists who left France at the time of the French Revolution.
18C. French, p.p. of *émigrer*, from Latin *emigrare* to depart.

éminence grise (eminās grēzˊ) *n.* (*pl.* **éminences grises** (eminās grēzˊ)) a man in the background exercising power unofficially.
mid-20C. French, lit. grey eminence.
• The term was originally a nickname applied to Cardinal Richelieu's private secretary, the Capuchin Père Joseph (originally François Joseph le Clerc du Tremblay), 1577–1638. He was so called by contrast with Richelieu himself, the *Éminence rouge* Red Eminence (from the colour of his cardinal's robes).

emir (imiəˊ) *n.* **1** in the Middle East and N Africa, a prince, chieftain, governor or commander. **2** a title given to the descendants of Muhammad through Fatima, his daughter.
16C. French *émir*, from Arabic *'amīr*. See AMIR.

Emmental (em´əntahl), **Emmenthal** *n.* a type of Swiss cheese with holes in it.
early 20C. German *Emmentaler*, from *Emmental*, a region in Switzerland.

emmer (em´ə) *n.* a variety of wheat, *Triticum dicoccum*, grown in Europe largely as livestock fodder.
early 20C. German, from Old High German *amer*.

empennage (impen´ij) *n.* the stabilizing parts at the rear of an aeroplane, including the rudder, the fin and the elevator.
early 20C. French feathering (of an arrow), from *empenner* to feather (an arrow), from *en* in + *penne*, from Latin *penna* feather.

emporium (impaw´riəm) *n.* (*pl.* **emporiums, emporia** (-riə)) **1** a large shop where many kinds of goods are sold. **2** a commercial centre, a market.
16C. Latin, from Greek *emporion*, from *emporos* merchant, from *en* in + verbal stem *por-*, *per-* to journey.

empressement (āpres´mā) *n.* cordiality, goodwill, eagerness.
18C. French, from *empresser* to urge.

en avant (ān avā´) *int.* forward!
19C. French forward, from *en* into + AVANT.

en barbette (ā bahbet´) *a.* (of guns) so mounted as to allow of their being fired over a parapet without embrasures or port-holes.
18C. French, from *en* in + BARBETTE.

en bloc (ā blok´) *adv.* as one unit, all together.
19C. French in a block, from *en* in + BLOC.

en brosse (ā bros´) *a.* (of hair) cut very short so that it stands on end.
early 20C. French in a brush, from *en* in + *brosse* brush.

en cabochon (ān kab´əshon) *a.* (of a precious stone) polished, but without facets.
19C. French in a cabochon, from *en* in + CABOCHON.

encaenia (insē´niə) *n.pl.* **1** a festival to commemorate the dedication of a church, the founding of a city etc. **2** the annual commemoration of founders and benefactors of Oxford University.
14–15C. Latin, from Greek *egkainia* dedication festival, from *en* in + *kainos* new, recent.

enceinte (āsīnt´) *a.* (*euphem.*) pregnant. ~*n.* the space within the ramparts of a fortification.
18C. French, from Latin *incincta*, fem. p.p. of *incingere* to gird in, from *in* in + *cingere* to gird.

enchanté (āshātā´), (*fem.*) **enchantée** *a.* delighted, pleased to meet you.
early 20C. French, p.p. of *enchanter* to delight, to enchant.

enchilada (enchilah´də) *n.* a Mexican dish of a meat-filled tortilla served with chilli sauce.
19C. American Spanish, fem. of *enchilado*, p.p. of *enchilar* to season with chilli. See CHILLI.

enchiridion (enkīrid´iən) *n.* (*pl.* **enchiridions, enchiridia** (-diə)) (*formal*) a handbook or manual, a small guide or book of reference.
14–15C. Late Latin, from Greek *egkheiridion*, from *en* in + *kheir* hand + dim. suf. *-idion*.

encierro (ensyer´o) *n.* (*pl.* **encierros** (-os)) the driving of bulls through the streets of a Spanish town as a festive sport.

19C. Spanish, lit. a shutting in, from *en-* in + *cierre* shutting.

• A famous *encierro* or bull run is the one held annually in Pamplona on 7 July, the feast day of San Fermín, the city's first bishop.

en clair (ā kleə´) *a., adv.* (of telegrams etc.) not in code or cipher.
19C. French in clear, from *en* in + *clair* clear.

enclave (en´klāv) *n.* **1** a territory completely surrounded by that of another state; an enclosure, as viewed from outside it. **2** a group of people whose behaviour and opinions differ from those of the people they live among.
19C. French, from Old French *enclaver* to enclose, to dovetail, from Popular Latin *inclavare*, from Latin *in* in + *clavis* key.

encomium (inkō´miəm) *n.* (*pl.* **encomiums, encomia** (-miə)) **1** a formal eulogy or panegyric. **2** high commendation. **3** high-flown praise.
16C. Latin, from Greek *egkōmion* eulogy, neut. (used as n.) of *egkōmios*, from *en* in + *kōmos* revel.

encore (ong´kaw) *int.* used as a call for a repetition at a concert, theatre etc. ~*n.* **1** a demand for a repetition of a song etc. **2** the repetition itself. ~*v.t.* **1** to call for a repetition of. **2** to call back (a performer). ~*v.i.* to call for an encore.
18C. French still, again, ? from Popular Latin *hinc-ad-horam* from then to this hour.

• The French equivalent word is BIS.

en effet (ān efe´) *adv.* in effect.
19C. French in effect, from *en* in + *effet* effect.

energumen (enəgū´mən) *n.* **1** an enthusiast, a fanatic. **2** a person possessed by a spirit, esp. an evil spirit, a demoniac.

18C. Late Latin *energumenus*, from Greek *energoumenos*, p.p. of *energein* to work upon, from *en* in + *ergon* work.

en face (ā fas´) *adv.* **1** opposite, facing. **2** facing forwards.
18C. French facing, from *en* in + *face* face.

en famille (ā famēy´) *adv.* **1** at home with one's family. **2** informally.
18C. French in the family, from *en* in + *famille* family.

enfant gâté (āfā gatā´) *n.* (*pl.* **enfants gâtés** (āfā gatā´)) someone whose character has been spoiled by over-indulgence.
19C. French spoilt child, from *enfant* child + *gâté*, p.p. of *gâter* to spoil, from Latin *vastare* to destroy.

enfant terrible (āfā terēbl´, terēb´lə) *n.* (*pl.* **enfants terribles** (āfā terēbl´, terēb´lə)) **1** a person who embarrasses people by behaving indiscreetly, unconventionally etc. **2** a child who makes embarrassing remarks.
19C. French terrible child, from *enfant* child + *terrible* terrible.

enfant trouvé (āfā troovā´) *n.* (*pl.* **enfants trouvés** (āfā troovā´)) a foundling, an abandoned child of unknown parents.
19C. French, lit. found child.

en fête (ā fet´) *adv.* dressed for a holiday, celebrating a holiday.
19C. French in a festival, from *en* in + FÊTE.

enfilade (enfilād´) *n.* **1** gunfire that may rake a position, line of works or body of troops, from end to end. **2** a position liable to raking gunfire. ~*v.t.* to pierce or rake with shot from end to end.
18C. French, from *enfiler* to thread on a string, from *en* in + *fil* thread.

engagé (āgazhā´, ong·gazh´ā) a. (of a writer, artist etc.) committed to a moral or political cause.
19C. **French**, p.p. of *engager* to commit.

en garde (ā gahd´) *int.* in fencing, used as a warning to be ready to receive attack. ~a. ready for attack.
19C. **French** on guard, from *en* on + *garde* guard.

en grande tenue (ā grād tənü´) *adv.* in full evening dress.
19C. **French** in grand dress, from *en* in + fem. of *grand* great, grand + *tenue*, from *tenir*, from Latin *tenere* to hold, to keep.

en grand seigneur (ā grā senyœ´) *adv.* like a lord, using or having a grand or arrogant manner.
19C. **French** in (the manner of a) grand lord, from *en* in + *grand* great, grand + SEIGNEUR.

enjambement (injamb´mənt) *n.* the continuation of a sentence or clause, without a pause in sense, from one line of verse or couplet into the next.
19C. **French**, from *enjamber* to stride over, to go beyond, from *en* in + *jambe* leg.

en masse (ā mas´) *adv.* in a group, all together.
18C. **French** in a mass, from *en* in + *masse* mass.

ennui (onwē´) *n.* lack of interest in things, boredom.
18C. **French**, from Latin *in odio* in phrase *mihi in odio est* it is hateful to me.

enosis (en´ōsis, enō´-) *n.* the proposal for the political union of Cyprus with Greece.
mid-20C. **Modern Greek** *henōsis*, from *hena* one.

en papillote (ā papēyot´) *adv.* baked in an envelope of foil or greased paper.
late 20C. **French** in a curlpaper, from *en* in + PAPILLOTE.

en passant (ā pas´ā) *adv.* **1** by the way. **2** in chess, applied to the taking of a pawn that has moved two squares as if it has moved only one.
17C. **French** in passing, from *en* in + pres.p. of *passer* to pass.

en pension (ā pāsyō´) *adv.* as a lodger, with meals provided.
19C. **French** in a lodging house, from *en* in + PENSION.

en plein air (ā plen eə´) *adv.* in the open air.
19C. **French**, lit. in full air.
• The phrase was used in association with the French Impressionist painters who rejected the studios of the academics in favour of work in the open air.

en principe (ā prīsēp´) *adv.* in principle.
early 20C. **French**.

en prise (ā prēz´) *a.* in chess, of or relating to a piece which is exposed to capture.
19C. **French** in (a position to be) taken, from *en* in + fem. p.p. (used as n.) of *prendre* to take.

en rapport (ā rapaw´) *adv.* in sympathy (with).
19C. **French**, lit. in rapport, from *en* in + RAPPORT.

en règle (ā regl´, reg´lə) *adv.* in order, according to form.
19C. **French**, lit. in rule.

en revanche (ā rəvāsh´) *adv.* in return, by way of compensation.
19C. **French**, from *en* in + REVANCHE.

en route (ā root´) *adv.* on the way; on the road.
   18C. French on the road, from *en* in + *route* road, way, route.

ens (enz) *n.* (*pl.* **entia** (en´shiə)) (*Philos.*)
   1 entity, being, existence. **2** any existing being or thing.
   16C. Late Latin, pres.p. (used as n.), formed from *esse* to be, on a supposed analogy of *absens* from *abesse* to be absent.
   ● Latin *esse* in fact has no present participle, but some compounds do, such as *absens* from *abesse*, *praesens* from *praeesse* to be before. Latin *ens* here thus renders Greek *on* as the noun of the present participle of *einai* to be.

ensemble (āsā´blə, onsom´bəl) *n.* **1** all the parts of anything taken together. **2** the general effect of things taken together. **3** an outfit consisting of several (matching) garments. **4** (*Mus.*) the joint effort of all the performers. **5** (*Mus.*) a combination of two or more performers or players. **6** a group of supporting players or performers. **7** (*Math., Physics*) a set of systems having the same constitution but behaving in different ways. ~*adv.* **1** all together. **2** all at once.
   14–15C. Old French, from Latin *insimul*, from *in* in + *simul* at the same time.

ensilage (en´silij, insī´lij) *n.* **1** a method of preserving forage crops whilst moist and succulent, without previously drying, by storing them en masse in pits or trenches. **2** fodder so preserved, silage. ~*v.t.* to preserve by the process of ensilage.
   19C. French, from *ensiler*, from Spanish *ensilar*, from *en-* in + *silo* silo.

en suite (ā swēt´) *adv.* in succession, as part of a set. ~*a.* forming a unit, as in *en suite bathroom*.
   18C. French in a suite, from *en* in + SUITE.

entasis (en´təsis) *n.* (*pl.* **entases** (-sēz)) (*Archit.*) the almost imperceptible convex curvature given to a shaft or a column.
   17C. Modern Latin, from Greek, from *enteinein* to strain.

entente (ātānt´, ontont´) *n.* **1** a friendly understanding. **2** a group of states having such an understanding.
   19C. French, obs. fem. p.p. (used as n.) of *entendre* to understand.

Entente Cordiale (ātānt´, ontont´ kawdiahl´) *n.* **1** the understanding between France and Britain reached in 1904. **2** (*also* **entente cordiale**) any such understanding between states or other powers.
   19C. French, lit. cordial understanding.

entêté (ātetā´), (*fem.*) **entêtée** *a.* obstinate, stubborn.
   19C. French, p.p. of *entêter* to be obstinate, from *en-* in + *tête* head. Cp. English *headstrong*.

entourage (ātoorahzh´, on-) *n.* **1** retinue, people following or attending on an important person. **2** surroundings, environment.
   19C. French, from *entourer* to surround. Cp. French *entours* surroundings, *à l'entour* around.

en tout cas (ā too kah´) *n.* a parasol that can also serve as an umbrella.
   19C. French, lit. in any case, in all emergencies.
   ● En-Tout-Cas is also the proprietary name of a hard tennis court, which can be used when wet or dry.

entr'acte (ātrakt´) *n.* **1** the interval between the acts of a play. **2** music, dancing or other performance between the acts of a play.
   19C. Obsolete French (now *entracte*), from *entre* between + *acte* act.

entrain (ātrī´) *n.* enthusiasm, high spirits.
19C. French, from Old French *entraîner*, from *en* in + *traîner* to drag.

en train (ā trī´) *adv.* in progress, under way.
18C. French, lit. in train, from *en* in + *train* movement, progress.

entrechat (ā´trəshah) *n.* a leap in dancing, esp. one including a striking of the heels together several times.
18C. French, from Italian (*capriola*) *intrecciata* complicated (capriole).

entrecôte (on´trəkōt, -kot) *n.* a beefsteak cut from between two ribs.
19C. French, lit. between rib, from *entre* between + *côte* rib.

entrée (ā´trā, on´-) *n.* **1** freedom or right of entrance. **2** (*orig. N Am.*) the main course of a meal. **3** a dish served between the fish and the meat courses.
18C. French, fem. p.p. of *entrer* to enter, to make an appearance.

entremets (ā´trəmā) *n.* (*pl.* **entremets**) **1** a light dish served between courses. **2** a sweet dish.
15C. French, from *entre* between + *mets* dish.

entre nous (ātrə noo´) *adv.* between ourselves, in private.
17C. French between us, from *entre* between + *nous* us.

entrepôt (ā´trəpō) *n.* **1** a warehouse for the temporary deposit of goods. **2** a free port where foreign merchandise is kept in bond till re-exported. **3** a commercial centre to which goods are sent for distribution.
18C. French (earlier *entrepost*), from *entreposer* to store, from *entre* among + *poser* to place.

entrepreneur (ātrəprənœ´, on-) *n.* **1** a person who undertakes a (financial) enterprise, esp. one with an element of risk. **2** a contractor, or commercial intermediary. **3** an organizer of entertainments for the public.
19C. French, from *entreprendre* to undertake. Cp. IMPRESARIO.

entresol (ā´trəsol) *n.* a low storey between two higher ones, usu. between the first and the ground floor, a mezzanine.
18C. French, from Spanish *entresuelo*, from *entre* between + *suelo* storey.

envoi (en´voi), **envoy** *n.* a postscript to a collection of poems, or a concluding stanza to a poem.
14–15C. Old French, from *envoyer* to send, from phr. *en voie* on the way.

épatant (āpatā´) *a.* shocking, daring.
early 20C. French, pres.p. of *épater* to astonish, from *é-* out + *patte* paw, leg.
● The French verb had the original sense of depriving of a leg and so flattening. Cp. English 'knocked flat'.

épater les bourgeois (āpatā lā buə´zhwah), **épater le bourgeois** (lə) *v.phr.* to shock the narrow-minded.
early 20C. French, lit. to astonish the bourgeois. See ÉPATANT, BOURGEOIS.
● The formula *Il faut épater les bourgeois* is attributed to the French poet Charles Baudelaire (1821–67).

epaulette (ep´əlet), (*N Am.*) **epaulet** *n.* **1** an ornamental badge worn on the shoulder in military, naval and certain civil full dress uniforms. **2** (*pl., fig.*) the rank of officer.
18C. French *épaulette*, dim. of *épaule* shoulder, from Latin *spatula* shoulder blade.

épée (ep´ā) *n.* **1** a duelling sword. **2** a fencing foil.
19C. French sword, from Old French *espee*, from Latin *spatha* long sword, from Greek *spathē* broad blade.

epergne (ipœn´) *n.* an ornamental stand, usu. branched, for the centre of a table etc.
18C. ? French *épargne* a saving, economy, from Germanic source of English *spare*.

ephebe (ifēb´, ef´ēb) *n.* in ancient Greece, a freeborn youth between the ages of 18 and 20, qualified for citizenship.
19C. Latin *ephebus*, from Greek *ephēbos*, from *epi* upon + *hēbē* early manhood.

ephod (ef´od, ē´-) *n.* **1** an emblematic short coat covering the shoulders and breast of the Jewish High Priest. **2** a similar but less splendid garment worn by the ordinary priests.
14–15C. Hebrew *'ēp̄ōḏ*.

ephor (ef´aw) *n.* (*pl.* **ephors, ephori** (-ərī)) any one of the five magistrates chosen at Sparta and invested with the highest power, controlling even the kings.
16C. Latin *ephorus*, or from Greek *ephoros* overseer, from *epi* upon + base of *horan* to see.

epi (ā´pē) *n.* (*pl.* **epis**) **1** a tuft of hair, esp. on a horse's forehead. **2** a cowlick.
19C. French *épi* tuft, spike.

epicedium (episē´diəm) *n.* (*pl.* **epicediums, epicedia** (-iə)) **1** a dirge. **2** a funeral ode.
16C. Latin, from Greek *epikēdeion*, neut. (used as n.) of *epikēdeios* funerary, from *epi* upon + *kēdos* care, grief.

epigone (ep´igōn) *n.* (*pl.* **epigones, epigoni** (ipig´ənī)) a person belonging to a later and less noteworthy generation.
18C. French *épigones* (pl.), from Latin *epigoni*, from Greek *epigonoi*, pl. of *epigonos* offspring, from *epi* upon + *-gonos*, from *gignesthai* to be born.

epithalamium (epithəlā´miəm) *n.* (*pl.* **epithalamiums, epithalamia** (-miə)) a song or poem celebrating a marriage.
16C. Greek *epithalamion*, neut. (used as n.) of *epithalamios* nuptial, from *epi* upon + *thalamos* bridal chamber.

epitome (ipit´əmi, ep-) *n.* **1** a brief summary of a book, document etc. **2** a perfect example, a person or thing that embodies the characteristics of a group, class etc. **3** (*fig.*) a representation in miniature of something else.
16C. Latin, from Greek *epitomē*, from *epitemnein* to cut into, to cut short, from *epi* upon + *temnein* to cut.

e pluribus unum (ā pluəribəs oo´nəm) *n.* one out of many (the motto of the USA).
18C. Latin one out of many, from *e*, form of *ex* out of + abl. pl. of *plus, pluris* more (see PLUS) + neut. sing. of *unus* one.
● The phrase was adapted from *e pluribus unum* in Virgil's *Minor Poems* and was adopted on June 20, 1782 for the motto on the face of the Great Seal of the United States.

epode (ep´ōd) *n.* **1** (in Greek lyric poetry) the part after the strophe and antistrophe. **2** lyric poetry in which a shorter line follows a longer one.
17C. French *épode* or Latin *epodos*, from Greek *epōidos*, from *epi* upon + *ōidē* ode.

epopee (ep´əpē), **epopoeia** (-pē´ə) *n.* **1** an epic or heroic poem. **2** epic poetry, the series of events forming the material for an epic.
17C. French *épopée*, from Greek *epopoiia*, from EPOS + *poiein* to make.

epos (ep´os) *n.* (*pl.* **eposes**) **1** an epopee. **2** unwritten narrative poetry embodying heroic traditions.
19C. Greek word, song, from *ep-*, stem of *eipein* to say.

eppur si muove (epuə sē mwō´vā) *int.* and yet it does move, the supposed words of Galileo used in reaffirmation of his belief in the Copernican theory of planetary motion.
early 20C. Italian.
• The words refer to the earth, which in the Copernican system was held to move around the sun, rather than vice versa. Galileo was forced by the Inquisition to recant this belief in 1633 after the theory was outlawed on the grounds that it conflicted with Catholic doctrine, which maintained that the earth was central to the universe and stationary. Galileo's statement is generally thought to be apocryphal.

épris (āprē´), (*fem.*) **éprise** (-prēz´) *a.* taken (with), enamoured (of).
18C. French, p.p. of (*s'*)*éprendre* to become attached, from *é-* out + *prendre* to take, from Latin *prehendere* to seize.

epsilon (ep´silon) *n.* the fifth letter of the Greek alphabet (E, ε).
18C. Greek *e psilon*, lit. bare e, i.e. short e.

épuisé (āpwē´zā) *a.* exhausted, worn out.
18C. French, p.p. of *épuiser* to exhaust, from *é-* out + *puits* well.
• The word is not recorded in English use in the 19C, but reappeared in the 20C.

epyllion (ipil´iən) *n.* (*pl.* **epyllia** (-iə)) a poem like an epic but shorter.
19C. Greek *epullion*, dim. of EPOS.

equilibrium (ēkwilib´riəm, ek-) *n.* (*pl.* **equilibriums, equilibria** (-riə))
1 a state of equal balance, equipoise.
2 equality of weight or force. **3** mental or emotional balance or stability. **4** due proportion between parts. **5** (*Physics*) a state of rest or balance due to the action of forces which counteract each other.
17C. Latin *aequilibrium*, from *aequus* level + *libra* balance.

équipe (ākēp´) *n.* (esp. in motor racing) a team.
mid-20C. French group, team, prob. ult. from Old Norse *skip* ship.

equivoque (ek´wivōk, ēk´-), **equivoke** *n.* **1** an ambiguous term or phrase, an equivocation. **2** a pun or other play upon words.
14–15C. Old French *équivoque* or Late Latin *aequivocus*, from *aequivocare*, from *aequus* equal + *vocare* to call.

Erdgeist (eəd´gīst) *n.* the Earth Spirit, the active spiritual force of the world.
early 20C. German, from *Erd* earth + *Geist* spirit, ghost.
• The *Erdgeist* is invoked by Faust in Part I of Goethe's *Faust* (1808).

erg (œg) *n.* (*pl.* **ergs, areg** (ah´reg)) an area of shifting sand dunes, esp. in the Sahara.
19C. French, from Arabic *'irḳ, 'erg*.

ergo (œ´gō) *adv.* (*formal*) **1** therefore. **2** consequently.
14–15C. Latin therefore.

erotica (irot´ikə) *n.pl.* erotic art or literature.
19C. Latin, from Greek *erōtika*, neut pl. of *erōtikos*, from *erōs, erōtos* sexual love, the source of English *erotic*.

erratum (irah´təm, er-) *n.* (*pl.* **errata** (-tə)) **1** an error or mistake in printing or writing. **2** (*pl.*) a list of corrections appended to a book.
16C. Latin error, neut. p.p. (used as n.) of *errare* to err.

ersatz (œ´zats, eə´-) *a.* **1** imitation. **2** artificial. ~*n.* a substitute (in a pejorative sense).
19C. German compensation, replacement.

escadrille (eskədril´) n. **1** a French squadron of aircraft. **2** a flotilla.
early 20C. French flotilla (alt. influ. by French *escadre* squadron), from Spanish *escuadrilla*, dim. of *escuadra* squadron, squad.

escalade (eskəlād´) n. an attack on a fortified place in which ladders are used to mount the ramparts etc. ~v.t. to storm by means of ladders.
16C. French, from Spanish *escalada*, from Medieval Latin *scalare*, from Latin *scalae* staircase, ladder.

escalope (es´kəlop, iskal´əp) n. a thin boneless slice of meat, esp. veal or pork.
19C. French, from Old French shell.
● The cut is so named from the shell-shaped pan in which it is cooked.

escamotage (escam´ətahzh) n. juggling, manipulation.
early 20C. French, from *escamoter* to make something disappear, prob. ult. from Latin *squama* scale.

escargot (iskah´gō) n. an edible snail.
19C. French, from Old French *escargol*, from Provençal *escaragol*.

escritoire (eskritwah´) n. a writing desk with drawers etc. for papers and stationery, a bureau.
16C. Old French study, writing box (Modern French *écritoire* writing desk), from Medieval Latin *scriptorium* writing room.

escroc (eskrok´) n. a swindler.
early 20C. French, from Italian *scrocco*, rel. to English *crook*.

escudo (eskū´dō) n. (pl. **escudos**) **1** the standard unit of currency in Portugal. **2** a coin representing an escudo.
19C. Spanish and Portuguese, from Latin *scutum* shield. Cp. ÉCU, SCUDO.

esker (es´kə), **eskar** n. (Geol.) a bank or long mound of glacial drift such as are found abundantly in Irish river valleys.
19C. Irish *eiscir*.

espada (espah´də) n. a matador.
19C. Spanish, lit. sword, from Latin *spatha*, rel. to English *spade*.

espadrille (espədril´, es´-) n. a rope-soled shoe with a cloth upper.
19C. French, from Provençal *espardilhos*, from *espart* ESPARTO.

espagnolette (ispanyəlet´) n. a bolt used for fastening a French window, one turn of the knob securing the sash both at top and bottom.
19C. French, dim. of *espagnol* Spanish.
● The bolt is so named as it is of Spanish origin.

espalier (ispal´iə) n. **1** a lattice-work on which shrubs or fruit trees are trained flat against a wall. **2** a tree so trained. ~v.t. to train (a tree or shrub) in this way.
17C. French, from Italian *spalliera*, from *spalla* shoulder, from Late Latin *spatula* shoulder blade.

esparto (ispah´tō) n. (pl. **espartos**) a kind of coarse grass or rush, *Stipa tenacissima,* growing in the sandy regions of N Africa and Spain, used largely for making paper, mats etc.
19C. Spanish, from Latin *spartum*, from Greek *sparton* rope.

espiègle (espiegl´, espieg´lə) a. roguish, frolicsome.
19C. French *Ulespiegle*, from Dutch *Uilenspiegel*, from *uil* owl + *spiegel* mirror, from Latin *speculum*.
● The reference is to Till *Eulenspiegel*, a German peasant of the 14C whose practical jokes were the subject of a 16C collection of satirical tales. His name was translated as English *Owlglass* to mean jester.

esplanade (esplənād´, -nahd´) *n.* **1** a level space, esp. a level walk or drive by the seaside etc. **2** a clear space between the citadel and the houses of a fortified town.
16C. French, from Italian *spianata*, from fem. of Latin *explanatus*, p.p. of *explanare* to flatten, to level.

espressivo (espresē´vō) *a.* (*Mus.*) with expression.
19C. Italian, from Latin *expressus*. See ESPRESSO.

espresso (ispres´ō), **expresso** (iks-) *n.* (*pl.* **espressos, expressos**) **1** very strong black coffee made by a machine which uses steam pressure. **2** a coffee-making machine using steam pressure for high extraction. **3** an espresso bar.
mid-20C. Italian (*caffè*) *espresso*, from *espresso* pressed out, from Latin *expressus*, p.p. of *exprimere* to squeeze out, to express.

esprit (isprē´, es-) *n.* **1** wit. **2** sprightliness.
16C. French, from Latin *spiritus* spirit.

esprit de corps (isprē´, es- də kaw´) *n.* the spirit of comradeship, loyalty and devotion to the body or association to which one belongs.
18C. French, lit. spirit of (the) body.

esprit de l'escalier (isprē´, es- də leskal´yā) *n.* **1** the thinking of an apt or witty answer after the moment for it has passed. **2** such an answer.
early 20C. French, lit. wit of the staircase.
● The phrase was coined by the French philosopher and writer Denis Diderot in his treatise on acting *Le Paradoxe sur le comédien* (*c.*1773).

esquisse (eskwēs´) *n.* (*pl.* **esquisses** (-kēs´)) a rough or preliminary sketch.
18C. French, from Italian *schizzo*, the source of English *sketch*.

estaminet (estam´inā) *n.* a small café in which wine etc. is sold.
19C. French, from Walloon *staminé* byre, from *stamo* pole to which a cow is tethered in a stall, ? from German *Stamm* stem, trunk.

estancia (istan´siə, -thiə) *n.* **1** in Spanish America, a cattle-farm, ranch or country estate. **2** the residence on this.
17C. Spanish station, from Medieval Latin *stantia*, from Latin *stans, stantis*, pres.p. of *stare* to stand.

estrade (istrahd´) *n.* a slightly raised platform, a dais.
17C. French, from Spanish *estrado*, from Latin STRATUM.

ETA (et´ə) *n.* a Basque separatist terrorist organization.
mid-20C. Abbr. of Basque *Euzkadi ta Azkatasuna* Basque Homeland and Liberty.

eta (ē´tə, ā´-) *n.* the seventh letter of the Greek alphabet (H, η).
14–15C. Greek *ēta*.

étagère (ātazheə´) *n.* a stand with open shelves for ornaments etc.
19C. French, from *étage* shelf, stage.

et al. (et al´) *abbr.* and others.
Abbr. of **Latin** *et alii* and others, from *et* and + masc. pl. of *alius* other.
● The *al.* could also represent fem. *aliae* or neut. *alia*. The abbreviation is typically found in bibliographies, e.g. 'William A. Craigie *et al.*'.

etalon (et´əlon) *n.* (*Physics*) a device which measures wavelengths by means of reflections from silvered glass or quartz plates.
early 20C. French *étalon* standard of measurement.

etcetera (itset´ərə, et-), **et cetera** *adv.* and the rest, and so on.

12–14C. Latin *et cetera* and the rest, from *et* and + *cetera*, neut. pl. of *ceterus* remaining over.

eth (edh), **edh** *n.* a letter (Đ, ð) used in Icelandic and in Old English to represent the speech sound th.
19C. Icelandic, prob. representing the sound of the letter.

ethos (ē´thos) *n.* the characteristic spirit, character, disposition or genius of a people, community, institution, system etc.
19C. Greek *ēthos* nature, disposition.

etiquette (et´iket) *n.* **1** the conventional rules of behaviour in polite society. **2** the established rules of precedence and ceremonial in a court. **3** the codes of formal behaviour between members of a profession etc.
18C. French *étiquette* ticket.
• The word is said to have originated in the directions for behaviour on a soldier's billet (ticket) for lodgings.

étourderie (ātuədərē´) *n.* thoughtlessness, carelessness.
18C. French, from *étourdi*, p.p. of *étourdir* to stun, to make giddy, from Popular Latin *exturditus*, from *ex-* out + *turdus* thrush.
• The allusion is to the giddy behaviour of a thrush after gorging on berries. The French say *soûl comme une grive* drunk as a thrush.

étrier (ā´triā) *n.* a small rope ladder used in mountaineering.
mid-20C. French stirrup.

et seq., et seqq. (et sek´) *abbr.* and the following (passage(s), page(s) etc.).
12–14C. Abbr. of **Latin** *et sequens* and the following, from *et* and + pres.p. of *sequi* to follow, or of *et sequentes* (m. and fem. pl. of *sequens*), *et sequentia* (neut. pl. of *sequens*) and the following things.

et tu Brute (et too broo´tā) *int.* an expression of reproach following a betrayal of trust.
16C. Latin and you, Brutus.
• The words are from a line spoken by Caesar in Shakespeare's *Julius Caesar* (III,i) (1599) immediately upon being stabbed, when he realises that his supposed friend Brutus is among the conspirators. In modern facetious usage the name Brutus is often exchanged for another.

étude (ātüd´, -tūd´) *n.* (*Mus.*) a short composition written mainly to test or develop a player's technical skill.
19C. French study.

etui (ātwē´, et-) *n.* a small case for pins, needles etc.
17C. French *étui*, from Old French *estui* prison, from *estuier* to shut up, to keep.

euchre (ū´kə) *n.* an orig. American card game for several persons, usu. four, with a pack from which the cards from the twos to the nines have been excluded. ~*v.t.* **1** to beat by taking three of the five tricks at euchre. **2** (*Austral., coll.*) to beat thoroughly, to ruin. **3** to outwit.
19C. German dial. *Juckerspiel*.

euphoria (ūfaw´riə) *n.* a feeling of well-being, supreme content, esp. exaggerated or baseless.
17C. Modern Latin, from Greek, from *euphoros* borne well, healthy, from *eu* well + *pherein* to bear.

eureka (ūrē´kə) *int.* used to express exultation over a discovery. ~*n.* **1** an exclamation of 'eureka'. **2** a discovery, an invention.
17C. Greek *heurēka* I have found (it), 1st pers. sing. perf. of *heuriskein* to find.
• The word represents an exclamation supposedly uttered by Archimedes when he hit on a method of establishing the purity of gold.

événement (āven´mã) n. (pl.
événements (-mã)) politically
motivated civil disorder.
mid-20C. French event, happening.
• The word's use in English sprang
from the French strikes and student
riots of 1968, described by the French
media as *les événements*.

evzone (ev´zōn) n. a member of an elite
Greek infantry regiment.
19C. Modern Greek *euzōnas*, from
Greek *euzōnos* dressed for exercise,
from *eu* well + *zōnē* girdle.

Ewigkeit (ā´vigkīt) n. eternity, infinity.
19C. German.
• The word is chiefly used in 'into the
Ewigkeit' meaning into thin air.

Ewig-Weibliche, das (das
āvigvīb´likh·ə) n. the eternal feminine,
the supposed unchanging power of
woman to inspire and spiritualize.
early 20C. German, from *ewig* eternal +
weiblich feminine, womanly.
• The phrase comes from the
conclusion of Part II of Goethe's *Faust*
(1832): *Das Ewig-Weibliche zieht uns
hinan* 'the eternal feminine draws us
on'.

ex (eks) prep. 1 from, out of, sold from.
2 without.
19C. Latin out of.

ex animo (eks an´imō) adv. heartily,
sincerely.
17C. Latin from the soul, from *ex* from
+ abl. of *animus* soul.

ex ante (eks an´ti) a. based on the
prediction of results.
mid-20C. Modern Latin, from *ex* out of
+ ANTE.

exarch (ek´sahk) n. 1 in the Greek
Church, a grade in the ecclesiastical
hierarchy instituted by Constantine the
Great, formerly equivalent to patriarch
or metropolitan, later a bishop in charge
of a province, and also a legate of a
patriarch. 2 a governor of a province
under the Byzantine Empire.
16C. Ecclesiastical Latin *exarchus*, from
Greek leader, chief, from *ex* out of +
arkhos chief.

ex cathedra (eks kəthē´drə) a.
authoritative, to be obeyed. ~adv.
authoritatively.
17C. Latin from the (teacher's) chair,
from *ex* out of + abl. sing. of
CATHEDRA.

excelsior (eksel´siaw, ik-) int. used to
express an intention of climbing
higher.
18C. Latin, comp. of *excelsus*, from *ex*
out of + *celsus* lofty + comp. suf. -*ior*.

excursus (ikskœ´səs, ek-) n. (pl.
excursuses, excursus) 1 a dissertation
appended to a work, containing an
exposition of some point raised or
referred to in the text. 2 a digression
during a narrative.
19C. Latin excursion, from *excursus*,
p.p. of *excurrere* to run out.

exeat (ek´siat) n. 1 leave of absence, as
to a student at school or university.
2 permission granted by a bishop to a
priest to go out of his diocese.
18C. Latin let him go out, 3rd pers. sing.
pres. subj. of *exire* to go out. Cp. EXIT²,
EXEUNT.

exedra (ek´sidrə, -sē´-) n. (pl. **exedrae**
(-drē)) 1 the portico of the Grecian
palaestra in which discussions were
held. 2 a hall for conversation. 3 an
elevated seat, a bishop's throne, a porch,
a projecting chapel. 4 a recess.
18C. Latin, from Greek, from *ek* out of
+ *hedra* seat.

exegesis (eksijē´sis) *n.* (*pl.* **exegeses**
(-sēz)) exposition, interpretation, esp. of
the Scriptures.
17C. Greek *exēgēsis*, from *exēgeisthai*,
from *ek* out of + *hēgeisthai* to guide.

exemplum (igzem´pləm) *n.* (*pl.*
exempla (-plə)) **1** an example. **2** a short
story or anecdote which illustrates a
moral.
19C. Latin example.

exequatur (eksikwā´tə) *n.* **1** a written
recognition of a consul or commercial
agent, given by the government to
which he is accredited. **2** official
authority or permission to execute
some act. **3** an authorization by a
sovereign or government for the exercise
of episcopal functions under papal
authority or the promulgation of a
papal bull.
17C. Latin let him perform, 3rd pers.
sing. pres. subj. of *exequi* to carry out, to
execute.

exergue (ek´sœg, -sœg´) *n.* **1** the small
space beneath the base line of a subject
engraved on a coin or medal. **2** the
name, date or inscription placed there.
17C. French, from Medieval Latin
exergum, from Greek *ek* out of + *ergon*
work.

exeunt (ek´siunt) *v.i.* they go off the
stage, they retire (stage direction).
15C. Latin they go out, 3rd pers. pl.
pres. ind. of *exire* to go out. Cp. EXIT².
• A variant form of stage direction
sometimes found is *exeunt omnes* they
all leave the stage.

ex gratia (eks grā´sha) *a., adv.* as an act
of favour, and with no acceptance of
liability.
18C. Latin from grace, from *ex* out of +
abl. sing. of *gratia* grace.

ex hypothesi (eks hīpoth´əsī) *adv.*
according to the hypothesis stated;
following the hypothesis.
17C. Modern Latin, from Latin *ex* out of
+ abl. of Late Latin HYPOTHESIS.

exigeant (egzēzhā´), (*fem.*) **exigeante**
(-ãt) *a.* exacting.
18C. French, pres.p. of *exiger*, from
Latin *exigere* to exact.

exit[1] (ek´sit, eg´zit) *n.* **1** a passage or door,
a way out. **2** a going out. **3** freedom to
go out. **4** a place where vehicles can
enter or leave a motorway, roundabout
etc. **5** the departure of an actor from the
stage. **6** departure, esp. from this life;
death, decease. ~*v.i.* **1** to depart, to leave
a place. **2** (*formal*) to die. **3** (in bridge,
whist etc.) to lose the lead deliberately.
4 (*Comput.*) to leave a subroutine, a
program etc. ~*v.t.* (*NAm.*) to leave.
16C. Latin *exitus*, p.p. of *exire*. See
EXIT².

exit[2] (ek´sit) *v.i.* (as a stage direction) goes
off the stage.
16C. Latin he goes out, 3rd pers. sing.
pres. ind. of *exire* to go out, from *ex-* out
+ *ire* to go. Cp. EXEAT.

ex-lib. (eks lib) *abbr.* ex-libris.
early 20C. Abbr. of **Latin** EX-LIBRIS.

ex-libris (ekslib´ris) *n.* (*pl.* **ex-libris**) a
bookplate, a label bearing an owner's
name, crest, device etc.
19C. Latin out of the books, from *ex* out
of + abl. pl. of *liber, libri* book.

ex nihilo (eks nī´hilō) *adv.* out of
nothing.
16C. Latin, from *ex* out of + abl. of *nihil*
nothing.

Exocet® (ek´səset) *n.* **1** a French-built
surface-skimming missile that can
be launched from surface or air.
2 (**exocet**) an exceptionally effective
weapon.

late 20C. **French** flying fish, from Latin *exocetus*, from Greek *exōkoitos* sleeping out, fish that comes out (onto the beach), from *exō* out of + *koitos* bed.

exodus (eks´ədəs) *n.* **1** a departure, esp. of a large group of people. **2** (**Exodus**) the departure of the Israelites from Egypt under Moses. **3** (**Exodus**) the second book of the Old Testament, narrating this event.
pre-1200. **Ecclesiastical Latin**, from Greek *exodos*, from *ek* out of + *hodos* way.
● Senses 1 and 2 arose in the 17C.

ex off. (eks of) *abbr.* ex officio.
19C. Abbr. of **Latin** EX OFFICIO.

ex officio (eks əfish´iō) *adv.* by virtue of one's office. ~*a.* official.
16C. **Latin** out of duty, from *ex* out of + abl. sing. of *officium* duty, office.

Exon (ek´son) *a.* of Exeter. ~*n.* Exeter (the official signature of the Bishop of Exeter).
18C. Abbr. of **Modern Latin** *Exoniensis*, from *Exonia* Exeter.

exordium (igzaw´diəm) *n.* (*pl.* **exordiums, exordia** (-diə)) the beginning of anything, esp. the introductory part of a literary work or discourse.
16C. **Latin**, from *exordiri* to begin, from *ex* out of + *ordiri* to begin.

ex parte (eks pah´tā, -ti) *adv.* (*Law*) **1** proceeding from one side only. **2** in the interests of one side.
17C. **Latin** from the side, from *ex* out of + abl. sing. of *pars, partis* side.

explication de texte (eksplikasyŏ də tekst´) *n.* (*pl.* **explications de texte** (-yŏ), **explications de textes** (tekst´)) a detailed textual examination of a literary work.

mid-20C. **French** explication of (the) text.

explicit (iksplis´it, ek-) *n.* (*Hist.*) a word formerly written at the end of manuscript books, and equivalent to 'finis', 'the end'.
12–14C. **Late Latin**, either *explicit* here ends, or abbr. of *explicitus est liber* the book is unrolled, respectively 3rd pers. sing. pres. indic. and p.p. of *explicare* to unfold.

exposé (ikspō´zā, ek-) *n.* **1** a formal declaration or recital of facts. **2** a disclosure, an exposure (of damning or sensational information).
19C. **French**, p.p. of *exposer* to set out, to display, to expose.

ex post (eks pōst´) *a.* based on actual results.
mid-20C. **Modern Latin**, from Latin *ex* out of + *post* after.

ex post facto (eks pōst fak´tō) *a., adv.* having retrospective force.
17C. Misdivision of **Latin** *ex postfacto* in the light of subsequent events, from *ex* out of + abl. of *postfactum* that which is done subsequently, from *post* after + FACTUM.

ex silentio (eks silen´shiō) *a., adv.* based on a lack of contrary evidence.
early 20C. **Latin** from silence, from *ex* out of + abl. of *silentium* silence.

extempore (ikstem´pəri, ek-) *adv.* without premeditation or preparation. ~*a.* unstudied, delivered without preparation.
16C. **Latin** *ex tempore* on the spur of the moment, from *ex* out of + abl. sing. of *tempus, temporis* time.

extrados (ikstrā´dos) *n.* (*pl.* **extrados** (-dōz), **extradoses**) (*Archit.*) the

exterior curve of an arch, esp. measured on the top of the voussoirs.
18C. French, from Latin *extra* outside + French *dos* back.

extra muros (ekstrǝ mūǝ´rōs) *adv.* concerned with the external policies or affairs of an institution etc.
early 20C. Latin, lit. outside the walls (of a city). Cp. INTRA MUROS.

exuviae (igzū´viē, eg-) *n.pl.* (*also constr. as sing.*) **1** the cast or shed skin, shells, teeth etc. of animals. **2** fossil remains of animals in a fragmentary state. **3** things cast off or relinquished.
17C. Latin clothing stripped off, skins of animals, from *exuere* to divest oneself of.

ex-voto (eksvō´tō) *adv.* in pursuance of a vow. ~*n.* (*pl.* **ex-votos**) anything offered to a divinity in gratitude for an exemplary favour.
18C. Latin *ex voto* from a vow, from *ex* out of + abl. sing. of *votum* vow.

F

fabliau (fab´liō) *n.* (*pl.* **fabliaux** (-ōz)) a metrical tale, dealing usually with ordinary life, composed by the trouvères in the 12th and 13th cents., and intended for recitation.
19C. French, from Old French (Picard) *fabliaux*, pl. of *fablel*, dim. of *fable* fable.

façade (fəsahd´), **facade** *n.* **1** the front of a building. **2** an outward appearance, esp. one put on for show or to deceive.
17C. French, from Old French *face* face, based on Italian *facciata*.

facetiae (fəsē´shiē) *n.pl.* **1** humorous or witty sayings. **2** curious, comic, or esp. indecent books.
16C. Latin, pl. of *facetia* jest, from *facetus* graceful, witty.

facies (fā´shiēz) *n.* (*pl.* **facies**) **1** the general aspect of an assembly of organisms characteristic of a particular locality. **2** (*Geol.*) the characteristics of a rock or a geological formation.
17C. Latin shape, appearance.

facile princeps (fasili prin´seps) *a.* easily first. ~*n.* an acknowledged leader or obvious winner in a contest.
19C. Latin easily first.

façon de parler (fas´ō də pah´lā) *n.* manner of speaking; phrase, phrasing.
19C. French way of speaking, from *façon* manner + *de* of + *parler* to speak.

facsimile (faksim´ili) *n.* **1** an exact copy of printing, a picture etc. **2** the transmission by electronic scanning and reproduction of written or pictorial material. ~*v.t.* (*pres.p.* **facsimileing**, *past, p.p.* **facsimiled**) to make a facsimile of.
16C. Modern Latin, from Latin *fac*, imper. of *facere* to do, to make + *simile*, neut. of *similis* similar.
● Sense 2 is usually abbreviated *fax* although some users of the system prefer the full form.

facta non verba (faktə non vœ´bə) *int.* deeds, not words, what one does is more important than what one says.
19C. Latin deeds not words.
● The moralizing tag is found as the motto of various families, educational establishments, etc.

factotum (faktō´təm) *n.* (*pl.* **factotums**) **1** a person employed to do all sorts of work, a handyman. **2** a servant who manages all their employer's concerns.
16C. Medieval Latin, from Latin *fac*, imper. of *facere* to do, to make + *totum* the whole. Cp. FAINÉANT.

factum (fak´təm) *n.* (*pl.* **factums**, **facta** (-tə)) **1** a thing done; an act or deed. **2** (*Law*) a deed, a sealed instrument. **3** a report of facts or points in a controversy.
18C. Latin, neut. p.p. (used as n.) of *facere* to do.

fade (fahd) *a.* insipid, colourless.
early 20C. French, from Popular Latin
fastidus, prob. blending Latin *fatuus*
insipid and *sapidus* sapid, the source of
English *fade*.

fado (fah´dō) *n.* (*pl.* **fados**) a type of esp.
melancholy Portuguese folk song.
early 20C. Portuguese, lit. fate.

faeces (fē´sēz), (*esp. N Am.*) **feces** *n.pl.*
excrement from the bowels.
14–15C. Latin, pl. of *faex* dregs.

faenza (fīent´sə) *n.* a type of glazed
pottery.
19C. Italian *Faenza*, a city in N Italy.
Cp. FAIENCE.
● The pottery was made in Faenza in
the 15C and 16C.

fagotto (fəgot´ō) *n.* (*pl.* **fagotti** (-ē)) a
bassoon.
19C. Italian bassoon, rel. to English
faggot.

faience (fayās´) *n.* **1** tin-glazed
earthenware of a particular kind.
2 glazed blocks of terracotta used as
facings.
17C. French *faïence*, from *Faïence*
Faenza, city in N Italy, where it was
originally made. Cp. FAENZA.

fainéant (fā´niənt, -ā) *a.* do-nothing; idle,
sluggish. *~n.* a do-nothing, an idler.
17C. French, from *fait*, 3rd pers. sing. of
faire to do + *néant* nothing. Cp.
FACTOTUM.
● In French history the *Rois fainéants*
('Do-nothing kings') were those of the
Merovingian dynasty from Theoderic
(Thierry) III (reigned 673–690) on, who
left government to their court advisers.

faire bonne mine (feə bon mēn´)
v.phr. to put a good face on it, to give
a favourable reception to something.
19C. French, lit. to make a good
expression.

fait accompli (fāt əkom´pli, fet) *n.* (*pl.*
faits accomplis (fāt əkom´pli, fet)) an
accomplished fact.
19C. French accomplished fact, from *fait*
fact + *accompli*, p.p. of *accomplir* to
accomplish.

faites vos jeux (fet vō zhœ´) *int.* place
your stakes! (in roulette, the words
spoken by the croupier to indicate that
play is about to begin).
early 20C. French, lit. make your bets.
Cp. RIEN NE VA PLUS.

fajita (fəhē´tə) *n.* a kind of tortilla
wrapped around meat, chillies, onions
etc.
late 20C. Mexican Spanish, lit. little
strip, little belt.

fakir (fā´kiə, fəkiə´) *n.* **1** a Muslim
religious mendicant. **2** a Hindu
mendicant, ascetic or wonder-worker.
3 a very holy man.
17C. Arabic *faḳīr* poor (man).

Falange (fəlanj´) *n.* the Fascist movement
in Spain, founded in 1933.
mid-20C. Spanish phalanx.

Falasha (fəlah´shə) *n.* (*pl.* **Falasha,
Falashas**) a member of an Ethiopian
people who practise a form of Judaism.
18C. Amharic exile, immigrant.

falbala (fal´bələ) *n.* **1** a trimming, a
flounce. **2** a furbelow.
18C. French, of unknown orig.
● According to some sources, the word
is from Provençal *farbello*, related to
Italian *faldella* carded cotton (for
linings).

falsetto (fawlset´ō) *n.* (*pl.* **falsettos**)
1 a pitch or range of (usu. the male)
voice higher than the natural register.
2 a singer using this range. *~a.* **1** of,
relating to or produced by such a voice.
2 artificial, affected.
18C. Italian, dim. of *falso* false.

fama clamosa (fahmə klamō´zə) *n.*
1 a rumour or scandal. **2** (*Sc.*) a rumour
ascribing immoral conduct to a minister
of the church.
19C. Latin, lit. noisy rumour.

famille (famē´, famēy´) *n.* a Chinese
enamelled porcelain.
19C. French family.

famulus (fam´ūləs) *n.* (*pl.* **famuli** (-lī))
an assistant or servant of a magician
or scholar.
19C. Latin servant.

fandango (fandang´gō) *n.* (*pl.*
fandangoes, fandangos) **1** a lively
Spanish dance in triple time, for two
people who beat time with castanets.
2 the musical accompaniment of such a
dance.
18C. Spanish, of unknown orig. ? From
African.

fanfaronade (fanfərənād´, -nahd´) *n.*
1 arrogant boasting, swaggering or
blustering. **2** a fanfare. ~*v.i.* to make a
flourish or noisy display.
17C. French *fanfaronnade*, from
fanfaron, from *fanfare* fanfare.

fan-tan (fan´tan) *n.* **1** a Chinese
gambling game involving guessing a
number of objects. **2** a card game in
which the cards are played in a
sequence.
19C. Chinese *fān tān*, from *fān* kind +
tān to spread out, to take a share.
● The name alludes to the payment of
stakes so many times the original
number of objects.

fantasia (fantā´ziə, -təzē´ə) *n.* a musical
or other composition that is not
governed by traditional fixed form; a
composition based on several popular
tunes.
18C. Italian fantasy.

farandole (farəndōl´) *n.* **1** a lively
Provençal dance. **2** a piece of music for
this dance.
19C. French, from Provençal *farandoulo*.

farceur (fahsœ´) *n.* **1** a joker, a jester, a
wag. **2** a performer in or writer of farces.
17C. French, from obs. *farcer* to act
farces.

faro (feə´rō) *n.* a game of cards in which
players bet against the dealer.
18C. French PHARAOH, ? as one of the
names of the king of hearts.

farouche (fəroosh´) *a.* **1** unsociable, shy,
sullen. **2** wild, untamed.
18C. French, alt. of Old French *faroche*,
from Medieval Latin *forasticus*, from
Latin *foras* out of doors.
● The original sense was sense 2.

farrago (fərah´gō) *n.* (*pl.* **farragos**,
(*N Am.*) **farragoes**) a confused mixture,
a medley.
17C. Latin mixed fodder for cattle, from
far spelt, corn.

farruca (fəroo´kə) *n.* a type of flamenco
dance.
early 20C. Spanish, fem. of *farruco*,
from *Farruco*, pet form of male
forename *Francisco* Francis.
● *Farruco* is a nickname for someone
from Galicia or Asturias, where the
dance originated.

fartlek (faht´lek) *n.* a method of athletic
training, mixing fast and slow running.
mid-20C. Swedish, from *fart* speed + *lek*
play.

fasces (fas´ēz) *n.pl.* **1** the ancient insignia
of the Roman lictors, consisting of a
bundle of elm or birch rods, in the
middle of which was an axe. **2** in
Fascist Italy, an emblem of authority.
16C. Latin, pl. of *fascis* bundle.

fascia (fā´shə, fash´iə) n. (pl. **fasciae**
(-shiē), **fascias**) 1 (Archit.) †a flat
surface in an entablature or elsewhere.
2 a band, stripe belt, sash, fillet.
3 (Anat.) a thin, tendon-like sheath
surrounding the muscles and binding
them in their places. 4 facia.
16C. Latin band, fillet, casing of a door.
Rel. to FASCES.

fata Morgana (fah´tə mawgah´nə) n.
1 a mirage observed from the harbour
of Messina and adjacent places, and
supposed by Sicilians to be the work of
the fairy Morgana. 2 a mirage; a figment
of the imagination.
19C. Italian fairy Morgan (Morgan le
Fay), sister of King Arthur.
• The legend of King Arthur was
brought to Sicily by Norman settlers
when they conquered the island in
the 11C.

Fatiha (fah´tiə, fat´-), **Fatihah** n. the
short first sura of the Koran, used by
Muslims as a prayer.
19C. Arabic al-Fātiḥa the opening
(sura), use as n. of fem. part. fātiḥa
opening, from fataḥa to open.

fatwa (fat´wah) n. a religious edict issued
by a Muslim leader.
17C. Arabic fatwā, from 'aftā to decide a
point of law. Cp. MUFTI.
• The term came into prominence in
the late 20C when Ayatollah Khomeini
of Iran issued a fatwa condemning the
Indian-born British writer Salman
Rushdie to death on account of his
novel The Satanic Verses (1988), which
many Muslims held to be blasphemous.

faubourg (fō´buəg) n. a suburb of a city
or town.
15C. French, from Old French fors borc
outside the town; from fors (Modern
French hors), from Latin foris outside,
+ borc (Modern French bourg), from

Late Latin burgus fortress, influ. by
French faux false.

fauna (faw´nə) n. (pl. **faunae** (-nē),
faunas) 1 the animals found in or
belonging to a certain region or time.
2 a treatise upon or list of these.
18C. Fauna, ancient Italian rural
goddess, sister of Faunus, ancient Italian
god identified with Greek god Pan.
• The name of the goddess was adopted
by Linnaeus for the title of his work
Fauna Suecica (1746), a companion
volume to his Flora Suecica ('Swedish
Flora') (1745). See FLORA.

faute de mieux (fōt də mjœ´) adv. for
lack of anything better.
18C. French (for) want of (anything)
better, from faute lack + de of + mieux
better, comp. of bien well.

fauteuil (fōtœy´) n. an easy, upholstered
armchair.
18C. French, from Old French
faudestuel, rel. to English faldstool a
type of folding chair or stool.

faux (fō) a. imitation, false.
late 20C. French false.

faux amis (fōz amē´) n.pl. two words in
different languages which appear
similar but have significantly different
meanings.
mid-20C. French, lit. false friends.
• The term was first used in Les Faux
Amis, ou les Trahisons du vocabulaire
anglais (1928), a collection of such pairs
of words by Maxime Kœssler and Jules
Derocquigny. Examples are French
actuel current and English actual,
French bribe fragment and English
bribe.

faux-naïf (fōnīēf´) a. self-consciously
artless. ~n. a person who pretends
naivety.
mid-20C. French, from FAUX + NAÏF.

faux pas (fō pah´) n. (pl. **faux pas** (pahz´)) **1** a blunder, a slip. **2** a social indiscretion.
17C. French false step, from FAUX + *pas* step.

favela (fav´elə) n. in Brazil, a shack or shanty town.
mid-20C. Portuguese.

fec. abbr. he/she made it.
Abbr. of **Latin** *fecit* he/she made (it).

fecula (fek´ūlə) n. (pl. **feculae** (-lē)) lees, sediment, from vegetable infusions, esp. starch.
17C. Latin *fecula* crust of wine, dim. of *faex* dregs, sediment. Cp. FAECES.

fedayee (fedah´yē) n. (pl. **fedayeen** (-yēn)) a member of an Arab commando group, esp. fighting against Israel.
19C. Arabic and Persian *fidā´ī* one who gives his life for another, from *fadā* to ransom.

féerie (feə´rē) n. a (theatrical) representation of fairyland, a landscape suggesting fairyland.
19C. French, from *fée* fairy.

felafel (felah´fəl), **falafel** n. a spicy ball or cake of mashed chickpeas or beans.
mid-20C. Arabic (coll. Egyptian) *falāfil*, pl. of Arabic *fulfil, filfil* pepper.

feldspar (feld´spah), **felspar** (fel´spah) n. (*Mineral.*) any of a group of silicates of aluminium combined with a mineral, e.g. potassium, sodium or calcium, that are the most important group of rock-forming minerals and the major constituent of igneous rocks.
18C. Alt. of **German** *Feldspath*, from *Feld* field + *Spath* spath, with substitution of synonymous English *spar*.
● The false association with German *Fels* rock gave the variant spelling *felspar*.

fellah (fel´ə) n. (pl. **fellahin** (-əhēn´)) an Egyptian agricultural labourer or peasant.
18C. Arabic *fallāḥ*, coll. pl. *fallāḥīn*, tiller of the soil, from *falaḥa* to split, to till the soil.

felo de se (fē´lō dā sā, fel´ō) n. (pl. **felones de se** (filō´nēz di sē), **felos de se** (fē´lōz, fel´ōz)) **1** a person who commits felony by suicide. **2** self-murder, suicide.
17C. Anglo-Latin felon of himself, from *felo* felon + *de* of + *se* himself.

felucca (felŭk´ə) n. a small vessel used in the Mediterranean, propelled by oars or lateen sails or both.
17C. Italian, prob. from obs. Spanish *faluca*, ? from Arabic word of unknown orig.

feme covert (fēm, fem kŭv´ət), **feme couvert** (fam koovea´) n. (*Law*) a married woman.
16C. Old French, lit. covered woman, i.e. a wife protected by her husband. Cp. FEME SOLE.

feme sole (fēm, fem sōl) n. (*Law*) **1** an unmarried woman, spinster or widow. **2** a married woman having rights of property or trade independent of her husband.
16C. Old French, lit. sole woman, i.e. one who is single or 'lone'.

femme (fem) n. (*sl.*) **1** a particularly feminine or effeminate person. **2** the less dominant or more feminine partner in a lesbian or male homosexual relationship.
mid-20C. French woman.

femme de chambre (fam də shābr´, shā´brə) n. (pl. **femmes de chambre** (fam)) **1** a chambermaid. **2** a lady's maid.
18C. French woman of the bedroom, from FEMME + *de* of + *chambre* chamber.

femme du monde (fam dü mōd, fem doo mond´) *n.* (*pl.* **femmes du monde** (fam, fem)) a sophisticated woman.
19C. French, lit. woman of the world.

femme fatale (fam fatahl´, fətahl´) *n.* (*pl.* **femmes fatales** (fam fatahl´, fətahl´)) a seductive woman, esp. one who lures men to their downfall.
early 20C. French fatal woman, from FEMME + fem. of *fatal* fatal.

fen (fŭn, fen) *n.* (*pl.* **fen**) a Chinese monetary unit worth one hundredth of a yuan; a coin of this value.
19C. Chinese *fēn* to divide, to distribute, fraction.

fenestella (fenistel´ə) *n.* (*Archit.*) a niche on the south side of the altar containing the piscina, and often the credence.
14–15C. Latin, dim. of *fenestra* window.

feng shui (feng shoo´i, fŭng, fung shwā´) *n.* in Chinese philosophy, a system of good and bad influences in the environment, used when deciding where to locate buildings, furniture etc.
18C. Chinese *fēng* wind + *shuǐ* water.

ferae naturae (fiə´rē nətū´rē, fer´ē) *a.* (of deer, hares, pheasants etc.) wild, as distinguished from domesticated.
17C. Latin of wild nature, from gen. sing. of *fera natura*, from fem. of *ferus* wild + *natura* nature.

fer de lance (feə də lās´) *n.* (*pl.* **fers de lance** (feə), **fer de lances** (lās´)) the yellow viper of Central and South America, *Bothrops atrox*.
19C. French iron (head) of lance, from *fer* iron + *de* of + *lance* lance.
● The name alludes to the shape of the snake's head.

fermata (fœmah´tə) *n.* (*pl.* **fermatas**) (*Mus.*) **1** a continuation of a note or rest beyond its usual length; pause. **2** a sign indicating this.
19C. Italian stop, pause, from *fermare* to stop.

fermeture (fœ´məchə) *n.* the mechanism for closing the breech of a gun or other firearm.
19C. French closure, from *fermer* to close, from Latin *firmare*, from *firmus* firm.

†ferrandine (fer´əndēn), **†farandine** (far´-) *n.* a mixed cloth of silk and other materials.
17C. French, from Italian *ferrandina*, from *ferro* iron.
● The name refers to the cloth's light grey colour.

festina lente (fes´tinə len´ti) *v.i.* (*imper.*) make haste slowly, do not be impetuous.
16C. Latin hasten slowly, from *festina*, imper. of *festinare* to hasten + *lente* slowly.
● The phrase was originally a Greek proverb, quoted by Suetonius in its Latin form as a favourite tag of Augustus Caesar.

Festschrift (fest´shrift), **festschrift** *n.* (*pl.* **Festschriften** (-tən), **Festschrifts**, **festschriften**, **festschrifts**) a collection of learned writings by various authors, published in honour of a scholar.
early 20C. German, lit. celebration writing, from *Fest* celebration + *Schrift* writing.

feta (fet´ə), **fetta** *n.* a firm white Greek cheese made from sheep's or goat's milk.
mid-20C. Modern Greek *pheta* slice (of cheese), from Italian *fetta*.

fête (fāt, fet), **fete** *n.* **1** an outdoor event with stalls and entertainments, usu. locally organized to raise money for charity. **2** a festival, an entertainment. **3** the festival of the saint after whom a person is named. ~*v.t.* to entertain, to honour lavishly.
14–15C. French, from Old French *feste* feast.

fettuccine (fetuchē´ni), **fettucini** *n.*
tagliatelle.
early 20C. Italian, pl. of *fettuccina*, dim.
of *fetta* slice. Cp. FETA.

feu de joie (fœ də zhwa´) *n.* (*pl.* **feux de
joie** (fœ də zhwa´)) the firing of guns in
token of public rejoicing.
17C. French fire of joy, from *feu* fire +
de of + *joie* joy.
● The original sense was bonfire. The
current sense arose in the 18C.

feu follet (fœ folā) *n.* (*pl.* **feux follets**
(fœ folā)) (*usu. fig.*) a will-o'-the-wisp.
19C. French, lit. frolicsome fire. Cp.
IGNIS FATUUS.

feuilleton (fœy´tō) *n.* **1** that part of a
newspaper which is devoted to light
literature, criticism or fiction. **2** an
article or a serial story in this part of
a newspaper.
19C. French, from *feuillet*, dim. of
feuille leaf.

feux d'artifice (fœ dahtifēs´) *n.pl.*
1 fireworks. **2** displays of wit.
19C. French, lit. fires of artifice.

fez (fez) *n.* (*pl.* **fezzes**) a flat-topped
conical usu. red cap without a brim,
fitting close to the head, with a tassel
of silk, wool etc., worn by men in the
Middle East.
19C. Turkish *fes*, from *Fez* (now Fès),
a town in Morocco, where it was
originally made.
● The fez was formerly the national
headgear of the Turks.

fiacre (fiah´krə) *n.* a small four-wheeled
horse-drawn carriage.
17C. French, from the Hôtel de St
Fiacre, rue St Antoine, Paris, where the
vehicles were first hired out.
● St Fiacre, d. *c.*670, was an Irish saint
who settled as a hermit near Meaux,
east of Paris.

fiançailles (fiãsī´) *n.pl.* a betrothal
ceremony, an engagement.
17C. French, from *fiancer* to promise in
marriage, to betroth. Cp. FIANCÉ.

fiancé (fiã´sā, -on´-), (*fem.*) **fiancée** *n.* the
person to whom one is engaged to be
married.
19C. French, from Old French *fiancer*
to betroth, from *fiance* promise,
engagement, from *fier* to trust.

fianchetto (fiənchet´ō, -ket´-) *n.* (*pl.*
fianchettoes) in chess, the
development of a bishop to a long
diagonal of the board. ~*v.t.* (*3rd pers.
sing. pres.* **fianchettoes**, *pres.p.*
fianchettoing, *past, p.p.* **fianchettoed**)
to develop (a bishop) in this way.
19C. Italian, dim. of *fianco* flank.

Fianna Fáil (fiana foil´) *n.* one of the
major political parties in the Republic of
Ireland.
early 20C. Irish, from *fianna*, pl. of *fian*
band of warriors + *Fáil*, gen. of *Fál*, an
ancient name of Ireland, lit. defensive
fortification, rel. to Latin VALLUM.
● The party name is conventionally
interpreted as Warriors of Destiny. *Fál*
itself is an ancient 'stone of destiny'
(Irish *lia fáil*) at Tara, Co. Meath.

fiasco (fias´kō) *n.* (*pl.* **fiascos**) a complete
and humiliating failure.
19C. Italian bottle, flask.
● The current sense derives from the
Italian phrase *far fiasco* literally to make
a bottle, with an unexplained allusion.

fiat (fī´ət, -at) *n.* **1** an order, command,
decree, esp. an arbitrary one. **2** (*Law*)
the order or warrant of a judge or other
constituted authority sanctioning or
allowing certain processes; an
authorization.
14–15C. Latin let it be done, 3rd pers.
sing. pres. subj. of *fieri* to be made, to
come about.

fiat justitia (fīat jŭstish´iə) *int.* let justice be done.
19C. Latin, from FIAT + *justitia* justice.
● The full phrase is *fiat justitia, ruat caelum* 'let justice be done, though the heavens fall', first cited in 1602 by the English conspirator William Watson (*c.*1559–1603).

fiat lux (fīat luks´) *int.* let there be light, a general command by which something comes into being.
16C. Latin, from FIAT + *lux* light.
● The phrase comes from the Latin version of Gen. i.3.

fiche (fēsh) *n.* (*pl.* **fiche, fiches**) a sheet of film bearing miniature photographs of documents etc.
mid-20C. French, abbr. of *microfiche*, from Greek *mikros* small + French *fiche* card, slip, alt. from Latin *figere* to fix.

fichu (fē´shoo) *n.* a light shawl or scarf worn by women over the neck and shoulders.
18C. Orig. unknown.
● According to some, the word is from the past participle of *ficher* to put (on in a hurry), from Latin *figere* to fix. Cp. English *throw* as a term for a shawl or stole.

†fico (fē´kō), **figo** (fē´gō) *n.* (*pl.* **ficoes, figoes**) **1** a fig; a worthless thing. **2** a gesture of contempt shown by putting the thumb between the second and third fingers.
16C. Italian, from Latin *ficus* fig.

fideicommissum (fidiīkəmis´əm) *n.* (*pl.* **fideicommissa**) **1** a testator's bequest to trustees. **2** a trust or trust estate.
18C. Latin *fidei-commissum*, neut. p.p. of *fidei-committere* to entrust something to a person's good faith, from *fidei*, dat. of *fides* faith + *committere* to entrust.

Fidei Defensor (fidiī difen´saw) *n.* Defender of the Faith.

16C. Latin Defender of the Faith, from *fidei*, gen. of *fides* faith + *defensor* defender, from *defendere* to defend.
● The title was first given to Henry VIII in 1521 by Pope Leo X for writing his *Assertio septem sacramentorum* (Declaration of the seven sacraments) against Luther. It was authorized as a royal title in 1544.

fidus Achates (fīdəs əkā´tēz) *n.* a trusty friend, a faithful companion.
17C. Latin faithful Achates, from *fidus* faithful + *Achates*, the name of the faithful friend of Aeneas in Virgil's *Aeneid* (1C BC).

fieri facias (fī´ərī fā´shias) *n.* (*Law*) a writ to a sheriff to order a levy on the goods and chattels of a defendant in order to pay a sum or debt.
14–15C. Latin cause (it) to be made, from *fieri* to come into being + 2nd pers. sing. pres. subj. of *facere* to make, to do.
● The phrase is often abbreviated as *fi. fa.*

fiesta (fies´tə) *n.* **1** a holiday or festivity. **2** (esp. in Spain and Latin America) a religious holiday or festival esp. on a saint's day.
19C. Spanish feast.

figura (figūə´rə) *n.* a person or thing that is representative or symbolic.
mid-20C. Latin shape, figure.

figurine (fig´ərēn, -ūə-) *n.* a statuette in clay or metal.
19C. French, from Italian *figurina*, dim. of *figura* figure.

filet (fil´ā, fil´it) *n.* **1** a kind of net or lace having a square mesh. **2** a fillet of meat.
19C. French, from dim. of Latin *filum* thread.

filet mignon (fē´lā mē´nyō) *n.* a small, very tender steak cut from the tail end of a fillet of beef.

early 20C. French small fillet. Cp.
MIGNON.

Filipino (filipē´nō) *n.* (*pl.* **Filipinos**) a
native or inhabitant of the Philippine
Islands. ~*a.* of or relating to the
Philippines or the Filipinos.
19C. Spanish, from (*las Islas*) *Filipinas*
(the) Philippine (Islands).

fille (fē) *n.* daughter, junior (used to
distinguish a daughter from a mother
with the same name).
19C. French. Cp. FILS², MÈRE.

fille de joie (fē də zhwah´) *n.* (*pl.* **filles
de joie** (fē də zhwah´)) a prostitute.
18C. French, lit. girl of pleasure, from
fille girl + *de* of + *joie* pleasure, joy.

fille d'honneur (fē donœ´) *n.* (*pl.* **filles
d'honneur** (fē)) maid of honour.
19C. French.

film noir (film nwah´) *n.* (*pl.* **films noirs**
(film nwah´)) a genre of film of a
pessimistic and sombre character, esp.
a black-and-white American crime film
of the 1940s or 50s with gloomy
photography, a grim urban setting and
sordid or cynical characters.
mid-20C. French, lit. black film.

filo (fē´lō), **phyllo** *n.* a kind of flaky
pastry, usually layered in thin leaves.
mid-20C. Modern Greek *phullo* leaf.

filoselle (filəsel´, fil´əsel) *n.* floss silk.
17C. French, from Italian *filosello*,
from Popular Latin *follicellus* cocoon,
dim. of *follis* bag, influ. by Italian *filo*
thread.

fils¹ (fils) *n.* (*pl.* **fils**) a monetary unit of
Bahrain, Iraq, Jordan, Kuwait and
Yemen.
19C. Coll. pronun. of **Arabic** *fals* small
copper coin, from Greek *phollis* follis,
small coin introduced by Diocletian,
AD 296.

fils² (fēs) *n.* the son, junior (added to a
French surname to distinguish a son
from a father with the same name).
19C. French son, from Latin *filius*. Cp.
PÈRE.

finale (finah´li) *n.* **1** the last section or
movement of a musical composition.
2 the last part, piece, scene or action in
any performance or exhibition. **3** the last
piece in a programme. **4** the end,
conclusion.
18C. Italian, n. of a. from Latin *finalis*
final, from *finis* end.

fin de siècle (fĩ də syekl´, syek´lə) *a.* **1**
of, relating to or characteristic of the
close of the nineteenth century. **2**
decadent. ~*n.* the end of the century,
esp. the nineteenth.
19C. French end of century, from *fin*
end + *de* of + *siècle* century.

fine (fēn), **fine champagne** (fēn
shāpahn´yə) *n.* old liqueur brandy.
early 20C. French fine (brandy from)
Champagne.
● The brandy comes from the Grande
Champagne and Petite Champagne
vineyards in the Charente region of
France.

Fine Gael (fēnə gāl´) *n.* one of the major
political parties in the Republic of
Ireland.
mid-20C. Irish tribe of Gaels, from *fine*
family group, race + *Gael* Gael.

fines herbes (fēnz eəb´) *n.pl.* a mixture
of chopped herbs used as flavouring.
19C. French fine herbs, from fem. pl. of
fin fine + pl. of *herbe* herb.
● The herbs are so called because finely
chopped.

finesse (fines´) *n.* **1** elegance, refinement.
2 artifice or artful manipulation. **3** skill,
dexterity, esp. in handling difficult
situations. **4** in whist etc., an attempt to
take a trick with a lower card, so as to

retain a higher one for later tricks. ~*v.i.*
1 to use artifice to gain an end. **2** to try
to win a trick with a lower card than a
card possibly in one's opponent's hand,
while one has a higher card in one's
own. ~*v.t.* **1** to play (a card) in this
manner. **2** to manipulate, to manage by
means of trickery or stratagem.
12–14C. French, from base of *fin* fine.

fini (finē´) *a.* finished, over, ruined.
early 20C. French, p.p. of *finir* to finish.

finis (fin´is, fē´-) *n.* **1** the end, finish,
conclusion (printed at the end of a
book). **2** the end of all things, death.
14–15C. Latin end.

finnesko (fin´əskō) *n.* (*pl.* **finnesko**) a
boot made of the tanned skin of
reindeer, having the hair on the outside.
19C. Norwegian *finnsko*, from *Finn* Finn
+ *sko* shoe.

fino (fē´nō) *n.* (*pl.* **finos**) a light-coloured
very dry sherry.
19C. Spanish fine.

fioritura (fyawrituə´rə) *n.* (*pl.* **fioriture**
(-rə)) (*Mus.*) a decorative phrase or turn,
a flourish added by the performer.
19C. Italian, from *fiorire* to flower.

firman (fœ´mən, -mahn) *n.* a decree,
mandate or order of an Eastern
monarch, issued for any purpose, such
as a passport, grant, licence etc.
17C. Persian *firmān*. Cp. Sanskrit
pramāṇa measure, standard, authority.

firn (fœn) *n.* névé, snow on the higher
slopes of lofty mountains, not yet
consolidated into ice.
19C. German of last year, from Old High
German *firni* old, rel. to Old Norse *forn*
ancient.

fjord (fyawd), **fiord** *n.* a long, narrow
inlet of the sea, bounded by high cliffs,
as in Norway.

17C. Norwegian, from Old Norse *fj"rthr*,
rel. to English *firth*.

flabellum (fləbel´əm) *n.* (*pl.* **flabella** (-ə))
1 a fan, esp. one used in the Greek
Church to drive away flies from the
chalice or in the Roman Catholic
Church to carry in religious processions.
2 (*Biol.*) a fan-shaped part or organ.
19C. Latin, dim. of *flabrum* gust, from
flare to blow.

flacon (flakō´) *n.* a small bottle, esp. a
scent-bottle.
19C. French, from Germanic source of
English *flask*.

flageolet¹ (flajəlet´, flaj´-) *n.* **1** a small
wind instrument blown from a
mouthpiece at the end, with two thumb
holes and producing a shrill sound
similar to but softer than that of the
piccolo. **2** an organ stop producing a
similar sound. **3** a tin whistle.
17C. French, dim. of Old French *flageol*,
from Provençal *flaujol*, of unknown
orig.
● According to some, the origin is in
Latin *flabrum* gust, from *flare* to blow.
Cp. FLABELLUM.

flageolet² (flajəlet´, -lā´) *n.* a kind of
French bean.
19C. French, ult. from Latin *phaseolus*
bean, from Greek.
● The French word has been influenced
by FLAGEOLET¹.

flak (flak), **flack** *n.* **1** fire from anti-
aircraft guns. **2** adverse criticism,
dissent.
mid-20C. German, abbr. of
Fliegerabwehrkanone, lit. aviator
defence gun.

flambé (flā´bā, flom´-) *v.t.* (*3rd pers. sing.
pres.* **flambés**, *pres.p.* **flambéing**, *past,
p.p.* **flambéed**) to sprinkle with brandy
etc. and ignite. ~*a.* served in ignited
brandy.

19C. French, p.p. of *flamber* to singe, to pass through flame, ult. from Latin *flamma* flame. Cp. FLAMBEAU.

flambeau (flam´bō) *n.* (*pl.* **flambeaus, flambeaux**) 1 a torch, esp. one made of thick wicks covered with wax or pitch. 2 a large ornamental candlestick.
17C. French, dim. of *flambe*, from Latin *flammula*, dim. of *flamma* flame.

flamboyant (flamboi´ənt) *a.* 1 exuberant, showy. 2 florid, highly decorated. 3 gorgeously coloured. 4 (of hair etc.) wavy or flamelike. 5 (*Archit.*) of or relating to the decorated French Gothic style, having flamelike tracery.
19C. French, pres.p. of *flamboyer* to blaze, to flame, from *flambe*. See FLAMBEAU.

flamenco (fləmeng´kō) *n.* (*pl.* **flamencos**) 1 a kind of music played on the guitar or sung by gypsies. 2 a dance performed to such music.
19C. Spanish Fleming, flamingo.
• The word is said to have first applied to the music and dancing of gypsies of Andalusia, whose colourful show suggested the ruddy complexion of the Flemings and the bright pink plumage of the flamingo.

flan (flan) *n.* 1 an open pastry or sponge base with fruit or savoury filling. 2 a plain metal disc from which a coin is made.
19C. French round cake, from Old French *flaon*, from Medieval Latin *flado, fladonis*, from Frankish, from Germanic. Cp. German *Fladen* a type of round flat dough cake.

flaneur (flanœ´) *n.* a lounger, an idler.
19C. French *flâneur*, from *flâner* to lounge, to saunter idly, from Scandinavian *flana* to wander about.

flèche (flāsh, flesh) *n.* 1 a spire, esp. a slender one, usu. of wood covered with lead, over the intersection of the nave and transepts of a church. 2 a simple kind of redan, usu. constructed at the foot of the glacis, consisting of a parapet with faces.
12–14C. Old French arrow, from Frankish. Cp. German *fliegen* to fly.

fleur-de-lis (flœdəlē´), **fleur-de-lys** *n.* (*pl.* **fleurs-de-lis** (flœdəlē´), **fleurs-de-lys**) 1 the iris flower. 2 (*Her.*) a a lily with three petals. b (*Hist.*) the royal arms of France.
12–14C. Old French *flour de lys*, from *flour* flower + *de* of + *lys* lily.

fleuret (fluə´rət, flœ´-) *n.* an ornament like a small flower.
19C. French *fleurette*, dim. of *fleur* flower.

fleuron (fluə´ron, flœ´-) *n.* a flower-shaped ornament, used for a tailpiece, in architecture, on coins etc.
14–15C. Old French *floron* (Modern French *fleuron*), from *flour* flower.

flic (flēk) *n.* a French policeman.
19C. French (*coll.*), of uncertain orig. ? Imit. of the crack of a whip or riding crop.
• There is a police officer Flick in the writings of the French humorist Georges Courteline (1858–1929).

flora (flaw´rə) *n.* (*pl.* **floras, florae** (-rē)) 1 the whole vegetation of a country, district or geological period. 2 a book dealing with the vegetation of a country or district.
16C. Latin, from *Flora*, the Roman goddess of flowers and gardens, from *flos, floris* flower. Cp. FAUNA.

Floréal (flor´āal) *n.* the eighth month of the French revolutionary calendar, from 21 April to 20 May.
19C. French, from Latin *floreus* flowery, from *flos, floris* flower.

floreat (flo´riat) *v.i.* may (a person, situation etc.) flourish.
19C. **Latin** may he flourish, 3rd pers. sing. pres. subj. of *florere* to flower, to flourish. Cp. FLORUIT.
• The word is often followed by the name of a person, institution or the like. Thus *Floreat Etona* 'May Eton flourish' is the motto of Eton College.

florilegium (florilē´jiəm, flaw-) *n.* (*pl.* **florilegia** (-jiə), **florilegiums**) an anthology.
17C. **Modern Latin**, lit. bouquet, from Latin *flori-*, comb. form of *flos* flower + *legere* to gather, translating Greek *anthologion* anthology.

floruit (flor´uit, flaw´-) *v.i.* (he or she) was alive and actively working; flourished, used to express the period during which a person, e.g. a painter or writer, was most active (in the absence of exact dates of birth and death). ~*n.* the period during which a person was alive and actively working.
19C. **Latin** he/ she flourished, 3rd pers. sing. perf. ind. of *florere* to flourish. Cp. FLOREAT.
• The word is usually found in the abbreviated form *fl.*, e.g. Hesiod *fl.* *c.*800 BC.

flos ferri (flos fe´ri) *n.* (*Mineral.*) a spicular variety of aragonite.
18C. **Latin**, lit. flower of iron, from *flos* flower + gen. of *ferrum* iron.

flotant (flō´tənt) *a.* (*Her.*) floating, as a flag, bird, or anything swimming.
17C. **French** *flottant*, pres.p. of *flotter* to float.

flotilla (flətil´ə) *n.* **1** a small fleet. **2** a fleet of small vessels.
18C. **Spanish**, dim. of *flota* fleet.

flugelhorn (floo´gəlhawn) *n.* a valved brass instrument resembling, but slightly larger than, a cornet.
19C. **German** *Flügelhorn*, from *Flügel* wing + *Horn* horn.
• The instrument is so named because it was originally used to signal the flanking riders in a hunt, especially when drawing game.

focaccia (fəkach´ə) *n.* (*pl.* **focaccias**)
1 a kind of Italian bread sprinkled before baking with olive oil, salt and often herbs. **2** a loaf of this.
mid-20C. **Italian**, ult. from Latin *focus* hearth.
• In ancient Rome the *panis focacius*, lit. hearth bread, was a type of flat bread cooked in the ashes. The French equivalent of the focaccia is the *fougasse*.

focus (fō´kəs) *n.* (*pl.* **focuses, foci** (fō´sī))
1 (*Physics*) a point at which rays of light, heat, electrons etc. meet after reflection, deflection or refraction, or from which they appear to diverge. **2** the relation between the eye or lens and the object necessary to produce a clear image. **3** a state of clear definition. **4** (*Med. etc.*) the point from which any activity (such as a disease or an earthquake wave) originates. **5** the point on which attention or activity is concentrated. **6** (*Geom.*) one of two points having a definite relation to an ellipse or other curve. ~*v.t.* (*pres.p.* **focusing, focussing**, *past, p.p.* **focused, focussed**) **1** to bring (rays) to a focus or point. **2** to adjust (eye or instrument) so as to be at the right focus. **3** to bring into focus. **4** to concentrate. **5** to cause to converge to a focus. ~*v.i.* **1** to concentrate. **2** to converge to a focus.
17C. **Latin** fireplace, domestic hearth.

föhn (fœn), **foehn** *n.* **1** the warm S wind in the Alps. **2** a warm dry wind on the lee side of mountains.
19C. **German**, ult. from Latin (*ventus*) *Favonius* mild W wind, rel. to *fovere* to warm.

foible (foi´bəl) *n.* **1** a weak point in a person's character. **2** the part of a sword blade between the middle and point.
16C. French, obs. var. of *faible* feeble.

foie gras (fwah grah´) *n.* pâté made of fatted goose liver.
19C. French, abbr. of *pâté de foie gras*, from PÂTÉ + *de* of + *foie* liver + *gras* fat.

folie (folē´) *n.* madness, folly.
19C. French, from *fou, fol* mad, from Latin *follis* bag, balloon.
• A balloon when released flies uncontrollably in different directions, as if crazed.

folie à deux (folē´ a dœ´) *n.* the presence of similar delusions in the minds of two closely associated people.
early 20C. French, lit. madness of two. Cp. FOLIE.

folie de grandeur (folē´ də grãdœ´) *n.* delusions of grandeur.
19C. French, lit. madness of greatness. Cp. FOLIE.

folio (fō´liō) *n.* (*pl.* **folios**) **1** a leaf of paper or other material for writing etc., numbered on the front. **2** a page of manuscript. **3** a sheet of paper folded once. **4 a** a book of the largest size, whose sheets are folded once. **b** any large volume or work. **5** a page in an account book, or two opposite pages numbered as one. **6** the number of a page. **7** 72 words of manuscript in legal documents, 90 words in Parliamentary proceedings. ~*a.* (of a book) of, relating to or having the format of a folio.
14–15C. Medieval Latin, from Latin (abl. of) *folium* leaf, or from Italian *foglio*.
• The Medieval Latin sense meant literally at leaf (so-and-so). In sense 4 (16C) the origin is in the phrase *in folio*, from Italian *in foglio*.

fomes (fō´mēz) *n.* (*pl.* **fomites** (-mitēz)) a substance of a porous kind liable to absorb and retain contagious substances and so spread disease.
17C. Latin tinder, touchwood.

fonctionnaire (fõksyoneə´) *n.* a French civil servant or local authority employee.
late 20C. French, lit. functionary.

fondant (fon´dənt) *n.* a sweet paste made of sugar and water.
19C. French, pres.p. (used as n.) of *fondre* to melt. Cp. FONDUE.

fondue (fon´doo, -dū) *n.* a dish consisting of a hot sauce (usu. of cheese and white wine) into which pieces of bread etc. are dipped, or of cubes of meat which are cooked by dipping into hot oil at table and eaten with a variety of spicy sauces.
19C. French, fem. p.p. of *fondre* to melt. Cp. FONDANT.

fons et origo (fonz et or´igō) *n.* the source and origin.
19C. Latin.
• The earliest use of the phrase is in *fons et origo mali* the source and origin of evil.

foo yong (foo yong´) *n.* a Chinese dish made with egg mixed with chicken, meat and other ingredients, cooked like an omelette.
mid-20C. Chinese (Cantonese) *foŏ yung*, lit. hibiscus.

force de frappe (faws də frap´) *n.* (*pl.* **forces de frappe** (faws)) a striking force, esp. a nuclear capability.
mid-20C. French striking force.

force majeure (faws mazhœ´) *n.*
1 superior power. **2** circumstances not under a person's control, so excusing them from fulfilling a contract.
19C. French superior strength, from *force* strength, force + fem. of *majeur* superior, greater.

forint (for´int) *n.* the standard unit of currency of Hungary since 1946, equivalent to 100 fillér.
mid-20C. Hungarian, from Italian *fiorino*.

formula (faw´mūlə) *n.* (*pl.* **formulas, formulae** (-lē)) **1** (*Chem.*) (*pl.* **formulae**) an expression by means of symbols of the elements of a compound. **2** (*Math.*) (*pl.* **formulae**) the expression of a rule or principle in algebraic symbols. **3** a prescribed form of words. **4** a conventional usage. **5** a formal enunciation of doctrine, principle etc. **6** a compromise solution to a dispute, an agreed form of words. **7** a prescription, a recipe. **8** a milk mixture or substitute used as baby food. **9** a technical specification which determines the class in which a racing car competes.
17C. Latin, dim. of *forma* form.

forte[1] (faw´tā, faw´ti, fawt) *n.* **1** a person's strong point. **2** that in which a person excels. **3** the strong part of a sword blade, i.e. from the hilt to the middle.
17C. French, use as n. of fem. of *fort* strong.
● The French feminine form was substituted for the masculine in English, as in LOCALE, MORALE. The pronunciation has been partly influenced by that of FORTE[2].

forte[2] (faw´ti) *adv.* (*Mus.*) with loudness or force. ~*a.* performed with loudness or force. ~*n.* a passage to be performed with loudness or force.
18C. Italian strong, loud, from Latin *fortis* strong.

fortissimo (fawtis´imō) *adv.* (*Mus.*) very loudly. ~*a.* performed very loudly. ~*n.* (*pl.* **fortissimos, fortissimi** (-mē)) a passage that is to be performed very loudly.
18C. Italian, superl. of FORTE[2].

forum (faw´rəm) *n.* (*pl.* **forums, fora** (-rə)) **1** a place of assembly for public discussion or judicial purposes. **2** a meeting to discuss matters of public interest. **3** a medium, e.g. a magazine, for open discussion. **4** a tribunal, a court of law. **5** a market place. **6** (*Hist.*) the public place in Rome in which were the courts of law, public offices etc. and where orations were delivered. **7** in the Roman Catholic Church, the sphere in which the Church exercises jurisdiction.
14–15C. Latin, rel. to *fores* (outside) door, orig. an enclosure surrounding a house.

fossor (fos´aw) *n.* (*Hist.*) a member of an order of inferior clergy charged with the burial of the dead.
19C. Latin digger, miner, from *fossus*, p.p. of *fodere* to dig.

foudroyant (foodroi´ənt) *a.* **1** (of a disease) beginning in a sudden and intense form. **2** †overwhelming, thundering or flashing, like lightning.
19C. French, pres.p. of *foudroyer* to strike (as if) by lightning, from *foudre*, from Latin *fulgur* lightning.

fouetté (fwet´ā) *n.* a step in ballet in which the dancer stands on one foot and makes a whiplike movement with the other.
19C. French, p.p. of *fouetter* to whip, from *fouet* whip.

foulard (foolah´, -lahd´, foo´-) *n.* **1** a soft, thin material of silk or silk mixed with cotton. **2** something made of this, e.g. a silk handkerchief.
19C. French, of unknown orig.
● According to some, the word is from Provençal *foulat* fulled (cloth). Cp. FOULÉ.

foulé (foolā´) *n.* a light woollen dress material.
19C. French pressed (cloth), p.p. of *fouler* to full.

fourchette (fuǝshet´) *n.* **1** (*Anat.*) a thin fold of skin at the back of the vulva. **2** a fork-shaped piece between the fingers of gloves. **3** a forked surgical instrument formerly used for cutting the fraenum in tongue-tied infants.
18C. French, dim. of *fourche* fork.

fourgon (fuǝ´gō) *n.* a French baggage-wagon.
19C. French, of unknown orig.
● The wagon may originally have been known as a *charrette à fourgon*, from *fourgon* poker (from Popular Latin *furicare*, from Latin *furari* to steal), with reference to its slatted sides, resembling pokers.

fou rire (foo riǝ´) *n.* a fit of wild or uncontrollable laughter.
early 20C. French, lit. mad laughter.

foyer (fo´yā, -yǝ) *n.* the entrance hall or other large public area where people meet or wait in a hotel, theatre etc.
18C. French hearth, home, from Latin *focus* hearth.

Fra (frah) *n.* brother, a title given to an Italian monk or friar.
16C. Abbr. of **Italian** *frate* monk, friar, from Latin *frater* brother.

fracas (frak´ah) *n.* (*pl.* **fracas** (-ahz)) a disturbance, a row, an uproar, a noisy quarrel.
18C. French, from *fracasser*, from Italian *fracassare* to make an uproar.

fraise (frāz) *n.* **1** a ruff. **2** a horizontal or sloping palisade round a rampart. **3** a tool for enlarging a drill hole etc.
17C. French mesentery of a calf.

Fraktur (frak´tuǝ) *n.* a style of typeface formerly used for typesetting German.
19C. German, from Latin *fractura* a breaking.
● The name refers to the curlicues that broke up the continuous line of a word.

franc (frangk) *n.* the standard unit of currency in France, Belgium, Switzerland and various other countries.
14–15C. Old French, from Latin *Francorum rex* King of the Franks.
● The legend was that on gold coins first struck in the reign of Jean le Bon (1350–64).

franc-tireur (frātērœ´) *n.* (*pl.* **francs-tireurs** (frāteroe´)) a French light-infantry soldier belonging to an irregular corps.
19C. French free shooter, from *franc* free + *tireur*, from *tirer* to shoot.
● The soldier was so called because he was free to shoot with any group of fighters.

frangipane (fran´jipān) *n.* **1** a kind of pastry made with cream, almonds and sugar; a flan filled with this. **2** frangipani.
17C. French.
● The word was originally the name of the perfume (sense 2), then (19C) that of the pastry or, more properly, the cream with which it is made. The pastry name is sometimes popularly said to mean Frank's bread, as if from Latin *Franci panis*.

franglais (frā´glā) *n.* an informal version of French which contains a high proportion of English words.
mid-20C. French, blend of *français* French and *anglais* English.
● The word was popularized by René Étiemble in his book *Parlez-vous franglais?* (1964). Cp. *Spanglish* (*Spanish* and *English*), *Japlish* (*Japanese* and *English*) and similar formations.

frankfurter (frangk´fœtǝ) *n.* a small, smoked sausage of beef and pork.
19C. German *Frankfurter Wurst* sausage of Frankfurt, a city in central Germany. Cp. HAMBURGER.

frappé (frap´ā) *a.* iced. ~*n.* **1** an iced drink. **2** a soft water ice.
19C. **French**, p.p. of *frapper* to ice (drinks) (lit. to strike).

frascati (fraskah´ti) *n.* (*pl.* **frascatis**) an esp. white wine from the Frascati region of Italy.
mid-20C. *Frascati*, a district in Latium, Italy, south-east of Rome.

Frau (frow) *n.* (*pl.* **Frauen** (frow´ən)) a German woman, wife or widow; Mrs.
19C. **German**, ult. rel. to English *free*.

Fräulein (froi´līn, fraw´-, frow´-) *n.* (*pl.* **Fräulein**) (*often offensive*) a young lady, a German spinster; Miss.
17C. **German**, dim. of FRAU.
● German *-lein* corresponds to English *-ling*, as in *Entlein*, English *duckling*.

frère (freə) *n.* brother (the title of a member of a religious community).
19C. **French**.

fresco (fres´kō) *n.* (*pl.* **frescos, frescoes**) a kind of watercolour painting on fresh plaster or on a wall covered with mortar not quite dry. ~*v.t.* (*3rd pers. sing. pres.* **frescoes,** *pres.p.* **frescoing,** *past, p.p.* **frescoed**) to paint (a picture) or decorate (a wall etc.) in fresco.
16C. **Italian** cool, fresh. Cp. ALFRESCO.
● The English word first occurs in the phrase *in fresco*, representing Italian *al fresco* on the fresh (plaster).

fricandeau (frik´andō) *n.* (*pl.* **fricandeaux** (-dōz)) **1** a larded veal cutlet, braised or roasted and glazed. **2** a dish made with this, served with a sauce. ~*v.t.* (*3rd pers. sing. pres.* **fricandeaus,** *pres.p.* **fricandeauing,** *past, p.p.* **fricandeaued**) to make into a fricandeau.
18C. **French**, ? from source of FRICASSEE.

fricassee (frik´əsē, -sē´) *n.* small pieces of meat, esp. chicken or veal, fried, stewed

and served in a usu. white sauce. ~*v.t.* (*3rd pers. sing. pres.* **fricassees,** *pres.p.* **fricasseeing,** *past, p.p.* **fricasseed**) to cook as a fricassee.
16C. **French** *fricassée*, fem. p.p. of *fricasser* to cut up and stew in sauce, ? from Popular Latin *frigicare*, from Latin *frigere* to fry, or a blend of French *frire* to fry and *casser* to break.

frijol (frihōl´) *n.* (*pl.* **frijoles** (-hō´les)) a bean resembling the kidney bean, used in Mexican cookery.
16C. **Spanish** bean, ult. from Latin *phaseolus*. Cp. FLAGEOLET².

Frimaire (frimeə´) *n.* the third month of the French revolutionary calendar, from 22 November to 21 December.
19C. **French**, from *frimas* hoarfrost, from Frankish *hrīm*, rel. to English *rime*.

frisée (frē´zā) *n.* endive.
late 20C. **French**, from *chicorée frisée* curly chicory. See FRISETTE.

frisette (frizet´) *n.* a front or band of artificial curls worn on the forehead.
19C. **French**, from *friser* to curl, to frizz.

friseur (frēzœ´) *n.* a hairdresser.
18C. **French**, from *friser* (see FRISETTE).

frisson (frē´sō) *n.* a shudder, a thrill.
18C. **French** shiver, thrill, from Late Latin *frictio, frictionis*, from *frictus*, p.p. of *frigere* to fry, assoc. with *frigere* to be cold.

frittata (fritah´tə) *n.* an Italian dish made with fried beaten eggs.
mid-20C. **Italian**, from *frittare* to fry, from *fritto*, p.p. of *friggere* to fry.

fritto misto (fritō mis´tō) *n.* a dish of fried food, esp. seafood.
early 20C. **Italian** mixed fry, from *fritto* (see FRITTATA) + *misto* mixed.

froideur (frwŭdœ´) *n.* coolness in a relationship between people.

early 20C. **French** coolness, from *froid*, from Latin *frigidus* cold.

fromage blanc (fromahzh blä´) *n.* a kind of soft French cheese made from cow's milk, with a creamy sour taste.
late 20C. **French** white cheese, from *fromage* cheese (from Popular Latin *formaticum*, from Latin *forma* form) + *blanc* white.

fromage frais (fromahzh frä´) *n.* a kind of smooth low-fat soft cheese with a light texture.
late 20C. **French** fresh cheese, from *fromage* (see FROMAGE BLANC) + *frais* fresh.
● This type of cheese is usually known in France as PETIT SUISSE.

Fronde (frond) *n.* **1** (*Hist.*) the French party, 1648–57, who attacked Mazarin and the Court during the minority of Louis XIV. **2** any party of malcontents.
18C. **French**, lit. sling.
● The name refers to a children's game played in the streets of Paris in defiance of the civil authorities.

frottage (frotahzh´) *n.* **1** the technique of producing images or textures by rubbing with e.g. a pencil on a sheet of paper placed on top of an object. **2** (*Psych.*) sexual gratification obtained by rubbing against another person's clothed body.
mid-20C. **French** rubbing, friction, from *frotter* to rub, from Old French *freter*, from Popular Latin *frictare*, freq. of Latin *fricare* to rub.

frou-frou (froo´froo) *n.* **1** a rustling, as of a silk dress. **2** elaborate dress, frills.
19C. **French**, imit.

Fructidor (frŭk´tidaw) *n.* **1** in the French Revolutionary calendar, the twelfth month of the republican year from 18 August to 16 September. **2** the coup d'état that occurred in Fructidor in 1797.

18C. **French**, from Latin *fructus* fruit + Greek *dōron* gift.

fruits de mer (frwē də meə´) *n.pl.*
1 seafood. **2** a dish containg a variety of different shellfish.
mid-20C. **French**, lit. fruits of the sea.
● The phrase is based on *fruits de la terre*, meaning vegetable products. Cp. English *fruits of the earth*.

frutti proibiti (frutē pro-ib´itē) *n.pl.*
anything desired but pronounced unlawful, forbidden fruit.
19C. **Italian** forbidden fruit.
● An Italian proverb runs *i frutti proibiti son' i più dolci* 'forbidden fruits are the sweetest'. The ultimate reference is to the Garden of Eden in the biblical story of Adam and Eve (Gen. iii).

fuero (fweə´rō) *n.* (*pl.* **fueros**) (*Hist.*)
1 in Spain, a code, charter, grant of privileges or custom having the force of law. **2** a tribunal or a place where justice is administered.
early 20C. **Spanish**, from Latin FORUM.

fughetta (fūget´ə) *n.* a short condensed fugue.
19C. **Italian**, dim. of *fuga* fugue.

führer (fū´rə, fü´-), **fuehrer** *n.* **1** a leader, esp. one who exerts tyrannical authority. **2** (**Führer, Fuehrer**) the head of the National Socialist German government, the title assumed by Adolf Hitler from 1934.
mid-20C. **German** leader.
● Sense 2 made the word widely known.

führerprinzip (fū´rəprintsip, fü´-) *n.*
the principle of government whereby unquestioning loyalty is shown by the people towards a single leader.
mid-20C. **German**, from FÜHRER + *Prinzip* principle.
● *Führerprinzip* was the dominant precept of Fascism and in particular of Nazism under Hitler.

fulcrum (ful´krəm, fŭl´-) *n.* (*pl.* **fulcra**
(-krə), **fulcrums**) **1** the fixed point on
which the bar of a lever rests or about
which it turns. **2** a means of making any
kind of force or influence effective.
3 (*Zool., Bot.*) an additional organ, such
as a stipule, scale, spine etc.
17C. Latin post or foot of a couch, from
base of *fulcire* to prop up, to support.

fumatorium (fūmətaw´riəm) *n.* (*pl.*
fumatoriums, fumatoria (-riə))
1 a room or apparatus for fumigating.
2 a chamber in a conservatory etc. for
destroying insects by chemical fumes.
19C. Latin, from *fumare* to smoke.

funèbre (foonebr´, fooneb´rə, fū-) *a.*
(*chiefly Mus.*) mournful, funerary, as in
marche funèbre.
19C. French funereal.

furioso (fūriō´sō, -zō) *adv.* (*Mus.*) with
fury or vehemence. ~†*n.* (*pl.* **furiosos**)
a furious or impetuous person.
17C. Italian, from Latin *furiosus* furious.

furore (fūraw´ri, fū´raw) *n.* **1** an outburst
of public indignation. **2** great excitement
or enthusiasm. **3** a craze, a rage.
18C. Italian, from Latin *furor*, from
furere to rage.

fusarole (fū´zərōl) *n.* a moulding placed
immediately under the echinus in Doric,
Ionic or composite capitals.

17C. French *fusarolle*, from Italian
fusaruola, ult. dim. of Latin *fusus*
spindle. Cp. FUSELAGE.

fuselage (fū´zəlahzh) *n.* the main body of
an aeroplane.
early 20C. French, from *fuseler* to shape
like a spindle, from *fuseau* spindle.

fusillade (fūzilād´) *n.* **1** a continuous,
rapid discharge of firearms. **2** a rapid
succession of blows, critical comments
etc. ~*v.t.* to shoot down or storm by
fusillade.
19C. French, from *fusiller* to shoot, from
fusil rifle, gun, ult. from Latin *focus* fire.

fusilli (fuzil´i) *n.pl.* pasta in the form of
short, thick spirals.
mid-20C. Italian, pl. of *fusillo*, dim. of
fuso spindle. Cp. FUSELAGE.

fustanella (fŭstənel´ə) *n.* a type of short
white kilt worn by men in Greece and
Albania.
19C. Italian, from Modern Greek
phoustani, phoustanela, and from
Albanian *fustan*, ? from Italian *fustagno*
fustian.

futon (foo´ton) *n.* **1** a Japanese floor-
mattress used as a bed. **2** a kind of low
wooden sofa bed with such a mattress.
19C. Japanese bedding.
● The word gained general use in
English only in the late 20C.

G

gabelle (gəbel´) *n.* a tax or duty, esp. the tax on salt in France before the Revolution, 1789.
14–15C. French, from Italian *gabella*, rel. to Spanish *alcabula*, from Arabic *al-kabāla* the tax.

gabion (gā´biən) *n.* a cylindrical basket of wickerwork or metal, filled with earth or stones, used for foundations etc. in engineering work and (esp. formerly) for shelter against an enemy's fire while trenches are being dug.
16C. French, from Italian *gabbione*, augm. of *gabbia* cage.

gaffe (gaf) *n.* a social blunder, esp. a tactless comment.
early 20C. French, lit. boat-hook, from Provençal *gafar*, from Gothic *gaffôn* to seize.

gaga (gah´gah) *a.* (*coll., derog.*) foolish, senile, fatuous.
early 20C. French, of imit. orig.

gagaku (gag´akoo) *n.* a traditional type of Japanese music mainly associated with ceremonial occasions.
mid-20C. Japanese, from *ga* noble, graceful + *gaku* music.

gaijin (gījin´) *n.* in Japan, a foreigner. ~*a.* foreign, alien.
mid-20C. Japanese, contr. of *gaikoku-jin*, from *gaikoku* foreign country + *jin* person.

gaine (gān) *n.* a metal tube containing explosive which is screwed to a fuse.
early 20C. French sheath, ult. from Latin *vagina* sheath.

gala (gah´lə, gā´-) *n.* **1** a festivity, a fête. **2** a sporting occasion involving several events. ~*a.* festive.
17C. French, or from Italian, from Spanish, from Old French *gale* merrymaking.

galanterie (galātrē´) *n.* courtesy, politeness.
early 20C. French gallantry.

galantine (gal´əntēn) *n.* a dish of white meat, freed from bone, tied up, sliced, boiled, covered with jelly and served cold.
12–14C. Old French, alt. of *galatine*, from Medieval Latin *galatina*, dial. var. of *gelatina* gelatin.

galette (gəlet´) *n.* a flat, round cake.
18C. French, dim. of Old French *gal* pebble.
● The cake is so named for its round shape.

galleria (galərē´a) *n.* a number of small independent shops in one building, on

one floor or arranged in galleries on several floors.
19C. Italian *gallery*.
● The concept of the shopping arcade on Italian principles in the English-speaking world dates only from the mid-20C and the word itself caught on in English only from the late 20C.

galop (gal´əp, gəlop´) *n.* **1** a lively dance in 2/4 time. **2** the music to the dance. ~*v.i.* (*pres.p.* **galoping**, *past, p.p.* **galoped**) to dance this.
19C. French *gallop*.

gamba (gam´bə) *n.* **1** a viola da gamba. **2** an organ stop with a tone like that of the violin or cello.
16C. Italian, shortening of VIOLA DA GAMBA.

gambade (gambād´), **gambado** (-dō) *n.* (*pl.* **gambades, gambados, gambadoes**) **1** a bound or spring of a horse. **2** a caper, a fantastic movement, a frolic.
16C. French, from Italian *gambata*, from *gamba* leg. Cp. GAMBADO.
● The form *gambado* is from Spanish (from Italian *gamba* leg) and dates from the 19C.

gambado (gambā´dō) *n.* (*pl.* **gambados, gambadoes**) a leather legging or large boot for horse riders.
17C. Spanish, from Italian *gamba* leg.

gamin (gam´in, -mī´) *n.* **1** a homeless child, an urchin. **2** a cheeky child.
19C. French, ? from base *gamm-* meaning good-for-nothing.

gamine (gam´ēn, -ēn´) *n.* **1** a small boylike girl or woman. **2** a female gamin. ~*a.* (esp. of a girl or woman) having a boyish look.
19C. French, fem. of GAMIN.

gamma (gam´ə) *n.* **1** the third letter of the Greek alphabet (Γ, γ). **2** a third-class

mark given for a student's work. **3** (*Astron.*) (**Gamma**) the third star (in brightness or position etc.) in a constellation.
14–15C. Latin, from Greek.

ganja (gan´jə) *n.* marijuana, a dried preparation of *Cannabis sativa* or Indian hemp, smoked as an intoxicant and narcotic.
19C. Hindi *gāṁjā*.

garage (gar´ahzh, -ij) *n.* **1** a building for housing or repairing motor vehicles. **2** an establishment where this is done as a business or where motor fuels etc. are sold. **3 a** garage rock. **b** a type of house music. ~*v.t.* to put or keep in a garage. ~*a.* (*coll.*) rough-and-ready, amateurish, improvised.
early 20C. French, from *garer* to shelter. Rel. to English *ware*.

garam masala (gŭrəm məsah´lə) *n.* a mixture of spices often used in Indian cookery.
early 20C. Urdu *garam maṣālaḥ* hot MASALA.

garçon (gah´son) *n.* a waiter (usu. used as a form of address: *Garçon!*).
17C. French *boy*, (male) servant, from Frankish.

garçonnière (gahsonyeə´) *n.* (*pl.* **garçonnières** (-yeə´)) a bachelor flat.
early 20C. French, from GARÇON bachelor.

Garda (gah´də) *n.* the police force of the Irish Republic.
early 20C. Irish *Garda Síochána* Civic Guard, lit. guard of peace.

garibaldi (garibawl´di, -bal´-) *n.* (*pl.* **garibaldis**) **1** a loose kind of blouse worn by women or children and popular in the 1860s, like the red shirts worn by Garibaldi and his men. **2** a sandwich-type biscuit with a layer of

currants. **3** a small red fish, *Hypsypops rubicundus*, of California.
19C. Giuseppe *Garibaldi*, 1807–82, Italian patriot, general and statesman.

garni (gah´nē) *a.* in cooking, garnished, trimmed, esp. with salad.
early 20C. French, p.p. of *garnir* to garnish.

garrotte (gərot´), **garotte**, (*N Am.*) **garrote** *n.* **1** (*Hist.*) a method of execution in which the victim was fastened by an iron collar to an upright post, and a knob operated by a screw or lever dislocated the spinal column, or a small blade severed the spinal cord at the base of the brain (orig. the method was strangulation by a cord twisted with a stick). **2** killing with a length of wire around the throat. **3** robbery with strangling of the victim. ~*v.t.* **1** to execute or kill by this means. **2** to render helpless or insensible by strangulation in order to rob.
17C. Spanish *garrote* cudgel, ? of Celtic orig.

Gastarbeiter (gast´ahbītə) *n.* (*pl.* **Gastarbeiters, Gastarbeiter**) a person with temporary permission to work in a foreign country.
mid-20C. German, from *Gast* guest + *Arbeiter* worker.

gasthaus (gast´hows) *n.* (*pl.* **gasthäuser** (-hoizə)) a German guest house or small hotel.
19C. German, from *Gast* guest + *Haus* house.

gasthof (gast´hof) *n.* (*pl.* **gasthöfe** (-hœfə)) a (relatively large) German hotel.
19C. German, from *Gast* guest + *Hof* hotel, large house.

gateau (gat´ō) *n.* (*pl.* **gateaus** (-ōz), **gateaux** (-ō, -ōz)) a rich cake filled with cream and decorated with icing etc.
19C. French *gâteau* cake, from Old French *gastel*, from Popular Latin *wastellum*, from Germanic. Cp. Frankish *wastil* food.

gauche (gōsh) *a.* **1** awkward, clumsy. **2** tactless, uncouth, boorish.
18C. French, lit. left-handed.

gaucho (gow´chō) *n.* (*pl.* **gauchos**) a cowboy of the pampas of Uruguay and Argentina, noted for their horse-riding skills.
19C. American Spanish, prob. from Araucanian *kaučú*.

gaudeamus igitur (gowdiah´mus ig´ituə) *int.* let us therefore rejoice.
18C. Latin let us be merry therefore, 1st pers. pl. pres. subj. of *gaudere* to rejoice + *igitur* therefore.
● The words open the Modern Latin students' song with the first line *Gaudeamus igitur, iuvenes dum sumus* Let us be merry therefore while we are still young.

gauleiter (gow´lītə) *n.* **1** the chief official of a district in Germany under the Nazi regime. **2** (*coll.*) someone in a position of petty authority who behaves in an overbearing and excessively authoritarian manner.
mid-20C. German, from *Gau* administrative district + *Leiter* leader.

gavotte (gəvot´) *n.* **1** a dance of a lively yet dignified character resembling the minuet. **2** the music for this. **3** a dance tune in common time and in two parts, each repeated.
17C. French, from Provençal *gavoto*, from *Gavot* an inhabitant of the Alps.
● The *Gavots* are so named from Provençal *gava* throat, goitre, with reference to the goitrous condition from which many mountain dwellers suffered.

gazette (gəzet´) *n.* **1** an official journal containing lists of appointments to any public office or commission, legal notices, lists of bankrupts etc. **2** a newspaper. ~*v.t.* (*usu. in p.p.*) to publish in a gazette, esp. to announce the appointment or bankruptcy of.
17C. French, or from Italian *gazzetta*, orig. Venetian *gazeta de la novità* 'ha'p'orth of news', from *gazeta*, a Venetian coin of small value.

gazpacho (gaspach´ō) *n.* (*pl.* **gazpachos**) a spicy Spanish soup made with tomatoes, chopped onion, cucumber, green peppers, garlic etc. and usu. served cold.
19C. Spanish, from Arabic word meaning soaked bread.

gefilte fish (gəfil´tə fish), **gefüllte fish** *n.* in Jewish cookery, cooked chopped fish mixed with matzo meal, egg and seasonings and then poached, either stuffed back into the skin of the fish or as dumplings.
19C. Yiddish stuffed fish, from *gefilte*, inflected p.p. of *filn* to fill + fish.

gegenschein (gā´gənshīn) *n.* a faint glow in the night sky at a position opposite to that of the sun, counterglow.
19C. German *gegen* opposite + *Schein* shine, glow.

geisha (gā´shə) *n.* (*pl.* **geisha, geishas**) **1** a Japanese girl or woman trained in the art of being a hostess for men, with skills in conversation, dancing, music. **2** a Japanese prostitute.
19C. Japanese entertainer, from *gei* (performing) arts + *sha* person.

Geist (gīst) *n.* the spirit, principle or tendency of an age or group.
19C. German spirit. Cp. ERDGEIST, ZEITGEIST.

Gemara (gəmah´rə) *n.* the second portion of the Talmud, consisting of a commentary on the first part of the Mishna, or text.
17C. Aramaic *gĕmārā* completion.

gemeinschaft (gəmīn´shahft) *n.* (*pl.* **gemeinschaften** (-tən)) a social group united by kinship, common beliefs etc.
mid-20C. German, from *gemein* common, general + *-schaft* -ship.

Gemeinschaft und Gesellschaft (gəmīn´shaft unt gəzel´shahft) *n.* kinship and association.
19C. German, from *gemein* common, general + *-schaft* -ship + *und* and + *Gesell* companion + *-schaft*.
● The two terms represent a form of social integration in German society, based respectively on personal and impersonal ties. The terms are also found individually.

gemütlich (gəmoot´likh) *a.* **1** comfortable, cosy. **2** friendly, genial.
19C. German.

gendarme (zhā´dahm) *n.* **1** an armed policeman, in France and some other Continental countries. **2** a pinnacle of rock blocking a mountain ridge.
16C. French, sing. n. from pl. *gens d'armes* men of arms.
● The word is popularly regarded as the general French word for policeman, which is really *agent* (*de police*).

gendarmerie (zhādahmərē´, -dah´-), **gendarmery** (-dah-´) *n.* (*pl.* **gendarmeries**) **1** the armed police of France. **2** a body of gendarmes. **3** the headquarters of a body or gendarmes.
18C. French, from GENDARME.

generalissimo (jenərəlis´imō) *n.* (*pl.* **generalissimos**) **1** the chief commander of a force furnished by several powers, or military and naval in combination. **2** a commander-in-chief. **3** (*coll.*) any esp. autocratic leader.
17C. Italian, superl. of *generale* general.

genius (jē´niəs) *n.* (*pl.* **geniuses, genii** (-niī)) **1** a person of extraordinary intellectual, imaginative, expressive or inventive ability. **2** an extraordinary endowment of ability. **3** the dominant character, spirit or sentiment (of). **4** natural bent or inclination of the mind. **5** a person who exercises powerful influence over another for good or ill. **6** in mythology, a guardian deity or spirit, supposed to preside over the destinies of an individual, place, nation etc. **7** in mythology, either of two spirits attendant on a person through life, one good, the other evil.
14–15C. Latin, from base of *gignere* to beget and Greek *gignesthai* to be born.
• The earliest sense is sense 7. The current sense 1 dates from the 17C.

genius loci (jē´niəs lō´sī, lo´kē) *n.* **1** the spirit or associations predominant in a locality, community or institution. **2** the presiding deity of a place.
17C. Latin genius of the place, from GENIUS + gen. of *locus* place.

genizah (gənē´zə) *n.* a room attached to a synagogue for storing old books, documents etc.
19C. Hebrew, lit. a hiding, from *gānaz* to set aside, to hide.

genre (zhã´rə, zhon´rə) *n.* **1** a kind, sort, class, particularly in the field of the arts. **2** a style, manner, esp. artistic. **3** a type of painting, the subject of which is some scene in everyday life.
19C. French kind, type, from Latin GENUS.

genro (genrō´) *n.pl.* (*Hist.*) elder statesmen in Japan who were on occasion consulted by the Emperor.
19C. Japanese principal elders, from *gen* origin + *rō* old.

gens (jenz) *n.* (*pl.* **gentes** (jen´tēz)) **1** in anthropology, a tribe, clan or group of families. **2** a clan, house, or sept among the ancient Romans or ancient Greeks.
19C. Latin, from base of *gignere* to beget.

gentilhomme (zhãtēyom´) *n.* a Frenchman of aristocratic birth, a French nobleman or squire.
19C. French, from *gentil* gentle + *homme* man. Cp. English *gentleman*.

genus (jē´nəs, je´-) *n.* (*pl.* **genera** (jen´ərə)) **1** (*Biol.*) a class or kind of objects containing several subordinate classes or species. **2** a group or class of plants or animals differentiated from all others by certain common characteristics and comprising one or more species. **3** a kind, group, class, order, family.
16C. Latin birth, family, nation.

georgette (jawjet´) *n.* a plain semi-transparent dress material usually of silk or crêpe.
early 20C. Mme *Georgette* de la Plante, *fl. c.*1900, French dressmaker.

gerah (giə´rə) *n.* the smallest ancient Hebrew weight and coin, equivalent to one twentieth of a shekel.
16C. Hebrew *gērāh*.

gesellschaft (gəzel´shahft) *n.* (*pl.* **gesellschaften** (-tən)) a social group, held together by practical concerns and not by ties of kinship, as distinct from *gemeinschaft*.
19C. German, from *Gesell* companion + *-schaft* -ship.

gesso (jes´ō) *n.* (*pl.* **gessoes**) **1** plaster of Paris used for painting, sometimes for sculpture. **2** a ground made of this.
16C. Italian, from Latin *gypsum* white lime plaster.

gestalt (gəshtalt´) *n.* (*Psych.*) an organized whole in which each part affects every other part.
early 20C. German form, shape.

Gestapo (gəstah´pō) *n.* **1** the body of secret police formed to secure strict obedience to the government of Nazi Germany. **2** (*derog.*) any similar organization.
mid-20C. **German**, acronym of *Geheime Staatspolizei* Secret State Police.

gesundheit (gəzunt´hīt) *int.* your health (said after someone has sneezed).
early 20C. **German** health.

geta (gā´tə) *n.* (*pl.* **geta**, **getas**) a Japanese wooden sandal.
19C. **Japanese**.

gharry (ga´ri), **gharri** *n.* (*pl.* **gharries**, **gharris**) a variety of wheeled carriage in the Indian subcontinent.
19C. **Hindi** *gārī*.

ghat (gaht, gawt), **ghaut** (gawt) *n.* (*Ind.*) **1** a flight of steps descending to a river, a landing-place. **2** a range of mountains. **3** a mountain pass.
17C. **Hindi** *ghāṭ*.

ghazal (gaz´əl) *n.* an Oriental lyric poem, usu. erotic, convivial or religious in subject, having a limited number of couplets, all with the same rhyme.
18C. **Persian**, from Arabic *ġazal*.

Ghazi (gah´zi) *n.* (*pl.* **Ghazis**) a person who has fought for Islam against non-Muslims.
18C. **Arabic** *al-ġāzī*, active part. of *ġazā* to raid, to invade.

ghee (gē), **ghi** *n.* butter, usu. prepared from buffalo-milk, clarified into an oil, which can be kept for a long time.
17C. **Hindi** *ghī*, from Sanskrit *ghṛta*, p.p. of *ghṛ-* to sprinkle.

gherao (gerow´) *n.* (*pl.* **gheraos**) in the Indian subcontinent, a form of industrial action in which a person, e.g. an employer, is imprisoned in a room, building etc. until certain demands are met.
mid-20C. **Hindi** *ghernā* to surround, to besiege.

ghetto (get´ō) *n.* (*pl.* **ghettos**, **ghettoes**) **1** a poor, densely populated area of a city, esp. inhabited by an ethnic minority. **2** the quarter of a town formerly inhabited by Jews. **3** a segregated area, a place apart. **4** a group confined to such an area. ~*v.t.* (*3rd pers. sing. pres.* **ghettoes**, *pres.p.* **ghettoing**, *past*, *p.p.* **ghettoed**) to confine to a ghetto.
17C. **Italian** of uncertain orig. ? Abbr. of *borghetto*, dim. of *borgo* borough, or from *getto* foundry (where first ghetto in Venice was sited, 1516).
• According to some, the word is from Latin *Aegyptus* Egypt.

giaour (jow´ə) *n.* (*derog.*) a non-Muslim, esp. a Christian.
16C. **Turkish** *gâvur*, from Persian *gaur*, var. of *gabr*, prob. from Arabic *kāfir* KAFFIR.

gigolo (jig´əlō, zhig´-) *n.* (*pl.* **gigolos**) **1** a young man paid by an older woman to be a sexual partner or escort. **2** a professional dance partner or escort.
early 20C. **French**, formed as m. of *gigole* dance hall woman. Rel. to English *jig*.

gigot (jig´ət) *n.* a leg of mutton or lamb.
16C. **French**, dim. of dial. *gigue* leg, from *giguer* to hop, to jump. Rel. to English *jig*.

gigue (zhēg) *n.* (*Mus.*) a piece of dance music, usu. in 6/8 time.
17C. **French**, from English *jig*.

gilet (jilā´) *n.* **1** a woman's light sleeveless top resembling a waistcoat. **2** a sleeveless padded jacket.
19C. **French** waistcoat, from Spanish *gileco*, from Spanish Arabic *jalaco*, from Turkish *yelek*.

gilgai (gil´gī) *n.* (*pl.* **gilgais**) in Australia, a saucer-shaped depression containing a pool of water, a water hole.
19C. Australian Aboriginal (Wiradhuri and Kamilaroi) *gilgaay*.

gillie (gil´i), **ghillie** *n.* **1** a man or boy who attends a person fishing or hunting, esp. in the Scottish highlands. **2** (*Hist.*) an attendant on a Highland clan chief.
17C. Gaelic *gille*, rel. to Irish *giolla* lad, servant.
• The Gaelic word is the source of the first syllable of surnames such as *Gillespie*, *Gilmore*, respectively meaning servant of the bishop, servant of (the Virgin) Mary.

ginseng (jin´seng) *n.* **1** any of several herbs belonging to the genus *Panax*, esp. *P. schinseng* of China and *P. quinquefolius* of North America, the root of which has a sharp, aromatic taste, and is highly esteemed as a medicine or tonic by the Chinese and others. **2** this root.
17C. Chinese *rénshēn*, from *rén* man + *shēn* kind of herb.
• The herb has a forked root suggesting a human body and resembling the Chinese ideogram for human being, man.

giocoso (jokō´sō, -zō) *adv., a.* (*Mus.*) (played) in a lively, joking manner.
19C. Italian merry, from Latin *iocosus* humorous.

girandole (jir´əndōl) *n.* **1** a revolving firework discharging rockets. **2** a branching chandelier or candlestick. **3** a rotating jet of water. **4** a pendent jewel, usu. for the ears, with a large set encircled by smaller ones.
17C. French, from Italian *girandola*, from *girare*, from Late Latin *gyrare* to gyrate.

giro (jī´rō) *n.* (*pl.* **giros**) **1** in the UK, a system operated by banks and post offices whereby, when the required instructions have been issued, payments can be made by transfers from one account to another. **2** a giro cheque.
~*v.t.* (*3rd pers. sing. pres.* **giroes**, *pres.p.* **giroing**, *past, p.p.* **giroed**) to pay by giro.
19C. German, from Italian circulation (of money), from Latin *gyrus* circle.

gitano (jitah´nō) *n.* (*pl.* **gitanos**) a male gypsy.
19C. Spanish, alt. of *Egiptano* Egyptian, from Popular Latin *Aegyptanus*.
• Gypsies were formerly believed to have originated in Egypt. Hence also English *gypsy*.

gîte (zhēt) *n.* in France, a privately-owned, self-contained, self-catering apartment or cottage available for holiday lets.
18C. French, from obs. fem. p.p. (used as n.) of *gésir* to lie. Cp. CI-GÎT.
• The original sense was stopping place, lodging. The current sense evolved in the mid-20C.

giusto (joos´tō) *a., adv.* (*Mus.*) (of musical tempo) regular(ly), strict(ly), accurate(ly).
19C. Italian regular, from Latin *iustus* just.

glacé (glas´ā) *a.* **1** (of fruit etc.) preserved in sugar, candied (and usu. glossy). **2** (of leather goods etc.) polished, smooth. **3** iced.
19C. French, p.p. of *glacer* to ice, to give a gloss to, from *glace* ice.
• The sense has apparently been influenced by English *glass*, *gloss*.

glacis (glas´is, -ē, glā´-) *n.* (*pl.* **glacis** (-is, -ēz)) a sloping bank in a fortification, e.g. in front of a rampart, where assailants would be exposed to fire.
17C. French, from Old French *glacier* to slip, to slide, from *glace* ice.

glasnost (glaz´nost, glahs´-) *n.* esp. of the Soviet government of the later 1980s, a willingness to be more open and accountable.
late 20C. Russian *glasnost'* the state of being public, openness, from Old Church Slavonic *glasŭ* voice + Russian *-nost'* -ness.

Gleichschaltung (glīkh´shaltung) *n.* the enforced standardization of political, cultural, economic institutions etc. in authoritarian states.
mid-20C. German coordination, from *gleich* like + *schalten* to govern.

glissade (glisahd´, -sād´) *n.* **1** a method of sliding down a steep snow slope, usu. with an ice axe or alpenstock held as rudder and support. **2** a gliding step in ballet. ~*v.i.* to slide down a steep snow slope using an ice axe etc. for support.
19C. French, from *glisser* to slip, to slide.

glissando (glisan´dō) *a., n.* (*pl.* **glissandos, glissandi** (-dē)) (*Mus.*) (of) an esp. rapid sliding up and down the musical scale.
19C. Italian, from French *glissant*, pres.p. of *glisser* to slip, to slide.

glissé (glē´sā) *n.* (*pl.* **glissés** (glē´sā)) in ballet, a sliding step esp. using the flat of the foot.
early 20C. French, p.p. of *glisser* to slip, to slide.

glockenspiel (glok´ənshpēl) *n.* a musical instrument consisting of hanging metal bars or tubes, to be struck with a hammer.
19C. German bell-play, chimes, from *Glocken* bells + *Spiel* play.

gloria (glaw´riə) *n.* (*pl.* **glorias**)
1 (**Gloria**) **a** a song or versicle of praise, forming part of the English Church service or the Mass, or the music to this, esp. *Gloria in excelsis Deo*. **b** a doxology. **2** a halo. **3** a closely-woven fabric of silk, cotton etc. used for umbrellas.
12–14C. Latin glory.

gloriole (glaw´riōl) *n.* a glory, halo or nimbus.
19C. French, from Latin *gloriola*, dim. of *gloria* glory.

glühwein (gloo´vīn) *n.* hot, spiced sweetened red wine, mulled wine, as prepared in Germany.
19C. German, from *glühen* to mull, to glow + *Wein* wine.

gneiss (nīs) *n.* a laminated metamorphic rock consisting of feldspar, quartz and mica.
18C. German, from Old High German *gneisto* spark, from Germanic.

gnocchi (nok´i, nyok´i) *n.* an Italian dish consisting of small potato or semolina dumplings, served with a sauce or used to garnish soup etc.
19C. Italian, pl. of *gnocco*, from *nocchio* knot (in wood).

gnomon (nō´mon) *n.* **1** a rod, pillar, pin or plate on a sundial, indicating the time of day by its shadow. **2** a vertical pillar used in analagous way for determining the altitude of the sun. **3** the index of the hour-circle of a globe. **4** (*Geom.*) the figure remaining when a parallelogram has been removed from the corner of a larger one of the same form.
16C. French, or from Latin, from Greek *gnōmōn* inspector, indicator, from *gnō-*, base of *gignōskein* to know.

gnosis (nō´sis) *n.* (*pl.* **gnoses** (-sēz))
1 knowledge, esp. of mysteries. **2** gnostic philosophy.
16C. Greek *gnōsis* investigation, knowledge, from *gnō-*, base of *gignōskein* to know.

go (gō) *n.* a Japanese board game for two people, its aim being to capture one's opponent's counters (or stones) in order to occupy a greater amount of the board.
19C. Japanese.

gobang (gōbang´) *n.* a game played on a chequer-board, with 50 coloured counters, the object being to get five into a row.
19C. Japanese *goban* board for playing GO.

gobemouche (gōb´moosh) *n.* (*pl.* **gobemouches** (gōb´moosh)) a gullible, credulous person, someone who will believe anything.
19C. French *gobe-mouches* flycatcher, from *gober* to swallow + *mouche* fly.

godown (gōdown´, gō´-) *n.* an E Asian or Indian warehouse.
16C. Portuguese *gudāo*, from Tamil *kiṭaṅku*, Malayalam *kiṭaṅṅu*, Kannada *gaḍaṅgu* store.

golem (gō´ləm) *n.* in Jewish legend, a figure constructed in the form of a human being and brought to life by supernatural means.
19C. Yiddish *goylem*, from Hebrew *gōlem* shapeless mass.

†Golgotha (gol´gəthə) *n.* a burial place, a charnel house.
17C. Late Latin, from Greek, from Aramaic *gōgolṭâ*, ? influ. by Hebrew *gulgōleṭ*.
● In the New Testament, Golgotha, the site of the crucifixion, is explained as meaning 'place of a skull' (Matt. xxvii.33).

gombeen (gombēn´) *n.* (*Ir.*) usury.
19C. Irish *gaimbín*.

gombroon (gombroon´) *n.* Persian semi-transparent white pottery imitated in Chelsea ware.
17C. *Gambroon* (now Bandar-e ʻAbbās), a seaport in S Iran.

Gomorrah (gəmor´ə) *n.* a dissolute town.
16C. *Gomorrah*, one of five biblical 'cities of the plain', destroyed together with Sodom by 'brimstone and fire' because of their wickedness (Gen. xix.24).

gomuti (gəmoo´ti) *n.* a black hairlike fibre, not decaying in water, obtained from the sago palm, and used for cordage, thatching etc.
19C. Malay *gemuti*.

gondola (gon´dələ) *n.* **1** a long, narrow Venetian boat with peaked ends, propelled by one oar. **2** the car of an airship, balloon, ski lift etc. **3** a free-standing block of shelves used to display goods in a supermarket etc. **4** (*N Am.*) **a** a large, light, flat-bottomed freight-boat. **b** (*also* **gondola car**) a flat railway wagon.
16C. Venetian Italian, from Old Italian *gondula*, of uncertain orig., ? from Greek *kondu* vase, drinking cup.

goonda (goon´də) *n.* a desperado, a hooligan.
early 20C. Hindi *guṇḍā* rascal.

gopak (gō´pak) *n.* a folk dance from Ukraine characterized by high leaps, performed by men.
early 20C. Russian, from Ukrainian *hopak*, from *hop!*, interjection used in lively dances.

Gorsedd (gaw´sedh) *n.* a meeting of bards and Druids in Wales, esp. associated with the eisteddfod.
18C. Welsh mound, throne, assembly.

Goshen (gō´shən) *n.* a land of plenty.
17C. Hebrew, name of the fertile land allotted to the Israelites in Egypt in which 'all the children of Israel had light' (Exod. x.23) during the plague of darkness.

Götterdämmerung (gœtədem´ərung)
n. in German mythology, the final
destruction of the world.
early 20C. German, lit. twilight of the
gods, from *Götter*, pl. of *Gott* god +
Dämmerung twilight, from *dämmern* to
fall (of dusk).
• The term was popularized as the title
of Wagner's opera (1876).

gouache (gooahsh´) *n.* a method of
painting with opaque colours mixed
with water, honey and gum.
19C. French, from Italian *guazzo*, ult.
from Latin *aqua* water.

goujon (goo´zhon) *n.* a small strip of
chicken or fish, usu. deep-fried in a
coating of breadcrumbs etc.
19C. French gudgeon, from Latin *gobius*
goby.

goulash (goo´lash) *n.* **1** a stew of meat
and vegetables highly seasoned with
paprika. **2** in contract bridge, a method
of dealing again with unshuffled cards
in threes and fours, used when no
player has bid on the previous deal.
19C. Hungarian *gulyáshús*, from *gulyás*
herdsman + *hús* meat.
• The stew is so named as it was eaten
by Hungarian cattlemen, shepherds and
pig herders.

gourmand (guə´mənd) *n.* **1** a glutton.
2 (*dated*) a person who loves delicate
fare, a gourmet. ~*a.* gluttonous, fond of
eating.
14–15C. Old French, of unknown orig.
Cp. GOURMET.

gourmet (guə´mā) *n.* a connoisseur of
good food, an epicure. ~*a.* **1** of or
relating to a gourmet. **2** of a standard
considered appropriate to a gourmet.
19C. French, orig. wine-taster, from
Old French *gromme* wine merchant,
of uncertain orig., ? from Old English
*grom manservant, source of English
groom.

goût (goo) *n.* **1** taste, relish. **2** good taste,
artistic discernment.
16C. French, earlier *goust*, from Latin
gustus taste. Cp. GUSTO.

goutte (goot) *n.* a drop of liquid, esp. as a
small drink or dram.
19C. French drop, from Latin *gutta*.

goutte à goutte (goot a goot´) *adv.* drop
by drop.
19C. French, from GOUTTE + *à* by.

goy (goy) *n.* (*pl.* **goyim**, (-im), **goys**) (*sl.*,
offensive) among Jews, a name for a
non-Jewish person.
19C. Hebrew *gōy* people, nation.

graben (grā´bən) *n.* (*Geol.*) an elongated
depression where the earth's surface has
subsided between two fault lines.
19C. German, orig. ditch.

gradatim (grədā´tim) *adv.* gradually, step
by step.
16C. Latin. Cp. LITERATIM, SERIATIM.

gradus (grā´dəs) *n.* (*pl.* **graduses**) a
dictionary of Greek or Latin prosody
formerly used in public schools.
18C. Latin *gradus* step, in *Gradus ad
Parnassum* Step(s) to Parnassus, title of
a manual of Latin prosody (1687).

Graf (grahf) *n.* a German nobleman.
17C. German, ult. from Greek *graphein*
to write, rel. to obs. English *grave*, as in
landgrave, *margrave* etc.
• The title corresponds to English
count.

graffiti (grəfē´ti) *n.pl.* (*sing.* **graffito**
(-tō)) **1** (*pl.*) drawings or words,
sometimes obscene, sometimes political,
painted or written on walls etc. in
public view. **2** (*pl.*) drawings or
inscriptions scratched on an ancient
wall or other surface. **3** a piece of
graffiti. **4** SGRAFFITO.
19C. Italian, pl. of *graffito*, from *graffio*
scratching.

grama (grah´mə), **grama grass** *n.* any of various species of low pasture grass in the W and SW US.
19C. **Spanish** grass.

grand coup (grã koo´) *n.* (*pl.* **grands coups** (grã koo´)) a bold or important stroke.
19C. **French** great stroke.

grand cru (grã krü´, grãd kroo´) *n., a.* (*pl.* **grands crus** (grã krü´), **grand crus** (grãd krooz´)) (a wine) from a top-ranking vineyard.
19C. **French** great growth, from *grand* great + CRU.

grande dame (grã dam´) *n.* (*pl.* **grandes dames** (grã dam´)) **1** an aristocratic lady. **2** a dignified and socially important old lady.
18C. **French** great lady, from fem. of *grand* + *dame* lady.

grande horizontale (grãd orizõtahl´) *n.* (*pl.* **grandes horizontales** (grãd orizõtahl´)) a courtesan or prostitute.
19C. **French**, lit. great horizontal.
• The allusion is to the position assumed.

grandeur (gran´dyə) *n.* **1** the quality of being grand. **2** greatness, nobility, impressiveness, sublimity, majesty. **3** splendour, magnificence, dignity, splendid or magnificent appearance or effect.
16C. **Old French** greatness, from *grand* great.

Grand Guignol (grã gēnyol´) *n.* a theatrical programme consisting of short sensational blood-curdling pieces.
early 20C. **French** Great Punch, name of a theatre in Paris.
• *Guignol* is an alteration of the puppet name *Chignol*, itself so called because its owner came from the village of *Chignolo*. The name is apparently not related to French *guigner* to eye surreptitiously.

grandioso (grandiõ´zō) *adv.* (*Mus.*) in a grand or imposing manner.
19C. **Italian**.

grand mal (grã mal´) *n.* a major epileptic attack, involving severe convulsions and loss of consciousness.
19C. **French**, lit. great sickness, from *grand* great + *mal* sickness. Cp. PETIT MAL.

Grand Marnier® (grã mah´niā) *n.* a French liqueur with an orange flavour, based on brandy.
early 20C. **French**, from *grand* great, fine + *Marnier*-Lapostolle, name of orig. manufacturer.

Grand Prix (grã prē´) *n.* (*pl.* **Grands Prix** (grã prē´)) **1** any of several international motor or motorcycle races taking place annually in locations round the world. **2** any of various other major international competitive events, e.g. in horse racing.
19C. **French** great prize, from *grand* great + *prix* prize.

grand seigneur (grã senyœ´) *n.* (*pl.* **grands seigneurs** (grã senyœ´)) **1** a person of high rank. **2** a noble gentleman.
17C. **French** great lord, from *grand* great + SEIGNEUR.

grand siècle (grã syekl´, syek´lə) *n.* the golden age, esp. the 17th cent. in France.
19C. **French** great century, great age, from *grand* great + *siècle* century, age.

granita (granē´tə) *n.* (*pl.* **granite** (granē´ti, -tā)) a flavoured water ice with a grainy texture.
19C. **Italian**, fem. of *granito* grainy.

Granth (grŭnt), **Granth Sahib** (sah´hib) *n.* the sacred scriptures of the Sikhs.
18C. **Sanskrit** *grantha* tying, literary composition, from *granth* to tie.

grappa (grap´ə) *n.* a coarse Italian brandy distilled from the residue of a wine press.
19C. Italian, from Italian dial. grape stalk.

gratin (grat´ĭ) *n.* **1** in cookery, a light crust on a dish, usu. made by browning breadcrumbs and cheese. **2** a dish prepared in this way with breadcrumbs and grated cheese.
17C. French, from *gratter*, earlier *grater* to grate. Cp. AU GRATIN.

gratis (grat´is, grā´-) *adv.* for nothing, without charge, free. ~*a.* available without payment or charge, costing nothing.
14–15C. Latin, contr. of *gratiis* out of kindness, abl. pl. of *gratia* grace, favour.

graupel (grow´pəl) *n.* soft hail, snow pellets.
19C. German, dim. of *Graupe* peeled grain, prob. from Slavonic. Cp. Russian *krupa* peeled grain.

gravamen (grəvā´men) *n.* (*pl.* **gravamens, gravamina** (-minə)) **1** the most serious part of a charge. **2** (*Law*) the part of an action which weighs most heavily against the defendant.
17C. Ecclesiastical Latin physical inconvenience, from Latin *gravare* to weigh on, to oppress, from *gravis* heavy, serious.

Graves (grahv) *n.* a light usu. white wine, pressed in the Graves district.
17C. *Graves*, a district of SW France.

grazioso (gratsiō´sō, -zō) *a.* (*Mus.*) graceful, elegant.
19C. Italian graceful, gracious.

grecque (grek) *n.* **1** (*Archit.*) an ornamental Greek fret. **2** a coffee-strainer or a coffee-pot fitted with a strainer.
19C. French, fem. of *grec* Greek.

greige (grāzh), **grège** (grezh) *a.* of a colour midway between grey and beige.
early 20C. French *grège* in *soie grège* raw silk, from Italian *greggio* raw, crude, unprocessed.

grenadine (gren´ədēn) *n.* a pomegranate syrup.
19C. French (*sirop de*) *grenadine*, from *grenade* pomegranate.

greywacke (grā´wakə), (*N Am.*) **graywacke** *n.* (*Geol.*) a gritstone or conglomerate, usu. consisting of small fragments of quartz, flinty slate etc. cemented together, occurring chiefly in Silurian strata.
18C. German *Grauwacke*, from *grau* grey + WACKE.

grillade (grilād´, grēyahd´) *n.* a grilled dish.
17C. French, from *griller* to grill.

grillage (gril´ij) *n.* a structure of sleepers and cross-beams forming a foundation in marshy soil for a pier, wharf or the like.
18C. French grating.

gringo (gring´gō) *n.* (*pl.* **gringos**) (*esp. N Am., derog.*) an English-speaking foreigner.
15C. Spanish foreign, foreigner, gibberish, of uncertain orig. ? From *griego* Greek (in sense gibberish).

grisaille (grizāl´, -zī´) *n.* a style of painting or staining in grey monochrome, esp. on stained glass, representing solid bodies in relief, such as ornament of cornices etc.
19C. French, from *gris* grey.

grisette (grizet´) *n.* **1** a lively and attractive girl or young woman of the French working classes. **2** †a grey woollen fabric, used for dresses by women of the working classes.
18C. French, from *gris* grey.
● The name refers to the cheap grey

dress fabric formerly worn by French working girls.

groschen (grō´shən) n. **1** an Austrian coin worth one hundredth of a schilling. **2** (coll.) a German 10-pfennig piece. **3** an old German silver coin.
17C. German, from Middle High German gros, from Medieval Latin denarius grossus thick penny.

grosgrain (grō´grān) n. a heavy ribbed silk, rayon etc. fabric or ribbon.
19C. French course grain, from gros large, coarse + grain grain.
● The French word is the source of English grogram.

gros point (grō pwī´) n. a stitch in embroidery covering two horizontal and two vertical threads.
19C. French large stitch, from gros large + point stitch. Cp. PETIT POINT.

Gruyère (groo´yeə, grē´-) n. a Swiss or French cheese made from cows' milk, pale-coloured, firm and full of cavities.
19C. Gruyère, a town in Switzerland.

GT n. a touring car, usu. a fast sports car. Abbr. of **Italian** gran turismo, lit. grand touring.
● The Italian phrase dates from the mid-20C.

guacamole (gwahkəmō´li) n. a Mexican dish of mashed avocado, citrus juice and seasonings.
early 20C. American Spanish, from Nahuatl ahuacamolli, from ahuacatl avocado + molli sauce.

guano (gwah´nō) n. (pl. **guanos**) **1** a valuable manure, composed chiefly of the excrement of seabirds found esp. on islands off South America and in the Pacific. **2** an artificial manure, esp. fish manure. ~v.t. (3rd pers. sing. pres. **guanoes**, pres.p. **guanoing**, past, p.p. **guanoed**) to manure or fertilize with guano.

17C. Spanish, or from American Spanish huano, from Quechua huanu dung.

guardia civil (gwahdia thibil´, sibil´) n. (pl. **guardias civiles** (gwahdias thibil´es, sibil´es)) the Spainsh police force.
19C. Spanish civil guard. Cp. GARDA.

guéridon (ger´idən, geridō´) n. a small ornamental table or stand, usu. with a central pedestal and ornately carved.
19C. French, name of a character in a 17C farce.
● The character held a candelabra while others danced round it.

guerite (gārēt´) n. (Mil.) a small loopholed tower, usu. on the point of a bastion, to hold a sentinel.
18C. French guérite sentry-box.

guerrilla (gəril´ə), **guerilla** n. a member of a small independent fighting band carrying out irregular warfare, esp. against an army, and usu. politically motivated.
19C. Spanish, dim. of guerra war.
● The word was introduced to English during the Peninsular War (1808–14).

guichet (gē´shā) n. a hatch, esp. one through which tickets are sold, as at a station, stadium etc.
19C. French wicket, from Old Scandinavian source of English wicket.

guilloche (gilōsh´) n. an ornament of intertwisted or interlaced bands.
19C. French guillochis guilloche, or guilloche the tool used in making it.

guillotine (gil´ətēn) n. **1** an apparatus for beheading a person at a stroke, consisting of an upright frame, down which a weighted blade slides in grooves. **2** a machine for cutting thicknesses of paper etc. **3** a surgical

instrument for cutting tonsils etc. **4** in
Parliament, the curtailment of debate by
fixing beforehand the hours when parts
of a bill must be voted on. ~*v.t.* **1** to
execute by guillotine. **2** to cut with a
guillotine.
18C. French, from Joseph-Ignace
Guillotin, 1738–1814, French physician,
who recommended it for executions in
1789.

guimpe (gimp, gīp), **guimp** *n.* a high-
necked chemisette, a blouse designed
for wearing under a low-necked dress.
19C. French, from Germanic source of
English *wimple*.

guipure (gipūə´) *n.* **1** a lace without a
ground or mesh, the pattern being held
in place by threads. **2** a kind of gimp.
19C. French, from *guiper* to cover with
silk, wool, etc, from Frankish v.
meaning to wind round.

gulag (goo´lag) *n.* the system of forced
labour camps in the former Soviet
Union, esp. as used to correct dissidents.
20C. Russian acronym, from *G*lavnoe
*u*pravlenie ispravitel'no-trudovykh
*lag*ereĭ Chief Administration for
Corrective Labour Camps.
● The camps were first made generally
known by Aleksandr Solzhenitsyň's
account, *The Gulag Archipelago*
(Russian *Arkhipelag Gulag*) (1973–76).

gulden (gul´dən) *n.* **1** any of various gold
coins of Germany or the Netherlands.
2 a silver coin, the florin of Austria and
Hungary, and the guilder of Holland.
15C. Dutch and German, use as n. of a.
corr. to obs. *gilden* (see GULDEN).

gung-ho (gŭnghō´) *a.* **1** uninhibited,
over-eager. **2** enthusiastic.
mid-20C. Chinese *gōnghé* to cooperate,
from *gōng* work + *hé* to join, to
combine.

● The term was adopted as a slogan by
US marines in World War II.

gunny (gŭn´i) *n.* (*pl.* **gunnies**) **1** a heavy
coarse sackcloth, usu. of jute or hemp,
of which bags etc. are made. **2** a bag
made of this.
18C. Marathi *gōnī*, from Sanskrit *goṇī*
sack.

gunyah (gŭn´yah) *n.* an Aboriginal bush
hut, usu. built of twigs and bark.
19C. Australian Aboriginal (Dharuk)
ganyi.

gurdwara (guə´dwahrə, gœdwah´ra) *n.*
a Sikh temple.
early 20C. Panjabi *gurduārā*, from
Sanskrit GURU + *dvāra* door.

guru (gur´oo) *n.* **1** a Hindu spiritual
teacher or guide. **2** a mentor with
particular expertise or knowledge.
17C. Sanskrit elder, teacher.

gusto (gŭs´tō) *n.* **1** zest, enjoyment,
pleasure. **2** flavour, relish.
17C. Italian, from Latin *gustus* taste.
Cp. GOÛT.

gutta-percha (gŭtəpœ´chə) *n.* a tough,
waterproof rubber substance obtained
from the latex of various Malaysian
trees.
19C. Malay *getah perca*, from *getah*
gum + *perca* strips of cloth (which it
resembles).

gymkhana (jimkah´nə) *n.* a meeting for
equestrian sports and games, orig. a
place for athletic sports.
19C. Alt. (by assim. to English
gymnasium) of **Urdu** *gendḵānah* racket
court, from Hindi *gēdṁ* ball + Persian
ḵānah house.

gyttja (yich´ə) *n.* (*Geol.*) a usu. black
organic sediment deposited in a lake.
19C. Swedish mud, ooze.

H

haaf (hahf) *n.* a deep-sea fishing ground (off Orkney and Shetland).
18C. **Old Norse** *haf* sea, ocean.

habanera (habəneəˊrə) *n.* **1** a Cuban dance in slow duple time. **2** the music for this dance.
19C. **Spanish**, short for *danza habanera* Havanan dance, fem. of *habanero* of Havana, the capital of Cuba.

habeas corpus (hābiəs kawˊpəs) *n.* (*Law*) a writ to produce a prisoner before a court, with details of the day and cause of the arrest and detention, in order that the justice of this may be determined.
14–15C. **Latin** thou (shalt) have the body, 2nd pers. sing. pres. subj. of *habere* to have + acc. sing. of *corpus* body.
• The fuller version of the formula is *habeas corpus ad subiiciendum* thou (shalt) have the body to be subjected (to examination).

habitat (habˊitat) *n.* **1** the natural home or locality of an animal or plant. **2** the place where a person or group is at home or usually found.
18C. **Latin**, lit. it inhabits, 3rd pers. sing. pres. indic. of *habitare* to dwell in.
• The term evolved from the first word of Latin descriptions in Floras and Faunas, such as (of the primrose): *Habitat in silvis sepibus et ericetis ubique* It is found in woods, hedges and heaths everywhere (William Hudson *Flora Anglica*, 1762).

habitué (həbitˊūā) *n.* a person who habitually frequents a place, esp. a place of amusement.
19C. **French**, p.p. of *habituer*, from Latin *habituare*, from *habitus* habit.

háček (hahˊchek) *n.* a diacritical mark (ˇ) placed above a letter to modify its pronunciation, esp. in Slavonic languages.
mid-20C. **Czech**, dim. of *hák* hook.

hacienda (hasienˊdə) *n.* **1** in Spain, Latin America etc., an estate, a farm or plantation, an establishment in the country for stock-raising etc., esp. with a residence for the proprietor. **2 a** (Spanish or Latin American) factory.
18C. **Spanish**, from Latin *facienda* things to be done, from *facere* to do.

Hadith (hadˊith) *n.* tradition, esp. the body of tradition relating to the sayings and doings of Muhammad.
18C. **Arabic** *ḥadīṯ* statement, tradition.

hadj (haj), **hajj**, **haj** *n.* (*pl.* **hadjes**, **hajjes**, **hajes**) a pilgrimage to Mecca.
18C. **Arabic** pilgrimage.

hadji (haj´i), **hajji**, **haji** *n.* (*pl.* **hadjis, hajjis, hajis**) (a title conferred on) a Muslim who has performed the pilgrimage to Mecca.
17C. Persian, from Turkish *ḥājjī* pilgrim, from Arabic *al-ḥajj* the HADJ.

haeremai (hī´rəmī), **haere mai** *int.* (*New Zeal.*) welcome!
18C. Maori, lit. come hither.

hafiz (hah´fiz) *n.* (a Muslim title for) a person knowing the Koran by heart.
17C. Persian, from Arabic *ḥāfiẓ*, pres.p. of *ḥāfiẓa* to guard, to know by heart.

Haggadah (həgah´də) *n.* **1** the legendary part of the Talmud. **2** a book recited at Seder.
18C. Hebrew *Haggāḏāh* tale, from biblical Hebrew *higgīḏ* to declare, to tell.

haiduk (hī´duk), **heyduck** *n.* a member of a class of mercenaries in Hungary who were granted lands and the rank of nobles in 1605.
17C. Czech, Polish and Serbo-Croat *hajduk*, from Hungarian *hajdú* robber, pl. *hajdúk*.

haik (hīk, hāk), **haick** *n.* a strip of woollen or cotton cloth worn as an upper garment by Arabs over the head and body.
18C. Arabic *ḥā'ik*.

haiku (hī´koo) *n.* (*pl.* **haiku**) **1** a Japanese verse of 17 syllables, in three parts. **2** an imitation of this in English etc.
19C. Japanese, abbr. of *haikai no ku* unserious verse.

haka (hah´kə) *n.* **1** a ceremonial Maori dance. **2** a similar display by a New Zealand rugby team before a match.
19C. Maori.

hakenkreuz (hah´kənkroits) *n.* the swastika, the Nazi symbol.

mid-20C. German, from *Haken* hook + *Kreuz* cross. Cp. SWASTIKA.

hakim¹ (həkēm´), **hakeem** *n.* (in Muslim countries) a physician.
17C. Arabic *ḥakīm* wise man, philosopher, physician. Cp. HAKIM².

hakim² (hah´kim) *n.* **1** (in Muslim countries) a governor. **2** a judge.
17C. Arabic *ḥakīm* ruler, governor, judge, from *ḥakama* to pass judgement.

Halachah (hələh´kə, halahkhah´), **Halakah** (-k-) *n.* a body of traditional laws, supposed to be of Mosaic origin, included in the Mishna.
19C. Hebrew *hălākāh* law.

halal (həlahl´) *n.* meat which is prepared in accordance with Muslim law. ~*v.t.* (*pres.p.* **halalling**, *past, p.p.* **halalled**) to prepare (meat) in this way. ~*a.* (of meat) prepared in this way.
19C. Arabic *ḥalāl* according to religious law.

haler (hah´lə) *n.* (*pl.* **haler, halers, haleru** (hah´ləroo)) a unit of currency of the Czech Republic.
mid-20C. Czech *haléř*, from Middle High German *haller*, from (*Schwäbisch*) *Hall*, town in Germany where the *haller* was first minted.

Hallstatt (hal´stat, -shtat), **Hallstattian** (-iən) *a.* denoting the first period of the Iron Age, typified by weapons found in the necropolis of Hallstatt which illustrate the transition from the use of bronze to that of iron.
19C. *Hallstatt*, a village in Upper Austria, the site of a prehistoric burial ground.
● More than 2000 graves were found at Hallstatt between 1846 and 1899.

halma (hal´mə) *n.* a game for two to four played on a board with 256 squares.
19C. Greek leap.
● Pieces advance on the board by moving over ('leaping') other pieces. The game was invented *c.*1880.

halva (hal´və, -vah), **halvah** n. a sweet made from sesame seeds and honey, typically from the E Mediterranean.
17C. **Yiddish**, also mod. Hebrew *ḥalḇāh*, mod. Greek *khalbas*, Turkish *helva* etc., from Arabic and Persian *halwā* sweetmeat.

hamartia (həmah´tiə) n. the tragic flaw which destroys the principal character in a Greek tragedy.
18C. **Greek** fault, failure, guilt.

hamba (ham´bə) int. (S Afr., offensive) go away.
19C. **Nguni**, imper. of *ukuhamba* to go.

hamburger (ham´bœgə) n. a flat cake of minced beef, fried or grilled and often served in a bun.
19C. German of *Hamburg*, a city in N Germany.
● A hamburger was originally a type of German sausage, named after the city where it was first made.

hammal (həmahl´) n. 1 an Oriental porter. 2 a palanquin-bearer.
18C. **Arabic** *ḥammāl*, from *ḥamala* to carry.

hammam (həmahm´) n. 1 an Oriental bathhouse. 2 a Turkish bath.
17C. **Turkish**, from Arabic *ḥammām* bath, from *ḥamma* to heat.

hamza (ham´zə), **hamzah** n. the sign used for a glottal stop in Arabic script.
19C. **Arabic**, lit. compression (i.e. of the larynx).

Hanukkah (han´əkə, -nukə), **Chanukah, Chanukkah** n. the Jewish festival of lights in commemoration of the rededication of the temple (165 BC).
19C. **Hebrew** *ḥănukkāh* consecration.

hapax legomenon (hapaks ligom´inon) n. (pl. **hapax legomena** (-minə)) a word or expression that has only been used once; a nonce-word.

17C. **Greek** (thing) said only once, from *hapax* once + *legomenon* said, from *legein* to say.

happi (hap´i) n. (pl. **happis**) a loose casual coat worn in Japan.
19C. **Japanese** *happi* kind of coat formerly worn by the followers of nobles.

hara-kiri (harəkē´ri, -kir´-), **hari-kari** (harikar´i) n. a Japanese method of suicide by disembowelling.
19C. **Japanese**, from *hara* belly + *kiri* cutting.
● *Hara-kiri* was long popularly understood to mean happy dispatch, a misinterpretation that may have arisen as a joke. Cp. SEPPUKU.

Hare Krishna (hari krish´nə, hahrā) n. 1 a sect devoted to the Hindu god Krishna. 2 a member of this sect.
late 20C. *Hare Krishna*, words of a Sanskrit devotional chant, from **Hindi** *hare Krishnā* O Lord Krishna.

harem (heə´rəm, hah´rēm, -rēm´), **hareem** (hah´rēm, -rēm´) n. 1 the apartments reserved for the women in a Muslim household. 2 the occupants of these. 3 a group of female animals that share the same mate.
17C. **Turkish**, from Arabic *ḥaram* (that which is) prohibited, (hence) inviolable place, sanctuary, women's apartments, wives, women, from *ḥarama* to be prohibited.

haricot (har´ikō) n. the kidney or French bean, often dried.
17C. **French**, prob. from Aztec *ayacotli*.

Harijan (hŭr´ijən, har´-) n. a member of a class of people in India, formerly known as the 'untouchables'.
mid-20C. **Sanskrit** *harijana* person devoted to the Hindi god Vishnu, from *Hari* Vishnu + *jana* person.

harmattan (hahmat´ən) *n.* a dry hot wind blowing from the interior of Africa to the west coast in December, January and February.
17C. **Twi** *haramata.*

hartal (hah´təl) *n.* (*Ind.*) a boycott or protest carried out by closing shops.
early 20C. **Hindi** *haṛtāl,* var. of *haṭṭāl,* lit. locking of shops, from Sanskrit *haṭṭa* shop + *tāla* lock.

haruspex (hərŭs´peks) *n.* (*pl.* **haruspices** (-pisēz)) an ancient Etruscan or Roman soothsayer who divined the will of the gods by inspecting the entrails of victims.
15C. **Latin,** from base seen in Sanskrit *hirā* artery + Latin *-spex,* from *specere* to look at.

hashish (hash´ēsh), **hasheesh** *n.* the tender tops and sprouts of the Indian hemp, *Cannabis indica,* used as a narcotic for smoking, chewing etc.
16C. **Arabic** *ḥašīš* dry herb, hay, powdered hemp leaves.

Hasid (has´id) *n.* (*pl.* **Hasidim** (-im)) a member of any of several mystical Jewish sects.
19C. **Hebrew** *ḥāsīḏ* pious, pietist.

hasta la vista (asta la vis´ta) *int.* goodbye, see you soon.
mid-20C. **Spanish,** lit. until the seeing. Cp. ARRIVEDERCI, AUF WIEDERSEHEN, AU REVOIR.

hatha yoga (hathə yō´gə) *n.* a form of yoga involving physical exercises and breathing control.
early 20C. **Sanskrit,** from *haṭha* force + YOGA.

hausfrau (hows´frow) *n.* a German housewife.
18C. **German,** from *Haus* house + *Frau* wife, woman.

haute bourgeoisie (ōt buəzhwahzē´) *n.* the upper middle class.
19C. **French,** lit. high bourgeoisie. See BOURGEOIS.

haute couture (ōt kutūə´, -tuə´) *n.*
1 the designing and making of exclusive trend-setting fashions. **2** the designers and houses creating such fashions.
early 20C. **French,** lit. high dressmaking, from fem. of *haut* high + COUTURE.

haute cuisine (ōt kwizēn´) *n.* cooking of a very high standard.
early 20C. **French,** lit. high cooking, from fem. of *haut* high + CUISINE.

haute école (ōt ākōl´) *n.* **1** difficult feats of horsemanship. **2** a method of teaching these.
19C. **French,** lit. high school, from fem. of *haut* high + *école* school.

haute époque (ōt epok´) *n.* the architecture and furniture of the reigns of Louis XIV, XV and XVI of France (1643–1793).
early 20C. **French,** lit. high period.

hauteur (ōtœ´) *n.* haughtiness, lofty manners or demeanour.
17C. **French** height, from *haut* high.

haut monde (ō mōd´) *n.* high society.
19C. **French,** lit. high world, from *haut* high + *monde* world. Cp. BEAU MONDE.

haut-relief (ōrilēf´) *n.* **1** high relief. **2** carving in high relief.
19C. **French,** lit. high relief, from *haut* + *relief* relief. Cp. ALTO-RELIEVO.

havildar (hav´ildah) *n.* a sergeant of an Indian regiment of infantry.
17C. **Urdu** *hawildār,* from Persian *ḥawāldār* charge holder, from *ḥawāl,* from Arabic *ḥawāl* charge, assignment + Persian *-dār* holding, holder.

Hegira (hej´irə), **Hejira, Hijra** (hij´rə) *n.*
1 the flight of Muhammad from Mecca to Medina, in AD 622, from which the Muslim era is computed. **2** a hurried escape from a dangerous situation.
16C. Medieval Latin, from Arabic *hijra* departure from one's home and friends, from *hajara* to separate, to emigrate.
● The abbreviation AH (*anno Hegirae*) is used in Islamic dates.

hegumen (higū´mən), **hegumenos** (-minōs) *n.* the head of a monastery in the Greek Church.
17C. Late Latin *hegumenus*, from Greek *hēgoumenos*, pres.p. (used as n.) of *hēgeisthai* to lead, to command.

Heimweh (hīm´vā) *n.* homesickness.
18C. German, from *Heim* home + *Weh*, lit. woe.

hei-tiki (hātik´i) *n.* (*New Zeal.*) a neck decoration made of greenstone.
19C. Maori, from *hei* to hang + TIKI.

Heldentenor (hel´dəntenə) *n.* (*pl.* **Heldentenors, Heldentenöre** (-nœ´rə)) (a singer with) a strong tenor voice, suitable for Wagnerian roles.
early 20C. German hero tenor, from *Held* hero + *Tenor* tenor.

hendiadys (hendī´ədis) *n.* a rhetorical figure representing one idea by two words connected by a conjunction rather than with subordination, e.g. 'go and find' rather than 'go to find'.
16C. Medieval Latin, from Greek *hen dia duoin* one through two.

heroin (her´ōin) *n.* a derivative of morphine, used in medicine and by drug addicts.
19C. German *Heroin*.
● The drug is so called from the effect on the user's self-esteem.

Herr (heə) *n.* (*pl.* **Herren** (her´ən)) **1** the German title corresponding to the English Mr. **2** a German man.
17C. German, from Old High German *hērro*, comp. of *hēr* exalted.

Herrenvolk (her´ənfolk) *n.* **1** the supposed Aryan race as conceived by Nazi ideology as a master race. **2** a group regarding itself as naturally superior.
mid-20C. German master race, from HERR + *Volk* race.

Herrnhuter (heən´hootə) *n.* a Moravian, a member of the sect calling themselves the United Brethren.
18C. German *Herrnhut* (the Lord's keeping), name of the first settlement of the Moravian Church.
● A group of the earlier Bohemian Brethren fled Moravia in 1722 and settled on the estate of Count Nikolaus Ludwig von Zinzendorf in Saxony, naming their new settlement *Herrnhut*.

Heshvan (hesh´vahn), **Hesvan** (hes´-) *n.* the second month of the Jewish civil year and the eighth month of the Jewish ecclesiastical year.
19C. Hebrew *ḥešwān*, from earlier *marḥešwān*, from Akkadian *araḥ samna* eighth month.

hetaera (hitiə´rə), **hetaira** (-ī´rə) *n.* (*pl.* **hetaeras, hetaerae** (-rē), **hetairas, hetairai** (-rī)) one of a class of highly educated courtesans in ancient Greece.
19C. Greek *hetaira*, fem. of *hetairos* companion.

hetman (het´mən) *n.* (*pl.* **hetmans, hetmen**) a commander or leader of Cossacks or Poles.
20C. Polish, ? from German *Hauptmann* (earlier *Heubtman*) headman, captain.
Cp. ATAMAN.

hexaemeron (heksəē´məron) *n.* **1** a period of six days, esp. the six days of the Creation in the biblical account. **2** a history of this period.

16C. Ecclesiastical Latin, from Greek use as n. of a. *hexaēmeros*, from *hex* six + *hēmera* day.

hexapla (hek´səplə) *n.* an edition of a book, esp. of the Bible, having six versions in parallel columns.
17C. Greek (*ta*) *hexapla* (the) sixfold (texts), neut. pl. of *hexaplous* sixfold.
● *Hexapla* was the title of Origen's edition of the Old Testament published in this form (3C AD).

Hezbollah (hezbol´ə, hezbolah´) *n.* an extremist Shiite Muslim group.
late 20C. Arabic *ḥizbullāh* party of God, from *ḥezb* party + ALLAH.
● The Hezbollah was created after the Iranian revolution of 1979.

hiatus (hīā´təs) *n.* (*pl.* **hiatuses**) **1** a gap, a break, a lacuna in a manuscript, connected series etc. **2** (*Gram.*) the coming together of two vowels in successive syllables or words. **3** a break or interruption in an activity.
16C. Latin gaping, opening, from *hiare* to gape.

hibachi (hibach´i, hib´əchi) *n.* **1** a large earthenware pan or brazier for heating. **2** a type of cooking apparatus similar to a barbecue.
19C. Japanese, from *hi* fire + *hachi* bowl, pot.

hic jacet (hik yak´et) *n.* an epitaph.
17C. Latin here lies, first two words of a Latin epitaph, from *hic* here + 3rd pers. sing. pres. of *iacere* to lie. Cp. CI-GÎT.

hidalgo (hidal´gō) *n.* (*pl.* **hidalgos**) a Spanish nobleman of the lowest class, a gentleman by birth.
16C. Spanish, formerly also *hijo dalgo*, contr. of *hijo de algo*, lit. son of something.

hin (hin) *n.* a Hebrew measure for liquids, equal to twelve pints or 3.5 litres.
14–15C. Biblical Hebrew *hīn*.

hinterland (hin´təland) *n.* **1** the region situated behind something, esp. a coast or the shore of a river. **2** the remote or underdeveloped areas of a country. **3** an area located near and dependent on a large city, esp. a port.
19C. German, from *hinter* behind + *Land* land.

hiragana (hērəgah´nə) *n.* the cursive form of Japanese syllabic writing.
19C. Japanese, from *hira* plain + KANA. Cp. KATAKANA.

hoi polloi (hoi pəloi´) *n.* (*often derog.*) **1** the common herd, the masses. **2** the majority.
17C. Greek the many, from *hoi*, pl. of *ho* the + *polloi* many, pl. of *polus* much.
● To speak of 'the hoi polloi' is strictly speaking a tautology as Greek *hoi* means 'the'.

holla (hol´ə) *int.* used to call attention. ~*n.* a call of 'holla!'. ~*v.i.* (*3rd pers. sing. pres.* **hollas**, *pres.p.* **hollaing**, *past, p.p.* **hollaed, holla'd**) to shout to call attention. ~*v.t.* to call to (hounds).
16C. French *holà*, from *ho* + *là* there.
● The original sense was stop!, cease!

hollandaise (holəndāz´) *n.* a sauce made with butter, egg yolk and lemon juice etc. often served with fish.
19C. French, fem. of *hollandais* Dutch, from *Hollande* Holland.

hombre (om´brā) *n.* (*N Am., sl.*) man.
19C. Spanish man, from Latin *homo*, *hominis* human being.

homer (hō´mə) *n.* **1** a Hebrew liquid measure of 75⅜ gallons (343.8 litres). **2** a Hebrew dry measure of 11⅜ bushels (four hectolitres).
16C. Hebrew *hōmer*, lit. heap.
● 'The seed of an homer shall yield an ephah' (Isa. v.10).

homme d'affaires (om dafeə´) *n.*
(*pl.* **hommes d'affaires** (om)) a
businessman or agent.
18C. French, lit. man of business.

homme moyen sensuel (om mwayã
sãsüel´) *n.* the average man, the man in
the street.
early 20C. French, lit. average sensual
man.
● The French expression implies a
person with normal appetites and
desires, neither an intellectual on the
one hand nor an idiot on the other.

homo homini lupus (homō homini
loop´əs) *int.* the contention that humans
are by their nature aggressive and
hostile towards each other.
19C. Latin, lit. man is a wolf to man,
from *homo* man + *lupus* wolf + dat.
sing. of *homo*.
● The phrase ultimately derives from
Plautus: *Lupus est homo homini, non
homo* 'A man is a wolf rather than a
man to another man' (*Asinaria*, 2C BC).

Homo sapiens (hō´mō sap´ienz) *n.* man
as a species.
19C. Modern Latin, lit. wise man.
● The term was introduced by Linnaeus
in his *Systema Naturae* (1758).

honcho (hon´chō) *n.* (*pl.* **honchos**)
(*N Am., sl.*) **1** a boss, leader or manager.
2 an important or able man. ~*v.t.* (*3rd
pers. sing. pres.* **honchoes**, *pres.p.*
honchoing, *past, p.p.* **honchoed**) to
be in charge of, to oversee.
mid-20C. Japanese *hanchō* group leader.

hong (hong) *n.* in China, a foreign factory,
warehouse or other mercantile
establishment.
18C. Chinese *háng* row, trade.

honi soit qui mal y pense (oni swah
kē mal ē pãs´) *int.* shame to him who
thinks evil of it (the motto of the Order
of the Garter).

16C. Obsolete French.
● The phrase was first used by Edward
III on 23 April 1348 or 1349. According
to a picturesque legend, the words
commemorate an occasion when
Edward was dancing with Joan of Kent,
Countess of Salisbury, when one of her
garters dropped to the floor. The King
gallantly picked it up and put it on his
own leg, admonishing the sniggering
courtiers with the phrase, now often
popularly rendered as 'Evil be to him
who evil thinks'.

honnête homme (onet om´) *n.* a
decent, sophisticated man of the world;
a gentleman.
17C. French honest man, from *honnête*
decent, honest + *homme* man.

honorarium (onəreə´riəm) *n.* (*pl.*
honorariums, honoraria (-riə)) a fee
or payment for the services of a
professional person.
17C. Latin gift made on being admitted
to a post of honour, use as n. of neut. of
honorarius honorary.

honoris causa (onawris kow´zə),
honoris gratia (grā´shə) *adv.* (esp. of an
honorary degree) as a token of esteem.
17C. Latin for the sake of honour, from
honoris, gen. of *honor* honour + abl. of
causa sake, cause.

hookah (huk´ə), **hooka** *n.* a tobacco
pipe in which the smoke passes through
water.
18C. Urdu, from Arabic *ḥuḳḳa* small
box, container, jar.

Hoolee (hoo´li) *n.* the great Hindu
festival in honour of Krishna.
17C. Hindi *holī*.

hoplite (hop´līt) *n.* in ancient Greece, a
heavily-armed soldier.
18C. Greek *hoplitēs*, from *hoplon*
weapon, *hopla* arms.

hornblende (hawn'blend) *n.* a dark-coloured mineral consisting of silica, magnesia, lime and iron.
18C. **German**, from *Horn* horn + *Blende* blende, lit. deceit.
• Blende, or sphalerite, was so called because it resembled galena but yielded no lead.

hornfels (hawn'felz) *n.* a compact rock formed by the action of heat on clay rocks.
19C. **German** horn rock, from *Horn* horn + *Fels* rock.

hornito (hawnē'tō) *n.* (*pl.* **hornitos**) a small smoking mound or fumarole produced by volcanic action.
19C. **American Spanish**, dim. of *horno* (from Latin *furnus*) oven, furnace.

horribile dictu (horibilā dik'too) *adv.* horrible to relate.
19C. **Modern Latin**.
• The phrase is based on MIRABILE DICTU.

hors (aw) *prep.* out of, beyond.
18C. **French** out of, outside, var. of *fors*, from Latin *foris* outside.

hors concours (aw kõ'kuə) *a.* 1 (*fig.*) unrivalled. 2 not in competition.
19C. **French** out of (the) competition.
• The phrase also has both senses in contemporary French.

hors de combat (aw də kõ'bah) *a.* out of the battle or the running.
18C. **French** out of the fight.

hors d'oeuvre (aw dœ'vrə) *n.* (*pl.* **hors d'oeuvres** (dœ'vrə, dœ'vrəz)) a dish not forming part of the main meal, served as an appetizer before or sometimes during a meal.
18C. **French**, lit. outside the work.
• The 'work' is the main meal.

horst (hawst) *n.* (*Geol.*) a raised block of land separated by faults from the surrounding land.
19C. **German** heap, mass.

hors texte (aw tekst') *n.* an illustration on a separate leaf tipped into a book.
early 20C. **French** outside (the) text.
• The illustration is not an integral part of the text.

hortus siccus (hawtəs sik'əs) *n.* 1 a collection of dried plants arranged systematically; a herbarium. 2 a collection of uninteresting facts.
17C. **Latin** dry garden, from *hortus* garden + *siccus* dry.

hosanna (hōzan'ə) *n., int.* 1 an acclamatory prayer for blessing. 2 a shout of praise and adoration.
pre-1200. **Ecclesiastical Latin** *osanna*, from Greek *hōsanna*, from Rabbinical Hebrew *hōša'nā*, abbr. of biblical *hōšī'ā-nnā* save, (we) pray (Ps. cxviii.25).

hospitium (hospish'iəm) *n.* (*pl.* **hospitia** (-shiə)) a hospice.
17C. **Latin** hospitality, lodgings, from *hospes, hospitis* guest.

hospodar (hos'pədah) *n.* (*Hist.*) a prince or governor of Wallachia and Moldavia under the Ottomans.
16C. **Romanian** *hospodár*, from Ukrainian *hospodar*, rel. to Russian *gospodar*, from *gospod'* lord, in turn rel. to Latin *hospes* host.

houri (hoo'ri) *n.* (*pl.* **houris**) 1 a nymph of the Muslim paradise. 2 a beautiful woman.
18C. **French**, from Persian *ḥūrī*, from Arabic *ḥūr*, pl. of *'aḥwar*, fem. *ḥawrā'* having eyes with marked contrast of black and white.

howdah (how'də), **houdah** *n.* a seat, usu. canopied, carried on an elephant's back.
18C. **Urdu** *haudah*, from Arabic *hawdaj* a litter carried by a camel.

hubris (hūˊbris) *n.* insolent pride or security, arrogance.
19C. Greek insolence, outrage.

Huguenot (hūˊgənō) *n.* (*Hist.*) a French Protestant.
16C. **French**, alt. (by assim. to name of Besançon *Hugues*, *c.*1491–1532, a Geneva burgomaster) of obs. *eiguenot*, from Dutch *eedgenot*, from Swiss German *Eidgenoss* confederate, from *Eid* oath + *Genoss* associate.

hula (hooˊlə), **hula-hula** *n.* a Hawaiian dance performed by women.
19C. **Hawaiian**.

hummus (hŭmˊəs, humˊəs), **hoummos** *n.* a kind of Middle Eastern hors d'oeuvre consisting of puréed chickpeas, sesame oil, garlic and lemon.
mid-20C. **Arabic** *ḥummuṣ*.

humpy (hŭmˊpi) *n.* (*pl.* **humpies**) (*Austral.*) a hut, shack, lean-to.
19C. **Australian Aboriginal** (Jagara) *yumpi*, influ. by English *hump*.

humus (hūˊməs) *n.* soil or mould, esp. that largely composed of decayed vegetation.
18C. **Latin**, rel. to Greek *khamai* on the ground.

hussar (huzahˊ) *n.* **1** a soldier of a light cavalry regiment in European armies. **2** (*Hist.*) a light horseman of the Hungarian cavalry in the 19th cent.
16C. **Hungarian** *huszár* freebooter, light horseman, from Old Serbian *husar*, *gusar*, from Italian *corsaro* corsair, pirate.

hwyl (hooˊil) *n.* passion or fervour, esp. in speech, recitation etc.
19C. **Welsh**.

hyperbole (hīpœˊbəli) *n.* a figure of speech expressing much more than the truth, rhetorical exaggeration.
14–15C. **Latin**, from Greek *huperbolē* excess, exaggeration, from *huper* over + *ballein* to throw.

hypostasis (hīposˊtəsis) *n.* (*pl.* **hypostases** (-sēz)) **1** that which forms the basis of anything. **2** in metaphysics, that by which a thing subsists, substance as distinct from attributes. **3** the essence or essential principle. **4** the personal subsistence as distinct from substance. **5** (*Theol.*) **a** one of the persons of the Trinity. **b** the person of Christ. **6** (*Med.*) the accumulation and congestion of blood in the lower parts of the body due to the effects of gravity in circumstances of poor circulation.
16C. **Ecclesiastical Latin**, from Greek *hupostasis* sediment, foundation, subject matter, from *hupo* under + *stasis* standing.

hypothesis (hīpothˊəsis) *n.* (*pl.* **hypotheses** (-sēz)) **1** a proposition assumed for the purpose of an argument. **2** a theory assumed to account for something not understood. **3** a mere supposition or assumption.
16C. **Late Latin**, from Greek *hupothesis* foundation, base, from *hupo* under + *thesis* placing.

hysteron proteron (histəron protˊəron) *n.* a figure of speech in which what should follow comes first, an inversion of the natural or logical order.
16C. **Ecclesiastical Latin**, from Greek *husteron proteron* latter (put in place of) former, from *husteron*, neut. of *husteros* latter + *proteron*, neut. of *proteros* before, former.

I

iambus (īam´bəs), **iamb** (ī´amb) *n.* (*pl.*
iambuses, iambi (-bī), **iambs**) a poetic
foot of one short and one long, or one
unaccented and one accented syllable.
16C. Latin, from Greek *iambos* iambus,
lampoon, from *iaptein* to assail in words.
● The iambic trimeter was first used by
Greek satirists. Hence the connection
with lampoons.

ibidem (ib´idem) *adv.* in the same place
(when referring to a book, page etc.
already cited).
18C. Latin in the same place, from *ibi*
there + demonstrative suf. *-dem*. Cp.
IDEM, TANDEM.
● The abbreviated form *ibid.* is generally
used in bibliographies and the like, e.g.
'30. Clarkson, I, 148. 31; ibid., 140'.

I Ching (ē ching´) *n.* an ancient Chinese
method of divination employing a set of
symbols, eight trigrams and 64
hexagrams, together with the text
known as the *I Ching* which serves to
interpret them.
19C. Chinese, lit. Book of Changes, from
yì change + *jīng* classics.

ichor (ī´kaw) *n.* **1** in Greek mythology, the
ethereal fluid which flowed in place of
blood in the veins of the gods. **2** a thin
watery liquid such as serum. **3** †a watery
acrid discharge from a wound etc.
17C. Greek *ikhōr*.

ici on parle français (ēsē ō pahl frãsā´)
int. French spoken here (used as a sign
in a shop etc. in a country where French
is not the native language).
early 20C. French, lit. here one speaks
French. Cp. MAN SPRICHT DEUTSCH.

icon (ī´kon), **ikon** *n.* **1** (*also* **eikon**) in the
Eastern Church, a sacred image, picture,
mosaic, or monumental figure of a holy
personage. **2** a symbol. **3** a hero figure,
esp. one who represents a particular
movement or belief. **4** (*Comput.*) a
pictorial representation of a facility
available to the user of a computer
system. **5** a linguistic sign that shares
something with or suggests what it
signifies.
16C. Latin, from Greek *eikōn* likeness,
image, similitude.

ictus (ik´təs) *n.* (*pl.* **ictuses, ictus**) **1** the
stress, or rhythmical accent on a syllable
in a line of verse. **2** (*Med.*) a stroke; a fit.
18C. Latin, from *ictus*, p.p. of *icere* to
strike.

id (id) *n.* (*Psych.*) the instinctive impulses
in the unconscious mind of the
individual.
early 20C. Latin it, translating German
es. Cp. EGO.
● The word was popularized by Freud
in *Das Ich und das Es* (1923), translated
as *Ego and Id*.

idée fixe (ēdā fēks′) *n.* (*pl.* **idées fixes** (ēdā fēks′)) a fixed idea, an obsession.
19C. French fixed idea, from *idée* idea + *fixe* fixed.

idée reçue (ēdā rəsū′) *n.* (*pl.* **idées reçues** (ēdā rəsū′)) a generally accepted idea.
mid-20C. French received idea, from *idée* idea + *reçue*, fem. p.p. of *recevoir* to receive.

idem (id′em) *n.* the same (word, author, book etc.). ~*adv.* in the same author, book etc.
14–15C. Latin the same.

ides (īdz) *n.pl.* in the ancient Roman calendar, the 15th day of March, May, July, October, and 13th day of the other months.
pre-1200. Old French, from Latin *idus* (pl.), of unknown orig.

idiot savant (ēdiō savā′) *n.* (*pl.* **idiot savants** (ēdiō savā′), **idiots savants**) a person who is considered to be mentally retarded but who has an outstanding ability in a specific area, such as mental arithmetic.
early 20C. French clever idiot, from *idiot* idiot + SAVANT.

idolum (īdō′ləm) *n.* (*pl.* **idola** (-lə)) **1** an image. **2** (*Philos.*) a fallacy.
17C. Latin, from Greek *eidōlon* image.

i.e. *abbr.* that is to say.
Abbr. of **Latin** *id est* that is, from *id* that + *est*, 3rd pers. sing. pres. of *esse* to be.

igloo (ig′loo) *n.* an Inuit hut, often built of snow.
19C. Inuit *iglu* house.

ignis fatuus (ignis fat′ūəs) *n.* (*pl.* **ignes fatui** (ignēz fat′ūī)) **1** an apparent flame, probably due to the spontaneous combustion of inflammable gas, floating above the ground in marshes etc. **2** a delusive object or aim.
16C. Modern Latin foolish fire, from *ignis* fire + *fatuus* foolish, fatuous.
● The phenomenon is so called because it flits erratically from place to place.

ignoramus (ignərā′məs) *n.* (*pl.* **ignoramuses**) an ignorant person.
16C. Latin we do not know, we take no notice of (it), 1st pers. pl. pres. indic. of *ignorare* not to know.
● The sense of ignorant person arose in the 17C and may have come from *Ignoramus*, the title of a comedy by George Ruggle (1615) satirizing lawyers. The word was originally used as an endorsement by a grand jury on an indictment which they rejected as it was not backed by sufficient evidence to bring before a petty jury.

IHS *abbr.* Jesus (often used as a Christian symbol).
19C. Abbr. (first two and last letters) of **Greek** *Iēsous* Jesus.
● The letters have been popularly interpreted as an abbreviation of various Latin phrases, e.g. *Iesus Hominum Salvator* Jesus Saviour of Men, *In Hoc Signo* (*vinces*) in this sign (thou shalt conquer), *In Hac Salus* in this (cross is) salvation. These take the second letter of the original Greek, eta, as a Roman *H*.

ikebana (ikibah′nə) *n.* the Japanese art of arranging flowers.
early 20C. Japanese, from *ikeru* to arrange + *hana* (*bana*) flower.

illuminati (iloominah′tē) *n.pl.* **1** a group of people claiming to possess knowledge or gifts. **2** (*Hist.*) (**Illuminati**) any of various sects and secret societies professing to have superior enlightenment.
16C. Pl. of **Italian** *illuminato*, or of Latin *illuminatus* enlightened.

ils ne passeront pas (ēl nə pasrō pah´)
int. they shall not pass.
early 20C. French.
- The words formed the Order of the
Day issued by Marshal Pétain at Verdun
in 1916. The phrase was taken up by the
Republicans in the Spanish Civil War in
the Spanish form *¡No pasarán!*,
popularized by the Spanish Communist
leader Dolores Ibarruri in a radio
broadcast of 19 July 1936.

imago (imā´gō) *n.* (*pl.* **imagoes**,
imagines (-jinēz)) **1** the adult,
fully-developed insect after its
metamorphosis. **2** (*Psych.*) an idealized
image of a parent or other person that
exercises a persistent influence in the
unconscious.
18C. Latin image, likeness, rel. to *imitari*
to imitate.

imam (imahm´) *n.* **1** a person who leads
congregational prayer in a mosque.
2 the title of various Muslim rulers and
founders.
17C. Arabic *'imām* leader, from *'amma*
to lead the way.

imbroglio (imbrō´liō), **embroglio** *n.*
(*pl.* **imbroglios, embroglios**) **1** a
perplexing or confused state of affairs.
2 a complicated plot, e.g. of a play or
novel. **3** a disorderly heap.
18C. Italian, from *imbrogliare* to
confuse, rel. to English *embroil*.

immer schlimmer (imə shlim´ə) *int.*
going from bad to worse.
early 20C. German, lit. ever worse, from
immer always, ever + comp. of *schlimm*
bad, poor.

immortelle (imawtel´) *n.* an everlasting
flower, esp. a helichrysum.
19C. French, from *fleur immortelle*
everlasting flower.
- The flowers so named have a papery
texture and retain their colour after
being dried.

impasse (am´pas, im´-) *n.* an
insurmountable obstacle; deadlock.
19C. French, from *in-* not, without +
stem of *passer* to pass.
- The word was adopted by Voltaire
in 1761 as a euphemistic synonym for
CUL-DE-SAC.

impasto (impas´tō) *n.* **1** the application
of a thick layer of paint, to give relief
etc. **2** the paint applied in this way.
18C. Italian, from *impastare*, from *im-*
in + *pasta* paste.

impedimenta (impedimen´tə) *n.pl.*
1 things that impede progress. **2** baggage,
esp. supplies for an army on the march.
17C. Latin, pl. of *impedimentum*, from
impedire to shackle the feet of, from
pes, pedis foot.

imperator (impərah´taw) *n.* (*Hist.*)
1 a title originally bestowed upon a
victorious Roman general. **2** under the
Roman Empire, the title bestowed on
the emperor.
16C. Latin, from *imperatus*, p.p. of
imperare to command, to rule.

imperium (imper´iəm) *n.* absolute
command, authority or rule, esp. that
of Rome during the Empire.
17C. Latin dominion.

impetus (im´pitəs) *n.* (*pl.* **impetuses**)
1 an impulse or driving force. **2** the
force with which a body moves or is
impelled.
17C. Latin assault, force, from *impetere*
to assail, from *in* in + *petere* to seek.

impi (im´pi) *n.* (*pl.* **impis**) a group of Zulu
fighters.
19C. Zulu regiment, army, military force.

imponderabilia (impondərəbil´iə) *n.pl.*
factors whose importance cannot be
assessed or evaluated, imponderables.
early 20C. Modern Latin, neut. pl. of
imponderabilis, lit. that which cannot
be weighed.

impresa (imprē´zə), **imprese** (imprēz´)
n. **1** a heraldic device. **2** a motto.
16C. Italian undertaking, device. Cp.
IMPRESARIO.

impresario (imprizah´riō) n. (pl.
impresarios) **1** a person who organizes
musical or theatrical performances. **2** a
director of an opera company, a ballet
company etc.
18C. Italian, from IMPRESA.

imprimatur (imprimā´tə, -ah´tə) n. **1** a
licence to print a book, granted by the
Roman Catholic Church. **2** official
sanction or approval.
17C. Latin let it be printed, 3rd pers.
sing. pres. subj. pass. of *imprimere* to
imprint. Cp. NIHIL OBSTAT.

imprimatura (imprēmətūə´rə) n. a
coloured transparent glaze used as a
primer in painting.
mid-20C. Italian *imprimatura*, from
imprimere to impress.

imprimis (imprī´mis) adv. in the first
place.
14–15C. Latin, assim. form of *in primis*
among the first (things), from *in* in +
primis, abl. pl. of *primus* first.

impromptu (impromp´tū) adv. off-hand,
without previous study. ~a. done or said
off-hand, extempore. ~n. (pl.
impromptus) **1** an extempore speech,
performance, act etc. **2** a short piece of
music, often for the piano, and
sometimes having the character of an
improvisation.
17C. French, from Latin *in promptu* at
hand, in readiness, from *in* in + abl. of
promptus readiness.

in absentia (in absen´tiə, -sen´shiə) adv.
in one's absence, while one is absent or
away.
19C. Latin in absence.

inamorato (inamərah´tō) n. (pl.
inamoratos) a man who is in love or is
beloved.
16C. Italian (now *innamorato*), p.p. of
inamorare to fall in love, from *in-* in +
amore love.

in camera (in kam´ərə) adv. **1** in private.
2 in a judge's chamber, or with the
public excluded from the court.
19C. Late Latin in the chamber.

incipit (in´sipit) n. the opening words of
a text.
19C. Latin, 3rd pers. pres. sing. indic. of
incipere to begin.
● The word was used by medieval
scribes to indicate the beginning of a
new treatise etc. Cp. EXPLICIT.

incognito (inkognē´tō, inkog´nitō) a.,
adv. with one's real name or identity
disguised or kept secret. ~n. (pl.
incognitos) **1** a person who is
incognito. **2** the state of being unknown
or in disguise. **3** an assumed identity.
17C. Italian, from Latin *incognitus*
unknown, from *in-* not, without +
cognitus, p.p. of *cognoscere* to know.

incommunicado (inkəmūnikah´dō)
a. **1** with no means of communication
with the outside world. **2** in solitary
confinement.
19C. Spanish *incomunicado*, p.p. of
incomunicar to deprive of
communication.

inconnu (inkənoo, īkonü´), (fem.)
inconnue n. an unknown person, a
stranger.
19C. French unknown. Cp. INCOGNITO.

incubus (ing´kūbəs) n. (pl. **incubi** (-bī))
1 a demon supposed to have sexual
intercourse with women at night.
2 a nightmare. **3** any person, thing or
influence that oppresses or disturbs.
12–14C. Late Latin, from Latin *incubo*
nightmare, from *incubare* to lie on.
Cp. SUCCUBA.

incunabulum (inkūnab´ūləm) *n.* (*pl.*
incunabula (-lə)) **1** an early printed
book, esp. one printed before AD 1500.
2 (*pl.*) the beginning or origins of
something.
19C. Latin *incunabula* (neut. pl.)
swaddling clothes, cradle, from *in* in +
cunae cradle.
● The books are so called because
produced in the 'infancy' of printing.

indaba (indah´bə) *n.* (*S Afr.*) **1** a council;
a conference. **2** a problem or matter for
discussion.
19C. Zulu discussion.

index (in´deks) *n.* (*pl.* **indexes, indices**
(-disēz)) **1** a list of names, subjects,
places etc. in alphabetical order, with
page references, usu. at the back of a
book. **2** a card index. **3** a thumb index.
4 a numerical scale indicating variations
in the cost of living, wages etc., by
reference to a given base level. **5** (*Math.*)
an exponent (indicating powers of
multiplication). **6** (*Med., Physics*) a
number expressing a ratio or property.
7 a pointer on a dial, watch etc. **8** a sign
or indicator. **9** (*Comput.*) a value that
identifies an element in a set of data.
10 (**Index**) a list of books prohibited by
the Roman Catholic Church. **11** a
printed symbol in the shape of a
pointing hand, used to point to a note,
paragraph etc. ~*v.t.* **1** to provide (a book)
with an index. **2** to enter (a word etc.) in
an index. **3** to relate (interest rates,
wages etc.) to an index.
14–15C. Latin *index, indicis* forefinger,
informer, from *in* in + *-dex, -dicis*, from
base represented by *dicere* to say.
● The earliest meaning was the
forefinger, used in pointing. Sense 1
dates from the 16C. Sense 10 is short for
Index Librorum Prohibitorum index of
prohibited books. The first such *Index*
was published in 1564 and the list was
not abolished until 1966.

indicia (indish´iə, -siə) *n.pl.*
1 distinguishing marks. **2** indications.
19C. Pl. of **Latin** *indicium.* See **INDEX.**

induna (indoo´nə) *n.* (*S Afr.*) **1** a leader
or tribal councillor, esp. of an impi.
2 an African overseer or foreman.
19C. Zulu, from nominal pref. *in-* +
duna councillor, headman, overseer.

in extenso (in eksten´sō) *adv.* at full
length.
19C. Latin, from *in* in + *extenso*, abl. of
extensus, p.p. of *extendere* to extend.

in extremis (in ikstrē´mis, -strā´-) *a.* **1** in
desperate circumstances, in extremity.
2 at the point of death.
16C. Latin, from *in* in + *extremis*, abl.
pl. of *extremus* outermost.

infanta (infan´tə) *n.* in Spain and
(formerly) Portugal, any royal princess
(usu. the eldest) except an heiress
apparent.
16C. Spanish and Portuguese, fem. of
infante, from Latin *infans, infantis*
infant.
● An infanta is so called because
although the oldest she is junior
to the heir to the throne. In 1999 the
heir to the Spanish throne was thus
Felipe, b.1968, but the eldest child of
King Juan Carlos I was Infanta Elena,
b.1963.

in flagrante (in fləgran´ti), **in flagrante
delicto** (dilik´tō) *adv.* whilst actually
committing the misdeed.
18C. Latin in the heat (of the crime),
from *in* in + abl. of *flagrans, flagrantis*
pres.p. of *flagrare* to burn.
● The fuller Latin form has *delicto* as
the ablative singular of *delictum*, the
neuter past participle (used as a noun)
of *delinquere* to offend (the sense of
English *delinquent*). *In flagrante delicto*
means literally 'in blazing crime'.

influenza (influen´zə) *n.* a highly contagious virus infection, often occurring in epidemics, often characterized by muscular aches and pains, catarrh and fever.
18C. **Italian**, lit. influence, from Medieval Latin *influentia*.
● The word originated from the epidemic that broke out in Italy in the 1740s and that spread to the rest of Europe. The Italians regarded it as a visitation by some evil force and named it accordingly. The word is generally abbreviated to *flu* in modern English.

in forma pauperis (in fawmə paw´pəris) *adv.* (*Law*) allowed on account of poverty to sue without paying costs.
16C. **Latin** in the form of a poor person, from *in* in + abl. of *forma* form + gen. of *pauper* poor person.

infra (in´frə) *adv.* (in a passage of a book etc.) below, further on.
19C. **Latin** below. Cp. SUPRA.

infra dig (infrə dig´) *a.* (*coll.*) beneath one's dignity.
19C. Abbr. of **Latin** *infra dignitatem* beneath (one's) dignity.
● The colloquial abbreviation may to some extent pun on English *dig*, as an action 'beneath' one. Cp. the biblical parable of the unjust steward: 'I cannot dig: to beg I am ashamed' (Luke xvi.3).

ingénue (īzhänü´) *n.* an ingenuous or naive girl, esp. such a character on the stage.
19C. **French**, fem. of *ingénu* ingenuous.
● There is no corresponding male **ingénu*.

in loco parentis (in lōkō pəren´tis) *adv.* in the place of a parent (used esp. of a teacher).
18C. **Latin** in place of a parent, from *in* in + abl. of *locus* place + gen. of *parens* parent.

in medias res (in mēdias rāz´) *adv.* in or into the middle of things or of a story.
18C. **Latin** into the midst of things, from *in* in + fem. acc. pl. of *medius* middle + acc. pl. of RES.

in memoriam (in mimaw´riam) *prep.* in memory of. ~*n.* an obituary.
19C. **Latin** to the memory (of), from *in* in + acc. of *memoria* memory.
● The phrase was popularized by Tennyson's sequence of poems, *In Memoriam A.H.H.* (1850).

innuendo (inūen´dō) *n.* (*pl.* **innuendos, innuendoes**) 1 an indirect or oblique hint, esp. one that is disapproving.
2 a suggestive remark. ~*v.t.* (*3rd pers. sing. pres.* **innuendoes**, *pres.p.* **innuendoing**, *past, p.p.* **innuendoed**) to insinuate. ~*v.i.* to make innuendoes.
16C. **Latin** by nodding at, by intimating, abl. ger. of *innuere* to nod, to signify, from *in* in + *nuere* to nod.

in propria persona (in prōpriə pœsō´nə) *adv.* in person.
17C. **Latin** in (one's) own person, from *in* in + fem. abl. of *proprius* own + abl. of PERSONA.

inquirendo (inkwiren´dō) *n.* (*Law*) authority given to inquire into something for the benefit of the Crown.
17C. **Latin** by inquiring, abl. ger. of *inquirere* to inquire.

INRI *abbr.* Jesus of Nazareth King of the Jews (the superscription on Christ's cross (John xix.19), found esp. in representations of the crucifixion in Renaissance art).
16C. Abbr. of **Latin** *Iesus Nazarenus Rex Iudaeorum* Jesus of Nazareth, King of the Jews.

in saecula saeculorum (in sekulə sekulaw´rəm) *adv.* to all eternity, for ever.

16C. Late Latin to the ages of ages, from *in* into + acc. pl. of *saeculum* period, age + gen pl. of *saeculum*, the source of English *secular*.

• In Christian Latin *saeculum* meant 'world'. Hence the closing words of the Doxology in the Latin Ordinary of the Mass, *in saecula saeculorum*, translated in English as 'world without end'. The phrase should not be confused with SANCTUM SANCTORUM.

inselberg (in´səlbœg, -zəl-) *n.* an isolated steep rocky hill in a flat plain.
early 20C. German, from *Insel* island + *Berg* mountain.

inshallah (inshal´ə) *int.* if Allah wills it.
19C. Arabic *in šā' Allāh* if God (Allah) wills it. Cp. DV.

insignia (insig´niə) *n.pl.* **1** (*often constr. as sing., N Am.*) badges of office or honour. **2** distinguishing marks or signs (of).
17C. Latin, pl. of *insigne* mark, sign, badge of office, use as n. of neut. of *insignis* distinguished, differentiated, from *in* in + *signum* sign.

in situ (in sit´ū) *adv.* **1** in its place. **2** in the original position.
18C. Latin in (its) place, from *in* in + abl. of *situs* position.

insouciance (insoo´siəns, īsoosyās´) *n.* carefreeness, lack of concern.
18C. French, from *insouciant*, from *in-* not + pres.p. of *soucier* to care, from Latin *sollicitare* to disturb.

• English has also adopted the corresponding adjective *insouciant* (19C) carefree, undisturbed.

inspan (inspan´) *v.t.* (*pres.p.* **inspanning**, *past, p.p.* **inspanned**) (*S Afr.*) **1** to yoke (horses, oxen etc.) to a wagon etc. **2** to harness animals to (a wagon). **3** (*fig.*) to harness into service. ~*v.i.* to harness or yoke up animals.

19C. Afrikaans, from Dutch *inspannen*, from *in-* in + *spannen* to span, to fasten.

instanter (instan´tə) *adv.* (*formal or facet.*) at once, immediately.
17C. Latin immediately, adv. from *instans, instantis*, pres.p. of *instare* to be present.

in statu pupillari (in statū pūpilah´ri) *a.* **1** in a state of wardship, esp. as a pupil. **2** in a junior position at a university.
19C. Latin in a state of guardianship, from *in* in + abl. of STATUS + abl. of *pupillaris*, from *pupillus* orphan.

intaglio (intah´lyō) *n.* (*pl.* **intaglios**) **1** a figure cut or engraved in a hard substance. **2** the act or process of producing this. **3** a gem with a figure cut or engraved into it, as distinct from a *cameo*. **4** an engraved design. **5** a method of printing from an etched or engraved design. ~*v.t.* (*3rd pers. sing. pres.* **intaglioes**, *pres.p.* **intaglioing**, *past, p.p.* **intaglioed**) **1** to cut or engrave (a substance) with a sunk design. **2** to engrave (a design) in this way.
17C. Italian, from *intagliare* to engrave, from *in-* in + *tagliare* to cut.

intarsia (intah´siə) *n.* **1** the practice or art of using wood to make decorative mosaics, as developed in 15th-cent. Italy. **2** similar work in stone, glass or metal. **3** in knitting, the working of a design using separate lengths of yarn for each coloured section.
19C. Italian *intarsio*, from *intarsiare* to inlay, from *in-* in + *tarsiare* to inlay. Cp. TARSIA.

intelligentsia (intelijent´siə) *n.* **1** the class of people who are considered to be cultured, educated and politically aware. **2** intellectuals.

early 20C. Russian *intelligentsiya*, from Polish *inteligencja*, from Latin *intelligentia* intelligence.

● The original reference of the word was to the cultured stratum of society in pre-Revolutionary Russia who opposed the existing political and social system.

inter alia (intər ah'liə, ā'liə) *adv.* among other things.
17C. Latin among other (things), from *inter* among + *alia*, acc. neut. pl. of *alius* another.

interim (in'tərim) *n.* the intervening time or period. ~*a.* temporary, provisional. ~†*adv.* meanwhile.
16C. Latin, from *inter* between + adverbial ending *-im*.

intermezzo (intəmet'sō) *n.* (*pl.* **intermezzi** (-si), **intermezzos**)
1 a short movement connecting the main divisions of an opera or a large musical composition. **2** a piece of this kind performed independently.
3 a short piece of music for a solo instrument. **4** a short dramatic or other entertainment between the acts of a play.
18C. Italian, from Late Latin *intermedium*, neut. sing. (used as n.) of Latin *intermedius*, from *inter* between + *medius* middle. Cp. MEZZO.

internuncio (intənun'shiō) *n.* (*pl.* **internuncios**) **1** a messenger between two parties. **2** an ambassador of the Pope sent to a court when there is no nuncio present or to minor states.
17C. Italian *internunzio*, from Latin *internuntius*, from *inter* between + *nuntius* messenger.

interregnum (intəreg'nəm) *n.* (*pl.* **interregnums, interregna** (-nə)) **1** the period between two reigns, ministries or governments. **2** a suspension or

interruption of normal authority, succession etc. **3** an interval, a pause.
16C. Latin, from *inter* between + *regnum* sovereignty.

interrex (in'təreks) *n.* (*pl.* **interreges** (-rējēz)) a person who governs during an interregnum; a regent.
16C. Latin *inter* between + *rex* king.

intifada (intifah'də) *n.* the Palestinian uprising in the Israeli-occupied West Bank and Gaza Strip, that began in 1987.
late 20C. Arabic *intifāḍa* a shaking off, a jumping up (in response to some external stimulus), from *intifaḍa* to be shaken, to shake oneself.

in toto (in tō'tō) *adv.* completely.
18C. Latin in entirety, from *in* in + neut. abl. (used as n.) of *totus* all.

intra muros (intrə muə'rōs) *adv.* concerned with the internal politics of an institution etc.
early 20C. Latin, lit. within the walls (of a city). Cp. EXTRA MUROS.

in utero (in ū'tərō) *adv.* in the womb.
18C. Latin in the womb, from *in* in + abl. of *uterus* womb.

in vacuo (in vak'ūō) *adv.* **1** in a vacuum. **2** in isolation; without reference to context.
17C. Latin in a vacuum, from *in* in + neut. abl. (used as n.) of *vacuus* empty.

in vino veritas (in vē'nō ver'itahs) *int.* alcohol loosens the tongue; when drunk, people are likely to tell the truth.
17C. Latin, lit. in wine (is) truth.

● The phrase has been traced back to Pliny's *Natural History* (AD 77) which has the line, *Vulgoque veritas iam attributa vino est* 'Now truth is commonly said to be in wine'.

in vitro (in vē´trō) *a., adv.* (*Biol.*) (of biological processes etc.) taking place outside a living organism, e.g. in a test tube.
19C. Latin in glass, from *in* in + abl. of *vitrum* glass.

in vivo (in vē´vō) *a., adv.* (*Biol.*) (of biological processes) occurring within a living organism.
early 20C. Latin in the living (body), from *in* in + abl. of *vivus*, from *vivere* to live.

iota (īō´tə) *n.* **1** the ninth letter of the Greek alphabet (I, ι). **2** (*usu. with neg.*) a very small quantity.
14–15C. Greek *iōta*, of Phoenician orig. Cp. YOD.
● Sense 2 dates from the 17C. Iota is the smallest letter of the Greek alphabet.

ipecacuanha (ipikakūan´ə) *n.* the dried root of *Cephaelis ipecacuanha*, a cinchonaceous plant from Brazil, used in medicine as an emetic and purgative.
17C. Portuguese, from Tupi-Guarani *ipekaaguéne*, from *ipe* small + *kaa* leaves + *guíne* to vomit.

ipse dixit (ipsi dik´sit) *n.* **1** a mere assertion. **2** a dogmatic statement.
16C. Latin (he) himself said (it), translating Greek *autos epha*, a phr. used of Pythagoras by his followers.

ipsissima verba (ipsisimə vœ´bə) *n.pl.* the precise words.
19C. Latin the very words, neut. pl. of *ipsissimus*, superl. of *ipse* self (cp. IPSE DIXIT) + pl. of *verbum* word.

ipso facto (ipsō fak´tō) *adv.* **1** by that very fact. **2** thereby.
16C. Latin by the fact itself, abl. of *ipse* self + abl. of *factum* deed, fact.

irade (irah´di) *n.* (*Hist.*) a written decree of a Muslim ruler.
19C. Turkish *ˀrade*, from Arabic *'irāda* will, decree, from *'arāda* to intend.

Islam (iz´lahm) *n.* **1** the Muslim religion, that teaches that there is only one God and that Muhammad is his prophet. **2** the Muslim world.
17C. Arabic *'islām*, from *'aslama* to submit, to surrender (i.e. to God). Cp. MUSLIM, SALAAM.

Ismaili (izmah·ē´li) *n.* (*pl.* **Ismailis**) a member of a sect of Shiite Muslims whose spiritual leader is the Aga Khan.
19C. Arabic, from *'Ismā'īl* (d.762), eldest son of Ja'far ibn Muḥammad, the sixth Shiite imam.
● The Ismailis hold that at the death (765) of Ja'far, the imamate should have descended to the posterity of his deceased eldest son, 'Ismā'īl, whereas it actually passed to his younger son, Mūsā al-Kāẓim (d.799).

issei (ē´sā) *n.* a Japanese immigrant to the USA or Canada.
early 20C. Japanese, lit. first generation, from *is-* one, first + *sei* generation. Cp NISEI, SANSEI.
● Many Japanese immigrated to California in the early 20C.

Italia irredenta (itahliə iriden´tə) *n.* the parts of Italy remaining under foreign domination after the war of 1866.
early 20C. Italian, lit. unredeemed Italy.
● The phrase gave the name of the Irredentists, the Italian patriots who sought to deliver Italian lands from foreign rule in the late 19C and early 20C. Many areas at that time were still controlled by Austria.

item (ī´təm) *n.* **1** any of a series of things listed or enumerated. **2** an individual entry in an account, schedule etc. **3** a piece of news in a newspaper, television

programme etc. **4** an article, esp. one of a number. **5** (*coll.*) two people who are in a romantic or sexual relationship.
~†*adv.* likewise, also. ~*v.t.* **1** to make a note of. **2** to itemize.
14–15C. Latin just so, similarly, moreover, from *ita* thus, so.
‡ The word was originally used as an introductory word in a list or formal document. The sense then passed (16C) to an individual component of the list itself.

Iyar (iyah´) *n.* in the Jewish calendar, the eighth month of the civil year and the second month of the religious year.
18C. Hebrew *'iyyār.*

izzat (iz´ūt), **izzut** *n.* honour, reputation, prestige.
19C. Persian, from Arabic *'izza* glory.

J

jabot (zhab´ō) *n.* **1** a lace frill worn at the neck of a woman's bodice. **2** a ruffle on a shirt front.
19C. **French** bird's crop, shirt frill, ? from Latin *gaba* cheek.

j'accuse (zhaküz´) *n.* an accusation, esp. against an authority.
mid-20C. **French** I accuse.
● The words are from the opening of Émile Zola's letter to the newspaper *L'Aurore* of 13 January 1898 in which he attacked the wrongful condemnation of the Jewish army officer Alfred Dreyfus (1859–1935) on a charge of treason (1894) and the subsequent attempt by the French military to suppress the truth.

jacquard (jak´ahd, -əd) *n.* **1** an apparatus with perforated cards used to weave intricate designs. **2** fabric so woven.
19C. Joseph-Marie *Jacquard*, 1752–1834, French inventor.

Jacquerie (jak´əri, zhakərē´) *n.* **1** a revolt of the peasants against the nobles in France, in 1357–8. **2** any peasant revolt.
16C. **Old French**, from male forename *Jacques*.
● French *Jacques* equates to English *James* as a name, but here corresponds in meaning to *Jack*. The similarity between the names is unexplained.

j'adoube (zhadoob´) *int.* in chess, used as a notification that a piece is being adjusted rather than moved.
19C. **French** I adjust, from *je, j'* I + 1st pers. sing. pres. indic. of *adouber* to move provisionally.

jai alai (hīəlī´) *n.* a game similar to pelota played by two or four players on a court, who wear woven baskets tied to their wrists and using these hurl a ball at the walls.
early 20C. **Spanish**, from Basque *jai* festival + *alai* merry.

Jain (jīn, jān), **Jaina** (-nə) *n.* an adherent of a non-Brahminical Indian religion.
~*a.* of or belonging to the Jains or Jainism.
18C. **Hindi**, from Sanskrit *jaina* pertaining to a Jina, from *jina*, lit. victor, overcomer, from *ji-* to conquer or *jyā-* to overcome.

jalapeño (haləpān´yō, -pē´nō) *n.* (*pl.* **jalapeños**) (*also* **jalapeño pepper**) a very hot green chilli pepper.
mid-20C. **Mexican Spanish** (*chile*) *jalapeño* Jalapa chilli, from *Jalapa*, a city in Mexico.

jalousie (zhal´uzi) *n.* a louvre blind, a Venetian shutter.
18C. **French**, lit. jealousy.
● One can look (jealously) through the blind without being seen. The ultimate

association is with the screening of women from view in the Middle East.

jambalaya (jambəlī´ə) *n*. a S US dish consisting of meat, seafood, rice, onions etc.
19C. Louisiana French, from Provençal *jambalaia* chicken and rice stew.

jampan (jam´pan) *n*. a sedan chair borne on two bamboo poles by four people.
19C. Bengali *jhămpān*, Hindi *jhappān*.

jardinière (zhahdinyeə´) *n*. **1** an ornamental pot or stand for growing flowers in a room etc. **2** a dish of mixed cooked vegetables.
19C. French, lit. female gardener.

jaspé (jas´pā) *a*. **1** (of ceramics) having an appearance like jasper. **2** (of cotton fabric) of mottled appearance.
19C. French, p.p. of *jasper* to marble.

jemadar (jem´ədah) *n*. in the Indian subcontinent, an army officer.
18C. Urdu *jama'dār*, from Persian, from Arabic *jama'*, *jamā'at* to muster + Persian *-dār* holder.

je ne sais quoi (zhə nə sā kwa´) *n*. an indefinable something.
17C. French, lit. I do not know what.

jereed (jirēd´), **jerid** *n*. **1** a javelin, used in Iran and Turkey, esp. in games. **2** a game with this.
17C. Arabic *jarīd* palm branch stripped of its leaves, javelin.

jet d'eau (zhe dō´) *n*. (*pl.* **jets d'eau** (zhe)) an ornamental jet of water from a fountain.
17C. French jet of water.

jeté (zhet´ā, -tā´) *n*. a leap from one foot to the other in ballet.
19C. French, p.p. of *jeter* to throw.
● The implied full French phrase is *pas jeté* thrown step.

jeu (zhœ) *n*. (*pl.* **jeux** (zhœ)) a game, a play, a jest.
18C. French play, game, from Latin *iocus* joke.

jeu d'esprit (zhœ desprē´) *n*. (*pl.* **jeux d'esprit** (zhœ)) a witticism, a play of wit, a witty sally.
18C. French, lit. play of wit.

jeune premier (zhœn prəmyā´), (*fem.*) **jeune première** (prəmyeə´) *n*. (*pl.* **jeunes premiers** (zhœn prəmyā´), **jeunes premières** (prəmyeə´)) an actor or actress who plays the part of a principal lover or young hero or heroine.
19C. French, lit. first young (one).

jeunesse dorée (zhœnes dor´ā, dorā´) *n*. a young, wealthy and fashionable clique within a society.
19C. French, lit. gilded youth, from *jeunesse* youth + fem. p.p. of *dorer* to gild.
● The original *jeunesse dorée* was a group of fashionable counter-revolutionaries in France during the Revolution (1789–95).

jibba (jib´ə), **jibbah, djibba, djibbah** *n*. **1** a long, loose coat worn by Muslims. **2** a loose overall or pinafore.
19C. Egyptian var. of Arabic *jubba*.

jihad (jihad´, -hahd´), **jehad** *n*. **1** a holy war proclaimed by Muslims against unbelievers or the enemies of Islam. **2** a war or crusade on behalf of a principle etc.
19C. Arabic *jihād*, lit. effort.

jinnee (jinē´), **jinn** (jin), **djinn** *n*. (*pl.* **jinn, djinn**) any of a race of spirits or demons in Muslim mythology supposed to have the power of assuming human or animal forms.
19C. Arabic *jinnī* (m. sing), *jinn* (pl.).

jinrickshaw (jinrik´shaw), **jinrickisha** (-shə) *n.* a rickshaw.
19C. Japanese *jin-riki-sha*, from *jin* man + *riki* strength, power + *sha* vehicle.
• Punsters equate the origin of the name with *Pullman car*.

joie de vivre (zhwa də vēvr´, vēv´rə) *n.* joy of living; exuberance.
19C. French joy of living, from *joie* joy + *de* of + *vivre* to live. Cp. German *Lebenslust*, lit. lust for life.

jolie laide (zholē led´) *n.* (*pl.* **jolies laides** (zholē led´)) a fascinating ugly woman.
19C. French, from *jolie* pretty + *laide* ugly (fem. aa.).
• The masculine equivalent, *joli laid*, is occasionally found.

jongleur (zhōglœ´) *n.* (*Hist.*) an itinerant minstrel or reciter of the Middle Ages, esp. in N France.
18C. French, alt. of *jougleur*, from Latin *ioculator* jester.

jour de fête (zhuə də fet´) *n.* (*pl.* **jours de fête** (zhuə)) a feast day, esp. that of a patron saint.
early 20C. French, lit. day of (the) feast.

jube (joo´bi) *n.* a rood-loft or gallery dividing the choir from the nave.
18C. French *jubé*, from Latin *iube*, imper. of *iubere* to bid, to order.
• The Latin word is the first word of the formula *Jube, domine, benedicere* Sir, bid a blessing, addressed by a deacon to a priest before the reading of the Gospel, which in some churches was done in the rood-loft.

jubilate (joobilah´ti, yoo-) *n.* **1** (**Jubilate**) the 100th Psalm used as a canticle in the morning service of the Church of England, from its Latin commencing words *Jubilate Deo*. **2** a shout of joy or exultation.
12–14C. Latin shout for joy!, imper. of *iubilare*.
• More fully, as the opening words of Ps. c, *Jubilate Deo*, translated in the Prayer Book as 'O be joyful in the Lord' and in the Bible as 'Make a joyful noise unto the Lord'.

judicium Dei (joodisiəm dā´ē) *n.* the judgement of God.
17C. Latin judgement of God, from *iudicium* judgement + gen. of *Deus* God.

judo (joo´dō) *n.* a modern sport derived from a form of ju-jitsu.
19C. Japanese *jū* gentle + *dō* way. Cp. JU-JITSU.

Jugendstil (yoo´gəntshtēl) *n.* art nouveau in Germany, Austria etc.
early 20C. German, from *Jugend* youth + *Stil* style.
• *Die Jugend* was a German satirical magazine, first published in 1896, in which the designs appeared.

ju-jitsu (joojit´soo), **jiu-jitsu**, **ju-jutsu** *n.* the Japanese art of wrestling, based on the principle of making one's opponent exert their strength to their own disadvantage.
19C. Japanese *jūjutsu*, from *jū* gentle + *jutsu* skill. Cp. JUDO.

ju-ju (joo´joo) *n.* **1** a fetish, an idol credited with supernatural power. **2** the ban or taboo worked by this.
17C. W African, prob. from French *joujou* plaything, reduplicated formation from *jouer* to play, from Latin *iocare*.

julienne (joolien´) *n.* **1** a clear soup made from meat with chopped or shredded vegetables. **2** any foodstuff, esp. vegetables, cut into short thin strips. **3** a variety of pear.
18C. French, from male forename *Jules* or *Julien*.
• The identity of the man so named is unknown.

jumelle (joomel´, zhoo-) *a.* twin, paired.
15C. French, fem. of *jumeau* twin,
from Latin *gemellus*, dim. of *geminus*
twin.

junker (yung´kə) *n.* (*Hist.*) **1** a young
German noble. **2** a member of the
German reactionary aristocratic party.
16C. German, earlier *Junkherr*, from
Middle High German *junc* young
+ *herre* (modern German *Herr*) lord,
HERR.

junta (jŭn´tə, hun´-) *n.* **1** a group, esp. of
military officers who take control of a
country e.g. after a coup. **2** a cabal. **3** a
legislative or administrative council,
esp. in Spain, Portugal, and South
America.
17C. Spanish and Portuguese, from
Italian *giunta*, from Latin *iuncta*, fem.
p.p. of *iungere* to join.

junto (jŭn´tō) *n.* (*pl.* **juntos**) **1** a secret
political or other council. **2** a cabal,
clique, a faction.
17C. Alt. of JUNTA, based on Spanish nn.
in *-o*.

jupe (joop, zhüp) *n.* a skirt.
19C. French, from Arabic *jubba*. Cp.
JIBBA.
● The word originally denoted a man's
loose jacket (12–14C). It then transferred
to a woman's jacket or gown (18C)
before becoming obsolete in this sense
in the early 20C.

jupon (joo´pən, zhoo´-) *n.* a skirt or
petticoat.
14–15C. Old French *juppon* (Modern
French *jupon*), from *jupe* skirt.

jus gentium (jŭs jen´shiəm) *n.*
international law.
16C. Latin law of nations.

jus primae noctis (jŭs prīmē nok´tis)
n. (*Hist.*) the supposed right of a feudal
overlord to have sexual intercourse with
the bride of any of his tenants on her
wedding night.
19C. Latin right of the first night. Cp.
DROIT DE SEIGNEUR.

jus sanguinis (jŭs sang´gwinis) n. the
principle that a person's nationality is
that of their natural parents.
19C. Latin, lit. right of blood.

juste milieu (zhüst miliœ´) *n.* a happy
medium, the golden mean.
19C. French, lit. right mean.
● The expression particularly applies to
judicious moderation in politics.

juvenilia (joovənil´iə) *n.pl.* writings etc.,
produced in youth.
17C. Latin, neut. pl. of *iuvenilis* juvenile.

K

ka (kah) *n.* (*pl.* **kas**) the spirit of a person or statue in ancient Egyptian mythology, born with but surviving the individual.
19C. Ancient Egyptian.

Kaaba (kah´bə, -əbə), **Caaba** *n.* a sacred building in Mecca, containing the black stone, which Muslims face when they pray.
17C. Arabic (*al-*)*ka'ba*, lit. the square house.

kabuki (kəboo´ki) *n.* a highly-stylized, traditional and popular form of Japanese drama, based on legend and acted only by men, in elaborate costumes.
19C. Japanese, orig. (as v.) to act dissolutely, but later interpreted as from *ka* song + *bu* dance + *ki* art, skill.

kachina (kəchē´nə) *n.* **1** any of the spirits of the ancestors of the Pueblo Indians. **2** a dancer representing a kachina in a ceremony.
19C. Hopi *kacina* supernatural, from Keresan.

Kaddish (kad´ish), **Qaddish** *n.* a form of thanksgiving and prayer used by Jews, esp. in mourning.
17C. Aramaic *qaddīš* holy.

Kaffeeklatsch (kaf´āklach) *n.* a gossip over coffee cups, a coffee party.
19C. German, from *Kaffee* coffee + *Klatsch* gossip, of imit. orig.

Kaffir (kaf´ə), **Kafir** *n.* (*offensive*) **1** a member of the South African Xhosa-speaking people. **2** their language, Xhosa. **3** (*S Afr.*) any black African. **4** (*pl.*) South African mining shares.
~*a.* of or relating to these people or their language.
16C. Arabic *kāfir* unbeliever, from active part. of *kafara* to be unbelieving.

kaftan (kaf´tan, -tən), **caftan** *n.* **1** a long belted tunic worn in the East. **2** a woman's long loose dress with wide sleeves.
16C. Turkish, from Persian *ḵaftān*.

kai (kī) *n.* (*New Zeal.*) food.
19C. Maori.

kaiser (kī´zə) *n.* **1** an emperor. **2** (*Hist.*) the Emperor of Germany or Austria. **3** (*Hist.*) the head of the Holy Roman Empire.
pre-1200. Old English *cāsere*, from Germanic, from Greek *kaisar*, from Latin family name *Caesar*. Cp. TSAR.
● In modern use, referring to Austrian or German emperors, the immediate source is German *Kaiser*.

kaizen (kīzen´) *n.* the concept of constant improvement in Japanese business and industry.
late 20C. Japanese improvement, from *kai* revision, change + *zen* (the) good.

kajawah (kəjah´wə) *n.* a pannier or frame carried in pairs on a camel, horse or mule, used as a litter by women and children in some Eastern countries.
17C. Urdu *kajāwah*.

kakemono (kakimō´nō) *n.* (*pl.* **kakemonos**) a Japanese wall picture mounted on rollers for putting away.
19C. Japanese, from *kake-* to hang + *mono* thing.

kaki (kah´ki) *n.* (*pl.* **kakis**) an Asian persimmon, *Diospyros kaki*.
18C. Japanese.

kala-azar (kahləəzah´) *n.* a chronic tropical disease with a high mortality, caused by a protozoan *Leishmania donovani*.
19C. Assamese, from *kālā* black + *āzār* disease.
• The disease is so called from the bronzing of the skin.

Kalashnikov (kalash´nikof) *n.* a type of sub-machine gun made in Russia.
late 20C. Mikhail T. *Kalashnikov*, 1919–, Russian weapons designer.

kalian (kahlyahn´) *n.* an Iranian form of hookah.
19C. Persian *ḳalyān*, from Arabic *ġalayān*.

kalpa (kal´pə) *n.* a day of Brahma, or a period of 4,320,000 years, constituting the age or cycle of a world.
18C. Sanskrit.

Kama (kah´mə) *n.* **1** the god of love in the puranas. **2** impure or sensual desire.
19C. Sanskrit *kāma* love, desire. Cp. KAMA SUTRA.

Kama Sutra (kah´mə soo´trə) *n.* an ancient Hindu book on erotic love.
19C. Sanskrit, from KAMA + SUTRA.

kameez (kəmēz´) *n.* a type of loose tunic with tight sleeves worn esp. by Muslim women in the Indian subcontinent and S Asia.
19C. Arabic *ḳamīṣ*, ? from Late Latin *camisia*. See CHEMISE.

kamerad (kamərahd´) *int.* comrade, a German form of surrender or appeal for quarter.
early 20C. German, lit. comrade, from French *camerade*, *camarade*.

kami (kah´mi) *n.* (*pl.* **kami**) **1** a Japanese title, equivalent to lord, given to nobles, ministers, governors etc. **2** in Shinto, a divinity, a god.
17C. Japanese.

kamikaze (kamikah´zi) *n.* a Japanese airman or plane performing a suicidal mission in World War II. ~*a.* **1** of or relating to a kamikaze. **2** (*coll.*) suicidal, self-destructive.
19C. Japanese divine wind, from KAMI + *kaze* wind.
• In Japanese tradition, the original 'divine wind' was the gale that destroyed the fleet of invading Mongols in 1281.

kampong (kam´pong, kampong´) *n.* a Malay village.
18C. Malay *kampung* enclosure, small village.
• The Malay word also gave English *compound* in the sense of a large open area enclosed by a fence.

kana (kah´nə) *n.* a Japanese syllabic system of writing.
18C. Japanese. Cp. HIRAGANA, KATAKANA.

kanaka (kənak´ə, kan´-) *n.* **1** an indigenous Hawaiian. **2** a South Sea Islander. **3** (*Hist.*) a Hawaiian or South Sea Islander employed as an indentured labourer on the Queensland sugar plantations.
19C. Hawaiian person, human being.

kanban (kan´ban) *n*. **1** (*also* **kanban system**) the Japanese system of printing orders on cards during manufacturing processes. **2** a card used in the kanban system.
late 20C. **Japanese** billboard, sign.

kanga (kang´gə), **khanga** *n*. a piece of brightly coloured cotton worn as a woman's dress in E Africa.
mid-20C. **Kiswahili.**

kanji (kan´ji) *n*. (*pl*. **kanjis**) a script for representing Japanese syllables derived from Chinese orthography.
early 20C. **Japanese**, from *kan* Chinese + *ji* letter, character.

kanoon (kənoon´) *n*. a kind of dulcimer or zither with 50 or 60 strings.
19C. **Persian** *ḳānūn*, from Arabic, ult. from Greek *kanōn*.

kantar (kan´tə), **cantar** *n*. an Oriental measure of weight, varying from 100–130 pounds (45.4–59.0 kilograms).
16C. **Arabic** *ḳinṭār*, pl. *ḳanāṭīr*, from Latin *centenarius* centenary.

kantikoy (kan´tikoi) *n*. **1** a North American Indian ceremonial dance. **2** a meeting for dancing, a dancing match.
17C. **Delaware** *kéntke:w*, lit. he dances.

kaolin (kā´əlin) *n*. a porcelain clay (also used medicinally as a poultice or internally) derived principally from the decomposition of feldspar, China clay.
18C. **French**, from Chinese *gāolĭng*, lit. high hill, a place in Jiangxi province where the clay is found.

kapellmeister (kəpel´mīstə), **capellmeister** *n*. (*pl*. **kapellmeister**, **capellmeister**) the musical director of a choir, band or orchestra, esp. a German one.
19C. **German**, from *Kapelle* court orchestra, from Medieval Latin *capella* chapel + *Meister* master.

kapok (kā´pok) *n*. a fine woolly or silky fibre enveloping the seeds of a tropical tree, *Ceiba pentandra*, used for stuffing cushions etc.
18C. **Malay** *kapuk*.

kappa (kap´ə) *n*. the tenth letter of the Greek alphabet (Κ, κ).
14–15C. **Greek.**

kaput (kəput´) *a*. (*coll*.) finished, done for, smashed up.
19C. **German** *kaputt*, from French (*être*) *capot* (to be) without tricks (in piquet etc.). Cp. CAPOT.

karabiner (karəbē´nə) *n*. a metal clip with a spring inside it, for attaching to a piton, used in mountaineering.
mid-20C. Abbr. of **German** *Karabinerhaken* spring hook.

karaoke (karəō´ki, kari-) *n*. a leisure activity in which members of an audience can sing solo with pre-recorded backing music.
late 20C. **Japanese**, from *kara* empty + *oke*, abbr. of *ōkesutora* orchestra.
• The orchestra is 'empty' until complemented by the singers. Japanese *ōkesutora* represents English *orchestra*.

karate (kərah´ti) *n*. a traditional Japanese martial art, based on blows and kicks.
mid-20C. **Japanese**, from *kara* empty + *te* hand.
• Karate is a form of unarmed combat.

karma (kah´mə) *n*. **1** in Buddhism and Hinduism, the results of action, ethical causation as determining future existence, esp. the cumulative consequence of a person's acts in one stage of existence as controlling their destiny in the next. **2** destiny.
19C. **Sanskrit** *karman* action, effect, fate.

Karoo (kəroo´), **Karroo** *n.* (*pl.* **Karoos**, **Karroos**) any of the waterless South African tablelands, esp. the Great and the Little Karoo in S Cape Province.
18C. Nama dry.

karoshi (kərō´shi) *n.* death through overwork.
late 20C. Japanese, from *karo* overwork, stress + *shi* death.

kaross (kəros´) *n.* a traditional South African garment made of skins with the hair left on.
18C. Afrikaans *karos*, ? from Nama *caro-s* skin blanket.

karst (kahst) *n.* the characteristic scenery of a limestone region with underground streams, caverns and potholes forming a drainage system.
19C. German *der Karst*, a limestone plateau region in Slovenia, SE Europe.

kasbah (kaz´bah), **casbah** *n.* **1** the castle or fortress in a N African city. **2** the area around this.
18C. French *casbah*, from Maghribi pronun. of Arabic *ḳaṣaba* fortress.

kasha (kash´ə) *n.* a type of porridge made from cooked buckwheat or other grains.
19C. Russian.

kashruth (kashroot´), **kashrut** *n.* **1** the state of being kosher. **2** the Jewish dietary rules.
early 20C. Hebrew legitimacy (in religion). See KOSHER.

kata (kat´ə) *n.* a martial arts exercise consisting of a sequence of movements.
mid-20C. Japanese.

katabasis (katab´əsis) *n.* a military retreat.
19C. Greek going down, from *katabainein*, from *kata* down + *bainein* to go.

katakana (katəkah´nə) *n.* an angular form of Japanese syllabary.
18C. Japanese from *kata* side + KANA.
● The characters so named originated as mnemonic symbols written alongside the Chinese characters that they represented.

kathak (kath´ək, kəthahk´) *n.* a type of Indian classical dance involving mime.
mid-20C. Sanskrit *kathaka* professional storyteller, from *kathā* story.

kathakali (katəkah´li) *n.* a type of S Indian drama consisting of dance and mime.
early 20C. Malayalam *kathakaḷi*, from Sanskrit *kathā* story + Malayalam *kaḷi* play.

katharevusa (kathərev´əsə, -us-), **katharevousa** *n.* a literary form of modern Greek, based on ancient Greek.
early 20C. Modern Greek *kathareuousa*, fem. of *kathareuōn*, pres.p. of Greek *kathareuein* to be pure, from *katharos* pure.
● The form of Greek was formerly that officially used by the state, as opposed to the popular and spoken demotic (from Greek *dēmos* the people).

katzenjammer (kat´zənjamə) *n.* **1** a hangover. **2** emotional distress.
19C. German, from *Katzen* (comb. form of *Katze* cat) + *Jammer* distress, wailing. Cp. coll. English 'cats' chorus'. The German word was popularized by *The Katzenjammer Kids*, a comic strip by Rudolph Dirks first drawn for the *New York Journal* in 1897.

kava (kah´və), **kaava** *n.* **1** a Polynesian shrub, *Piper methysticum*. **2** a beverage prepared from the chewed or pounded roots of this.
18C. Tongan.

kayak (kī´ak), **kaiak** *n.* **1** the Inuit and Alaskan canoe, made of sealskins stretched on a light wooden framework. **2** a small covered canoe resembling this. ~*v.i.* (*pres.p.* **kayaking**, *past, p.p.* **kayaked**) to travel in a kayak, to paddle a kayak.
18C. Inuit *qayaq.* Cp. UMIAK.

kebab (kibab´), **cabob** (kəbob´) *n.* small pieces of meat, vegetables etc., cooked on skewers.
17C. Arabic *kabāb,* ? ult. from Persian. See also DONER KEBAB, SHISH KEBAB.

kedgeree (kej´ərē) *n.* **1** a stew of rice, pulse, onions, eggs etc., a common Indian dish. **2** a dish of fish, rice, hard-boiled eggs etc.
17C. Hindi *khichṛī,* from Sanskrit *khiccā* dish of boiled rice and sesame.

keeshond (kās´hond, kēs´-) *n.* a Dutch breed of dog, with a heavy coat, pointed muzzle, and erect ears.
early 20C. Dutch *Kees,* pet form of male forename *Cornelius* + *hond* dog.

kef (kēf, kef), **kief** (kēf), **kif** (kif) *n.* **1** the drowsy, dreamy, trancelike condition produced by the use of marijuana etc. **2** dreamy repose, happy idleness. **3** Indian hemp, smoked to produce this condition.
19C. Arabic *kayf.*

keffiyeh (kefē´yə), **kaffiyeh** (kafē´yə) *n.* a Bedouin Arab's kerchief headdress.
19C. Arabic *kūffiyya,* coll. *keffiyya.*

kenaf (kənaf´) *n.* the fibre from an Asian hibiscus, used in ropes.
19C. Persian, var. of *kanab* hemp.

kendo (ken´dō) *n.* the Japanese martial art of fencing, usu. with pliable bamboo staves, occasionally with swords.
early 20C. Japanese, from *ken* sword + *dō* way.

kenosis (kənō´sis) *n.* (*Theol.*) Christ's relinquishment of the divine nature at the Incarnation.
19C. Greek *kenōsis* an emptying.
● The reference is to Phil. ii.7, where Paul says that Christ 'made himself of no reputation'. In the Revised Version, the original Greek words, *heauton ekenōse,* are translated 'emptied himself'.

kepi (kā´pē, kep´ē) *n.* (*pl.* **kepis**) a French flat-topped military hat with a horizontal peak.
19C. French *képi,* from Swiss German *Käppi,* dim. of *Kappe* cap.

kermes (kœ´mēz) *n.* **1** the dried bodies of the females of an insect, *Kermes ilicis,* yielding a red or scarlet dye. **2** dye from this source.
16C. French *kermès,* from Arabic *ḳirmiz.*

kermis (kœ´mis), **kirmess** *n.* **1** in the Netherlands, a fair or outdoor festival or merrymaking, orig. a church festival. **2** (*N Am.*) a charity fair.
16C. Dutch, from *kerk* church + *misse* mass.
● The word was originally the term for a mass held on the annual anniversary of a church's dedication, with an accompanying fair.

kerygma (kərig´mə) *n.* in the early Christian Church, the teaching of the Gospel.
19C. Greek *kērugma,* from *kērussein* to proclaim.

khaddar (kah´də), **khadi** (-di) *n.* Indian hand-woven cloth.
early 20C. Punjabi.

khaki (kah´ki) *a.* dust-coloured, dull brownish yellow. ~*n.* (*pl.* **khakis**) **1** a dull brownish-yellow colour. **2** a twilled cloth of this colour, used for army uniforms.
19C. Urdu *ḳākī* dust-coloured, from *ḳāk* dust, from Persian.

khalasi (kəlas´i) *n.* (*pl.* **khalasis**) a labourer or servant in the Indian subcontinent.
18C. Urdu *k̲alāṣī.*

khamsin (kam´sin), **hamsin** (ham´sin) *n.* a hot southerly wind blowing in Egypt for some 50 days between March and May.
17C. Arabic *k̲amāsīn,* from *k̲amsīn* fifty.

khan[1] (kahn, kan) *n.* **1** a title given to officials and rulers in central Asia etc., equivalent to 'esquire'. **2** (*Hist.*) a king or emperor, esp. the chief ruler of a Tartar, Turkish, and Mongol tribe, or the Chinese emperor in the Middle Ages.
14–15C. Old French *chan* or Medieval Latin *canus,* from Turkic *k̲ān* lord, prince.
● The title was originally popularized in Europe by the Mongol warrior Genghis Khan, *c.*1162–1227, and was later associated with the Aga Khan as spiritual head of the Ismaili Muslim sect. (Aga Khan I was granted his title in 1818.)

khan[2] (kahn, kan) *n.* a caravanserai.
14–15C. Persian *k̲ān.*

kheda (ked´ə) *n.* an enclosure used in India etc., for catching elephants.
18C. Assamese and Bengali *khedā.*

Khedive (kidēv´) *n.* (*Hist.*) the official title of the governor of Egypt when under Turkish rule, 1867–1914.
19C. French *khédive,* from Ottoman Turkish *k̲ediv,* from Persian *k̲adiw* prince, var. of *k̲udaiw* petty god, from *k̲udā* god.

khus-khus (kŭs´kŭs), **cuscus** *n.* the fibrous, aromatic root of an Indian grass, used for making fans, baskets etc.
19C. Urdu, from Persian *k̲ask̲as.*

kia ora (kēə aw´rə) *int.* (*New Zeal.*) greetings!, your health!
19C. Maori.
● The phrase is familiar as the brand name of a fruit squash, originally sold in Australia.

kibbutz (kibuts´) *n.* (*pl.* **kibbutzim** (-im)) a communal agricultural settlement in Israel.
mid-20C. Modern Hebrew *qibbūṣ* gathering.

kibitka (kibit´kə) *n.* **1** a Russian wheeled vehicle with a tentlike covering, used as a sledge in snowy weather. **2** a Tartar circular tent, usu. made of lattice-work and felt. **3** a Tartar family.
18C. Russian, from Turkic *kebit, kibit* + Russian suf. *-ka.*

kibitzer (kib´itsə) *n.* (*N Am., coll.*) **1** an interfering onlooker, esp. at a card game. **2** a meddler, a person who offers unwanted advice.
early 20C. Yiddish, from *kibitz,* from German *kiebitzen,* from *Kiebitz* lapwing, peewit.
● The lapwing is a noisy, fussy bird.

kiblah (kib´lə), **qibla** *n.* **1** the direction of the Kaaba at Mecca, to which Muslims turn during prayer. **2** a mihrab.
17C. Arabic *k̲ibla* that which is opposite.

kiddush (kid´ush) *n.* a Jewish ceremony of prayer and blessing over wine, performed at a meal ushering in the Sabbath or a holy day.
18C. Hebrew *qiddūš* sanctification.

kieselguhr (kē´zəlguə) *n.* a type of diatomite.
19C. German, from *Kiesel* gravel + *Guhr* fermentation.

kilim (kil´im, kē´lim) *n.* a pileless woven carpet made in the Middle East.
19C. Turkish *kilim,* from Persian *gelīm.*

kimchi (kim´chi) *n.* a type of strongly flavoured cabbage pickle.
19C. Korean *kimch'i*.
● Kimchi is a Korean national dish.

kimono (kimō´nō) *n.* (*pl.* **kimonos**)
1 a loose robe fastened with a sash, the principal outer garment of Japanese costume. **2** a dressing gown resembling this.
17C. Japanese, from *ki* wearing + *mono* thing.

kina (kē´nə) *n.* the standard monetary unit of Papua New Guinea.
late 20C. Tolai, lit. clam, mussel (orig. used as currency).

kincob (king´kob) *n.* a rich Indian fabric interwoven with gold or silver thread.
18C. Urdu and Persian *kamk̠āb* gold or silver brocade, alt. of *kamk̠ā* damask silk, from Chinese.

kindergarten (kin´dəgahtən) *n.* a school for infants and children below official school age, in which knowledge is imparted chiefly by simple object lessons, by toys, games, singing and work.
19C. German, lit. children's garden, from pl. of *Kind* child + *Garten* garden.
● The word was originally the term for a school teaching young children according to the principles proposed by Friedrich Froebel, and it was he who coined it in 1840.

kiosk (kē´osk) *n.* **1** an open-fronted structure for the sale of newspapers etc. **2** a public telephone booth. **3** an open pavilion or summerhouse in Turkey, Iran etc. **4** (*Austral.*) a café in the grounds of a park, zoo etc. **5** a bandstand.
17C. French *kiosque*, from Turkish *köşk*, from Persian *kušk* pavilion.

kip (kip) *n.* (*pl.* **kip**, **kips**) the standard monetary unit of Laos.
mid-20C. Thai.

Kir® (kiə), **kir** *n.* a drink made from white wine and cassis.
mid-20C. Canon Félix *Kir*, 1876–1968, mayor of Dijon, France, said to have devised its recipe.

Kirche, Küche, Kinder (kiə´khə kü´khə kin´də) *int.* church, cooking, children.
early 20C. German.
● The words enumerate the occupations regarded as fitting for a woman under the Nazi regime. The order is sometimes varied as *Kinder, Kirche, Küche*, and a late 19C version added *Kleider* clothes to this.

kirsch (kiəsh), **kirschwasser** (kiəsh´vasə) *n.* an alcoholic liqueur distilled from the fermented juice of the black cherry.
19C. German, abbr. of *Kirschenwasser*, from *Kirsche* cherry + *Wasser* water.

Kislev (kis´lef, -lef´) *n.* the third month of the civil, and the ninth of the ecclesiastical Jewish year, corresponding roughly to December.
14–15C. Hebrew *kislēw*.

kismet (kiz´mət, kis´-) *n.* fate, destiny.
19C. Turkish *k̠smet*, from Arabic *k̠ismat* division, portion, lot, fate.

kitsch (kich) *n.* art or literature that is considered to be inferior or in bad taste, esp. that designed to appeal to popular sentimentality.
early 20C. German, prob. from German dial. *kitschen* to smear.

klepht (kleft) *n.* **1** any of the Greeks who refused to submit to the Turks after the Turkish conquest (15th cent.), and took refuge in the mountains. **2** any of their descendants, many of whom lived as bandits. **3** a bandit, a brigand.
19C. Modern Greek *klephtēs*, from Greek *kleptēs* thief.

klong (klong) *n.* a canal in Thailand.
19C. Thai.

kloof (kloof) *n.* (*S Afr.*) a ravine, gully or mountain gorge.
18C. Dutch cleft, rel. to English *cleave*.

klutz (klŭts) *n.* (*N Am., sl.*) a clumsy or foolish person.
mid-20C. Yiddish, from German *Klotz* wooden block, rel to English *clot*.

knackwurst (nak´wœst) *n.* a type of short, fat, spicy German sausage.
mid-20C. German, from *knacken* to make a cracking noise + WURST.

Knesset (knes´it, -et) *n.* the single-chamber parliament of the modern state of Israel.
mid-20C. Hebrew, lit. gathering.

knish (kənish´) *n.* a filled dumpling that is baked or fried.
mid-20C. Yiddish, from Russian, kind of bun or dumpling.

knout (nowt) *n.* (*Hist.*) a whip or scourge formerly used as an instrument of punishment in Russia. ~*v.t.* to punish with the knout.
17C. French, from Russian *knut*, from Old Norse *knútr*, rel. to English *knot*.

koan (kō´an) *n.* a problem with no logical answer, used for meditation by Zen Buddhists.
mid-20C. Japanese *kōan*, from Chinese *gōngàn* official business.

kobold (kō´bōld) *n.* in Germanic folklore, an elf or sprite frequenting houses; also a gnome or goblin haunting mines and hidden lodes.
19C. German.
• The German word gave the English name of the metallic element *cobalt*, so called by miners from their belief that it was a worthless substance put in silver ore by goblins after stealing the silver.

koeksister (kuk´sistə) *n.* (*S Afr.*) a cake made with sweetened dough.
early 20C. Afrikaans, ? from *koek* cake + *sissen* to sizzle.

kofta (kof´tə, kō´-) *n.* in Indian cookery, a spiced ball of meat, vegetables etc.
19C. Urdu and Persian *koftah* pounded meat.

kohl (kōl) *n.* fine black powder, usu. of antimony or lead sulphide used to darken the eyelids.
18C. Arabic *kuḥl*.

kohlrabi (kōlrah´bi) *n.* (*pl.* **kohlrabies**) a variety of cabbage, *Brassica oleracea caulorapa*, with an edible swollen stem resembling a turnip.
19C. German, from (with assim. to *Kohl* cabbage) Italian *cauli rape* or *cavoli rape*, pl. of *cavolo rapa* cabbage turnip, from Medieval Latin *caulorapa*.

koine (koi´nē) *n.* **1** a Greek dialect used as a common language in the E Mediterranean during the Hellenistic and Roman periods. **2** a lingua franca.
19C. Greek *koinē*, fem. sing. of *koinos* common, ordinary.

kolkhoz (kolkhoz´, kŭlk´hawz) *n.* (*pl.* **kolkhozy** (-zi)) a cooperative or collective farm in the former Soviet Union.
early 20C. Russian, abbr. of *kollektivnoe khozyaĭstvo* collective farm.

Kol Nidre (kol nid´ri) *n.* **1** the service marking the beginning of Yom Kippur. **2** the opening prayer of this service.
19C. Aramaic *kol niḏrē* all the vows (the first words of the opening prayer).

Komsomol (kom´səmol) *n.* **1** the Young Communist League of the former Soviet Union. **2** a member of this.
mid-20C. Russian, abbr. of *Kommunisticheskiĭ soyuz molodëzhi* Communist Union of Youth.

kop (kop) *n.* **1** (*S Afr.*) a prominent hill. **2** (*Hist.*) a high terrace for standing spectators at a football stadium.
19C. Afrikaans, from Dutch head.
● Sense 2 derives from *Spion Kop*, a mountain in Natal that was the site of a battle (1900) in the Boer War.

kopi (kō´pi) *n.* (*Austral.*) powdered gypsum.
19C. Australian Aboriginal (Bagandji) *yabi.*

kopje (kop´i), **koppie** *n.* (*S Afr.*) a small hill.
19C. Afrikaans, from Dutch, dim. of *kop* head. Cp. KOP.

koradji (kor´əji, kəraj´i) *n.* (*Austral.*) an Aboriginal medicine man.
18C. Australian Aboriginal (Dharuk) *garraaji.*

Koran (kərahn´), **Quran**, **Qur'an** *n.* the Muslim sacred scriptures consisting of the revelations delivered orally by Muhammad and collected after his death.
17C. Arabic *ḳur'ān* recitation, reading, from *ḳara'a* to read, to recite.

korfball (kawf´bawl) *n.* a game similar to basketball, with teams each consisting of six men and six women.
early 20C. Dutch *korfbal*, from *korf* basket + *bal* ball.

korma (kaw´mə) *n.* an Indian dish composed of braised meat or vegetables cooked in spices and a yogurt or cream sauce.
19C. Urdu *ḳormā*, from Turkish *kavurma*, lit. cooked meat.

korrigan (kor´igən) *n.* a fairy or witch in Breton folklore, noted esp. for stealing children.
19C. Breton (dial.), fem. of *korrig* gnome, dim. of *korr* dwarf. Cp. Welsh *cor* dwarf.

koruna (koroo´nə) *n.* the standard currency unit of the Czech Republic and Slovakia, equal to 100 haler.
early 20C. Czech crown.

kosher (kō´shə) *a.* **1** (of food or a shop where it is sold) fulfilling the requirements of the Jewish law. **2** (*coll.*) genuine, above board. **3** permitted, right. ~*n.* **1** kosher food. **2** a kosher shop.
19C. Hebrew *kāšēr* fit, proper.

koto (kō´tō) *n.* (*pl.* **kotos**) a Japanese stringed instrument with a wooden body and 13 silk strings.
18C. Japanese.

kourbash (kuə´bash), **kurbash** *n.* a hide whip used as an instrument of punishment in Turkey and Egypt.
19C. Arabic *kurbāj*, from Turkish *k´rbaç* whip.

kowtow (kowtow´), **kotow** (kōtow´) *n.* the ancient Chinese method of obeisance by kneeling or prostrating oneself, and touching the ground with the forehead. ~*v.i.* **1** to act obsequiously. **2** (*Hist.*) to perform the kowtow.
19C. Chinese *kētóu*, from *kē* to knock, to strike + *tóu* head.

kraal (krahl) *n.* (*S Afr.*) **1** a South African village or group of huts enclosed by a palisade. **2** an enclosure for cattle or sheep.
18C. Afrikaans, from Portuguese *curral*, from Nama.

kraft (krahft), **kraft paper** *n.* strong, brown, wrapping paper.
early 20C. Swedish strength, from *kraftpapper* kraft paper.

Kraft durch Freude (kraft duəkh froi´də) *n.* strength through joy.
mid-20C. German.
● The words originated as a German Labour Front slogan, first used on 2 December 1933.

kraken (krah´kən) *n.* a fabulous sea monster, said to have been seen at different times off the coast of Norway. **18C. Norwegian** dial., from *krake* kraken + Norwegian *-n*, definite article suf.

krans (krahns), **krantz** (krahnts), **kranz** *n.* (*S Afr.*) a precipitous upward slope, esp. of crags walling in a valley. **18C. Afrikaans**, from Dutch coronet, chaplet, from Germanic base meaning ring. Cp. German *Kranz* coronet, circle.

Kraut (krowt) *n.* (*sl., offensive*) a German. **19C. German** vegetable, cabbage. Cp. SAUERKRAUT.

kremlin (krem´lin) *n.* **1** the citadel of a Russian town. **2** (**the Kremlin**) **a** the citadel of Moscow enclosing the old imperial palace, now government buildings etc. **b** the Russian Government. **17C. French**, from Russian *kreml'* citadel.

kreuzer (kroit´sə) *n.* (*Hist.*) a copper coin (earlier silver), formerly a unit of currency in Germany and Austria. **16C. German** *Kreuz* cross.
• The coin is so named from the two crosses with which it was originally stamped.

kriegspiel (krēg´spēl) *n.* **1** a war game played on maps. **2** a form of chess in which each player has their own board, and does not see that of the opponent, with whom they communicate through an umpire. **19C. German**, from *Krieg* war + *Spiel* game.

krimmer (krim´ə) *n.* the tightly curled black or grey fleece from a type of lamb found in the Crimea. **19C. German**, from *Krim* Crimea, a peninsula between the sea of Azov and the Black Sea.

kris (krēs), **crease**, **creese**, **cris** *n.* a Malaysian or Indonesian dagger with a wavy edge. **16C. Malay** *keris*.

kromesky (krəmes´ki) *n.* (*pl.* **kromeskies**) a roll or ball of minced meat or fish wrapped in bacon, then fried. **19C. Polish** *kromeczka* small slice, dim. of *kromka* slice.

krona (krō´nə) *n.* **1** (*pl.* **kronor**) the basic monetary unit of Sweden. **2** (*pl.* **kronur**) the basic monetary unit of Iceland. **19C. Swedish** crown.

krone (krō´nə) *n.* **1** (*pl.* **kroner**) the monetary unit of Denmark and Norway. **2** (*Hist.*) (*pl.* **kronen**) a German gold coin. **3** (*Hist.*) (*pl.* **kronen**) an Austrian silver coin and monetary unit. **19C. Danish and Norwegian**, from German crown.

krugerrand (kroo´gərand) *n.* a coin minted in South Africa containing one troy ounce of gold. **mid-20C.** Stephanus Johannes Paulus *Kruger*, 1825–1904, President of the Transvaal (1883–99) + RAND.

krummhorn (krum´hawn, krŭm´-), **crumhorn** *n.* **1** a medieval wind instrument with a curved tube and a tone like that of a clarinet. **2** an organ stop consisting of reed pipes, with a similar tone. **17C. German**, from *krumm* crooked, curved + *Horn* horn.

Kshatriya (kshat´riyə) *n.* a member of the warrior caste in the Hindu caste system. **18C. Sanskrit** *kṣatriya*, from *kṣatra* rule.

kudos (kū´dos) *n.* **1** glory, fame, credit. **2** (*N Am.*) praise, acclaim. **18C. Greek** praise, renown.

kukri (kuk´ri) *n.* (*pl.* **kukris**) a curved knife broadening at the end, used by the Gurkhas.
19C. Nepali *khukuri.*

kulak (koo´lak) *n.* (*Hist.*) a prosperous Russian peasant of the class owning their own farms.
19C. Russian, lit. fist, i.e. tight-fisted person, from Turkic *ķol* hand.

Kultur (kul´tuǝ) *n.* (*often derog.*) German culture, esp. in its authoritarian and militaristic aspects.
early 20C. German, from Latin *cultura* or French *culture* culture.

Kulturkampf (kultuǝ´kampf) *n.*
1 (*Hist.*) a conflict between the German government and the Catholic Church at the end of the 19th cent. **2** a conflict between secular and religious authorities over e.g. education.
19C. German, from *Kultur* culture + *Kampf* struggle.

kumiss (koo´mis), **koomis**, **koumiss**, **kumis** *n.* an alcoholic liquor made by Tartars from fermented mare's milk.
16C. French *koumis*, Russian *kumys*, from Tartar *kumiz.*

kümmel (kum´ǝl) *n.* a liqueur flavoured with caraway seeds made in Germany and Russia.
19C. German, representing Middle High German, Old High German *kumil*, var. of *kumîn* cumin.

kung fu (kŭng foo´, kung) *n.* a Chinese martial art resembling karate.
19C. Chinese *gōngfù* skill, from *gōng* merit + *fù* man.

Kuomintang (kwōmintang´) *n.* (*Hist.*) the Chinese Nationalist party founded by Sun Yat Sen and holding power from 1928 until replaced by the Communist Party in 1949.
early 20C. Chinese *guómíndǎng* national people's party, from *guó* nation + *mín* people + *dǎng* party.

Kuo-yü (kwōyü´, gwaw-) *n.* a form of Mandarin taught all over China.
mid-20C. Chinese *guó* nation + *yǔ* language.

kurdaitcha (kǝdī´tshǝ), **kadaitcha** *n.*
1 in some Australian Aboriginal tribes, the practice of using a bone to cast spells. **2** a man who does this.
19C. Australian Aboriginal (Aranda) *gwedaje.*

kuri (koo´ri) *n.* (*pl.* **kuris**) (*New Zeal.*) a mongrel dog.
19C. Maori dog.

kursaal (kuǝ´zahl) *n.* **1** a public room for the use of visitors, esp. at German health resorts. **2** a casino.
19C. German *Kur* cure + *Saal* hall, room.

kurta (kuǝ´tǝ), **kurtha** *n.* a loose tunic worn by Hindus.
early 20C. Urdu and Persian *kurtah.*

kvass (kvahs) *n.* beer made from rye, esp. in Russia.
16C. Russian *kvas*, rel. to *kislyĭ* sour, Latin *caseus* cheese.

kvetch (kvech) *v.i.* (*esp. N Am., sl.*) to whine, to complain.
mid-20C. Yiddish *kvetsh* (n.), *kvetschn* (v.), from German *Quetsche* crusher, presser, *quetschen* to crush, to press.

kwacha (kwah´chǝ) *n.* the standard unit of currency in Zambia and Malawi.
mid-20C. Bantu dawn.
● The name represents a Zambian nationalist slogan calling for a new 'dawn' of freedom.

kwanza (kwan´zǝ) *n.* (*pl.* **kwanza**, **kwanzas**) the standard unit of currency of Angola.

late 20C. Prob. from River *Kwanza* (now *Cuanza*), Angola.
● The river name means 'first', 'prime' and this sense is probably shared by the currency, as the basic monetary unit.

kwashiorkor (kwashiaw´kaw) *n.* a nutritional disease caused by lack of protein.
mid-20C. Ghanaian local name.
● The word is said to mean deposed child (i.e. deposed from the mother's breast by a newborn sibling) in one African dialect and red boy in another. The latter would refer to the reddish-orange discoloration of the hair that the disease causes.

kwela (kwā´lə) *n.* a type of jazzlike pop music of central and southern Africa.
mid-20C. Afrikaans, from Zulu *khwela* to climb, to mount.

kyat (kyaht) *n.* (*pl.* **kyat**, **kyats**) the standard unit of currency of Burma (Myanmar).
mid-20C. Burmese.

kylin (kē´lin) *n.* a mythical animal of composite form, shown on Chinese and Japanese pottery.
19C. Chinese *qílín*, from *qí* male + *lín* female.

Kyrie (kir´iā, kiə´riā), **Kyrie eleison** (ilā´izon, -son) *n.* **1** this phrase used as a short petition in the liturgies of the Eastern and Western Churches, esp. at the beginning of the Eucharist or Mass. **2** a musical setting of this.
12–14C. Medieval Latin, from Greek *Kuriē eleēson* Lord, have mercy.

kyu (kyoo) *n.* (*pl.* **kyus**) each of the grades for beginners in judo, karate etc.
mid-20C. Japanese *kyū* class.

L

laager (lah´gə) *n.* **1** (*Hist.*) in South
Africa, a defensive encampment, esp.
one formed by wagons drawn into a
circle. **2** (*Mil.*) a park for armoured
vehicles etc. **3** (the mental attitude of) a
group of people who draw together in
defence of established ideas and
institutions and to resist change.
~*v.t.* **1** to form into a laager. **2** to encamp
(a body of people) in a laager. ~*v.i.* to
encamp.
19C. Afrikaans. Cp. German *Lager*
camp.

labarum (lab´ərəm) *n.* **1** the imperial
standard of Constantine the Great
(bearing the cross and a monogram of
the Greek name of Christ), adopted by
him after his conversion to Christianity.
2 a banner resembling this used in
religious processions.
17C. Late Latin, of unknown orig.

laborare est orare (laborah´ri est
orah´ri) *int.* to work is to pray (a motto
of the Benedictine Order).
19C. Latin.

lachryma Christi (lakrima kris´tē) *n.* a
wine from S Italy, orig. a sweet white
wine made from grapes grown on the
slopes of Mt Vesuvius.
17C. Modern Latin Christ's tear, from
lachryma tear + gen. of *Christus* Christ.
Cp. LIEBFRAUMILCH.

lacrimae rerum (lakrimē reə´rəm) *n.*
the sadness of life.
early 20C. Latin, lit. tears (for the
nature) of things.
● The words come from Virgil's *Aeneid*
(I) (1C BC): *Sunt lacrimae rerum et
mentem mortalia tangunt* 'There are
tears shed for things and mortality
touches the heart'. The spelling
lachrymae rerum is also
(unetymologically) found.

lacrimoso (lakrimō´zō) *a.* (*Mus.*) tearful.
19C. Italian.

lacuna (ləkū´nə) *n.* (*pl.* **lacunas,
lacunae** (-nē)) **1** a gap, blank or hiatus,
esp. in a manuscript or text. **2** (*Anat.*) a
cavity, small pit or depression, e.g. in a
bone.
17C. Latin, from *lacus* lake.

Ladino (lədē´nō) *n.* (*pl.* **Ladinos**)
1 a dialect based on Spanish with an
admixture of Hebrew, written in Hebrew
characters, spoken by Sephardic Jews.
2 a Spanish American of mixed (white
and Indian) descent.
19C. Spanish, from Latin *Latinus*
Latin.

ladino (lədē´nō) *n.* (*pl.* **ladinos**) a white
clover, *Trifolium repens*, used as
fodder.
early 20C. Italian.

la donna è mobile (la dona e mob´ilā)
int. woman is fickle.
19C. Italian.
● The phrase comes from an aria sung
by the Duke of Mantua in Verdi's opera
Rigoletto (1851).

lager (lah´gə) *n.* a light beer, blond in
colour and effervescent, the ordinary
beer of Germany.
19C. German *Lager-Bier* beer brewed for
keeping, from *Lager* storehouse.

lagniappe (lan´yap), **lagnappe** *n.*
(*NAm.*) **1** a small gift, esp. to a
customer. **2** a gratuity, a bonus.
19C. Louisiana French, from Spanish
la ñapa the gift, from Quechua *yapa*
something given extra.

lahar (lah´hah) *n.* a landslide or mudflow
consisting mainly of volcanic debris and
usu. occurring after heavy rain.
early 20C. Javanese.

laissez-aller (lesāal´ā), **laisser-aller**
n. **1** absence of restraint. **2** absence of
conventionality, unconstrainedness.
19C. French, lit. allow to go.

laissez-faire (lesāfeə´), **laisser-faire** *n.*
the principle of non-interference, esp.
by the Government in industrial and
commercial affairs. ~*a.* operating on this
principle.
19C. French, lit. allow to do.
● The maxim *laissez-faire et laissez-
passer* is particularly associated with
18C French free-trade economists.

laissez-passer (lesāpas´ā), **laisser-
passer** *n.* a pass or permit allowing one
unrestricted access or movement.
early 20C. French, lit. allow to pass.

lakh (lahk), **lac** *n.* in the Indian
subcontinent, the number 100,000 (usu.
of a sum of rupees).
17C. Hindi *lākh*, from Sanskrit *lakṣa*
mark, token, 100,000.

lama (lah´mə) *n.* a Tibetan or Mongolian
Buddhist priest or monk.
17C. Tibetan *bla-ma* (with silent *b*), lit.
superior. Cp. DALAI LAMA.

lambada (lambah´də) *n.* **1** an erotic
Brazilian dance performed by couples
in close contact with one another who
gyrate their hips in synchronized
movements. **2** the music to accompany
this dance.
late 20C. Portuguese, lit. beating,
lashing, from *lambar* to beat, to whip.

lambda (lam´də) *n.* **1** the eleventh letter
of the Greek alphabet (Λ, λ)
transliterated as Roman *l*. **2** a symbol
denoting wavelength. **3** a symbol
denoting celestial longitude.
17C. Greek.

lambrequin (lam´brikin, -bəkin) *n.*
1 (*esp. NAm.*) an ornamental strip of
drapery over a door, window,
mantelshelf etc. **2** a strip of cloth or
other material worn as covering over
a helmet for protection from heat.
3 (*Her.*) the floating wreath of a helmet.
18C. French, from Dutch dim. of *lamper*
veil.

lamé (lah´mā) *n.* a fabric containing
metallic, usu. gold or silver threads.
~*a.* made of such a fabric.
early 20C. French, lit. laminated, from
lame metal leaf, from Latin *lamina*.

lamia (lā´miə) *n.* **1** in classical mythology,
a lascivious evil spirit in the form of
a serpent with a woman's head.
2 a sorceress, a witch.
14–15C. Latin, from Greek mythical
monster, carnivorous fish.

lampion (lam´piən) *n.* an oil lamp with
a small coloured globe or cup, used in
illuminations.
19C. French, from Italian *lampione*,
augm. of *lampa* (from French *lampe*)
lamp.

Land (lant, land) *n.* (*pl.* **Länder** (len´də))
a federal state in Germany; a province in
Austria.
early 20C. German land.

landammann (lan´dəmən) *n.* the
chairman of the governing body in some
of the Swiss cantons.
17C. Swiss German, from *Land* land +
Ammann, var. of German *Amtmann*,
from *Amt* office + *Mann* man.

landau (lan´daw, -dow) *n.* a four-wheeled
horse-drawn carriage with folding hoods
at the front and back which can be
raised to cover the occupants.
18C. *Landau*, a town in W Germany,
where orig. made.

landdros (land´ros), **landdrost** (-rost)
n. (*Hist.*) a district magistrate, civil
commissioner, fiscal agent etc., in
South Africa.
18C. Afrikaans, from Dutch *land* land
+ *drost* bailiff.

ländler (lend´lə) *n.* **1** an Austrian or
S German dance, similar to a slow
waltz, in which the couples spin and
clap. **2** a piece of music in the rhythm
or style of this dance.
19C. German, from *Landel*, a district of
Austria, north of the River Ems.

landsknecht (lants´knekht) *n.* (*Hist.*) a
mercenary foot soldier, esp. a German
pikeman, in the late 15th, 16th and 17th
cents.
17C. German, from gen. of LAND +
Knecht soldier.

Landsturm (lant´shtooəm) *n.* **1** the
legislative assembly in a German-
speaking country. **2** general conscription
in time of war.
19C. German, lit. land storm.

Landtag (lant´tahk) *n.* **1** the legislative
assembly of a German or Austrian Land.

2 (*Hist.*) the diet of the Holy Roman
Empire or the German Federation.
16C. German, lit. land day.

Landwehr (lant´veər) *n.* the army
reserve in German-speaking countries.
19C. German, lit. land defence.

langlauf (lang´lowf) *n.* cross-country
skiing; a cross-country skiing race.
early 20C. German, lit. long run.

langouste (lãgoost´) *n.* the spiny lobster.
19C. French, from Old Provençal
lagosta, from Popular Latin alt. of Latin
locusta lobster.

langue (lãg) *n.* (in linguistics) language
regarded as an abstract system tacitly
shared by a speech community.
12–14C. French, from Latin *lingua*
tongue, language.

langue de chat (lãg də sha´) *n.* a thin,
finger-shaped biscuit or piece of
chocolate.
19C. French, lit. cat's tongue.

lansquenet (lans´kənet) *n.* **1** a
landsknecht. **2** a card game of German
origin, consisting largely of betting.
17C. French. See LANDSKNECHT.

lapilli (ləpil´ī) *n.pl.* volcanic ashes,
consisting of small, angular, stony or
slaggy fragments.
18C. Latin, pl. of *lapillus*, dim. of *lapis*
stone.

lapis lazuli (lapis laz´ūlī) *n.* **1** a rich blue
mineral, used as a gemstone, containing
sodium aluminium silicate and sulphur.
2 a pigment made from this. **3** its colour.
14–15C. Latin *lapis* stone + Medieval
Latin *lazuli*, gen. of *lazulum*, from
Persian *lā™ward* lapis lazuli.

lapsus (lap´səs) *n.* (*pl.* **lapsus**) (*formal*)
a lapse, a slip.
17C. Latin, p.p. of *labi* to slip.

lapsus calami (lapsəs kal´əmī) *n.* a slip of the pen.
  19C. Latin, from LAPSUS + gen. sing. of *calamus* reed, reed-pen.

lapsus linguae (lapsəs ling´wī, -gwē) *n.* a slip of the tongue.
  17C. Latin, from LAPSUS + gen. sing. of *lingua* tongue.

lar (lah) *n.* (*pl.* **lares** (lah´rēz)) an ancient Roman tutelary god, usu. a deified ancestor or hero.
  16C. Latin. Cp. LARES ET PENATES.

lares et penates (lah´rēz et pinah´tēz) *n.pl.* **1** the home, the household or the valued possessions contained in a home. **2** in ancient Rome, the household gods. **3** the statues representing these gods kept in a Roman house.
  16C. Latin, from pl. of LAR + *et* and + PENATES.
  • The semi-anglicized variant *lares and penates* is also found.

larghetto (lahget´ō) *adv.* (*Mus.*) somewhat slow.
  19C. Italian, dim. of LARGO.

largo (lah´gō) *adv.* (*Mus.*) slowly, broadly, in an ample, dignified style. ~*n.* (*pl.* **largos**) a piece of music played in this manner.
  17C. Italian broad, from Latin *largus* abundant, large.

larva (lah´və) *n.* (*pl.* **larvae** (-vē)) **1** the first condition of an insect on its issuing from the egg, when it is usu. in the form of a grub, caterpillar or maggot. **2** the half-developed state of other invertebrates that undergo metamorphosis.
  17C. Latin ghost, mask.
  • The stage was so called by Linnaeus because it is a 'ghost' form of the fully developed imago.

lasagne (ləsan´yə, -zan´-, -sahn´-),
  lasagna *n.* **1** pasta in the form of wide flat strips. **2** a baked dish consisting of this pasta, esp. layered with bolognese and béchamel sauces.
  19C. Italian, pl. of *lasagna*, ult. from Latin *lasanum* chamber pot, ? also cooking pot.

lasciate ogni speranza, voi ch'entrate (lashah´tā onyi speran´za voi kentrah´tā) *int.* abandon hope, all ye who enter here.
  early 20C. Italian.
  • The words are the inscription over the gates of Hell in Dante's *Inferno* (III) (*c.*1309–21).

La Tène (la ten´) *a.* of the later European Iron Age from the 5th–1st cents. BC.
  19C. *La Tène*, district at eastern end of Lake Neuchâtel, Switzerland, where remains of the culture were first discovered.

lathi (lah´ti) *n.* a long, heavy stick used as a weapon in India, esp. by police.
  19C. Hindi *lāṭhī*.

latifundium (latifŭn´diəm) *n.* (*pl.* **latifundia** (-diə)) a large landed or agricultural estate, esp. in ancient Rome.
  17C. Latin, from *latus* broad + *fundus* landed estate.

latke (lŭt´kə) *n.* a pancake made with grated potato in Jewish cookery.
  early 20C. Yiddish, from Russian *latka* earthenware cooking vessel.

latria (lat´riə, lətrī´ə) *n.* in the Roman Catholic Church, that supreme worship which can lawfully be offered to God alone.
  16C. Ecclesiastical Latin, from Greek *latreia*, from *latreuein* to wait on, to serve with prayer.

lava (lah´və) n. (pl. **lavas**) **1** molten matter flowing in streams from volcanic vents. **2** the solidified rock formed from the same matter by cooling.
18C. Italian (orig. Neapolitan dial.), from Latin *lavare* to wash.
• Italian etymologists derive the word from Latin *labes* a fall, from *labi* to fall.

lavabo (ləvah´bō, -vā´-) n. (pl. **lavabos**) **1** the washing of the celebrant's hands, in the Roman Catholic and other Churches, after the offertory and before the Eucharist. **2** the towel used in this ceremony, also the basin. **3** a washing trough or basin, often with running water, in monasteries.
18C. Latin I will wash, 1st pers. sing. fut. of *lavare* to wash.
• The word comes from the opening sentence of Ps. xxvi.6: *Lavabo inter innocentes manus meas* I will wash mine hands in innocency.

lavage (lā´vij, lavahj´) n. (Med.) the flushing out of a hollow organ with water or a medicated solution.
19C. French, from *laver* to wash.

lava-lava (lahvəlah´və) n. a rectangular piece of printed cloth worn as a shirtlike garment by both sexes in Polynesia.
19C. Samoan.

lavolta (ləvol´tə) n. (Hist.) an old Italian dance for two persons, with much high leaping, popular in the 16th cent.
16C. Italian, from *la* the + *volta* turn. Cp. VOLTA as an alternative name for the same dance.

layette (lāet´) n. the outfit or set of outfits for a newborn infant.
19C. French, dim. of Old French *laie* drawer, box, from Dutch *laege*.

lazaretto (lazəret´ō), **lazaret** (-ret´) n. (pl. **lazarettos**, **lazarets**) **1** a hospital (chiefly abroad) for persons suffering from some contagious disease, esp. leprosy. **2** a ship or other place of quarantine. **3** a storeroom or locker for provisions in ships or boats.
16C. Italian, dim. of *lazzaro* diseased person, lazar.

Lebensraum (lā´bənzrowm) n. territory considered necessary for a country's expanding population in terms of trade and settlement.
early 20C. German, lit. living space, from gen. of *Leben* life + *Raum* space, room.
• The concept of *Lebensraum* was adopted by Nazi Germany to justify the racist and expansionist policies of the Third Reich. In the mid-20C many German nationalists claimed *Lebensraum* was needed for the proper development of the country.

lechaim (ləkhay´im), **lehaim**, **l'chaim** int. a drinking toast. ~n. a small drink for toasting.
mid-20C. Hebrew *lĕ-ḥayyīm* to life!

lecythus (les´ithəs) n. (pl. **lecythi** (-thī)) in ancient Greece, a narrow-necked vase or flask for oil, unguents etc.
19C. Late Latin, from Greek *lēkuthos*.

lederhosen (lā´dəhōzən) n.pl. leather shorts with braces, the traditional male dress of Austria and Bavaria.
mid-20C. German, from *Leder* leather + pl. of *Hose* trouser.

legato (ligah´tō) adv., a. (Mus.) in an even gliding manner without a break. ~n. (pl. **legatos**) **1** this style of playing. **2** a legato passage.
18C. Italian, p.p. of *legare*, from Latin *ligare* to bind.

legerdemain (lejədimān´) n. **1** sleight of hand, a trick in which the eye is deceived by the quickness of the hand, conjuring. **2** jugglery, sophistry.
14–15C. French *légerdemain*, from *léger* light + *de* of + *main* hand.

legionnaire (lējəneə´) *n*. **1** a member of a foreign legion. **2** a member of the British or American Legions.
19C. French *légionnaire*, from *légion* legion.

lei (lā´i) *n*. a garland or necklace of flowers.
19C. Hawaiian.

leitmotiv (līt´mōtēf), **leitmotif** *n*. (*Mus.*) a leading, representative or recurring theme in a composition, orig. a musical theme invariably associated with a certain person, situation or idea throughout an opera etc.
19C. German, from *leit-* leading + *Motiv* motif.
• The term was first used in *c*.1865 by the Austrian composer A.W. Ambros in an article about Wagner's operas.

lek (lek) *n*. the chief currency of Albania.
early 20C. Abbr. of **Albanian** *Aleksandr* Alexander, from Alexander III (the Great), 356–323 BC, King of Macedonia.

lemma (lem´ə) *n*. (*pl.* **lemmas**, **lemmata** (-mətə)) **1** an auxiliary proposition taken to be valid in order to demonstrate some other proposition. **2** a theme, a subject, esp. when prefixed as a heading. **3** a dictionary headword. **4** in linguistics, the principal form of a word together with its variants and inflections. **5** a motto appended to a picture.
16C. Latin, from Greek *lēmma* something taken for granted, theme, argument, from base also of *lambanein* to take.

lempira (lempiə´rə) *n*. the standard unit of currency of Honduras, equivalent to 100 centavos.
mid-20C. *Lempira*, 1497–1537, an Indian chieftain killed when leading an army against the Spanish conquistadors.

lenis (lē´nis) *n*. (*pl.* **lenes** (lē´nēz)) a consonant, such as English *b* or *v*, articulated without muscular tension or force of breath. ~*a*. articulated in this way.
early 20C. Latin gentle.

lento (len´tō) *a., adv.* (*Mus.*) (to be played) slowly. ~*n*. (*pl.* **lentos**, **lenti** (-tē)) a piece of music played in this way.
18C. Italian slow, from Latin *lentus*.

Leo (lē´ō) *n*. **1** (*Astron.*) one of the twelve zodiacal constellations, the Lion. **2** (*Astrol.*) **a** the fifth sign of the zodiac, which the sun passes through between approx. 23 July and 22 August. **b** a person born under this sign.
pre-1200. Latin lion.

leone (lēō´ni) *n*. the standard unit of currency of Sierra Leone, equivalent to 100 cents.
mid-20C. Sierra *Leone*, a country on the coast of W Africa.

lepton (lep´ton) *n*. (*pl.* **lepta** (-tə)) **1** a modern Greek coin and monetary unit worth one hundredth of a drachma. **2** the smallest ancient Greek coin, the mite of the New Testament parable (Mark xii.42).
18C. Greek, neut. of *leptos* small.

lese-majesty (lēzmaj´əsti), **lèse-majesté** (lāzmazh´əstā) *n*. **1** an offence against the sovereign power or its representative, high treason. **2** an insult to a ruler or authority. **3** presumption.
14–15C. French *lèse-majesté*, from Latin *laesa maiestas* hurt majesty, from *laesa*, fem. p.p. pf *laedere* to injure, to hurt + *maiestas* majesty.

l'état c'est moi (lātah se mwah´) *n*. an expression used to imply that all power belongs to the speaker.
early 20C. French, lit. I am the state.
• The words were originally those of Louis XIV of France to the Parlement de Paris on 13 April 1655.

lettre de cachet (letrə də kash´ā) *n.*
(*pl.* **lettres de cachet** (letrə)) a royal
warrant for the imprisonment or exile
of a person without trial, in France
before the Revolution.
18C. French, lit. letter of seal, from
lettre letter + *de* of + *cachet* seal
(CACHET).

leu (lā´oo) *n.* (*pl.* **lei** (lā)) the standard
unit of currency of Romania.
19C. Romanian lion.

lev (lef) *n.* (*pl.* **leva** (lev´ə)) the standard
unit of currency of Bulgaria.
19C. Bulgarian, var. of *lăv* lion.

lex (leks) *n.* (*pl.* **leges** (lē´jēz)) **1** a body of
law. **2** a law.
16C. Latin law.

lexicon (lek´sikən) *n.* **1** a dictionary. **2** the
vocabulary of a language, an individual,
an area of study etc.
17C. Modern Latin, from Greek *lexikon*,
neut. sing. of *lexikos* pertaining to
words, from *lexis* phrase, word, diction,
from *legein* to speak.

li (lē) *n.* a Chinese measure of distance,
rather more than one third of a mile
(0.5 kilometres).
16C. Chinese *lĭ*.

liaison (liā´zon) *n.* **1** communication
and contact between units, groups
etc., esp. between military units.
2 a sexual or romantic relationship,
often of a clandestine or adulterous
nature. **3** in cooking, a thickening of
a sauce or soup, usu. made of yolk
of egg. **4** the carrying on of the
sound of a final consonant to a
succeeding word beginning with
a vowel or *h* mute. **5** a bond, a
connection.
17C. French, from *lier* to bind, from
Latin *ligare*.

liang (lyang) *n.* **1** a Chinese weight, equal
to about one twelfth of an ounce
avoirdupois (38 grams). **2** this weight of
silver as money of account.
19C. Chinese *liăng*.

libeccio (libech´ō), **libbecchio** (-ek´iō)
n. (*pl.* **libeccios**, **libecchios**) the SW
wind, esp. blowing on to the western
coast of Corsica.
17C. Italian, from Latin *Libs*, *Libis*, from
Greek *Lips*, *Libos*.

libero (lē´bərō) *n.* (*pl.* **liberos**) in football,
a sweeper.
mid-20C. Italian, abbr. of *battitore
libero*, from *battitore*, lit. beater (i.e.
defender) + *libero* free.

liberté, égalité, fraternité (lēbeətā´
egalitā´ frateənitā´) *n.* liberty, equality,
fraternity.
early 20C. French.
• The words were the slogan of the
French Revolution (1793) but are of
earlier origin.

libido (libē´dō) *n.* (*pl.* **libidos**) (*Psych.*)
1 the sexual drive. **2** in psychoanalysis,
the life force deriving from biological
impulses.
early 20C. Latin desire, lust, from *libere*
to be pleasing.

Libra (lē´brə) *n.* **1** (*Astron.*) one of the
twelve zodiacal constellations, the
Scales and Balance. **2** (*Astrol.*) **a** the
seventh sign of the zodiac which the
sun passes through between approx.
23 September and 22 October. **b** a
person born under this sign.
pre-1200. Latin *libra* pound, balance,
Libra.

libra (lī´brə) *n.* (*pl.* **librae** (-brē)) **1** an
ancient Roman pound, equal to about
twelve ounces (240 grams). **2** a pound
weight (*lb*), a pound sterling (£).
14–15C. Latin *libra* pound.

libretto (libret´ō) *n.* (*pl.* **libretti** (-ti), **librettos**) **1** the words of an opera, oratorio etc. **2** a book containing such words.
18C. **Italian**, dim. of *libro* book.

lictor (lik´tə) *n.* in ancient Rome, a civil officer who attended the chief magistrates, and bore the fasces as a sign of authority.
14–15C. **Latin**, ? rel. to *ligare* to bind.

lido (lē´dō) *n.* (*pl.* **lidos**) a bathing beach, an outdoor swimming pool.
17C. **Italian** *Lido*, a bathing beach near Venice, from *lido* shore, beach, from Latin *litus* shore.

Liebchen (lēb´shən) *n.* a dear person, a darling, a sweetheart, usu. as a term of address.
19C. **German**, lit. little loved one.

Liebfraumilch (lēb´frowmilsh, -milkh) *n.* a light white wine from the Rhine region of Germany.
19C. **German**, from *lieb* dear + *Frau* lady + *Milch* milk.
● The 'dear lady' is the Virgin Mary, patroness of the convent where the wine originated. The 'milk' is the white wine that she (it) produces.

lied (lēd, -t) *n.* (*pl.* **lieder** (-də)) a type of German song, often a poem set to music and usu. for solo voice with piano accompaniment.
19C. **German** *Lied* song.

lignum vitae (lignəm vī´tē, vē´tī) *n.* the very hard and heavy wood of various tropical American trees, esp. *Guaiacum officinale*.
16C. **Latin** wood of life.
● The wood is so called because the resin obtained from it was at one time believed to have medicinal properties.

limbo (lim´bō) *n.* (*pl.* **limbos**) **1** the edge or uttermost limit of hell, the abode of those who died unbaptized through no fault of their own, such as the just before Christ and infants. **2** an uncertain or transitional state. **3** a place of neglect or oblivion. **4** prison, confinement.
14–15C. **Latin**, abl. sing. of *limbus* edge, border, in phrs. such as *in limbo* on the edge, *e limbo* from the edge (i.e. of Hell).

Limburger (lim´bœgə) *n.* a white cheese with a strong taste and smell.
19C. **Dutch and German**, from *Limburg*, a province of NE Belgium.

limen (lī´mən) *n.* (*Psych.*) the stage of consciousness at which a given stimulus begins to produce sensation and below which it is imperceptible.
17C. **Latin** threshold.

limes (lī´mēz) *n.* (*pl.* **limites** (lim´itēz)) the fortified boundary of the Roman Empire.
16C. **Latin** boundary.

lingam (ling´gəm), **linga** (ling´gə) *n.* the phallus, representative of the god Siva in Hindu mythology.
18C. **Sanskrit** *liṅga* sign, (sexual) characteristic, influ. by Tamil *iliṅkam*.

lingerie (lã´zhəri) *n.* women's underwear and nightclothes.
19C. **French**, from *linge* linen.
● The original sense was linen articles in general, or all such articles in a woman's wardrobe or trousseau.

lingua franca (ling·gwə frang´kə) *n.* (*pl.* **lingua francas**) **1** a language serving as a medium of communication between different peoples. **2** any means of communication with this function. **3** (*Hist.*) a mixture of Italian with French, Greek, Arabic etc., used in Mediterranean ports.
17C. **Italian** Frankish tongue.
● 'Frankish' probably meant European to Arabs and other users of the original lingua franca.

linguine (lingwē´ni) *n.pl.* pasta in the form of long flat ribbons.
mid-20C. Italian, pl. of *linguina*, dim. of *lingua* tongue, from Latin.

liqueur (likūə´) *n.* **1** an alcoholic cordial sweetened or flavoured with an aromatic substance and drunk in small quantities, usu. after a meal. **2** (*in full* **liqueur chocolate**) a hollow chocolate sweet containing a small quantity of liqueur as its centre. ~*v.t.* to treat or flavour with this.
18C. French liquor.

lira (liə´rə) *n.* (*pl.* **lire** (liə´rə, -rā, -ri), **liras**) **1** the standard unit of currency of Italy. **2** the standard unit of currency of Turkey.
17C. Italian, from Provençal *liura*, from Latin *libra* pound. Cp. LIVRE.

literae humaniores (litərī hūmaniaw´rēz) *n.* at Oxford University, a faculty and honours course concerned with Greek and Latin literature, ancient history and philosophy.
18C. Latin, lit. more humane letters.
● The course is secular, devoted to humans, as opposed to divinity (theology), devoted to God.

literati (litərah´ti) *n.pl.* **1** men and women of letters. **2** the learned.
17C. Latin, pl. of *literatus* literate.

literatim (litərah´tim) *adv.* letter for letter, literally.
17C. Medieval Latin, from *litera* letter, based on GRADATIM. Cp. VERBATIM.

litotes (lītō´tēz) *n.* an understatement by which an affirmative is expressed by negation of its contrary, as in 'not a little' for 'very' or a weaker expression used to suggest a stronger one.
16C. Late Latin, from Greek *litōtes*, from *litos* single, simple, meagre.

littérateur (litəratœ´) *n.* an author, a professional writer.
19C. French, from Latin *litterator* teacher of letters, grammarian, from *litera* letter.

livre (lēv´rə) *n.* an old French coin, replaced by the franc in 1795.
16C. French, from Latin *libra* pound. Cp. LIRA.

llano (lah´nō) *n.* (*pl.* **llanos**) a level, treeless steppe or plain in the northern part of South America.
17C. Spanish, from Latin *planum* plain.

lobola (ləbō´lə, lawbaw´lə) *n.* a southern African custom whereby the bridegroom's family makes a payment of cash or cattle to the bride's family shortly before a marriage.
19C. Bantu (Nguni) *ukulobola* to give a dowry.

locale (lōkahl´) *n.* a place, site, esp. with reference to an event taking place there.
18C. French *local* local, respelt to indicate the stress. Cp. MORALE.

loc. cit. (lok sit´) *adv.* in the place cited.
19C. Abbr. of **Latin** *loco citato* or *locus citatus* (in) the place cited.

loco (lō´kō) *a.* **1** (*esp. N Am., sl.*) insane, mad. **2** affected with loco disease. ~*n.* (*also* **loco-plant**, **loco-weed**) any of several leguminous plants of the genus *Astragalus* of NW America which cause loco disease in livestock when ingested.
19C. Spanish insane.

locum (lō´kəm), **locum tenens** (tē´nenz, ten´-) *n.* (*pl.* **locums**, **locum tenentes** (tinen´tēz)) a deputy or substitute, esp. one acting in the place of a doctor or member of the clergy.

early 20C. Abbr. of **Medieval Latin** *locum tenens*, from Latin *locum*, acc. of *locus* place + *tenens*, pres.p. of *tenere* to hold.

• *Locum tenens* has now been generally superseded by *locum* in everyday English usage.

locus classicus (lōkəs klas´ikəs) *n.* (*pl.* **loci classici** (lōsī klas´isī, lōkē klas´ikē)) the best or most authoritative passage that can be quoted as an instance or illustration.

19C. **Latin**, lit. classical place.

loden (lō´dən) *n.* **1** a thick soft waterproof woollen cloth used for making coats. **2** a greyish-green colour typical of this cloth.

early 20C. **German**, from Old High German *lodo* thick cloth.

loess (lō´is, lœs) *n.* a wind-borne deposit of clay, loam, sand etc., in the Rhine, Mississippi and other river valleys.

19C. **German** *Löss*, from Swiss German *lösch* loose, from *lösen* to loosen.

loge (lōzh) *n.* a box in the theatre.

18C. **French**, from Old French arbour, hut, from Medieval Latin *laubia*, from Germanic source of English *lobby*.

loggia (loj´iə) *n.* (*pl.* **loggias**, **loggie** (loj´e)) **1** an open corridor, gallery or arcade along the front of a large building. **2** an open balcony in a theatre or concert hall.

18C. **Italian** lodge. Cp. LOGE.

logion (log´iən) *n.* (*pl.* **logia** (-giə)) a traditional saying, revelation or truth, esp. one of those ascribed to Christ but not recorded in the Gospels.

19C. **Greek** oracle, from *logos* word (LOGOS).

Logos (log´os) *n.* **1** in Greek philosophy, the divine reason implicit in and

governing the cosmos. **2** in Christian theology, the Divine Word, the Son of God, the Second Person of the Trinity.

16C. **Greek** account, relation, reasoning, argument, discourse, saying, speech, word, rel. to *legein* to choose, to collect, to gather, to say.

• The word was used in a mystic sense by Hellenistic and Neoplatonist philosophers and by St John, in whose Gospel and Book of Revelation it is translated in English by 'Word' as a title of Christ.

Lok Sabha (lōk sŭb´ə) *n.* the lower chamber of the Indian parliament.

mid-20C. **Sanskrit** *lok* people + *sabhā* assembly, council.

longeron (lon´jərən) *n.* a longitudinal spar of an aeroplane's fuselage.

early 20C. **French** longitudinal girder, from *allonger* to make long, from *long* long.

longueur (lō´gœ) *n.* a lengthy or tedious passage of writing, music etc.; a tedious stretch of time.

18C. **French** length.

lorgnette (lawnyet´) *n.* a pair of eyeglasses or opera glasses with a long handle.

19C. **French**, from *lorgner* to squint, to ogle.

• The form of the French word was influenced by LUNETTE.

louche (loosh) *a.* **1** morally suspect. **2** seedy. **3** sinister.

19C. **French** cross-eyed, squinting, from Latin *luscus* one-eyed.

louis (loo´i), **louis d'or** (daw´) *n.* (*pl.* **louis** (-iz), **louis d'or** (-i)) an old French gold coin issued from the reign of Louis XIII to Louis XVI, worth at different times 20 or 23 francs, superseded by the 20-franc piece.

17C. French, from *Louis* XIII, 1601–43, in whose reign it was first issued (1640).
● The coin retained the name through the reigns of subsequent kings Louis until that of Louis XVI (1774–93). It was withdrawn following his execution in 1793.

Luftwaffe (looft´wahfə, -vah-) *n.* the German Air Force before and during World War II.
mid-20C. German, from *Luft* air + *Waffe* weapon.

luge (loozh) *n.* a small toboggan for one or two people. ~*v.i.* to toboggan in one of these.
19C. Swiss French, ult. rel. to English *slide*.

Luger (loo´gə) *n.* a type of German automatic pistol.
early 20C. George *Luger*, 1849–1923, German engineer and firearms specialist.

luminaire (loomineə´) *n.* a light fitting.
early 20C. French, from *lumière* light, from Latin *lumen, luminis*.

lumpenproletariat (lŭm´pən prōləteə´riət, -at) *n.* the very poorest section of the urban population, made up of criminals, vagabonds etc.
early 20C. German, from *Lumpen* rag + PROLETARIAT.
● The term was introduced by Karl Marx in *Die Klassenkämpfe in Frankreich* (1850).

lunette (loonet´) *n.* **1** a semicircular aperture in a concave ceiling. **2** a crescent-shaped or semicircular space or panel for a picture or decorative painting. **3** a flattened watch-glass. **4** a ring on a vehicle to enable it to be towed by a towing hook. **5** a temporary fortification which has two

faces and two flanks. **6** a crescent-shaped holder for the consecrated host in a monstrance.
16C. French, dim. of *lune* moon, from Latin *luna*.
● French *lunettes* is now the standard word for spectacles. Cp. LORGNETTE.

lungi (lung´gi) *n.* (*pl.* **lungis**) a long cloth used as a loincloth or sash, sometimes as a turban.
17C. Hindi *lungī*.

lupus in fabula (loo´pəs in fab´ūlə) *n.* a person who appears just as they were being spoken of.
16C. Latin, lit. the wolf in the story.
● The phrase comes from Cicero's *Ad Atticum* (XIII) (1C BC).

lur (luə), **lure** *n.* a trumpet with long, curved tube, of prehistoric origin and used in Scandinavia for calling cattle home.
19C. Danish, Norwegian and Swedish.

lusus (loo´səs, lū´-), **lusus naturae** (natū´rē, -rī) *n.* (*pl.* **lusus**, **lususes**, **lusus naturae**) a freak of nature.
17C. Latin *lusus naturae* a sport of nature, from *lusus*, from *ludere* to play + gen. of *natura* nature.

lutz (luts) *n.* in figure skating, a jump from one skate with one, two or three rotations and a return to the other skate.
early 20C. From the Austrian figure skater Alois *Lutz* who was the first to perform the jump in Vienna in 1913.

luxe (luks) *n.* luxury, sumptuousness, superfine elegance.
16C. French, from Latin *luxus* excess.

lycée (lē´sā) *n.* a French state secondary school.
19C. French, from Latin LYCEUM.
● The French word was introduced in France in the early 19C, replaced by

collège royal in 1815 following the Restoration, then readopted in 1848 in the Second Republic.

lyceum (līsē´əm) *n.* **1** (**Lyceum**) the garden at Athens in which Aristotle taught. **2** (**Lyceum**) the Aristotelian philosophy or philosophic school. **3** (*N Am.*) an institution for literary instruction or mutual improvement by means of lectures, libraries etc. **4** a place or building devoted to literary studies, lectures etc.

16C. Latin, from Greek *Lukeion*, neut. of *Lukeios*, lit. wolfslayer, an epithet of Apollo.

● The original garden at Athens in which Aristotle taught philosophy was named from the neighbouring temple of Apollo Lukeios. Cp. ATHENAEUM.

M

maar (mah) *n.* a volcanic crater without a cone of lava, caused by a single explosion.
19C. German dial.

macaroni (makərō´ni) *n.* (*pl.* **macaronies, macaronis**) **1** an Italian pasta made of fine wheat flour formed into long slender tubes. **2** (*Hist.*) a fop, a dandy. **3** a crested variety of penguin. **4** (*pl.*) a medley. ~†*a.* foppish, fashionable, affected.
16C. Obsolete Italian *maccaroni*, later *maccheroni*, pl. of obs. *maccarone*, from Late Greek *makaria* barley food.

macédoine (masədwan´) *n.* **1** a dish of mixed vegetables. **2** a medley.
19C. French, from *Macédoine* Macedonia.
• The vegetables are mixed, like the mixed races in the Macedonian empire of Alexander the Great.

machair (makh´ə) *n.* a strip of land just above the high-water mark along a sandy shore, used for pasturage.
17C. Gaelic plain. Cp. Irish *machaire*.

machan (məchahn´) *n.* an elevated platform for hunting or watching game.
19C. Hindi *macān*, from Sanskrit *mañcaka*.

machete (məshet´i, -shā´ti), **matchet** (mach´it) *n.* a broad knife or cutlass used in tropical America as a weapon, to cut down sugar canes etc.
16C. Spanish, from *macho* hammer, from Latin *marcus*.

machismo (məkiz´mo, -chiz´-) *n.* aggressive arrogant assertiveness, often associated with masculinity.
mid-20C. Mexican Spanish, from MACHO.

macho (mach´ō) *a.* masculine, virile, esp. in an ostentatious or exaggerated way. ~*n.* (*pl.* **machos**) **1** a macho man. **2** machismo.
early 20C. Mexican Spanish male animal, masculine, vigorous, from Latin *masculus* male.

Machtpolitik (makht´politēk) *n.* power politics, esp. the advocacy of force by a state to attain its ends.
early 20C. German, from *Macht* power, strength + *Politik* policy, politics.

macramé (məkrah´mā) *n.* **1** a fringe or trimming of knotted thread or cord. **2** knotted work. **3** the art of making knotted work.
19C. Turkish *makrama* handkerchief, tablecloth, towel, from Arabic *miḵrama* bedcover, bedspread.

Madame (mədahm´) *n.* (*pl.* **Mesdames** (mādahmz´)) **1** the French title for married women and polite form of

address to a woman. **2** †the title of a French princess, esp. the eldest daughter of the king or the dauphin.
12–14C. Old French, from *ma dame*, lit. my lady.
● The Old French phrase is also the source of English *madam*.

madeleine (mad´əlin) *n.* a small sponge cake, often coated with jam and coconut.
19C. Appar. from *Madeleine* Paulmier, 19C French pastrycook.

Mademoiselle (madəmwəzel´) *n.* (*pl.* **Mesdemoiselles** (mādəmwəzəl´))
1 the French title for unmarried women or girls and polite form of address to an unmarried woman or a girl.
2 (**mademoiselle**) a young Frenchwoman. **3** (**mademoiselle**) a French governess or teacher.
14–15C. Old French, from *ma*, fem. of *mon* my + *demoiselle* damsel.

Madonna (mədon´a) *n.* **1** the Virgin Mary. **2** (*usu.* **madonna**) a picture or statue of the Virgin Mary.
16C. Italian, from *ma*, old unstressed form of *mia* my (from Latin *mea*) + *donna* lady (from Latin *domina*).

maduro (mədoo´rō) *n.* (*pl.* **maduros**) a type of dark, strong cigar.
19C. Spanish ripe, mature.

maelstrom (māl´strəm, -om) *n.* **1** a dangerous whirlpool, dangerously swirling water. **2** a turmoil, an overwhelming situation.
17C. Early Modern Dutch (now *maalstroom*), from *maalen* to grind, to whirl round + *stroom* stream. Cp. Swedish *malström*, Danish *malstrøm*.

maestoso (mīstō´sō, -zō) *a., adv.* (*Mus.*) with dignity, grandeur and strength. ~*n.* (*pl.* **maestosos**) a piece of music to be played this way.

18C. Italian majestic, from *maestà*, from Latin *maestas, maestatis* majesty.

maestro (mīs´trō) *n.* (*pl.* **maestros, maestri** (-ē)) **1** a master in any art, esp. in music. **2** a great composer or conductor.
18C. Italian, from Latin *magister* master.

Mafia (maf´iə) *n.* **1** a secret criminal society based on active hostility to the law and its agents, engaged in international organized crime, esp. in Sicily and the US. **2** any group of people considered to be using power for their own ends.
19C. Italian (Sicilian) bragging, bravado.
● The name alludes to the society's hostility to the law and those who uphold it, especially by means of vindictive crimes.

Mafioso (mafiō´so, -zō) *n.* (*pl.* **Mafiosi** (-sē, -zē)) **1** a member of the Mafia. **2** a member of a group who in some way resemble the Mafia.
19C. Italian, from MAFIA.

Magna Carta (magnə kah´tə), **Magna Charta** (chah´tə) *n.* **1** the Great Charter of English liberties sealed by King John on 15 June 1215. **2** any fundamental constitution guaranteeing rights and privileges.
15C. Medieval Latin, lit. great charter.

magna cum laude (magnə kum law´di, low´dā) *adv.* with great distinction.
19C. Latin, lit. with great praise, from fem. abl. sing. of *magnus* great + *cum* with + abl. of *laus, laudis* praise. Cp. SUMMA CUM LAUDE.

Magnificat (magnif´ikat) *n.* **1** the song of the Virgin Mary (Luke i.46–55). **2** a setting of this to music. **3** (**magnificat**) a song of praise.

12–14C. Latin (it) magnifies, 3rd pers. sing. pres. ind. of *magnificare* to magnify.
• The opening words of the song in the Vulgate (Latin version) are: *Magnificat anima mea Dominum* My soul doth magnify the Lord.

magnifico (magnif´ikō) *n.* (*pl.* **magnificoes**) a magnate, a grandee, orig. of Venice.
16C. Italian magnificent, from Latin *magnificus*, from *magnus* great + *-ficus*, from base of *facere* to make.

magnum (mag´nəm) *n.* (*pl.* **magnums**) **1** a wine bottle containing the equivalent of two normal bottles (about 1.5 litres). **2** a bottle containing two quarts (about 2.3 litres). **3** two quarts. **4** a large-calibre pistol. **5** a particularly powerful cartridge or shell.
18C. Latin, use as n. of neut. sing. of *magnus* large.

magnum opus (magnəm ō´pəs, op´-) *n.* (*pl.* **magnum opuses**, **magna opera** (magnə ō´pərə, op´-)) the greatest work of a writer, painter etc.
18C. Latin great work. See MAGNUM, OPUS.

magus (mā´gəs) *n.* (*pl.* **magi** (-jī)) **1** a member of the priestly caste among the Medes and Persians. **2** a magician, a sorcerer. **3** (*pl.* **the Magi**) the three 'wise men' of the East who brought presents to the infant Christ.
12–14C. Latin, from Greek *magos*, from Old Persian *maguš*.

maharaja (mah·hərah´jə), **maharajah** *n.* a title assumed by some Indian princes.
17C. Sanskrit *mahārājā*, from *mahā* great + *rājan* RAJA.
• Sanskrit *mahā* is ultimately related to English *much*.

maharani (mah·hərah´ni), **maharanee** *n.* **1** the wife or widow of a maharaja. **2** an Indian princess.
19C. Hindi *mahārānī*, from Sanskrit *mahā* great + RANEE.

maharishi (mah·hərish´i, -rē´shi) *n.* a Hindu religious teacher.
18C. Alt. of **Sanskrit** *maharṣi*, from *mahā* great + *ṛṣi* RISHI.

mahatma (məhat´mə) *n.* **1** in the Indian subcontinent, a much revered person. **2** an adept or sage of the highest order in some Indian and Tibetan religious thinking. **3** such a person supposed to have supernatural powers.
19C. Sanskrit *mahātman*, from *mahā* great + *ātman* soul. See ATMAN.

Mahayana (mah·həyah´nə) *n.* the most widespread tradition of Buddhism, practised esp. in China, Japan and Tibet.
19C. Sanskrit *mahāyāna*, from *mahā* great + *yāna* vehicle.

Mahdi (mah´di) *n.* (*pl.* **Mahdis**) the Muslim messiah, a title once assumed by leaders of insurrection in Sudan.
19C. Arabic (*al-*)*mahdī*, lit. he who is rightly guided, from pass. part. of *hadā* to lead on the right way, to guide aright.

mah-jong (mahjong´), **mah-jongg** *n.* a Chinese table game played with 136 or 144 tiles.
early 20C. Chinese dial. *ma jiang* sparrows (lit. hemp birds).
• The game is so called from a design on the tiles.

mahout (məhowt´) *n.* an elephant driver or keeper.
17C. Hindi *mahāut*, *mahāvat*, from Sanskrit *mahāmātra* high official, elephant keeper, from *mahā* great + *mātra* measure.

maidan (mīdahn´) *n.* an open space used as a sports or parade ground in India, Pakistan etc.
17C. Urdu and Persian *maidān*, from Arabic *maydān*.

maigre (mā´gə) *a.* **1** (of a day) that is designated a fast day in the Roman Catholic Church. **2** (of food, esp. soup) suitable for fast days, not made from meat or containing gravy.
16C. Old French thin.

maillot (mī´yō) *n.* (*pl.* **maillots** (-yō)) **1** tights for dancing, exercising etc. **2** a tight-fitting swimsuit for women. **3** a jersey.
19C. French, from *maille* stitch, mesh.

maillot jaune (mīyō zhōn´) *n.* yellow jersey, as worn by the overall leader in the *Tour de France* cycle race.
mid-20C. French, from *maillot* jersey, from *maille* mail + *jaune* yellow.
● The rider who achieved the fastest time over the previous day's stage wears a *maillot vert* green jersey.

maiolica (məyol´ikə), **majolica** (-jol´-) *n.* tin-glazed earthenware having metallic colours on a white ground (orig. from Italy).
16C. Italian, from former name of island of *Majorca*.

maison (mezō´) *n.* house.
16C. French, rel. to English *mansion*.
● The word is chiefly used of a fashion house.

maisonette (māzənet´, -sə-), **maisonnette** *n.* **1** part of a house or block of flats let separately, usu. having two floors and with a separate entrance. **2** a small house.
18C. French *maisonnette*, dim. of *maison* house.

maître d'hôtel (metrə dōtel´) *n.* (*pl.* **maitres d'hôtel** (metrə)) **1** the manager, chief steward etc. of a hotel. **2** a head waiter.
16C. French, lit. master of house.
● The original meaning was majordomo, steward, butler. The sense hotel manager, head waiter evolved in the 19C.

maja (makh´a) *n.* a woman who dresses showily in Spain and Spanish-speaking countries.
19C. Spanish, fem. of *majo* dandy.
● The word is familiar from Goya's twin paintings *La maja vestida* ('The clothed maja') and *La maja desnuda* ('The naked maja') (*c.*1800).

Majlis (majlis´, maj´-) *n.* **1** the Iranian legislative assembly. **2** the legislative assembly of various other N African and Middle Eastern countries.
19C. Arabic place of session, from *jalasa* to be seated.

makimono (makimo´no, makimō´nō) *n.* a Japanese scroll containing a narrative, usually in pictures with accompanying writing.
19C. Japanese scroll, from *maki* roll + *mono* thing.

maladroit (malədroit´) *a.* awkward, clumsy.
17C. French, from *mal* bad + *adroit* skilful.

mala fide (malə fī´di, mālə fē´dā) *a., adv.* (acting or done) in bad faith.
17C. Latin with bad faith, abl. of *mala fides* bad faith.

malagueña (maləgā´nyə) *n.* a Spanish dance or folk tune similar to the fandango.
19C. Spanish of *Málaga*, a port in S Spain.

malaise (malāz´) *n.* **1** a feeling of uneasiness, esp. as premonition of a serious malady. **2** a mild feeling of sickness or depression.
18C. French, from Old French *mal* bad, ill (from Latin *malus*) + *aise* ease.

malapropos (malaprəpō´) *adv.* unseasonably, unsuitably, out of place. ~*a.* unseasonable etc. ~*n.* an unseasonable or inopportune thing, remark, event etc.
17C. French *mal à propos*, from *mal* ill + *à* to + *propos* purpose. See APROPOS.

mal de mer (mal də meə´) *n.* seasickness.
18C. French, from *mal* sickness + *de* of + *mer* sea.

mal du pays (mal dü pāi´) *n.* homesickness.
19C. French, lit. sickness of the country. Cp. HEIMWEH.

mal du siècle (mal dü syekl´, syek´lə) *n.* world-weariness.
early 20C. French, lit. sickness of the century.
● The expression was used in 1833 by the critic and writer Charles Sainte-Beuve of the early French Romantic poets.

malentendu (malātā´dü) *n.* a misunderstanding.
18C. French, from *mal* badly + *entendu*, p.p. of *entendre* to hear, to understand.
● The word was earlier used adjectivally to mean mistaken, misapprehended.

malgré (mal´grā) *prep.* in spite of.
16C. French, lit. bad will, from *mal* bad + *gré* will, wish. Cp. BON GRÉ, MAL GRÉ.

mali (mā´lē, mah´-) *n.* (*pl.* **malis**) a member of the gardener caste in the Indian subcontinent.
18C. Hindi *mālī*, from Sanskrit *mālin*, from *mālā* garland.

mambo (mam´bō) *n.* (*pl.* **mambos**) a West Indian syncopated dance or dance tune, like the rumba. ~*v.i.* (*3rd pers. sing. pres.* **mamboes**, *pres.p.* **mamboing**, *past, p.p.* **mamboed**) to dance the mambo.
mid-20C. American Spanish, prob. from Haitian creole, from Yoruba, lit. to talk.

mamma mia (mamə mē´ə) *int.* an exclamation of surprise, wonder, frustration etc.
early 20C. Italian, lit. my mother.

mañana (mənyah´nə, man-) *n., adv.* **1** tomorrow. **2** presently, later on, in the indefinite future.
19C. Spanish morning, tomorrow, ult. from Latin *mane* in the morning.
● The Spanish sense tomorrow derives from Old Spanish *cras mañana*, lit. tomorrow early.

manche (mahnsh) *n.* **1** a sleeve, with long hanging ends. **2** (*Her.*) a bearing representing such a sleeve. **3** the neck of a violin etc.
14–15C. Old French, from Latin *manica*, from *manus* hand.

mandala (man´dələ, -dah´-) *n.* **1** any of various symbols used to represent the universe in Buddhism or Hinduism, used as an aid to meditation. **2** (*Psych.*) a circular symbol seen in dreams, supposed to represent personal wholeness.
19C. Sanskrit *maṇḍala* disc, circle.

mandamus (mandā´məs) *n.* (*pl.* **mandamuses**) (*Law*) a writ or (now) order issued from a higher court directed to a person, corporation or inferior court, requiring them to do a particular thing relating to their office or duty.
16C. Latin we command, 1st pers. pl. pres. ind. of *mandare* to command.

mandorla (mandaw´lə) *n.* an area of light, oval but pointed in shape, surrounding a painting or sculpture of the risen Christ or of the Virgin at the Assumption.
19C. **Italian** almond.

manège (manāzh´, -nezh´), **manege** *n.* **1** a school for training horses or teaching horsemanship. **2** the training of horses. **3** the movements of a trained horse. **4** horsemanship.
17C. **French**, from Italian *maneggio*, from *maneggiare*, ult. from Latin *manus* hand.

manes (mā´nēz, mah´nāz) *n.pl.* **1** the spirits of the dead, esp. of ancestors worshipped as guardian divinities. **2** (*as sing.*) the shade of a deceased person regarded as an object of reverence.
14–15C. **Latin**, ? rel. to *manus* good.

manet (man´et) *int.* he or she remains on stage.
18C. **Latin**, 3rd pers. sing. pres. indic. of *manere* to remain.

manga (mang´gə) *n.* a type of Japanese comic book or strip, usu. containing erotic or violent material.
late 20C. **Japanese** cartoon, comic.

mangetout (mãzh´too, mãzhtoo´) *n.* (*pl.* **mangetout**, **mangetouts** (mãzh´too, mãzhtoo´)) a type of pea which is eaten complete with the pod.
19C. **French**, lit. eat-all, from *manger* to eat + *tout* all, everything.

manifesto (manifes´tō) *n.* (*pl.* **manifestos**) a public declaration, esp. by a political party, government, sovereign or other authoritative body, of opinions, motives or intentions.
16C. **Italian**, from *manifestare*, from Latin *manifestus* apparent.

manilla (manil´ə) *n.* **1** a metal ring worn by some Africans on the legs or arms. **2** a piece of metal shaped like a ring or horseshoe formerly used as a medium of exchange among the indigenous peoples of the W African coast.
16C. **Spanish**, prob. dim. of *mano* hand, from Latin *manus*.

manille (mənil´) *n.* in ombre or quadrille, the highest but one trump or honour.
17C. **French**, from Spanish *malilla*, dim. of *mala*, fem. of *malo* bad.
● The second best trump card is not the best, and is relatively thus a *mala carta*, Spanish bad card.

manna (man´ə) *n.* **1** the food miraculously supplied to the Israelites in the wilderness. **2** divine food, spiritual nourishment, esp. the Eucharist. **3** a sweetish exudation, of a slightly laxative nature, from certain species of ash, esp. the manna ash.
pre-1200. **Late Latin**, from Hellenistic Greek, from Aramaic *mannā*, from Hebrew *mān*.
● The original word corresponds to Arabic *mann* exudation of the tamarisk. In the Old Testament the word is explained as meaning 'what is it?' (Exod. xvi.15), as if from Hebrew *mān hû'*.

mannequin (man´ikin, -kwin) *n.* **1** a woman employed to wear and display clothes. **2** a window dummy.
18C. **French**, from Dutch *manneken* manikin.
● A mannequin was originally a dummy figure for the display of clothes. The current sense dates from the early 20C.

manoeuvre (mənoo´və), (*N Am.*) **maneuver** *n.* **1** a tactical movement or change of position by troops or warships. **2** (*pl.*) tactical exercises in

imitation of war. **3** a contrived plan or action. ~*v.i.* **1** to perform manoeuvres. **2** to manage with skill. **3** to employ a stratagem. ~*v.t.* **1** to move or effect by means of strategy or skilful management. **2** to cause (troops) to perform manoeuvres. **3** to manipulate.
15C. French *manœuvre*, from *manœuvrer*, from Medieval Latin *manuoperare*, from Latin *manu operari* to work with the hand, from *manus* hand.

ma non troppo (mah non trop´ō) *adv.* (*Mus.*) but not too much.
early 20C. Italian, from *ma* but + *non* not + TROPPO.

manqué (mã´kā) *a.* having the potential to be, but not actually being, something specified.
18C. French, p.p. of *manquer* to fall short of, to lack, to fail.

man spricht Deutsch (man shprikht doich´) *int.* German spoken (here), esp. used as a sign in a shop etc. in a country where German is not the native language.
early 20C. German, lit. one speaks German. Cp. ICI ON PARLE FRANÇAIS.

mantilla (mantil´ə) *n.* **1** a veil for the head and shoulders, worn in Spain and Italy. **2** a woman's light cloak or cape.
18C. Spanish, dim. of *manta* mantle.

mantra (man´trə) *n.* **1** a word or phrase chanted inwardly in meditation, orig. a Hindu formula or charm. **2** a Vedic hymn of praise.
18C. Sanskrit, lit. thought, from *man* to think.

mantua (man´tūə) *n.* (*Hist.*) a woman's loose gown worn in the 17th and 18th cents.
16C. Alt. of **French** *manteau* gown, cloak, from Old French *mantel*, from

Latin *mantellum*, influ. by name of *Mantua*, a city in N Italy.

manzanilla (manzənil´ə, -thənē´lyə) *n.* a very dry sherry.
19C. Spanish, lit. camomile, dim. of *manzana* apple.

maquette (maket´) *n.* **1** a sculptor's preliminary model in clay, wax etc. **2** a preliminary sketch.
early 20C. French, from Italian *macchietta* speck, little spot, dim. of *macchia* spot, from *macchiare* to spot, to stain, from Latin *maculare* to stain.

maquillage (makēyahzh´) *n.* **1** make-up, cosmetics. **2** the technique of applying cosmetics.
19C. French, from *maquiller* to make up one's face, from Old French *masquiller* to stain, alt. of *mascurer* to darken.

Maquis (makē´) *n.* (*pl.* **Maquis**) **1** those surreptitiously resisting the German invaders of France etc., in 1940–45. **2** a member of the French resistance. **3** (**maquis**) scrub or bush in Corsica and other Mediterranean coastal regions.
19C. French, from Corsican Italian *macchia* thicket, from Latin *macula* spot.
• The maquis scrub was the traditional hiding place for fugitives. Hence the connection between senses 1 and 2 and sense 3.

marabout (mar´əboot, -boo) *n.* **1** a Muslim hermit or saint, esp. one of a priestly caste in N Africa. **2** the tomb or dwelling of such a saint.
17C. French, from Portuguese *marabuto*, from Arabic *murābiṭ*, from *ribāṭ* frontier station. Cp. MARAVEDI.
• The frontier station during a holy war was where the holy man would earn his status.

maraca (mərak´ə) *n.* a hollow gourd or shell containing beads, shot etc. shaken, usu. in a pair, as a percussive accompaniment to music, esp. in Latin America.
17C. Portuguese *maracá*, from Tupi *maráka*.

maraschino (marəskē´nō, -shē´-) *n.* (*pl.* **maraschinos**) a cordial or liqueur distilled from bitter cherries grown in Dalmatia.
18C. Italian, from *marasca* variety of cherry, from *amarasca*, from *amaro* bitter.

maravedi (marəvā´di) *n.* (*pl.* **maravedis**) (*Hist.*) **1** a former Spanish copper coin of low value. **2** a former Spanish gold coin.
14–15C. Spanish *maravedí*, from Arabic *murābiṭīn*, oblique case of *murābiṭ* MARABOUT.
● The coin is named after the N African Berber rulers of Muslim Spain, 1087–1145.

marc (mahk) *n.* **1** the compressed residue of grapes left after pressing, in the making of wine or oil. **2** brandy made from this.
17C. French, from *marcher* in its orig. sense to tread, to trample, ult. from Latin *marcus* hammer.

marcato (mahkah´tō) *a.* (*Mus.*) (of notes) heavily accented. ~*adv.* (played) with a heavy accent.
19C. Italian, p.p. of *marcare* to mark, to accent, of Germanic orig.

Mardi Gras (mahdi grah´) *n.* **1** Shrove Tuesday. **2** the carnival celebrated at this time.
17C. French, lit. fat Tuesday, from *Mardi* Tuesday + *gras* fat.
● Mardi Gras is so named as the last day before Ash Wednesday and the start of Lent, the 'feast before the fast'.

maremma (mərem´ə) *n.* (*pl.* **maremme** (-mā)) a marshy and usu. unhealthy region by the seashore.
19C. Italian, from Latin *maritima*, fem. of *maritimus* maritime. Cp. French *marnis* marsh.
● As a proper name, the Maremma is a coastal area in Tuscany, central Italy, along the Tyrrhenian Sea. It flourished in early Roman times but was largely abandoned in the Middle Ages because of malaria. It has now been successfully reclaimed.

margarita (mahgərē´tə) *n.* a cocktail made from tequila and lemon (or other fruit) juice.
early 20C. Spanish *Margarita* Margaret.

marginalia (mahjinā´liə) *n.pl.* marginal notes.
19C. Latin, neut. pl. (used as n.) of *marginalis* marginal.

mariage blanc (mariahzh blã´) *n.* (*pl.* **mariages blancs** (mariahzh blã´)) an unconsummated marriage.
early 20C. French, lit. white marriage.

mariage de convenance (mariahzh´ de kõvənãs) *n.* (*pl.* **mariages de convenance** (mariahzh´)) a marriage of convenience.
19C. French marriage of convenience, from *mariage* marriage + *de* of + *convenance* convenience.

mari complaisant (mari komplezã´) *n.* (*pl.* **maris complaisants** (mari komplezã´)) a husband who tolerates his wife's adultery.
19C. French, lit. obliging husband.

marijuana (mariwah´nə), **marihuana** *n.* **1** dried leaves, flowering tops and stems of Indian hemp, usu. used to make cigarettes smoked as a narcotic. **2** Indian hemp.
19C. American Spanish, of unknown orig.

marimba (mərim´bə) *n.* a musical instrument similar to a xylophone.
18C. Congolese.

marina (mərē´nə) *n.* a system of sheltered moorings designed mainly for pleasure boats.
19C. Italian and Spanish, fem. of *marino*, from Latin *marinus* marine.

marinade (marinād´) *n.* **1** a mixture of vinegar, oil etc. flavoured with wine, spices etc., for soaking fish or meat prior to cooking. **2** fish or meat soaked in this.
~*v.t.* to marinate.
18C. French, from Spanish *marinada*, from *marinar* to pickle in brine, from *marino* (MARINA).

marionette (mariənet´) *n.* a puppet moved by strings.
17C. French *marionnette*, from *Marion*, dim. of *Marie* Mary.
• *Marie* was a common name for female characters in old French plays.

marivaudage (marivodahzh´) *n.* exaggeratedly sentimental or affected style or language.
18C. French, from Pierre Carlet de Marivaux (1688–1763), French dramatist, whose plays employed such language.

markka (mah´kə) *n.* the standard unit of currency in Finland.
early 20C. Finnish.
• The coin is the equivalent of the German *Mark*.

marmite (mah´mīt, -mēt´) *n.* an earthenware cooking pot.
19C. French, orig. meaning hypocrite, from blend of base of *marmouser* to murmur + *mite*, name of the cat in the *Roman de Renart* (12–13C), of imit. orig.
• Both a hypocrite and a cooking pot conceal their content. *Marmite* as a

proprietary name for a savoury extract dates from the early 20C. An illustration of a cooking pot on the label is a reminder of the origin of the name.

marocain (mar´əkān) *n.* a cloth similar in structure to crêpe de Chine, but made from coarser yarns.
early 20C. French from *Maroc* Morocco. Cp. MAROQUIN.

maroquin (mar´əkin, -kēn´) *n.* morocco leather.
16C. French alt. (prob. based on Spanish *marroquín*) of *Maroc* Morocco. Cp. MAROCAIN.

marque[1] (mahk) *n.* a brand, esp. a make of motor car as distinct from a specific model of car.
early 20C. French, back-formation from *marquer* to mark, to brand, alt. of Old French *merchier*, from *merc* limit, of Scandinavian orig. Rel. to English *mark*.

marque[2] (mahk) *n.* (*Hist.*) reprisals.
14–15C. French, from Provençal *marca*, from *marcar* to seize as a pledge, ? ult. from Germanic base of English *mark*.

marquisette (mahkizet´) *n.* a finely-woven mesh fabric used for clothing, net curtains and mosquito nets.
early 20C. French, dim. of *marquise* marchioness.

marron glacé (marõ glas´ā) *n.* (*pl.* **marrons glacés** (marõ glas´ā)) a preserved chestnut coated with sugar.
16C. French, lit. iced chestnut, from *marron* chestnut + GLACÉ.

Marsala (mahsah´lə) *n.* a sweet white fortified dessert wine.
19C. *Marsala*, a town and port on the western coast of Sicily.

Marseillaise (mahsāez´, -səlāz´) *n.* the national anthem of the French Republic.

18C. French, fem. of *Marseillais* of Marseilles, from *Marseille* Marseilles, a city and port in SE France.
• The Marseillaise was composed in 1792 on the declaration of war against Austria and first sung in Paris by patriots from Marseilles.

martellato (mahtelah´tō) *a.* (*Mus.*) with notes heavily accented.
19C. Italian, p.p. of *martellare* to hammer.
• The direction usually applies to the heavy staccato bowing of a stringed instrument.

masala (məsah´lə) *n.* **1** any of several spice mixtures used in Indian cookery. **2** a dish prepared with such a mixture.
18C. Urdu *maṣālaḥ*, from Persian and Urdu *masāliḥ*, from Arabic *maṣāliḥ* ingredients.

mascara (maskah´rə) *n.* a dark cosmetic for eyelashes.
19C. Italian *mascara*, *maschera* mask.

mascarpone (maskəpō´ni) *n.* a soft mild cream cheese made in Italy.
mid-20C. Italian, earlier *mascarpa* a type of ricotta.
• According to some, the derivation may be in Latin *manuscarpere* to take in the hand, to masturbate, as an analogy with the S Italian phrase *far ricotta* to masturbate, literally to make RICOTTA.

mashallah (mashal´ə, mahshahlah´) *int.* an expression of praise or compliance among Muslims.
19C. Arabic *mā šā'llāh* what God wills. Cp. ALLAH.

masjid (mŭs´jid) *n.* a mosque.
19C. Arabic, from *sajada* he worshipped.
• The Arabic word is the ultimate source of English *mosque*.

Masorah (məsaw´rə), **Massorah** *n.* a mass of traditional information and illustrative matter on the text of the Hebrew Bible, compiled before the 10th cent.
17C. Hebrew, var. of *māsōreṭ* bond, from *'āsar* to bind, but later interpreted as meaning tradition, as if from *māsar* to hand down.
• The biblical ref. is to Ezek. xx.37: 'I will bring you into the bond of the covenant'.

masque (mahsk) *n.* (*Hist.*) a play or dramatic entertainment, usu. presented by amateurs at court or in noblemen's houses, the performers wearing masks, orig. in dumb show, later with dialogue, poetical and musical accompaniments.
16C. French mask.
• The word was originally the same as *mask*, but was retained in its French form to denote the play or entertainment presented in noblemen's houses.

massage (mas´ahzh, -ahj, -sahzh´) *n.* **1** treatment by rubbing or kneading the muscles and body, usu. with the hands. **2** an instance of this. ~*v.t.* **1** to subject to massage. **2** to manipulate or misrepresent (esp. statistics). **3** to flatter.
19C. French, from *masser* to apply massage to, ? from Portuguese *amassar* to knead.

massé (mas´ā) *n.* in billiards, a stroke with the cue held almost vertically.
19C. French, p.p. of *masser* to play a massé stroke, from *masse* mace.

masseur (masœ´) *n.* a person skilled in massage.
19C. French, from *masser* to apply massage to. Cp. MASSAGE.

massif (mas´ēf, masēf´) *n.* the main or central mass of a mountain or range.
16C. French, use as n. of a. *massif* massive.

mastaba (mas´təbə) *n.* **1** an ancient Egyptian tomb or chapel covering a sepulchral pit, used for the deposit of offerings. **2** a stone bench attached to an Eastern house.
17C. Arabic *maṣṭaba*.

matador (mat´ədaw) *n.* **1** in Spanish bullfights, the person who has to kill the bull. **2** one of the three principal cards at ombre and quadrille. **3** a game played with dominoes in which each played must give a total of seven.
17C. Spanish, from *matar* to kill.

Mata Hari (mahtə hah´ri) *n.* a beautiful female spy.
mid-20C. *Mata Hari*, name taken by Margaretha Gertruida Zelle, 1876–1917, Dutch courtesan and spy, from Malay *matahari* sun, from *mata* eye + *hari* day.
● It is a curious coincidence that the name *Margaretha* (*Margaret*) has the French equivalent *Marguerite* which gave *marguerite* as the word for a daisy, and that this flower's English name literally means day's eye, the exact equivalent of Malay *matahari*.

maté (mat´ā), **mate** *n.* **1** an infusion of the leaves of *Ilex paraguayensis*, a Brazilian holly. **2** this shrub. **3** the leaves of this shrub. **4** the vessel in which the infusion is made.
18C. Spanish *mate*, from Quechua *mati*.

matelassé (matəlas´ā) *a.* having a raised pattern as in quilting.
19C. French, p.p of *matelasser* to quilt, from *matelas* mattress.

matelot (mat´lō), **matlo**, **matlow** *n.* (*coll.*) a sailor.
early 20C. French sailor, from Middle Dutch *mattenoot*, lit. bed companion, from *matte* mat, bed + *noot* companion.

matelote (mat´əlōt) *n.* a dish of fish with wine, onions etc.

18C. French, from *matelot* sailor. See MATELOT.

mater (mā´tə) *n.* (*pl.* **matres** (-trēz)) (*sl.*) a mother.
19C. Latin mother.

materfamilias (mātəfəmil´ias) *n.* (*pl.* **matresfamilias** (mahtrāz-)) the mother of a family, the female head of a household.
18C. Latin, from MATER + *familias*, old gen. of *familia* family.

materia medica (mətiəriə med´ikə) *n.* **1** the different substances employed in medicine. **2** the scientific study of such substances.
17C. Modern Latin, translating Greek *hulē iatrikē* healing material.

materiel (mətiəriel´) *n.* the material, supplies, machinery or instruments, as distinct from the personnel, employed in an art, business, military or naval activity etc.
19C. French *matériel*, use as n. of a.

matinée (mat´inā), **matinee** *n.* an afternoon performance of a play, film etc.
19C. French morning, that which occupies a morning, from *matin* morning. Cp. SOIRÉE.

matryoshka (matriosh´kə) *n.* a type of Russian doll.
mid-20C. Russian, dim. of pers. name *Matrona*, rel. to English *matron*.
● The doll contains a set of figures of different sizes, each nesting inside the next largest.

matte (mat) *n.* an impure metallic product containing sulphur, from the smelting of ore, esp. copper.
19C. French, use as n. of fem. of *mat* matt.

matzo (mat´sō) *n.* (*pl.* **matzoth** (-ōt), **matzos**) (a thin wafer of) unleavened bread, eaten esp. at the Passover.
19C. Yiddish *matse*, from Hebrew *maṣṣāh*.

mausoleum (mawzəlē´əm) *n.* (*pl.* **mausolea** (-ə), **mausoleums**) a sepulchral monument of considerable size or architectural pretensions.
14–15C. Latin, from Greek *Mausōleion*, from *Mausōlos* Mausolos, king of Caria, whose magnificent tomb was erected in the 4C BC at Halicarnassus by his queen, Artemisia.

mauvais goût (mōvā goo´) *n.* bad taste, lack of good taste.
early 20C. French, from *mauvais* bad + *goût* taste.

mauvais quart d'heure (mōvā kah dœ´) *n.* a brief unpleasant experience.
18C. French, lit. bad quarter of an hour.
● The phrase was formerly associated with the time between the arrival of guests and the start of dinner.

mauvais ton (mōvā tō´) *n.* bad taste.
19C. French, from *mauvais* bad + *ton* tone. Cp. BON TON.

maven (mā´vən) *n.* (*N Am.*, *coll.*) an expert, a connoisseur.
mid-20C. **Hebrew** *mēḇīn* understanding.

mavourneen (məvuə´nēn) *n.* (*Ir.*) my dear one, darling.
19C. Irish *mo mhuirnín*, from *mo* my + *muirnín*, dim. of *muirn* affection.

maxixe (maksēks´, məshish´ə) *n.* a dance of Brazilian origin resembling the polka.
early 20C. Portuguese.

maya (mī´ə) *n.* in Hinduism, the world as perceived by the senses, regarded as illusory.
18C. Sanskrit *māyā*, from *mā* to create.

mayonnaise (māənāz´) *n.* **1** a thick sauce or salad dressing made of egg yolk, vinegar etc. **2** a dish with this as a dressing.
19C. French, ? fem. of *mahonnais* (a.), from *Mahon*, the capital of Minorca.
● Mahon was captured in 1756 by the Duc de Richelieu, and his cook is said to have created the sauce in honour of his master's victory.

mazel tov (maz´əl tov, tof) *int.* good luck, congratulations, used esp. by Jews.
19C. Modern Hebrew *mazzāl ṭōḇ*, lit. good star, from Hebrew *mazzāl* star.

mazuma (məzoo´mə) *n.* (*sl.*) money, cash.
early 20C. Yiddish, from Hebrew *mĕzummān*, from *zimmēn* to prepare.

mazurka (məzœ´kə) *n.* **1** a lively Polish dance like the polka. **2** the music for this.
19C. French, or from German *Masurka*, from Polish *mazurka* woman from (the province of) Mazovia.

mea culpa (māə kŭl´pə, kul´-) *int.* used to acknowledge responsibility for a mistake. ~*n.* an acknowledgement that one has made a mistake.
14–15C. Latin, lit. (through) my fault.
● The words come from the prayer of confession in the Latin liturgy of the Church, more fully: *Mea culpa, mea culpa, mea maxima culpa* Through my fault, through my fault, through my most grievous fault. The expression is now often used as a jocular admission of guilt. Cp. PECCAVI.

mealie (mē´li), **mielie** *n.* (*S Afr.*) **1** (*usu. pl.*) maize. **2** a cob of corn.
19C. Afrikaans *mielie*, from Portuguese *milho* maize, millet, from Latin *milium*. Not rel. to English *meal*.

medico (med´ikō) n. (pl. **medicos**) (coll.)
1 a physician, a doctor. **2** a medical
student.
17C. Italian, from Latin *medicus*
physician.

medina (midē´nə), **Medina** n. the
ancient Arab quarter of N African cities.
early 20C. Arabic, lit. town.
• The Arabic word gave the name of
Medina, the second of the two most
sacred cities of Islam, in W Saudi Arabia.

Medjidie (məjē´diə) n. **1** a Turkish order
of knighthood established by Sultan
Abdul-Medjid in 1851. **2** a Turkish coin
first minted by Sultan Abdul-Medjid.
19C. Turkish *mecidiye* silver coins, from
Sultan Abdul-*Medjid*, 1823–61.

Medoc (mādok´) n. a red claret wine.
19C. *Médoc*, an area along the left bank
of the Gironde estuary, SW France.

meerschaum (miə´shəm, -shawm) n.
1 a white compact hydrous magnesium
silicate, used for tobacco pipes. **2** a pipe
made of this.
18C. German, from *Meer* sea + *Schaum*
foam, translating Persian *kef-i-daryā*
foam of sea.
• The reference is to the mineral's
lightness and whiteness, evoking froth
in the sea or surf.

megaron (meg´əron) n. (pl. **megara**
(-rə)) the central room of a large
Mycenaean house.
19C. Greek, from *megas* great, large.

Megillah (məgil´ə) n. **1** a scroll
containing a book of Hebrew scripture
designated for reading on a specific day.
2 (**megillah**) a long, tedious or
complicated story, a rigmarole.
mid-20C. Hebrew *mĕğillāh*, lit. roll,
scroll.
• Sense 1 refers particularly to the Book
of Esther, which is read at the festival of
Purim.

Meissen (mī´sən) n. a type of fine
German porcelain.
19C. *Meissen*, a town near Dresden in
Germany.

meistersinger (mī´stəsingə) n.
(pl. **meistersinger**) a German burgher
poet and musician of the 14th–16th
cents., one of the successors of the
minnesingers.
19C. German, from *Meister* master +
Singer singer.

melancholia (melənkō´liə) n. a mental
disorder, often preceding mania,
characterized by depression, frequently
with suicidal tendencies.
17C. Late Latin, from Greek
melankholia, from *melas*, *melanos* black
+ *kholē* bile.
• The condition was originally thought
to have been caused by an excess of
black bile.

mélange (mālāzh´) n. a mixture, medley
or miscellany.
17C. French, from *mêler* to mix.
Cp. MÊLÉE.

mêlée (mel´ā), (N Am.) **melee** n. **1** a
confused hand-to-hand fight, an affray.
2 a muddle.
17C. French, from Old French *mellée*,
p.p. of *meller*, var. of *mesler* to mix.

melisma (miliz´mə) n. (pl. **melismata**
(-mətə), **melismas**) (Mus.) a melodic
embellishment, consisting of a group of
notes sung to a single syllable.
19C. Greek, lit. song.

†membrum virile (membrəm virī´li,
-ē´li) n. the penis.
19C. Latin male member.

memento (mimen´tō) n. (pl. **mementos**,
mementoes) a souvenir.
14–15C. Latin remember!, imper. of
meminisse to remember, with redupl. of
base of English *mind*.

memento mori (mimen´tō maw´ri) *n.* an emblem of mortality, esp. a skull. **16C. Latin** remember that you have to die, from MEMENTO + *mori* to die.

memoir (mem´wah) *n.* **1** (*usu. pl.*) an account of events or transactions in which the narrator took part. **2** an autobiography or a biography. **3** a communication to some learned society on a special subject. **4** (*pl.*) the published proceedings of a learned society. **16C. French** *mémoire*, from Latin *memoria* memory.

memorabilia (memərəbil´iə) *n.pl.* **1** souvenirs of past events, people etc. **2** †things worthy to be remembered. **18C. Latin**, neut. pl. of *memorabilis* memorable.

memorandum (meməran´dəm) *n.* (*pl.* **memorandums**, **memoranda** (-də)) **1** a note to help the memory. **2** a short informal letter, usu. unsigned, with the sender's name etc. printed at the head, often sent internally within a company etc. **3** a brief record or note. **4** (*Law*) a summary or draft of an agreement etc. **14–15C. Latin**, neut. sing. of *memorandus*, ger. of *memorare* to bring to mind, from *memor* mindful.

memsahib (mem´sahb) *n.* (*Hist.*) a term of address formerly applied by Indians in speaking to or of European married women living in the Indian subcontinent. **19C. Anglo-Indian**, from *mem*, var. of English *ma'am* + SAHIB.

ménage (mānahzh´) *n.* **1** a household. **2** housekeeping, household management. **12–14C. Old French** *menaige* (Modern French *ménage*), from Latin *mansio*, *mansionis* dwelling, from *manere* to stay, to remain.

ménage à trois (mānahzh a trwah´) *n.* (*pl.* **ménages à trois** (mānahzh a trwah´)) a household of three adults living together, usu. a married couple and the lover of one of them. **19C. French** household of three, from MÉNAGE + *à* of, by + *trois* three.

menagerie (mənaj´əri) *n.* **1** a collection of wild animals. **2** a place or enclosure where wild animals are kept. **17C. French** *ménagerie*, from MÉNAGE.

mene mene tekel upharsin (meeni meeni tekəl yoofah´sin) *int.* formula written on the wall by a mysterious disembodied hand at the feast of Belshazzar (Dan. v.25–28), interpreted by Daniel as signalling the downfall of the king and his realm. **early 20C. Aramaic** numbered, numbered, weighed, divided. ● The words were taken to mean that the kingdom would be divided between the Medes and the Persians. The words themselves were perhaps originally the names of weights or coins. The biblical story is the origin of the English expression 'the writing on the wall'.

menhir (men´hiə) *n.* a prehistoric monument consisting of a tall upright stone. **19C. Breton** *maen-hir*, from *maen* stone + *hir* long. Cp. DOLMEN.

meno mosso (menō mos´ō) *adv.* (*Mus.*) less quickly. **19C. Italian**, from *meno* less + MOSSO. Cp. PIÙ MOSSO.

menorah (minaw´rə) *n.* a candelabrum with several branches, used in Jewish worship. **19C. Hebrew** *měnōrāh* candlestick.

mensch (mensh) *n.* a person of integrity, an honourable person. **mid-20C. Yiddish**, from German *Mensch* person.

Menshevik (men´shəvik) *n.* (*Hist.*) a member of the moderate party in the Russian Revolution, as distinct from *Bolshevik*.
early 20C. Russian *men'shevik* member of the minority, from *men'shiĭ* less, comp. of *malyĭ* little.

mens rea (menz rē´ə) *n.* criminal intent, the knowledge that an act is wrong.
19C. Latin guilty mind.

mens sana in corpore sano (menz sah´nə in kawpərā sah´nō) *n.* a healthy mind in a healthy body.
17C. Latin, lit. sound mind in sound body.
• The words are from Juvenal's *Satires* (X) (2C AD).

menu (men´ū) *n.* (*pl.* **menus**) **1** a list of dishes available at a restaurant etc. **2** a list of dishes to be served at a meal. **3** (*Comput.*) a list of alternative operations, topics etc., usu. displayed on-screen, which the user can choose from.
17C. French detailed list, use as n. of a. meaning small, from Latin *minutus*.

mère (meə) *n.* mother, used to distinguish a mother from a daughter of the same name.
19C. French. Cp. FILLE, PÈRE.

meringue (mərang´) *n.* **1** a baked confection of white of eggs, sugar etc. **2** a cake made of this, usu. filled with cream etc.
18C. French, of unknown orig.
• The word is popularly but erroneously traced to the name of a Swiss chef.

merino (mərē´nō) *n.* (*pl.* **merinos**) **1** a breed of sheep valuable for their fine wool. **2** a fine woollen dress fabric, orig. of this wool. **3** a fine woollen yarn used for hosiery. ~*a.* **1** of or relating to this breed of sheep. **2** made of merino.
18C. Spanish, of unknown orig.

mesa (mā´sə) *n.* a plateau with steep sides, a tableland.
18C. Spanish table, from Latin *mensa*.

mésalliance (māzaliãs´, -zal´-) *n.* marriage with a person of inferior social position.
18C. French from *més-* mis- + *alliance* alliance.

meseta (mes´etə) *n.* a plateau in Spain or a Spanish-speaking country, esp. that in central Spain.
early 20C. Spanish, dim. of MESA.

meshuga (mishug´ə), **meshugga** *a.* mad, crazy, stupid.
19C. Yiddish *meshuge*, from Hebrew *měshugga'*.

mesquin (meskĭ) *a.* sordid, shabby.
18C. French, from Italian *meschino*, from Arabic *mesqīn* poor.

Messiah (misī´ə) *n.* **1** an expected saviour or deliverer. **2** the anointed one, Christ, as the promised deliverer of the Jews.
12–14C. Old French *Messie*, from Popular Latin *Messias*, from Greek, from Aramaic *měšīḥā*, Hebrew *māšīăḥ* anointed, from *māšaḥ* to anoint.
• The Latin form of the word *Messias* was rejected by the 1560 Geneva Bible translators in favour of the more Hebraic-looking *Messiah*. Cp. the many Old Testament names ending in *-iah*, as *Isaiah, Jeremiah, Josiah, Nehemiah*, etc.

Messieurs (mesyœ´), **Messrs** (mes´əz) *n.pl.* sirs, gentlemen.
18C. French, pl. of MONSIEUR.

mestizo (mestē´zō) *n.* (*pl.* **mestizos**) **1** a person of mixed Spanish or Portuguese and American Indian blood. **2** a person of mixed Chinese and Philippine blood.
16C. Spanish, from Latin *mixtus*, p.p. of *miscere* to mix.

métier (met´iā, mā´-) *n.* **1** trade, profession. **2** an area of activity in which one is skilled, feels comfortable etc., one's forte.
18C. French, from alt. of Latin *ministerium* service, ministry, prob. influ. by *mysterium* mystery.

Metis (mā´tēs, mātēs´), **Métis** *n.* (*pl.* **Metis**, **Métis**) a person of mixed blood, esp. (in Canada) the offspring of a person of European descent and an American Indian.
19C. French *métis*, from Old French *mestis*, from Latin *mixtus*. See MESTIZO.

metro (met´rō) *n.* (*pl.* **metros**) an underground railway network in a city.
early 20C. French *métro*, abbr. of (*Chemin de Fer*) *Métropolitain* Metropolitan (Railway).

meunière (mœnyeə´) *a.* (of fish) cooked or served in butter with lemon juice and herbs, esp. parsley.
19C. French (*à la*) *meunière*, lit. (in the manner of a) miller's wife.

mezuzah (məzoo´zə), **mezuza** *n.* (*pl.* **mezuzoth** (-zōt)) a small case containing extracts from religious texts fixed to the doorpost by Jews as a sign of their piety.
17C. Hebrew *mĕzūzāh*, lit. doorpost.
• The practice is prescribed in Deut. vi.9 'And thou shalt write them [God's commandments] upon the post of thy house'.

mezzanine (mez´ənēn, met´sə-) *n.* **1** a storey intermediate in level between two main storeys, usu. between the ground and first floors. **2** a window in such a storey. **3** a floor beneath the stage of a theatre from which the traps etc. are worked. **4** (*N Am.*) the dress circle in a theatre. ~*a.* of or relating to unsecured high-interest loans of intermediate status between secured loans and equities.

18C. French, from Italian *mezzanino*, dim. of *mezzano*, from Latin *medianus* middle, medium.

mezza voce (metsə vō´chi) *a., adv.* (*Mus.*) **1** (singing or sung) softly. **2** quiet(ly).
18C. Italian *mezza*, fem. of MEZZO + *voce* voice.

mezzo (met´sō) *a.* half or medium. ~*n.* (*pl.* **mezzos**) (*Mus.*) a mezzo-soprano.
18C. Italian middle, half, from Latin *medius* medium.

mezzo forte (metsō faw´ti) *a., adv.* (*Mus.*) moderately loud(ly).
19C. Italian, from MEZZO + FORTE².

mezzo piano (metsō pyah´nō) *a., adv.* (*Mus.*) moderately soft(ly).
19C. Italian, from MEZZO + PIANO.

mezzo-relievo (metsōrəlyā´vō) *n.* (*pl.* **mezzo-relievos**) half relief; a sculpture in which the figures stand out from the background to a half of their proportions.
16C. Italian, from MEZZO + RELIEVO.

mezzo-soprano (metsōsəprah´nō) *n.* **1** a female singing voice lower than a soprano and higher than a contralto. **2** a singer with such a voice. **3** a part written for such a voice.
18C. Italian, from MEZZO + SOPRANO.

miasma (miaz´mə) *n.* (*pl.* **miasmata** (-tə), **miasmas**) **1** an infectious or poisonous vapour. **2** an unwholesome atmosphere.
17C. Greek defilement, pollution, rel. to *miainein* to pollute.

midinette (midinet´) *n.* a shop girl in Paris, esp. in a milliner's shop.
early 20C. French, from *midi* midday + *dînette* light dinner.
• The girls are so called because they originally had a light meal at midday.

Midrash (mid´rash, -ŭsh) *n.* (*pl.*
Midrashim (-im)) a commentary on
part of the Hebrew scriptures.
17C. **Hebrew** *miḏrāš* commentary, from
dāraš to study, to expound.

mignon (mēn´yon) *a.* delicate and small,
dainty.
16C. **French**, from *minet*, the popular
word for a cat in medieval tales and
plays.
• The ultimate source of the French
word is imitative. Cp. MARMITE,
MISTIGRIS.

mignonette (minyənet´) *n.* **1** any annual
plant of the genus *Reseda*, esp. *R.
odorata*, which has fragrant greenish
flowers. **2** the greenish colour of its
flowers. **3** a type of fine narrow
pillowlace.
18C. **French** *mignonette*, dim. of
MIGNON.

mihrab (mē´rahb) *n.* a niche etc. in a
mosque indicating the direction of
Mecca.
19C. **Arabic** *miḥrāb.*

mikado (mikah´dō) *n.* (*pl.* **mikados**)
(*Hist.*) the emperor of Japan.
18C. **Japanese**, from *mi* august + *kado*
gate.

miladi (milā´di), **milady** *n.* (*pl.* **miladies**)
(*Hist.*) **1** an English gentlewoman or
noblewoman. **2** (in France) my lady
(used as a form of address or reference).
18C. **French**, from English *my lady.*
Cp. MILORD.

miles gloriosus (mēlāz glawriō´səs,
mīlēz) *n.* (*pl.* **milites gloriosi** (mēlitāz
glawriō´sē, mīlitēz glawriō´sī)) a soldier
who boasts about his exploits, esp. a
stock character in Renaissance comedy.
early 20C. Latin boastful soldier.
• The words were originally the title of
a comedy by Plautus (*c.*250–184 BC).

milieu (mēlyœ´, mē´-) *n.* (*pl.* **milieux**,
milieus (-yœz)) environment,
surroundings.
19C. **French**, from *mi* (from Latin
medius middle) + *lieu* place.

militia (milish´ə) *n.* **1** a supplementary
military force consisting of the body
of citizens not enrolled in the regular
army. **2** (*Hist.*) the former constitutional
force of England, consisting usu. of
volunteers enrolled and disciplined, but
called out only in case of emergency,
superseded by the Territorial Army in
1907.
16C. **Latin** military service, warfare,
from *miles, militis* soldier.

millefeuille (mēlfœy´) *n.* a cake of puff
pastry filled with jam and cream.
19C. **French**, lit. thousand leaves, from
mille thousand + *feuille* leaf.
• The French name refers to the
many layers (leaves) of puff pastry.
(A conventionally made sheet of puff
pastry comprises 729 laminations, and
millefeuille may have two to five layers,
giving 1458 to 3645 leaves. These
figures, numbering literally thousands,
entirely justify the name.)

millefiori (mēlifyaw´ri) *n.* a kind of
ornamental glass made by fusing
together glass rods of different sizes and
colours and cutting the resultant mass
into sections.
19C. **Italian**, from *mille* thousand + *fiori*,
pl. of *fiore* flower.

milord (milawd´) *n.* (*Hist.*) my lord
(formerly applied to aristocratic
Englishmen).
16C. **French**, from *my lord.* Cp. MILADI.

mimbar (mim´bah), **minbar** (min´-) *n.*
the pulpit of a mosque.
19C. **Arabic** *minbar*, from *nabara* to
raise.

mina (mī´nə) *n.* (*pl.* **minas**, **minae** (-ē))
1 an ancient Greek weight of 100
drachmae, or about one pound
avoirdupois (0.454 kilograms). **2** an
ancient coin worth 100 drachmae.
16C. Latin, from Greek *mna*, prob. ult.
from Akkadian.

minestrone (ministrō´ni) *n.* a thick soup
of mixed vegetables with pasta or rice.
19C. Italian, from *minestra* vegetable
soup, from *minestrare* to serve, to dish
out + augm. suf. *-one*.
• Italian *minestra* is one of two general
words for soup, the other being *zuppa*.

minnesinger (min´ising·ə, min´ə-) *n.*
any of a body of German lyric poets and
singers, 1138–1347, whose chief theme
was love.
19C. German, from *Minne* love + obs.
Singer (now *Sänger*) singer.

minutia (minū´shiə, mī-) *n.* (*pl.*
minutiae (-iē)) (*usu. in pl.*) a small
and precise or trivial particular.
18C. Latin smallness, from *minutus*
small.

mirabelle (mirəbel´) *n.* **1** a European
plum tree, *Prunus institia*, bearing small
firm yellow fruit. **2** the fruit of this tree.
3 a liqueur made from this fruit.
18C. French, alt. (influ. by female
forename *Mirabelle*, from Latin *mirabilis*
wonderful, lovely) of Latin *myrobalanus*
myrobalan.

mirabile dictu (mirahbilā dik´too) *int.*
wonderful to relate.
19C. Latin, from *mirabile*, neut. of
mirabilis wonderful + *dictu*, supine of
dicere to say.
• The phrase is generally applied
sarcastically.

mirador (mirədaw´) *n.* a belvedere turret
or gallery, commanding an extensive
view.
17C. Spanish, from *mirar* to look, to
observe.

mirage (mirahzh´) *n.* **1** an optical illusion
by which images of distant objects are
seen as if inverted, esp. in a desert
where the inverted sky appears as a
sheet of water. **2** an illusory thing, a
delusion.
19C. French from *se mirer* to be
reflected, to be mirrored, from Latin
mirari to gaze in wonder at.

mirepoix (miəpwah´, miə´-) *n.* (*pl.*
mirepoix) a sauce of sautéd chopped
vegetables.
19C. French, from the Duc de *Mirepoix*,
1699–1757, French diplomat and
general.
• The sauce was reputedly devised by
the duke's cook.

mirliton (mœ´liton) *n.* a musical
instrument resembling a kazoo.
19C. French reed pipe, prob. of imit.
orig.

mirza (mœ´zə) *n.* **1** an Iranian title for a
doctor, scholar or other learned person.
2 a Persian (Iranian) prince.
17C. Persian *mīrzā*, from *mīr* prince
(from Arabic *'amīr* AMIR) + *zād* son.

miscellanea (misəlā´niə) *n.pl.* **1** a
collection of miscellaneous literary
compositions. **2** a collection of
miscellaneous items.
16C. Latin, neut. pl. of *miscellaneus*,
from *miscellus* mixed.

misch metal (mish´ metəl) *n.* an alloy
of cerium with other rare earth metals,
used for cigarette-lighter flints.
early 20C. German *Mischmetall*, from
mischen to mix + *Metall* metal.

mise en scene (mēz ā sen´) *n.* **1** the
settings, properties etc. of a play, film
etc. **2** the art of achieving this. **3** the
environment of an event.
19C. French *mise en scène*, lit. (a)
putting onto the stage, from fem. p.p.
(used as n.) of *mettre* to put + *en* on +
scène stage, scene.

misère (mizeə´) *n.* a declaration in solo whist etc. by which a player undertakes not to take a single trick.
19C. French poverty, misery.

miserere (mizəreə´ri) *n.* **1** a prayer or cry for mercy. **2** the 51st Psalm. **3** a musical setting of this psalm. **4** a misericord.
12–14C. Latin have mercy!, imper. sing. of *misereri* to have pity, to have mercy, from *miser* wretched.
• The word begins the Latin version of Ps. li, more fully: *Miserere mei Deus* Have mercy upon me, O God.

Mishnah (mish´nə), **Mishna** *n.* the second or oral Jewish law, the collection of traditions etc. forming the text of the Talmud.
17C. Post-biblical Hebrew *mišnāh* repetition, instruction.

miso (mē´sō) *n.* a food paste made from soya beans fermented in brine, used for flavouring.
18C. Japanese.

missa solemnis (misə solem´nis) *n.* a High Mass.
early 20C. Latin solemn Mass.
• The phrase is familiar as the title of various musical compositions based on the Roman Mass, such as that by Beethoven (composed 1819–22).

mistico (mis´tikō) *n.* (*pl.* **misticos**) a small coasting vessel used in the Mediterranean.
19C. Spanish, ? ult. from Arabic *musaṭṭaḥ* armed vessel.

mistigris (mis´tigris) *n.* **1** the joker or a blank card used as a wild card in a form of draw poker. **2** the game using this.
19C. French *mistigri* jack of clubs, orig. a pop. word for a cat, from *miste*, var. of *mite*, of imit. orig. (cp. MARMITE) + *gris* grey.

mistral (mistrahl´) *n.* a cold dry NW wind of S France.

17C. French, from Provençal, from Latin *magistralis* (*ventus*) dominant (wind).

mitrailleuse (mitrahyœz´) *n.* a breech-loading machine-gun consisting of several barrels united, for firing simultaneously or in succession.
19C. French, fem. of *mitrailleur*, from *mitrailler* to fire mitraille, from *mitaille* small money, pieces of metal, from *mite*, rel. to English *mite*.

mittimus (mit´iməs) *n.* (*pl.* **mittimuses**) **1** (*Law*) a warrant of commitment to prison. **2** †a writ to remove records from one court to another.
14–15C. Latin we send, 1st pers. plur. pres. indic. of *mittere* to send, first word of the writ in Latin.

mitzvah (mits´və) *n.* (*pl.* **mitzvoth** (-vōt)) **1** in Judaism, a commandment or rule. **2** a good deed done by a Jew for religious reasons.
17C. Hebrew *miṣwāh* commandment.
See also BAR MITZVAH, BAT MITZVAH.

Mizpah (miz´pə) *a.* of a trinket etc., given as a keepsake.
19C. Hebrew *Miṣpah*, a place in ancient Palestine.
• *Mizpah* was originally the name given to the cairn of stones made in token of the covenant between Jacob and Laban (Gen. xxxi.43–55).

modena (mod´inə) *n.* a deep crimson or purple.
19C. *Modena*, a city in N Italy.

moderato (modərah´tō) *a., adv.* (*Mus.*) in moderate time. ~*n.* (*pl.* **moderatos**) a piece of music in moderate time.
18C. Italian moderate.

moderne (mədœn´, modeən´) *a.* of a style of architecture and design popular in the 1920s and characterized by bright colours and austere geometric forms.
mid-20C. French modern.

modicum (mod´ikəm) *n.* a little, a small amount, a scanty allowance.
15C. Latin little way, short time, neut. sing. of *modicus* moderate, from *modus* measure.

modiste (modēst´) *n.* **1** a milliner. **2** a dressmaker.
19C. French, from *mode* fashion.

modus (mō´dəs) *n.* (*pl.* **modi** (-dī))
1 mode, manner, way. **2** (*Hist.*) money compensation in lieu of tithe.
16C. Latin manner, measure.

modus operandi (mōdəs operan´dī, opəran´dē) *n.* (*pl.* **modi operandi** (mōdī, -dē)) **1** a method of working. **2** the way something operates.
17C. Latin mode of operating, from MODUS + gen. of *operandum*, ger. of *operare* to operate.

modus vivendi (mōdəs viven´dī, viven´dē) *n.* (*pl.* **modi vivendi** (mōdī, -dē)) **1** a way of living, or life. **2** an arrangement by means of which people who are in dispute carry on in a situation pending a settlement.
19C. Latin mode of living, from MODUS + gen. of *vivendum*, ger. of *vivere* to live.

moeurs (mœ, mœz) *n.pl.* the behaviour or customs of a people or group of people.
early 20C. French, from Latin MORES.

mofette (mofet´) *n.* **1** a fissure in the earth giving vent to noxious gas, a fumarole. **2** an exhalation of noxious gas from this.
19C. French, from Neapolitan Italian *mofetta*, from *muffa* mould, mildew, from Germanic base *muff-*, of imit. orig.

mogul¹ (mō´gəl) *n.* **1** a powerful and influential entrepreneur. **2** (**Mogul**) **a** a Mongolian, a Mughal. **b** a follower of Baber, descendant of Tamerlane, or of Genghis Khan.
16C. Urdu *muġal*, from Persian and Urdu *muġul*, rel. to English *Mongol*.

mogul² (mō´gəl) *n.* a mound of packed snow on a ski slope.
mid-20C. Prob. from **Southern German** dial. *Mugel, Mugl.*

moi (mwah) *pron.* (*usu. facet.*) me.
late 20C. French.

moidore (moi´daw) *n.* (*Hist.*) a Portuguese gold coin.
18C. Portuguese *moeda d'ouro* money of gold.

moire (mwah), **moire antique** (ätēk) *n.* **1** watered silk. **2** a watered appearance on textile fabrics or metals.
17C. French, later form of *mouaire* mohair (+ *antique* ancient, antique).

moksha (mok´shə) *n.* in Hindu and Jain religions, release from the cycle of rebirth.
18C. Sanskrit *mokṣa*, from *muc* to set free, to release.

molto (mol´tō) *adv.* (*Mus.*) much, very, as in *molto allegro.*
19C. Italian, from Latin *multus* much.

momentum (məmen´təm) *n.* (*pl.* **momenta** (-tə)) (*Physics*) **1** impetus, power of overcoming resistance to motion. **2** the quantity of motion in a body, the product of the mass and the velocity.
17C. Latin movement.

mondaine (mōden´, mon-) *a.* **1** of fashionable society. **2** worldly. ~*n.* a person of fashionable society.
19C. French, fem. of *mondain* worldly.
Cp. DEMI-MONDAINE.

mondo (mon´dō) *adv.* very, extremely.
late 20C. Italian world.
● The colloquial use of the word derives from the Italian film *Mondo Cane* ('A Dog's Life') (1961), which depicts violently eccentric human behaviour.

Monegasque (monegask´) *a.* of or relating to the principality of Monaco. ~*n.* a native or inhabitant of Monaco. **19C. French** *monégasque* of Monaco, an independent principality forming an enclave on the south coast of France, from Provençal *mounegasc*, from *Mounegue* Monaco.

monocoque (mon´əkok) *n.* **1** in an aircraft, a form of streamlined fuselage shaped like an elongated egg. **2** an aeroplane with such a fuselage. **3** a car or vehicle with a body and chassis manufactured as an integrated structure. **4** a boat with a hull all made of one piece. **early 20C. French**, from *mono-* single + *coque* eggshell.

Monseigneur (monsenyœ´, mõ-) *n.* (*pl.* **Messeigneurs** (māsenyœ´)) a French title of honour given to high dignitaries, esp. in the Church. **17C. French**, from *mon* my + *seigneur* lord.

Monsieur (məsyœ´, mis-) *n.* (*pl.* **Messieurs**) **1** the French title of address corresponding to *Mr* or *Sir*. **2** a Frenchman. **16C. French**, from *mon* my + *sieur* lord.

Monsignor (monsē´nyə) *n.* (*pl.* **Monsignori** (-yaw´ri)) a title given to Roman Catholic prelates, officers of the Pope's court and others. **16C. Italian**, based on French MONSEIGNEUR.

montage (montahzh´) *n.* **1** the cutting and assembling of shots taken when making a film, video etc. **2** a sequence of such shots. **3** an artistic, literary or musical work consisting of heterogeneous elements in juxtaposition. **early 20C. French**, from *monter* to mount.

montagnard (mõtanyah´) *n.* (*pl.* **montagnard, montagnards**) **1** an inhabitant of a mountainous region. **2** (*Hist.*) a member of the 'Mountain' or extreme democratic wing in the French Revolutionary Legislative Assembly (1791–92). **19C. French**, from *montagne* mountain.

monte (mon´ti) *n.* **1** a Spanish game of chance with 45 cards, resembling faro. **2** in Latin America, a tract of wooded country. **19C. Spanish** mountain, pile of cards left after dealing.

montero (monteə´rō) *n.* (*pl.* **monteros**) a Spanish huntsman's cap with flaps and a round crown. **17C. Spanish** mountaineer, hunter, from *monte* mount.

moolvi (mool´vi), **moolvie** *n.* (*pl.* **moolvis, moolvies**) **1** a Muslim doctor of law. **2** a learned or respected person, a teacher. **17C. Urdu** *maulvī*, from Arabic *mawlawī* judicial, from *mawlā* MULLAH.

moonshee (moon´shi), **munshi** *n.* a secretary, teacher of languages or interpreter in the Indian subcontinent. **18C. Persian and Urdu** *munšī*, from Arabic *munši'* writer, author, active p. of *'anša'a* to write (a book).

moped (mō´ped) *n.* a motorized pedal cycle, of less than 50 cubic centimetres. **mid-20C. Swedish**, from trampcykel med *mo*tor och *ped*aler, pedal cycle with engine and pedals.
● The word was popularly derived in English from *mo*tor + *ped*al.

moquette (moket´) *n.* a woven fabric of wool and hemp or linen with a velvety pile, used for carpets and upholstery. **19C. French**, of unknown orig. ? Rel. to (or from) obs. Italian *mocaiardo* mohair.

moraine (mərān´) *n.* the debris of rocks brought down by glaciers.
18C. French, from Savoyard Italian *morena*, from S French *mor*, *morre* muzzle, snout, from a word rel. to English *morion* a type of 16C helmet.

morale (mərahl´) *n.* **1** mental or moral condition. **2** courage and endurance in supporting threats to one's mental well-being.
18C. French *moral*, from Latin *moralis* moral, respelt to indicate the stress. Cp. LOCALE.

moratorium (mərətaw´riəm) *n.* (*pl.* **moratoriums**, **moratoria** (-riə)) **1** a deferment, delay or temporary suspension. **2** a legal act authorizing a debtor or bank to defer or suspend payment for a time. **3** the period of such a suspension.
19C. Modern Latin, neut. sing. (used as n.) of Late Latin *moratorius* that which delays, from *moratus*, p.p. of *morari* to delay.

morceau (mawsō´) *n.* (*pl.* **morceaux** (-sō´)) **1** a small piece. **2** a short literary or musical composition.
18C. French, from Old French *morsel*, dim. of *mors*, from Latin *morsus* bite, from p.p. of *mordere* to bite.

mores (maw´rāz) *n.pl.* the customs and conduct which embody the fundamental values of a social group.
19C. Latin, pl. of *mos*, *moris* manner, custom.

Moresque (məresk´, maw-) *a.* Moorish in style and decoration. ~*n.* Moorish decoration, as the profusely ornamented work in the Alhambra.
14–15C. French, from Italian *moresco*, from *Moro* Moor. Cp. MORISCO.

morgen (maw´gən) *n.* in SE Africa, the Netherlands and parts of the US, a unit of land measurement, about 0.8 hectares (just over two acres).
17C. Dutch and German, lit. morning, appar. meaning the area of land that can be ploughed in a morning.

morgue (mawg) *n.* **1** a mortuary. **2** a building or room where the bodies of unknown persons found dead are exposed for identification. **3** a stock of files, clippings etc., esp. future obituaries, kept by a newspaper for reference.
19C. French, proper name of a Paris mortuary, orig. a place in a Paris prison where bodies were viewed to establish their identity, prob. from *morgue* haughtiness, orig. sad expression, solemn look, of unknown orig.

†**Morisco** (məris´kō), **Moresco** (-es´-) *n.* (*pl.* **Moriscos**, **Morescos**, **Moriscoes**, **Morescoes**) **1** a Moor, esp. one of the Moors remaining in Spain after the conquest of Granada by the Christians. **2** the language of the Moors. **3** a morris dance. ~*a.* Moorish.
16C. Spanish, from *Moro* Moor. Cp. MORESQUE.

morituri te salutant (morituri tā saloo´tant, -tū-) *int.* an expression used by someone about to face a difficult or dangerous situation.
18C. Latin, those who are about to die salute you.
● A variant is *morituri te salutamus* 'we who are about to die salute you', in Roman times the words addressed by gladiators to the emperor as they entered the arena.

mortadella (mawtədel´ə) *n.* (*pl.* **mortadelle** (-i)) a type of large spicy pork sausage, sold ready to eat.
17C. Italian, from Latin *murtatum* (sausage) seasoned with myrtle berries, from *murtus* myrtle.

Moselle (məzel´), **Mosel** *n.* a white wine
made in the valley of the river Moselle.
17C. *Moselle*, a river of NE France and
W Germany.
● *Moselle* is the French form of the
river name, *Mosel* the German.

moshav (mō´shav, -shav´) *n.* (*pl.*
moshavim (-im)) a co-operative
association of small farms in Israel.
mid-20C. **Hebrew** *mōšāḇ* dwelling,
colony.

mosso (mos´ō) *adv.* (*Mus.*) with liveliness
and speed.
19C. **Italian**, p.p. of *muovere* to move.
Cp. PIÙ MOSSO, MENO MOSSO.

mot (mō) *n.* (*pl.* **mots** (mō)) **1** a witty or
pithy saying. **2** †a motto.
16C. **French** word, saying, from alt. of
Popular Latin *muttum*, rel. to Latin
muttire to murmur. Cp. MOTTO.

motif (mōtēf´) *n.* **1** the dominant feature
or idea in a literary, musical or other
artistic composition. **2** an ornamental
piece of lace etc. sewn on a dress.
3 (*Mus.*) a theme in music.
19C. **French** motive, from Medieval
Latin *motivus*, from Latin *movere* to
move.

mot juste (mō zhoost´) *n.* the
appropriate or felicitous word or phrase.
early 20C. **French** exact word.

motocross (mō´təkros) *n.* the sport of
racing on motorcycles over rough
ground.
mid-20C. **French** *moto-cross*, from *moto*
motorcycle (from *motocyclette*) + *cross*,
shortening of *cross-country*, from
English.

moto perpetuo (mōtō pœpet´ūō) *n.*
(*Mus.*) a short fast-moving instrumental
piece.
19C. **Italian** perpetual motion. Cp.
PERPETUUM MOBILE.

motte (mot) *n.* a mound on which a
castle, camp etc. is situated.
19C. **French** mound, from Old French
mote hillock, mound, castle.

motto (mot´ō) *n.* (*pl.* **mottoes**) **1** a short
pithy sentence or phrase expressing a
sentiment. **2** a principle or maxim
adopted as a rule of conduct. **3** a joke
or maxim contained in a paper cracker.
4 (*Her.*) a word or sentence used with a
crest or coat of arms.
16C. **Italian**, from Latin *muttum* grunt,
word. See MOT.

mouche (moosh) *n.* a beauty spot on the
face.
17C. **French**, lit. fly.
● The beauty spot originally took the
form of a small patch of black plaster
worn on the face as an ornament, the
aim being to draw attention to the
unblemished countenance that it
discreetly marred.

moue (moo) *n.* a small pouting grimace.
19C. **French**, from Frankish, of imit.
orig. Cp. English *mope*.

mouflon (moo´flon), **moufflon** *n.* a wild
sheep, *Ovis orientalis*, of Sardinia and
Corsica.
18C. **French**, from Italian dial. *muflone*,
from Popular Latin dial. *mufro*.

mouillé (moo´yā) *a.* (of a consonant)
palatalized (as *gn* in *lasagne*, *ñ* in *señor*).
19C. **French**, p.p. of *mouiller* to wet, to
moisten, from Popular Latin *molliare* to
soften by dipping, from Latin *mollis*
soft.

moulage (moolahzh´) *n.* **1** the taking of
plaster casts of footprints etc. **2** a plaster
cast made in this way. **3** in the US, a
section of a police force that specializes
in this.
early 20C. **French** moulding, moulded
reproduction, from *mouler* to mould.

moulin (moo´li) *n.* a vertical pit in a glacier created and maintained by a constant stream of water from the surface.
19C. French, lit. mill.

mousquetaire (mooskəteə´) *n.* (*Hist.*) a musketeer.
18C. French, from *mousquet* musket.

moussaka (moosah´kə), **mousaka** *n.* a Greek dish of minced meat, aubergines and tomatoes, topped with a cheese sauce.
mid-20C. Turkish *musakka*, ult. from Arabic *musakkā*.

mousse (moos) *n.* **1** a dish of flavoured cream whipped and frozen. **2** any of various light, stiff, liquid preparations, e.g. used for hairstyling or cosmetic purposes. **3** oil and sea water forming a froth after a spillage of oil.
19C. French moss, froth.

mousseline (moos´lēn, -lēn´) *n.* **1** fine French muslin. **2** a light sauce made by whipping cream with hollandaise sauce.
17C. French muslin.

mousseux (moosœ´) *a.* sparkling (of wine).
19C. French, from MOUSSE.

Mozarab (mōzar´əb) *n.* (*Hist.*) any of those Christians in Spain after the Moorish conquest who were allowed the exercise of their religion in return for allegiance to the Moors.
17C. Spanish *mozárabe*, from Arabic *musta'rib*, lit. making oneself an Arab.

mozzarella (motsərel´ə) *n.* a soft white unsalted Italian curd cheese.
early 20C. Italian, dim. of *mozza* a kind of cheese, from *mozzare* to cut off.

mozzetta (məzet´ə, motset´ə), **mozetta** *n.* a short cape with a small hood worn by cardinals, bishops, abbots etc. in the Roman Catholic Church.

18C. Italian, shortening of *almozzetta*, from Medieval Latin *almucia* amice.

muchacha (muchah´chə) *n.* a Spanish girl or young woman.
19C. Spanish, fem. of MUCHACHO.

muchacho (muchah´chō) *n.* a Spanish boy or young man.
16C. Spanish, from obs. Spanish *mochacho*, from *mocho* cropped, shorn.

mudir (moodiə´) *n.* **1** a governor of a village or canton in Turkey. **2** a governor of a province in Egypt.
19C. Turkish *mud´r*, from Arabic *mudīr* active part. of *'adāra* to direct, to manage.

muesli (mūz´li) *n.* (*pl.* **mueslis**) a dish of crushed cereals, dried fruit and nuts, usu. eaten as a breakfast cereal.
mid-20C. Swiss German, dim. of *mus* pulpy food, purée, rel. to Old English *mōs* food.

muezzin (mooez´in) *n.* a Muslim crier of the hour of prayer.
16C. Arabic, dial. var. of Arabic *mu'aḍḍin*, active part. of *'aḍḍana* to call to prayer, from *'uḍn* ear.

mufti (mŭf´ti) *n.* **1** an official interpreter or expounder of the Koran and Muslim law. **2** civilian dress worn by members of the armed service off duty. **3** ordinary dress as distinct from that worn on state or ceremonial occasions.
16C. Arabic *muftī*, active part. of *'aftā* to decide a point of law, rel. to FATWA.
● Sense 2 dates from the 19C and may allude to the costume formerly traditional for the stage role of a mufti, viz. dressing gown, cap and slippers.

Muharram (mŭhŭr´əm), **Moharram** (mō-) *n.* **1** the first month (30 days) of the Muslim year. **2** the first ten days of this observed as a fast in memory of the martyrdom of Husain, the son of Ali.
19C. Arabic *muḥarram* inviolable.

mujahedin (mŭjah·hidēn´),
mujahideen, mujahidin *n.pl.*
fundamentalist Muslim guerrilla
fighters.
mid-20C. Persian and Arabic
mujāhidīn, collect. pl. of *mujāhid*
person who fights a JIHAD.

mulatto (mŭlat´ō) *n.* (*pl.* **mulattos,
mulattoes**) the offspring of a white
person and a black person. ~*a.* of the
skin colour of a mulatto, tawny, esp.
when intermediate in colour between
the parents.
16C. Spanish and Portuguese *mulato*
young mule, mulatto, from *mulo* mule.

mullah (mŭl´ə), **mollah** (mol´ə) *n.* an
honorary title among Muslims for
persons learned in theology and sacred
law, and for Muslim ecclesiastical and
civil dignitaries.
17C. Persian and Urdu *mullā*, Turkish
molla, from Arabic *mawlā* master.

mulligatawny (mŭligətaw´ni) *n.* a
highly-flavoured curry soup.
18C. Tamil *miḷaku-taṇṇi*, lit. pepper-
water.

multum in parvo (multəm in pah´vō)
n. much in little, a lot in a small space
(the motto of Rutland).
18C. Latin much in little.
● Rutland is England's smallest county.

mung (mŭng), **mung bean** *n.* (the seed
of) an E Asian bean plant of the genus
Vigna, used as a forage plant and as the
main source of beansprouts.
19C. Hindi *mūng*.

Muscadet (mŭs´kədā) *n.* **1** a light dry
white wine from the Loire region of
France. **2** the grape from which this
wine is made.
early 20C. French, from *muscade*
nutmeg, from *musc* musk.

muscardine (mŭs´kədin) *n.* a disease
fatal to silkworms, caused by a fungoid
or parasitic growth.
19C. French from *muscadin, muscardin*,
lit. musk-comfit, from Italian *moscado*
musk.
● The disease is so called because the
fungus resembles *muscadin*.

muscovado (mŭskəvah´dō) *n.* (*pl.*
muscovados) a moist, dark-coloured,
unrefined sugar left after evaporation
from the juice of sugar cane and the
draining off from the molasses.
17C. Portuguese *mascabado*, p.p. (used
as n.) of *mascabar* to make badly.

musette (mŭzet´) *n.* **1** (*Hist.*) a small
bagpipe formerly used in France.
2 (*Hist.*) a soft pastoral melody imitating
the sound of the bagpipe. **3** (*Hist.*) a
French instrument resembling the oboe.
4 †a French rustic dance. **5** (*N Am.*) a
small knapsack.
14–15C. Old French, dim. of *muse*
bagpipe.

museum (mūzē´əm) *n.* a room or
building for the preservation or
exhibition of objects illustrating
antiquities, art, natural science etc.
17C. Latin library, study, from Greek
mouseion seat of the Muses, use as n. of
neut. of *mouseios*, from *mousa* muse.

musique concrète (mūzēk kōkret´,
kon-) *n.* music consisting of pieces of
pre-recorded music or other sound put
together and electronically modified,
concrete music.
mid-20C. French concrete music.
● The term was coined in 1948 by the
French composer Pierre Schaeffer to
describe his first electronic studies.

Muslim (muz´lim, mŭz´-), **Moslem**
(moz´ləm) *n.* a person of the Islamic
faith. ~*a.* of or relating to the Islamic
faith, culture etc.

17C. **Arabic** *muslim*, active p. of *'aslama*. See ISLAM.

must (mŭst), **musth** *a.* (of male elephants and camels) in a dangerous state of frenzy, connected with the mating season. ~*n.* this state.
19C. **Urdu** *mast*, from Persian, lit. intoxicated.

mustachio (məstah´shiō) *n.* (*pl.* **mustachios**) a moustache, esp. a large one.
16C. **Italian** *mostaccio*, ult. from Greek *mustax*, *mustakos* upper lip, moustache.

mutatis mutandis (mūtahtis mūtan´dis) *adv.* the necessary alterations having been made.
15C. **Latin**, lit. things being changed that have to be changed, abl. pl. respectively of p.p. and ger. of *mutare* to change.

muu-muu (moo´moo) *n.* a loose brightly-coloured dress worn by women in Hawaii.

early 20C. **Hawaiian** *mu'u mu'u*, lit. cut off.
● The dress is so called because the yoke was originally omitted.

muzhik (moo´zhik), **moujik** *n.* (*Hist.*) a Russian peasant, a serf.
16C. **Russian**, dim. of *muzh* man, husband.
● Russian peasants were called 'little men' because they were regarded as minors under old Russian law.

mynheer (mīnhiə´) *n.* **1** the Dutch title of address equivalent to Mr or Sir. **2** a Dutchman.
17C. **Dutch** *mijnheer*, from *mijn* my + *heer* lord, master.

mystique (mistēk´) *n.* **1** professional skill or technique that impresses the layperson. **2** the mystery surrounding some creeds, professions etc. **3** any mysterious aura surrounding a person or thing.
19C. **French** mystic.

N

nabi (nah´bē) *n.* **1** (*Theol.*) a prophet, esp. a prophetical writer of the Old Testament and the Hebrew scriptures. **2** a member of a group of French painters in the 1890s, whose work was inspired by the theories of the artist Paul Gauguin (1848–1903).
19C. Hebrew *nābī.*

nabob (nā´bob) *n.* **1** (*Hist.*) a deputy-governor or prince under the Mughal empire in India. **2** a very rich person, esp. one who amassed wealth in India.
17C. Portuguese *nababo,* or from Spanish *nabab,* from Urdu *nawwāb, nawāb* deputy governor. See NAWAB.

nacarat (nak´ərat) *n.* **1** a pale red colour tinged with orange. **2** a fine linen or crêpe dyed this colour.
18C. French, ? from Spanish and Portuguese *nacarado,* from *nacar* nacre.

nacelle (nəsel´) *n.* **1** the basket suspended from a balloon. **2** a small, streamlined body on an aircraft, distinct from the fuselage, housing engines, crew etc.
15C. French, from Late Latin *navicella,* dim. of Latin *navis* ship.

nacho (nah´chō) *n.* (*pl.* **nachos**) a crisp corn chip used as an appetizer in Mexican cuisine, often served with melted cheese, a chilli dip etc.
mid-20C. Orig. uncertain. ? Mexican Spanish *Nacho,* pet form of male forename *Ignacio.*
● The name of the dish may be that of the chef who created it, reputedly Ignacio Anaya, who worked in the Piedras Negras area of Mexico in the 1940s.

nada (nad´a, nah´də) *n.* nothing, non-existence.
mid-20C. Spanish, from Latin (*res*) *nata,* lit. (thing) born.

nadir (nā´diə, nad´-) *n.* **1** the point of the heavens directly opposite to the zenith or directly under our feet. **2** the lowest point or stage (of decline, degradation etc.).
14–15C. Old French, from Arabic *naẓīr* (*as-samt*) opposite (the zenith).

Nagari (nah´gəri) *n.* Devanagari.
18C. Sanskrit *nāgarī,* from *nagara* town. Cp. DEVANAGARI.

naïf (nīēf´) *a.* naive. ~*n.* a naive person.
16C. French, from Latin *nativus* native, the source also of English *naive.* Cp. FAUX-NAÏF.

nainsook (nān´suk) *n.* a thick muslin, formerly made in India.
18C. Urdu (Hindi) *nainsukh,* from *nain* eye + *sukh* pleasure.

naira (nī´rə) *n.* the standard unit of currency of Nigeria.
late 20C. Alt. of *Nigeria*.

nan (nahn), **naan** *n.* in Indian cookery, a type of slightly leavened bread.
early 20C. Persian and Urdu *nān*.

nankeen (nangkēn´) *n.* **1** a cotton fabric, usu. of a buff or yellow colour, exported from Nanjing. **2** a fabric made in imitation of this. **3** a yellowish-buff colour. **4** (*pl.*) clothes, esp. trousers, made of nankeen.
18C. *Nanking* (Nanjing), the capital of Kiangsu province, E central China.

naos (nā´os) *n.* (*pl.* **naoi** (nā´oi)) in ancient Greece, the inner part of a temple.
18C. Greek temple.

nappe (nap) *n.* (*Geol.*) a large sheet of rock which has been moved from its original position by thrusting.
19C. French, lit. tablecloth.

narghile (nah´gilā, -li) *n.* a hookah or tobacco pipe in which the smoke is drawn through water.
18C. Persian *nārgīl* coconut, hookah, from Sanskrit *nārikela* coconut.
• The hookah's reservoir was originally made out of coconut.

Narrenschiff (nar´ənshif) *n.* a poorly run organization or enterprise.
mid-20C. German, lit. ship of fools, from *Narren*, pl. of *Narr* fool + *Schiff* ship.
• The ultimate source of the word is Sebastian Brant's social satire *Das Narrenschiff* (1494), using a ship's voyage to highlight the foibles of the age. The work was translated by Alexander Barclay as *Ship of Fools* (1509). Modern use of the term was revived by Katherine Anne Porter's allegorical novel *Ship of Fools* (1962).

narthex (nah´theks) *n.* (*pl.* **narthexes**)
1 a vestibule or porch across the western end in early Christian churches, to which catechumens, women and penitents were admitted. **2** a similar vestibule in a modern church.
17C. Latin, from Greek *narthēx* giant fennel, stick, casket, narthex.

nartjie (nah´chi) *n.* (*S Afr.*) a small sweet orange like a mandarin.
18C. Afrikaans *naarjie*, from Tamil *nārattai* citrus.

nascitur (nash´itœ, -tuə) *int.* he or she was born.
18C. Latin, 3rd pers. sing. pres. of *nasci* to be born.
• The word is frequently found on old gravestones, often abbreviated as *nasc.* or simply *n.* Cp. OBIIT.

nasi goreng (nahsi gəreng´) *n.* a Malaysian dish of fried rice with meat or fish.
late 20C. Malay fried rice.

naturelle (natūrel´) *a.* of a pale pink or beige colour, skin-coloured.
19C. French, fem. of *naturel* natural. Cp. AU NATUREL.

nature morte (natūə mawt´) *n.* a still life.
early 20C. French, lit. dead nature.
• The term has been used in French art since the 18C. A still life is a painting of an arrangement of inanimate objects such as fruit, dead animals etc.

nautch (nawch) *n.* an Indian exhibition of dancing by girls.
19C. Hindi *nāc*, from Prakrit *nachcha*, from Sanskrit *nṛtya* dancing.

navarin (nav´ərin) *n.* a lamb casserole with vegetables.
19C. French, prob. from *Navarin* Navarino, from name of battle (1827) in which a Turkish–Egyptian fleet was destroyed by the allied naval forces of Britain, France and Russia.
● The battle was fought in the Bay of Navarin in the SW Peloponnese.

nawab (nəwahb´) *n.* **1** in Pakistan, a distinguished Muslim. **2** (*Hist.*) an Indian governor or nobleman; a nabob.
18C. Urdu *nawāb*, from Urdu and Persian *nawwāb*, var. of *nuwwāb*, pl. (used as sing.) of Arabic *nā'ib* deputy. Cp. NABOB.

Nazi (naht´si) *n.* (*pl.* **Nazis**) **1** (*Hist.*) a member of the German National Socialist Party. **2** (*derog.*) a racist, extremist or authoritarian person. **3** a person who belongs to any extreme right-wing organization. ~*a.* of or relating to the Nazis.
mid-20C. German, representation of the pronun. of the first two syllables of *Nationalsozialist* National Socialist.
● The full name of the party was *Nationalsozialistiche Deutsche Arbeiterpartei* National Socialist German Workers' Party, in power under Hitler in Germany, 1933–45.

nazir (nah´ziə) *n.* **1** (*Hist.*) a non-European official formerly employed in Anglo-Indian courts. **2** a title of various Muslim officials.
17C. Persian and Urdu *nāzir*, from Arabic *nāẓir* superintendent, inspector, from *naẓar* sight, vision.

NB *int.* note well.
Abbr. of **Latin** *nota bene*, from *nota* note + *bene* well.
● The full Latin phrase dates from the 18C.

né (nā) *a.* born (used with a man's original name), as in *Elton John, né Reginald Dwight*.
mid-20C. French born, m. p.p. of *naître* to be born. Cp. NÉE.

nebelwerfer (nā´bəlvœfə, -veəfə) *n.* a type of rocket mortar used by German forces in World War II.
mid-20C. German, lit. fog-thrower, from *Nebel* mist, fog + *Werfer* thrower, mortar, from *werfen* to throw.
● The mortar was nicknamed by US and British troops 'Screaming Meemie' or 'Moaning Minnie', from the sound of the rockets in flight.

nécessaire (neseseə´) *n.* a small case for pencils, scissors, tweezers etc.
19C. French, lit. necessary.

née (nā), (*N Am.*) **nee** *a.* born (used with the maiden name of a married woman), as in *Joanna Murphy, née Smith*.
18C. French born, fem. p.p. of *naître* to be born. Cp. NÉ.

nef (nef) *n.* **1** an ornamental piece of plate shaped like a boat or ship, formerly used for holding the salt cellars, table napkins etc. of people of great distinction. **2** †the nave of a church.
17C. French ship, nave.

negligée (neg´lizhā), **negligee**, **négligé** *n.* **1** a woman's loose dressing gown of flimsy material. **2** a lady's loose gown worn in the 18th cent. **3** a state of undress or free-and-easy attire. **4** a long necklace of irregular beads or coral.
18C. French *négligé*, p.p. of *négliger* to neglect.
● Sense 1 dates from the mid-20C.

Negrillo (nigril´ō) *n.* (*pl.* **Negrillos**) a member of a black people of small stature in central and southern Africa.
19C. Spanish, dim of NEGRO.

Negrito (nigrē´tō) *n.* (*pl.* **Negritos**) a member of a black people in some islands of the Malay Archipelago etc.
19C. Spanish, dim. of NEGRO.

Negro (nē´grō) *n.* (*pl.* **Negroes**) (*offensive*) a person belonging to, or descended from, one of the dark-skinned African peoples. ~*a.* of or relating to these peoples.
16C. Spanish and Portuguese, from Latin *niger*, *nigris* black, of unknown orig.

negro (nē´grō) *a.* (*Zool.*) black, dark.
19C. Spanish and Portuguese black. See NEGRO.

nek (nek) *n.* (*S Afr.*) a mountain pass.
19C. Dutch neck.

nem. con. (nem kon´) *adv.* with no one dissenting.
16C. Abbr. of **Latin** *nemine contradicente* (with) no one contradicting, abl. of *nemo* no one + abl. of *contradicens*, pres.p. of *contradicere* to oppose.

nemesis (nem´əsis) *n.* (*pl.* **nemeses** (-sēz)) **1** retributive justice. **2** an instance or agent of this.
16C. Greek righteous indignation, personified as *Nemesis*, the goddess of retribution or vengeance, from *nemein* to deal out what is due, rel. to *nomos* custom, law.

nemo me impune lacessit (nāmō mā impūnā lakes´it) *int.* no one provokes me with impunity.
17C. Latin.
● The words are the motto of the Crown of Scotland and of all Scottish regiments and were inscribed round the milled edge of a Scottish one-pound coin from 1984.

ne plus ultra (nā plus ul´trə) *n.* the most perfect or uttermost point.
17C. Latin not further beyond.
● The Latin words were said to be inscribed on the Pillars of Hercules

(Strait of Gibraltar) to prohibit ships from sailing westward.

n'est-ce pas? (nes pah´) *int.* is it not? isn't that so? right?
early 20C. French.
● The phrase is the standard French tag question, corresponding to English variable 'aren't I?', 'don't you?', 'hasn't she?' 'can't we?' etc. Cp. NICHT WAHR?

netsuke (net´suki) *n.* (*pl.* **netsuke**, **netsukes**) a small piece of carved wood or ivory worn or attached to various articles, as a toggle or button, by the Japanese.
19C. Japanese.

Neufchâtel (nœshatel´) *n.* a soft white cheese, similar to cream cheese but with less fat.
19C. *Neufchâtel*, a town in N France near Rouen.

névé (nev´ā) *n.* consolidated snow above the glaciers, in the process of being converted into ice.
19C. Swiss French, from Latin *nix*, *nivis* snow.

nexus (nek´səs) *n.* (*pl.* **nexuses**) **1** a connected group. **2** a link, a connection.
17C. Latin, from *nexus*, p.p. of *nectere* to bind.

ngultrum (neg·gul´trəm) *n.* (*pl.* **ngultrums**) the standard unit of currency of Bhutan, central Asia.
late 20C. Dzongkha, from *ngul* silver + *trum*, shortening of *tram-ka*, dim. of *tram* tram.

niche (nich, nēsh) *n.* **1** a recess in a wall for a statue, vase etc. **2** one's proper place or natural position. **3** in business, a small, specialized, but profitable area of the market. ~*v.t.* **1** to put in a niche. **2** to settle (oneself) in a comfortable place.

17C. Old French from *nichier* (Modern French *nicher*) to make a nest, to nestle, from Latin *nidus* nest.

nicht wahr? (nikht vah´) *int.* isn't it? isn't that so? right?
early 20C. German, lit. not true?
Cp. N'EST-CE PAS?

niello (niel´ō) *n.* (*pl.* **nielli** (-lē), **niellos**)
1 a black alloy used to fill the lines of incised designs on metal plates. **2** an example of this work.
19C. Italian, from Latin *nigellus*, dim. of *niger* black.

Niersteiner (niə´shtīnə) *n.* a white Rhine wine.
19C. *Nierstein*, a town in W Germany.

nihil (nī´hil) *n.* nothing.
16C. Latin nothing. Cp. NIL.

nihil obstat (nīhil ob´stat, nihil) *n.*
1 the official certificate of the Roman Catholic Church that a written work contains nothing morally or doctrinally offensive and is suitable for publication.
2 a statement of official approval.
mid-20C. Latin, lit. nothing hinders (the publication). Cp. IMPRIMATUR.

nil (nil) *n.* nothing; zero.
19C. Latin, contr. of NIHIL.

nil desperandum (nil despəran´dəm) *int.* do not despair.
17C. Latin, no need to despair.
• The words open a quotation from Horace's *Odes* (1C BC): *Nil desperandum Teucro duce et auspice Teucro* 'No need to despair with Teucer as your leader and Teucer to protect you'.

nimbus (nim´bəs) *n.* (*pl.* **nimbi** (-bī), **nimbuses**) **1** a halo or glory surrounding the heads of divine or sacred personages in paintings etc.
2 a rain cloud, a dark mass of cloud, usu. with ragged edges, from which rain is falling or likely to fall.
17C. Latin cloud, rain, aureole.

ninja (nin´jə) *n.* (*pl.* **ninjas**) a person who is skilled in ninjutsu.
mid-20C. Japanese spy, from *nin* stealth, invisibility + *ja* person.

ninjutsu (ninjŭt´soo) *n.* a Japanese martial art involving stealth and camouflage.
mid-20C. Japanese, from *nin* stealth, invisibility + *jutsu* art, science.

nirvana (niəvah´nə) *n.* **1** absorption of individuality into the divine spirit with extinction of personal desires and passions, the Buddhist state of beatitude. **2** (*coll.*) bliss, heaven.
19C. Sanskrit *nirvāṇa*, p.p. (used as n.) of *nirvā-* to be extinguished, from *nis-* out + *vā-* to blow.

nisei (nē´sā, -sā´), **Nisei** *n.* an American whose parents were immigrants from Japan.
mid-20C. Japanese, from *ni* second + *sei* generation. Cp. SANSEI.

nisi (nī´sī) *a.* (*Law*) taking effect on certain conditions.
14–15C. Latin unless.
• The word is usually found in the phrase *decree nisi*, denoting a provisional order for divorce that will be made absolute after a specified period of time unless a good reason to prevent it can be produced.

nisi Dominus frustra (nīsī dominəs frus´trah) *int.* in vain without the Lord (the motto of the city of Edinburgh).
18C. Latin, lit. unless the Lord in vain.
• The words are taken from the Latin version of Ps. cxxvii.1, in English: 'Except the Lord build the house, they labour in vain that build it: except the Lord keep the city, the watchman waketh but in vain'.

nisus (nī´səs) *n.* (*pl.* **nisus**) (*formal*) an effort, striving.
17C. **Latin**, p.p. of *niti* to strive, to endeavour.

nizam (nīzam´) *n.* (*pl.* **nizam**) **1** a soldier in the Turkish regular army. **2** (**Nizam**) the title of the ruler of Hyderabad.
18C. **Turkish**, **Persian and Urdu** *nizām*, from Arabic *niẓām* good order, disposition, arrangement.
● In sense 1 the word is an abbreviation of *nizām askeri* regular soldier; in sense 2 of *nizām al-mulk* administrator of the realm.

noblesse (nōbles´) *n.* the nobility (of a foreign country).
12–14C. **Old French** nobility, from *noble*, from Latin *nobilis* noble. Cp.
NOBLESSE OBLIGE.

noblesse oblige (nōbles əblēzh´) *n.* the idea that privileged people are obliged to behave honourably and to help less privileged people.
19C. **French**, lit. nobility obliges.

nocturne (nok´tœn) *n.* **1** (*Mus.*) a dreamy piece of music suited to the night or evening. **2** a painting or drawing of a night scene.
19C. **French** nocturnal.
● The term was invented, and the form popularized, in *c.*1814 by the Irish pianist and composer John Field.

nodus (nō´dəs) *n.* (*pl.* **nodi** (-dī)) **1** a knotty point, a complication, a difficulty. **2** a node.
18C. **Latin** knot, and the source of English *node*.

Noh (nō), **No** *n.* the Japanese drama developed out of religious dance.
19C. **Japanese** talent, faculty, accomplishment.

noisette¹ (nwazet´) *n.* **1** a small round piece of mutton, veal, etc. **2** a chocolate made with chopped hazelnuts.
19C. **French**, dim. of *noix* nut.

noisette² (nwazet´) *n.* a variety of rose, a cross between the China rose and the musk-rose.
19C. Philippe *Noisette*, brother of Louis Claude *Noisette*, d.1849, French gardener.

nolens volens (nōlenz vō´lenz) *adv.* willingly or unwillingly, willy-nilly.
16C. **Latin**, pres.pp. of *nolo, nolle* to be unwilling, *volo, velle* to be willing.

noli-me-tangere (nō´limātang´gəri) *n.* **1** the touch-me-not, *Impatiens noli tangere*. **2** an ulcerous disease of the skin, lupus.
14–15C. **Latin** do not touch me.
● The words are from the Vulgate (Latin version of the Bible) and are those spoken by Christ to Mary Magdalene at the sepulchre after the Resurrection: (AV) 'Touch me not' (John xx.17).

nolle prosequi (noli pros´ikwī) *n.* (*Law*) **1** the act by a plaintiff discontinuing a suit. **2** the recording of a nolle prosequi.
17C. **Latin** to be unwilling to pursue.

nolo contendere (nō´lō konten´dəri) *n.* I will not contest it, a plea which accepts conviction without pleading guilt.
19C. **Latin** I do not wish to contend.

nom de guerre (nom də geə´) *n.* (*pl.* **noms de guerre** (nom)) an assumed name, a pseudonym.
17C. **French** war name.

nom de plume (nom də ploom´) *n.* (*pl.* **noms de plume** (nom)) a pen-name.
19C. **French** pen name, based on NOM DE GUERRE.

nomen (nō´men) *n.* in ancient Rome, a person's second name, designating the gens.
18C. Latin name.

nomenklatura (nomenklatūə´rə) *n.* (*constr. as pl.*, *Hist.*) the elite class of politicians, bureaucrats and industrialists appointed by the Communist Party to occupy the most important posts in the former Soviet Union.
mid-20C. Russian, from Latin *nomenclatura* list of names.

non compos mentis (non kompos men´tis), **non compos** (non kom´pos) *a.* not in one's right mind.
17C. Latin not master of one's mind, from *non* not + *compos* controlling + gen. of *mens* mind.

nonpareil (nonpərā´) *a.* having no equal; peerless, unrivalled, unique.
~*n.* **1** a paragon or thing of unequalled excellence. **2** (*Hist.*, *Print.*) a size of type equal to six point. **3** a fine variety of apple.
14–15C. French, from *non-* not + *pareil* like, equal, from Popular Latin *pariculus*, dim. of Latin *par* equal.

non placet (non plā´set) *n.* the formula used in university and ecclesiastical assemblies in giving a negative vote.
16C. Latin, lit. it does not please, from *non* not + 3rd pers. sing. pres. indic. of *placere* to please.

non possumus (non pos´ūməs) *n.* a plea of inability.
19C. Latin, lit. we cannot, from *non* not + 2nd pers. pl. pres. indic. of *potere* to be able.

non sequitur (non sek´witə) *n.* a conclusion which cannot be logically deduced from the premises.
14–15C. Latin, lit. it does not follow, from *non* not + 3rd pers. sing. pres. indic. of *sequi* to follow.

noria (naw´riə) *n.* an endless chain of buckets on a wheel for raising water from a stream or similar.
18C. Spanish, from Arabic *nāy'ūra*.

nostalgie de la boue (nostalzhē də la boo´) *n.* a desire for degradation and depravity.
19C. French, lit. yearning for mud.
● The expression was introduced by Émil Augier in the play *Le Mariage d'Olympe* (1855).

nostrum (nos´trəm) *n.* (*pl.* **nostrums**) **1** a medicine based on a secret formula; a quack remedy. **2** a scheme for political or social reform.
17C. Latin *nostrum* (*remedium*) our (remedy), from *nostrum* neut. sing. of *noster* our.
● In sense 1 the medicine was so called as it was presumably prepared by the person recommending it.

notabilia (nōtəbil´iə) *n.pl.* notable things.
19C. Latin, neut. pl. of *notabilis* notable.
● The word was based on MEMORABILIA.

notandum (nōtan´dəm) *n.* (*pl.* **notanda** (-də)) something to be noted, a memorandum.
17C. Latin, neut. ger. of *notare* to note.

notitia (nōtish´iə) *n.* (*pl.* **notitias**) a list, register, or catalogue.
18C. Latin knowledge, from *notus* known.

nougat (noo´gah, nŭg´ət) *n.* a confection made of nuts and sugar.
19C. French, from Provençal *nogat*, from *noga* nut, from Latin *nux*.

noumenon (noo'minən, now'-, -non) *n.* (*pl.* **noumena** (-nə)) **1** the substance underlying a phenomenon. **2** an object or the conception of an object as it is in itself, or as it appears to pure thought.
18C. German, from Greek neut. pres.p. pass. (used as n.) of *noein* to apprehend, to conceive.
● The term was introduced by the German philosopher Immanuel Kant, 1724–1804, in contrast to *phenomenon*.

nous (nows) *n.* **1** (*coll.*) sense, wit, intelligence. **2** (*Philos.*) mind, intellect.
17C. Greek.

nous avons changé tout cela (nooz avō shāzhā too səla') *int.* we have changed all that, things are different now.
18C. French we have changed all that.
● The words are those spoken by the pretended doctor in Molière's play *Le Médecin malgré lui* (1666) when it is pointed out that he has located the heart and the liver on the wrong side of the body.

nouveau (noo'vō), (*fem.*) **nouvelle** (-vel) *a.* new.
early 20C. French new, from Latin *novus*.

nouveau riche (noovō rēsh') *n.* (*pl.* **nouveaux riches** (noovō rēsh')) a person who has recently acquired wealth but who has not acquired good taste or manners.
19C. French, lit. new rich.

nouvelle cuisine (noovel kwizēn') *n.* a style of simple French cooking which does not involve rich food, creamy sauces etc. and relies largely on artistic presentation.
late 20C. French, lit. new cooking.
● The fashion for such cooking spread beyond France in the late 1970s and early 1980s, when it appealed to advocates of healthy eating.

nouvelle vague (noovel vahg') *n.* a movement in the French cinema, dating from just before 1960, which aimed at imaginative quality in films.
mid-20C. French, lit. new wave.

nova (nō'və) *n.* (*pl.* **novae** (-ē), **novas**) a star which flares up to great brightness and subsides after a time.
17C. Latin, fem. of *novus* new.
● The word was originally used for a new star or nebula.

novalia (nōvā'liə) *n.pl.* (*Sc. Law*) waste lands newly brought into cultivation.
19C. Latin, pl. of *novale* fallow land, land ploughed for the first time, from *novus* new.

novella (nōvel'ə, nəv-) *n.* (*pl.* **novellas**) **1** a tale, a short story. **2** a short novel.
early 20C. Italian.
● The term was originally applied to the tales in Boccaccio's *Decameron* (1348–58).

novena (nōvē'nə) *n.* (*pl.* **novenas**) in the Roman Catholic Church, a devotion consisting of a prayer or service repeated on nine successive days.
19C. Medieval Latin, from *novem* nine, based on Latin *novenarius* of nine days.

noyade (nwah·yahd') *n.* a mode of executing political prisoners by drowning, esp. during the Reign of Terror in France in 1794.
19C. French, from *noyer* to drown, from Latin *necare* to kill without a weapon, to drown, from *nex, necis* slaughter.

noyau (nwah·yō') *n.* (*pl.* **noyaux** (-yōz')) brandy cordial flavoured with bitter almonds etc.
18C. French, earlier *noiel* kernel, from Popular Latin *nodellus*, from Late Latin *nucalis*, from *nux, nucis* nut.

nuance (nū´ahns) *n.* **1** a delicate gradation in colour or tone. **2** a fine distinction between things, feelings, opinions etc. ~*v.t.* to give a nuance to.
18C. French, from *nuer* to show cloudlike variations in colour, from *nue* cloud, from Popular Latin var. of Latin *nubes*.

nudnik (nud´nik) *n.* a nagging or annoying person, a bore.
mid-20C. Yiddish, from Russian *nudnyĭ* tedious, boring + agent suf. -*nik*.

nuée ardente (nūā ahdăt´, -dont´) *n.* (*Geol.*) a hot cloud of ash, gas and lava fragments ejected from a volcano.
early 20C. French, lit. burning cloud.
• The term was introduced in 1903 by the French mineralogist Alfred Lacroix, who said that by *ardent* he meant *brûlant* burning rather than *incandescent* glowing. The term is usually rendered in English as glowing cloud rather than burning cloud.

nuevo sol (nwāvō sol´) *n.* the standard unit of currency of Peru.
late 20C. Spanish new sol, from *nuevo* new + *sol* sol.
• The earlier currency *sol* derived its name from Latin SOLIDUS.

nugae (nū´gē, -jē) *n.pl.* trifles, esp. literary compositions of a trifling kind.
18C. Latin jests, trifles.

nullah (nŭl´ə) *n.* (*Ang.-Ind.*) a ravine, gully or watercourse.
18C. Hindi *nālā*.

nulli secundus (nuli sekun´dəs), **nulli secundum** (-dəm) *a.* second to none.
19C. Latin, from dat. of *nullus* none + *secundus* second.

numdah (nŭm´də) *n.* an embroidered felt rug from India etc.
19C. Urdu *namdā*, from Persian *namad* felt, carpet, rug. Cp. NUMNAH.

numen (nū´mən) *n.* (*pl.* **numina** (-minə) a deity or spirit presiding over a place.
17C. Latin, rel. to *nuere* to nod, Greek *neuein* to incline the head.

numero uno (nūmərō oo´nō) *n.* the best or most important person.
late 20C. Italian and Spanish number one.

numnah (nŭm´nə) *n.* a fabric or sheepskin pad placed under a saddle to prevent chafing.
19C. Urdu *namdā* NUMDAH.

nunatak (nŭn´ətak) *n.* a mountain peak which projects through an ice sheet.
19C. Inuit *nunataq*.

Nunc Dimittis (nŭngk dimit´is) *n.* the canticle 'Lord, now lettest thou thy servant depart in peace'.
16C. Latin now you let (your servant) depart, opening words of the Song of Simeon (Luke ii.29–32), in the Vulgate (Latin version of the Bible) beginning: *Nunc dimittis servum tuum, Domine, secundum verbum tuum in pace* (AV) Lord, now lettest thou thy servant depart in peace: according to thy Word.

nunc est bibendum (nunk est biben´dəm) *int.* now is the time to drink.
early 20C. Latin.
• The phrase comes from Horace's *Odes* (I) (1C BC). The name Bibendum was adopted for the 'Michelin man', a fat and jolly figure made of tyres as an advertisement for the Michelin Tyre Co. The founders of this company, André (1853–1931) and Édouard (1859–1940)

Michelin, made notes about restaurants when touring France to sell their tyres and in 1900 published their first restaurant guide.

nuncio (nŭn´siō, -shiō) *n.* (*pl.* **nuncios**) a papal envoy or ambassador to a foreign power.

16C. Obsolete Italian *nuncio* (now *nunzio*), from Latin *nuncius*, from *nunciare* to announce.

nux vomica (nŭks vom´ikə) *n.* **1** a S Asian tree, *Strychnos nux-vomica.*

2 the seed of the nux vomica, which yields strychnine.
14–15C. Medieval Latin, lit. emetic nut, from Latin *nux* nut + a. from *vomere* to vomit.

nyet (nyet) *int.* no.
early 20C. Russian.
• The word came to express a blunt refusal, especially as uttered by A.A. Gromyko, nicknamed 'Mr Niet', Soviet foreign minister from 1957 to 1985, in response to requests from the West for concessions.

obang (ō´bang) *n.* an oblong gold coin formerly current in Japan.
17C. **Japanese** *ō-ban*, from *ō* great, major + *ban* part, share, division.

obbligato (obligah´tō), **obligato** *a.* (*Mus.*) **1** not to be omitted. **2** indispensable to the whole. ~*n.* (*pl.* **obbligatos**, **obligatos**, **obbligati** (-tē), **obligati**) an instrumental part or accompaniment that forms an integral part of the composition or is independently important (usu. by a single instrument).
18C. **Italian** obliged, obligatory.

obeah (ō´biə), **obi** (ō´bi) *n.* **1** a form of sorcery practised by blacks, esp. in the West Indies. **2** a magical charm.
18C. **Twi** *o-bayifo* sorcerer, from *bayi* sorcery.

obelus (ob´ələs) *n.* (*pl.* **obeli** (-lī, -lē)) **1** a mark (-, ÷, or †), used to mark spurious or doubtful passages in ancient manuscripts. **2** in printing, a dagger symbol (†) indicating a cross-reference, footnote or death date.
14–15C. **Latin** spit, critical obelus, from Greek *obelos* spit.

obi (ō´bi) *n.* (*pl.* **obi**, **obis**) a coloured sash worn around a Japanese kimono.
19C. **Japanese** belt.

obiit (ob´iit) *int.* he or she died, used esp. on gravestones and in epitaphs.

18C. **Latin**, 3rd pers. sing. perf. of *obire* to die, lit. to go towards.
● The word is often abbreviated as *ob*. Cp. NASCITUR.

obiter (ob´itə) *adv.* incidentally, by the way.
16C. **Latin** *ob iter* by the way.

obiter dictum (obitə dik´təm) *n.* (*pl.* **obiter dicta** (-tə)) **1** a passing remark. **2** a judge's personal opinion on a point of law, as distinct from the decision of a court.
19C. **Latin**, from OBITER + DICTUM.

objet (ob´zhā) *n.* (*pl.* **objets** (-zhā)) an object.
19C. **French** object.

objet d'art (obzhā dah´) *n.* (*pl.* **objets d'art** (obzhā)) a small decorative object.
19C. **French**, lit. object of art.

objet trouvé (obzhā troo´vā) *n.* (*pl.* **objets trouvés** (obzhā)) a natural object or an artefact taken as possessing artistic significance.
early 20C. **French**, lit. found object.
● The concept of the *objet trouvé* was taken up by the Dadaists and particularly Marcel Duchamp (1887–1968), inventor of the associated 'ready-made'.

oblast (ob´last, -lahst) *n.* (*pl.* **oblasts**, **oblasti** (-sti)) an administrative district or province in Russia.

19C. Russian *oblast'* power, province, from Old Church Slavonic *obvolst'*, from *ob-* around + *volst'* possession.

obol (ob´ol), **obolus** (-ləs) *n.* (*pl.* **obols**, **oboli** (-lī)) a small coin of ancient Greece weighing and worth one sixth of a drachma.
14–15C. Latin *obolus*, from Greek *obolos*, var. of *obelos* spit.

ocarina (okərē´nə) *n.* a musical instrument of terracotta with finger-notes and a mouthpiece, giving a mellow whistling sound.
19C. Italian, from *oca* goose.
• The instrument is so called with reference to its shape.

octavo (oktā´vō) *n.* (*pl.* **octavos**) 1 a book in which a sheet is folded into eight leaves or 16 pages. 2 the size of such a book or paper (written *8vo*). ~*a.* of this size, having this number of leaves per sheet.
16C. Latin (*in*) *octavo* (in) an eighth (of a sheet), from *octavus* eighth.

octodecimo (oktōdes´imō) *n.* (*pl.* **octodecimos**) 1 a book having 18 leaves to the sheet. 2 the size of such a book (written *18mo*). ~*a.* having 18 leaves to the sheet.
19C. Latin (*in*) *octodecimo* (in) an eighteenth (of a sheet), from *octodecimus* eighteenth.

octroi (ok´trwah) *n.* 1 a tax levied at the gates of some European, esp. French, towns on goods brought in. 2 the barrier or place where this is levied. 3 the body of officials collecting it. 4 a road toll for cars.
16C. French, from *octroyer* to grant, from Medieval Latin *auctorizare* to authorize.

odalisque (ō´dəlisk), **odalisk** *n.* (*Hist.*) an Oriental female slave or concubine, esp. in a harem.

17C. French, from Turkish *ōdalik*, from *ōda* chamber, hall + *-lik*, suf. expressing a function.

odi et amo (ōdē et am´ō) *int.* I hate and I love.
early 20C. Latin.
• The phrase, deriving from Catullus' *Carmina* (1C BC), is the classic expression of the modern 'love-hate syndrome'.

odium (ō´diəm) *n.* 1 general dislike, reprobation. 2 repulsion.
17C. Latin hatred, from *odi* I hate.

oeuvre (œvr´, œ´vrə) *n.* the works of an author, painter etc.
19C. French *œuvre* work, from Latin *opera* (OPERA). Cp. CHEF-D'OEUVRE.

ohne Hast, ohne Rast (ōnə hast ōnə rast´) *int.* without haste, without rest.
19C. German.
• The phrase comes from Goethe's *Zahme Xenien* (1796) and originally referred to the sun.

Oireachtas (er´əkhtəs) *n.* the legislature of the Republic of Ireland.
early 20C. Irish assembly, convocation.

olé (ōlā´) *int.* used to express approval or victory at a bullfight.
19C. Spanish, from Arabic *wa-llāh*, from *wa-* and + ALLAH.

olim (ō´lim) *adv.* formerly, at one time.
17C. Latin.

olla (ol´ə) *n.* 1 a mixed dish. 2 an olla podrida.
17C. Spanish, from Latin.

ollamh (ol´əv), **ollav** *n.* among the ancient Irish, a learned man, a doctor, a scholar.
18C. Irish and Old Irish *ollam* learned man, doctor.

olla podrida (olə pədrē´də) *n.* **1** a Spanish dish consisting of meat chopped fine, stewed with vegetables. **2** a multifarious or incongruous mixture. **16C. Spanish**, lit. rotten pot, from OLLA + *podrida* putrid. Cp. POT-POURRI.
● Sense 2 arose in the 17C.

oloroso (olərō´sō) *n.* (*pl.* **olorosos**) a medium-sweet golden sherry. **19C. Spanish** fragrant.

ombré (om´brā) *a.* (of a fabric etc.) with colours shading into each other from light to dark. **19C. French**, p.p. of *ombrer* to shade.

ombudsman (om´budzmən) *n.* (*pl.* **ombudsmen**) an official investigator of complaints against government bodies or employees; in the UK, the Parliamentary Commissioner for Administration. **mid-20C. Swedish**, from *ombud* commissioner, from Old Norse *umboth* charge, commission, *umbothsmathr* commissary, manager.
● The office of ombudsman originated in Sweden in 1809 and was subsequently introduced to other countries, including Britain in 1967.

omega (ō´migə, om´-) *n.* **1** the last letter of the Greek alphabet (Ω, ω). **2** the last of a series. **3** the conclusion, the end, the last stage or phase. **16C. Greek** *ō mega*, lit. great O.
● The Greek phrase is opposed to *o mikron* small O, i.e. omicron (O, o), the 15th letter of the Greek alphabet.

omelette (om´lit), **omelet** *n.* a flat dish made with beaten eggs cooked in fat, eaten plain or seasoned and filled with herbs, cheese etc. **17C. French**, earlier *amelette*, alt. of *alemette*, from *alemelle* knife blade (with *la lemelle* misdivided as

l'alemelle), from Latin *lamella* metal plate.
● The reference is probably to the thin flat shape of an omelette.

omer (ō´mə) *n.* a Hebrew measure of capacity, 5⅕ pints (about 2.8 litres). **17C. Hebrew** *'ōmer*.

omertà (ōmœtah´, om-) *n.* a conspiracy of silence, part of the Mafia code of honour. **19C. Italian**, dial. var. of *umiltà* humility.
● The term originally referred to the Mafia code which obliged members to submit to their leader.

omnia vincit amor (omniə ving·kit amaw´) *int.* love conquers all things. **19C. Latin**, from acc. neut. pl. of *omnis* all + 3rd pers. sing. pres. of *vincere* to conquer + *amor* love.
● The words come from Virgil's *Eclogues* (X) (1C BC) and are also found in the variant *amor vincit omnia*.

omnium gatherum (omniəm gadh´ərəm) *n.* (*coll.*) a miscellaneous collection or assemblage, a medley. **16C. Pseudo-Latin**, from gen. pl. of *omnis* all + English *gather* + Latin ending -*um*.

ondes martenot (ōd mah´tənō) *n.* (*pl.* **ondes martenot**) (*Mus.*) an electronic keyboard instrument producing one note of variable pitch. **mid-20C. French** *ondes* (*musicales*) (musical) waves + Maurice *Martenot*, 1898–1980, French inventor.
● The instrument was patented in 1922 by Martenot, who himself named it *ondes musicales*.

on dit (ō dē´) *n.* (*pl.* **on dits** (dē´)) **1** hearsay, gossip. **2** a bit of gossip. **19C. French** they say, from *on* one + 3rd pers. sing. pres. of *dire* to say.

onus (ō´nəs) *n.* (*pl.* **onuses**) **1** a duty or obligation. **2** a burden.
19C. Latin load, burden.

oolong (oo´long) *n.* a kind of China tea.
19C. Chinese *wūlóng*, from *wū* black + *lóng* dragon.

op. cit. (op sit´) *adv.* in the work cited, used esp. in bibliographic references.
19C. Abbr. of Latin OPERE CITATO.

opera (op´ərə) *n.* **1** a dramatic entertainment in which singing and instrumental music form an essential part. **2** a composition comprising words and music for this. **3** the branch of the musical and dramatic arts concerned with this. **4** a company which performs opera. **5** an opera house. **6** a libretto, a score.
17C. Italian, from Latin labour, exertion, rel. to OPUS, *operis* work. Cp. OEUVRE.

opera bouffe (opərə boof´) *n.* a type of 19th-cent. French satirical opera.
19C. French *opéra bouffe*, from Italian OPERA BUFFA.

opera buffa (opərə boo´fə) *n.* a type of 17th-cent. Italian comic opera.
19C. Italian comic opera, from OPERA + fem. of *buffo* comical, rel. to English *buffoon*. Cp. OPERA SERIA.

opéra comique (opərə komēk´) *n.*
1 a type of opera having some spoken dialogue. **2** comic opera.
18C. French comic opera.
• The genre was originally humorous, then romantic.

opera seria (opərə seə´riə) *n.* a serious type of opera of the 18th cent. involving elaborate arias and having a heroic or mythical plot.

early 20C. Italian serious opera. Cp. OPERA BUFFA.

opere citato (opere kitah´tō, sī-) *adv.* in the work cited.
19C. Latin in the work cited, abl. of *opus citatum* the work quoted, from OPUS + p.p. of *citare* to call upon, to quote.

operetta (opəret´ə) *n.* a short opera of a light character.
18C. Italian, dim. of OPERA.

opprobrium (əprō´briəm) *n.* **1** disgrace, infamy, ignominy, obloquy. **2** a cause of this.
17C. Latin infamy, reproach, from *ob* against + *probrum* shameful deed, disgrace.

optimum (op´timəm) *n.* (*pl.* **optima** (-mə), **optimums**) **1** the most favourable condition. **2** the best compromise. *~a.* (of conditions, circumstances etc.) best or most favourable.
19C. Latin, use as n. of neut. of *optimus* best.

opus (ō´pəs, op´-) *n.* (*pl.* **opera** (op´ərə), **opuses**) (*esp. Mus.*) **1** a work, esp. a musical composition. **2** a work numbered in order of publication.
18C. Latin work. Cp. OPERA.

opus Dei (ō´pəs dā´ē, op´-) *n.* **1** liturgical worship; the duty of prayer. **2** (**Opus Dei**) a Roman Catholic organization founded in Spain in 1928 with the aim of re-establishing Christian ideals and principles.
19C. Medieval Latin work of God, from OPUS + gen. of *Deus* God.

orarium (əreə´riəm) *n.* (*pl.* **oraria** (-riə), **orariums**) **1** a scarf sometimes wound round the handle of the medieval crozier. **2** an ecclesiastical stole.
18C. Latin napkin, from *os*, *oris* mouth, face.

oratorio (orətaw´riō) *n.* (*pl.* **oratorios**) a musical composition for voices and instruments, usually semi-dramatic in character, having a scriptural theme.
17C. Italian, from Ecclesiastical Latin *oratorium* oratory.
• The form of composition originated in the musical services held in the church of the Oratory of St Philip Neri in Rome.

ordinaire (awdineə´) *n.* everyday drinking wine, *vin ordinaire*.
19C. French ordinary.

ordonnance (aw´dənəns) *n.* the arrangement of the elements of a picture, building, literary composition etc.
17C. French, alt. of Old French *ordenance*, based on French *ordonner* to set in order.

öre (œ´rə) *n.* (*pl.* **öre**) a monetary unit in Sweden.
17C. Swedish, from Old Norse *aurar* (pl.), prob. from Latin *aureus* golden.

øre (œ´rə) *n.* (*pl.* **øre**) a monetary unit in Norway and Denmark.
17C. Norwegian and Danish, from Old Norse *aurar* (ÖRE).

oregano (origah´nō, əreg´ənō) *n.* (*pl.* **oreganos**) the (usu. dried) leaves of wild marjoram, *Origanum vulgare*, used as a culinary herb.
18C. Spanish and American Spanish var. of ORIGANUM.

organdie (aw´gəndi), (*NAm.*) **organdy** *n.* (*pl.* **organdies**) a stiff, light transparent muslin.
19C. French *organdi*, of unknown orig.
• According to some, the word is an alteration of *Organzi*, a variant form of *Urgench*, a city in Uzbekistan in central Asia, where the muslin was first made.

organon (aw´gənon) *n.* a system of principles and rules of investigation, deduction and demonstration regarded as an instrument of knowledge.
16C. Greek instrument, organ.
• The word is familiar as the title of Aristotle's logical treatises (4C BC).

orienteering (awrientiə´ring) *n.* a sport in which the contestants race cross-country following checkpoints located by a map and compass.
mid-20C. Swedish *orientering* orienteering, orig. orientating.

oriflamme (or´iflam) *n.* **1** (*Hist.*) the ancient royal banner of France, orig. the red silk banderole of the Abbey of St Denis handed to the early kings in setting out for war. **2** a symbol of lofty endeavour. **3** a bright or glorious object.
14–15C. Old French *oriflambe*, from Medieval Latin *auriflamma*, from *aurum* gold + *flamma* flame.

origami (origah´mi) *n.* the (traditionally Japanese) art of paper folding.
mid-20C. Japanese, from *oru*, *orori* to fold + *kami* paper.

origanum (orig´ənəm) *n.* any plant of the genus *Origanum*, esp. wild marjoram.
12–14C. Latin, from Greek *origanon*, prob. from *oros* mountain + *ganos* brightness, joy. Cp. OREGANO.

ormolu (aw´məloo) *n.* **1** a gold-coloured alloy of copper, zinc and tin, used for cheap jewellery. **2** gold leaf ground and used as a pigment for decorating furniture etc. **3** metallic ware, furniture etc. decorated with this.
18C. French *or moulu*, lit. powdered gold.

osso bucco (osō boo´kō) *n.* a stew made from knuckle of veal and marrowbone.

mid-20C. Italian *ossobuco* marrowbone, from *osso* bone + *buco* hole.

ostinato (ostinah´tō) *n.* (*pl.* **ostinatos, ostinati** (-ti)) a musical figure continuously reiterated throughout a composition.
19C. **Italian** obstinate, persistent.

Ostmark (ost´mahk) *n.* (*Hist.*) the standard unit of currency in the former Democratic Republic of Germany.
mid-20C. **German**, from *Ost* east + *Mark* mark.

Ostpolitik (ost´politēk) *n.* (*Hist.*) the foreign policy of establishing normal relations with the Communist bloc.
mid-20C. **German**, from *Ost* east + *Politik* politics. Cp. WESTPOLITIK.

O tempora! O mores! (ō tem´pərə ō maw´rēz) *int.* (*also facet.*) an expression of dismay at contemporary social standards.
16C. **Latin** O times, O manners!
● The words come from Cicero's *In Catilinam* (I.i) (63 BC), the first speech in which he denounced the senator Catiline, who led an abortive coup in the same year, as a dangerous and immoral traitor.

ottava rima (otahvə rē´mə) *n.* a form of versification consisting of stanzas of eight lines, of which the first six rhyme alternately, and the last two form a couplet (as in Byron's *Don Juan* (1819–24)).
18C. **Italian** eighth rhyme.

ouabain (wahbah´in) *n.* a poisonous white crystalline glycoside extracted from certain trees.
19C. **French**, from Somali *wabayo* tree yielding arrow poison containing ouabain.

oubliette (oobliet´) *n.* an underground dungeon in which persons condemned

to perpetual imprisonment or secret death were confined.
18C. **French**, from *oublier* to forget.
● The French word itself dates from the 14C. Its use in England was popularized by Sir Walter Scott, e.g. in *Ivanhoe* (1819).

outré (oo´trā) *a.* **1** extravagant, exaggerated, eccentric. **2** outraging convention or decorum.
18C. **French**, p.p. of *outrer* to overdo.

ouzo (oo´zō) *n.* (*pl.* **ouzos**) an aniseed-flavoured spirit from Greece.
19C. **Modern Greek**, of unknown orig.
● According to some, the word is derived from Italian *uso Massalia* for the (commercial) use of Marseilles, words formerly stamped on packages of silkworm cocoons exported from Greece. The designation came to imply superior quality, which the spirit claimed to possess. But this is probably a popular etymology.

ovolo (ō´vəlō) *n.* (*pl.* **ovoli** (-lē)) (*Archit.*) a convex moulding; in Roman architecture, a quarter-circle in outline; in Greek, elliptical with the greatest curve at the top.
17C. **Italian**, dim. of *uovo*, obs. *ovo*, from Latin *ovum* egg.

Oxon (ok´son) *a.* of Oxford (University). ~*n.* Oxford (the official signature of the Bishop of Oxford).
18C. Abbr. of **Modern Latin** *Oxoniensis*, from *Oxonia* Oxford.

oyez (ō´yes, ōyez´, ōyā´), **oyes** *int.* a cry repeated three times as introduction to any proclamation made by an officer of a court of law or public crier.
14–15C. **Old French** hear ye! imper. pl. of *oïr* (Modern French *ouïr*), from Latin *audire* to hear.

oy vey (oi vā´) *int.* an expression of dismay or grief, used esp. by Jews.
19C. **Yiddish**, lit. oh woe.

P

pabulum (pab´ūləm) *n.* **1** food; nourishment. **2** nutriment of a physical, mental or spiritual kind. **3** bland or intellectually uninspiring material.
17C. Latin, from stem of *pascere* to feed.
● Sense 3 arose in the late 20C, perhaps partly influenced by *Pablum*, the proprietary name of a children's breakfast cereal, itself from PABULUM in sense 1.

pace (pā´si, pah´chā) *prep.* with the permission of; with due respect to (someone who disagrees).
18C. Latin, abl. sing. of *pax* peace, as in *pace tua* by your leave.

pachinko (pəching´kō) *n.* a Japanese form of pinball.
mid-20C. Japanese, from *pachin* with a click.

pachisi (pəchē´zi) *n.* an Indian game played on a board with cowries for dice, named after the highest throw.
19C. Hindi *pacīsī* (throw of) twenty-five (the highest throw in the game), ult. from Sanskrit *pañcaviṃśati* twenty-five.

paco (pah´kō) *n.* (*pl.* **pacos**) the alpaca.
17C. Spanish, from Quechua *pako* red, reddish yellow.

paddy (pad´i) *n.* (*pl.* **paddies**) **1** a paddy field. **2** rice in the straw or in the husk.
17C. Malay *pādī*, corr. to Javanese *pari*, Kannada *bhatta*.

Padishah (pah´dishah) *n.* (*Hist.*) the title of the Shah of Iran, also in India of the British sovereign and of the Great Mogul.
17C. Persian *pādišāh*, Pahlavi *pātaḳsāh*, from *pati* lord + *šāh* SHAH.

padre (pah´drā) *n.* **1** father (used in addressing a priest in Italy, Spain and Spanish America). **2** a chaplain in the armed forces.
16C. Italian, Spanish and Portuguese, from Latin *pater, patris* father.

padrone (pədrō´ni) *n.* **1** a master, an Italian employer or house owner. **2** the proprietor of an inn in Italy.
17C. Italian, from Latin *patronus* patron.

paduasoy (pad´ūəsoi) *n.* **1** a kind of silk material, frequently used in the 18th cent. **2** a garment made of paduasoy.
16C. French *pou-de-soie* (earlier *pout de soie*), of unknown orig., alt. by assoc. with earlier *Padua say* say (a cloth resembling serge) from Padua, Italy.
● French *pou-de-soie* has also become associated with *soie* silk. Cp. PEAU-DE-SOIE.

paean (pē´ən) *n.* **1** a choral song addressed to Apollo or some other deity. **2** a song of triumph or rejoicing.

16C. Latin, from Greek *paian, paiōn* hymn to Apollo evoked by the name of *Paian, Paiōn,* orig. the Homeric name of the physician of the gods. Cp. PAEON.

paella (pīel´ə) *n.* a Spanish dish of rice, seafood, meat and vegetables, flavoured with saffron.
19C. Catalan, from Old French *paele* (Modern French *poêle*), from Latin *patella* pan, dish.

paeon (pē´ən) *n.* a metrical foot of four syllables, one long and the others short in different order.
17C. Latin, from Greek *paiōn.* See PAEAN.

pagoda (pəgō´də) *n.* **1** a sacred temple, usu. in the form of a pyramidal tower in many receding storeys, all elaborately decorated, in China, Japan and other countries in the Far East. **2** a building imitating this. **3** a gold coin formerly current in India.
16C. Portuguese *pagode,* prob. ult. from Persian *butkada* idol temple, from *but* idol + *kada* habitation, alt. by assoc. with Prakrit *bhagodī* divine, holy.

paillette (palyet´) *n.* **1** a small piece of metal or foil used in enamel painting. **2** a spangle.
19C. French, dim. of *paille* straw, chaff. Cp. PAILLON.

paillon (pal´yən) *n.* a bright metal backing for enamel or painting in translucent colours.
19C. French, deriv. of *paille* scale of chaff. Cp. PAILLETTE.

paisa (pī´sah) *n.* (*pl.* **paise** (-sā)) a monetary unit of countries of the Indian subcontinent, equal to one hundredth of a rupee.
19C. Hindi *paisā.* Cp. PICE.

pakora (pəkaw´rə) *n.* an Indian dish of pieces of vegetable, chicken etc. dipped in spiced batter and deep-fried.
mid-20C. Hindi *pakoṛā* a dish of vegetables in gram flour.

paktong (pak´tong) *n.* a Chinese alloy of zinc, nickel and copper, like silver.
18C. Chinese *bái tóng* white copper.

palaestra (pəlēs´trə), **palestra** (-les´-) *n.* in ancient Greece, a place where athletic exercises were taught and practised; a gymnasium or wrestling school.
14–15C. Latin, from Greek *palaistra,* from *palaiein* to wrestle.

palafitte (pal´əfit) *n.* a prehistoric house built on piles, a lake-dwelling.
19C. French, from Italian *palafitta* fence of stakes, from *palo* stake + *fitto* fixed.

palais (pal´ā) *n.* (*coll.*) a dance hall.
early 20C. French, abbr. of PALAIS DE DANSE.

palais de danse (palā də dās´) *n.* (*pl.* **palais de danse**) a dance hall.
early 20C. French, lit. palace of dancing.

palampore (pal´əmpaw) *n.* a decorated chintz bedspread, formerly made in India.
17C. Prob. from **Portuguese** *palangapuzes* (pl.), from Urdu and Persian *palangpoš* bed cover (cp. Hindi *palang* bed, Persian *poš* cover), or from *Pālanpur,* a town and former market centre in Gujarat, India.

palanquin (palənkēn´), **palankeen** *n.* a couch or litter in India and the East carried by four or six people on their shoulders.
16C. Portuguese *palanquim,* from Oriya *pālaṅki,* Hindi *pālkī,* prob. through Malay *palangki,* ult. from Sanskrit *palyaṅka* bed, litter.

palazzo (palat´sō) *n.* **1** (*pl.* **palazzi** (-si)) a palatial mansion. **2** (*pl.* **palazzos** (palat´sōz)) a type of loose wide-legged women's trousers.
17C. **Italian** palace.
• Sense 2 dates from the late 20C, the name denoting the trousers' 'palatial' fitting.

paletot (pal´tō) *n.* a loose overcoat for men or women.
19C. **French**, of unknown orig. ? From Middle English *paltok* a kind of jacket.

palette (pal´it) *n.* **1** a flat board used by artists for mixing colours on. **2** the colours or arrangement of colours used for a particular picture or by a particular artist.
18C. **French** pallet.

pallium (pal´iəm) *n.* (*pl.* **palliums**, **pallia** (-iə)) **1** a scarflike vestment of white wool with red crosses, worn by the Pope and certain metropolitans and archbishops. **2** (*Hist.*) a man's square woollen cloak, worn esp. by the ancient Greeks. **3** (*Zool.*) the mantle of a bivalve.
12–14C. **Latin** covering.

pallone (pahlō´nā) *n.* an Italian game like tennis, in which the ball is struck with the arm protected by a wooden guard.
19C. **Italian**, augm. of *palla* ball. Cp. PELOTA.

palmette (palmet´) *n.* (*Archit.*) a carved or painted ornament in the form of a palm leaf.
19C. **French**, dim. of *palme* palm.

palmier (pal´miā) *n.* (*pl.* **palmiers** (-miā)) a sweet pastry shaped like a palm leaf.
early 20C. **French**, lit. palm tree.

palomino (paləmē´nō) *n.* (*pl.* **palominos**) a cream, yellow or gold horse with a white mane and tail.
early 20C. **American Spanish**, from Spanish, from Latin *palumbinus* like a dove, from *palumba* ring dove.
• The horse is so called because of its dovelike colouring.

pampas (pam´pəs) *n.pl.* the open, far-extending, treeless plains in South America, south of the Amazon.
18C. **Spanish**, pl. of *pampa*, from Quechua a plain.

pampero (pampeə´rō) *n.* (*pl.* **pamperos**) a violent westerly or south-westerly wind blowing over the pampas.
18C. **Spanish** from *pampa* (PAMPAS) + *-ero*.

pan (pan) *n.* **1** a betel leaf. **2** a betel leaf wrapped around sliced betel nut mixed with spices, used for chewing.
17C. **Hindi** *pān* betel leaf, from Sanskrit *parṇa* leaf.

panacea (panəsē´ə) *n.* (*pl.* **panaceas**) a universal remedy.
16C. **Latin**, from Greek *panakeia*, from *panakēs* all-healing, from *pan-* all + base of *akos* remedy.

panache (pənash´) *n.* **1** show, swagger, bounce; style; airs. **2** a tuft or plume, esp. on a headdress or helmet.
16C. **French**, from Italian *pennacchio*, from Late Latin *pinnaculum*, dim. of *pinna* feather.
• The original sense was sense 2. Sense 1 dates from the 19C.

panada (pənah´də) *n.* **1** a paste made of flour, water etc. **2** bread boiled to a pulp, sweetened and flavoured.
16C. **Spanish and Portuguese**, ult. from Latin *panis* bread.

panatella (panətel´ə) *n.* a type of long, slender cigar.
19C. **American Spanish** *panatela* long thin biscuit, sponge cake, from Spanish, from Italian *panatella* small loaf, dim. of *panata*. See PANADA.

Panathenaea (panathənē´ə) n. (Hist.) in ancient Greece, the chief annual festival of the Athenians, celebrating with games and processions the union of Attica under Theseus.
17C. Greek panathēnaia, neut. pl. a., from pan- all + Athēnaios Athenian, from Athēnai Athens or Athēnē Athene.

panchayat (pŭnchī´yət) n. a village council in India.
19C. Hindi pañcāyat, prob. from Sanskrit pañcāyatta, from pañca five + āyatta depending on.
• The word originally denoted a council consisting of five members.

Panchen Lama (panchən lah´mə) n. a Grand Lama of Tibet, next in rank after the Dalai Lama.
18C. Tibetan, abbr. of pandi-tachen-po great learned one (cp. PUNDIT) + LAMA.

pancratium (pankrā´shiəm) n. (pl. **pancratia** (-iə)) in ancient Greece, an athletic contest including both boxing and wrestling.
17C. Latin, from Greek pagkration, from pan- all + kratos strength.

pandore (pandaw´), **pandora** (pandaw´rə) n. a lutelike musical instrument, a bandore.
16C. Italian pandora, from Latin pandura, from Greek pandoura, of unknown orig.

pandour (pan´dooə), **pandoor** n. (Hist.) any one of a body of Croatian foot soldiers, noted for their ferocity, who were enrolled in the Austrian army.
18C. French, and from German Pandur, from Serbo-Croat pandur constable, bailiff, prob. from Medieval Latin banderius guard of cornfields and vineyards.

panem et circenses (panem et sœken´zēz, kœken´sāz) n. food and entertainment provided by the state as a means of winning public support.
18C. Latin, lit. bread and circuses, from acc. of panis bread + et and + acc. of circenses (ludi) (games) of the circus.
• The phrase derives from Juvenal's Satires (X) (2C AD): Duas tantum res anxius optat / Panem et circenses 'Only two things does he [the modern citizen] anxiously wish for, bread and circuses'.

panga (pang´gə) n. (pl. **pangas**) a broad, heavy, African knife.
mid-20C. Kiswahili.

panne (pan), **panne velvet** n. a soft, long-napped fabric.
18C. French, of unknown orig. ? From Latin penna feather.

panzer (pan´zə) n. 1 (pl.) armoured troops, esp. an armoured division, in the German army. 2 a vehicle in such a division, esp. a tank. ~a. heavily armoured.
mid-20C. German mail, coat of mail, ult. rel. to English paunch.

papabile (pəpah´bilā) a. suitable for high office.
mid-20C. Italian suitable to be a pope, from papa pope.

paparazzo (papərat´sō) n. (pl. **paparazzi** (-sē)) a freelance professional photographer who specializes in photographing celebrities at private moments, usu. without their consent.
mid-20C. Italian, from Paparazzo, name of a freelance photographer in the Italian film La Dolce Vita (1960).
• The word has become popularly associated with English paper (i.e. newspaper).

papeterie (pap´ətri) n. an ornamental case for storing writing materials.
19C. French paper manufacture, stationer's shop, writing case, from papetier papermaker.

papier collé (papiā kol´ā) n. (pl.
papiers collés (papiā kol´ā)) a collage
made from paper.
mid-20C. French glued paper, from
papier paper + p.p. of *coller* to glue.
Cp. COLLAGE.

papier mâché (papiā mash´ā) n. a
material made from pulped paper,
moulded into trays, boxes etc. ~a. made
of papier mâché.
18C. French, lit. chewed paper, from
papier paper + *mâché*, p.p. of *mâcher* to
chew, from Latin *masticare*.
• The material was promoted
commercially under this name in
Britain apparently in the belief that it
meant mashed paper. It may thus not
actually have been of genuine French
origin.

papillon (pap´ilon, pap´iyō) n. a breed of
toy spaniel with large butterfly-shaped
ears.
early 20C. French butterfly.

papillote (pap´ilōt) n. a paper frill round
a cutlet etc.
18C. French, from *papillot*, dim. of
papillon butterfly.

paprika (pap´rika, pəprē´kə) n. 1 (Bot.)
a sweet variety of red pepper. 2 a
powdered condiment made from
paprika.
19C. Hungarian, from Serbo-Croat *pàpar*
pepper, from Latin *piper* pepper.

parador (par´ədaw) n. (pl. **paradors**,
paradores (-daw´rez)) a Spanish state-
owned hotel.
19C. Spanish inn, hostel.

parados (par´ədos) n. (pl. **paradoses**)
(Mil.) a rampart or earthwork to protect
against fire from the rear.
19C. French, from *para-*, from Greek
para beside, against, + *dos* back.

paramo (par´əmō) n. (pl. **paramos**) a
high plateau with no trees in South
America.
18C. Spanish and Portuguese *páramo*,
from Latin *paramus* plain.

parang (pah´rang) n. a heavy sheath
knife.
19C. Malay.

parasang (par´əsang) n. an ancient
Persian measure of length, about 3¼
miles (5.25 kilometres).
16C. Latin *parasanga*, from Greek
parasaggēs, from Persian.

parasol (pa´rəsol) n. 1 a small umbrella
used to give shelter from the sun, a
sunshade. 2 any of several fungi of the
genus *Lepiota*, having an umbrella-
shaped cap.
17C. French, from Italian *parasole*, from
para-, from Greek *para* beside, against +
sole sun. Cp. French *parapluie* umbrella
(from *para-* + *pluie* rain).

paratha (pərah´tə) n. in Indian cookery, a
piece of flat, round, unleavened bread
fried on a griddle.
mid-20C. Hindi *parāṭhā*.

par avion (pahr avyō´) adv. by airmail.
early 20C. French by aeroplane.
• French *avion* comes from the name of
two early aircraft, *Avion I* and *Avion II*,
first flown in 1890 by the French
engineer Clément Ader (1841–1925).
The name itself is from Latin *avis* bird.

Parcae (pah´sē) n.pl. in Roman
mythology, the Fates.
16C. Latin, sing. of *Parcae*, prob. from
parere to produce, rather than *parcere*
to spare.

par excellence (pahr ek´sələns) adv.
above all others, pre-eminently.
17C. French, from Latin *per
excellentiam* by virtue of excellence.

parfait (pahfã´) *n.* **1** a rich, cold dessert made with whipped cream, eggs, fruit etc. **2** a dessert made of layers of ice cream, meringue, fruit and sauce, served in a tall glass.
19C. French, lit. perfect.

parfleche (pahflesh´) *n.* **1** a hide, usu. of buffalo, stripped of hair and dried on a stretcher. **2** a tent, wallet or other article made of this.
19C. Canadian French *parflèche*, from French *parer* to ward off + *flèche* arrow.

pargana (pəgŭn´ə), **pergunnah**, **pergana** *n.* in India, a subdivision of a district.
17C. Persian and Urdu *parganah* district.

pari-mutuel (parimū´tūəl) *n.* **1** a system of betting in which the winners divide the losers' stakes less a percentage for management. **2** a totalizator.
19C. French mutual stake, mutual wager, from *pari* stake, wager + *mutuel* mutual.

pari passu (pahri pas´oo) *adv.* (esp. in legal contexts) with equal pace, in a similar degree, equally.
16C. Latin, lit. with equal step, from abl. of *par passus* equal step.

parka (pah´kə) *n.* a hooded jacket edged or lined with fur.
18C. Aleut, from Russian skin jacket, prob. from Nenets.

parlando (pahlan´dō) *adv.* (*Mus.*) in an expressive or declamatory manner.
19C. Italian, pres.p. of *parlare* to speak.

parleyvoo (pahlivoo´) *v.i.* (*dated, sl.*) to speak French. ~*n.* **1** the French language. **2** a Frenchman.
18C. French *parlez-vous* (*français*)? do you speak (French)?

parquet (pah´kā) *n.* **1** inlaid woodwork for floors. **2** a flooring made of this. **3** (*N Am.*) the part of the floor of a theatre between the orchestra and the row immediately under the front of the gallery. ~*a.* made of parquet. ~*v.t.* (*pres.p.* **parqueting**, *past, p.p.* **parqueted**) to floor (a room) with parquet.
19C. Old French small marked-off space, dim. of *parc* park.

parramatta (parəmat´ə), **paramatta** *n.* a light twilled dress fabric of merino wool and cotton.
19C. *Parramatta*, a settlement (now a city) in New South Wales, Australia, where orig. made.

Parsee (pah´sē) *n.* **1** a Zoroastrian, a descendant of the Persians who fled to India from the Muslim persecution in the 7th and 8th cents. **2** the Pahlavi language.
17C. Persian *Pārsē* Persian, from *Pārs* Persia.

parterre (pahteə´) *n.* **1** an ornamental arrangement of flower beds, with intervening walks. **2** (*N Am.*) the ground floor of a theatre or the part of this behind the orchestra.
17C. French, use as n. of *par terre* on the ground, along the ground.

parti (pahtē´) *n.* (*pl.* **partis**) a person regarded as eligible for marriage.
18C. French choice, from Old French *partie* part, share, side in a contest, from Latin *partita*, fem. p.p. (used as n.) of *partiri* to part.

partim (pah´tim) *adv.* partly.
18C. Latin in part, from *pars, partis* part + adv. suf. *-im*.

parti pris (pahti prē´) *n.* (*pl.* **partis pris** (pahti)) a preconceived view, bias, prejudice. ~*a.* biased, prejudiced.
19C. French, lit. side taken, from *parti* (PARTI) + *pris*, p.p. of *prendre* to take.

partita (pahtē´tə) *n.* (*pl.* **partitas**, **partite** (-tā)) (*Mus.*) **1** a suite of music. **2** an air with variations.
19C. **Italian**, fem. pp. of *partire* to divide, from Latin *partiri*.
• The suite is so called as it is divided into parts, originally as a set of variations (sense 2).

parure (pəruə´) *n.* a set of jewels or other personal adornments.
12–14C. **Old French**, from *parer* to adorn, to arrange, from Latin *parare* to prepare.
• The original sense was an ornament for an alb or amice, also a paring or peeling. The current sense dates from the 19C.

parvenu (pah´vənoo, -nū), (*fem.*) **parvenue** *n.* (*pl.* **parvenus**) **1** a person who has risen socially or financially. **2** an upstart. ~*a.* of or relating to a parvenu or parvenue.
19C. **French**, use as n. of p.p. of *parvenir* to arrive, from Latin *pervenire*, from *per-* through + *venire* to come. Cp. ARRIVISTE.

pas (pah) *n.* (*pl.* **pas** (pah)) **1** a dance step, esp. in ballet. **2** precedence.
18C. **French** step, pace.

pas de deux (pah də dœ´) *n.* (*pl.* **pas de deux**) a dance for two people.
18C. **French**, lit. step of two.
• The dance is especially found in classical ballet.

pas devant les enfants (pah dəvā lāz ā´fā) *int.* not in front of the children, used with reference to a remark or action that is regarded as inappropriate for children (or other present company) to hear or see.
mid-20C. **French**.
• The warning is expressed in French so as not to be understood by the person(s) in question. It is often shortened to *pas devant*.

pasha (pah´shə), **bashaw** (bəshaw´), **pacha** *n.* (*Hist.*) a Turkish title of honour, usu. conferred on officers of high rank, governors etc.
17C. **Turkish** *paşa*, from Persian *pādšāh*. See PADISHAH.
• According to some, the word is from Turkish *başa*, from *baş* head, chief.

pashm (pash´əm) *n.* the under-fur of various Tibetan animals, esp. goats, used to make cashmere shawls.
19C. **Persian** *pašm* wool. See PASHMINA.

pashmina (pashmē´nə) *n.* **1** a fine quality woollen fabric made from Tibetan goat hair. **2** a garment, esp. a shawl, made from this.
19C. **Persian** *pašm* wool. See PASHM.

paskha (pahs´kə) *n.* a Russian dessert made from curd cheese and dried fruit, traditionally eaten at Easter.
early 20C. **Russian** Easter, rel. to English *paschal*.

paso doble (pasō dō´blā) *n.* **1** a Latin American ballroom dance in fast 2/4 time, based on a march step. **2** this march step.
early 20C. **Spanish** double step.

pas op (pas op´) *int.* be careful, watch out.
mid-20C. **Afrikaans**, from Dutch *oppassen* to be on one's guard.

passacaglia (pasəkah´liə) *n.* (*Mus.*) an instrumental piece with a ground bass.
17C. **Italian**, from Spanish *pasacalle*, from *pasar* to pass + *calle* street.
• The piece was originally one often played in the streets.

†passade (pasād´) *n.* in dressage, a turn or course of a horse backwards or forwards on the same spot.
17C. **French**, from Italian *passata* or Provençal *passada*, from Medieval Latin *passare* to pass.

passé (pas´ā) *a.* **1** old-fashioned, behind the times. **2** †past one's prime, faded.
18C. **French**, p.p. of *passer* to pass.

passementerie (pas´məntri) *n.* a trimming for dresses, esp. of gold and silver lace.
17C. **French**, from *passement*, from *passer* to pass.
• The ornament is presumably so called from the passing of the thread.

passepartout (paspah´too) *n.* **1** a master key. **2** a simple frame for a picture, photograph etc. **3** the sticky tape or paper used for such a frame.
17C. **French**, from *passer* to pass + *partout* everywhere.

passepied (paspyā´) *n.* a Breton dance resembling a minuet, popular in the 17th cent.
17C. **French**, from *passer* to pass + *pied* foot.

passim (pas´im) *adv.* here and there, throughout (indicating the occurrence of a word, allusion etc. in a cited work).
19C. **Latin**, lit. scatteredly, from *passus* scattered, p.p. of *pandere* to spread out, + adv. suf. *-im*.

pasta (pas´tə) *n.* **1** a flour and water dough, often shaped and eaten fresh or in processed form, e.g. spaghetti. **2** a dish made with this dough. **3** a particular type or shape of this dough.
19C. **Italian**, from Late Latin small square piece of medicinal preparation, from Greek *pastē*.

pastiche (pastēsh´), **pasticcio** (-tich´ō) *n.* (*pl.* **pastiches, pasticcios**) a medley, musical work, painting etc. composed of elements drawn from other works or which imitates the style of a previous work.
19C. **French**, from Italian *pasticcio* pie, pasty, from Late Latin *pasta*. See PASTA.

pastille (pas´təl, -til) *n.* **1** an aromatic lozenge. **2** a roll, cone or pellet of aromatic paste for burning as a fumigator or disinfectant.
17C. **French**, from Latin *pastillus* little loaf, roll, lozenge, dim. of *panis* loaf.

pastis (pas´tis, pastēs´) *n.* (*pl.* **pastis**) an aniseed-flavoured alcoholic drink.
early 20C. **French**, orig. pie, pasty.

pastorale (pastərahl´, -rah´li) *n.* (*pl.* **pastorales** (-ahlz´), **pastorali** (-ah´li)) **1** a simple rustic melody. **2** a cantata on a pastoral theme. **3** a symphony dealing with a pastoral subject.
18C. **Italian**, use as n. of a., pastoral.

pastrami (pastrah´mi) *n.* a highly seasoned smoked beef.
mid-20C. **Yiddish**, from Romanian *pastramă*, prob. of Turkish orig.

pataca (pətah´kə) *n.* (*pl.* **patacas**) the standard unit of currency of Macao.
19C. **Spanish and Portuguese**, from Portuguese *pataea* piece of eight, dollar.

patchouli (pach´uli, pəchoo´-) *n.* **1** an Indian shrub of the genus *Pogostemon*, yielding a fragrant oil. **2** a perfume prepared from this.
19C. **Tamil** *pacçuli*.

pâte (paht) *n.* the paste from which porcelain is made.
19C. **French** paste.

pâté (pat´ā) *n.* **1** a spread made of cooked, diced meat, fish or vegetables blended with herbs etc. **2** a pie, a patty.
18C. **French**, from Old French *pasté*.
• The original sense was sense 2. Sense 1 dates from the 19C.

pater (pā´tə) *n.* (*sl.*, *usu. facet.*) a father.
12–14C. **Latin** father.
• The word was originally a shortening of PATERNOSTER. The current usage dates from the 17C, first in the sense spiritual father.

patera (pat´ərə) n. (pl. **paterae** (-rē)) **1** a round dish used for wine in ancient Rome. **2** a flat, round ornament on a frieze or in bas-reliefs.
17C. Latin, from *patere* to be open.

paterfamilias (pātəfəmil´ias, pa-) n. (pl. **patresfamilias** (pahtrāz-)) the father of a family, the male head of a household.
15C. Latin, from PATER + old gen. of *familia* family.

paternoster (patənos´tə) n. **1** the Lord's Prayer, esp. in Latin. **2** every eleventh bead of a rosary, indicating that the Lord's Prayer is to be said. **3** a rosary. **4** a type of lift with compartments attached to a continuous, circular belt. **5** a fishing line with a weight at the end and short lines with hooks extending at intervals.
pre-1200. Latin *pater noster*, lit. our father, the first two words of the Lord's Prayer in Latin.

patha patha (patə pat´ə) n. **1** a sensuous Black African dance. **2** sexual intercourse.
mid-20C. Xhosa, lit. touch-touch.
• Sense 2 evolved in the late 20C.

pathos (pā´thos) n. a quality or element in events or expression that excites emotion, esp. pity or sorrow.
16C. Greek suffering, feeling, rel. to *paskhein* to suffer, *penthos* grief.

patina (pat´inə) n. (pl. **patinas**) **1** the green incrustation that covers ancient bronzes. **2** a similar film on any surface. **3** a soft shine produced by age on woodwork.
18C. Latin shallow dish, pan.

patio (pat´iō) n. (pl. **patios**) **1** a paved area beside a house, used for outdoor meals, sunbathing etc. **2** the open inner court of a Spanish or Spanish–American house.

19C. Spanish court of a house, prob. from Old Provençal *patu*, *pati* untilled land, place of pasture, from Latin *pactum* agreement, pact.

patisserie (pətē´səri) n. **1** a pastry-cook's shop. **2** pastries collectively.
16C. French *pâtisserie*, from Medieval Latin *pasticium*, from *pasta*. See PASTA.

patois (pat´wah) n. (pl. **patois** (-wahz)) a non-standard dialect of a district.
17C. Old French rough speech, ? from *patoier* to handle roughly, to trample, from *patte* paw, of unknown orig.

patroon (pətroon´) n. (N Am.) a proprietor of land with manorial privileges and right of entail under a Dutch grant, esp. in New York and New Jersey (abolished 1850).
18C. Dutch patron.

pavane (pəvan´), **pavan** (pav´ən) n. **1** a slow and stately dance, usu. in elaborate dress, in vogue in the 16th and 17th cents. **2** music for this.
16C. French, prob. from Italian dial. *pavana*, fem. of *pavano* of Padua, from *Pavo*, dial. name of Padua (Italian *Padova*), a city in NE Italy.
• According to some, the word is from (or has been influenced by) Latin *pavo*, *pavonis* peacock.

pavé (pav´ā) n. **1** a pavement. **2** a stone-paved road. **3** a setting of gems placed close together.
14–15C. French, use as n. of p.p. of *paver*, back-formation from *pavement*, from Latin *pavimentum* beaten floor, from *pavire* to beat, to tread down.

pavlova (pavlō´və, pav´ləvə) n. a dessert consisting of a meringue base topped with fruit and whipped cream.
early 20C. Anna *Pavlova* (1881–1931), Russian ballerina.
• The dessert was so named in the dancer's honour when she visited

Australia and New Zealand in the 1920s.

pavonazzo (pavənat´sō) *n.* (*pl.* **pavonazzos**) a variety of marble with brilliant markings.
19C. **Italian**, from Latin *pavonaceum*, from *pavo, pavonis* peacock.
● The marble is so named from its markings, which resemble the colours of a peacock.

pax (paks) *n.* **1** the kiss of peace. **2** a tablet or plaque bearing a representation of the Crucifixion or other sacred subject which was formerly kissed by the priest and congregation at Mass; an osculatory. ~*int.* (*sl.*) used to express a call for a truce (in children's games).
14–15C. **Latin** peace.

†**paysage** (pāzazh´) *n.* **1** a rural scene or landscape. **2** a landscape painting.
17C. **French**, from *pays* country.

péage (pāahzh) *n.* a toll paid to travel on a French motorway.
late 20C. **French**, from Medieval Latin *pedaticum*, from Latin *pes, pedis* foot.
● In medieval times the French word was in general use for a toll paid for passing through a place or country.

peau-de-soie (pōdəswah´) *n.* a rich, finely ribbed fabric of silk or rayon.
19C. **French**, lit. silk skin, from *peau* skin + *de* of + *soie* silk. Cp. PADUASOY.

pébrine (pābrēn´) *n.* an epidemic disease, characterized by black spots, attacking silkworms.
19C. **French**, from Provençal *pebrino*, from *pebre* pepper.

peccadillo (pekədil´ō) *n.* (*pl.* **peccadilloes**, **peccadillos**) a minor sin or offence.
16C. **Spanish** *pecadillo*, dim. of *pecado* sin.

peccavi (pekah´vē) *int.* (also *facet.*) used to express contrition. ~*n.* (*pl.* **peccavis**) a confession of guilt.
16C. **Latin** I have sinned, 1st pers. sing. perf. ind. of *peccare* to sin. Cp. MEA CULPA.

pecorino (pekərē´nō) *n.* (*pl.* **pecorinos**) an Italian ewe's-milk cheese.
mid-20C. **Italian**, from *pecora* sheep.

peignoir (pān´wah) *n.* a loose robe or dressing gown worn by a woman.
19C. **French**, from *peigner* to comb.
● The garment was originally worn by a woman while her hair was being combed.

peine forte et dure (pen fawt ā dūə´) *n.* the punishment of being pressed to death under heavy weights, formerly imposed on those refusing to plead on a charge of felony.
16C. **French**, lit. severe and hard punishment.

pekoe (pē´kō) *n.* a fine black tea.
18C. **Chinese** (Amoy) *pekho*, from *pek* white + *ho* down, hair.
● The tea is so called because its leaves when picked are covered in white down.

pelerine (pel´ərēn) *n.* a lady's long narrow fur cape.
18C. **French** *pèlerine*, fem. of *pèlerin* pilgrim.
● The garment is so called from its resemblance to the type of cape worn by pilgrims.

pelisse (pilēs´) *n.* (*Hist.*) **1** a woman's long cloak or mantle. **2** a fur-lined cloak worn by a hussar. **3** a garment worn over other clothes by a child.
18C. **Old French**, from Medieval Latin *pellicia* cloak, from Latin *pellicea*, fem. of *pelliceus* made of skin, from *pellis* skin.

pelota (pilot´ə, -lō´-) *n.* (*pl.* **pelotas**)
1 a game similar to squash played with
a ball and a curved racket fitting upon
the hand, popular in Spain and the
Basque country. **2** the ball used in
pelota.
19C. Spanish ball, augm. of *pella*, from
Latin *pila* ball.

pelta (pel´tə) *n.* (*pl.* **peltae** (-tē)) **1** (*Hist.*)
a small light shield or target used by the
ancient Greeks and Romans. **2** (*Bot.*) a
structure or part like a shield in form or
function.
17C. Latin, from Greek *peltē* a small
light leather shield.

penates (pinah´tēz) *n.pl.* (*Hist.*) the
Roman household gods, orig. of the
storeroom and kitchen.
16C. Latin *Penates* (pl.), from *penus*
provision of food, rel. to *penes* within.
See also LARES ET PENATES.

penchant (pā´shā) *n.* a strong inclination
or liking.
17C. French, pres.p. (used as n.) of
pencher to incline, to lean.

pendente lite (pendenti lī´ti) *adv.* (*Law*)
while a suit is in progress.
18C. Latin, lit. with the lawsuit pending,
from abl. sing. of *pendens*, *pendentis*,
pres.p. of *pendere* to hang, to be
undecided + abl. sing. of *lis*, *litis*
lawsuit.

penetralia (penitrā´liə) *n.pl.* **1** the inner
part of a house, palace, temple or
shrine. **2** secrets, mysteries.
17C. Latin (pl.) from *penetralis* interior,
innermost, from stem of *penetrare* to
penetrate.

penne (pen´i) *n.* pasta quills, pasta in
short, thick, ridged tube shapes.
late 20C. Italian, pl. of *penna* quill.

pensée (pā´sā) *n.* a thought, a reflection.
14–15C. French thought, from Old
French *pensee*.
● The original sense was thoughtfulness,
anxiety, care. The current sense dates
from the 19C.

penseroso (pensərō´sō, pensərō´zō) *a.*
pensive, brooding melancholy.
19C. Obsolete Italian (now *pensieroso*),
from *pensiere* thought, ult. from Latin
pensare to ponder, to consider.
● The use of the word in English was
popularized by Milton's poem *Il
Penseroso* (1632), invoking the goddess
Melancholy.

pension (pāsyŏ´) *n.* a boarding house.
17C. French, from Latin *pensio*,
pensionis payment, rent.
● The current sense evolved from the
payment made to keep a child at a
boarding school.

pentimento (pentimen´tō) *n.* (*pl.*
pentimenti (-tē)) (a part of) a painting
that has been painted over and later
becomes visible.
early 20C. Italian, lit. repentance, regret.
● The work is so called because the
artist has changed his mind or
concealed a mistake.

peperino (pepərē´nō) *n.* a porous
volcanic rock, composed of sand,
cinders etc. cemented together.
18C. Italian, from *peper* (PEPPERONI)
+ dim. suf. *-ino*.
● The rock is so called because it
consists of small grains.

peplum (pep´ləm), **peplus** (-ləs) *n.*
(*pl.* **peplums**, **pepluses**) **1** a flared
extension attached to the waist of a
tight-fitting jacket or bodice. **2** an outer
robe or gown worn by women in ancient
Greece. **3** an overskirt supposed to
resemble the ancient peplum.
early 20C. Latin, from Greek *peplos*.

pepo (pē´pō) *n.* (*pl.* **pepos**) any of various fruits of the gourd family, e.g. cucumber, melon, with a hard rind, watery pulp, and many seeds.
14–15C. Latin *pepo, peponis* pumpkin, from Greek *pepōn*, use as *n.* of *a.*, ripe.

pepperoni (pepərō´ni), **peperoni** *n.* a dry sausage of pork and beef that is heavily seasoned, esp. with pepper.
mid-20C. Italian *peperone* chilli, from *pepe* pepper, from Latin *piper* pepper + augm. suf. *-one*.

per (pœ) *prep.* **1** for each. **2** by, through, by means of. **3** according to. **4** (*Her.*) in the direction of.
14–15C. Latin through, by, ult. rel. to English *for*.

per annum (pər an´əm) *adv.* yearly, each year.
17C. Modern Latin, from PER + acc. of Latin *annus* year.
• The expression is often abbreviated as *p.a.*

per ardua ad astra (pœr ahdūə ad as´trə) *int.* through difficulties to the stars (the motto of the Royal Air Force).
early 20C. Latin.
• The phrase, originally the motto of the Mulvany family, was adopted as the motto of the RAF (then the Royal Flying Corps) in 1914. The headquarters of the former Air Ministry (now part of the Ministry of Defence) was set up at Adastral House, London, in 1955.

percale (pəkāl´) *n.* a closely woven cotton cambric.
17C. French of unknown orig.
• The fabric was originally imported from India.

per capita (pə kap´itə), **per caput** (kap´ut) *adv.* for each person.
17C. Modern Latin, from PER + acc. pl. of Latin *caput* head.

percheron (pœ´shəron) *n.* a breed of heavy and powerful horses.
19C. French, *a.* from *le Perche*, a region in N France, where orig. bred.

per contra (pœ kon´trə) *adv.* on the opposite side.
16C. Latin on the contrary.

per diem (pœ dē´em) *a., adv.* by the day, for each day. ~*n.* a per diem payment or allowance.
16C. Modern Latin, from PER + acc. of Latin *dies*.

père (peə) *n.* father, senior, added to a surname to distinguish a father from a son of the same name.
17C. French father, from Latin *pater, patris* father. Cp. FILS[2].

perestroika (peristroi´kə) *n.* in the former Soviet Union, the policy of restructuring and reforming Soviet institutions initiated in the 1980s by Mikhail Gorbachev.
late 20C. Russian *perestroĭka* restructuring, from *pere-* again, across + *stroĭka*, from *stroit'* to build.

perfecto (pəfek´tō) *n.* (*pl.* **perfectos**) a large cigar which tapers at both ends.
19C. Spanish perfect.

pergola (pœ´gələ) *n.* (*pl.* **pergolas**) a covered walk or arbour with climbing plants trained over posts, trellis-work etc.
17C. Italian, from Latin *pergula* projecting roof, vine arbour, from *pergere* to come forward, to go forward.

peri (piə´ri) *n.* **1** a being represented as a descendant of fallen angels, excluded from paradise until some penance is accomplished. **2** a beautiful being, a fairy.
18C. Persian *perī*.

periplus (per´ipləs) *n.* (*pl.* **peripli** (-plī))
a circumnavigation.
18C. Latin, from Greek *periplous*, from
peri around + *plous* voyage.

perique (pərēk´) *n.* a strong, dark-
coloured variety of tobacco grown and
manufactured in Louisiana, used chiefly
in mixtures.
19C. Louisiana French, appar. from
Perique, nickname (or pseudonym) of
Pierre Chenet, who first grew the
tobacco.

perpetuum mobile (pœpetūəm
mō´bili, -lā) *n.* **1** perpetual motion.
2 (*Mus.*) moto perpetuo.
17C. Latin perpetual motion, from
perpetuus perpetual + *mobilis* movable,
mobile, based on PRIMUM MOBILE. Cp.
MOTO PERPETUO.

per se (pœ sā´) *adv.* by itself, in itself.
16C. Latin by itself.

persicot (pœ´sikō) *n.* a cordial made
from peaches, nectarines etc., macerated
in spirit and flavoured with their
kernels.
18C. French, dim. of Savoy dial. *perse*
peach, from Latin *persicum*.

persienne (pœsien´) *n.* **1** an Oriental
cambric or muslin. **2** (*pl.*) window
blinds or shutters like Venetian blinds.
19C. French, fem. of *persien* Persian.

persiflage (pœ´siflahzh) *n.* banter,
raillery, frivolous treatment of any
subject.
18C. French, from *persifler* to banter,
from *per-* through + *siffler* to whistle.

persona (pəsō´nə) *n.* (*pl.* **personas**,
personae (-nē)) **1** a person's social
façade, as distinct from *anima*. **2** (*often
pl.*) a character in a play, novel etc.
early 20C. Latin mask used by an actor.

persona grata (pəsō´nə grah´tə) *n.* (*pl.*
personae gratae (pəsō´nē grah´tē)) an
acceptable person, esp. in diplomatic
circles.
19C. Late Latin, from PERSONA + fem. of
gratus pleasing.

persona non grata (pəsō´nə non
grah´tə) *n.* an unacceptable person.
early 20C. Late Latin, from PERSONA
+ *non* not + fem. of *gratus* pleasing.
Cp. PERSONA GRATA.

personnel (pœsənel´) *n.* **1** the body of
persons engaged in some service, esp.
a public institution, military or naval
enterprise etc. **2** the staff of a business
firm etc. **3** a personnel department.
19C. French, use as n. of a. personal, as
distinct from MATERIEL.

Pesach (pā´sahkh) *n.* Passover.
17C. Hebrew *pesaḥ*.

pesade (pesahd´) *n.* in dressage, the
motion of a horse when raising the
forequarters without advancing.
18C. French, alt. of *posade*, from Italian
posata, lit. pause, resting, from *posare*
to pause, from Latin *pausare*.

pesante (pizan´tā) *adv.* (*Mus.*) heavily,
gravely.
19C. Italian heavily.

peseta (pəsā´tə) *n.* (*pl.* **pesetas**) **1** the
standard unit of currency of Spain and
Andorra. **2** (*Hist.*) a silver coin.
19C. Spanish, dim. of *pesa* weight, from
Latin *pensa*, pl. of *pensum*, neut. p.p. of
pendere to weigh. Cp. PESO.

pesewa (pəsā´wah) *n.* a unit of currency
of Ghana, worth one hundredth of a
cedi.
mid-20C. Akan penny.

Peshito (pəshē´tō) *n.* the Syriac version
of the Holy Scriptures.
18C. Syriac *pšīṭā*, lit. the simple, the
plain.

peshwa (pāsh´wa), **peishwa** *n.* **1** the hereditary ruler of the Marathas. **2** orig. the chief minister of the Marathas.
17C. Persian *pīšwā* chief.

peso (pā´sō) *n.* (*pl.* **pesos**) the standard unit of currency of several Central and South American countries and the Philippines.
16C. Spanish weight, from Latin *pensum*. See PESETA.

pesto (pes´tō) *n.* an Italian sauce made of basil, garlic, pine nuts etc.
mid-20C. Italian, contr. of *pestato*, p.p. of *pestare* to pound, to crush.

pétanque (pətangk´) *n.* a game similar to boules, played esp. in Provence.
mid-20C. French, from Provençal *pèd tanco*, lit. foot fixed (to the ground).
● The reference is to the start position.

petasus (pet´əsəs) *n.* **1** a broad-brimmed, low-crowned hat worn by the ancient Greeks. **2** the winged cap of Hermes.
16C. Latin, from Greek *petasos*.

pétillant (pā´tēyā) *a.* (of wine) slightly sparkling.
19C. French, from *pétiller*, dim. of *péter* to break wind.

petit beurre (pəti bœ´, peti) *n.* (*pl.* **petits beurres** (pəti bœ´, peti)) a sweet butter biscuit.
early 20C. French little butter.

petit bourgeois (peti buə´zhwah) *n.* (*pl.* **petits bourgeois** (peti buə´zhwah)) a member of the lower middle classes.
19C. French, lit. little citizen. Cp. BOURGEOIS.

petite (pətēt´) *a.* **1** (of a woman) slight, dainty, graceful. **2** designed for a small woman.
16C. French, fem. of *petit* small.

petit four (peti faw´) *n.* (*pl.* **petits fours** (fawz´)) a small fancy cake or biscuit.
19C. French, lit. little oven.
● The confections were formerly baked in small ovens.

petitio principii (pətishiō prinsip´iī, pit-, -kip-) *n.* (*Logic*) begging the question.
16C. Latin assuming a principle, from *petitio* request + gen. of *principium* principle.

petit maître (pətimātr´, -mā´trə) *n.* a fop, a coxcomb.
18C. French, lit. little master.

petit mal (pəti mal´, peti) *n.* **1** a mild form of epilepsy. **2** a mild epileptic fit.
19C. French, lit. little sickness. Cp. GRAND MAL.

petit pain (pəti pī´, peti) *n.* (*pl.* **petits pains** (pəti pī´, peti)) a small bread roll.
18C. French, lit. little loaf.

petit point (pəti pwī´) *n.* **1** a fine kind of embroidery. **2** tent stitch.
19C. French, lit. little stitch. Cp. GROS POINT.

petits pois (pəti pwah´) *n.pl.* small, sweet green peas.
19C. French, lit. small peas.

petit suisse (pəti swēs´, peti) *n.* a type of small round cream cheese.
early 20C. French, lit. little Swiss.

pétroleur (pātrəlœ´) *n.* an arsonist who uses petroleum.
19C. French, from *pétrole* petroleum.

petuntse (pātŭnt´sə) *n.* (*Geol.*) a fusible substance similar to feldspar used for the manufacture of porcelain.
18C. Chinese *báidūnzǐ*, from *bái* white + *dūnzǐ* block of stone, mound of earth (from *dūn* block, heap + *zǐ* son).

pfennig (pfen´ig) *n.* (*pl.* **pfennigs**, **pfennige** (-igə)) a German unit of currency, worth one hundredth of a mark.
16C. German penny.

Pharaoh (feə´rō) *n.* any one of the ancient Egyptian kings.
12–14C. Ecclesiastical Latin *Pharao, Pharaonis*, from Greek *Pharaō*, from Hebrew *par ʻōh*, from Egyptian *pr-ʻo* great house.
● The English final *-h* is from Hebrew.

physique (fizēk´) *n.* the physical structure or constitution of a person.
19C. French, use as *n.* of *a.*, physical.

pi (pī) *n.* **1** the 16th letter of the Greek alphabet (Π, π). **2** the symbol representing the ratio of the circumference of a circle to the diameter, i.e. 3.14159265.
14–15C. Greek.
● In sense 2 the letter stands for Greek *periphereia* or English *periphery*. The mathematical symbol was adopted by the Swiss mathematician Leonhard Euler in his *Introductio in analysin infinitorum* (1748).

pianino (pēənē´nō) *n.* (*pl.* **pianinos**) a small piano.
19C. Italian, dim. of *piano* piano.

pianissimo (piənis´imō) *adv.* (*Mus.*) very softly. ~*a.* to be played very softly. ~*n.* (*pl.* **pianissimos**, **pianissimi** (-mi)) a passage to be played pianissimo.
18C. Italian, superl. of PIANO.
● As a musical direction the word is usually abbreviated to *pp*.

piano (pyah´nō) *adv.* **1** (*Mus.*) softly. **2** in a subdued manner. ~*a.* **1** (*Mus.*) to be played softly. **2** subdued. ~*n.* (*pl.* **pianos**, **piani** (-ni)) a passage to be played piano.

17C. Italian, from Latin *planus* flat, later (of sound) soft, low.
● As a musical directiond the word is usually abbreviated to *p*.

piano nobile (piahnō nō´bilā) *n.* (*Archit.*) the main floor of a large house.
19C. Italian, from *piano* floor, storey + *nobile* noble, great.

piano piano (pyahnō pyah´nō) *adv.* little by little, in a quiet and leisurely manner.
17C. Italian, lit. softly softly. See PIANO.

piassava (pēəsah´və) *n.* **1** a coarse stiff fibre obtained from Brazilian palms, used esp. to make ropes and brushes. **2** a Brazilian palm yielding piassava.
19C. Portuguese, from Tupi *piaçába*.

piastre (pias´tə), (*NAm.*) **piaster** *n.* **1** a small coin of Turkey and several former dependencies. **2** the Spanish dollar or silver peso.
16C. French, from Italian *piastra* (*d'argento*) plate (of silver), from Latin *emplastra, emplastrum* plaster.

piazza (piat´sə) *n.* (*pl.* **piazzas**) **1** a square open space, public square or market place, esp. in an Italian town. **2** any open space surrounded by buildings or colonnades. **3** (*NAm.*) the veranda of a house. **4** (*loosely*) a colonnade, or an arcaded or colonnaded walk.
16C. Italian, rel. to French *place* place. Cp. PLAZA.
● The sense was extended in the 17C to a covered gallery or walk around a square, as the Piazza, Covent Garden, London.

pibroch (pē´brokh) *n.* a series of variations, chiefly martial, played on the bagpipes.
18C. Gaelic *pìobaireachd* the art of playing the bagpipes, from *pìobair* piper (from *pìob* pipe, from English *pipe*) + *-achd*, suf. of function.

picador (pik´ədaw) *n.* in Spanish bullfights, a horseman with a lance who goads the bull.
18C. Spanish, from *picar* to prick, to pierce.

picaresque (pikəresk´) *a.* describing the exploits and adventures of rogues or vagabonds, of or relating to a style of fiction describing the episodic adventures of an errant rogue.
19C. French, from Spanish *picaresco*, from *pícaro* roguish, knavish.

piccolo (pik´əlō) *n.* (*pl.* **piccolos**) **1** a small flute, with the notes one octave higher than the ordinary flute. **2** a piccolo player.
19C. Italian small.

pice (pīs) *n.* (*pl.* **pice**) (*Hist.*) an Indian copper coin worth a quarter of an anna.
17C. Hindi *paisā.* Cp. PAISA.

pickelhaube (pik´əlhowbə) *n.* (*Hist.*) the spiked helmet of a German soldier.
19C. German, alt. (influ. by *Pickel* pickaxe) of Middle High German *beckelhūbe* from *becken* basin + *hūbe* cap.

picot (pē´kō) *n.* a small loop of thread forming part of an ornamental edging.
17C. French, dim. of *pic* peak, point, prick.

pie (pī) *n.* (*Hist.*) an Indian copper coin worth one-twelfth of an anna.
19C. Hindi *pāī*, from Sanskrit *pādikā*, from *pāda* quarter. Cp. PICE.

pièce de résistance (pyes də rezis´tās, rā-) *n.* (*pl.* **pièces de résistance** (pyes)) **1** an outstanding item. **2** the main dish of a meal.
18C. French, lit. piece of resistance (orig. the most substantial dish in a meal).

pied-à-terre (pyādəteə´) *n.* (*pl.* **pieds-à-terre** (pyādəteə´)) a flat or house for occasional use, e.g. a city apartment for a country dweller.
19C. French, lit. foot to earth.

pied noir (pyā nwah´) *n.* (*pl.* **pieds noirs** (pyā nwah´)) (*often derog.*) a person of European, esp. French, origin living in Algeria during French rule (1842–1962).
mid-20C. French, lit. black foot.
● The expression may have arisen on French steamers where Algerians traditionally worked barefoot as stokers.

pierrot (pyer´ō, piə´-) *n.* a buffoon or itinerant minstrel, orig. French and usu. dressed in loose white costume with the face whitened.
18C. French *Pierrot*, pet form of *Pierre* Peter.

pietà (piātah´, pyā-) *n.* a pictorial or sculptured representation of the Virgin Mary and the dead Christ.
17C. Italian, from Latin PIETAS.

pietas (pī´ətahs) *n.* respect due to an ancestor.
early 20C. Latin dutifulness, from *pius* pious, dutiful.

pietra dura (pietra du´ra) *n.* semi-precious stones.
19C. Italian, lit. hard stone.

piffero (pif´ərō) *n.* (*pl.* **pifferos**) a small flute like an oboe.
18C. Italian, rel. to Spanish *pifaro*, French *fifre*, English *fife*.

pilaf (pilaf´), **pilaff**, **pilau** (-low´), **pilaw** (-law´), **pillau** (-low´) *n.* a Middle Eastern or Indian mixed dish consisting of rice boiled with meat, poultry, or fish, together with raisins, spices etc.
17C. Turkish *pilâv* cooked rice.

Pilsner (pilz´nə, pils´-), **Pilsener** *n.* a
pale beer with a strong flavour of hops.
19C. German, from *Pilsen* (Czech *Plzeň*),
a province and city in Bohemia (now in
Czech Republic).

pimento (pimen´tō) *n.* (*pl.* **pimentos**)
1 a pimiento. **2** (*esp. W Ind.*) allspice.
17C. Spanish PIMIENTO.

pimiento (pimien´tō) *n.* (*pl.* **pimientos**)
a red pepper.
17C. Spanish, from Latin *pigmentum*
pigment, paint, unguent, (in Medieval
Latin) scented confection or drink.

piña (pē´nyə), **piña cloth**, **piña muslin**
n. a delicate cloth made in the
Philippines from the fibres of the
pineapple leaf.
16C. South American Spanish, rel. to
Portuguese *pinha* pineapple, (orig.) pine
cone, from Latin *pinea* pine cone.

pina colada (pēnə kəlah´də) *n.* a cocktail
made from rum, pineapple juice and
coconut juice.
early 20C. Anglicized form of **Spanish**
PIÑA + *colada* strained.

pince-nez (pīsnā´) *n.* (*pl.* **pince-nez**) a
pair of armless eyeglasses held in place
by a spring clipping the nose.
19C. French, from *pincer* to pinch + *nez*
nose.

pincette (pinset´, pīset´) *n.* a pair of
small tweezers or forceps.
16C. French, dim. of *pince* a pair of
pincers.

pindari (pindah´ri) *n.* (*pl.* **pindaris**) a
mounted marauder employed as an
irregular soldier by princes in central
India during the 17th and 18th cents.
18C. Marathi *pēḍhārā* marauding band,
Hindi *piṇḍārā*, Marathi *pēḍhārī*
marauder.

pineal (pin´iəl, pī´niəl) *a.* shaped like a
pine cone.
17C. French *pinéal*, from Latin *pinea*
pine cone.
● The pineal body is so called from its
shape in humans.

pinto (pin´tō) *a.* (*N Am.*) piebald. ~*n.* (*pl.*
pintos) a horse or pony with patches of
white and another colour.
19C. Spanish painted, mottled.

pinxit (pingk´sit) *v.i.* (he or she) painted it
(in the signature to a picture).
19C. Latin (he) painted, 3rd pers. sing.
perf. indic. of *pingere* to paint.

Pinyin (pinyin´) *n.* a system of romanized
spelling used to transliterate Chinese
characters.
mid-20C. Chinese *pīnyīn* transcription,
from *pīn* to put together + *yīn* sound.

piolet (pyōlā´) *n.* a climber's ice axe.
19C. French (Savoy dial.), dim. of *piolo*,
appar. rel. to French *pioche*, *pic* pick,
pickaxe.

pipette (pipet´) *n.* a fine tube for
removing quantities of a fluid, esp. in
chemical investigations. ~*v.t.* to transfer
or measure with a pipette.
19C. French, dim. of *pipe* pipe.

piquant (pē´kənt) *a.* **1** having an
agreeably pungent taste. **2** stimulating,
lively.
16C. French, pres.p. of *piquer*. See
PIQUE¹.

pique¹ (pēk) *v.t.* (*pres.p.* **piquing**, *past*,
p.p. **piqued**) **1** to irritate. **2** to touch the
envy, jealousy or pride of. **3** to stimulate
or excite (curiosity etc.). **4** to plume or
congratulate (oneself on). ~*n.* ill feeling,
resentment.
16C. French *piquer* to prick, to pierce, to
sting, to irritate.

pique² (pēk) *n.* in the game of piquet, the scoring of 30 points before one's opponent begins to count, entitling one to 30 more points. ~*v.t.* (*pres.p.* **piquing**, *past, p.p.* **piqued**) to score a pique against. ~*v.i.* to score a pique. **17C. French** *pic*, from Old French stabbing blow.

piqué (pē´kā) *n.* a heavy cotton fabric with a corded surface, quilting. **19C. French**, use as n. of p.p. of *piquer* to backstitch, PIQUE¹.

piquet (piket´) *n.* a game of cards for two persons, with a pack of cards from which all below the seven have been withdrawn. **17C. French**, of unknown orig.

piragua (pirag´wə) *n.* (*pl.* **piraguas**) a pirogue. **17C. Spanish**, from Carib dug out. Cp. PIROGUE.

pirogue (pirōg´) *n.* **1** a large canoe made from a hollowed trunk of a tree. **2** a large, flat-bottomed boat or barge for shallow water, usu. with two masts rigged fore-and-aft. **17C. French**, prob. from Carib. Cp. PIRAGUA.

piroshki (pirosh´ki) *n.pl.* small Russian pastries or patties filled with meat, fish, rice etc. **early 20C. Russian** *pirozhki*, pl. of *pirozhok*, dim. of *pirog* pie, prob. from *pir* feast.

pirouette (piruet´) *n.* a rapid whirling round on the point of one foot, in dancing. ~*v.i.* to dance or perform a pirouette. **17C. French**, of unknown orig. ? Influ. by *rouet*, dim. of *roue* wheel.

pis aller (pēz al´ā) *n.* a makeshift, a last resort. **17C. French**, from *pis* worse + *aller* to go.

Pisces (pī´sēz) *n.* (*pl.* **Pisces**) **1** (*Astron.*) a large constellation resembling two fishes joined by their tails. **2** (*Astrol.*) **a** the Fishes, the twelfth sign of the zodiac. **b** a person born under the sign of Pisces. **pre-1200. Latin**, pl. of *piscis* fish.

piscina (pisē´nə) *n.* (*pl.* **piscinae** (-nē), **piscinas**) **1** a stone basin with outlet beside the altar in some churches to receive the water used in purifying the chalice etc. **2** a fish pond. **3** (*Hist.*) a Roman bathing pond. **16C. Latin** fish pond, from *piscis* fish. ● The original sense was sense 2. Sense 1 dates from the 18C.

pisé (pē´zā) *n.* rammed clay forming a wall. **18C. French**, use as n. of p.p. of *piser* to beat, to pound (earth), from Latin *pinsare*.

pissaladière (pisaladyeə´) *n.* a Provençal open tart similar to a pizza. **mid-20C. French**, from Provençal *pissaladiero*, from *pissala* salt fish, from Latin *piscis* fish + *sal* salt.

pissoir (pēs´wah, pis´-, -wah´) *n.* a public urinal. **early 20C. French**, from *pisser* to urinate.

pistachio (pistah´shiō) *n.* **1** an Asian tree, *Pistacia vera*, having a reddish fruit with an edible pale greenish kernel. **2** (*also* **pistachio nut**) the edible pale greenish kernel of the fruit of the pistachio. **3** the flavour of the pistachio nut. **4** a pale green colour. **14–15C. Old French** *pistace* (Modern French *pistache*), superseded by forms from Italian *pistaccio*, both from Latin *pistacium*, from Greek *pistakion*, *pistakē*.

piste (pēst) *n.* **1** a slope prepared for skiing. **2** a rectangular area on which a fencing contest is held.

18C. French track, from Latin *pista* (*via*) beaten (track), from fem. p.p. of *pinsere* to pound, to stamp.

pistole (pistōl´) *n.* (*Hist.*) a foreign gold coin, esp. a 16th–17th cent. Spanish coin.
16C. French, shortening of *pistolet*, of unknown orig.

pithos (pith´os) *n.* (*pl.* **pithoi** (pith´oi)) in archaeology, a large storage jar.
19C. Greek.

piton (pē´ton) *n.* a bar, staff or stanchion used for fixing ropes on precipitous mountainsides etc.
19C. French eye bolt, of unknown orig.

pitta (pit´ə), **pita** *n.* a flat, round, slightly leavened bread, hollow inside so that it can be filled with food.
mid-20C. Modern Greek *pētta*, *pitta* bread, cake, pie.

più (pū) *adv.* (*Mus.*) more.
18C. Italian more, from Latin PLUS.

più mosso (pū mos´ō) *adv.* (*Mus.*) more animatedly.
18C. Italian, from PIÙ + MOSSO. Cp. MENO MOSSO.

pizza (pēt´sə) *n.* (*pl.* **pizzas**) a flat, round piece of baked dough covered with cheese and tomatoes, and also often with anchovies, mushrooms, slices of sausage etc.
19C. Italian pie.

pizzicato (pitsikah´tō) *a.* (*Mus.*) played by plucking the strings of a violin etc. with the fingers. ~*adv.* in this manner. ~*n.* (*pl.* **pizzicatos**, **pizzicati** (-ti)) a passage or work so played.
19C. Italian, p.p. of *pizzicare* to pinch, to twitch, from *pizzare*, from *pizza* point, edge.

placebo (pləsē´bō) *n.* (*pl.* **placebos**)
1 a medicine having no physiological

action, given to humour the patient, to provide psychological comfort or as a control during experiments to test the efficacy of a genuine medicine. **2** something said or done to placate someone without addressing the cause of their anxiety. **3** in the Roman Catholic Church, the first antiphon in the vespers for the dead.
12–14C. Latin I shall please, I shall be acceptable, 1st pers. sing. fut. indic. of *placere* to please.
● The Latin word is the first word of the first antiphon in the Latin rite of Vespers of the Office of the Dead: *Placebo Domino in regione vivorum* (Ps. cxiv.9) I will walk before the Lord in the land of the living (AV) (Ps. cxvi.9).

placer (plā´sə) *n.* **1** an alluvial or other deposit containing valuable minerals. **2** a place where deposits are washed for minerals. **3** any mineral deposit not classed as a vein.
19C. American Spanish deposit, shoal, rel. to *placel* sandbank, from *plaza* place.

placet (plā´set) *n.* permission, assent, sanction.
16C. Latin it pleases, 3rd pers. sing. pres. ind. of *placere* to please.

†placitum (plas´itəm) *n.* (*pl.* **placita** (-tə)) a decree, judgement or decision, esp. in a court of justice or a state assembly.
17C. Latin, neut. p.p. of *placere* to please, (Medieval Latin) court sentence, trial, plea.

plafond (plaf´ō) *n.* **1** a ceiling, esp. one of a richly decorated kind. **2** a painting on a ceiling. **3** an early form of contract bridge.
17C. French ceiling, from *plat* flat + *fond* bottom.
● As its source suggests, the original meaning of the French word was floor.

plage (plahzh) *n*. **1** (*Astron.*) a light or dark spot on a spectroheliogram, associated with hot or cool gas on the earth's surface. **2** a beach, a shore at a seaside resort.
14–15C. Old French region (Modern French beach), from Medieval Latin *plaga* open space.
● The original sense (to the 17C) was region, district. Sense 2 arose in the 19C, and sense 1 in the mid-20C, the latter with reference to a region usually associated with sunspots (as on a beach).

planchette (plahnshet´) *n*. a small, usu. heart-shaped, board resting on two castors, and a pencil which makes marks as the board moves under the hands of the person resting upon it (believed by spiritualists to be a mode of communicating with the unseen world).
19C. French, dim. of *planche* board.

plaque (plahk) *n*. **1** a plate, slab or tablet of metal, porcelain, ivory etc., usu. of an artistic or ornamental character. **2** a filmy deposit on the surface of the teeth consisting of mucus and bacteria. **3** (*Med.*) a patch or spot on the surface of the body. **4** a small plate worn as a badge or personal ornament.
19C. French, from Dutch *plak* tablet, from *plakken* to stick.

plastique (plastēk´) *n*. **1** the art of statuesque poses or slow graceful movements in dance. **2** a plastic substance used for modelling. **3** plastic explosive.
19C. French plastic, from Latin *plasticus.*
● Sense 2 arose in the early 20C and sense 3 in the mid-20C.

plat du jour (plah doo zhuə´) *n*. (*pl.* **plats du jour** (plah)) the dish of the day on the menu of a restaurant etc.
early 20C. French dish of the day, from *plat* dish + *du* of the + *jour* day.

plateau (plat´ō) *n*. (*pl.* **plateaux** (-ōz), **plateaus**) **1** a tableland, an elevated plain. **2** a period of stability after or during an upward progression, a levelling-off. **3** a large ornamental centre dish. **4** an ornamental plaque. **5** a woman's flat-topped hat. ~*v.i.* (*3rd pers. sing. pres.* **plateaus**, *pres.p.* **plateauing**, *past, p.p.* **plateaued**) to level off after an upward progression.
18C. French, from Old French *platel*, from *plat* flat.

plateresque (platəresk´) *a*. (*Archit.*) in a richly ornamented style resembling silverware.
19C. Spanish *plateresco*, from *platero* silversmith, from *plata* silver.

platteland (plat´əland) *n*. (*S Afr.*) rural areas.
mid-20C. Afrikaans, from Dutch *plat* flat + *land* country.

playa (plī´ə) *n*. (*pl.* **playas**) a dried-up lake in a desert basin.
19C. Spanish shore, beach, coast, from Late Latin *plagia*. See PLAGE.

plaza (plah´zə) *n*. (*pl.* **plazas**) **1** a public square or open paved area. **2** (*esp. N Am.*) a shopping mall.
17C. Spanish, from Latin *platea* courtyard, broad street.

plectrum (plek´trəm) *n*. (*pl.* **plectrums**, **plectra** (-trə)) a small implement of ivory etc., with which players pluck the strings of the guitar, harp, lyre etc.
14–15C. Latin, from Greek *plēktron* thing to strike with, from *plēssein* to strike.

pleidiol wyf i'm gwlad (plādyol ooiv ēm glahd´) *int.* loyal am I to my country.
late 20C. Welsh.
● The words are from the Welsh national anthem *Hen Wlad Fy Nhadau* Land of my Fathers, thought to have been written in 1856 by Evan James, a

weaver from Mid Glamorgan. The song was adopted as the national anthem in the late 19C. The phrase was also inscribed round the milled edge of a Welsh one-pound coin from 1985.

plein-air (plenee´) *a.* (done) out of doors, esp. in relation to the principles and practice of the Impressionist school of painting.
19C. Shortening of **French** *en plein air* in the open air (lit. in full air).

plethora (pleth´ərə) *n.* **1** superabundance, excess. **2** (*Med.*) **a** excessive fullness of blood. **b** an excess of any body fluid.
16C. Late Latin, from Greek *plēthōrē* fullness, reputation, from *plēthein* to be full.

plié (plē´ā) *n.* (*pl.* **pliés**) a ballet movement in which the knees are bent outwards while the back remains straight.
19C. French, p.p. of *plier* to bend.

plissé (plē´sā) *a.* (of a fabric) having a wrinkled finish. ~*n.* (a fabric having) a wrinkled finish.
19C. French, p.p. of *plisser* to pleat.

plombière (plombieə´) *n.* a type of dessert made with ice cream and glacé fruits.
19C. French, from *Plombières*-les-Bains, a resort in E France.

plongeur (plŏzhœ´) *n.* (*pl.* **plongeurs** (plŏzhœ´)) a person employed to wash dishes in a restaurant or hotel.
mid-20C. French, from *plonger* to plunge, to immerse in liquid.

plus (plŭs) *prep.* **1** (*Math.*) with the addition of. **2** (of temperature) above zero. **3** (*coll.*) having gained. ~*a.* **1** at least (after a number). **2** better than (after an exam grade). **3** (*Math.*) above zero, positive. **4** electrified positively. **5** additional, extra, esp. additional

and advantageous. ~*n.* **1** a plus sign. **2** an addition, a positive quantity. **3** an advantage, a positive feature. **4** a surplus. ~*conj.* (*coll.*) and in addition, and what is more.
16C. Latin more.

plus ça change (plü sa shāzh´) *int.* used to express the view that superficial changes cannot alter the essential nature of something, esp. human nature.
early 20C. French, in full *plus ça change, plus c'est la même chose* the more it changes, the more it stays the same.
● The expression is first recorded in the words of the French journalist Alphonse Karr in his satirical paper *Les Guêpes*: *On change quelquefois le prix, quelquefois le bouchon, mais c'est toujours la même piquette qu'on nous fait boire.* — *Plus ça change* — *plus c'est la même chose.* They sometimes change the price, sometimes the cork, but it's always the same plonk we're given to drink. The more they change it, the more it stays the same (1849).

p.m. *adv.* in the afternoon or evening. Abbr. of **Latin** *post meridiem* after midday, from *post* after + acc. of *meridies* noon, midday. Cp. A.M.
● The Latin phrase dates from the 17C.

pneuma (nū´mə) *n.* breath, spirit, soul.
14–15C. Greek wind, breath, spirit, that which is blown or breathed, from *pneein, pnein* to blow, to breathe.

pochette (poshet´) *n.* a small handbag shaped like an envelope.
19C. French, dim. of *poche* pocket.

poco (pō´kō) *adv.* (*Mus.*) a little.
18C. Italian (a) little, from Popular Latin *paucum*, neut. of Latin *paucus* few.

pococurante (pōkōkūran´ti) *n.* a careless or apathetic person. ~*a.* indifferent.
18C. Italian, from *poco* little + *curante* caring.

podestà (podes'tə, -stah´) *n.* a subordinate municipal judge in an Italian city.
16C. **Italian**, from Latin *potestas*, *potestatis*, power, authority, magistrate.

podium (pō´diəm) *n.* (*pl.* **podiums**, **podia** (-diə)) 1 a low projecting wall or basement supporting a building etc. 2 a platform encircling the arena in an amphitheatre. 3 a continuous structural bench round a hall etc. 4 a small raised platform (for a conductor, lecturer etc.).
18C. **Latin** elevated place, balcony, from Greek *podion*, dim. of *pous*, *podos* foot.

podzol (pod´zol), **podsol** (-sol) *n.* an infertile soil, with a greyish-white upper layer, like ash, and a brown subsoil.
early 20C. **Russian**, from *pod-* under + *zola* ash.
● The variant form has been influenced by Latin *solum* soil.

pogrom (pog´rəm, pəgrom´) *n.* an organized attack, usu. with pillage and massacre, upon a class of the population, esp. Jews.
early 20C. **Russian** devastation, from *gromit'* to destroy by violent means, rel. to *grom* thunder.

poi (pō´ē) *n.* a Hawaiian dish made of a paste of fermented taro root.
19C. **Polynesian**.

poilu (pwa´lü) *n.* (*pl.* **poilus** (-lü)) (*Hist.*, *coll.*) a French private soldier.
early 20C. **French** hairy, virile, from *poil* hair, from Latin *pilus*.

point d'appui (pwī dapwē´) *n.* 1 a fulcrum. 2 a strategic point.
19C. **French** point of support.
● The phrase typically has a military application.

pointe (pwīt) *n.* (*pl.* **pointes** (pwīt)) 1 (in ballet) the extreme tip of the toe. 2 a position in which the dancer balances on this.
19C. **French** point.

pointillism (pwī´tilizm) *n.* (in painting) delineation by means of dots of various pure colours which merge into a whole in the viewer's eye.
early 20C. **French** *pointillisme*, from *pointiller* to mark with dots, from *pointille*, from Italian *puntiglio*, dim. of *punto* point.

polder (pōl´də) *n.* a tract of land below sea or river level, that has been drained and cultivated, esp. in the Netherlands.
17C. **Dutch**, from Middle Dutch *polre*.

polenta (pəlen´tə) *n.* a kind of porridge made of maize meal, or less commonly from barley or chestnut meal, a common food in Italy.
pre-1200. **Latin** (later directly from Italian, from Latin) pearl barley.

polis (pol´is) *n.* (*pl.* **poleis** (-īs)) a Greek city state.
19C. **Greek** city.

politburo (pol´itbūrō) *n.* (*pl.* **politburos**) the political bureau of the Central Committee of the Communist Party of the former Soviet Union.
early 20C. **Russian** *politbyuro*, from *politicheskiĭ* political + *byuro* bureau.

politesse (polites´) *n.* formal politeness.
18C. **French**, from Italian *pulitezza*, from *pulito* clean, neat, polished.

politico (pəlit´ikō) *n.* (*pl.* **politicos**, **politicoes**) (*coll.*) a politician.
17C. **Italian** *politico*, Spanish *político* politic, politician.

politique (politēk´) *n.* a political concept or doctrine.
mid-20C. **French**, use as n. of a. *politique* political.

polka (pōl´kə, pol´-)` n. (pl. **polkas**) **1** a
lively round dance of Bohemian origin.
2 a piece of music in duple time for
this. **3** (*Hist.*) a woman's tight-fitting
jacket, usu. made of knitted wool. ~*v.i.*
(*3rd pers. sing. pres.* **polkas**, *pres.p.*
polkaing, *past, p.p.* **polkaed**, **polka'd**)
to dance a polka.
19C. German and French, from Czech,
? rel. to *Polka*, fem. of *Polák* Pole.
● It is possible that Czech *polka* is an
alteration of *pŭlka* half, referring to the
half steps of the original Bohemian
peasant dance.

polo (pō´lō) *n.* (*pl.* **polos**) a game of Asian
origin resembling hockey but played on
horseback.
19C. Balti ball.
● The game came to England from
India.

polonaise (polənāz´) *n.* **1** a slow dance of
Polish origin. **2** a piece of music in 3/4
time for this. **3** (*Hist.*) an article of dress
for women, consisting of a bodice and
short skirt in one piece. **4** a similar
garment for men worn in the early 19th
cent. ~*a.* cooked in a Polish style.
18C. French, use as n. of fem. of
polonais Polish, from Medieval Latin
Polonia Poland.

poltergeist (pōl´təgīst, pol´-) *n.* an
alleged spirit which makes its presence
known by noises and moving objects.
19C. German, from *poltern* to make a
noise, to create a disturbance + *Geist*
ghost.
● The word was popularized in English
by spiritualists.

polynya (pəlin´iə), **polynia** *n.* an open
place in water that is for the most part
frozen over, esp. in the Arctic.
19C. Russian, from base of *pole*,
polyana field.

pompadour (pom´pəduə) *n., a.* (*Hist.*) a
method of wearing the hair brushed up
from the forehead or (in women) turned
back in a roll from the forehead.
18C. French, from Jeanne-Antoinette
Poisson, marquise de *Pompadour*
(1721–64), mistress of Louis XV of
France.
● Pompadour is a location in the
Limousin region of S central France.

pompon (pom´pon), **pompom** (-pom)
n. **1** an ornament in the form of a tuft
or ball of feathers, ribbon etc., worn on
women's and children's hats, shoes etc.,
on the front of a soldier's shako, on a
French sailor's cap etc. **2** a small
compact chrysanthemum or dahlia.
18C. French, of unknown orig. ? From
Old French *pompe* pomp.

poncho (pon´chō) *n.* (*pl.* **ponchos**) **1** a
woollen cloak, worn in South America,
with a slit in the middle through which
the head passes. **2** a cycling cape of this
pattern.
18C. South American Spanish, from
Araucanian.

pone (pōn, pō´ni) *n.* **1** the player to the
dealer's right who cuts the cards. **2** in a
two-handed card game, the non-dealer.
19C. Latin, imper. sing. of *ponere* to
place.

pongal (pong´gəl) *n.* **1** the Tamil festival
celebrating New Year, in which new rice
is cooked. **2** a dish of cooked rice.
18C. Tamil *poṅkal*, lit. swelling,
boiling.

pongee (pŭnjē´, pon-) *n.* **1** a soft
unbleached kind of Chinese silk. **2** a
fine cotton fabric resembling this.
18C. Chinese *běnjī*, lit. own loom, or
běnzhì, lit. home-woven.

pons asinorum (ponz asinaw´rəm) *n.*
any severe test for a beginner.

18C. Latin bridge of asses, from *pons* bridge + gen. pl. of *asinus* ass.

• The allusion is to the fifth proposition of the first book of Euclid's *Elements of Geometry* (*c*.300 BC), notoriously difficult for beginners ('asses') to understand or 'get over'. The proposition is in fact quite simple — that the base angles of an isosceles triangle are equal.

pont (pont) *n.* (*S Afr.*) a small ferry boat, esp. one guided across a river by a cable.

17C. Dutch, from Middle Dutch *ponte*.

pood (pood) *n.* a Russian unit of weight of about 36 pounds (16 kilograms).

16C. Russian *pud*, from Low German or Old Norse *pund* pound.

poppadom (pop´ədəm), **poppadum**, **popadum**, **popadam**, **popadom** *n.* a crisp, thin Indian bread, spiced and fried or roasted, often served with chutneys.

19C. Tamil *pappaṭam*, ? from *paruppa aṭam* lentil cake.

portamento (pawtəmen´tō) *n.* (*pl.* **portamentos**, **portamenti** (-tē)) (*esp. Mus.*) 1 a smooth, continuous glide from one note to another across intervening tones. 2 a style of piano playing between legato and staccato.

18C. Italian, lit. a carrying, from *portare* to carry.

Porte (pawt) *n.* (*Hist.*) the old Imperial Turkish Government in Constantinople; also *Sublime Porte*, *Ottoman Porte*.

17C. French (*la Sublime*) *Porte* (the exalted) gate, translating Turkish Arabic *bāb i-āli* high gate, eminent gate, official title of the central office of the Ottoman government.

porte cochère (pawt kosheə´) *n.* 1 a carriage entrance leading into a courtyard. 2 (*esp. N Am.*) a roof extending from the entrance of a building over a drive to shelter people entering or alighting from vehicles.

18C. French, from *porte* port + *cochère*, fem. a. from *coche* coach.

portfolio (pawtfō´liō) *n.* (*pl.* **portfolios**) 1 a portable case for holding papers, drawings etc. 2 a collection of such papers, esp. samples of recent work etc. 3 the office and duties of a minister of state. 4 the investments made, or securities held, by an investor.

18C. Italian *portafogli*, from *porta*, imper. of *portare* to carry + *fogli* leaves, sheets of paper, pl. of *foglio*, from Latin *folium* leaf.

portico (paw´tikō) *n.* (*pl.* **porticoes**, **porticos**) 1 a colonnade, a roof supported by columns. 2 a porch with columns.

17C. Italian, from Latin *porticus* porch.

portière (pawtyeə´) *n.* 1 a door-curtain. 2 a woman porter, a concierge.

19C. French, from *porte* door.

portmanteau (pawtman´tō) *n.* (*pl.* **portmanteaus**, **portmanteaux** (-tōz)) a travelling bag which opens out flat, for carrying clothes. ~*a.* combining several uses or qualities.

16C. French *portemanteau*, from *porte-*, stem of *porter* to carry + *manteau* coat.

portolan (paw´tələn), **portolano** (pawtəlah´nō) *n.* (*pl.* **portolans**, **portolanos**) (*Hist.*) a sailing manual containing charts, descriptions of ports, coastlines etc.

18C. Italian *portolano*, from *porto* harbour.

Port Salut (paw səloo´) *n.* a type of mild cheese, made in a round flat shape.

19C. *Port Salut*, a Trappist monastery in NW France.

• The monastery name (properly *Port-du-Salut*) means haven of salvation.

posada (pəsah´də) *n.* (*pl.* **posadas**) an inn, in a Spanish-speaking country.
18C. **Spanish**, from *posar* to lodge.

posaune (pōzow´nə) *n.* a rich and powerful reed-stop in an organ.
18C. **German** trombone, ult. from Old French *buisine*, from Latin *buccina* trumpet.

poseur (pōzœ´) *n.* an affected person.
19C. **French**, from *poser* to pose.

posse (pos´i) *n.* **1** a body or force (of persons). **2** (*N Am.*) a group of men called on by a sheriff to help with law enforcement. **3** a posse comitatus. **4** (*sl.*) a criminal gang. **5** (*sl.*) a group of people from the same area, or sharing a background or interest. **6** (*Law*) possibility.
17C. Abbr. of **Medieval Latin** *posse comitatus* force of the county.
• The word was originally the term for the body of men in a county who could be summoned by the sheriff to repress a riot or for some other purpose (sense 3).

poste restante (pōst res´tont) *n.* **1** a department in a post office where letters are kept until called for. **2** an address on a letter to a poste restante department.
18C. **French** post remaining.
• The term was originally a direction written on a letter indicating that it was to remain at a particular post office until called for. The name passed to the department itself in the 19C.

post hoc (pōst hok´) *n.* (*Logic*) the fallacy of assuming that if something happened after something else, it must have happened because of it.
19C. **Latin** after this.
• The full form of the Latin term is *post hoc, ergo propter hoc* after this, therefore because of this.

postiche (postēsh´) *n.* **1** a hairpiece. **2** an imitation, a sham. ~*a.* artificial, superadded (of superfluous ornament).
18C. **French**, from Italian *posticcio* counterfeit, feigned.

post-mortem (pōstmaw´təm) *adv.* after death. ~*a.* made or occurring after death. ~*n.* **1** an examination of a dead body to determine the cause of death. **2** an analysis or review after a game etc., esp. after defeat or failure.
18C. **Latin** after death.

post-obit (pōstō´bit, -ob´it) *a.* taking effect after death; post-mortem. ~*n.* a bond securing payment of a sum of money to a lender on the death of a specified person from whose estate the borrower has expectations.
18C. Abbr. of **Latin** *post obitum* after decease.

post-partum (pōstpah´təm) *a.* of or relating to the period immediately after childbirth.
19C. **Latin** after childbirth.

potage (potahzh´) *n.* thick soup.
12–14C. Orig. from **Old French**, lit. that which is put in a pot, from *pot* pot, later (17C) readopted from French.
• The Old French word also gave English *pottage* and (as an alteration of this) *porridge*.

potager (pot´əjə) *n.* a vegetable garden.
17C. **French** (*jardin*) *potager* (garden) for the kitchen.
• The literal sense of the French word, dating from the 14C, is 'one who cooks potage'. The present English sense was introduced by the diarist John Evelyn (1620–1706).

pot-au-feu (potōfœ´) *n.* (*pl.* **pot-au-feu**) **1** a traditional French stew of beef and vegetables. **2** the type of pot used for this stew. **3** the broth from this stew.
18C. **French**, lit. pot on the fire.

potiche (potēsh´) *n.* a kind of oriental pot or vase, round or polygonal, narrowing towards the top and with a detachable lid.
19C. **French**, deriv. of *pot* pot.

pot-pourri (pōpərē´, pōpoo´ri) *n.* (*pl.* **pot-pourris**) 1 a mixture of dried flower petals and spices, usu. kept in a bowl for perfuming a room. 2 a literary miscellany, a musical medley etc.
17C. **French**, lit. rotten pot, from *pot* pot + *pourri*, p.p. of *pourrir* to rot, translating Spanish OLLA PODRIDA.
● The word was originally used for a stew made of different kinds of meat. The current sense dates from the 18C.

potrero (potreə´rō) *n.* (*pl.* **potreros**) 1 (*N Am., S Am.*) a paddock or pasture for horses etc. 2 (*N Am.*) a steep-sided, narrow plateau.
19C. **Spanish**, from *potro* colt, pony.

pouf (poof), **pouffe** *n.* 1 a large solid cushion used as a seat or footstool. 2 a part of a woman's dress gathered into a kind of knot or bunch. 3 a mode of dressing women's hair fashionable in the 18th cent.
19C. **French**, ult. imit.

pourboire (puəbwah´) *n.* a gratuity, a tip.
19C. **French**, lit. for drinking, from *pour* for + *boire* to drink. Cp. German *Trinkgeld*.

pour encourager les autres (puər ākuərazhā lāz ō´trə) *adv.* as an example to others.
19C. **French**, lit. to encourage the others.
● The phrase was first used by Voltaire in *Candide* (1759), in reference to the execution two years earlier of Admiral John Byng for neglect of duty in failing to relieve Minorca: *Dans ce pays-ci il est bon de tuer de temps en temps un amiral pour encourager les autres* In this country [England] it is thought a good idea to kill an admiral from time to time to encourage the others.

pour-parler (puəpah´lā) *n.* a preliminary discussion with a view to formal negotiation.
18C. **French**, use as n. of Old French *porparler*, from *por-*, from Latin *pro* before, + *parler* to speak.

pousse-café (pooskafā´) *n.* (*pl.* **pousse-cafés** (-kafā´)) a glass of liqueurs or cordials poured in successive layers and taken straight after coffee.
19C. **French**, lit. push-coffee.

poussette (pooset´) *v.i.* (of partners in a country dance) to move up or down the set with hands joined. ~*n.* this figure.
19C. **French**, dim. of *pousse* push.

poussin (poo´sī) *n.* a young chicken reared for eating.
mid-20C. **French** chick, from Popular Latin *pullicinus*, dim. of Latin *pullus* chicken.

pozzolana (potsōlah´nə), **pozzuolana** (-swō-), **puzzolana** (puts-) *n.* a volcanic ash used in hydraulic cements.
18C. **Italian** *pozzuolana* (*terra*) (earth) belonging to Pozzuoli, a town near Naples, where the ash is found.

pp *adv.* by proxy.
Abbr. of **Latin** *per procurationem*.
● The abbreviation is used to indicate that a letter has been signed by someone other than the writer and as such is popularly understood to mean 'on behalf of'. The Latin expression dates from the 19C.

PPC *adv.* to bid farewell.
Abbr. of **French** *pour prendre congé*, lit. to take leave.
● The abbreviation was formerly written on a card left on the occasion of a farewell visit and is now sometimes put on an invitation to a farewell party. The French phrase dates from the 19C.

practicum (prak´tikəm) *n.* a practical section of a course of study.
early 20C. Late Latin, neut. (used as n.) of *practicus* practical.
• The term is mainly used in the US.

praecipe (prē´sipē) *n.* **1** a writ requiring something to be done, or a reason for its non-performance. **2** an order requesting a writ.
14–15C. Latin, imper. of *praecipere* to enjoin.

praemunire (prēmūnī´ri, -niə´-),
premunire *n.* (*Hist.*) **1** a writ or process against a person charged with obeying or maintaining the papal authority in England. **2** an offence against the Statute of Praemunire (1393) on which this is based. **3** the penalty incurred by it.
14–15C. Latin to fortify or protect in front.
• In Medieval Latin the word was confused with and used instead of *praemonere* to forewarn, to admonish. The words in the 1393 writ were: *precipimus quod per bonos et legales homines de balliua tua premunire facias prefatum propositum [A.B.] quod tunc sit coram nobis* We command that through good and loyal men of thy jurisdiction thou do [or cause to] warn the aforesaid [A.B.] that he appear before us.

praline (prah´lēn) *n.* a confection of almond or other nut with a brown coating of sugar.
18C. French, from Marshal de Plessis-*Praslin* (1598–1675), French general, whose cook invented it.

pralltriller (prahl´trilə) *n.* (*Mus.*) an ornament in which a note is preceded by itself and the note immediately above it, an inverted mordent.
19C. German, from *prallen* to bounce + *Triller* trill.

prana (prah´nə) *n.* **1** in Hinduism, the breath of life. **2** breath, breathing.
19C. Sanskrit *prāṇa*.

pratique (prat´ēk, -ēk´) *n.* a licence to a ship to hold communication with a port after quarantine, or upon certification that the vessel has not come from an infected place.
17C. French practice, intercourse, corr. to (or from) Italian *pratica*, from Medieval Latin *practica*, use as n. of fem. of *practicus*, from Greek *praktikos*, from *prattein* to do.

praxis (prak´sis) *n.* (*pl.* **praxises**, **praxes** (-ēz)) **1** use, practice, accepted practice. **2** the practice of an art; the practical as distinct from the theoretical side. **3** (*Gram.*) a collection of examples for practice.
16C. Medieval Latin, from Greek, from *prattein* to do.

précieux (presyœ´), (*fem.*) **précieuse** (-œz´) *a.* over-refined, affectedly fastidious. *n.* a person affecting over-refinement.
18C. French precious.
• The use of the word in English was influenced by Molière's play *Les Précieuses ridicules* (1659) satirizing the circle of people surrounding Mme de Rambouillet (1588–1665).

précis (prā´sē) *n.* (*pl.* **précis** (-sēz)) **1** an abstract, a summary. **2** the act or practice of drawing up abstracts. ~*v.t.* (*3rd pers. sing. pres.* **précises** (prā´sēz), *pres.p.* **précising** (prā´sēing), *past, p.p.* **précised** (prā´sēd)) to make a précis of.
18C. French, use as n. of *précis* precise.

predella (pridel´ə) *n.* (*pl.* **predelle** (-lā)) **1** the platform on which an altar stands or the highest of a series of altar steps. **2** a painting on the face of this. **3** a painting on a steplike or shelflike

appendage, usu. at the back of the altar, at the foot of an altarpiece, a gradine.
19C. Italian bench, of Germanic orig. Cp. German *Brett* board, plank.

predikant (pred´ikənt, -kant) *n.* a minister of the Dutch Reformed Church, esp. in South Africa.
19C. Dutch predicant.

premier cru (prəmyā krü´, premiə kroo´) *n.* (*pl.* **premiers crus** (prəmyā krü´), **premier crus** (premiə krooz)) a wine of the best quality.
19C. French, lit. first growth. Cp. GRAND CRU.

premiere (prem´ieə, -iə), **première** *n.* a first performance of a play or film. ~*v.t.* to give a first performance of (a play or film). ~*v.i.* (of a play or film) to have its first performance.
19C. French *première*, fem. of *premier* first.

première danseuse (prəmyeə dāsœz´) *n.* (*pl.* **premières danseuses** (prəmyeə dāsœz´)) a leading female dancer in a ballet company.
19C. French, fem. of *premier danseur*, lit. first (male) dancer.
● The French masculine equivalent is also used in English.

presidio (prisid´iō) *n.* (*pl.* **presidios**) **1** a fort or fortified settlement, in areas under Spanish control. **2** a Spanish penal colony.
18C. Spanish, from Latin *praesidium* garrison, fort, from *praesidere* to protect.

presidium (prisid´iəm), **praesidium** *n.* (*pl.* **presidiums**, **presidia** (-diə), **praesidiums**, **praesidia** (-diə)) a permanent executive committee in a Communist country.
early 20C. Russian *prezidium*, from Latin *praesidium*. See PRESIDIO.

prestissimo (prestis´imō) *adv.* (*Mus.*) very fast indeed. ~*a.* very fast. ~*n.* (*pl.* **prestissimos**) a very fast movement or passage.
18C. Italian, superl. of PRESTO.

presto (pres´tō) *adv.* (*Mus.*) quickly. ~*a.* quick. ~*n.* (*pl.* **prestos**) a quick movement or passage. ~*int.* (*also* **hey presto**) immediately (to indicate the speed with which e.g. a conjuring trick is done).
16C. Italian quick, quickly, from Late Latin *praestus* ready, from Latin *praesto* at hand.

prêt-à-porter (pretapaw´tā) *a.* (of clothes) ready-to-wear. ~*n.* (a collection of) such clothes.
mid-20C. French ready to wear, from *prêt* ready + *à* to + *porter* to wear.

pretzel (pret´səl) *n.* a crisp biscuit of wheaten flour flavoured with salt, usu. in the shape of a stick or a knot.
19C. German, from Old High German *brezitella*, from Medieval Latin *brachitellum*, dim. of Latin *bracchiatus* having branches, from *bracchium* arm.
● The biscuit was probably so called from its resemblance to a pair of folded arms.

prie-dieu (prēdyœ´) *n.* (*pl.* **prie-dieux** (-dyœ´)) a kneeling-desk for prayers.
18C. French, lit. pray God.

prima (prē´mə) *a.* first, chief, principal.
18C. Italian, fem. of *primo* first.

prima donna (prē´mə don´ə) *n.* (*pl.* **prima donnas**, **prime donne** (-mē don´ē)) **1** a chief female singer in an opera or an opera company. **2** a person who is temperamental, self-important and given to histrionics.
18C. Italian first lady.
● Sense 2 dates from the 19C.

prima facie (prīmə fā´shi, -shii) *adv.* at first sight, on the first impression. ~*a.* **1** based on first impressions. **2** (*Law*) (of evidence) that apparently establishes the truth of a case until disproved.
15C. Latin at first sight, from fem. abl. of *primus* first + abl. of *facies* appearance.

primero (primeə´rō) *n.* a game of cards fashionable in the 16th and 17th cents., the precursor of poker.
16C. Alt. of **Spanish** *primera*, fem. of *primero* first, from Latin *primarius* of the first.

primeur (primœ´) *n.* (*pl.* **primeurs** (primœ´)) **1** a new or early thing. **2** new wine. **3** (*pl.*) fruit or vegetables grown to be available early in the season.
19C. French newness, a new thing, from *prime* first.

primo (prē´mō) *n.* (*pl.* **primos**) (*Mus.*) the first part (in a duet etc.).
18C. Italian first, from Latin PRIMUS. Cp. PRIMA.

primum mobile (prīməm mō´bili) *n.* **1** the first source of motion, the mainspring of any action. **2** (*Astron.*) in the Ptolemaic system, a sphere believed to revolve from east to west in 24 hours, carrying the heavenly bodies with it.
15C. Medieval Latin, lit. first moving thing, from Latin, neut. of PRIMUS + *mobilis* mobile.

Primus® (prī´məs) *n.* a portable paraffin cooking stove used esp. by campers.
early 20C. Latin PRIMUS, ? punningly as 'first in the field'.

primus (prī´məs) *n.* the presiding bishop in the Scottish Episcopal Church. ~*a.* first, eldest (of the name, among boys in a school).
16C. Latin first.

primus inter pares (prē´məs intə pah´rēz, prī´-), (*fem.*) **prima inter pares** (prē´mə, prī´-) *n.* the first among equals; the senior member of a group.
19C. Latin, from PRIMUS + *inter* between, among, + acc. pl. of *par* equal.

princeps (prin´seps) *a.* (*pl.* **principes** (-sipēz)) first. ~*n.* **1** a chief or head man. **2** the title of the Roman emperor as constitutional head of the state.
17C. Latin leader, emperor, prince.

principia (prinsip´iə) *n.pl.* beginnings, origins, elements, first principles.
17C. Latin, pl. of *principium*, from PRINCEPS, *principis*.

privatdozent (privatdotsent´) *n.* in a German university, a recognized teacher or lecturer not on the regular staff.
19C. German private teacher, from *privat* private + *Dozent* teacher, lecturer, from Latin *docens*, *docentis*, pres.p. of *docere* to teach.

prix fixe (prē fēks´) *n.* (*pl.* **prix fixes** (fēks)) in a restaurant, (a menu at) a fixed price.
19C. French, lit. fixed price.

pro bono (prō bō´nō) *a.* (*Law, N Am.*) of or relating to legal work done without charge for poor clients, or to a lawyer who does such work.
mid-20C. Latin, shortening of *pro bono publico* for the public good.

procès-verbal (prosāvœbal´) *n.* (*pl.* **procès-verbaux** (-bō´)) **1** in French law, a written statement of particulars relating to a charge. **2** an official record of proceedings, minutes.
17C. French, lit. verbal trial.

profiterole (prəfit´ərōl) *n.* a small, hollow ball of choux pastry with a sweet filling, usu. served with chocolate sauce.

16C. **French**, dim. of *profit* profit.
• The pastry is presumably so called as it was originally regarded as a small welcome addition, a 'bonus'.

pro forma (prō faw´mə) *a., adv.* (done) as a matter of form, as a formality. ~*n.* a pro forma invoice.
16C. **Latin** for the sake of form.

pro hac vice (prō hak vī´sē) *adv.* for this occasion only.
17C. **Latin** for this occasion (only).

proletariat (prōləteə´riət, -at) *n.* the working class, wage earners collectively.
19C. **French** *prolétariat*, from Latin *proletarius* a Roman citizen of the lowest class, from *proles* offspring.
• The Roman citizens were so called as the only useful function they were thought to serve within the state was that of reproduction.

prolonge (prəlonj´) *n.* a rope in three pieces connected by rings with a hook at one end and a toggle at the other, used for moving a gun etc.
19C. **French**, from *prolonger* to extend.

prominenti (prominen´tē) *n.pl.* distinguished or important people.
mid-20C. **Italian**, pl. of *prominente* prominent.

pronaos (prōnā´os) *n.* (*pl.* **pronaoi** (-nā´oi)) 1 (*Hist.*) the area immediately before a Greek or Roman temple enclosed by the portico. 2 a vestibule.
17C. **Latin**, from Greek, from *pro* before + NAOS.

proneur (prōnœ´) *n.* a flatterer.
19C. **French** *prôneur*, from *prôner* to address a congregation, to eulogize, from *prône* the grating or railing separating the chancel of a church from the nave (where notices were given and addresses delivered).

pronto (pron´tō) *adv.* (*coll.*) without delay; quickly.
early 20C. **Spanish**, from Latin *promptus* ready.

pronunciamento (prənŭnsiəmen´tō) *n.* (*pl.* **pronunciamentos**) a manifesto, a proclamation, esp. one issued by revolutionaries in Spanish-speaking countries.
19C. **Spanish** *pronunciamiento*, from *pronunciar*, from Latin *pronuntiare* to pronounce.

pro-nuncio (prōnŭn´siō, -shō) *n.* (*pl.* **pro-nuncios**) a papal ambassador of lower status than a nuncio.
mid-20C. **Italian** *pro-nunzio*, from *pro-*, from Latin *pro* instead of + *nunzio* NUNCIO.

propaganda (propəgan´də) *n.* 1 (*often derog.*) information, ideas, opinions etc. propagated as a means of winning support for, or fomenting opposition to, a government, cause, institution etc. 2 an organization, scheme or other means of propagating such information etc. 3 (**Propaganda**) in the Roman Catholic Church, a congregation of cardinals charged with all matters connected with foreign missions.
18C. **Italian**, from Modern Latin *congregatio de propaganda fide* congregation for propagating the faith.
• The Modern Latin title was originally (sense 3) that of a committee of cardinals responsible for foreign missions, founded by Pope Gregory XV in 1622. Sense 1 dates from the early 20C.

pro patria (prō pat´riə) *adv.* for one's country.
19C. **Latin** for one's country. Cp. DULCE ET DECORUM EST PRO PATRIA MORI.

propositus (prəpoz´itəs) *n.* (*pl.* **propositi** (-tī)) a person with a distinctive characteristic who serves as the starting point for a genetic study of a family etc., a proband.
18C. Latin, p.p. of *proponere* to put forward.

propraetor (prōprē´tə), (*N Am.*) **propretor** *n.* (*Hist.*) a praetor who at the expiration of his term of office was made governor of a province.
16C. Latin, orig. *pro praetore* (person acting) for the praetor.

proprium (prō´priəm) *n.* (*pl.* **propria** (-iə)) (*Logic*) a property.
16C. Latin, use as n. of neut. sing. of *proprius* one's own.

propylaeum (propilē´əm) *n.* (*pl.* **propylaea** (-lē´ə)) 1 the entrance, esp. one of imposing architectural character, to a temple. 2 (**Propylaeum**) the entrance to the Acropolis in Athens.
18C. Latin, from Greek *propulaion*, use as n. of neut. of *propulaios* before the gate, from *pro* before + *pulē* gate. Cp. PROPYLON.

propylon (prop´ilon) *n.* (*pl.* **propylons**, **propyla** (-lə)) a propylaeum, esp. to an Egyptian temple.
19C. Latin, from Greek *propulon*, from *pro* before + *pulē* gate.

pro rata (prō rah´tə, rā´-) *a.* proportional. ~*adv.* proportionally, in proportion.
16C. Latin according to the rate.
● In ancient and Medieval Latin *pro rata* was a short form of *pro rata parte* or *pro rata portione* according to the fixed part, with *rata* the feminine ablative singular of *ratus* fixed, established, agreeing with (the ablative of the feminine noun) *pars* or *portio*, and itself the past participle of *reri*. It was this phrase that gave English *rate*.

proscenium (prəsē´niəm) *n.* (*pl.* **prosceniums**, **proscenia** (-niə)) 1 the part of a stage between the curtain and the orchestra. 2 (*also* **proscenium arch**) the frame through which the audience views the traditional type of stage. 3 in a Roman or Greek theatre, the space in front of the scenery, the stage.
17C. Latin, from Greek *proskēnion*, from *pro* before + *skēnē* stage.

prosciutto (proshoo´tō) *n.* (*pl.* **prosciutti** (-tē), **prosciuttos**) cured Italian ham, usu. eaten as an hors d'oeuvre.
mid-20C. Italian ham, ult. from Latin *exsuctus* lacking juice, p.p. of *exsugere* to suck out.

prost (prōst), **prosit** (prō´sit) *int.* used as a (German) drinking toast.
19C. German, from Latin *prosit* may it benefit, 3rd pers. sing. pres. subj. of *prodesse* to be useful, to benefit.

prospectus (prəspek´təs) *n.* (*pl.* **prospectuses**) a descriptive circular announcing the main objects and plans of a commercial scheme, institution, literary work etc.
18C. Latin view, prospect, use as n. of p.p. of *prospicere* to look forward.

protégé (prot´ezhā, prō´-), (*fem.*) **protégée** (-zhā) *n.* a person under the protection, care, or patronage of another.
18C. French, p.p. of *protéger*, from Latin *protegere* to protect.

pro tem (prō tem´), **pro tempore** (tem´pəri) *a.* temporary. ~*adv.* for the time being.
19C. Abbr. of Latin *pro tempore* (14–15C) for the time.

Provençal (provāsahl´) *n.* 1 a native or inhabitant of Provence (France). 2 the Romance language of Provence.

~*a.* of or relating to Provence, its language, or inhabitants.
16C. French, from Latin *provincialis* provincial.
● Provence, a region and former province of SE France, derives its name from Latin *provincia* province. This was a nickname for S Gaul under Roman rule, as the first Roman province to be founded beyond the Alps. Its actual name was *Gallia Transalpina* Transalpine Gaul.

proviso (prəvī´zō) *n.* (*pl.* **provisos**)
1 a provisional condition, a stipulation.
2 a clause in a covenant or other document rendering its operation conditional.
14–15C. Latin, neut. abl. sing. of *provisus*, p.p. of *providere* to provide, as in Medieval Latin *proviso ut* it being provided that.

provocateur (prəvokatœ´) *n.* a political agitator.
early 20C. French provoker, from *provoquer* or Latin *provocare* to provoke.

provolone (prōvəlō´ni) *n.* a soft, pale yellow kind of Italian cheese made from cow's milk.
mid-20C. Italian, from *provola* buffalo's milk cheese.

proxime accessit (proksimā akses´it) *n.* (*pl.* **proxime accessits**) the person who comes second in an examination, or who gains the second prize.
19C. Latin, lit. (he) came very near.

proximo (prok´simō) *a.* in or of the month succeeding the present, next month (in old commercial use).
19C. Latin in the next (month), abl. sing. of *proximus* next.

PS *n.* postscript.
Abbr. of **Latin** *postscriptum*, from neut. p.p. (used as n.) of *postscribere* to

write after, from *post* after + *scribere* to write.
● The Latin word dates from the 16C and gave English *postscript*, sometimes popularly (but wrongly) regarded as additional writing to be sent in the *post* (in a letter).

pschent (pskent, skent) *n.* the double crown of ancient Egypt, combining the white pointed mitre of Upper Egypt and the red crown with square front of Lower Egypt.
19C. Greek *pskhent*, from Egyptian *p-skhent*, from *p* the + *skhent*, from (hieroglyphic) *sekhent, sekhet, sekhte* the double crown of ancient Egypt.

psyche (sī´ki) *n.* **1** the soul, the spirit, the mind. **2** the principles of emotional and mental life.
17C. Latin, from Greek *psukhē* breath, life, soul, mind, rel. to *psukhein* to breathe.

pudendum (pūden´dəm) *n.* (*pl.* **pudenda** (-də)) (*often pl.*) the genitals, esp. those of a woman. ~*a.* of or relating to the pudenda.
17C. Latin, neut. of *pudendus*, ger. of *pudere* to be ashamed.

pueblo (pweb´lō) *n.* (*pl.* **pueblos**) **1** a village, town or settlement, esp. of the Indians of New Mexico etc. **2** (**Pueblo**) a member of a North American Indian people who live in pueblos, in New Mexico etc. ~*a.* (**Pueblo**) of or relating to the Pueblos.
19C. Spanish, from Latin *populus* people.

pugaree (pŭg´əri), **puggaree**, **puggree** *n.* (*Ang.-Ind.*) **1** a light turban. **2** a long piece of muslin wound round a hat or helmet in hot climates as protection against the sun.
17C. Hindi *pagṛī* turban.

puissance (pū´isəns, pwē´sās) *n.* **1** a
show-jumping event that tests a horse's
power to jump high obstacles. **2** (*formal*)
power, strength.
14–15C. French power, ult. from Latin
posse to be able.
● Sense 1 dates from the mid-20C.

puja (poo´jə), **pooja** *n.* a Hindu act of
worship.
17C. Sanskrit *pūjā* worship.

pukka (pŭk´ə), **pucka**, **pukkah** *a.*
(*Ang.-Ind.*) **1** genuine. **2** superior.
3 durable, substantial. **4** of full weight.
17C. Hindi *pakkā* cooked, ripe,
substantial.
● The word was frequently found in the
phrase *pukka sahib* a true gentleman, in
allusion to the former British Indian
Empire. See SAHIB.

pulque (pul´ki, -kā) *n.* a Mexican vinous
beverage made by fermenting the sap of
a species of agave.
17C. American Spanish, from Nahuatl
puliúhki decomposed.

puna (poo´nə) *n.* (*pl.* **punas**) **1** a cold
high plateau between the two ranges of
the Andes. **2** the cold wind prevalent
there. **3** mountain sickness.
17C. American Spanish, from
Quechua.

Punchinello (pŭnchinel´ō) *n.* (*pl.*
Punchinellos) **1** a buffoon, a Punch, a
grotesque person. **2** the chief character
in an Italian puppet show.
17C. Alt. of Neapolitan dial. *Polecinella*,
literary Italian *Pulcinella*, prob. from
dim. of *pollecena*, young of the
turkeycock, from *pulcino* chicken, from
Latin *pullus* chicken.
● The turkeycock's hooked beak bears
some resemblance to the character's
nose. Like the modern Punch, the
original stock character of the Italian

commedia dell'arte had a hooked
nose, humped back, and short, stout
figure.

punctilio (pŭngktil´iō) *n.* (*pl.*
punctilios) **1** a nice point in conduct,
ceremony or honour. **2** precision in form
or etiquette. **3** petty formality.
16C. Italian *puntiglio*, Spanish *puntillo*,
dim. of *punto* point, later assim. to Latin
punctum.

pundit (pŭn´dit) *n.* **1** (*also* **pandit**) a
Hindu learned in the Sanskrit language
and the science, laws and religion of
India. **2** a learned person. **3** (*iron.*) a
pretender to learning.
17C. Sanskrit *paṇḍita* learned,
conversant with.

punkah (pŭng´kə) *n.* (*Ind.*) **1** a large
portable fan made from a palm leaf.
2 a large screenlike fan suspended from
the ceiling and worked by a cord.
17C. Hindi *paṅkhā* fan, from Sanskrit
pakṣaka, from *pakṣa* wing.

punt (punt) *n.* the standard unit of
currency of the Republic of Ireland.
late 20C. Irish *púnt* pound.

punto (pŭn´tō) *n.* (*pl.* **puntos**) a thrust or
pass in fencing.
16C. Italian or Spanish, from Latin
punctum point.

Purana (poorah´nə) *n.* (*pl.* **Puranas**)
any of a great class of Sanskrit poems
comprising the whole body of Hindu
mythology.
17C. Sanskrit *purāṇa* belonging to
former times, from *purā* formerly.

purdah (pœ´də) *n.* **1** the custom in
some Muslim and Hindu societies of
secluding women from the view of
strangers. **2** a curtain or screen, esp. one
keeping women secluded.

19C. **Persian and Urdu** *parda* veil, curtain.

purée (pūˊrā) *n.* (*pl.* **purées**) **1** a smooth thick pulp of fruit, vegetables etc. obtained by liquidizing, sieving etc. **2** a thick soup made by boiling meat or vegetables to a pulp and straining it. ~*v.t.* (*3rd pers. sing. pres.* **purées**, *pres.p.* **puréeing**, *past, p.p.* **puréed**) to reduce to a purée.

18C. **Old French**, in form fem. p.p. of *purer*, from Medieval Latin *purare* to refine (ore, metal), from Latin *purus* pure.

puri (pooˊri) *n.* (*pl.* **puris**) an unleavened wholewheat bread, deep-fried and sometimes containing a spicy vegetable etc. mixture.

mid-20C. **Hindi** *pūrī*, from Sanskrit *pūrikā*.

Purim (puəˊrim, purēmˊ) *n.* a Jewish festival instituted in commemoration of the deliverance of the Jews from the destruction threatened by Haman's plot (Esther ix.20–32).

14–15C. **Hebrew**, pl. of *pūr*, a foreign word explained in the Old Testament as meaning lot, with ref. to the casting of lots by Haman.

● 'In the first month ... they cast Pur, that is, the lot, before Haman' (Esther iii.7); 'Because Haman ... had devised against the Jews to destroy them, and had cast Pur, that is, the lot, to consume them' (Esther ix.24).

putsch (puch) *n.* a sudden rising, revolt; a coup d'état.

early 20C. **Swiss German** thrust, blow, prob. ult. of imit. orig.

puttee (pŭtˊi, -ē) *n.* **1** a long strip of cloth wound spirally round the leg, usu. from ankle to knee, as a form of gaiter. **2** (*N Am.*) a leather legging.

19C. **Hindi** *paṭṭī* band, bandage, from Sanskrit *paṭṭikā*.

putto (putˊō) *n.* (*pl.* **putti** (-ē)) a figure of a small boy, cherub or cupid in Renaissance and baroque art.

17C. **Italian**, from Latin *putus* boy.

puy (pwē) *n.* a conical hill of volcanic origin, esp. in the Auvergne, France.

19C. **French** hill, from Latin PODIUM.

QED which was to be proved (used to conclude a mathematical or other proof).
Abbr. of **Latin** *quod erat demonstrandum*, translating Greek *hoti edei deixai*.
● The Latin phrase dates from the 17C.

qindar (kindah´), **qintar** (-tah´) *n.* a unit of Albanian currency equal to one hundredth of a lek.
early 20C. Albanian, from *qind* hundred.

qua (kwā, kwah) *conj.* in the character of, by virtue of being, as.
17C. Latin, abl. sing. fem. of *qui* who.

quadriga (kwodrē´gə) *n.* (*pl.* **quadrigae** (-jē)) (*pl.*) an ancient Roman two-wheeled chariot drawn by four horses abreast.
17C. Latin, sing. of *quadrigae* (pl.), contr. of *quadriiugae*, from *quadri-*, comb. form of *quattuor* + *iugum* yoke.

quadrille¹ (kwədril´, kwod-) *n.* **1** a dance consisting of five figures executed by four sets of couples. **2** a piece of music for such a dance. ~*v.i.* **1** to dance a quadrille. **2** to play music for a quadrille.
18C. French, from Spanish *cuadrilla*, from *cuadro* square.

quadrille² (kwədril´, kwod-) *n.* a game of cards played by four persons with 40 cards, fashionable in the 18th cent.
18C. French, ? from Spanish *cuartillo* (from *cuarto* fourth), assim. to QUADRILLE¹.

quadrivium (kwodriv´iəm) *n.* in the Middle Ages, an educational course consisting of arithmetic, music, geometry, and astronomy.
19C. Latin place where four ways meet, from *quadri-*, comb. form of *quattuor* four + *via* way.

quaere (kwiə´rē) *int.* used to introduce a question. ~*n.* a question, a query.
16C. Latin, imper. sing. of *quaerere* to ask. See QUAESTOR.

quaestor (kwēs´tə), **questor** *n.* an ancient Roman magistrate having charge of public funds, a public treasurer, paymaster etc.
14–15C. Latin, from old form of *quaesitus*, p.p. of *quaerere* to ask, to inquire, to seek.

quai (kā) *n.* a public street or path along an embankment by a stretch of navigable water, esp. the River Seine in Paris.
19C. French, from Medieval Latin *caiagium*, ult. from Gaulish *caio* and the source of English *quay*.

quantum (kwon´təm) *n.* (*pl.* **quanta** (-tə)) **1** (*Physics*) the smallest possible amount into which a physical property

such as energy or momentum can be subdivided and by which the value of that property can change. **2** a quantity, an amount. **3** a portion, a proportion, a share. **4** an amount required, allowed or sufficient.
16C. Latin, neut. of *quantus?* how much?

quarant' ore (kwarǝnt aw´rā, kwor-) *n.* in the Roman Catholic Church, 40 hours' exposition of the Blessed Sacrament.
17C. Italian, contr. of *quaranta ore* forty hours.

quark (kwahk) *n.* a low-fat soft cheese made from skimmed milk.
mid-20C. German curds, cottage cheese, from Slavonic. Cp. Russian *tvorog*.

quartier (kahtiā´) *n.* (*pl.* **quartiers** (kahtiā´)) a district or area, esp. of a French city.
19C. French, from Latin *quartarius* fourth part of a measure, from *quartus* fourth, the source also of English *quarter*.

quarto (kwaw´tō) *n.* (*pl.* **quartos**) **1** a size obtained by folding a sheet of paper twice, making four leaves or eight pages (usu. written *4to*). **2** a book, pamphlet etc. having pages of this size. ~*a.* having the sheet folded into four leaves.
14–15C. Latin (*in*) *quarto* (in) a fourth (of a sheet), from *quartus* fourth.

quasi (kwā´zī, -sī, kwah´zi) *adv.* as if; as it were.
15C. Latin as if, almost.

Quattrocento (kwatrōchen´tō, kwah-) *n.* the 15th cent., regarded as a distinctive period in Italian art and literature.
19C. Italian four hundred (i.e. the 1400s).

quel dommage (kel domahzh´) *int.* what a shame, what a pity.
early 20C. French, lit. what damage.

quenelle (kǝnel´) *n.* a ball of savoury paste made of meat or fish, usu. served as an entrée.
19C. French, of unknown orig.
● According to some, the word is from German *Knödel* dumpling.

quercetum (kwœsē´tǝm) *n.* a collection of living oaks, an arboretum of oak trees.
19C. Latin oak wood, from *quercus* oak.

quesadilla (kāsǝdē´yǝ) *n.* a tortilla filled, fried and topped with cheese.
mid-20C. Spanish, dim. of *quesada* cheese turnover, from *queso* cheese, from Latin *caseus*.

que sais-je? (kǝ sezh´ǝ) *int.* what do I know?
early 20C. French.
● The phrase was the motto of the French writer Montaigne (1533–92).

questionnaire (kweschǝneǝ´) *n.* a series of questions seeking information from a particular group of people.
19C. French, from *questionner* to question.

queue (kū) *n.* **1** a line of people, vehicles etc. waiting their turn. **2** a sequence of items to be dealt with in order. **3** a waiting list. **4** a plaited tail hanging at the back of the head, either of the natural hair or a wig, a pigtail. ~*v.t.* (*pres.p.* **queuing**, **queueing**, *past*, *p.p.* **queued**) to arrange or place in a queue. ~*v.i.* to form into a waiting queue, to take one's place in a queue.
16C. French, ult. from Latin *cauda* tail.
● The original sense was a heraldic term for the tail of an animal. The current sense arose in the 19C.

quiche (kēsh) *n.* a pastry shell filled with a savoury egg custard to which cheese, onion or other vegetables, bacon etc. have been added.
mid-20C. French, from Alsatian dial. *Küchen* (German *Kuchen* cake).

quidnunc (kwid´nŭngk) *n.* a person who is curious to know or pretends to know everything that goes on, a newsmonger, a gossip.
18C. **Latin** *quid nunc?* what now?

quid pro quo (kwid prō kwō´) *n.* (*pl.* **quid pro quos**) something in return or exchange (for something), an equivalent.
16C. **Latin** something for something.

quién sabe? (kyen sah´bā) *int.* who knows?
early 20C. **Spanish**.
• The phrase came into American English from its frequent use in Mexico.

quietus (kwīē´təs) *n.* (*pl.* **quietuses**) **1** a final discharge or settlement. **2** release from life, death. **3** something that represses or quietens.
14–15C. Abbr. of **Medieval Latin** *quietus est*, lit. (he) is quiet.

quillon (kēyō´) *n.* either of the arms forming the cross-guard of a sword.
19C. **French**, appar. from *quille* ninepin.

quina (kē´nə) *n.* quinine.
19C. **Spanish**, from Quechua *kina* bark.

quincunx (kwin´kŭngks) *n.* (*pl.* **quincunxes**) an arrangement of five things in a square or rectangle, one at each corner and one in the middle, esp. such an arrangement of trees in a plantation.
17C. **Latin** five twelfths, from *quinque* five + *uncia* twelfth.
• The Latin word originally denoted an arrangement of five dots or dashes in this pattern to represent five twelfths of an *as*, a coin originally of twelve ounces.

quinta (kin´tə, kwin´-) *n.* a country house or villa in Portugal, Madeira and Spain.

18C. **Spanish and Portuguese**, from *quinta parte* fifth part.
• The word originally applied to a house and farm let out at a rent of one fifth of the farm's produce.

quinze (kwinz, kīz) *n.* a card game of chance analogous to vingt-et-un, the object being to score nearest to 15 points without exceeding it.
18C. **French**, from Latin *quindecim* fifteen.

quipu (kē´poo, kwip´oo) *n.* a contrivance of coloured threads and knots used by the ancient Peruvians in place of writing.
18C. **Quechua** *khípu* knot.

quis custodiet? (kwis kustō´diet) *int.* who is to control those in authority?
19C. **Latin**.
• The words are a shortened form of a sentence from Juvenal's *Satires* (VI) (2C AD): *Quis custodiet ipsos custodes?* Who shall guard the guardians themselves?

qui s'excuse, s'accuse (kē seksküz saküz´) *int.* a person who makes excuses is admitting responsibility.
19C. **French**, lit. (he) who excuses himself, accuses himself.

qui tam (kwē tam´) *n.* an action brought by an informer under a penal statute.
18C. **Latin**, lit. who as well (beginning the clause of the action).

qui va là? (kē va la´) *int.* who goes there?
early 20C. **French**.
• The phrase became familiar as a military challenge in World War I.

qui vive (kē vēv´) *int.* who lives, who goes there?
16C. **French**, lit. (long) live who?
• The French phrase is a sentry's challenge, made to discover the loyalty of an approaching person. A typical answer might be *vive le roi* (long) live

the king, or *vive la France* (long) live
France. Cp. VIVAT.

quodlibet (kwod´libet) *n.* **1** a fantasia,
a medley of popular tunes. **2** (*dated
or formal*) a scholastic discussion or
argument.
14–15C. Medieval Latin, from Latin,
from *quod* what + *libet* it pleases.
● The original sense (2) was a question
proposed as an exercise in a
philosophical or theological debate.
Sense 1 arose in the 19C.

quondam (kwon´dam, -dəm) *a.* having
formerly been, sometime, former.
16C. Latin formerly.

quorum (kwaw´rəm) *n.* (*pl.* **quorums**)
the minimum number of officers or
members of a society, committee etc.
that must be present to transact
business.
14–15C. Latin, lit. of whom, as in phr.
quorum vos ... unum esse volumus of
whom we wish that you ... be one.
● The phrase was originally used in
the wording of commissions specifying
one or more persons as always to be
included.

quota (kwō´tə) *n.* (*pl.* **quotas**) **1** a
proportional share, part or contribution.
2 a prescribed number or quantity, e.g.
of students to be admitted to a given
college at the beginning of each year.
17C. Medieval Latin *quota* (*pars*) how
great (a part), fem. of *quotus*, from Latin
quot how many.

quot homines, tot sententiae (kwot
hom´ināz tot senten´tiī) *int.* there are as
many opinions as there are men.
16C. Latin, lit. as many men, so many
opinions.
● The phrase comes from Plautus's
comedy *Phormio* (2C BC).

quo warranto (kwō woran´tō) *n.* (*Law*)
a writ requiring a person or body to
show by what authority some office or
franchise is claimed or exercised.
16C. Law Latin by what warrant, abl.
sing. of *quod* what + abl. sing. of
warrantum warrant.

q.v. *abbr.* an instruction to look up a
cross-reference.
Abbr. of **Latin** *quod vide*, from *quod*
which + imper. sing. of *videre* to see.
● The Latin phrase dates from the 18C.

R

rabbi (rab´ī) *n.* (*pl.* **rabbis**) **1** a Jewish doctor or teacher of the law, esp. one ordained and having certain legal and ritual functions. **2** the leader of a Jewish congregation.
pre-1200. Ecclesiastical Latin and Ecclesiastical Greek, from Hebrew *rabbī* my master, from *raḇ* master.

rabi (rŭb´i) *n.* the grain crop reaped in the spring, the chief of the three crops in India, Pakistan etc.
19C. Persian and Urdu, from Arabic *rabī'* spring.

racloir (raklwah´) *n.* in archaeology, a flint implement used for scraping sideways.
19C. French scraper.

raconteur (rakontœ´) *n.* a (good, skilful etc.) storyteller.
19C. French, from *raconter* to relate.

radicchio (rədē´kiō) *n.* (*pl.* **radicchios**) a type of chicory from Italy with purple and white leaves eaten raw in salads.
late 20C. Italian chicory.

rafale (rafal´) *n.* (*pl.* **rafales** (rafal´)) repeated bursts of gunfire.
early 20C. French, lit. gust of wind, from *r-* + *affaler* to bowl over, to cause to collapse, influ. by Italian *raffica* gust, squall.

raga (rah´gə), **rag** (rahg) *n.* **1** in traditional Indian music, a form or a mode which forms the basis for improvisation. **2** a composition following such a pattern.
18C. Sanskrit *rāga* colour, passion, melody.

ragi (rah´gi, rag´i), **ragee**, **raggee**, **raggy** *n.* an Indian food-grain, *Eleusine coracana*.
18C. Sanskrit and Hindi *rāgī*, from Telugu *rāgi*.

ragout (ragoo´) *n.* a highly seasoned dish of small pieces of stewed meat and vegetables. ~*v.t.* to make into a ragout.
17C. French *ragoût*, from *ragoûter* to revive the taste of (from Old French *re-* back + *à* to + *goût* taste). Cp. GUSTO.

rai (rī) *n.* a form of popular music originating in Algeria that incorporates elements of traditional Bedouin music and Western rock.
late 20C. Algerian French *raï*, of uncertain orig.
● According to some, the word is from the dialect Arabic expression *ha er-ray*, literally here is the view, that's the thinking, frequently found in songs.

raison d'être (rāzon det´rə) *n.* (*pl.* **raisons d'être** (rāzon det´rə)) the reason for a thing's existence.
19C. French reason for being.

raisonné (rā´zənā) *a.* (of a catalogue) arranged systematically.
18C. French, p.p. of *raisonner* to reason, from *raison* reason.

raita (rah·ē´tə, rāē´tə, rīē´tə, rī´ta) *n.* an Indian side dish of chopped cucumber or other salad vegetables in yogurt.
mid-20C. Hindi *rāytā.*

raj (rahj) *n.* **1** (in the Indian subcontinent) rule, government. **2** (**the Raj**) the British rule of India before 1947.
19C. Hindi *rāj*, from Sanskrit *rājya.* Cp. RAJA.

raja (rah´jə), **rajah** *n.* **1** an Indian king, prince or tribal chief, a dignitary or noble. **2** a Malayan or Javanese chief.
16C. Prob. from **Portuguese**, from Sanskrit *rājan* king, from *rāj* to reign, to rule, rel. to Latin *rex, regis* king.

Rajput (rahj´put), **Rajpoot** *n.* **1** a member of a Hindu warrior caste who claim descent from the Kshatriyas. **2** a member of a Hindu aristocratic class.
16C. Hindi *rājpūt*, from Sanskrit *rājan* king + *putra* son. See RAJ.

raki (rahkē´, rak´i), **rakee** *n.* (*pl.* **rakis, rakees**) an aromatic liquor made from spirit or grape juice, usu. flavoured with mastic, used in the E Mediterranean region.
17C. Turkish *rāqī* (now *rakˀ*) brandy, spirits.

raku (rah´koo) *n.* Japanese lead-glazed pottery used esp. for tea bowls.
19C. Japanese, lit. ease, relaxed state, enjoyment.

rale (rahl), **râle** *n.* (*Med.*) a rattling sound in addition to that of respiration, heard with the stethoscope in lungs affected by disease.
19C. French *râle*, from *râler* to rattle in the throat, of unknown orig.

rallentando (raləntan´dō) *adv., a.* (*Mus.*) gradually slower. ~*n.* (*pl.* **rallentandos, rallentandi** (-dē)) **1** a gradual slowing in the speed at which music is played. **2** a passage to be played in this way.
19C. Italian, pres.p. of *rallentare* to slow down.

Ramadan (ram´ədan, -dan´, -dahn´), **Ramadhan** *n.* the ninth and holiest month of the Islamic year, the time of the great annual fast.
15C. Arabic *ramaḍān*, from *ramida* to be parched, to be hot.
● The reason for the name is uncertain.

rambutan (ramboo´tən) *n.* **1** the red, hairy, pulpy fruit of a Malaysian tree, *Nephelium lappaceum.* **2** this tree.
18C. Malay, from *rambut* hair, with ref. to the covering of the fruit.

rand (rand, rant) *n.* **1** the standard unit of currency of South Africa. **2** (*S Afr.*) the high land bordering a river valley.
19C. Afrikaans, from Dutch *rand* edge.
● Sense 1 refers to *the Rand*, i.e. the Witwatersrand, the chief gold-mining area of the Transvaal. Cp. KRUGERRAND.

ranee (rah´ni), **rani** *n.* (*pl.* **ranees, ranis**) **1** a Hindu queen. **2** the consort of a raja.
17C. Hindi *rānī*, from Prakrit, from Sanskrit *rājñī*, fem. of *rājan* RAJA.

rangatira (rŭng·gətiə´rə) *n.* a Maori chief of either sex.
19C. Maori.

rangé (rā´zhā), (*fem.*) **rangée** (rā´zhā) *a.* **1** orderly. **2** (of a number of heraldic charges) set in order.
18C. French, p.p. of *ranger* to put in order.

ranz-des-vaches (rãdāvash´) *n.* a melody played by Swiss cowherds on the Alpine horn.
18C. Swiss French (dial.), from *ranz*,

from Germanic, rel. to German *Rang*
rank + *des vaches* of the cows.
● The term alludes to the rows of cows
that respond to the call.

rapido (rap´idō) *adv.* (*Mus.*) in rapid time.
19C. **Italian** rapid.

rappel (rapel´) *n.* **1** abseiling. **2** (*Hist.*) the
beat of a drum calling soldiers to arms.
~*v.i.* (*pres.p.* **rappelling**, *past, p.p.*
rappelled) to abseil.
19C. **French**, from *rappeler* to recall.
● The original sense was sense 2. Sense
1 dates from the mid-20C. A climber
who abseils is one 'recalled' to the
ground.

rapport (rapaw´, rəp-) *n.* **1** sympathetic
relationship, harmony. **2** communication
via a spiritualist.
16C. **French**, from *rapporter*, from *re-*
back + *apporter* to bring.

rapprochement (raprosh´mä) *n.*
reconciliation, re-establishment of
friendly relations, esp. between nations.
19C. **French**, from *rapprocher*, from *re-*
back + *approcher* to approach.

rara avis (rahrə ah´vis, reərə ā´vis) *n.*
(*pl.* **rarae aves** (-rē, -vēz)) a rarity,
something very rarely met with.
17C. **Latin** rare bird.
● The phrase comes from Juvenal's
Satires (VI) (2C AD): *Rara avis in terris
nigroque simillima cycno* A rare bird on
earth, comparable to a black swan.
The passage in Juvenal refers to a
hypothetical woman who possesses all
possible virtues.

ras (ras) *n.* an Ethiopian governor or
administrator.
17C. **Amharic** *rās* head, from Arabic *ra's*
(coll. *rās*).

raskolnik (raskol´nik) *n.* a dissenter from
the Orthodox or Greek Church in Russia.
18C. **Russian** *raskol'nik*, from *raskol*
separation, schism.

rassolnik (rasol´nik, ras·sol´-) *n.* a
Russian soup of brine, salted dill
cucumbers and pickled vegetables, meat
and fish, served cold.
early 20C. **Russian** *rassol'nik*, from
rassol' brine, from *sol'* salt + -*nik*.

raster (ras´tə) *n.* the pattern of scanning
lines which appears as a patch of light
on a television screen and which
reproduces the image.
mid-20C. **Greek** screen, frame, from
Latin *rastrum* rake, from *rasus*, p.p. of
radere to scrape, to shave.

ratafia (ratəfē´ə) *n.* **1** a liqueur or cordial
flavoured with the kernels of cherry,
peach, almond or other kinds of fruit.
2 a sweet almond-flavoured biscuit
eaten with this.
17C. **French**, ? rel. to TAFIA.

rataplan (rat´əplan) *n.* a noise like the
rapid beating of a drum. ~*v.t.* (*pres.p.*
rataplanning, *past, p.p.* **rataplanned**)
1 to beat (a drum). **2** to beat out (a tune)
on or as if on a drum. ~*v.i.* to make a
rataplan on a drum.
19C. **French**, of imit. orig.

ratatouille (ratətwē´) *n.* a vegetable
casserole from Provence, France, made
with aubergines, tomatoes, peppers etc.,
stewed slowly in olive oil.
19C. **French** dial., appar. from *ratouiller*,
var. of *touiller* to stir up, to stir round.

Rathaus (raht´hows) *n.* the town hall of
a German town.
early 20C. **German** *Rat* council + *Haus*
house.

ravioli (raviō´li) *n.* small pasta cases with
a savoury filling.
19C. **Italian**, pl. of *raviolo*, dim. of some
n. now unknown.
● Some authorities take *raviolo* as a
diminutive of *rava* turnip, perhaps with
reference to the shape of the cases rather
than their contents.

Rayah (rī´ə) *n.* (*Hist.*) a non-Muslim subject in Turkey.
19C. Turkish *râya*, from Arabic *ra'āyā*, pl. of *ra'iyya*. See RYOT.

razzia (raz´iə) *n.* (*pl.* **razzias**) (*Hist.*) a foray or incursion for the purpose of capturing slaves etc., as practised by African Muslims.
19C. French, from Algerian Arabic *ġāziya* raid, from Arabic *ġazā* to go forth to fight, to make a raid.

re (rē, rā) *prep.* **1** in the matter of. **2** (*coll.*) as regards, about.
18C. Latin, abl. of *res* thing.

real (rā´al, -ahl) *n.* (*pl.* **reals**, **reales** (-lēz)) **1** the standard unit of currency of Brazil. **2** (*Hist.*) a Spanish silver coin or money of account.
16C. Spanish, use as n. of *real* royal.

realpolitik (rāahl´politēk) *n.* politics based on practical reality rather than moral or intellectual ideals.
early 20C. German *Realpolitik*, from *real* objective, practical + *Politik* politics.

rebus (rē´bəs) *n.* (*pl.* **rebuses**) **1** a picture or figure enigmatically representing a word, name or phrase, usu. by objects suggesting words or syllables. **2** (*Her.*) a device representing a proper name or motto in this way.
17C. French *rébus*, from Latin *rebus*, abl. pl. of *res* thing.
● Latin *rebus* has its origin in *de rebus quae geruntur*, literally concerning the things that are taking place, a title given in 16C Picardy to satirical pieces containing riddles in picture form. The pieces were composed by clerics at the annual carnival and related to current topics, follies etc.

réchauffé (rāshō´fā) *n.* **1** a dish warmed up again. **2** a rehash.
19C. French, p.p. of *réchauffer* to warm

up again, from *re-* back + *échauffer* to warm up.

recherché (rəshœ´shā) *a.* **1** out of the common, rare, choice, exotic. **2** affected, precious, far-fetched.
17C. French, p.p. of *rechercher*, from *re-* back + *chercher* to seek.

recipe (res´ipi) *n.* **1** a list of ingredients and directions for preparing a dish. **2** a remedy, expedient, device or means for effecting some result. **3** a formula or prescription for compounding medical or other mixtures.
14–15C. Latin, imper. sing. of *recipere* to take, to receive.
● The word was originally used at the beginning of medical prescriptions (sense 3). It then became the term for the prescription itself. Sense 1 dates from the 18C.

recitativo (rechitatē´vō, resitətē´vō) *n.* (*pl.* **recitativi** (rechitatē´vi), **recitativos** (resitətē´vōz)) (*Mus.*) **1** a style of musical declamation between singing and speech. **2** a passage delivered in this way
17C. Italian, from Latin *recitatus*, p.p. of *recitare* to recite.
● The style is traditionally found in Italian opera. It also exists in French opera, when it is known as *récitatif*. English *recitative* is also used for either.

réclame (rāklahm´) *n.* **1** public attention, publicity or notoriety. **2** self-advertisement, puffing.
19C. French, from *réclamer* to demand.

reconnaissance (rikon´əsəns, -is-) *n.* **1** a preliminary examination or survey. **2** an exploratory survey of a tract of country or a coastline in wartime to ascertain the position of the enemy, the strategic features etc.
19C. French, from *reconnaître*, *reconnaiss-* to recognize.

recto (rek´tō) *n.* (*pl.* **rectos**) **1** the right-hand page of an open book (usu. bearing an odd number) as distinct from *verso*. **2** the front of a printed sheet of paper.
19C. Latin, abl. of *rectus* right.

reculer pour mieux sauter (rekülā puə myœ sō´tā) *n.* the use of a withdrawal or setback as a basis for an advance or success.
19C. French, lit. to draw back in order to leap better.
● The full French proverb is *Il faut reculer pour mieux sauter*. An English equivalent is recorded in *c.*1500 as 'Wyse men goo abacke for to lepe the ferther'.

redingote (red´ing·gōt) *n.* **1** a woman's long double-breasted coat. **2** a similar coat worn by men in the 18th cent.
18C. French, from English *riding-coat*.

†redivivus (redivī´vəs, -vē´-) *a.* (*usu. following n., formal*) come to life again, revived.
16C. Latin, from *re-* back + *vivus* living, alive.

redowa (red´əvə) *n.* a Bohemian round dance of two forms, one resembling a waltz, the other a polka.
19C. French or German, from Czech *rejdovák*, from *rejdovat* to turn round, to whirl.

reductio ad absurdum (ridŭktiō ad absœ´dəm) *n.* **1** proof of the falsity of a proposition by showing the absurdity of its logical consequence. **2** proof of the truth of a proposition by showing that its contrary has absurd consequences. **3** (*coll.*) an absurd conclusion.
18C. Latin, lit. reduction to the absurd.

referendum (refərən´dəm) *n.* (*pl.* **referendums**, **referenda** (-də)) **1** the submission of a political question to the whole electorate for a direct decision by general vote. **2** a vote taken in this manner.
19C. Latin, ger. of *referre* to refer.

reflet (rəflā´) *n.* a metallic lustre or glow, esp. on pottery.
19C. French reflection.

regalia[1] (rigā´liə) *n.pl.* **1** the insignia of royalty, esp. the emblems worn or displayed in coronation ceremonies etc. **2** the emblems or insignia of an office or order. **3** finery in general.
16C. Medieval Latin royal residence, royal rights, use as n. of neut. pl. of Latin *regalis* regal.

regalia[2] (rigā´liə) *n.* a Cuban cigar of superior quality.
19C. Spanish royal privilege.

regatta (rigat´ə) *n.* a sporting event comprising a series of yacht or boat races.
17C. Italian (Venetian dial.) *regatta*, *rigatta* fight, struggle, contest, from *regattare* to compete, to contend for mastery, to sell by haggling, ? from *recatare* to buy and sell in order to resell, from Popular Latin *recaptare* to capture, from *re-* back + *captare* to try to catch.

Régie (rāzhē´) *n.* the revenue department in some European countries having sole control of the importation of tobacco and sometimes of salt.
18C. French, fem. p.p. of *régir* to rule.

regime (rāzhēm´), **régime** *n.* **1** a prevailing system of government or management. **2** the prevailing social system or general state of things. **3** a prevailing set of conditions. **4** a regimen.
15C. French *régime*, from Latin REGIMEN.

regimen (rej´imən) *n.* **1** (*Med.*) a systematic plan or course of diet, exercise etc. for the preservation or restoration of health. **2** †rule, government. **3** a government, a regime, a prevailing system of government. **4** (*Gram.*) the syntactical dependence of one word on another.
14–15C. **Latin**, from *regere* to rule.

Regina (rijī´nə) *n.* a reigning queen.
18C. **Latin** queen. Cp. REX.

régisseur (rezhēsœ´) *n.* an official in a dance company whose responsibilities include directing.
19C. **French** director, from *régir*, *régiss*- to direct.

regius (rē´jiəs) *a.* **1** royal. **2** appointed by the sovereign.
17C. **Latin** royal, from *rex*, *regis* king.

Reich (rīkh) *n.* the German realm considered as an empire made up of subsidiary states.
early 20C. **German** kingdom, empire, state.

relievo (relē´vō, rəlyā´vō) *n.* (*pl.* **relievos**) raised or embossed work, relief.
17C. **Italian** *rilievo*, from *rilevare* to raise, ult. from Latin *relevare* to raise again.

religieuse (rilēzhyœz´) *n.* a nun.
17C. **French**, fem. of *religieux* religious.

reliquiae (rilik´wiē) *n.pl.* **1** remains. **2** (*Geol.*) fossil remains of organisms.
17C. **Latin**, use as n. of fem. pl. of *reliquus* remaining, from *re-* back + *liq-*, stem of *linquere* to leave.

remblai (rä´blā) *n.* the material used to form a rampart or embankment.
18C. **French**, from *remblayer* to embank, from *re-* back + *emblayer* to heap up.

rémoulade (remulahd´, rem´-) *n.* a sauce, often made with mayonnaise,

flavoured with herbs, mustard and capers and served with fish, cold meat, salads etc.
19C. **French**, from Italian *remolata*, of unknown orig.
● According to some, the word is from Picardy dialect *ramolas* horseradish, from Latin *armoracea*.

remuage (rəmüahzh´, remūahzh´) *n.* the periodic turning or shaking of bottled wine in order to move the sediment towards the cork.
early 20C. **French**, lit. moving about, from *remuer* to move.

Renaissance (rinā´səns) *n.* **1** the revival of art and letters in the 14th–16th cents. **2** the period of this. **3** the style of architecture, painting, literature and science that was developed under it. **4** (**renaissance**) any revival of a similar nature, a rebirth.
19C. **French**, from *re-* again + *naissance* birth, from Latin *nascentia*, from *nasci* to be born, or from French *naître*, *naiss*- to be born.

rendezvous (ron´dāvoo, rä´-) *n.* (*pl.* **rendezvous** (-vooz)) **1** a place agreed upon for meeting. **2** a meeting at an arranged place and time. **3** a place appointed for assembling, esp. of troops or warships. **4** an arranged meeting of two spacecraft in preparation for docking. **5** a place of common resort. ~*v.i.* (*3rd pers. sing. pres.* **rendezvouses** (-vooz), *pres.p.* **rendezvousing** (-vooing), *past, p.p.* **rendezvoused** (-vood)) to meet or assemble at a rendezvous.
16C. **French**, use as n. of *rendez-vous* present yourselves, imper. of *se rendre*.
● The earliest sense is sense 3.

rendzina (rendzē´nə) *n.* a dark rich soil containing lime, found in grassy regions overlying chalk.
early 20C. **Russian**, from Polish *r†dzina*.

rente (rāt) *n.* (*pl.* **rentes** (rāt)) **1** annual income or revenue from capital investment. **2** (*pl.*) **a** interest or annuities from French and other European government stocks. **b** the stocks themselves.
19C. French, from Old French, from Popular Latin *rendita*, fem. p.p. (used as n.) of Latin *rendere*, alt. of *reddere* to give back.

rentier (rā´tiā) *n.* a person drawing income from rentes or investment.
19C. French, from RENTE.

renvoi (rāvwah, ren´voi) *n.* (*Law*) referral of a legal question or dispute to another jurisdiction.
19C. French, from *renvoyer* to send back, from *re-* back + *envoyer* to send.

repechage (rep´əshahzh) *n.* a heat, esp. in rowing or fencing, where contestants beaten in earlier rounds get another chance to qualify for the final.
early 20C. French *repêchage*, from *repêcher*, lit. to fish out, to rescue.

repertoire (rep´ətwah) *n.* **1** a stock of plays, musical pieces, songs etc., that a person, company etc. is ready to perform. **2** a stock or range of items, techniques, skills etc. available or regularly used.
19C. French *répertoire*, from Late Latin *repertorium* inventory, from *repertus*, p.p. of *reperire* to discover.

répétiteur (repetitœ´, rāpātētœ´) *n.* a person who coaches opera singers.
mid-20C. French tutor, coach, from Latin *repetitus*, p.p. of *repetere* to repeat.

replica (rep´likə) *n.* (*pl.* **replicas**) **1** a duplicate of a picture, sculpture etc. by the artist who executed the original. **2** an exact copy, a facsimile. **3** a copy on a smaller scale.

18C. Italian, from Latin *replicare* to repeat, to reply.

repoussé (ripoo´sā) *a.* (of ornamental metalwork) formed in relief by hammering from behind. ~*n.* metalwork ornamented in this way.
19C. French, p.p. of *repousser*, from *re-* back + *pousser* to push.

reprise (riprēz´) *n.* (*Mus.*) a repeated phrase, theme etc., a refrain. ~*v.t.* **1** to repeat (an earlier phrase, theme etc.). **2** to repeat or restage the performance of.
14–15C. Old French, fem. p.p. (used as n.) of *reprendre*, from *re-* again + *prendre* to take.
● The original sense was amount taken back, loss, expense. The musical sense dates from the 18C.

requiem (rek´wiəm) *n.* **1** (**Requiem**) in the Roman Catholic Church, a mass for the repose of the soul of a dead person. **2** (*Mus.*) the musical setting of this, a dirge. **3** a memorial (for). ~*a.* (**Requiem**) of or relating to a Requiem.
12–14C. Latin, acc. of *requies* rest, first word of the introit in the Mass for the dead in the Latin liturgy.
● The introit begins: *Requiem aeternam dona eis, Domine: et lux perpetua luceat eis* Give them eternal rest, O Lord: and let light perpetual shine upon them.

requiescat (rekwies´kat) *n.* a wish or prayer for the repose of the dead.
19C. Latin, from *requiescat in pace* may he rest in peace. Cp. RIP.

res (rās) *n.* (*pl.* **res**) a thing, property.
17C. Latin thing.

res gestae (rās jes´tē) *n.pl.* **1** achievements. **2** exploits. **3** (*Law*) relevant facts or circumstances admissible in evidence.
17C. Latin things done.

res judicata (rās joodikah´tə) *n.* (*Law*) an
issue that has already been settled in
court and cannot be raised again.
17C. Latin thing judged.

restaurant (res´təront, -trənt, -trǎ) *n.* a
place for refreshment, a public eating
house.
19C. French, use as n. of pres.p. of
restaurer to restore.

résumé (rez´ūmā), **resumé** *n.* **1** a
summary, a recapitulation, a condensed
statement. **2** (*esp. N Am.*) a curriculum
vitae.
19C. French, p.p. (used as n.) of *résumer*
to sum up.

retiarius (retiah´riəs) *n.* (*pl.* **retiarii**
(-riī)) (*Hist.*) a Roman gladiator armed
with a net and trident.
17C. Latin, from *rete* net.

retroussé (ritroo´sā, rət-) *a.* (of the nose)
turned up at the end.
19C. French, p.p. of *retrousser* to turn
up, from *re-* back + *trousser* to truss.

retsina (retsē´nə) *n.* a resin-flavoured
white wine from Greece.
early 20C. Modern Greek, from *retsini*,
from Greek *rētinē* pine resin.

revanche (rivahnch´) *n.* a policy directed
towards restoring lost territory or
possessions.
19C. French, earlier *revenche*, from (*se*)
revencher to revenge (oneself), from Late
Latin *revindicare* to avenge.

reveille (rival´i) *n.* a morning signal by
drum or bugle to awaken soldiers or
sailors.
17C. French *réveillez*, imper. pl. of
réveiller to awaken, from *ré-* back +
veiller, from Latin *vigilare* to keep
watch.

revenant (rev´ənənt) *n.* a person who
returns from the grave or from exile,
esp. a ghost.
19C. French, pres.p. of *revenir* to return.

revenons à nos moutons (rəvenō a
nō moo´tō) *int.* let's get back to the point
at issue, let's get back to the subject.
19C. French, lit. let us return to our
sheep.
● The French phrase comes from the
15C farce *Maistre Pierre Pathelin*, where
it is spoken by a judge to focus the
attention of a witness who is confusing
two different law suits. The words are
sometimes given a jocular anglicization
as 'Let us return to our muttons'.

reverie (rev´əri) *n.* **1** listless musing, a
daydream, a loose or irregular train of
thought. **2** †a wild or fantastic conceit,
a vision, a delusion. **3** (*Mus.*) a dreamy
musical composition.
12–14C. Old French *reverie* rejoicing,
revelry, from *rever* to be delirious
(Modern French *rêver* to dream), of
unknown orig.
● The original sense (to the 16C) was
joy, delight, revelry. Sense 1 dates from
the 17C and derives from French
resverie (now *rêverie*), from Old French
reverie.

revers (riviə´) *n.* (*pl.* **revers** (-viəz´)) a
part of a coat, esp. a lapel, turned back
so as to show the lining.
19C. French, from Latin *reversus* p.p. of
revertere to turn back.

reversi (rivœ´si) *n.* **1** a game played by
two people on a draughtboard with
pieces differently coloured above and
below, which may be reversed. **2** †a card
game in which the player who takes
fewest tricks wins.
19C. French, alt., based on REVERS, of
earlier *reversion*, from Italian *rovescina*,
from *rovesciare* to reverse.

revue (rivū´) *n.* a light entertainment with songs, dances etc., representing topical characters, events, fashions etc.
19C. French review.

Rex (reks) *n.* a reigning king (the official title used by a king, esp. on documents, coins etc.).
17C. Latin king. Cp. REGINA.

rhetor (rē´tə) *n.* **1** in ancient Greece, a teacher or professor of rhetoric. **2** (*often derog.*) a professional orator, a mere orator.
12–14C. Late Latin *rhethor*, var. of Latin *rhetor*, from Greek *rhētōr* orator.

ria (rē´ə) *n.* (*pl.* **rias**) a long, narrow inlet into the sea coast.
19C. Spanish *ría* estuary.

ricercar (rēchəkah´), **ricercare** (-kah´rā) *n.* (*Mus.*) an elaborate, contrapuntal, instrumental composition in a slow tempo.
18C. Italian *ricercare* to search out, to seek.
● The composition arose as a form of musical 'research'.

†richesse (rishes´) *n.* (*usu. in pl.*) abundant possessions, wealth, opulence, affluence.
12–14C. Old French *richeise* (Modern French *richesse*), from *riche* rich. Cp. EMBARRAS DE RICHESSE.
● English *riches* as in *rags to riches* was originally a variant of RICHESSE, not a plural form of *rich*.

rickshaw (rik´shaw), **ricksha** (-shah) *n.* a light two-wheeled hooded carriage drawn by one or two people, or attached to a bicycle etc.
19C. Abbr. of Japanese JINRICKSHAW.

ricochet (rik´əshā) *n.* **1** a rebounding or skipping of a stone, projectile or bullet off a hard or flat surface. **2** the act of aiming so as to produce this, or a hit so made. ~*v.i.* (*pres.p.* **richocheting** (-shāing), **richochetting** (-sheting), *past, p.p.* **ricocheted** (-shād), **richochetted** (-shetid)) to skip or bound in this way.
18C. French the skipping of a shot or of a flat stone on water, of unknown orig.
● According to some, the origin is in the Medieval French *chanson du ricochet* song of the *ricochet*, from some dialect word ultimately deriving from Latin *recalcare* to reshoe, the song itself being an endless succession of questions and answers. But popular etymology bases the song title on French *coq* cock, with reference to the *fable du rouge coquelet* fable of the little red cockerel, whose Italian equivalent is *la favola dell'uccellino* the fable of the little bird.

ricotta (rikot´ə) *n.* a soft white Italian cheese made from sheep's milk.
19C. Italian recooked, from Latin *recocta*, fem. p.p. of *recoquere*, from *re-* again + *coquere* to cook.
● The name refers to the process of manufacture. The milk is 'cooked' once to separate the curd from the whey, then the whey is 'cooked' again to produce the cheese.

rictus (rik´təs) *n.* (*pl.* **rictuses**, **rictus**) **1** (*Zool., Anat.*) the expanse of a person's or animal's open mouth, gape. **2** the opening of a two-lipped corolla.
18C. Latin, lit. open mouth, from *rictus*, p.p. of *ringi* to gape.

ridotto (ridot´ō) *n.* (*pl.* **ridottos**) (*Hist.*) an entertainment consisting of singing and dancing, esp. a masked ball.
18C. Italian, corr. to French *réduit*, from Medieval Latin *reductus*, use as n. of p.p. of Latin *reducere* to reduce.
● The entertainment was apparently so called as it was originally held among select company, 'reduced' to the best.

riel (rē′əl) *n.* the standard unit of currency of Cambodia.
mid-20C. Khmer.

riem (rēm) *n.* (*S Afr.*) a rawhide strap or thong.
19C. Dutch, from Middle Dutch *rieme*.

rien ne va plus (ryĭ nə va plü′) *int.* no more bets; in roulette, spoken by the croupier once the wheel is spinning to indicate that no more bets can be taken.
19C. French, lit. nothing goes any more. Cp. FAITES VOS JEUX.

Riesling (rēz′ling, rēs′-) *n.* a dry white wine, or the grape that produces it.
19C. German alt. of obs. *Rüssling*, of unknown orig.

rifacimento (rēfahchimen′tō) *n.* (*pl.* **rifacimenti** (-tē)) a recast of a literary work etc.
18C. Italian, from *rifac-*, stem of *rifare* to remake.

rigor mortis (rig′ə maw′tis) *n.* the stiffening of the body following death.
19C. Latin stiffness of death.

Rigsdag (rigz′dag) *n.* (*Hist.*) the Danish parliament.
19C. Danish, from gen. of *rige* realm + *dag* day. Cp. *Reichstag* (REICH), RIKSDAG.

Rig-Veda (rigvā′də) *n.* the oldest and most original of the Hindu Vedas.
18C. Sanskrit *ṛgveda*, from *ṛc* sacred stanza + *veda* VEDA.

rijsttafel (rīs′tahfəl, rīst′tahfəl) *n.* a SE Asian meal of different foods (such as eggs, meat, fish, fruit etc.) mixed with rice and served in separate dishes.
19C. Dutch, from *rijst* rice + *tafel* table.
● The dish dates from Dutch colonial times

rikishi (rik′ish-i) *n.* a sumo wrestler.
late 20C. Japanese, from *riki* strength + *shi* warrior.

Riksdag (riks′dag) *n.* the Swedish parliament.
19C. Swedish, from gen. of *rike* realm + *dag* day. Cp. RIGSDAG.

rille (rill) *n.* (*Astron.*) a furrow, trench or narrow valley on Mars or the moon.
19C. German, prob. of Low German orig.

rinderpest (rin′dəpest) *n.* a malignant contagious disease attacking ruminants, esp. cattle.
19C. German, from *Rinder* cattle (pl. of *Rind*) + *Pest* plague.

rinforzando (rinfawtsan′dō) *adv.* (*Mus.*) with a sudden stress or crescendo.
19C. Italian, pres.p. of *rinforzare* to strengthen, rel. to English *reinforce*.

ringgit (ring′git) *n.* the standard unit of currency of Malaysia, the Malaysian dollar.
late 20C. Malay, lit. serrated, jagged (with ref. to the coin's edge).

Rioja (riokh′ə) *n.* a Spanish table wine from Rioja.
early 20C. *Rioja*, a district of N Spain.

RIP *int.* may he, she or they rest in peace. Abbr. of **Latin** *requiescat in pace* (REQUIESCAT) or its pl. equivalent, *requiescant in pace*.
● The abbreviation is sometimes popularly taken to represent the initial letters of English *rest in peace*. The full Latin phrase dates from the 16C.

ripieno (ripiā′nō) *a.* additional, supplementary. ~*n.* (*pl.* **ripienos**, **ripieni** (-nē)) (*Mus.*) **1** in baroque concerto music, a number of additional accompanying instruments. **2** a ripieno player or instrument.
18C. Italian, from *ri-* again + *pieno* full.

riposte (ripost´) n. **1** a quick reply, a retort. **2** in fencing, a quick lunge or return thrust. ~v.i. to make a riposte.
18C. French, from Italian *risposta*, fem. p.p. (used as n.) of *rispondere* to respond, from Latin *respondere*, from *re-* again + *spondere* to pledge.

rishi (rish´i) n. (pl. **rishis**) a seer, a saint, an inspired poet, esp. each of the seven sages said to have communicated the Hindu Vedas to humankind.
18C. Sanskrit *ṛṣi*.

Risorgimento (risawjimen´tō) n. the rising of the Italian peoples against Austrian and papal rule, culminating in the unification of Italy in 1870.
19C. Italian renewal, renaissance, lit. resurgence.

risotto (rizot´ō) n. (pl. **risottos**) an Italian dish of rice cooked in butter and stock or broth, with onions, cheese, chicken, ham etc.
19C. Italian, from *riso* rice.

risqué (rēs´kā, -kā´) a. suggestive of indecency, indelicate.
19C. French, p.p. of *risquer* to risk.

rissole (ris´ōl) n. a ball or flat cake of minced meat, fish etc., coated with breadcrumbs and fried.
18C. French, later form of Old French *ruissole*, dial. var. of *roisole*, *roussole*, from use as n. of fem. of Late Latin *russeolus* reddish, from Latin *russus* red.

ritardando (ritahdan´dō) adv., a., n. (pl. **ritardandos**, **ritardandi** (-dē)) (Mus.) (a) slowing down.
19C. Italian, pres.p. of *ritardare* to slow down.

rite de passage (rēt də pasahzh´) n. a ceremony marking an individual's change of status, esp. into adulthood or matrimony.

early 20C. French, lit. rite of passage.
● The phrase was coined by Arnold van Gennep in his book *Les Rites de passage* (1909).

ritenuto (ritənoo´tō) a., adv. (Mus.) restrained, held back. ~n. (pl. **ritenutos**) a passage played in this way.
19C. Italian, p.p. of *ritenere*, from Latin *retinere* to hold back.

ritornello (ritawnel´ō) n. (pl. **ritornellos**, **ritornelli** (-lē)) (Mus.) a brief prelude, interlude or refrain.
17C. Italian, dim. of *ritorno* return.

riviera (riviəə´rə) n. a coastal strip with a subtropical climate.
18C. Italian seashore, coast.
● The word was originally the name of the coast either side of Genoa, NW Italy (now known as the Italian Riviera, for distinction from the French Riviera, SE France).

rivière (riviəə´) n. a necklace of gems, usu. of several strings.
19C. French river, stream.
● The necklace is so called as it 'streams'.

robe de chambre (rob də shābr´, shā´brə) n. (pl. **robes de chambre** (rob)) a dressing gown or morning dress.
18C. French, lit. robe of (the) chamber.

robot (rō´bot) n. **1** a machine capable of acting and speaking in a human manner; a humanoid, an automaton. **2** a programmable machine capable of carrying out a series of functions, esp. used in industry as an alternative to human labour. **3** a brutal, mechanically efficient person who has no sensitivity. **4** (S Afr.) a traffic light.
early 20C. Czech, from *robota* forced labour. Cp. Russian *rabota* work.
● The word originated as a term for the mechanical men in Karel Čapek's play

R.U.R. (standing for *Rossum's Universal Robots*, the firm that manufactured the men) (1920).

rocaille (rōkī´) *n.* decorative work of rock, shell or a similar material.
19C. French, from Old French *roche* rock. Cp. ROCOCO.

roche moutonnée (rosh mooton´ā) *n.* (*pl.* **roches moutonnées** (rosh mooton´ā)) (*Geol.*) rock ground down by glacial action so as to present a rounded appearance on the side from which the flow came.
19C. French, from Old French *roche* rock + French *moutonnée*, from *mouton* sheep.
● The rock is so called as it is rounded like a sheep's back.

rococo (rəkō´kō) *n.* **1** a florid style of ornamentation (in architecture, furniture etc.) flourishing in the 18th cent. **2** design or ornament of an eccentric and over-elaborate kind. ~*a.* in this style.
19C. French, fanciful alt. of ROCAILLE.
● The style is so called from its use of rocaille. The term arose as artists' jargon.

rodeo (rō´diō, rədā´ō) *n.* (*pl.* **rodeos**) **1** a driving together or rounding-up of cattle. **2** a place they are rounded up in. **3** an outdoor entertainment or contest exhibiting the skills involved in this. **4** an exhibition of motorcycling skills etc.
19C. Spanish, from *rodear* to go round, based on Latin *rotare* to rotate.

rodomontade (rodōmontād´, -tahd´) *n.* **1** brag, bluster. **2** an instance of bragging. ~*a.* bragging, boastful. ~*v.i.* to boast, to bluster.
17C. French, from obs. Italian *rodomontada*, from *Rodomonte*, the

boastful Saracen leader in Ariosto's *Orlando Furioso* (1516).
● The character's name itself literally means 'roll mountain'.

roentgen (rŭnt´yən, rœnt´-), **röntgen** *n.* the international unit of quantity of X- or gamma-rays.
19C. Wilhelm Conrad *Roentgen*, 1845–1923, German physicist, discoverer of X-rays.

rogan josh (rōgən jōsh´) *n.* a dish of curried meat cooked in a rich sauce.
mid-20C. Urdu *roġan još*, from Persian *rauġan* oil, ghee + *još* stew.

role (rōl), **rôle** *n.* **1** a part or character taken by an actor. **2** any part or function one is called upon to perform.
17C. French *rôle* roll, orig. the roll or paper containing an actor's part.

Rom (rom) *n.* (*pl.* **Romas, Roma** (-ə)) a male gypsy, a Romany.
19C. Romany man, husband.
● The word is popularly regarded as an abbreviation of English *Romany*.

romaine (rōmān´) *n.* (*N Am.*) a cos lettuce.
early 20C. French, fem. of *romain* Roman.
● The name may have been given because the cos reached W Europe through Rome.

romaji (rō´məji) *n.* a system of romanized spelling for the transliteration of Japanese.
early 20C. Japanese, from *rōma* Roman + *ji* letter.

romal (rōmahl´), **rumal** (roo-) *n.* **1** a handkerchief worn as a headdress. **2** in the Indian subcontinent, a silk or cotton fabric.
17C. Persian and Urdu *rūmāl*, from *rū* face + *māl* (base of Persian *mālidan* to wipe) wiping.

roman-à-clef (rōmahnaklā´) *n.* (*pl.* **romans-à-clef** (rōmahnaklā´)) a novel in which a knowing reader is expected to identify real people under fictitious names, or actual events disguised as fictitious.
19C. French, lit. novel with a key, from *roman* romance, novel + *à* at, with + *clef* key, CLEF.

roman à thèse (romã a tez´) *n.* (*pl.* **romans à thèse** (romã)) a type of novel that seeks to expound or promote a theory.
19C. French, lit. novel with a thesis.

Romanes (rom´ənis) *n.* the Romany language.
19C. Romany, adv. from *Romano*.

roman-fleuve (rōmahnflœv´) *n.* (*pl.* **romans-fleuves** (rōmahnflœv´)) a novel sequence or saga chronicling a family history, and thereby a social period.
mid-20C. French, lit. river-novel, from *roman* novel + *fleuve* river.
● The sequence is so called because the narrative flows through a series of novels like a river.

Romano (rōmah´nō) *n.* a strong-tasting, hard Italian cheese.
early 20C. Italian Roman.

romanza *n.* (roman´sa, -mant´sa, -man´za) (*Mus.*) **1** a romantic song or melody. **2** a lyrical piece of music. **3** a romance.
19C. Spanish or Italian, from Popular Latin, from Latin *Romanicus*, from *Romanus* Roman.

rondavel (rondah´vəl) *n.* a round hut or building in South Africa.
19C. Afrikaans *rondawel*, ? from Dutch *rondeel* round bastion.

ronde (rond) *n.* **1** a dance in which the dancers move round in a circle.

2 a course of talk etc. **3** an upright angular form of type imitating handwriting.
19C. French, fem. of *rond* round.

rondeau (ron´dō) *n.* (*pl.* **rondeaux** (ron´dōz, ron´dō)) **1** a poem in iambic verse of eight or ten syllables and ten or thirteen lines, with only two rhymes, the opening words coming twice as a refrain. **2** (*Mus.*) a rondo.
16C. Old French, later form of *rondel*, from *rond* round.

rondo (ron´dō) *n.* (*pl.* **rondos**) a musical composition having a principal theme which is repeated after each subordinate theme, often forming part of a symphony etc.
18C. Italian, from French RONDEAU.

ronin (rō´nin) *n.* (*pl.* **ronin, ronins**) **1** (*Hist.*) in Japan, a lordless samurai. **2** a Japanese student retaking an examination.
19C. Japanese.

rooinek (roi´nek) *n.* (*S Afr., sl., offensive*) an English-speaking South African.
19C. Afrikaans, from *rooi* red + *nek* neck.
● British troops were highly susceptible to sunburn in South Africa when engaged in the Boer War (1899–1902).

Roquefort (rok´faw) *n.* **1** a French blue cheese made from ewes' milk. **2** a salad dressing made from Roquefort.
19C. *Roquefort*, a village in SW France.

roquelaure (rok´əlaw) *n.* a short cloak for men worn in the 18th cent.
18C. Antoine-Gaston, duc de *Roquelaure*, 1656–1738, Marshal of France.

rosé (rō´zā) *n.* a pink-coloured wine, having had only brief contact with red grape skins.
19C. French, from *rose* pink.

roseau pensant (rōzō pāsā´) *n.* a human being regarded as physically frail but mentally superior.
19C. French, lit. thinking reed, from *roseau* reed + pres.p. of *penser* to think.
• The expression comes from Pascal's *Pensées* (1670): *L'homme n'est qu'un roseau, le plus faible de la nature, mais c'est un roseau pensant* Man is only a reed, the weakest in nature, but he is a thinking reed.

rosemaling (rō´səmahling) *n.* the art of painting furniture with flower motifs.
mid-20C. Norwegian rose-painting.

Rosh Hashana (rosh həshah´nə), **Rosh Hashanah** *n.* the Jewish New Year.
18C. Hebrew *rō's haššānāh*, lit. head of the year.

Roshi (rō´shi) *n.* (*pl.* **Roshis**) the spiritual leader of a community of Zen Buddhist monks.
mid-20C. Japanese, from *rō* old + *shi* teacher.

rosolio (rōzō´liō), **rosoglio** *n.* (*pl.* **rosolios**, **rosoglios**) a cordial made from raisins, spirits etc. in Italy and S Europe.
19C. Italian, var. of *rosoli*, from Latin *ros* dew + *solis*, gen. of *sol* sun.

rota (rō´tə) *n.* (*pl.* **rotas**) **1** a list of names, duties etc., a roster. **2** (**Rota**) in the Roman Catholic Church, the supreme court deciding on ecclesiastical and secular causes.
17C. Latin wheel.
• The word in sense 1 was originally the name of a political club, founded in 1659 by James Harrington, that advocated rotation in the offices of government. Harrington also first used *rotation* in this sense in 1656.

roti (rō´ti) *n.* unleavened bread, food.
early 20C. Hindi *roṭī*.

rotisserie (rōtis´əri, rət-) *n.* **1** a device with a spit on which food, esp. meat, is roasted or barbecued. **2** a restaurant specializing in meat cooked in this way.
19C. French *rôtisserie*, from *rôtir* to roast.

roturier (rotoor´yā) *n.* a plebeian.
16C. French, from *roture* land tenure of a person not of noble birth, from Latin *ruptura*, from *ruptus*, p.p. of *rumpere* to break.
• The evolution of meaning here is: broken land (i.e. land recently cleared), tax due to a lord for such land, land subject to tax, land held by a person not of noble birth.

rouble (roo´bəl), **ruble** *n.* the standard unit of currency of Russia, Belarus and Tajikistan.
16C. French, from Russian *rubl'*, from *rubit'* to chop, to hack.
• The reference is to a coin originally 'chopped' from a silver bar.

roué (roo´ā) *n.* a rake, a debauchee.
19C. French, use as n. of p.p. of *rouer* to break on the wheel.
• The reference is to the punishment said to be deserved by such a person.

rouge (roozh) *n.* **1** a cosmetic used to colour the cheeks red. **2** red oxide of iron used for polishing metal, glass etc. ~*v.t.* to colour with rouge. ~*v.i.* **1** to colour one's cheeks etc. with rouge. **2** to blush.
14–15C. Old French, from Latin *rubeus* red.

rouge-et-noir (roozhānwah´) *n.* a gambling card game played by a 'banker' and a number of people on a

table marked with four diamonds, two red and two black.
18C. French red and black.

roulade (rulahd´) n. **1** a rolled piece of veal or pork. **2** a thin slice of meat spread with a stuffing and rolled into a sausage shape. **3** (*Mus.*) a run of notes on one syllable, a flourish.
18C. French, from *rouler* to roll.

rouleau (roo´lō) n. (*pl.* **rouleaux** (-lōz), **rouleaus**) **1** a small roll, esp. a pile of coins done up in paper. **2** a trimming of decorative piping.
17C. French, from obs. *roule* (now *rôle*). See ROLE.

roulette (rulet´) n. **1** a gambling game played with a ball on a table with a revolving disc. **2** a wheel with points for making dotted lines, used in engraving, for perforating etc. **3** (*Math.*) a curve that is the locus of a point rolling on a curve.
18C. French, dim. of *rouelle* wheel, from Late Latin *rotella*, dim. of *rota* wheel.

roux (roo) n. (*pl.* **roux**) a sauce base, the thickening element in a sauce made from melted fat (esp. butter) and flour cooked together.
19C. French browned (i.e. butter).

RSVP abbr. please reply.
Abbr. of **French** *répondez, s'il vous plaît* reply, please.
● The French phrase dates from the 19C.

rubaiyat (roo´bīyat) n. in Persian poetry, a verse form consisting of quatrains.
19C. Arabic *rubā'iyāt*, pl. of *rubā'ī* quadripartite.

rubato (rubah´tō) n. (*pl.* **rubatos**, **rubati** (-tē)) (*Mus.*) **1** flexibility of rhythm, fluctuation of tempo within a musical piece. **2** an instance of this. ~a. to be performed in this manner.
18C. Italian, lit. robbed.

● The manner of performance is so called because the strict time is 'robbed' from a note or notes, to be 'paid' back later.

ruche (roosh) n. a pleated strip of gauze, lace, silk or the like used as a frill or trimming. ~v.t. to trim with a ruche.
19C. French, from Medieval Latin *rusca* tree bark, of Gaulish orig.
● Tree bark was used by the Gauls to form a rudimentary shelter for bees, and this 'edging' eventually gave the present sense.

rufiyaa (roofē´yah) n. the standard unit of currency of the Maldives.
late 20C. Maldivian, from source of RUPEE.

rumba (rŭm´bə), **rhumba** n. **1** a complex and rhythmic Cuban dance. **2** a ballroom dance developed from this dance. **3** a piece of music for this dance. ~v.i. (*3rd pers. sing. pres.* **rumbas**, **rhumbas**, *pres.p.* **rumbaing**, **rhumbaing**, *past, p.p.* **rumbaed**, **rumba'd**, **rhumbaed**, **rhumba'd**) to dance the rumba.
early 20C. American Spanish, orig. spree, carousal, party.

rupee (rupē´) n. the standard unit of currency of various Asian countries including India, Pakistan, Sri Lanka, Nepal, Mauritius and the Seychelles.
17C. Hindi *rupiyā*, *rūpiyā*, from Sanskrit *rūpya* wrought silver.

rupiah (roopē´ə) n. the standard unit of currency of Indonesia.
mid-20C. Indonesian, from source of RUPEE.

ruse de guerre (rooz də geə´) n. a war stratagem.
19C. French, lit. ruse of war.

rusée (roozā´) a. (of a woman) wily, sly, cunning.

18C. French, fem. of *rusé*, from *ruse* cunning.
● The French masculine form is also used in English.

rus in urbe (rus in œ´bā) *n.* an illusion of countryside created within a city.
18C. Latin, lit. country in city, from *rus* country + *in* in + abl. sing. or *urbs* city.
● The expression comes from Martial's *Epigrammata* (XII) (1C AD).

ryokan (riō´kan) *n.* a traditional Japanese inn.
mid-20C. Japanese, from *ryo* to travel + *kan* building.

ryot (rī´ət) *n.* in the Indian subcontinent, a peasant.
17C. Persian, from Persian and Urdu *ra'īyat*, Urdu *raiyat*, from Arabic *ra'īyya* flock, herd, subjects of a ruler, from *ra'ā* to pasture. Cp. RAYAH.

S

sabot (sab´ō) *n.* **1** a simple wooden shoe, usu. made in one piece. **2** a wooden-soled shoe. **3** a wooden disc fastened to a spherical projectile, or a metal cap on a conical one, to make these fit a gun bore. **4** a cap or shoe for protecting the end of a beam or pile etc. **5** (*Austral.*) a small sailing boat.
early 20C. French, from Old French *çabot*, blend of *çavate* (Modern French SAVATE) and *bote* (Modern French *botte*) boot.

sabotage (sab´ətahzh) *n.* **1** malicious damage to a railway, industrial plant, machinery etc., as a protest by discontented workers, or as a non-military act of warfare. **2** the operation of cutting shoes or sockets for railway lines. **3** any action designed to hinder or undermine. ~*v.t.* **1** to commit sabotage on. **2** to hinder or undermine.
early 20C. French, from *saboter* to make a noise with sabots, to execute badly, to destroy, from SABOT.
● The word is popularly said to refer to the action of striking workers who threw their sabots into machinery to damage it, but this origin is not sustainable. They may well have kicked the machinery with their sabots, however.

sabra (sab´rə) *n.* an Israeli born in Israel.
mid-20C. Modern Hebrew *ṣabbār* or Arabic *ṣabr* prickly pear.
● The prickly pear is widespread in the Negev and Jews born in the region regard themselves as possessing its qualities of strength and endurance.

sabretache (sab´ətash) *n.* a cavalry officer's leather pocket suspended on the left side from the sword-belt.
19C. French, from German *Säbeltasche*, from *Säbel* sabre + *Tasche* pocket.

sacellum (səsel´əm) *n.* (*pl.* **sacella** (-lə)) **1** a small, usu. roofless sanctuary containing an altar in an ancient Roman building. **2** a chapel, a shrine.
19C. Latin, dim. of *sacrum* shrine, from *sacer* holy.

sachem (sā´chəm) *n.* **1** a chief of certain tribes of North American Indians. **2** (*N Am., coll.*) a magnate, a prominent person. **3** (*N Am.*) any of the governing officers of the Tammany Society in New York City.
17C. Narragansett *sâchimau* chief, ruler. Cp. SAGAMORE.

sachet (sash´ā) *n.* **1** a small ornamental bag or other receptacle containing perfumed powder for scenting clothes etc. **2** a small packet of shampoo etc.
15C. French, dim. of *sac* bag.

sacrarium (səkreə´riəm) *n.* (*pl.* **sacraria** (-riə)) **1** the sanctuary of a church. **2** in the Roman Catholic Church, a piscina.

3 (*Hist.*) a sacred place where sacred things were kept in ancient Rome, esp. the room in the house where the penates were kept, or the adytum of a temple.
18C. Latin, from *sacer* sacred.

sadhu (sah´doo), **saddhu** *n.* a Hindu usu. mendicant holy man.
19C. Sanskrit *sādhu* good (man).

safari (səfah´ri) *n.* (*pl.* **safaris**) **1** a hunting or scientific expedition, esp. in E Africa. **2** a sightseeing trip to see African animals in their natural habitat.
19C. Kiswahili, from Arabic *safar* journey, trip, tour.

saffian (saf´iən) *n.* leather prepared from goatskin or sheepskin tanned with sumac and dyed yellow or red.
16C. Russian *saf'yan*, alt. of Romanian *saftian*, ult. from Persian *saktiyān*.

saga (sah´gə) *n.* **1** a medieval prose narrative recounting family or public events in Iceland or Scandinavia, usu. by contemporary or nearly contemporary native writers. **2** a story of heroic adventure. **3** a series of books relating the history of a family. **4** a long involved story or account.
18C. Old Norse (Icelandic), rel to English *saw* (proverb, maxim) and *say*.

sagamore (sag´əmaw) *n.* a North American Indian chief, a sachem.
17C. Eastern Abnaki *sāngman* chief, ruler. Cp. SACHEM.

sagan (sā´gən) *n.* the deputy of the Jewish high priest.
17C. Late use of **Hebrew** *sāgān*, from Akkadian *šaknu* governor.

sagene[1] (səjēn´) *n.* a fishing net.
19C. Latin, from Greek *sagēnē*.

sagene[2] (sah´zhen) *n.* a Russian measure of length, about seven feet (two metres).
18C. Russian *sazhen'*, rel. to obs. *syagat'* to reach.
● A sagene is regarded as the length of the span of both arms. Cp. English *fathom*, literally 'length of the outstretched arms'.

sagum (sā´gəm) *n.* (*pl.* **saga** (-gə)) the military cloak worn by ancient Roman soldiers.
18C. Latin, from Late Greek *sagos*.

sahib (sah´ib) *n.* (in India) a polite form of address for a man; a gentleman.
17C. Urdu, through Persian, from Arabic *ṣāḥib* friend, lord, master. Cp. MEMSAHIB. See also PUKKA.

saic (sā´ik) *n.* a sailing vessel of the E Mediterranean.
17C. French *saïque*, from Turkish *şayka*.

sake (sak´ā, sah´ki), **saké**, **saki** *n.* a fermented liquor made from rice.
17C. Japanese.

sakieh (sak´iə) *n.* an apparatus used in Egypt for raising water, consisting of a vertical wheel or wheel and chain carrying pots or buckets.
17C. Arabic *sāḳiya*, use as n. of fem. active part. of *saḳā* to irrigate.

Sakti (shak´ti), **sakti** *n.* in Hinduism, the female principle esp. as personified as the wife of a god.
19C. Sanskrit *śakti* power, divine energy.

salaam (səlahm´) *n.* a ceremonious salutation or obeisance in Eastern countries. ~*v.i.* to make a salaam. ~*v.t.* to make a salaam to (a person).
17C. Arabic *salām*, rel. to SHALOM.

salade niçoise (salad nēswahz´) *n.*
(*pl.* **salades niçoises** (salad nēswahz´))
a salad dish garnished with tomatoes,
hard-boiled eggs, capers, anchovies etc.
19C. **French** salad of Nice, from *salade*
salad + fem. of *Niçois* of Nice, a town in
S France.

salami (səlah´mi), **salame** *n.* (*pl.*
salamis, **salames**) a highly-seasoned
Italian sausage.
19C. **Italian**, pl. of *salame*, from Popular
Latin *salamen*, from *salare* to salt, from
Latin *sal* salt.

salep (sal´əp) *n.* a farinaceous meal made
from the dried roots of *Orchis mascula*
and other orchidaceous plants.
18C. **French**, from Turkish *sālep*, from
Arabic *ṭa‘lab* fox, shortening of *ḵuṣa-
’ṭ-ṭa‘lab* orchid, lit. testicles of the fox.

salmagundi (salməgŭn´di) *n.* (*pl.*
salmagundis) **1** a dish of chopped
meat, anchovies, eggs, oil, vinegar etc.
2 a multifarious mixture, a medley, a
miscellany.
17C. **French** *salmigondis*, obs.
salmigondin, of unknown orig.
• The first element may represent
French *sel* salt and the last be related
to English *condiment*.

salmi (sal´mē), **salmis** *n.* (*pl.* **salmis**) a
ragout, esp. of game birds stewed with
wine.
18C. Abbr. of **French** *salmigondis*
SALMAGUNDI.

salon (sal´on) *n.* **1** a reception room, esp.
in a great house in France. **2** the
business premises of a hairdresser,
beautician etc. **3** (*Hist.*) a periodical
reunion of eminent people in the house
of someone socially fashionable, esp. a
lady. **4** (*NAm.*) a meeting of esp.
intellectuals in the house of a celebrity
or socialite. **5** (*pl.*) fashionable circles.
6 a hall for exhibiting paintings etc.

7 (**Salon**) an annual exhibition of
paintings etc. held in Paris.
17C. **French**, from Italian *salone*, augm.
of *sala* hall.

salopettes (saləpets´) *n.pl.* thick usu.
quilted trousers with shoulder straps,
worn by skiers.
late 20C. Pl. of **French** *salopette*
dungarees, from *salope* slut, from *sale*
dirty + *huppe* hoopoe (a bird noted for
its dirty habits) + dim. suf. *-ette*.
• The trousers are worn by Frenchmen
as overalls.

salpicon (sal´pikon) *n.* a stuffing or thick
sauce made with chopped meat and
vegetables.
18C. **French**, from Spanish, from
salpicar to sprinkle (with salt).

salsa (sal´sə) *n.* **1** a Puerto Rican dance or
the music for this. **2** a spicy sauce, esp.
served with Mexican food.
19C. **Spanish** sauce.
• The dance music is a blend of
different styles, like the sauce, which is
specifically a relish containing a variety
of chopped-up ingredients.

saltarello (saltərel´ō) *n.* (*pl.* **saltarellos**,
saltarelli (-li)) **1** an Italian or Spanish
dance characterized by sudden skips.
2 the music for such a dance.
16C. **Italian** *salterello*, Spanish *salterelo*,
rel. to Italian *saltare*, Spanish *saltar* to
leap, to dance, from Latin *saltare*.

saltimbocca (saltimbok´ə) *n.* a dish of
rolled pieces of veal or poultry cooked
in herbs, bacon and other flavourings.
mid-20C. **Italian**, lit. leaps into the
mouth, from *saltare* to leap + *in* into
+ *bocca* mouth.

saltus (sal´təs) *n.* (*pl.* **saltus**) a sudden
starting aside, breach of continuity or
jumping to a conclusion.
17C. **Latin** leap.

salut (salü´) *int.* hello, goodbye.
early 20C. French, lit. salute, from Latin
salus, salutis health, salute. Cp. SALVE.

salve (sal´vā, -vi), **Salve Regina** (rigī´nə)
n. **1** a Roman Catholic antiphon
beginning with the words *Salve Regina,*
'Hail, holy Queen', addressed to the
Virgin. **2** music for this.
14–15C. Latin hail, greetings, imper.
sing. of *salvere* to be well.

salvo[1] (sal´vō) *n.* (*pl.* **salvoes**, **salvos**)
1 a discharge of guns etc. as a salute.
2 a concentrated fire of artillery, release
of missiles etc. **3** a volley of cheers etc.
16C. French *salve*, Italian *salva*
salutation, with substitution of -*o* for -*a*.

salvo[2] (sal´vō) *n.* (*pl.* **salvos**) **1** a saving
clause, a proviso. **2** a mental reservation,
an evasion, an excuse. **3** an expedient to
save one's reputation etc.
17C. Latin, abl. neut. sing. of *salvus*
safe, as in Medieval Latin phr. *salvo iure*
without prejudice to the right of (a
particular person).

sal volatile (sal vəlat´ili) *n.* an aromatic
solution of ammonium carbonate,
smelling salts.
17C. Latin, lit. volatile salt.

samadhi (səmah´di) *n.* **1** in Buddhism
and Hinduism, a state of concentration
induced by meditation. **2** in Buddhism
and Hinduism, a state into which a
perfected holy man is believed to pass
when he dies.
18C. Sanskrit *samādhi* contemplation,
lit. a putting together.

Sama-Veda (sah´məvādə) *n.* the third of
the four Vedas, mainly made up of
extracts from hymns in the Rig-Veda.
18C. Sanskrit *sāman* chant + VEDA.

samba (sam´bə) *n.* **1** a Brazilian dance.
2 a ballroom dance in imitation of this.
3 music for this. ~*v.i.* (*pres.p.* **sambaing**,
past, p.p. **sambaed**, **samba'd**) to dance
the samba.
19C. Portuguese, of African orig.

sambal (sam´bal) *n.* a side dish eaten
with Malayan and Indonesian curries.
19C. Malay.

sambuca (sambū´kə) *n.* an ancient
musical stringed instrument of high-
pitched tone.
14–15C. Latin *sambuca*, from Greek
sambukē, rel. to Aramaic *śabbĕka*.

samfu (sam´foo), **samfoo** *n.* an outfit
worn esp. by Chinese women,
consisting of a blouse or jacket and
trousers.
mid-20C. Chinese (Cantonese) *shaam
foò*, from *shaam* coat + *foò* trousers.

Samhain (sown, sow´in, saw´in) *n.*
1 November, celebrated as a festival
marking the beginning of winter by the
ancient Celts.
19C. Irish, from Old Irish *samain* (feast
of) All Saints.

samiel (sā´miəl) *n.* the simoom.
17C. Turkish *samyeli* hot wind, from
Arabic *samm* poison + Turkish *yel*
wind.

samisen (sam´isen) *n.* a Japanese three-
stringed guitar-like instrument played
with a plectrum.
17C. Japanese, from Chinese *sānxián*,
from *sān* three + *xián* string.

samizdat (sam´izdat, -miz´-) *n.* **1** the
clandestine publishing of banned
literature in the former Communist
countries of E Europe. **2** this literature.
mid-20C. Russian, from *samo-* self +
izdatel'stvo publishing house.
• A Russian punning colloquialism
tamizdat also existed, for banned
literature published *tam* there, i.e. in
the West.

samosa (səmō´sə) *n.* (*pl.* **samosas,
samosa**) an Indian savoury of spiced
meat or vegetables in a triangular pastry
case.
mid-20C. **Persian and Urdu**.

samovar (sam´əvah) *n.* a Russian tea urn
heated by burning charcoal in an inner
tube.
19C. **Russian**, from *samo-* self + *varit'*
to boil.
• The samovar is a 'self-boiler' as it
heats the water itself, without the use of
an external stove. Cp. Latin *authepsa*,
literally 'self-cooker', from Greek.

sampan (sam´pan) *n.* a Chinese flat-
bottomed river boat, frequently used as
a houseboat.
17C. **Chinese** *sānbǎn*, from *sān* three +
bǎn board.

samsara (səmsah´rə) *n.* **1** in Hinduism,
the cycle of birth, death and rebirth.
2 in Buddhism, the transmigration or
rebirth of a person.
19C. **Sanskrit** *saṃsāra* a wandering
through.

samshu (sam´shoo), **samshoo** *n.* a
Chinese alcoholic drink made from
fermented rice.
17C. **Pidgin English**, ult. of unknown
orig.

samskara (samskah´rə) *n.* **1** in
Hinduism, a purificatory ceremony
or rite. **2** in Hinduism, a mental
impression, instinct or memory.
19C. **Sanskrit** *saṃskāra* preparation,
a making perfect.

samsoe (sam´zō) *n.* a firm-textured
Danish cheese with a mild flavour.
mid-20C. *Samsoe*, a Danish island.

samurai (sam´urī) *n.* (*pl.* **samurai**)
1 a Japanese army officer. **2** (*Hist.*) a
member of the military caste under the
Japanese feudal regime, or a military
retainer.
18C. **Japanese** warrior, knight.

sanbenito (ṣanbənē´tō) *n.*
(*pl.* **sanbenitos**) (*Hist.*) a penitential
garment painted with a red St Andrew's
cross worn by heretics who recanted, or
painted over with flames and figures of
devils, worn at an auto-da-fé by persons
condemned by the Inquisition.
16C. **Spanish** *sambenito*, from *San
Benito* St Benedict.
• The garment is so called ironically
from its resemblance to the Benedictine
scapular.

sancho (sang´kō) *n.* (*pl.* **sanchos**) a
W African musical instrument like a
guitar.
19C. **Twi** *o-sanku*.

sanctum (sangk´təm) *n.* (*pl.* **sanctums,
sancta** (-tə)) **1** a sacred or private place.
2 (*coll.*) a private room, retreat.
16C. **Latin**, neut. of *sanctus* holy.

sanctum sanctorum (sangk´təm
sangktaw´rəm) *n.* (*pl.* **sancta
sanctorum** (-tə), **sanctum
sanctorums**) **1** the holy of holies in the
Jewish temple. **2** (*coll.*) one's sanctum.
14–15C. **Latin**, neut. sing. and gen. pl.
of *sanctus* holy, translating Hebrew
qōḏeš haqqŏḏāšīm holy of holies.
Cp. KIDDUSH.

sanctus (sangk´təs), **Sanctus** *n.* **1** the
liturgical phrase 'Holy, holy, holy', in
Latin or English. **2** the music for this.
14–15C. **Latin** holy, the first word of the
hymn.
• The full version of the hymn that
forms the conclusion of the Eucharistic
preface in the Latin Ordinary of the
Mass is: *Sanctus, sanctus, sanctus,
Dominus Deus Sabaoth. Pleni sunt coeli
et terra gloria tua. Hosanna in excelsis.
Benedictus qui venit in nomine Domini.*

Holy, holy, holy, Lord God of Hosts.
Heaven and earth are full of thy glory.
Hosanna in the highest. Blessed is he
that cometh in the name of the Lord.

sandarac (san´dərak), **sandarach** *n.* **1** a
whitish-yellow gum resin obtained from
a NW African tree, *Tetraclinis articulata.*
2 this tree. **3** realgar.
14–15C. Latin *sandaraca*, from Greek
sandarakē, of Asiatic orig.

sanga (sŭng´gə), **sangar** *n.* a breastwork
or wall of loose stones built for
defensive purposes in the Himalayas.
19C. Persian and Pashto *sangar*, prob.
from Persian *sang* stone.

sangaree (sang-gərē´) *n.* wine and water
sweetened, spiced and usu. iced.
18C. Spanish *sangría* SANGRIA.

sang-de-boeuf (sādəbœf´) *n.* a dark-red
colour such as that of some old Chinese
porcelain. ~*a.* of this colour.
19C. French, lit. ox's blood.

sang-froid (sāfrwah´) *n.* calmness,
composure in danger etc.
18C. French, lit. cold blood.

sangre azul (sang-grā athul´, asul´) *n.*
the purity of blood claimed by certain
ancient Castilian families.
19C. Spanish blue blood.
• Such families professed to be free
from Moorish or Jewish ancestry.

sangria (sang·grē´ə) *n.* a Spanish drink of
diluted (red) wine and fruit juices.
mid-20C. Spanish *sangría*, lit. bleeding.

Sanhedrin (san´idrin, -hē´-, -hed´-),
Sanhedrim (-rim) *n.* (*Hist.*) the supreme
court of justice and council of the Jewish
nation, until AD 425, consisting of 71
priests, elders and scribes.
16C. Post-biblical Hebrew *sanhedrīn*,
from Greek *sunedrion* council, from *sun*
together + *hedra* seat.

sanjak (san´jak) *n.* (*Hist.*) an
administrative subdivision of a Turkish
vilayet or province.
16C. Turkish *sancak*, lit. banner.

sannyasi (sŭnyah´si), **sanyasi** *n.*
(*pl.* **sannyasi**, **sanyasi**) a Hindu
religious man who lives by begging.
17C. Sanskrit *saṃnyāsī*, nom. sing. of
saṃnyāsin laying aside, abandoning,
ascetic, from *saṃ* together + *ni* down
+ *as* to throw.

sans (sanz, sā) *prep.* (*Shak.*, also *facet.*)
without.
12–14C. Old French *san, sanz* (Modern
French *sans*), from var. of Latin *sine*
without, partly influ. by Latin *absentia*
absence. Cp. SENZA.
• The word is especially associated
with Shakespeare's *As You Like It* (1599)
in which Jaques's famous speech
beginning 'All the world's a stage'
concludes with the line: 'sans teeth,
sans eyes, sans taste, sans everything'
(II.vii).

sans-culotte (sākulot´, sanzkū-) *n.*
1 (*Hist.*) a republican in the French
Revolution. **2** a radical extremist, a
revolutionary. **3** a person without
breeches. ~*a.* republican, revolutionary.
18C. French, from *sans* without +
culotte knee breeches, from *cul*
backside, bottom.
• The historical *sans-culottes* refused
to wear knee breeches, favoured by the
aristocracy, and instead wore ordinary
trousers.

sansei (san´sā) *n.* an American whose
grandparents were immigrants from
Japan.
mid-20C. Japanese, from *san* three + *sei*
generation. Cp. NISEI.

santal (san´təl) *n.* sandalwood.
18C. French, from Medieval Latin
santalum, from Late Greek *santalon*.

santir (santiə´) *n.* an Eastern form of dulcimer played with two sticks.
19C. Arabic *sanṭīr, sinṭīr*, alt. of Greek *psaltērion* psaltery.

santon (san´ton) *n.* a Muslim hermit, a dervish.
16C. French, from Spanish, from *santo* saint.

sapsago (sap´səgō) *n.* (*pl.* **sapsagos**) a greenish hard cheese flavoured with melilot, made in Switzerland.
19C. Alt. of **German** *Schabziger*, from *schaben* to grate + *Ziger* a kind of cheese.
• The cheese is also known by its German name, although *sapsago* is preferred in the US. A mistaken belief exists that the cheese is made from goat's milk, from a false association with *Ziege* goat.

saraband (sar´əband), **sarabande** *n.*
1 a slow and stately Spanish dance.
2 a piece of music for this in strongly accented triple time.
17C. French *sarabande*, from Spanish, Italian *zarabanda*.

sarangi (sərang´gi, -rŭng´-) *n.*
(*pl.* **sarangis**) an Indian stringed instrument similar to a violin.
19C. Sanskrit *sāraṅgī*.

sari (sah´ri), **saree** *n.* (*pl.* **saris**, **sarees**) a Hindu woman's traditional dress, formed from a length of material draped around the body.
18C. Hindi *sāṛī*, from Sanskrit *śāṭikā*.

sarod (sar´od) *n.* an Indian instrument like a cello, that may be played with a bow or plucked.
19C. Urdu, from Persian *surod* song, melody.

sarong (sərong´) *n.* a loose, skirtlike garment traditionally worn by men and women in the Malay Archipelago.
19C. Malay, lit. sheath, quiver.

sarpanch (sœ´pŭnch) *n.* an elected head of an Indian village council.
mid-20C. Urdu *sar-panch*, from *sar* head + *panch* five (from Sanskrit *pañca*). Cp. PANCHAYAT.

sarsaparilla (sahspəril´ə) *n.* **1** the dried roots of various species of smilax, used as a flavouring and formerly in medicine as an alterative and tonic.
2 a plant yielding this. **3** a carbonated drink flavoured with sassafras.
16C. Spanish *zarzaparilla*, from *zarza* bramble + dim. of *parra* vine, twining plant.

sartor resartus (sahtaw risah´təs) *n.*
a human being being regarded as refashioned by the trappings of society and the world about him.
19C. Latin, lit. the tailor retailored, from *sartor* tailor + p.p. of *resarcire* to patch again, to repair.
• The phrase comes from the title of a book by Thomas Carlyle (1833) in which he develops his philosophy of clothing.

Sarum (seə´rəm) *n.* **1** (**Sarum use**) the rites used at Salisbury cathedral before the Reformation. **2** the official signature of the Bishop of Salisbury.
16C. Medieval Latin *Sarum* Salisbury, prob. from abbr. of Latin *Sarisburia*.
• The name is used for Old Sarum, the site of the original city of Salisbury, just outside the modern city, and for New Sarum, the official title of modern Salisbury.

sash (sash) *n.* an ornamental band or scarf worn round the waist or over the shoulder, frequently as a badge or part of a uniform.
16C. Arabic *šāš* muslin, (length of cloth for a) turban.

sashimi (sashim´i) *n.* a Japanese dish of thin slices of raw fish.

19C. **Japanese**, from *sashi* to pierce + *mi* flesh.

sastrugi (sastroo´gi), **zastrugi** (zas-) *n.pl.* wavelike ridges on snow-covered plains caused by winds.
19C. **German**, pl. of *Sastruga*, from Russian *zastruga* small ridge, furrow in snow, from *zastrugat'* to plane, to smooth, from *strug* plane (the tool).

satara (sat´ərə, sətah´-) *n.* a heavy, horizontally-ribbed woollen fabric or broadcloth.
19C. *Satara*, a town and district in western India.

satay (sat´ā), **satai**, **saté** *n.* a Malaysian and Indonesian dish of cubed meat served with a spicy peanut sauce.
mid-20C. **Malay** *satai*, *sate*, Indonesian *sate*.

satori (sətaw´ri) *n.* in Zen Buddhism, an intuitive enlightenment.
18C. **Japanese** awakening.

satrap (sat´rap) *n.* **1** a governor of a province under the ancient Persian empire, a viceroy. **2** a governor, a ruler of a dependency etc., esp. one who affects despotic ways.
14–15C. **Old French** *satrape* or Latin *satrapa*, *satrapes*, from Greek *satrapēs*, from Old Persian *kšatra-pāvan* protector of the country, from *kšatra-* country + *pā-* to protect.

satsuma (satsoo´mə, sat´sumə, -sū-) *n.* **1** a seedless type of mandarin orange. **2** a tree that bears such fruit.
19C. *Satsuma*, a former province on the island of Kyushu, Japan.

saturnalia (satənā´liə) *n.*
(*pl.* **saturnalia**, **saturnalias**) **1** (*Hist.*) (*usu.* **Saturnalia**) an ancient Roman annual festival held in December in honour of Saturn, regarded as a time of unrestrained licence and merriment.

2 (*sing. or pl.*) a season or occasion of unrestrained revelry.
16C. **Latin**, neut. pl. (used as n.) of *Saturnalis* of *Saturnus* Saturn, the Roman god of agriculture.
● Sense 2 dates from the 18C.

satyagraha (sŭt´yəgrah·hə, -tyah´-) *n.* non-violent resistance to authority as practised orig. by Mahatma Gandhi.
early 20C. **Sanskrit** *satyāgraha* force born of truth, from *satya* truth + *āgraha* obstinacy.

saucisse (sōsēs´), **saucisson** (-sō´) *n.*
1 a long tube of gunpowder etc., for firing a charge. **2** a long fascine.
17C. **French** sausage.
● The variant *saucisson* is an augmentative of *saucisse*.

sauerkraut (sow´əkrowt) *n.* finely chopped cabbage compressed with salt until it ferments.
17C. **German**, from *sauer* sour + *Kraut* cabbage. Cp. KRAUT.

sault (soo) *n.* (*N Am.*) a rapid in a river.
12–14C. **Old French**, earlier spelling of *saut*, from Latin *saltus*, from *salire* to leap.
● The word is familiar from the names of the twin cities *Sault Sainte Marie*, opposite each other on St Mary's River, one in Ontario, Canada, the other in Michigan, USA.

sauna (saw´nə) *n.* **1** a Finnish-style steam or hot-air bath. **2** a building or room used for saunas. **3** a period spent in a sauna.
19C. **Finnish**.

sauté (sō´tā) *a.* lightly fried. ~*v.t.* (*pres.p.* **sautéing**, *past*, *p.p.* **sautéd**, **sautéed**) to fry lightly. ~*n.* a dish of sautéed food.
19C. **French**, p.p. of *sauter* to leap.
● The term refers to the tossing action while cooking, done to ensure that the food being cooked does not lie on the surface of the pan continuously.

Sauternes (sōtœn´, sət-) *n.* a sweet white Bordeaux wine.
18C. *Sauternes*, a district near Bordeaux in SW France.

sauve qui peut (sōv kē pœ´) *n.* a state of panic or chaos.
19C. French, lit. save-who-can.

savannah (səvan´ə), **savanna** *n.* an extensive treeless plain covered with low vegetation, esp. in tropical America.
16C. Obsolete Spanish *zavana, çavana* (now *sabana*), from Taino *zavana*.

savant (sav´ənt) *n.* a person of learning, esp. an eminent scientist.
18C. French, use as n. of a., orig. pres.p. of *savoir* to know.

savarin (sav´ərin) *n.* a ring-shaped cake containing nuts and fruit, often flavoured with rum.
19C. French, from Anthelme Brillat-*Savarin*, 1755–1826, French gastronome.

savate (savaht´, səv-) *n.* a style of boxing in which the feet are used as well as the hands.
19C. French, orig. a kind of shoe. Cp. SABOT.

saveloy (sav´əloi) *n.* a highly-seasoned dried sausage of salted pork (orig. of brains).
19C. Alt. of **obsolete French** *cervelat* (Modern French *cervelas*), from Italian *cervellata*. See CERVELAT.

savoir faire (savwah feə´) *n.* quickness to do the right thing, esp. in social situations.
19C. French, lit. to know (how) to do. Cp. SAVOIR VIVRE.

savoir vivre (savwah vē´vrə) *n.* knowledge of the world and the ways of society.

18C. French, lit. to know (how) to live. Cp. SAVOIR FAIRE.

savonette (sav´ənet) *n.* a toilet preparation of various kinds.
18C. French (now *savonnette*), dim. of *savon* soap.

sayyid (sī´id) *n.* **1** a Muslim title of respect. **2** a descendant of certain members of Muhammad's family.
17C. Arabic lord, prince.

sbirro (zbē´rō) *n.* (*pl.* **sbirri** (-rē)) **1** an Italian police officer. **2** a police spy.
17C. Italian, now coll., alt. of *birro*, from Medieval Latin *birrus* reddish-brown, from Greek *purrhos* flame-coloured, from *pur* fire.
● The reference is probably to the red police tunic, although some see an association with red as a 'devil's' colour. Cp. French slang *rousse* secret police, literally russet, and also perhaps English slang *rozzer* police officer.

scampi (skam´pi) *n.* **1** (*pl.*) large prawns such as the Norway lobster or Dublin (Bay) prawn, esp. when fried in breadcrumbs or batter. **2** (*sing.*) (*pl.* **scampi**, **scampis**) a dish of these.
19C. Italian, pl. of *scampo* a kind of lobster, of Venetian orig.

scena (shā´nə) *n.* (*pl.* **scene** (-nā)) (*Mus.*) a long elaborate solo piece or scene in opera.
19C. Italian, from Latin.

scenario (sinah´riō) *n.* (*pl.* **scenarios**) **1** a sketch or outline of the scenes and main points of a play etc. **2** the script of a film with dialogue and directions for the producer during the actual shooting. **3** an account or outline of projected or imagined future events.
19C. Italian, from Latin *scena*, alt. of *scaena* stage.

schadenfreude (shah´dənfroidə) *n.*
pleasure in others' misfortunes.
19C. German, from *Schaden* harm +
Freude joy.

schappe (shap, shap´ə) *n.* a fabric or yarn
made from waste silk.
19C. German silk waste.

schema (skē´mə) *n.* (*pl.* **schemata** (-tə),
schemas) **1** a scheme, summary, outline
or conspectus. **2** a chart or diagram.
3 the abstract figure of a syllogism. **4** a
figure of speech. **5** in Kant's philosophy,
the form, type or rule under which the
mind applies the categories to the
material of knowledge furnished by
sense perception.
18C. German, from Greek *skhēma* form,
figure.

scherzando (skeətsan´dō) *adv.* (*Mus.*)
playfully. ~*n.* (*pl.* **scherzandi** (-dē),
scherzandos) a passage or movement
played in this way.
19C. Italian, pres.p. of *scherzare* to joke,
from SCHERZO.

scherzo (skeət´sō) *n.* (*pl.* **scherzi** (-sē),
scherzos) (*Mus.*) a light playful
movement in music, usu. following a
slow one, in a symphony or sonata.
19C. Italian, lit. sport, jest.

schiavone (skyavō´nā) *n.* a 17th-cent.
basket-hilted broadsword.
19C. Italian, lit. Slavonian.
● The sword is so called because it was
used by the Slavonian guards of the
doge of Venice.

schiedam (skēdam´) *n.* a type of Dutch
gin.
19C. *Schiedam*, a town in the
Netherlands.

schiller (shil´ə) *n.* the peculiar bronzelike
sheen or iridescence characteristic of
certain minerals.
19C. German play of colours.

schilling (shil´ing) *n.* **1** the standard unit
of currency of Austria. **2** a coin of this
value.
18C. German, rel. to English *shilling*.

schipperke (skip´əki, ship´-, -kə) *n.* a
small black variety of lapdog.
19C. Dutch dial., lit. little boatman.
● The dog is so called from its use as a
watchdog on barges.

schläger (shlā´gə) *n.* a German student's
duelling sword, pointless, but with
sharpened edges towards the end.
19C. German, from *schlagen* to beat.

schlemiel (shləmēl´), **schlemihl**,
shlemiel *n.* (*esp. N Am., coll.*) a bungling
clumsy person who is easily victimized.
19C. Yiddish *shlemihl*, prob. from
biblical name of *Shelumiel* chief of the
tribe of Simeon (Num. vii.36).
● Shelumiel has been identified in the
Talmud with the Simeonite prince Zimri
ben Salu, killed while committing
adultery with a Midianite woman
(Num. xxv.6–15). Modern use of the
word has been influenced by Adelbert
von Chamisso's fairy tale *Peter
Schlemihls wundersame Geschichte*
(Peter Schlemihl's wonderful story)
(1814), whose eponymous hero sells his
shadow.

schlepp (shlep) *v.t.* (*pres.p.* **schlepping**,
past, p.p. **schlepped**) (*esp. N Am., coll.*)
to drag, pull. ~*n.* **1** a tedious journey.
2 an unlucky or incompetent person.
early 20C. Yiddish *shlepn*, from German
schleppen to drag.

schlieren (shlē´rən) *n.* **1** (*Geol.*) small
streaks of different composition in
igneous rock. **2** streaks in a transparent
fluid caused by regions of differing
density and refractive index.
19C. German, pl. of *Schliere* stria,
streak, from earlier *Schlier* marl, from
Middle High German *slier* mud.

schlimazel (shlimaz′əl), **shlimazel** *n.*
(*N Am., sl.*) an unlucky person; a born
loser.
mid-20C. Yiddish, from Middle High
German *slim* crooked + Hebrew *mazzāl*
luck.

schlock (shlok) *n.* (*N Am., coll.*) shoddy,
cheap goods; trash. ~*a.* shoddy, cheap,
trashy.
early 20C. Appar. from **Yiddish** *shlak*
apoplectic stroke, *shlog* wretch, untidy
person, from *shlogn* to strike.
• According to some, the word is from
German *Schlacke* dregs, scum, dross.

schloss (shlos) *n.* a castle (in Germany).
19C. German, rel. to English *slot*.

schlump (shlump) *n.* (*esp. N Am., sl.*) a
slovenly person, a slob.
mid-20C. Appar. rel. to **Yiddish**
shlumperdik dowdy, rel. to German
Schlumpe slattern.

schmaltz (shmawlts, shmolts), **schmalz**
n. (*esp. N Am., coll.*) over-sentimentality,
esp. in music.
mid-20C. Yiddish, from German
Schmalz dripping, lard.

schmatte (shmat′ə) *n.* a rag, a garment,
esp. a ragged one.
mid-20C. Yiddish, from Polish *szmata*
rag.

schmelze (shmelt′sə) *n.* any one of
various kinds of coloured glass, esp. that
coloured red and used to flash white
glass.
19C. Pl. of **German** *Schmelz* enamel.

schmo (shmō), **schmoe**, **shmo** *n.*
(*pl.* **schmoes, shmoes**) (*N Am., sl.*) a
stupid or boring person.
mid-20C. Alt. of SCHMUCK.

schmooze (shmooz), **schmoose**,
shmooze *v.i.* (*esp. N Am., sl.*) to gossip,
chat. ~*n.* chitchat.

19C. Yiddish *schmuesn* to talk, to chat,
from Hebrew *šĕmū′ōṭ*, pl. of *šĕmū′āh*
rumour.

schmuck (shmŭk) *n.* (*esp. N Am., sl.*) a
fool.
19C. Yiddish *shmok* fool, penis, ? from
Polish *smok* grass snake.

schnapps (shnaps) *n.* any of various
spirits resembling genever gin.
19C. German *Schnaps* dram of drink,
liquor, from Low German and Dutch
snaps gulp, mouthful, from *snappen* to
seize, to snatch.

schnauzer (shnow′zə, -tsə) *n.* a breed of
wire-haired German terrier.
early 20C. German, from *Schnauze*
snout, muzzle. Cp. SCHNOZZLE.
• The dog is so called from its
'moustache' and beard, which
accentuate its muzzle.

schnitzel (shnit′səl) *n.* an escalope of
meat, esp. veal.
19C. German cutlet, slice, from *Schnitz*
cut, slice. Cp. WIENER SCHNITZEL.

schnorrer (shnor′ə, shnaw′-) *n.* (*esp.
N Am., sl.*) a beggar.
19C. Yiddish var. of German
Schnurrer, from slang *schnurren* to go
begging.

schnozzle (shnoz′əl) *n.* (*esp. N Am., coll.*)
a nose.
mid-20C. Yiddish *shnoytzl*, dim. of
shnoytz, from German *Schnauze* snout.
Cp. SCHNAUZER.
• The word was popularized by the
US comedian Jimmy 'Schnozzle'
Durante (1893–1980), also known as
'Da Schnozz' and 'Schnozzola', in
allusion to his large nose.

schorl (shawl) *n.* black tourmaline.
18C. German *Schörl*, of unknown orig.

schottische (shotēsh´, shot´ish) n.
1 a dance resembling a polka. 2 the
music for it.
19C. German (der) Schottische(tanz)
(the) Scottish (dance).

schout (skowt) n. a municipal officer in
the Netherlands and Dutch colonies.
15C. Dutch, rel. to German Schulze.

schuss (shus) n. 1 a straight fast ski
slope. 2 a run made on this. ~v.i. to
make such a run.
mid-20C. German, lit. a shot.

schwa (shwah, shvah) n. 1 the symbol (ə)
used to represent a neutral unstressed
vowel sound in speech. 2 this speech
sound.
19C. German. See SHEVA.

Schweinhund (shvīn´hunt) n. a
despicable character.
early 20C. German, lit. pig dog, from
Schwein pig + Hund dog.
● The word became popular in English
as a mock (or real) term of abuse from
the time of World War I.

scienter (sīen´tə) adv. (Law) with
knowledge, wittingly, deliberately.
19C. Latin knowingly, from sciens,
scientis, pres.p. of scire to know + adv.
suf.

scilicet (sī´liset, skē´liket) adv. to wit,
videlicet, namely.
14–15C. Latin, from scire licet one may
understand, it is permitted to know,
from scire to know + 3rd pers. sing.
pres. ind. of licere to be permitted.
Cp. VIDELICET.
● As a term used to supply a missing
word or explain an ambiguity, the word
is usually abbreviated to sc.

scintilla (sintil´ə) n. (pl. **scintillas**)
1 a spark. 2 a trace, hint.
17C. Latin spark, glittering speck.

sciolto (shol´tō) adv. (Mus.) 1 freely, to
one's taste. 2 staccato.
19C. Italian, p.p. of sciogliere to loosen.

scire facias (sīəri fā´shias) n. (Law) a
writ to enforce the execution of or annul
judgements etc.
14–15C. Law Latin let (him) know, from
scire to know + 2nd pers. sing. pres.
subj. of facere to make, to do.

scordato (skawdah´tō) a. (Mus.) put out
of tune.
19C. Italian, p.p. of scordare to be out of
tune.

scoria (skaw´riə) n. (pl. **scoriae** (-riē))
1 cellular lava or ashes. 2 the refuse of
fused metals, dross.
14–15C. Latin, from Germanic skōria
refuse, from skōr dung.

scotia (skō´shə) n. a hollow moulding in
the base of a column.
16C. Latin, from Greek skotia, from
skotos darkness.
● The feature is so called from the dark
shadow inside the moulding.

scudo (skoo´dō) n. (pl. **scudi** (-dē)) an
old Italian silver coin and money of
account.
17C. Italian, from Latin scutum shield.
Cp. ESCUDO.

Seanad (shan´ədh), **Seanad Eireann**
(eə´rən) n. the upper house, or senate,
of the parliament of the Republic of
Ireland.
early 20C. Irish Seanad (Éireann) senate
(of Ireland).

seance (sā´ons, -äs), **séance** n. 1 a
meeting for exhibiting, receiving or
investigating spiritualistic
manifestations. 2 a session, as of a
society, deliberative body etc.
18C. French séance, from Old French
seoir, from Latin sedere to sit.
● The original sense was sense 2. Sense
1 arose in the 19C.

sec (sek) *a.* (of wine) dry.
   12–14C. French, from Latin *siccus* dry. Cp. SEKT.
   ● The word is only rarely found before the 19C.

secateurs (sekətœz´) *n.pl.* pruning scissors.
   19C. Pl. of **French** *sécateur*, from Latin *secare* to cut.
   ● The French word posits a non-existent Latin *secator (instead of *sector*) and is based on agent nouns in *-teur* or *-ateur* such as PROVOCATEUR.

secco (sek´ō) *n.* (*pl.* **seccos**) tempera-painting on dry plaster. ~*a.* (*Mus.*) plain, unadorned.
   19C. Italian, from Latin *siccus* dry.
   ● The sense painting on dry plaster derives from Italian *fresco secco*, literally dry fresco.

seconde (sikond´, səgōd´) *n.* in fencing, a position in parrying or lungeing.
   17C. French second.
   ● The position is the second of eight, the first being *prime*. Cp. SIXTE.

secondo (sikon´dō) *n.* (*pl.* **secondi** (-di)) (*Mus.*) the second part or the second performer in a duet.
   18C. Italian second.

secretaire (sekrəteə´) *n.* an escritoire, a bureau.
   18C. French *sécretaire*, from Late Latin *secretarius* confidential officer, use as n. of a. from Latin *secretus* secret.

secundum (sikŭn´dəm) *prep.* according to.
   16C. Latin according to.

Seder (sā´də) *n.* a ceremonial meal eaten on the first night (or the first two nights) of Passover.
   19C. Hebrew *sēḏer* order, procedure.

sederunt (sideə´rənt) *n.* (*Sc.*) **1** a sitting of a court etc. **2** a list of persons present. ~*v.i.* (*Sc. Law*) were present at the sitting of a court etc.
   17C. Latin (there) were sitting (the following persons), 3rd pers. pl. perf. indic. (used as n.) of *sedere* to sit.

sedile (sidī´li) *n.* (*pl.* **sedilia** (-dil´iə)) (*usu. pl.*) each of usu. three stone seats, usu. canopied and decorated, on the south side of the chancel in churches, for the priest, deacon and subdeacon.
   14–15C. Latin seat, from *sedere* to sit.
   ● The original sense was seat in general. The current specialized sense dates from the 18C.

seer (siə) *n.* an Indian weight of about one kilogram or liquid measure of about one litre.
   17C. Hindi *ser*, from Prakrit *satera*, from Greek *statēr* hundredweight, STATER.

segno (sā´nyō) *n.* (*pl.* **segni** (-nyē), **segnos**) (*Mus.*) a sign marking the beginning or end of a section to be repeated.
   19C. Italian sign. Cp. DAL SEGNO.

segue (seg´wā) *v.i.* (3rd pers. sing. pres. **segues**, pres.p. **seguing**, past, p.p. **segued**) (*Mus.*) to move without interruption from one song or melody to another. ~*n.* an act or result of seguing.
   mid-20C. Italian, 3rd pers. sing. pres. ind. of *seguire* to follow.
   ● The word was in earlier use (from the 18C) as a musical direction to proceed to the next movement without a break.

seguidilla (segidēl´yə) *n.* **1** a lively Spanish dance in triple time. **2** the music for this.
   18C. Spanish, from *seguida* following, sequence, from *seguir* to follow.

Sehnsucht (zān´zookht) *n.* yearning.
   19C. German, from *sehen* to see + *suchen* to seek.

seicento (sāchen´tō) *n.* the 17th cent. in Italian art, architecture or literature.
early 20C. Italian six hundred (i.e. 1600s).

seiche (sāsh) *n.* an undulation, somewhat resembling a tidal wave, in the water of Lake Geneva and other Swiss lakes, usu. due to disturbance of atmospheric pressure or to subterranean movements.
19C. Swiss French, ? from German *Seiche* sinking (of water).

seif (sēf, sāf), **seif dune** *n.* a long sand dune in the form of a ridge.
early 20C. Arabic *sayf*, lit. sword.

seigneur (senyœ´), †**seignior** (sān´yə) *n.* **1** (*Hist.*) a feudal lord. **2** (*Can.*) the holder of a seigneury.
16C. Old French, from Latin *senior* older.

seilbahn (zīl´bahn) *n.* a cable railway.
mid-20C. German, from *Seil* cable, rope + *Bahn* road way. Cp. ABSEIL, AUTOBAHN.

Sekt (zekt, sekt) *n.* a German sparkling white wine.
early 20C. German. Cp. SEC.

selah (sē´lə) *n.* a word occurring in the Psalms and in Habakkuk, always at the end of a verse, variously interpreted as indicating a pause, a repetition, the end of a strophe etc.
16C. Hebrew *selāh*.

Seljuk (sel´jook) *n.* a member of any of various Muslim dynasties in central and W Asia during the 11th and 13th cents., descended from the Turkish chieftain Seljuk. ~*a.* of or relating to the Seljuks.
19C. Turkish *seljūq, Selčük*, reputed ancestor of the Seljuk dynasties.

selva (sel´və) *n.* tropical rain forest in the Amazon basin.
19C. Spanish or Portuguese, from Latin *silva* wood.

semé (sem´ā), **semée** *a.* (*Her.*) (of a field or charge) strewn over with figures, such as stars, crosses etc.
14–15C. French, p.p. of *semer* to sow.

semester (simes´tə) *n.* a college half-year in German, some American and other universities.
19C. German, from Latin *semestris* of six months, from *sex* six + *mensis* month.

seminar (sem´inah) *n.* **1** a group of students undertaking an advanced course of study or research together, usu. under the guidance of a professor. **2** such a course. **3** a discussion group, or a meeting of it.
19C. German, from Latin *seminarium* nursery, seed-plot.

semolina (semələē´nə) *n.* the hard grains of wheat left after bolting, used for puddings etc.
18C. Alt. of **Italian** *semolino*, dim. of *semola* bran, based on Latin *simila* flour.

semper (sem´pə) *adv.* always.
17C. Latin always.

semper eadem (sempər āah´dem) *a.* always the same.
17C. Latin, fem. of *semper idem*.
● The phrase was the motto of Queen Elizabeth I (reigned 1558–1603) and Queen Anne (reigned 1702–14). As Latin *eadem* is feminine the phrase can only apply to women.

semper fidelis (sem´pə fidā´lis) *a.* always faithful.
early 20C. Latin, from *semper* always + *fidelis* faithful.
● The phrase is found as a motto borne by many families and several organizations.

semplice (sem´plichā) *adv.* (*Mus.*) simply, plainly, without embellishment.
18C. Italian simple.

sempre (sem´prā) *adv.* (*Mus.*) in the same manner throughout.
19C. Italian always, from Latin SEMPER.

semuncia (simŭn´shə) *n.* (*Hist.*) a Roman coin equal to half an uncia.
19C. Latin half-ounce, from *semi-* half + *uncia* twelfth, ounce.

sen (sen) *n.* (*pl.* **sen**) a Japanese monetary unit, one hundredth of a yen.
18C. Japanese.

senhor (senyaw´) *n.* **1** a man, in a Portuguese-speaking country. **2** the Portuguese or Brazilian title corresponding to the English *Mr* or *sir*.
18C. Portuguese, from Latin *senior* older. Cp. SEÑOR, SIGNOR.

senhora (senyaw´rə) *n.* **1** a lady (in Portugal, Brazil etc.). **2** a form of address to a married woman, corresponding to *Mrs* or *madam*.
19C. Portuguese, fem. of SENHOR. Cp. SEÑORA, SIGNORA.

senhorita (senyawrē´tə) *n.* **1** a young unmarried girl (in Portugal, Brazil etc.). **2** a form of address to an unmarried girl or woman, corresponding to *Miss*.
19C. Portuguese, dim. of SENHORA. Cp. SEÑORITA, SIGNORINA.

señor (senyaw´) *n.* (*pl.* **señores** (-riz))
1 a man, in a Spanish-speaking country. **2** the Spanish form of address corresponding to the English *Mr* or *sir*.
17C. Spanish, from Latin *senior* older. Cp. SENHOR, SIGNOR.

señora (senyaw´rə) *n.* **1** a lady (in Spain etc.). **2** the Spanish form of address to a married woman, corresponding to *Mrs* or *madam*.
16C. Spanish, fem. of SEÑOR.

señorita (senyawrē´tə) *n.* **1** a young unmarried girl (in Spain etc.). **2** the

Spanish form of address to an unmarried girl or woman, corresponding to *Miss*.
19C. Spanish, dim. of SEÑORA.

sensu stricto (sensoo strik´tō) *adv.* strictly speaking, in the narrow sense.
19C. Latin in the restricted sense.

senza (sent´sə) *prep.* (*Mus.*) without.
18C. Italian without, prob. from Latin *absentia* absence, influ. by Latin *sine* without. Cp. SANS.

Sephardi (sifah´di) *n.* (*pl.* **Sephardim** (-dim)) a Jew of Spanish, Portuguese or N African descent.
19C. Modern Hebrew, from *sĕpāraḍ*, a country mentioned in Obad. xx and taken to be Spain.

sepoy (sē´poi) *n.* (*Hist.*) an Indian soldier under European discipline, esp. one in the former British Indian army.
18C. Persian and Urdu *sipāhī* horseman, soldier, from *sipāh* army. Cp. SPAHI.

seppuku (sepoo´koo) *n.* hara-kiri.
19C. Japanese, from *setsu* to cut + *fuku* abdomen. Cp. HARA-KIRI.

septemvir (septem´viə) *n.* (*pl.* **septemviri** (-virī)) each of seven people forming a government, committee etc.
18C. Latin, sing. of *septemviri*, from *septem* seven + *viri* men.

serac (serak´, ser´-) *n.* any of the large angular or tower-shaped masses into which a glacier breaks up at an icefall.
19C. Swiss French *sérac*, orig. the name of a kind of compact white cheese, prob. from Latin *serum* whey.

seraglio (siral´yō) *n.* (*pl.* **seraglios**)
1 a harem. **2** (*Hist.*) a walled palace, esp. the old palace of the Turkish Sultan, with its mosques, government offices etc., at Istanbul.
16C. Italian *serraglio*, from Turkish *saray* (SERAI), with assim. to Italian

serraglio cage, from Medieval Latin
serraculum, dim. of Latin *sera* bolt.

serai (sərī´) *n.* a caravanserai.
17C. **Turkish** *saray* palace, mansion,
from Persian. Cp. SERAGLIO.

serang (sərang´) *n.* a boatman; the leader
of a Lascar crew.
18C. **Persian and Urdu** *sar-hang*
commander, from *sar* head + *hang*
authority.

serape (sərah´pā), **sarape** (sar-), **zarape**
(zar-) *n.* a Mexican blanket or shawl.
19C. **Mexican Spanish**.

seraskier (sərəskiə´) *n.* (*Hist.*) a Turkish
commander, esp. the commander-in-
chief or minister of war.
17C. **Turkish** *serasker*, *sarasker*, from
Persian *sar'askar*, from *sar* head +
Arabic *'askar* army, from Latin *exercitus*.

serein (sərān´) *n.* a fine rain falling from
a clear sky after sunset, esp. in tropical
regions.
19C. **French**, from Latin *serum* evening,
use as n. of *serus* late.

seriatim (siəriā´tim) *adv.* **1** in regular
order. **2** one point etc. after the other.
14–15C. **Medieval Latin**, from Latin
series chain, row, series + *-atim*.
• The word is based on Latin
GRADATIM. Cp. LITERATIM.

serrano (serah´nō) *n.* a member of a
Native American people of S California.
19C. **Spanish** highlander, from SIERRA.

serviette (sœviet´) *n.* a table napkin.
15C. **Old French** towel, napkin, from
servir to serve.

se-tenant (sēten´ənt) *a.* (of postage
stamps) joined together as when printed.
early 20C. **French**, lit. holding together,
from *se* oneself, themselves + pres.p. of
tenir to hold.

Sèvres (sevr´, sev´rə) *n.* porcelain made
at Sèvres.

18C. *Sèvres*, a town in N France (now a
suburb of Paris), where it was originally
made.

sexto (sek´stō) *n.* (*pl.* **sextos**) a book
formed by folding sheets into six leaves
each.
19C. **Latin**, abl. of *sextus* sixth. Cp.
OCTAVO, QUARTO.

sforzando (sfawtsan´dō), **sforzato**
(-tsah´tō) *adv.* (*Mus.*) emphatically, with
sudden vigour. ~*a.* emphatic, vigorous.
~*n.* (*pl.* **sforzandos**, **sforzandi** (-dē),
sforzatos, **sforzati** (-tē)) **1** a note or
group of notes emphasized in this way.
2 an increase in emphasis.
19C. **Italian**, pres.p. of *sforzare* to use
force.

sfumato (sfumah´tō) *a.* (of art) with
misty outlines. ~*n.* (*pl.* **sfumatos**) **1** the
technique of blending areas of different
colours. **2** this effect.
19C. **Italian**, p.p. of *sfumare* to shade
off, from *s-*, representing Latin *ex-* out
+ *fumare* to smoke.

sgraffito (sgrafē´tō) *n.* (*pl.* **sgraffiti** (-tē))
1 decoration by means of scratches
through plaster or slip, revealing a
differently coloured ground. **2** an
example of this.
18C. **Italian**, from *sgraffiare* to scratch
away, with *s-* representing Latin *ex-* out
of. Cp. GRAFFITI.

shabrack (shab´rak) *n.* (*Hist.*) the housing
or saddle-cloth of a cavalry saddle.
19C. **German** *Schabracke*, French
schabraque, of E European orig.
Cp. Turkish *çaprak*.

shabu-shabu (shaboo shab´oo) *n.* a
Japanese dish of pieces of thinly sliced
beef or pork cooked quickly with
vegetables in boiling water.
late 20C. **Japanese**.
• The name is said to represent the
swishing noise made by the morsels of

meat as they are moved in the boiling broth.

shadoof (shədoof´) *n.* a water-raising contrivance consisting of a long pole with bucket and counterpoise, used on the Nile etc.
19C. Egyptian Arabic *šādūf.*

shah (shah) *n.* (*Hist.*) a sovereign of Iran.
16C. Persian *šāh,* from Old Persian *kšāyatiya* king.
• The Old Persian word gave the name of Xerxes I (519–465 BC), king of Persia.

shako (shak´ō, shā´-) *n.* (*pl.* **shakos**) a military cylindrical hat, usu. flat-topped, with a peak in front, usu. tilting forward, and decorated with a pompom, plume or tuft.
19C. French *schako,* from Hungarian *csákó,* prob. from German *Zacken* peak, point, spike.

shakuhachi (shakuhach´i) *n.*
(*pl.* **shakuhachis**) a Japanese bamboo flute.
19C. Japanese, from *shaku* a unit of length (approximately 0.33 metres) + *hachi* eight (tenths).

shalom (shəlom´) *n., int.* peace (a greeting used esp. by Jewish people).
19C. Hebrew *šālōm* peace.

shalwar (shŭl´vah) *n.* a type of loose trousers worn in some S Asian countries and by some Muslims elsewhere.
19C. Persian and Urdu *šalwār.*
Cp. Russian *sharovary.*
• When worn by women with a KAMEEZ, the matching outfit is known as a *shalwar-kameez.*

shaman (shah´mən, shā´-) *n.* a priest, exorcist or medicine man among some Siberian and N African peoples.
17C. German *Schamane* or Russian *shaman,* from Tungus *šaman.*

shampoo (shampoo´) *v.t.* (*3rd pers. sing. pres.* **shampoos**, *pres.p.* **shampooing**, *past, p.p.* **shampooed**) 1 to wash with shampoo. 2 to wash the hair of with shampoo. ~*n.* (*pl.* **shampoos**) 1 a liquid soap or detergent used for washing the hair. 2 a similar cleaner for a car, carpet, upholstery etc. 3 an act of shampooing.
18C. Hindi *cǎpo,* imper. of *cǎpnā* to press, to knead.
• The original sense was to massage (as part of the process of a Turkish bath). Sense 1 evolved in the 19C.

shanghai (shanghī´) *v.t.* (*3rd pers. sing. pres.* **shanghais**, *pres.p.* **shanghaiing**, *past, p.p.* **shanghaied**) 1 to drug and ship as a sailor while stupefied. 2 to kidnap. 3 (*coll.*) to trick into performing an unpleasant task. 4 (*Austral.*) to shoot with a catapult. ~*n.* (*pl.* **shanghais**) (*Austral.*) a catapult.
19C. *Shanghai,* a city and seaport in E China.
• The reference is to the former practice of kidnapping sailors to serve on ships bound for the Far East.

shantung (shantŭng´) *n.* a plain fabric woven in coarse silk yarns.
19C. *Shantung,* a province in NE China, where orig. manufactured.

sharia (shərē´ə), **shariah** *n.* the body of Islamic religious law.
19C. Arabic *šarī'a.*

shashlik (shash´lik) *n.* a lamb kebab.
early 20C. Russian *shashlyk,* from Crimean Turkish *şişlik,* from *şiş* skewer.
Cp. SHISH KEBAB.

Shastra (shas´trə), **Shaster** (-tə), **Sastra** (sah´strə) *n.* any of the Vedas and other sacred scriptures of Hinduism.
17C. Sanskrit *śāstra,* lit. instruction, from *śāsti* he punishes, he instructs.

Shavuoth (shəvoo´əs, shahvuot´),
Shavuot *n.* the Jewish Pentecost.
19C. Hebrew *šāḇū´ōṯ*, pl. of *šāḇūă‘*
week.
● The name refers to the weeks
between Passover and Pentecost.
Hence the festival's English name,
Feast of Weeks.

shchi (shchē) *n.* cabbage soup.
19C. Russian, ? rel. to BORSCH.

Shebat (shebat´), **Sebat** (seb-) *n.* the
eleventh ecclesiastical month, or fifth
civil month, of the Jewish year
(corresponding to parts of January and
February).
16C. Hebrew *šĕḇaṭ*.

shebeen (shibēn´) *n.* **1** (*Ir.*) a low public
house. **2** an unlicensed house where
excisable liquors are sold.
18C. Irish *síbín*, ? var. of *séibín*, dim. of
séibe bottle, mug, liquid measure.

shechita (shehē´ta), **schechita**,
shehita, **schechitah**, **shehitah** *n.* the
Jewish manner of killing animals for
food.
19C. Hebrew *šĕḥīṭāh*, from *šāḥaṭ* to
slaughter.

sheikh (shāk, shēk), **sheik**, **shaikh** *n.*
1 the head of a Bedouin family, clan or
tribe. **2** a Muslim leader.
16C. Ult. from **Arabic** *šayḵ* old man,
elder, from *šāḵa* to be old, to grow old.
● A sense 'dashing male lover' (early
20C) arose from E.M. Hull's novel *The
Sheik* (1919) and was popularized by
the film of 1921 based on it, starring
Rudolph Valentino, and especially by
its sequel, *Son of the Sheik* (1926).

shekel (shek´əl) *n.* **1** the standard unit of
currency of Israel. **2** (*pl., coll.*) money,
riches. **3** a Hebrew weight of one fiftieth
of a mina. **4** (*Hist.*) a silver coin of this
weight.
16C. Hebrew *šeqel*, from *šāqal* to weigh.

Shekinah (shikī´nə), **Shechinah** *n.* the
visible presence of Jehovah above the
mercy-seat in the Tabernacle and
Solomon's Temple.
17C. Late Hebrew *šĕḵīnāh*, from *šākan*
to rest, to dwell.

Sheol (shē´ōl, -əl) *n.* the Hebrew place of
the dead, often translated 'hell' in the
Authorized Version of the Bible.
16C. Hebrew *šĕ’ōl*.

sherbet (shœ´bit, -bət) *n.* **1** an
effervescent powder used in sweets or
to make fizzy drinks. **2** (*esp. N Am.*) a
water ice. **3** an oriental cooling drink,
made of diluted fruit juices. **4** (*Austral.*,
facet.) beer.
17C. Turkish *şerbet*, Persian *šerbet*,
from Arabic *šarbat* draught, drink, from
šariba to drink. Cp. SHRUB.

sherif (shərēf´), **shereef**, **sharif** *n.* **1** a
descendant of Muhammad through his
daughter Fatima and Hassan Ibn Ali.
2 the chief magistrate of Mecca.
16C. Arabic *šarīf* noble, high-born.

Sherpa (shœ´pə) *n.* (*pl.* **Sherpa**,
Sherpas) a member of a mountaineering
people living on the southern slopes of
the Himalayas.
19C. Tibetan *sharpa* inhabitant of an
Eastern country.

sheva (shəvah´) *n.* **1** the Hebrew sign (:)
put under a consonant to denote the
absence of a following vowel sound.
2 SCHWA.
16C. Hebrew *šĕwā’*, appar. arbitrary alt.
of *šāw’* emptiness, variety.
● The Hebrew word was formerly spelt
Schwa in German books, giving SCHWA.

Shia (shē´ə), **Shiah**, **Shi'a** *n.* (*pl.* **Shia**,
Shias, **Shiah**, **Shiahs**, **Shi'a**, **Shi'as**)
1 one of the two main branches of Islam
(see also SUNNA), which regards Ali
(Muhammad's cousin and son-in-law)
as the first rightful imam or caliph and

rejects the three Sunni caliphs.
2 a Shi'ite. ~*a.* belonging to, or
characteristic of, the Shia branch of
Islam.
17C. Arabic *sī'a* faction, party (i.e. of
Ali).

shiatsu (shiat´soo) *n.* a massage in which
pressure is applied to the acupuncture
points of the body.
mid-20C. Japanese, lit. finger pressure.

shibboleth (shib´ələth) *n.* **1** a criterion,
test or watchword of a party etc. **2** an
old-fashioned or discredited doctrine
etc.
17C. Hebrew *šibbōleṭ* ear of corn, stream
in flood, used as a test of nationality for
foreigners who have difficulty in
pronouncing *sh*.
● The word was said to have been used
by the Gileadites to distinguish their
own men from the fleeing Ephraimites:
'Then said they unto him, Say now
Shibboleth: and he said Sibboleth: for
he could not frame to pronounce it
right' (Judg. xii.6).

shicer (shī´sə) *n.* (*Austral.*) **1** (*sl.*) a crook,
a welsher. **2** (*Mining*) a useless mine.
3 (*sl.*) a useless thing.
19C. German *Scheisser*, lit. shitter,
contemptible person.

shicker (shik´ə) *a.* (*Austral., New Zeal.,*
sl.) drunk. ~*n.* drink, excessive
drinking.
19C. Yiddish *shiker*, from Hebrew
šikkōr, from *šākar* to be drunk.

shih-tzu (shētsoo´) *n.* a small dog with
long silky hair, of a Tibetan and Chinese
breed.
early 20C. Chinese *shīzigŏu*, from *shīzi*
lion + *gŏu* dog.

shiitake (shitah´kā) *n.* a mushroom,
Lentinus edodes, used in Oriental
cookery.

19C. Japanese, from *shii* a kind of oak
+ *take* mushroom.

shikar (shikah´) *n.* (*Ang.-Ind.*) hunting,
sport, game.
17C. Persian and Urdu *šikār*.

shiksa (shik´sə), **schicksa**, **shikse** *n.*
(*offensive*) a non-Jewish woman.
19C. Yiddish *shikse*, from Hebrew
šiqṣāh, from *šeqeṣ* detested thing + fem.
suf. -*āh*.

Shinto (shin´tō) *n.* the indigenous
religion of the people of Japan existing
along with Buddhism, incorporating
nature- and ancestor-worship.
18C. Japanese *shin* gods + *tō* way.

shish kebab (shish kibab´) *n.* a skewer
of marinated and cooked meat and
vegetables.
early 20C. Turkish *şiş kebab*, from *şiş*
skewer + KEBAB. Cp. SHASHLIK.

shochet (shokh´ət) *n.* (*pl.* **shochetim**
(-tim)) a slaughterer who is qualified to
prepare meat and poultry according to
Jewish ritual.
19C. Hebrew *šōḥēṭ*, pres.p. of *šāḥaṭ* to
slaughter. Cp. SHECHITA.

shofar (shō´fah) *n.* (*pl.* **shofars**,
shofroth (-frō´)) a trumpet made from
a ram's horn used in Jewish religious
ceremonies and as a battle-signal in
ancient times.
19C. Hebrew *šŏpār*, pl. *šŏpārōṭ*.

shogun (shō´gun) *n.* (*Hist.*) the hereditary
commander-in-chief of the army and
virtual ruler of Japan under the feudal
regime, abolished in 1868.
17C. Japanese *shōgun*, from Chinese
jiāng jūn army general.

shoji (shō´jē) *n.* (*pl.* **shoji**, **shojis**) a paper
screen forming a wall or partition in a
Japanese home.
19C. Japanese *shōji*.

shoyu (shō´yoo) *n.* a type of sauce made from fermented soya beans.
18C. Japanese *shōyu*, from Chinese *jiàngyóu*, from *jiàng* bean paste + *yóu* oil. Cp. SOY.

shrub (shrŭb) *n.* a drink composed of the sweetened juice of lemons or other fruit with spirit.
18C. Arabic *šurb*, *šarāb*. Cp. SHERBET.

shtetl (shtet´əl, shtāt´-) *n.* a small Jewish town or village in E Europe.
mid-20C. Yiddish little town, from German *Stadt* town.

shtick (shtik), **schtick**, **schtik** *n.* (*sl.*) a comedian's or performer's routine, patter etc.
mid-20C. Yiddish, from German *Stück* piece, play.

shtoom (shtum), **schtoom**, **shtum**, **shtumm** *a.* (*sl.*) quiet, silent.
mid-20C. Yiddish, from German *stumm* silent.

shubunkin (shubŭng´kin) *n.* a type of large-finned goldfish with black spots and red patches.
early 20C. Japanese, from *shu* vermilion + *bun* pattern + *kin* gold.

shufti (shŭf´ti, shuf´-), **shufty** *n.* (*pl.* **shuftis**, **shufties**) (*sl.*) a (quick) look (at something).
mid-20C. Colloquial Arabic *šuftī* have you seen?, from *šāfa* to see.

shul (shool) *n.* a synagogue.
19C. Yiddish, from German *Schule* school.

sic (sēk, sik) *adv.* thus, so (usu. printed after a doubtful word or phrase to indicate that it is quoted exactly as in the original).
19C. Latin so, thus.

sic semper tyrannis (sik sempə tiran´ēs) *int.* such is the fate of tyrants (the motto of the state of Virginia).

early 20C. Latin, thus always to tyrants, from *sic* thus + *semper* always + dat. pl. of *tyrannus* tyrant.
• The words were quoted by John Wilkes Booth as he assassinated Abraham Lincoln on 14 April 1865.

sic transit gloria mundi (sik tranzit glawriə mŭn´di, mun´-) *int.* thus the glory of the world passes away, a reflection on the transitoriness of worldly success.
16C. Latin.
• The phrase comes from Thomas à Kempis's *On the Imitation of Christ* (*c.*1415–24).

siddhi (sid´i) *n.* (in Indian religions) fulfilment.
19C. Sanskrit.
• A person who has attained such spiritual perfection is known as a *siddha*.

siddur (sid´uə) *n.* (*pl.* **siddurim** (siduə´rim)) the Jewish prayer book used for daily worship.
19C. Hebrew *siddūr*, lit. order.

Sieg Heil (zēk hīl´, zēg) *int.* a victory salute at a Nazi political rally.
mid-20C. German, lit. hail victory, from *Sieg* victory + *Heil* hail. Cp. *Heil Hitler*.
• The phrase became familiar from World War II films.

sienna (sien´ə) *n.* **1** a pigment composed of a native clay coloured with iron and manganese. **2** the colour of this pigment, raw or burnt sienna.
18C. Italian (*terra di*) *Sienna* (earth of) *Siena*, a city and province in Tuscany, W Italy.

sierra (sieə´rə) *n.* (*pl.* **sierras**) in Spanish-speaking countries and the US, a long mountain chain, jagged in outline.
16C. Spanish, from Latin *serra* saw.

siesta (sies´tə) *n.* (*pl.* **siestas**) a short midday sleep, esp. in hot countries.
17C. Spanish, from Latin *sexta* (*hora*) sixth (hour) (of the day), i.e. midday.

siffleur (sēflœ´) *n.* a whistling artiste.
18C. French whistler, from *siffler* to whistle.
• The word was originally the term for an animal that makes a whistling noise. The current sense dates from the 19C.

siglum (sig´ləm) *n.* (*pl.* **sigla** (-lə)) a symbol, sign or abbreviation used in a manuscript or document.
18C. Late Latin *sigla* (pl.), ? from *singula*, neut. pl. of *singulus* single.

sigma (sig´mə) *n.* the 18th letter of the Greek alphabet (Σ, σ or, when final, ς, or, in uncial form, C or c).
14–15C. Latin, from Greek.

signor (sēn´yaw, -yaw´) *n.* (*pl.* **signori** (sēnyaw´rē)) **1** an Italian man. **2** the Italian form of address corresponding to *sir* or *Mr*.
16C. Italian, reduced form of *signore*, from Latin *senior* older.

signora (sēnyaw´rə) *n.* (*pl.* **signore** (-yaw´rā)) **1** a married Italian woman. **2** the Italian form of address to a married woman, corresponding to *madam* or *Mrs*.
17C. Italian, fem. of *signore* (see SIGNOR).

signorina (sēnyərē´nə) *n.* (*pl.* **signorine** (-nā)) **1** an unmarried Italian girl. **2** the Italian form of address to an unmarried girl or woman corresponding to *Miss* or to French *mademoiselle*.
19C. Italian, dim. of SIGNORA.

Sikh (sēk) *n.* a member of a monotheistic religion that takes the Granth as its scripture, founded in the 16th cent. in the Punjab. ~*a.* of or relating to Sikhs or Sikhism.
18C. Punjabi and Hindi, from Sanskrit *śiṣya* discipline.

silenus (sīlē´nəs) *n.* (*pl.* **sileni** (-nī)) a woodland satyr in the shape of a riotous and drunken old man.
17C. Latin *Silenus*, from Greek *Seilēnos*, in Greek mythology the foster-father of Bacchus and leader of the satyrs.

silhouette (siluet´) *n.* **1** a portrait in profile or outline, usu. black on a white ground or cut out in paper etc. **2** the outline of a figure as seen against the light or cast as a shadow. ~*v.t.* (*usu. in pass.*) to represent or cause to be visible in silhouette.
18C. French, from Étienne de *Silhouette*, 1709–67, French writer and politician.
• The portrait is said to be so called because it was inexpensive to produce, evoking the petty economies introduced by Silhouette in 1759 to finance the Seven Years' War. Others claim the portraits resembled those made by Silhouette to decorate the walls of his château at Bry-sur-Marne.

s'il vous plaît (sēl voo plā´) *adv.* please.
early 20C. French, lit. if it pleases you. Cp. RSVP.
• The phrase is sometimes misunderstood in English as meaning 'if you please'.

similia similibus curantur (similiə similibəs kooran´tə, kuə-) *int.* like cures like.
19C. Latin, lit. like things are cured by like things.
• The words express the principle of homoeopathy, which prescribes for patients drugs or other treatments that would produce in healthy persons symptoms of the disease being treated.

simoom (simoom´), **simoon** (-moon´) *n.*
a hot dry wind blowing over the desert,
esp. of Arabia, raising great quantities of
sand and causing intense thirst.
18C. Arabic *samūm*, from *samma* to
poison.

simpatico (simpat´ikō) *a.* congenial,
agreeable, likeable.
19C. Spanish *simpático*, from *simpatía*,
or Italian *simpatico*, from *simpatia*, both
from Latin *sympathia* sympathy, from
Greek *sumpatheia*, from *sumpathēs*
having a fellow feeling.

simpliciter (simplis´itə) *adv.* wholly,
absolutely, unconditionally.
16C. Latin.

simulacrum (simūlā´krəm) *n.*
(*pl.* **simulacra** (-krə)) **1** an image or
likeness. **2** a deceptive or superficial
likeness, a spurious substitute. **3** a mere
semblance or pretence.
16C. Latin, from *simulare* to imitate.

simurg (simœg´), **simorg** (-mawg´),
simurgh *n.* an enormous fabulous bird
of Persian mythology with the ability to
think and speak.
18C. Persian *sīmurġ*, from Pahlavi *sēn*
eagle + *murġ* bird.

sine (sin´i, sī´-) *prep.* without, lacking.
17C. Latin without.

sine die (sin´i dī´ē, sī´-, dē´ā) *adv., a.*
without any day (being fixed).
17C. Latin, from *sine* without + abl.
sing. of *dies* day.

sine qua non (sīni kwā non´, sini kwah
nōn´) *n.* (*pl.* **sine qua nons**) an
essential condition or indispensible
requirement.
17C. Latin (*causa*) *sine qua non* lit.
(cause) without which not, from *sine*
without + *qua* abl. sing. fem. of *qui*
which + *non* not.

sinfonia (sinfō´niə) *n.* (*Mus.*) **1** a
symphony. **2** an orchestral piece
introducing a baroque opera, suite etc.
3 a symphony orchestra.
18C. Italian symphony.

sinfonia concertante (sinfōniə
konchœtan´ti) *n.* a symphonic work with
parts for a number of solo instruments.
early 20C. Italian, from SINFONIA +
CONCERTANTE.

sinfonietta (sinfōniet´ə) *n.* **1** a short or
light symphony. **2** a small symphony
orchestra.
early 20C. Italian, dim. of SINFONIA.

singspiel (sing´shpēl, zing´-) *n.* a
dramatic entertainment in which the
action is expressed alternately in
dialogue and song.
19C. German, from *singen* to sing
+ *Spiel* play.

Sinn Fein (shin fān´) *n.* Irish political
party formed in 1905 with the aim of
creating a united republican Ireland
and closely associated with the Irish
Republican Army.
early 20C. Irish *sinn féin*, lit. we
ourselves.

sinsemilla (sinsəmē´lyə) *n.* **1** an
especially potent type of marijuana.
2 the seedless variety of cannabis plant
from which it is obtained.
late 20C. American Spanish, lit. without
seed.

sirdar (sœ´dah), **sardar** (sœ´dah) *n.* **1** a
military leader or commander in the
Indian subcontinent or in other Eastern
countries. **2** (**Sirdar**) the former
commander-in-chief of the Egyptian
army. **3** a title used before the names of
Sikh men. **4** a leader, chief, foreman etc.
16C. Persian and Urdu *sar-dār*, from
Persian *sar* position of head or chief
+ *dār* holding.

sirocco (sirok´ō), **scirocco** (shi-) *n.* (*pl.*
siroccos, sciroccos) **1** a hot oppressive
wind blowing from N Africa across to
Italy etc., often carrying dust or rain.
2 a sultry southerly wind in Italy.
17C. Italian *scirocco*, ult. from Spanish
Arabic *šalūḳ, šulūḳ* SE wind.

sirop (sirō´) *n.* a drink made from a
syrupy preparation of sweetened fruit
juice.
19C. French syrup.

sirvente (sœvāt´) *n.* a form of ballad or
lay, usu. satirical, used by the medieval
trouvères and troubadours.
19C. French, from Provençal *sirventes*,
of unknown orig.
● The final *-s* of the Provençal word
was mistaken as a plural ending.

sistrum (sis´trəm) *n.* (*pl.* **sistrums,**
sistra (-trə)) a jingling instrument used
by the ancient Egyptians in the worship
of Isis.
14–15C. Latin, from Greek *seistron*, from
seiein to shake.

sitar (sitah´, sit´-) *n.* an Indian stringed
musical instrument with a long neck.
19C. Persian and Urdu *sitār*, from *sih*
three + *tār* string.

sitzfleisch (zits´flīsh) *n.* the ability to
persist in an endeavour or endure in an
activity.
early 20C. German, from *sitzen* to sit
+ *Fleisch* flesh.

sitzkrieg (zits´krēg) *n.* a war or period of
a war characterized by a relative or
complete absence of fighting.
mid-20C. Pseudo-German, based on
Blitzkrieg (see BLITZ), as if from German
sitzen to sit + *Krieg* war.
● The term specifically referred to
the early months of World War II in
the period known as the 'phoney war'
(1939–40).

Siva (sē´və), **Shiva** (shē´-) *n.* the god who
is associated with Brahma and Vishnu
in the Hindu triad, known as the
destroyer and reproducer of life.
18C. Sanskrit *śiva*, lit. auspicious one.

Sivan (sivahn´) *n.* the third month of the
Jewish ecclesiastical year and ninth of
the civil year, comprising parts of May
and June.
14–15C. Hebrew *sīwān*.

sixte (sikst) *n.* a parry in fencing (the
sixth of eight parrying positions) in
which the hand is opposite the right
breast and the point of the sword raised
and a little to the right.
19C. French sixth. Cp. SECONDE.

sjambok (sham´bok), **jambok** (jam´-)
n. (*S Afr.*) a short heavy whip, usu. of
rhinoceros hide. ~*v.t.* (*pres.p.*
sjambokking, sjamboking,
jambokking, jamboking, *past, p.p.*
sjambokked, sjamboked,
jambokked, jamboked) to flog with
this kind of whip.
18C. Afrikaans, from Malay *sambuk,*
chambuk, from Persian and Urdu
chābuk horsewhip.

skat (skat) *n.* a three-handed card game
resembling piquet.
19C. German, from Italian *scarto* cards
laid aside, from *scartare* to discard.
Cp. ÉCARTÉ.

ski (skē) *n.* (*pl.* **skis, ski**) **1** either of a pair
of long narrow runners of waxed wood,
metal, plastic etc., usu. pointed and
curved upwards at the front, fastened
one to each foot and used for sliding
over snow. **2** a similar piece of apparatus
fitted to the underside of a vehicle or
aircraft. **3** a water-ski. ~*a.* for use or wear
while skiing. ~*v.i.* (*3rd pers. sing. pres.*
skis, *pres.p.* **skiing, ski-ing,** *past, p.p.*
skied (skēd), **ski'd**) to move on skis.
~*v.t.* to ski at (a certain venue) or on (a
certain route, slope etc.).

18C. Norwegian, from Old Norse *skith* billet of cleft wood, snowshoe.

ski-joring (skē´jawring, shē´yœring) *n.* a winter sport in which a skier is towed by a horse or a vehicle.
early 20C. Norwegian *skikjøring*, from *ski* ski + *kjøring* driving.

skol (skōl), **skoal** *int.* cheers! good health! (usu. as a toast).
17C. Danish *skaal*, Swedish *skål* toast, from Old Norse *skál* bowl.
● The Old Norse word gave English *scale* as one of the weighing pans on a pair of scales.

skyr (skiə) *n.* a dish of curds.
19C. Icelandic.

slainte (slahnch´ə) *int.* your health, here's to you (used as a drinking toast).
19C. Gaelic *slàinte* (*mhór*) (good) health. Cp. À VOTRE SANTÉ.

slalom (slah´ləm) *n.* **1** a downhill ski race on a zigzagged course marked with artificial obstacles. **2** a similarly zigzagged obstacle race in canoes or vehicles, or on water-skis or skateboards.
early 20C. Norwegian *slalåm*, from *sla* sloping + *låm* track.

slaw (slaw) *n.* (*N Am.*) sliced cabbage served as a salad, coleslaw.
18C. Dutch *sla*, contr. of *salade* salad.

slivovitz (sliv´əvits) *n.* a dry plum brandy.
19C. Serbo-Croat *šljivovica*, from *šljiva* plum.

sloot (sloot), **sluit** *n.* (*S Afr.*) **1** an irrigation ditch, a drainage channel. **2** a channel or gully formed by heavy rain.
19C. Afrikaans ditch, from Germanic.

smalt (smawlt) *n.* a blue glass coloured with cobalt, used in a pulverized state as a pigment.

16C. French, from Italian *smalto*, from Germanic, rel. to English *smelt*.

smetana (smet´ənə) *n.* sour cream.
early 20C. Russian, from *smetat'* to sweep together, to collect.

smorgasbord (smaw´gəsbawd) *n.* **1** a buffet or hors d'oeuvre of open sandwiches. **2** a buffet comprising an assortment of hors d'oeuvres and other dishes.
19C. Swedish *smörgåsbord*, from *smörgås* (slice of) bread and butter (from *smör* butter + *gås* goose, lump of butter) + *bord* board, table.
● The word is apt to be confused in English with *smørbrod* or *smørrebrod*, literally bread and butter (actually hors d'oeuvres served on slices of buttered bread), from Norwegian and Danish *smør* butter + *brød* bread.

smorzando (smawtsan´dō), **smorzato** (-sah´tō) *a., adv.* (*Mus.*) with a gradual fading or dying away. ~*n.* (*pl.* **smorzandos, smorzandi** (-dē), **smorzatos, smorzati** (-tē)) a smorzando or smorzato passage.
19C. Italian, pres.p. of *smorzare* to extinguish.

smriti (smrit´i) *n.* a body of Hindu religious teachings from the Vedas.
19C. Sanskrit *smṛiti*, lit. that which is remembered, from *smarati* he remembers.

snoek (snook) *n.* (*S Afr.*) **1** a barracouta. **2** a snook.
18C. Dutch pike.

sobriquet (sō´brikā), **soubriquet** (soo´-) *n.* **1** a nickname. **2** an assumed name.
17C. French chuck under the chin, of unknown orig.
● According to some, the word is from *sous* under + an element of unknown origin.

sofa (sō´fə) *n.* a long stuffed couch or seat with raised back and ends.
17C. French, ult. from Arabic *ṣuffa* long (stone) bench.

softa (sof´tə) *n.* a student of Muslim theology and sacred law.
17C. Turkish, from Persian *sūḵta* burnt, parched, scorched.
• The student is so called as he is inspired ('fired') by the teacher, or because he is ardent in study.

soi-disant (swahdēzā´) *a.* self-styled, pretended, so-called.
16C. French, from *soi* oneself + *disant*, pres.p. of *dire* to say.

soigné (swahn´yā), (*fem.*) **soignée**
a. **1** well-turned-out, well-groomed. **2** elegant, tasteful.
19C. French, p.p. of *soigner* to care for, from *soin* care.

soirée (swah´rā) *n.* an evening party or gathering for conversation and social intercourse etc., usu. with music.
18C. French, from *soir* evening.
Cp. MATINÉE.

soixante-neuf (swasātnœf´) *n.* (*sl.*) sixty-nine, a sexual position or activity in which a couple engage in oral stimulation of each other's genitals at the same time.
19C. French sixty-nine.
• The activity is so called because the position of the couple involved resembles the figures 6 and 9.

Sol (sol) *n.* (*poet.*) the sun personified.
14–15C. Latin sun.

solano (sōlah´nō) *n.* a hot oppressive SE wind in Spain.
18C. Spanish, from Latin *solanus*, from *sol* sun.

solarium (səleə´riəm) *n.* (*pl.* **solaria** (-riə), **solariums**) a room or building constructed for the enjoyment of, or therapeutical exposure of the body to, the rays of the sun.
19C. Latin, from *sol* sun.

solatium (səlā´shiəm) *n.* (*pl.* **solatia** (-shiə)) something given as compensation for suffering or loss.
19C. Latin, alt. of *solacium* solace.

solera (səleə´rə, soler´ə) *n.* a blend of sherry or Malaga wine produced by systematically introducing small amounts of younger wines into casks containing more mature wine.
19C. Spanish, lit. stone base, from *suelo* ground, floor, dregs, from Latin *solum* soil.

solfatara (solfətah´rə) *n.* a volcanic vent emitting sulphurous gases.
18C. Italian *Solfatara*, a sulphurous volcano near Naples, from Italian *solfo* sulphur.

solfeggio (solfej´ō), **solfège** (-fezh´) *n.* (*pl.* **solfeggi** (-fej´i) **solfeggios**, **solfèges** (-fezh´)) **1** a singing exercise in solmization. **2** solmization.
18C. Italian *solfeggio*, from *sol-fa* sol-fa.
• The French equivalent *solfège* derived from the Italian original and dates from the early 20C.

solidus (sol´idəs) *n.* (*pl.* **solidi** (-dī)) **1** the stroke (/) formerly denoting a shilling (as in 2/6), also used in writing fractions (e.g. 1/4), separating numbers (e.g. in dates) or alternative words (as in *him/ her*) etc. **2** (*in full* **solidus curve**) in a graph representing the composition and temperature of a mixture, a curve below which the mixture is completely solid. **3** a Roman gold coin introduced by Constantine.
12–14C. Latin solid.

solitaire (sol′iteə, -teə′) *n.* **1** a gem, esp. a diamond, set singly in a ring or other jewel. **2** a jewel, esp. a ring, set with a single gem. **3** a game for one player, played on a board with hollows and marbles or holes and pegs, in which marbles or pegs are removed from the board as others are jumped over them, till only one remains. **4** (*esp. N Am.*) a card game for one player, patience. **5** an American or West Indian rock-thrush. **6** an extinct flightless bird, *Pezophaps solitarius,* related to the dodo.
18C. French, from Latin *solitarius* solitary.

solo (sō′lō) *n.* (*pl.* **solos, soli** (-lē))
1 a composition or passage played by a single instrument or sung by a single voice, usu. with an accompaniment. **2 a** solo whist. **b** a bid in this game to win five tricks, or the accomplishment of this. **3** a solo flight. **4** any unaided or unaccompanied effort by one person. ~*a., adv.* unaccompanied, alone. ~*v.i.* (*3rd pers. sing. pres.* **soloes**, *pres.p.* **soloing**, *past, p.p.* **soloed**) **1** to perform a musical solo. **2** to fly an aircraft unaccompanied.
17C. Italian, from Latin *solus* sole, alone.

solus (sō′ləs), (*fem.*) **sola** (-lə) *a., adv.* in stage directions etc., alone.
16C. Latin *solus* sole, alone.

soma¹ (sō′mə) *n.* (*pl.* **somata** (sō′mətə))
1 the body as distinguished from soul and spirit. **2** the body of an organism excluding its reproductive cells.
19C. Greek *sōma* body.

soma² (sō′mə) *n.* **1** an intoxicating liquor used in connection with ancient Vedic worship. **2** the plant whose juice it is made from.
18C. Sanskrit.
● In his novel *Brave New World* (1932), Aldous Huxley gave the name *soma* to the narcotic drug distributed by the state to promote content and social harmony.

sombrero (sombreə′rō) *n.*
(*pl.* **sombreros**) a wide-brimmed hat worn esp. in Mexico.
16C. Spanish, from *sombra* shade.

sommelier (som′əlyā, sŭm′-, səmel′-) *n.* a wine waiter.
19C. French wine steward, orig. pack animal driver, from Provençal *sauma* pack animal, load of a pack animal.

sonata (sənah′tə) *n.* a musical composition for one instrument, or for one instrument accompanied on the piano, usu. of three or four movements in different rhythms.
17C. Italian, fem. p.p. of *sonare* to sound.
● In Italian the word means 'played', as distinct from a CANTATA, which is sung.

sonatina (sonətē′nə) *n.* a short or simple sonata.
18C. Italian, dim. of SONATA.

sondage (sondahzh′, sō-) *n.* (*pl.* **sondages** (-dahzh′)) in archaeology, a trial excavation or inspection trench.
mid-20C. French sounding, borehole.

sonde (sond) *n.* a scientific device for gathering information about atmospheric conditions at high altitudes, a radiosonde.
early 20C. French sounding line, sounding.

son et lumière (son ā loomieə′) *n.* an outdoor entertainment at a historic location which recreates past events associated with it using sound effects, a spoken narration, music, and special lighting.
mid-20C. French, lit. sound and light.

Sophy (sō´fi), **Sophi** n. (pl. **Sophies**)
(*Hist.*) the title of a Persian sovereign,
the shah.
16C. Arabic *ṣafī-ud-dīn* pure of religion,
epithet given to the ancestor of the
dynasty of Persia, *c*.1500–1736.
• The dynasty itself is the *Safavid*,
from Arabic *ṣafawī* descended from
Safī-ud-dīn. Its founder was Ismail I,
1486–1524.

soprano (səprah´nō) n. (pl. **sopranos**,
soprani (-nē)) (*Mus.*) **1** the highest
singing voice, treble. **2** a boy or female
singer with this voice. **3** a musical part
for this voice. **4** an instrument that has
the highest range within a family of
instruments. **5** the player of such an
instrument. ~a. (*Mus.*) of, or having, a
treble part, voice or pitch.
18C. Italian, from *sopra* above, from
Latin *supra*.

sorbet (saw´bā) n. **1** an ice flavoured
with fruit juice, spirit etc., a water ice.
2 sherbet.
16C. French, from Italian *sorbetto*, from
Turkish *ṣerbet* SHERBET.

sordino (sawdē´nō) n. (pl. **sordini** (-nē))
(*Mus.*) a contrivance for deadening the
sound of a bowed instrument or wind
instrument, a mute, a damper.
16C. Italian, from *sordo*, from Latin
surdus deaf, mute.

sortie (saw´ti) n. **1** a sally, esp. of troops
from a besieged place in order to attack
or raid. **2** a mission or attack by a single
aircraft. ~v.i. (*3rd pers. sing. pres.*
sorties, *pres.p.* **sortieing**, *past, p.p.*
sortied) **1** to sally. **2** to make a sortie.
17C. French, fem. p.p. of *sortir* to go out.

sostenuto (sostinoo´tō, -tən-) a., adv.
(*Mus.*) (played) in a steadily sustained
manner. ~n. (pl. **sostenutos**) a passage
to be played thus.
18C. Italian, p.p. of *sostenere* to sustain.

sottise (sotēz´) n. a foolish remark or
action.
17C. French, from *sot* fool, from
Medieval Latin *sottus*.

sotto voce (sotō vō´chi) adv. under one's
voice, in an undertone.
18C. Italian *sotto* under + *voce* voice.

sou (soo) n. (pl. **sous**) **1** (*Hist.*) a French
copper coin worth one-twelfth of a
livre. **2** (*Hist.*) the five-centime piece.
3 (*with neg.*) a very small amount of
money.
15C. French, sing. form deduced from
sous, pl. of Old French *sout*, from Latin
solidus gold coin. See SOLIDUS.

soubise (soobēz´), **soubise sauce** n. a
white sauce made from onions, butter,
béchamel sauce and consommé.
18C. French, from Charles de Rohan
Soubise, 1715–87, French general and
courtier.

soubrette (soobret´) n. **1** a lady's maid.
2 a mischievous coquettish scheming
female character in a comedy, esp. the
role of a lady's maid, or an actress or
singer practised in such roles.
3 a person who displays similar
characteristics, a flirt, a coquette.
18C. French, from Provençal *soubreto*,
fem. of *soubret* coy, from *soubra* to set
aside, from Latin *superare* to be above,
to surmount.

souchong (soo´shong) n. a black China
tea made from the youngest leaves.
18C. Chinese *siú chúng* small sort.

soufflé (soo´flā) n. any of various savoury
or sweet, cooked or uncooked dishes
made of beaten whites of eggs etc. ~a.
made light and frothy by beating etc.
19C. French, p.p. of *souffler* to puff up,
from Latin *sufflare*, from *sub* under +
flare to blow.

souk (sook) *n.* an outside, often covered market in a Muslim country (esp. in N Africa and the Middle East).
19C. Arabic *sūḳ.*

soupçon (soop´sō) *n.* a mere trace, taste or flavour (of).
18C. French, from Old French *souspeçon*, from Medieval Latin *suspectio, suspectionis* mistrust.

sourdine (suədēn´) *n.* **1** a soft stop on an organ etc. **2** SORDINO.
17C. French, from *sourd* deaf, dull.

sous- (soo) *pref.* (used before French-derived nouns) under-, subordinate, assistant etc.
12–14C. Old French *sous*, from Latin *subtus* under.

sous-chef (sooshef´) *n.* a head chef's assistant and deputy.
17C. French, from SOUS- + CHEF.

soutache (sootash´) *n.* a narrow, ornamental braid.
19C. French, from Hungarian *sujtás.*

soutane (sootahn´) *n.* a cassock.
19C. French, from Italian *sottana*, from *sotto*, from Latin *subtus* under.
● The garment is so called as it is worn under the vestments in a religious service.

souteneur (sootənœ´) *n.* a pimp.
early 20C. French protector, from *soutenir* to sustain.

souterrain (soo´tərān) *n.* an esp. Iron Age underground chamber.
18C. French, from *sous* under + *terre* earth, based on Latin *subterraneus* underground.

souvenir (soovəniə´) *n.* a keepsake, a memento. ~*v.t.* (*Austral., New Zeal., sl.*) to pilfer, to steal.
18C. French, use as n. of v. to remember, from Latin *subvenire* to come into the mind, from *sub* under + *venire* to come.

souvlaki (soovlah´ki) *n.* (*pl.* **souvlakis, souvlakia** (-kiə)) a Greek dish consisting of small pieces of meat grilled on a skewer.
mid-20C. Modern Greek *soublaki*, from *soubla* skewer.

soviet (sō´viət, sov´-) *n.* **1** a local council elected by workers and inhabitants of a district in the former Soviet Union. **2** a regional council selected by a number of these. **3** the national congress consisting of delegates from regional councils. **4** (*pl.*) (*usu.* **Soviet**) the government or people of the former Soviet Union. ~*a.* **1** (*usu.* **Soviet**) of or relating to the former Soviet Union, its government or its people. **2** of or relating to a soviet.
early 20C. Russian *sovet* council, trans. of Greek *sumboulion* advice, counsel, from *sun-* together + *boulē* project, plan.

sovkhoz (sov´koz, sŭvkawz´) *n.* (*pl.* **sovkhoz, sovkhozes** (sov´koziz), **sovkhozy** (sov´kozi)) a state-owned farm in the former Soviet Union.
early 20C. Russian, abbr. of *sovetskoe khozyaĭstvo* Soviet farm. Cp. KOLKHOZ.

soy (soi) *n.* **1** (*also* **soy sauce**) a thin brown salty sauce made from fermented soya beans, used extensively in Japanese and Chinese cookery. **2** the soya plant.
17C. Japanese, var. of *shōyu*, from Chinese *jiàngyóu*, from *jiàng* bean paste + *yóu* oil. Cp. SHOYU.

soya (soi´ə) *n.* **1** a leguminous herb, *Glycine soja*, native to SE Asia, grown for its seeds. **2** (*also* **soya bean**) the seed of this plant, used as a source of oil and flour, as a substitute for animal protein and to make soy sauce and tofu. **3** (*also* **soya sauce**) soy.
17C. Dutch *soja*, from Japanese *shōyu*. See SOY.

spadille (spədil´) *n.* **1** in the card games ombre and quadrille, the ace of spades. **2** the highest trump, esp. the ace of spades, in various card games.
17C. French, from Spanish *espadilla*, dim. of *espada* sword, from Latin *spatha*, from Greek *spathē* broad, flat instrument.

spaghetti (spəget´i) *n.* a variety of pasta made in long thin cylindrical strings.
19C. Italian, pl. of dim. of *spago* string.

spahi (spah´hē), **spahee** *n.* (*pl.* **spahis**, **spahees**) **1** a Turkish irregular cavalryman. **2** (*Hist.*) an Algerian cavalryman in the French army.
16C. French, from Turkish *sipahi*, from Persian *sipāhī*. See SEPOY.

Spätlese (shpet´lāzə) *n.* (*pl.* **Spätleses**, **Spätlesen** (-zən)) a (German etc.) white wine made from late-harvested grapes.
mid-20C. German, from *spät* late + *Lese* picking, vintage.

spatula (spat´ūlə) *n.* a broad knife or trowel-shaped tool used for spreading plasters, working pigments, mixing foods etc.
16C. Latin, var. of *spathula*, dim. of *spatha* broad, flat instrument.

spécialité (spesyalitā´) *n.* an unusual or distinctive thing.
19C. French speciality.
• In culinary terms the word is short for *spécialité de la maison*, lit. speciality of the house, as a term for a dish peculiar to or characteristic of a particular restaurant.

specie (spē´shē) *n.* coin as distinct from paper money.
17C. Latin, abl. sing. of *species* kind.
• The word was earlier found in the Latin phrase *in specie* in the (real) form.

specimen (spes´imən) *n.* **1** a part or an individual intended to illustrate or typify the nature of a whole or a class. **2** (*Med.*) a sample of blood, urine etc. taken for medical analysis. **3** (*coll.*) a person or animal.
17C. Latin, from *specere* to look (at).

spectrum (spek´trəm) *n.* (*pl.* **spectra** (-trə)) **1** the rainbow-like range of colours into which white light is dispersed, according to the degrees of refrangibility of its components, when passing through a prism, from violet (with the shortest wavelength) to red (with the longest wavelength). **2** the complete range of wavelengths of electromagnetic radiation. **3** any particular distribution of electromagnetic radiation, esp. as characteristic of a particular substance when emitting or absorbing radiation. **4** any similar range, e.g. of sound frequencies, or of particles distributed according to energy. **5** a complete range, of e.g. opinion, interests, activities, abilities etc. **6** an ocular spectrum.
17C. Latin image, appearance, apparition.

speiss (spīs) *n.* a compound of arsenic, nickel, copper etc., produced in the smelting of various ores such as lead.
18C. German *Speise*, orig. food.

spiccato (spikah´tō) *n.* (*Mus.*) a staccato style on a stringed instrument in which the player makes the bow rebound lightly from the strings. ~*a., adv.* (played) in this style.
18C. Italian detailed, distinct.

spiegeleisen (spē´gilīzən) *n.* a white variety of cast iron containing manganese, used in making Bessemer steel.
19C. German, from *Spiegel* mirror (from Latin *speculum*) + *Eisen* iron.

spiel (shpēl, spēl) *n.* the sales patter of a practised dealer, or anyone's well-rehearsed or familiar tale. ~*v.i.* to talk with glib or practised ease. ~*v.t.* to reel off (patter).
19C. German *spielen* to play, to gamble.

spitz (spits) *n.* a sharp-muzzled breed of dog, also called *Pomeranian*.
19C. German *Spitz, Spitzhund*, special use of *spitz* pointed, peaked.
• The dog is so called from its pointed nose and ears.

spoor (spuə) *n.* the track of a wild animal. ~*v.i.* to follow a spoor.
19C. Afrikaans, from Middle Dutch *spoor, spor*, from Germanic. Cp. German *Spur*.

sportif (spawtēf´) *a.* active or interested in athletic sports.
mid-20C. French sporting, sportive.
• The word is also used of a garment suitable for sport or informal wear.

SPQR *n.* (*Hist.*) the Senate and the people of Rome.
Abbr. of **Latin** *Senatus Populusque Romanus*, from *senatus* senate + *populus* people + *-que* and + *Romanus* Roman, of Rome.
• The abbreviation was displayed on Roman military standards etc. and is now to be seen on drain covers and buses in Rome.

Sprechgesang (shprekh´gəzang) *n.* (*Mus.*) a style of vocalization between singing and speaking.
early 20C. German, lit. speech song.

Sprechstimme (shprekh´shtimə) *n.* (*Mus.*) **1** the type of voice used in Sprechgesang. **2** Sprechgesang.
early 20C. German, lit. speech voice.

springbok (spring´bok) *n.* **1** a southern African gazelle, *Antidorcas marsupialis*, that runs with a high leaping movement. **2** (**Springbok**) a sportsman or sportswoman representing South Africa in international competitions.
18C. Afrikaans, from Dutch *springen* to spring + *bok* goat, antelope.

spritz (sprits) *v.t.* (*N Am.*) to squirt or spray. ~*n.* an act of spritzing.
early 20C. German *spritzen* to squirt, to splash.

spritzer (sprit´sə) *n.* a drink made from white wine and soda water.
mid-20C. German splash. Cp. SPRITZ.

spruit (sprāt) *n.* (*S Afr.*) a small tributary stream, esp. one that is dry in summer.
19C. Dutch sprout.

spumante (spooman´ti, -tā) *n.* (*pl.* **spumantes** (-tiz, -tāz)) a sparkling Italian wine.
early 20C. Italian sparkling.

sputnik (spŭt´nik, sput´-) *n.* any of a series of Russian artificial earth satellites, the first of which was launched in 1957.
mid-20C. Russian, lit. travelling companion, from *s* with + *put'* way, journey.

Stabat Mater (stahbat mah´tə, stā´bat mā´tə) *n.* **1** a Latin hymn reciting the seven dolours of the Virgin at the Cross, beginning with these words. **2** a musical setting of this.
19C. Latin, from the opening words of the hymn, *Stabat mater dolorosa* Stood the mother full of grief.
• The original hymn is ascribed to Jacopone du Todi, *c.*1230–1306, and others and has the full verse: *Stabat Mater dolorosa, / Iuxta crucem lacrimosa, / Dum pendebat filius* The mother stood in grief, weeping beside the cross while her son was hanging.

staccato (stəkah´tō) *a., adv.* (*Mus.*)
(played) with each note sharply distinct
and detached, as opposed to *legato*.
~*n.* (*pl.* **staccatos**) **1** a passage of music
played in this way. **2** a staccato style of
playing.
18C. Italian, p.p. of *staccare*, shortening
of *distaccare* to detach.

stacte (stak´tē) *n.* one of the spices used
by the ancient Jews in the preparation
of incense.
14–15C. Latin, from Greek *staktē*, fem.
of *staktos* distilling in drops, from
stazein to drip.

stadium (stā´diəm) *n.* (*pl.* **stadiums**,
stadia (-diə) **1** a sports arena with tiers
of benches for spectators. **2** (*Hist.*) a race
course for foot races or chariot races.
3 an ancient measure of length, about
185 metres (607 feet). **4** a stage of
development, e.g. in geology, or in the
course of a disease.
14–15C. Latin, from Greek *stadion*.
● The original sense was sense 3. Sense
2 evolved in the 17C, and sense 1 in the
19C.

stadtholder (stat´hōldə, stad´-),
stadholder (stad´-) *n.* (*Hist.*) **1** the chief
magistrate of the United Provinces. **2** a
viceroy, governor or deputy governor of
a province or town in the Netherlands.
16C. Dutch *stadhouder*, translating Latin
locum tenens (see LOCUM), from *stad*
place + *houder* holder, from *houden* to
hold.

staffage (stəfahzh´) *n.* additional or
accessory objects in a painting, such as
sheep or cattle in a landscape painting.
19C. German, pseudo-French formation,
from *staffieren* to fit out, to decorate,
? from Old French *estoffer*, from *estoffe*
stuff.

Stalag (stah´lag) *n.* a German prisoner-of-
war camp, esp. for men from the ranks
and non-commissioned officers.

mid-20C. German, contr. of *Stammlager*
main camp.
● The equivalent camp for officers was
the *Oflag*, a contraction of German
Offizierlager officers' camp.

stamina (stam´inə) *n.* **1** strength, vigour.
2 power of endurance, ability to tolerate
long periods of mental or physical
stress.
17C. Latin, pl. of *stamen*.
● The sense derives partly from Latin
stamen warp, since the warp of a fabric
provides its underlying foundation,
partly from Latin *stamina* (pl.) threads,
with reference to the threads spun by
the Fates at a person's birth to
determine how long they will live.

stanza (stan´zə) *n.* **1** a recurring group of
lines of poetry adjusted to each other in
a definite scheme, often with rhyme.
2 in classical prosody, a group of four
lines in some metres.
16C. Italian standing, stopping-place,
room, strophe, from Latin *stans, stantis*,
pres.p. of *stare* to stand.

Stasi (shtah´zi) *n.* in the German
Democratic Republic before 1989, the
internal security force.
mid-20C. German, acronym of
*Sta*ats*si*cherheits(dienst) state security
(service).

stasis (stā´sis, stas´-) *n.* (*pl.* **stases** (-sēz))
1 a state of equilibrium or inaction.
2 stagnation of the blood, esp. in the
small vessels or capillaries, or any
stoppage in the flow of a bodily fluid.
18C. Modern Latin, from Greek, lit.
standing, stoppage, from *sta-*, base of
histanai to stand.

stater (stā´tə) *n.* a coin of ancient Greece,
esp. the standard gold coin of 20
drachmas.
14–15C. Late Latin, from Greek *statēr*,
from *sta-*, base of *histanai* (in the sense
to weigh).

status (stā´təs) *n.* **1** relative standing or position in society. **2** (*Law*) a person's legal identity, e.g. whether alien or citizen. **3** the current situation or state of affairs.
17C. Latin, from *status* position.
● The original sense was the crisis of a disease. The current sense dates from the 18C.

status quo (stātəs kwō´) *n.* the existing state of affairs.
19C. Latin the state in which, from *status* state + abl. of *qui* which.

stein (stīn) *n.* a large, usu. earthenware beer mug, often with a hinged lid.
19C. German stone.

stela (stē´lə) *n.* (*pl.* **stelae** (-lē)) an upright stone slab or column, usu. with sculptured figures and an inscription.
18C. Latin, from Greek *stēlē*.
See STELE.

stele (stēl, stē´li) *n.* **1** (*Bot.*) the central cylinder in stems and roots of the higher plants, consisting of vascular bundles with pith and pericycle. **2** a stela.
19C. Greek *stēlē* standing block.
Cp. STELA.

stemma (stem´ə) *n.* (*pl.* **stemmata** (-tə)) **1** pedigree, a family tree. **2** a diagrammatical representation of the lines of descent of the surviving manuscripts of a text. **3** (*Zool.*) **a** a simple eye, an ocellus. **b** any one of the facets of a compound eye.
17C. Latin, from Greek garland, from *stephein* to crown.

steppe (step) *n.* a vast plain devoid of forest, esp. in Russia and Siberia.
17C. Russian *step'*, ? rel. to English *stipe*, with ref. to the feather grass that is characteristic of the steppes.

stet (stet) *v.i.* (*pres.p.* **stetting**, *past, p.p.* **stetted**) in proof-reading etc., to let the original stand (cancelling a previous correction), usu. as an instruction 'let it stand'. ~*v.t.* to write 'stet' against.
18C. Latin let it stand, 3rd pers. sing. pres. subj. of *stare* to stand.

stigma (stig´mə) *n.* (*pl.* **stigmas**, **stigmata** (-mətə, -mah´tə)) **1** a mark of discredit or infamy. **2** a distinguishing mark (of), a typical characteristic (of). **3** (*Bot.*) the part of a pistil of a flower that receives the pollen. **4** (*pl.*) in Christian dogma, the marks left on Christ's body from the process of crucifixion, believed also to have been divinely imprinted on the body of St Francis of Assisi and other saintly people. **5** a natural mark on the skin; a pore. **6** a mark or spot on a butterfly's wing. **7** a visible sign of a disease. **8** an insect's spiracle. **9** a mark branded on to the skin (e.g. of a slave or criminal).
16C. Latin, from Greek *stigma*, *stigmatos*, from base of *stizein* to prick.
● Sense 9 is the oldest. Sense 4 dates from the 17C, sense 3 from the 18C and sense 2 from the 19C.

stiletto (stilet´ō) *n.* (*pl.* **stilettos**) **1** a small dagger. **2** a pointed instrument for making eyelet-holes etc. **3** a stiletto heel. **4** a shoe with a stiletto heel. ~*v.t.* (*3rd pers. sing. pres.* **stilettoes**, *pres.p.* **stilettoing**, *past, p.p.* **stilettoed**) to stab with a stiletto.
17C. Italian, dim. of *stilo* dagger, ult. from Latin *stilus* stake.

stimulus (stim´ūləs) *n.* (*pl.* **stimuli** (-lī)) **1** something that stimulates one to activity, or energizes one; an incitement, a spur. **2** something that excites reaction in a living organism. **3** (*Med.*) a stimulant.
17C. Latin goad, spur, incentive, prob. from base also of *stilus* stylus.

stoep (stoop) *n.* (*S Afr.*) an open, roofed platform in front of a house, a veranda.
18C. Afrikaans, from Dutch, rel. to English *step*.

Stollen (shtol´ən) *n.* a spicy German bread containing dried fruit and coated with icing sugar.
early 20C. German, from Old High German *stollo* post, support.

stornello (stawnel´ō) *n.* (*pl.* **stornelli** (-lē)) an Italian form of short improvised song.
19C. Italian, prob. from *stornare* to turn aside.

Storting (staw´ting), **Storthing** *n.* the Norwegian parliament.
19C. Norwegian, from *stor* great + *ting* assembly. Cp. THING.

strafe (strāf, strahf) *v.t.* **1** to bombard heavily. **2** to rake with machine-gun fire from the air. **3** to reprimand or punish severely. **4** to abuse or do a serious and deliberate injury to. ~*n.* **1** an act of strafing. **2** an attack from the air.
early 20C. From **German** *Gott strafe England* may God punish England, a catchphrase in Germany in World War I.

strappado (strəpā´dō, -pah´-) *n.* (*pl.* **strappados**) (*Hist.*) **1** a punishment involving drawing up an offender by a rope and letting them fall to the end of this. **2** the rope etc. used in this. ~*v.t.* (*3rd pers. sing. pres.* **strappadoes**, *pres.p.* **strappadoing**, *past, p.p.* **strappadoed**) to torture or punish in this way.
16C. French *estrapade*, from Italian *estrapada*, from *strappare* to snatch.

strass (stras) *n.* paste for making false gems.
19C. German, from Josef *Strasser*, its 18C inventor.
● According to some sources the name is that of G.F. *Stras*, 1700–73, a French jeweller.

stratum (strah´təm, strā´-) *n.* (*pl.* **strata** (-tə)) **1** a horizontal layer of any material. **2** a bed of sedimentary rock. **3** a layer of tissue or cells. **4** a layer of sea or atmosphere. **5** a social level, a class. **6** in statistics, each of the bands into which a population is divided for the purpose of stratified sampling.
16C. Modern Latin, use of Latin *stratum*, lit. something spread, something laid down, neut. p.p. of *sternere* to lay down, to throw down.
● Sense 5 dates from the 19C and sense 6 from the early 20C.

strepitoso (strepitō´sō) *adv.* (*Mus.*) in a noisy, impetuous manner.
19C. Italian, lit. noisy, loud.

stretto (stret´ō) *adv.* (*Mus.*) at a quicker tempo.
18C. Italian, lit. narrow.

stria (strī´ə) *n.* (*pl.* **striae** (strī´ē)) **1** a superficial furrow, a thin line or groove, mark or ridge. **2** (*Archit.*) each of the fillets between the flutes of a column.
16C. Latin furrow, grooving.

stringendo (strinjen´dō) *adv.* (*Mus.*) in accelerated time.
19C. Italian, pres.p. of *stringere* to press, to squeeze, to bind together, from Latin *stringere* to bind.

strophe (strō´fi) *n.* **1** the turning of the chorus from right to left in ancient Greek drama. **2** a part of the ode (consisting of strophe, antistrophe and epode) sung whilst so turning, esp. the first part, the strophe proper. **3** a number of lines constituting a section of a lyric poem.
17C. Greek *strophē*, lit. turning, from *stroph-*, var. of base of *strephein* to turn.

strudel (stroo´dəl) *n.* a thin pastry rolled up with a filling (e.g. apple) and baked.
19C. German, lit. eddy, whirlpool.

stucco (stŭk´ō) *n.* (*pl.* **stuccoes, stuccos**) **1** fine plaster for coating walls or moulding into decorations in relief. **2** any plaster used for coating the outside of buildings. *~v.t.* (*3rd pers. sing. pres.* **stuccoes**, *pres.p.* **stuccoing**, *past, p.p.* **stuccoed**) to coat with stucco.
16C. Italian, ult. from Germanic. Cp. German *Stück* piece.

studio (stū´diō) *n.* (*pl.* **studios**) **1** the working room of a sculptor, painter, photographer etc. **2** the room in which records, radio and television programmes are recorded, or films made. **3** the place from which television and radio programmes are broadcast. **4** (*pl.*) the buildings used for making films by a television or film company.
19C. Italian, from Latin *studium* eagerness, painstaking application.

stupa (stoo´pə) *n.* a domed Buddhist shrine, a tope.
19C. Sanskrit *stūpa.* Cp. TOPE².

Sturm und Drang (shtuəm unt drang´) *n.* a late 18th-cent. German literary and artistic genre typified by stirring action, and the expression of strong passion or emotional unrest.
19C. German, lit. storm and stress, title of a 1776 play by Friedrich Maximilian Klinger.

suave (swahv) *a.* agreeable, bland, gracious, polite.
14–15C. Old French, or from Latin *suavis* sweet, agreeable.
● The original sense (to the 16C) was gracious, kindly. The current sense dates from the 19C.

subito (soo´bitō) *adv.* (*Mus.*) suddenly, immediately.
18C. Italian suddenly, from Latin *subitus* sudden, unexpected.

sub judice (sŭb joo´disi, yoo´dikā) *a.* (*Law*) under consideration, esp. by a court or judge.
17C. Latin, lit. under a judge, from *sub* under + abl. sing. of *iudex* judge.

subpoena (səpē´nə) *n.* (*Law*) a writ commanding a person's attendance in a court of justice under a penalty. *~v.t.* (*pres.p.* **subpoenaing**, *past, p.p.* **subpoenaed** (-nəd), **subpoena'd**) to serve with such a writ.
14–15C. Latin *sub poena* under penalty, the first words on the writ.

sub rosa (sŭb rō´zə) *adv.* **1** secretly. **2** in confidence.
17C. Latin, lit. under the rose.
● The rose was formerly an emblem of secrecy, a concept that may have arisen in Germany.

succès de scandale (suksā də skondahl´) *n.* success owing to notoriety.
19C. French, lit. scandalous success.

succès d'estime (suksā destēm´) *n.* a critical as opposed to a popular or commercial success.
19C. French, lit. success of esteem.

succès fou (suksā foo´) *n.* a success marked by wild enthusiasm.
19C. French, lit. mad success.

Succoth (sukōt´, sŭk´əth) *n.* the Jewish harvest festival commemorating the Israelites' sheltering in the wilderness.
19C. Hebrew *sukkōṭ*, pl. of *sukkāh*, lit. hut.
● The festival's alternative English name is *Feast of Tabernacles*.

succuba (sŭk´ūbə), **succubus** (-bəs) *n.* (*pl.* **succubae** (-bē), **succubi** (-bī)) a demon believed to assume the shape of a woman and have sexual intercourse with men in their sleep.

16C. **Late Latin** prostitute, from *succubare*, from *sub* under + *cubare* to lie.

• The variant form *succubus* dates from the 14–15C as a Medieval Latin masculine form (with feminine meaning) corresponding to *succuba*, based on INCUBUS.

sucre (soo´krə) *n.* the standard unit of currency of Ecuador.
19C. Antonio José de *Sucre*, 1795–1830, South American popular leader, who fought under Simón Bolívar (BOLIVAR) against Spanish rule.

sudd (sŭd) *n.* a floating mass of vegetation, trees etc. obstructing navigation in the White Nile.
19C. **Arabic** obstruction, dam, from *sadda* to obstruct, to block, to congest.

Sudra (soo´drə) *n.* (*pl.* **Sudras**) a member of the lowest of the four great Hindu castes.
17C. **Sanskrit** *śūdra*.

Sufi (soo´fi) *n.* (*pl.* **Sufis**) a Muslim pantheistic philosopher and mystic.
17C. **Arabic** *ṣūfī*, lit. woollen, prob. from *ṣūf* wool.

• The mystic is so called from the rough woollen garment associated with ascetics.

sui generis (sooī jen´əris, sooē) *a.* unique, of its own kind.
18C. **Latin** of its own kind, gen. of *suus genus* own kind.

sui juris (sooī juə´ris, sooē) *a.* (*Law*) of age; legally competent.
17C. **Latin**, lit. of one's own right, gen. of *suus ius* own law.

suite (swēt) *n.* **1** a set (of connecting rooms, matching furniture etc.). **2** (*Mus.*) a series of instrumental compositions. **3** (*Mus.*) a set of selected musical pieces played as one instrumental work. **4** a company, a retinue.
17C. **French** following.

suivez (swē´vā) *v.i.* (*imper., Mus.*) follow (a direction to the accompanist to adapt their time to the soloist).
19C. **French** follow, 2nd pers. pl. imper. of *suivre* to follow.

sukiyaki (sukiyak´i) *n.* a Japanese dish of thin slices of meat and vegetables cooked together with soy sauce, saki etc.
early 20C. **Japanese**, from *suki* spade + *yaki* roasting.

summa (sum´ə, sŭm´ə) *n.* (*pl.* **summae** (-mē)) a comprehensive survey of a subject.
14–15C. **Latin** main thing, whole amount.

summa cum laude (sŭmə kŭm law´dē, sumə kum low´dā) *adv., a.* (*esp. N Am.*) with the highest distinction.
19C. **Latin**, lit. with the highest praise, from *cum* with + abl. of *summa laus* highest praise. Cp. MAGNA CUM LAUDE.

summum bonum (suməm bon´əm) *n.* the highest or supreme good.
16C. **Latin** highest good.

summum genus (suməm jen´əs, jē´nəs) *n.* a genus which cannot be considered as a species of another genus.
16C. **Latin** highest kind.

summum jus (suməm jŭs´) *n.* the utmost rigour of the law.
16C. **Latin** highest law.

sumo (soo´mō) *n.* traditional Japanese wrestling in which a contestant attempts to force his opponent out of the designated area or to touch the ground with a part of the body other than the feet. ~*a.* of or relating to sumo.
19C. **Japanese** *sūmo* wrestling.

sumpitan (sŭm´pitan), **sumpit** *n.* a Malay blowpipe.

17C. **Malay**, from *sumpit* shooting with a blowpipe.

sunn (sŭn) *n.* a hemplike fibre obtained from a S Asian plant.
18C. **Hindi** *san*, from Sanskrit *śáṇá* hempen.

Sunna (sun´ə, sŭn´ə) *n.* the traditional part of the Muslim law, based on the sayings or acts of Muhammad, accepted as of equal authority to the Koran by one branch of Islam, the Sunni, but rejected by the Shiites.
18C. **Arabic** custom, normative rule.

supra (soo´prə) *adv.* above; earlier on.
16C. **Latin**.

suprême (sooprem´) *n.* a rich, creamy sauce or a dish served in this.
19C. **French** supreme.
● The name may also have been intended literally for a sauce that was poured over the dish.

supremo (suprē´mō) *n.* (*pl.* **supremos**) a supreme leader or head.
mid-20C. **Spanish** (*generalísimo*) *supremo* supreme general.
● Earl Mountbatten of Burma (1900–79) was nicknamed *supremo* during his time as Supreme Allied Commander, SE Asia (1943–45).

sura (suə´rə), **surah** *n.* a chapter of the Koran.
17C. **Arabic** *sūra*, prob. from Syriac *ṣūrṭā* scripture.

surah (sūə´rə) *n.* a soft, twilled, usu. self-coloured silk material.
19C. Representation of French pronun. of SURAT.

surat (sūrat´) *n.* (*Hist.*) **1** coarse, short cotton grown near Surat, India. **2** cloth made from this.
17C. *Surat*, a port and district in NW India.

Sûreté (sūə´tā) *n.* the French criminal investigation department before 1966.
early 20C. **French**, short form of *La Sûreté nationale*, lit. the national safety.
● The *Sûreté* was replaced in 1966 by *La Police nationale*, lit. the national police.

surra (suə´rə) *n.* a serious disease of horses, cattle etc. in Asia and NE Africa, transmitted by horseflies.
19C. **Marathi** *sūra* air breathed through the nostrils.

Sursum corda (sœsəm kaw´də) *int.* lift up your hearts (spoken by the priest in a Roman mass at the beginning of the Eucharistic Prayer).
16C. **Latin**, from *sursum* upwards + pl. of *cor* heart.

surtout (sœ´too) *n.* (*Hist.*) a man's overcoat, esp. one like a frock coat.
17C. **French**, from *sur* above + *tout* everything. Cp. English 'overall'.

surveillance (səvā´ləns, -vā´əns) *n.* observation, close watch, supervision.
19C. **French**, from *surveiller* to watch over, from *sur* over + *veiller* to keep watch, from Latin *vigilare*.

sushi (soo´shi) *n.* a Japanese dish of cold rice cakes with a vinegar dressing and garnishes of raw fish etc.
19C. **Japanese**.

Sutra (soo´trə) *n.* **1** in Hindu literature, a rule, a precept, an aphorism. **2** (*pl.*) Brahminical books of rules, doctrine etc.
19C. **Sanskrit** *sūtra* thread, string, rule. Cp. KAMA SUTRA.

suttee (sŭtē´, sŭt´i), **sati** (sŭt´i) *n.* (*pl.* **suttees**, **satis**) (*Hist.*) **1** a Hindu custom by which the widow was burnt on the funeral pyre with her dead husband. **2** a widow so burnt.
18C. **Sanskrit** *satī* faithful wife, fem. of *sat* good.

svelte (svelt) *a.* (esp. of a woman's figure) slender, lissom.
19C. **French**, from Italian *svelto*, lit. pulled out, lengthened, p.p. of *svellere* to pluck out, to root out, from Popular Latin *exvellere*, var. of Latin *evellere*, from *e*, *ex* out of + *vellere* to pluck, to pull, to stretch.

Swadeshi (swədā´shi) *n.* (*Hist.*) a movement in India for self-government, and agitation until this was obtained.
early 20C. **Hindi** *svadeśī*, from Sanskrit *svadeśīya* of one's own country, from *sva* own + *deśa* country. Cp. SWARAJ.

swami (swah´mi) *n.* (*pl.* **swamis**) a Hindu religious teacher.
18C. **Sanskrit** *svāmin*, nom. *svāmī* master, prince.

Swaraj (swərahj´) *n.* (*Hist.*) home rule for India.
early 20C. **Hindi** *svarāj*, from Sanskrit *svarājya*, from *sva* own + *rājya* rule. Cp. SWADESHI, RAJ.

swastika (swos´tikə) *n.* an ancient symbol in the form of a cross with arms bent at a right angle, appropriated by the Nazis and used as a symbol of anti-Semitism or Nazism.
19C. **Sanskrit** *svastika*, from *svasti* well-being, luck, from *su* good + *asti* being.
● The cross is so called because it was originally believed to bring good luck.

swy (swī) *n.* (*Austral.*) the game of two-up.
early 20C. **German** *zwei* two.

syce (sīs), **sice** *n.* esp. in the Indian subcontinent, a groom.
17C. **Persian and Urdu** *sā'is*, from Arabic.

sycee (sīsē´), **sycee silver** *n.* pure uncoined silver cast into ingots, usu. bearing the seal of a banker or assayer, and formerly used in China by weight as a medium of exchange.
18C. **Cantonese** pronun. of Chinese *xī sī*, lit. fine silk.
● The silver is so called because, if pure, it can be drawn out into fine threads.

sympathique (sīpatēk´) *a.* agreeable, likeable.
19C. **French** sympathetic. Cp. SIMPATICO.
● The word implies that the thing or person so described is in accord with one's own taste or mood. The French themselves often use the shortened form *sympa* to mean simply 'nice'.

T

taal (tahl) *n.* (*S Afr.*) the Afrikaans
language.
19C. Dutch language, speech, from
Middle Dutch *tāle*, rel. to English *tale*.

tabbouleh (təbooʹlā) *n.* a type of
Mediterranean salad made from
cracked wheat, tomatoes and cucumber
and flavoured with mint, lemon juice
and olive oil.
mid-20C. Arabic *tabbūla*.

tabla (tabʹlə) *n.* a pair of small Indian
drums with variable pitch, played with
the hands.
19C. Persian and Urdu *tabla*, Hindi
tablā, from Arabic *ṭabl* drum.

tableau (tabʹlō) *n.* (*pl.* **tableaux** (-lōz,
-lō)) **1** a presentation resembling
a picture. **2** a striking or vivid
representation or effect.
17C. French, from Old French *tablel*,
dim. of *table* table, from Latin *tabula*
plank, tablet.

tableau vivant (tablō vēʹvã) *n.*
(*pl.* **tableaux vivants** (-lō vēʹvã)) a
motionless group of performers dressed
and arranged to represent some scene or
event.
19C. French, lit. living picture.

table d'hôte (tahbəl dōtʹ) *n.*
(*pl.* **tables d'hôte** (tahbəl)) a hotel or
restaurant meal at a fixed price, limited
to certain dishes arranged by the
proprietor.
17C. French host's table.
● The converse is À LA CARTE.

tablier (tabʹliā) *n.* (*Hist.*) a small apron or
apron-like part of a woman's dress.
12–14C. Old French, ult. from Latin
tabula plank, tablet.
● The original sense (to the 15C) was
backgammon board. The sense apron
dates from the 19C.

taboo (təbooʹ), **tabu** *n.* (*pl.* **taboos**,
tabus) **1** something which is very
strongly disapproved of in a particular
society etc. **2** a custom among the
Polynesians etc., of prohibiting the use
of certain persons, places or things.
3 (*fig.*) ban, prohibition. **4** any ritual
restriction, usu. of something
considered to be unclean or unholy. *~a.*
banned, prohibited, by social, religious
or moral convention. *~v.t.* (*3rd pers. sing.
pres.* **taboos**, **tabus**, *pres.p.* **tabooing**,
tabuing, *past, p.p.* **tabooed**, **tabued**)
1 to put under taboo. **2** to forbid the use
of (something).
18C. Tongan *tabu*.

tabouret (tabʹərit, -ret), (*N Am.*) **taboret**
n. **1** a small seat, usu. without arms or
back. **2** an embroidery frame.
17C. French, dim. of *tabour*, prob. rel. to
Arabic *ṭabl* drum. Cp. TABLA, TAMBOUR.

tabula rasa (tabūlə rah´zə) *n.* (*pl.* **tabulae rasae** (-lē rah´zē)) **1** the mind in its supposed original state, before any impressions have been made on it. **2** a fresh start. **3** a writing tablet.
16C. Latin, lit. scraped tablet, from *tabula* tablet + fem. p.p. of *rader* to scrape.

tabun (tah´boon) *n.* an organic phosphorus compound, formula $C_2H_5OP(O)(CN)N(CH_3)_2$, used as a lethal nerve gas in chemical warfare.
mid-20C. German, of unknown orig.

tacamahac (tak´əməhak) *n.* **1** a resin obtained from various South American trees, esp. of the genus *Calophyllum*. **2** the balsam poplar. **3** the resin of this tree.
16C. Obsolete Spanish *tacamahaca* (now *tacamaca*), from Aztec *tecomahiyac*.

tac-au-tac (takōtak´) *n.* **1** in fencing, the parry combined immediately with the riposte. **2** a series of attacks and parries in swift succession.
early 20C. French, lit. clash for clash, from imit. *tac*.

tacet (tas´it) *v.i.* (*Mus.*) to be silent (used in the imperative as an instruction to a particular voice or instrument).
18C. Latin is silent, 3rd pers. sing. pres. ind. of *tacere* to be silent.

tachism (tash´izm), **tachisme** *n.* a form of action painting with haphazard blobs of colour.
mid-20C. French *tachisme*, from *tache* spot, blot.
● The French word is first recorded in 1951, when it is said to have been coined by the French critics Charles Estienne and Pierre Guéguen. It was given wide currency by Michel Tapié in his book *Un Art autre* (1952).

taco (tah´kō) *n.* (*pl.* **tacos**) a type of thin pancake or tortilla from Mexico, usually with a spicy meat or vegetable filling.
mid-20C. Mexican Spanish.

taedium vitae (tēdiəm vē´tī, vī´tē) *n.* weariness of life.
18C. Latin, from *taedium* weariness + gen. sing. of *vita* life.

tae kwon do (tī kwon dō´) *n.* a type of Korean martial art, similar to karate, involving kicks and punches.
mid-20C. Korean, lit. art of hand and foot fighting, from *tae* kick + *kwon* fist + *do* art, method.

tael (tāl) *n.* **1** a Chinese and Far Eastern weight of 1½ ounces (38 grams) or a weight close to this. **2** (*Hist.*) a monetary unit equal to a tael of silver.
16C. Portuguese, from Malay *tahil* weight.

Tafelwein (tah´fəlvīn) *n.* ordinary German wine of unexceptional quality.
late 20C. German, lit. table wine. Cp. VIN DE TABLE.

tafia (taf´iə), **taffia** *n.* a variety of rum distilled from molasses.
18C. French, from West Indian creole, alt. of RATAFIA.

tagliatelle (talyətel´i, -ā) *n.* pasta in the form of thin strips.
19C. Italian, from *tagliare* to cut.

tahini (təhē´ni) *n.* a thick paste made from ground sesame seeds.
mid-20C. Modern Greek *takhini*, from Arabic *ṭaḥīnā*, from *ṭaḥana* to grind, to crush, to pulverize.

tahsil (tahsēl´) *n.* a division for revenue and other administrative purposes in some Indian states.
19C. Persian and Urdu *taḥṣīl*, from Arabic collection, levying of taxes.

taiaha (tī´əhah) *n.* a Maori carved long-handled club, now ceremonial.
19C. Maori.

t'ai chi ch'uan (tī chē chwahn´), **t'ai chi** (chē´) *n.* a Chinese form of exercise and self-defence based on slow controlled movements.
mid-20C. Chinese *tàijí quán*, from *tài* great + *jí* limit + *quán* fist.

taiga (tī´gə) *n.* the spruce-dominated coniferous forests found in subarctic North America and Eurasia.
19C. Russian *taĭga*, from Mongolian.

taipan (tī´pan) *n.* the head of a foreign business in China.
19C. Chinese *tài* great + *bān* team.

taj (tahj) *n.* a crown, a head-dress of distinction, esp. a tall cap worn by Muslim dervishes.
19C. Persian *tāj* crown.

talapoin (tal´əpoin) *n.* **1** a Buddhist priest or monk in Burma (Myanmar), Sri Lanka etc. **2** an African monkey, *Miopithecus talapoin*.
16C. French, from Portuguese *talapão*, from Mongolian *tula pói*, lit. lord of merit, a respectful title for a Buddhist monk.

tales (tā´lēz) *n.* (*Law*) **1** a writ for summoning jurors to make up a deficiency. **2** a list of people who can be summoned for this purpose.
15C. Latin, pl. of *talis* such, in *talis de circumstantibus* such of the bystanders, the opening words of the writ.

Taliban (tal´iban), **Taleban** *n.pl.* members of a fundamentalist Islamic militia in Afghanistan.
late 20C. Persian, lit. students.

tallith (tal´ith) *n.* a fringed scarf worn over the head and shoulders by Jewish men during prayer.

17C. Rabbinical Hebrew *ṭallīt*, from biblical Hebrew *ṭillel* to cover.

Talmud (tal´mud) *n.* the body of Jewish civil and religious law not included in the Pentateuch, including the Mishna and the Gemara.
16C. Post-biblical Hebrew *talmūḏ* instruction, from Hebrew *lāmaḏ* to learn.

Tamagotchi® (taməgoch´i) *n.* a small electronic toy mimicking the demands for food, etc. of a pet.
late 20C. Japanese, lit. lovable egg, from *tamago* egg.
● The name relates to the shape of the toy.

tamale (təmah´li) *n.* a Mexican dish of highly seasoned maize and meat.
17C. Mexican Spanish *tamal*, pl. *tamales*, from Nahuatl *tamalli*.

tamari (təmah´ri) *n.* a concentrated wheat-free sauce made from soya beans.
late 20C. Japanese.

tamasha (təmah´shə) *n.* in the Indian subcontinent, a show, a public function.
17C. Persian and Urdu *tamāšā* walking about for amusement, from Arabic *tamāšā* to walk about together, from *mašā* to walk.

tambour (tam´buə) *n.* **1** a drum, esp. a bass drum. **2** a circular frame on which silk etc., is embroidered. **3** silk or other fabric embroidered thus. **4** (*Archit.*)
a a cylindrical stone, such as one of the courses of the shaft of a column.
b a vestibule with a ceiling and folding doors in a porch etc., for preventing draughts. **5** a palisade defending an entrance. **6** a sliding door, or rolling top, on cabinets and desks etc. **7** a sloping buttress that allows the ball in a game of real tennis or fives to be deflected. ~*v.t.*, *v.i.* to embroider with or on a tambour.
15C. French drum, prob. rel. to Arabic *ṭabl* drum. Cp. TABLA, TABOURET.

tambourine (tambərēn´) *n.* a small percussion instrument composed of a hoop with parchment stretched across one head and loose jingling discs in the sides, played by striking with the hand etc.
16C. French *tambourin*, dim. of TAMBOUR.

Tammuz (tam´uz) *n.* the fourth month in the Jewish calendar according to biblical reckoning, the tenth in the civil year, usually falling in June and July.
16C. Hebrew *tammūz*.

tam-tam (tam´tam) *n.* a large metal gong.
19C. ? Hindi *ṭam-ṭam* TOM-TOM.

tandem (tan´dəm) *n.* **1** a bicycle or tricycle for two riders one behind the other. **2** a vehicle with two or more horses harnessed one behind the other. **3** an arrangement of two things one behind the other. ~*adv.* **1** with horses harnessed one behind the other. **2** (harnessed) one behind the other. ~*a.* harnessed or arranged in this way.
18C. Latin at length, as a punning use of the Latin word, originally applied in sense 2.

tandoor (tanduə´) *n.* a clay oven as used in N India and Pakistan.
19C. Urdu *tandūr*, Persian *tanūr*, ult. from Arabic *tannūr* oven, furnace.
• Hence *tandoori* (mid-20C) as a style of Indian cooking based on the use of a tandoor.

tanga (tang´gə) *n.* pants, briefs or bikini bottoms that consist of two small joined triangular pieces, held in place by a string or thong waistband.
early 20C. Portuguese, ult. of Bantu orig.

tango (tang´gō) *n.* (*pl.* **tangos**) **1** a Latin American dance that is characterized by highly stylized, often erotic, body movements punctuated by glides and pauses. **2** a piece of music for this dance. ~*v.i.* (*3rd pers. sing. pres.* **tangoes**, *pres.p.* **tangoing**, *past, p.p.* **tangoed**) to dance the tango.
19C. American Spanish, ? of African orig.

tanka (tang´kə) *n.* a Japanese verse form with five lines and 31 syllables, the first and third lines having five syllables and the others having seven.
19C. Japanese, from *tan* short + *ka* song.

tant mieux (tõ myœ´) *int.* so much the better.
18C. French so much (the) better.
Cp. TANT PIS.

tanto (tan´tō) *adv.* (*Mus.*) too much.
19C. Italian, from Latin *tantum* so much.

tant pis (tõ pē´) *int.* so much the worse.
18C. French so much (the) worse.
Cp. TANT MIEUX.

tantra (tan´trə) *n.* any of a class of later Sanskrit Hindu and Buddhist textbooks dealing chiefly with magical powers.
18C. Sanskrit loom, warp, groundwork, system, doctrine.

Tao (tow) *n.* in Taoism, the principle of creative harmony in the universe, the relation between human life and eternal truth.
18C. Chinese *dào* way, path, right way.

Taoiseach (tē´shəkh, -shək) *n.* the Prime Minister of the Republic of Ireland.
mid-20C. Irish, lit. chief, leader.

tapa (tah´pə) *n.* **1** a kind of tough clothlike paper made from the bark of a tree, used by Polynesians for clothes, nets etc. **2** the bark this material is made from.
19C. Polynesian.

tapadero (tapədeə´rō) *n.* (*pl.* **tapaderos**) a leather guard worn in front of the stirrup in California and other parts of the W US.

19C. Spanish cover, lid, stopper, from *tapar* to stop up, to cover.

tapas (tap´as) *n.pl.* various light savoury snacks or appetizers, as served in Spain.
mid-20C. Spanish, pl. of *tapa*, lit. cover, lid.

tapioca (tapiō´kə) *n.* a starchy, granular substance produced by beating cassava, forming a light farinaceous food.
18C. Tupi-Guarani *tipioca*, from *tipi* residue, dregs + *ok*, *og* to squeeze out.

tapis (tap´ē) *n.* (*pl.* **tapis**) a tapestry, a thick table covering.
15C. Old French *tapiz* (Modern French *tapis*), from Late Latin *tapetium*, from Greek *tapētion*, dim. of *tapēs*, *tapētos* tapestry.

tapotement (təpōt´mənt) *n.* (*Med.*) the use of light rapid tapping as a form of massage.
19C. French, from *tapoter* to tap.

tapu (tah´poo) *a.* (*esp. New Zeal.*) sacred, taboo.
18C. Var. of **Tongan** *tabu*. See TABOO.

taramasalata (tarəməsəlah´tə), **tarama** (tar´əmə) *n.* a pale pink creamy Greek pâté, made from smoked cod roe or, less commonly, the roe of other fish, blended with olive oil and garlic.
early 20C. Modern Greek *taramosalata*, from *taramas* preserved roe + *salata* salad.

tarantass (tarəntas´) *n.* a large four-wheeled Russian carriage without springs.
19C. Russian *tarantas*.

tarantella (tarəntel´ə), **tarantelle** (-tel´) *n.* **1** a rapid S Italian dance in triplets for one couple. **2** the music for such a dance.
18C. Italian, dim. of *Taranto* (Latin *Tarentum*), a seaport in S Italy.

Pop. assoc. with Old Italian *tarantola* tarantula.
● The dance was attributed to the bite of the tarantula, which was believed to cause tarantism.

tarboosh (tahboosh´), **tarboush**, **tarbush** *n.* a brimless cap or fez, usu. red.
18C. Egyptian Arabic *ṭarbūš*, from Ottoman Turkish *terpōṣ*, *tarbuṣ*, from Persian *sarpūš*, from *sar* head + *pūš* cover.

targa (tah´gə) *n.* a sports car that has a removable hard roof which fits over a roll bar or goes into the boot when not in use. ~*a.* relating to this kind of sports car.
late 20C. Italian plate, shield.
● The word was originally the name of a model of Porsche car (introduced in 1965) with a detachable hood, probably itself named after the *Targa Florio* (Florio Shield), an annual motor time trial held in Sicily.

Targum (tah´gəm) *n.* any of various ancient Aramaic versions or paraphrases of the Old Testament Scriptures.
16C. Hebrew, from Aramaic *targūm* interpretation, from *targēm* to interpret. See DRAGOMAN.

tariff (tar´if) *n.* **1** a table of charges. **2** a list or table of duties or customs payable on the importation or export of goods. **3** a duty on any particular kind of goods. **4** a law imposing such duties. **5** a method of charging for gas and electricity. **6** the charges imposed on these. ~*v.t.* **1** to draw up a list of duties or charges on (goods etc.). **2** to price, to put a valuation on.
16C. French *tarif*, from Italian *tariffa*, from Turkish *tarife*, from Arabic *ta'rifa*, from *'arrafa* to notify, to apprise.
● The original sense was sense 2. Sense 1 arose in the 18C.

tarlatan (tah´lətən) *n.* a fine, transparent muslin.
18C. French *tarlatane*, alt. of *tarnatane*, prob. of Indonesian orig.

taro (tah´rō) *n.* (*pl.* **taros**) a tropical plant of the arum family, esp. *Colocasia esculenta* and *C. macrorhiza*, the roots of which are used as food by Pacific islanders.
18C. Polynesian.

tarot (tar´ō) *n.* **1** a figured playing card, one of a pack of 78, used in an old (orig. Italian) card game. **2** a pack of such cards, consisting of four suits of 14 plus a fifth suit of 22 permanent trump cards, used for fortune-telling. **3** (any of) these 22 cards. **4** any game played with tarot cards. ~*a.* belonging or relating to these cards or to fortune-telling using them.
16C. French, from Italian *tarocchi*, pl. of *tarocco*, of unknown orig.

tarsia (tah´siə) *n.* an Italian mosaic or inlaid woodwork.
17C. Italian INTARSIA.

Tass (tas) *n.* (*Hist.*) the official news agency of the former Soviet Union.
early 20C. Russian, acronym of *T*elegrafnoe *a*gentstvo *S*ovetskogo *S*oyuza Telegraphic Agency of the Soviet Union.

tatami (tətah´mi) *n.* (*pl.* **tatamis**) a traditional woven straw or rush mat of standard size, used as a floor covering in Japanese houses.
17C. Japanese.

tâtonnement (taton´mā) *n.* experimentation, tentative exploration.
19C. French, from *tâtonner* to feel one's way. Cp. À TÂTONS.

tatty (tat´i) *n.* (*pl.* **tatties**) in the Indian subcontinent, a matting of khus-khus for hanging in doorways and other openings, usu. kept wet to cool the air.
18C. Hindi *ṭaṭṭī* wicker frame.

tau (taw, tow) *n.* **1** the 19th letter of the Greek alphabet (T, τ). **2** a tau cross.
12–14C. Greek. Cp. *taw* final letter of the Hebrew alphabet, from Hebrew *tāw*.
• *Tau* was originally the final letter of the Greek alphabet.

taupe (tōp) *n.* a brownish-grey colour. ~*a.* of this colour.
early 20C. French, from Latin *talpa* mole.

tazza (tat´sə) *n.* (*pl.* **tazze** (-sā)) a flattish or saucer-shaped cup, esp. one on a high foot.
19C. Italian, from Arabic *ṭasa*.

teapoy (tē´poi) *n.* a small three- or four-legged table for holding a tea service etc.
19C. Hindi *ti-* three + Urdu and Persian *pāī* foot.
• The sense and spelling have been influenced by English *tea*.

Tebeth (teb´əth) *n.* the fourth month of the civil and tenth month of the Jewish ecclesiastical year, comprising parts of December and January.
14–15C. Hebrew *ṭēḇēṭ*.

technique (teknēk´) *n.* **1** a mode of artistic performance or execution. **2** mechanical skill in art, craft etc. **3** proficiency in some skill. **4** a particular way of carrying out or performing something.
19C. French, use as n. of a., from Latin *technicus*, from Greek *tekhnikos* relating to art, from *tekhnē* art, craft.

Te Deum (tē dē´əm) *n.* **1** a hymn of praise sung at morning service or as a special thanksgiving. **2** a musical setting for this. **3** a thanksgiving service at which it is sung.
pre-1200. Latin *Te Deum laudamus* We praise thee, O God, opening words of the hymn.

téléférique (teleferēk´) *n.* a cableway.
early 20C. French, from Italian *teleferica*, from Greek *tēle-* far + *pherein* to carry.
● The English word *teleferic* also exists.

telega (tilā´gə) *n.* a four-wheeled springless Russian cart.
16C. Russian.

tell (tel) *n.* in Middle Eastern archaeology, a mound that is composed of the remains of successive settlements.
19C. Arabic *tall* hill, hillock.

temblor (temblaw´) *n.* (*N Am.*) an earthquake or tremor.
19C. American Spanish.

tempeh (tem´pā) *n.* an Indonesian dish made by deep-frying fermented soya beans.
mid-20C. Indonesian *tempe*.

tempera (tem´pərə) *n.* **1** a method of artistic painting that uses an emulsion of powdered pigment mixed with egg yolk and water. **2** the emulsion itself.
19C. Italian, in phr. *pingere a tempera* to paint in distemper.

tempo (tem´pō) *n.* (*pl.* **tempi** (-pē), **tempos**) **1** (*Mus.*) the specified speed at which a piece of music is or should be played. **2** pace or rate.
17C. Italian, from Latin *tempus* time.

tempora mutantur (tempərə mootan´tə, mū-) *int.* times change.
19C. Latin.
● The full Latin sentence is *tempora mutantur, nos et mutamur in illis* 'Times change and we change with them'. The saying is ascribed to the Roman emperor Lothair I (795–855).

tempura (tem´purə) *n.* a Japanese dish of vegetables, seafood and fish coated in batter and deep-fried.
early 20C. **Japanese**, prob. from Portuguese *têmpêro* seasoning.

tempus fugit (tempəs fū´jit) *int.* time flies.
19C. Latin.
● The Latin words are based on Virgil's *Georgics* (III) (1C BC): *sed fugit interea, fugit inreparabile tempus* 'But meanwhile it is flying, irretrievable time is flying'.

temura (temur´ah), **temurah** *n.* a cabbalistic method of interpreting the Hebrew scriptures by systematically replacing the letters of a word with other letters.
early 20C. Hebrew *tĕmūrāh* exchange.

tendresse (tãdres´) *n.* a fondness or affection.
14–15C. French, from *tendre* tender.

Tenebrae (ten´ibrē) *n.pl.* **1** in the Roman Catholic Church, the offices of matins and lauds for the last three days in Holy Week. **2** these offices set to music.
17C. Latin darkness.
● The offices are so called as candles were formerly extinguished one by one in memory of the darkness during the crucifixion (Matt. xxvii.45 etc.).

tenet (ten´it, tē´-) *n.* an opinion, principle, doctrine or dogma held by a person, school or organization.
16C. Latin, lit. he holds, 3rd pers. sing. pres. of *tenere* to hold.

tenné (ten´i), **tenny** *n.* (*Her.*) a brownish-orange colour. ~*a.* having this colour.
16C. Obsolete French, var. of Old French *tané* tawny.

tenno (ten´ō) *n.* (*pl.* **tennos**) the Emperor of Japan, esp. in his capacity as divine ruler.
19C. Japanese *tennō*, from *ten* heavenly + *nō* power.

tenore (tinaw´rā) n. (pl. **tenori** (-rē)) a tenor voice or singer.
18C. **Italian** tenor.

tenue (tənü´) n. deportment, propriety, dress.
19C. **French**, fem. p.p. (used as n.) of *tenir* to hold, to keep.

tenuto (tinoo´tō) a., adv. (Mus.) sustained, held on for the full time. ~n. (pl. **tenutos**) a note or chord played in this way.
18C. **Italian**, p.p. of *tenere* to hold.

teocalli (tēōkal´i, tā-) n. (pl. **teocallis**) a pyramidal mound or structure, usu. surmounted by a temple, used for worship by the ancient peoples of Mexico, Central America etc.
17C. **American Spanish**, from Nahuatl *teo:kalli*, from *teòtl* god + *kalli* house.

tepee (tē´pē), **teepee**, **tipi** n. (pl. **tepees**, **teepees**, **tipis**) a North American Indian tent, usu. cone-shaped and made by stretching animal skins over a framework of poles.
18C. **Sioux** *típi* dwelling.

teppan-yaki (tep´anyaki) n. a Japanese dish of meat or fish (or both) fried with vegetables on a hot steel plate that forms the centre of the dining table.
late 20C. **Japanese**, from *teppan* steel plate + *yaki* to fry.

tequila (tikē´lə) n. 1 a Mexican spirit distilled from agave which forms the basis of many drinks. 2 the plant from which this spirit is distilled.
19C. **Mexican Spanish**, from *Tequila*, a district of central Mexico.

terai (ter´ī), **terai hat** n. a wide-brimmed felt hat, often with ventilation holes and a double crown, worn in subtropical regions.
19C. **Hindi** *Terai*, a belt of marshy jungle between the southern foothills of the Himalayas and the plains.

teriyaki (teriyah´ki) n. a Japanese dish of fish or meat marinated in soy sauce and grilled.
mid-20C. **Japanese**, from *teri* gloss, lustre + *yaki* to grill.

terminus (tœ´minəs) n. (pl. **termini** (-nī), **terminuses**) 1 the point where a railway or bus route ends. 2 the town, building or buildings at this point. 3 a storage place at the end of an oil pipeline etc. 4 a final point, a goal. 5 a starting point. 6 (*Archit.*) a sculpted figure, usu. of an animal or of the armless bust of a human, placed on top of a square pillar so that the figure seems to be springing from the post, orig. as a boundary marker. 7 (*Math.*) the end point of a vector etc.
16C. **Latin** end, limit, boundary.
● The original sense was sense 4. Sense 1 dates from the 19C.

terminus ad quem (tœminəs ad kwem´) n. the end or finishing point of an argument, period of time, particular policy etc.
16C. **Latin**, lit. the end to which.
Cp. TERMINUS A QUO.
● The phrase was originally part of the specific vocabulary of 13C philosophers such as Albertus Magnus and Thomas Aquinas.

terminus ante quem (tœminəs anti kwem´) n. the specified time or date before which something must have been achieved or done.
mid-20C. **Latin**, lit. the end before which.

terminus a quo (tœminəs ah kwō´) n. the beginning or starting point of an argument, period of time, particular policy etc.
16C. **Latin**, lit. the end from which.
● The phrase was originally part of the vocabulary of medieval philosophy.
Cp. TERMINUS AD QUEM.

terminus post quem (tœminəs pōst kwem´) *n.* the specified time or date before which something cannot or should not be started.
mid-20C. Latin, lit. the end after which.

terra (ter´ə) *n.* (*pl.* **terrae** (-rē)) in legal contexts, earth or land.
17C. Latin earth.

terracotta (terəkot´ə) *n.* **1** a hard, unglazed earthenware used as a decorative building material and for making pottery, models etc. **2** a statue or figure in this. **3** the brownish-orange colour of terracotta. ~*a.* **1** made of this earthenware. **2** having a brownish-orange colour.
18C. Italian *terra cotta* baked earth, from Latin *terra cocta*.

terra firma (terə fœ´mə) *n.* dry land, firm ground.
17C. Latin firm land.
• The phrase originally denoted a mainland or continent, as distinct from an island or lesser land mass.

terrain (tərān´) *n.* **1** a region, a tract, an extent of land of a definite geological character or as thought of in terms of military operations. **2** a field or sphere of interest, influence or knowledge.
18C. French, from Popular Latin var. of Latin *terrenum,* use as *n.* of neut. of *terrenus,* from *terra* earth.

terra incognita (terə inkognē´tə) *n.* unknown country, unexplored territory.
17C. Latin unknown land.
• Australia was known as *terra australis incognita,* southern unknown land, by voyagers who suspected its existence from the 2C AD and this formed the basis for its present name, given in the 19C.

terramare (terəmah´ri), **terramara** (-rə) *n.* (*pl.* **terramares,** **terramare** (-rā)) **1** a dark earthy deposit found at the sites of some prehistoric lakeside settlements, esp. in Italy. **2** a dwelling or settlement that once stood at such a site.
19C. French, from Italian dial. *terramara,* from *terra marna,* from *terra* earth + *marna* marl.

terrazzo (terat´sō) *n.* (*pl.* **terrazzos**) a mosaic floor-covering made by setting marble or other chips into cement, which is then polished.
early 20C. Italian terrace, balcony.

terreplein (teə´plān) *n.* **1** the upper surface of a rampart where guns are mounted. **2** the level surface around a fieldwork.
16C. French *terre-plein,* from Italian *terrapieno,* from *terrapienare* to fill with earth, from *terra* earth + *pieno* (from Latin *plenus*) full.

terre-verte (teəveət´) *n.* a soft green mineral used by artists as a pigment.
17C. French green earth.

terrine (tərēn´) *n.* **1** a type of coarse pâté, usu. made by incorporating vegetables into a meat or fish base. **2** an earthenware container, esp. one that this type of pâté is cooked in and which is sometimes sold along with the pâté.
18C. French large earthenware pot, fem. of Old French *terrin* earthen, from Latin *terra* earth.

tertium quid (tœshəm kwid´) *n.* a third (or intermediate) something.
18C. Late Latin, translating Greek *triton ti* some third thing.
• The entity is so termed as it is related in some way to two definite or known things, but distinct from both.

terza rima (teətsə rē´mə, tœt-) *n.* in prosody, an arrangement of tercets with a linking rhyme scheme of aba, bcb, cdc etc.
19C. Italian third rhyme.
• The form of verse is best known as the metre of Dante's *Divina Commedia* (*c.*1309–20).

terzetto (tœtset´ō, teət-) *n.* (*pl.* **terzettos**, **terzetti** (-tē)) (*Mus.*) a group of three performers or singers.
18C. Italian, from *terzo* third.

tessera (tes´ərə) *n.* (*pl.* **tesserae** (-rē))
1 a small cubical piece of marble, earthenware etc., used in mosaics. **2** in ancient Greece and Rome, a small piece of bone etc. used as a token.
17C. Latin, from Greek, neut. of *tesseres*, var. of *tessares* four.

tessitura (tesituə´rə) *n.* (*Mus.*) **1** the range that encompasses most of the tones of a voice part. **2** the natural pitch of a voice or piece of vocal music.
19C. Italian, lit. texture.

testudo (testū´dō) *n.* (*pl.* **testudos**, **testudines** (-dinēz)) **1** (*Hist.*) a type of protective barrier formed by attacking Roman soldiers who raised their shields above their heads so that they overlapped and made a screen. **2** (*Hist.*) a moveable screen used for protecting besieging Roman troops. **3** any similar screen, esp. one used by miners working in places liable to cave in.
14–15C. Latin, from *testa* pot, shell, *testu* pot lid.

tête-à-tête (tātahtāt´, tetahtet´) *n.* (*pl.* **tête-à-tête**, **tête-à-têtes** (tātahtāts´, tetahtets´)) **1** a private interview, a close or confidential conversation. **2** a sofa for two persons, esp. with seats facing in opposite directions so that the occupants face one another. ~*a.* private, confidential. ~*adv.* in private or close intimacy.
17C. French, lit. head to head.

tête-bêche (tātbesh´, tet-, -bāsh´) *a.* (of a postage stamp) printed so that it is upside down or facing the other way in comparison to the other stamps on a sheet.
19C. French, from *tête* head + *bêche* (reduced form of *béchevet*), lit. double bedhead.

TGV *n.* any of the high-speed electric trains or train services introduced in France in 1981.
Abbr. of **French** *train à grande vitesse* high-speed train.

thaler (tah´lə) *n.* (*Hist.*) an old German silver coin.
18C. German (now *Taler*) dollar.

thalweg (tahl´veg), **talweg** *n.* **1** the longitudinal line where the opposite slopes of a river, valley or lake meet. **2** (*Law*) a state boundary that follows the course of a valley or river at its centre.
19C. German, from *Thal* (now *Tal*) valley + *Weg* way.

thé dansant (tā dāsā´) *n.* (*pl.* **thés dansants** (tā dāsā´)) a dance held during afternoon tea, popular in the 1920s and 1930s.
19C. French, lit. dancing tea.

Theravada (therəvah´də) *n.* a form of Buddhism practised esp. in SE Asia.
19C. Pali *theravāda*, lit. doctrine of the elders.

thermae (thœ´mē) *n.pl.* (*Hist.*) public baths in ancient Greece and Rome.
16C. Latin (pl.), from Greek *thermai* hot baths, from *thermē* heat.

thesis (thē´sis) *n.* (*pl.* **theses** (-sēz))
1 a proposition advanced or maintained. **2** an essay or dissertation, esp. one submitted by a candidate for a degree etc. **3** a school or college exercise. **4** (*Logic*) an affirmation, as opposed to a hypothesis. **5** (the´sis) in prosody, the unaccented part of a metrical foot, as opposed to *arsis*.
14–15C. Late Latin, from Greek putting, placing, proposition, affirmation, from *the-*, base of *tithenai* to put, to place.

thing (thing) *n.* a Scandinavian public assembly, esp. a legislative body.
18C. Old Norse *thing*, Danish, Norwegian and Swedish *ting*.
Cp. STORTING.

thug (thŭg) *n.* **1** a violent or brutal ruffian. **2** (**Thug**) a member of a fraternity of religious assassins in India (suppressed 1828–35).
19C. Hindi *ṭhag* cheat, swindler.
● The word was originally (sense 2) the name of a member of an organization of professional robbers in India, who strangled their victims.

thyrsus (thœ´səs) *n.* (*pl.* **thyrsi** (-sī))
1 (*Hist.*) in ancient Greece and Rome, a spear or shaft wrapped with ivy or vine branches and tipped with a fir cone, an attribute of Bacchus. **2** (*Bot.*) an inflorescence consisting of a panicle with the longest branches in the middle.
16C. Latin, from Greek *thursos* stalk of a plant, Bacchic staff.

tiara (tiah´rə) *n.* **1** a jewelled coronet or headband worn as an ornament by women. **2** the headdress of the ancient Persian kings, resembling a lofty turban. **3** the triple crown worn by the Pope as a symbol of his temporal, spiritual, and purgatorial power. **4** the papal dignity.
16C. Latin, from Greek, partly through Italian.

tic (tik) *n.* a habitual convulsive twitching of muscles, esp. of the face.
19C. French, from Italian *ticchio*.

tic douloureux (tik doolərœ´, -roo´) *n.* trigeminal neuralgia characterized by spasmodic twitching.
19C. French painful tic.

tika (tē´kah, tik´ah), **tikka** *n.* **1** a mark on the forehead of a Hindu woman indicating caste or status. **2** a similar mark worn by both sexes as an ornament.
19C. Hindi *ṭīkā*.

tiki (tē´ki, tik´-) *n.* (*pl.* **tikis**) a Maori neck ornament or figurine, a stylized representation of an ancestor etc.
18C. Maori image. Cp. HEI-TIKI.

tikka (tik´ə, tē´-) *n.* an Indian dish of kebabs (esp. chicken or lamb) marinated in spices and dry-roasted in a clay oven.
mid-20C. Punjabi *ṭikkā*.

tilde (til´də, tild) *n.* a diacritical sign (˜) in Spanish put over *n* to indicate the sound *ny* as in *señor*, in Portuguese and phonetics put over vowels to indicate nasalization.
19C. Spanish, from Latin *titulus* title.

timbale (tambahl´) *n.* a dish of meat or fish pounded and mixed with white of egg, cream etc., and cooked in a drum-shaped mould.
19C. French kettledrum.

timbre (tam´bə) *n.* the quality of tone distinguishing particular voices, instruments etc., due to the individual character of the sound waves.
19C. French, from Medieval Greek *timbanon* timbrel, kettledrum, from Greek *tumpanon* drum.

timoroso (timərō´sō) *adv.* (*Mus.*) with hesitation.
19C. Italian, from Medieval Latin *timorosus* fearful.

timpani (tim´pəni), **tympani** *n.pl.* (*Mus.*) orchestral kettledrums.
19C. Italian, pl. of *timpano* kettledrum, from Latin *tympanum* drum.

tirailleur (tērahyœ´, tirəlœ´) *n.* **1** a skirmisher. **2** a sharpshooter.
18C. French, from *tirailler* to fire in skirmishing order, from *tirer* to draw, to shoot.

tiramisu (tiramisoo´) *n.* an Italian dessert consisting of layers of sponge cake soaked in coffee and brandy or Marsala and covered with mascarpone cheese and chocolate.
late 20C. Italian, from *tira mi sù* pick me up. Cp. English 'pick-me-up'.

tisane (tizan´), **ptisan** *n.* **1** herbal tea. **2** a medicinal infusion of dried leaves or flowers, orig. made with barley.
14–15C. Old French *tisane*, *ptisane*, from Latin *ptisana*, from Greek *ptisanē* peeled barley, barley water, rel. to *ptissein* to peel.

Tishri (tish´ri) *n.* the first month of the Hebrew civil year and the seventh of the ecclesiastical year, corresponding to parts of September and October.
17C. Late Hebrew *tišrī*, from Aramaic *šĕrā* to begin.

tobacco (tǝbak´ō) *n.* (*pl.* **tobaccos**)
1 a plant of American origin of the genus *Nicotiana,* with narcotic leaves which are used, after drying and preparing, for smoking, chewing, snuff etc. **2** the leaves of this, esp. prepared for smoking.
16C. Spanish *tabaco*, said to come from a Carib word meaning a pipe through which smoke was inhaled, or from a Taino word for a primitive cigar, but poss. actually from Arabic.

toccata (tǝkah´tǝ) *n.* (*Mus.*) a keyboard composition orig. designed to exercise or display the player's touch.
18C. Italian, fem. p.p. (used as n.) of *toccare* to touch.

toddy (tod´i) *n.* (*pl.* **toddies**) **1** a beverage of spirit and hot water sweetened. **2** the fermented juice of various palm trees.
17C. Marathi *tāḍī*, Hindi *tāṛī*, from Sanskrit *tāḍī* palmyra.

tofu (tō´foo) *n.* unfermented soya bean curd.
18C. Japanese *tōfu*, from Chinese *dòufŭ*, from *dòu* beans + *fŭ* to rot, to turn sour.

toga (tō´gǝ) *n.* a loose flowing robe, the principal outer garment of an ancient Roman citizen.
17C. Latin, rel. to *tegere* to cover.

toile (twahl) *n.* **1** cloth, esp. for clothes. **2** a model of a garment made up in cheap cloth.
14–15C. Old French, from Latin *tela* web, from base also of *texere* to weave.

toilette (twahlet´) *n.* the process of washing, dressing etc.
18C. French, dim. of TOILE, and the source of English *toilet*.

tokamak (tō´kǝmak) *n.* (*Physics*) a toroidal reactor used in thermonuclear experiments involving magnetic effects on hot plasma.
mid-20C. Russian, from *to*roidal'naya *ka*mera s *ma*gnitnym polem toroidal chamber with magnetic field.

tola (tō´lǝ) *n.* a unit of weight for gold and silver, usu. about 180 grains troy.
17C. Hindi *tolā*, from Sanskrit *tolaka*.

tolu (tǝloo´) *n.* a balsam derived from the South American trees *Myroxylon balsamum* and *M. toluifera.*
17C. Santiago de *Tolú*, a town in NW Colombia, from where it was exported.

toman (tǝmahn´) *n.* (*Hist.*) a former Persian gold coin worth about 10,000 dinars.
16C. Persian *tūmān*, from Old Turkish *tümen*, from Tocharian A *tmān*, prob. ult. from base of Chinese *wàn* ten thousand.

tomatillo (tomǝtil´yō, -til´ō) *n.* (*pl.* **tomatillos**) **1** a Mexican ground cherry, *Physalis philadelphica.* **2** the edible berry of this.
early 20C. Spanish, dim. of *tomate* tomato.

tombac (tom'bak) *n.* any one of various copper and zinc alloys, used for making cheap jewellery.
17C. French, from Portuguese *tambaca*, from Malay *tembaga* copper, brass, ? from Sanskrit *tāmraka* copper.

tombola (tombō'lə) *n.* an instant lottery at a fête etc.
19C. French or Italian, from Italian *tombolare* to turn a somersault, to tumble.
• The lottery is so called from the revolving container from which the tickets are drawn.

tombolo (tombō'lō) *n.* (*pl.* **tombolos**) a narrow spit joining an island to the mainland or to another island.
19C. Italian sand dune.

tom-tom (tom'tom) *n.* a long, narrow, hand-beaten drum used in India, Africa etc. ~*v.i.* (*pres.p.* **tom-tomming**, *past*, *p.p.* **tom-tommed**) to beat this.
17C. Telugu *ṭamaṭama*, Hindi *ṭam ṭam*, of imit. orig. Cp. TAM-TAM.

ton (tō) *n.* the prevailing fashion or mode.
18C. French, from Latin *tonus* tone.

tondo (ton'dō) *n.* (*pl.* **tondi** (-di)) **1** a circular easel painting, relief carving etc. **2** a maiolica plate with a wide decorated rim.
19C. Italian a round, circle, compass, shortened from *rotondo* round.

tong (tong) *n.* a Chinese secret society.
19C. Chinese *táng* hall, meeting place.

tonga (tong'gə) *n.* a light two-wheeled horse-drawn cart for four persons used in India.
19C. Hindi *tāgā*.

tonne (tŭn) *n.* the metric ton.
19C. French.

tonneau (ton'ō) *n.* the rear part of a car containing the back seats, esp. of an open car.

18C. French barrel, cask.
• The original sense was a unit of capacity for French wine. The term for the rear part of a car evolved in the early 20C.

tontine (ton'tēn, -tēn') *n.* a form of annuity in which the shares of subscribers who die are added to the profits shared by the survivors, the last of whom receives the whole amount.
18C. French, from Lorenzo *Tonti* (1630–95), Neapolitan banker, who started such a scheme to raise government loans in France in *c.*1653.

tope[1] (tōp) *n.* a grove, esp. of mango trees.
17C. Telugu *tōpu*, Tamil *tōppu*.

tope[2] (tōp) *n.* a Buddhist monument in the form of a dome, tower or mound, usu. containing relics, a stupa.
19C. Punjabi *thūp*, *thop* barrow, mound, appar. rel. to Sanskrit *stūpa* STUPA.

Tophet (tō'fit) *n.* in the Bible, hell.
14–15C. Hebrew *tōpeṭ*, a place in the valley of Hinnom near Jerusalem, used for idolatrous worship including the sacrifice of children (Jer. xix.6).

topi (tō'pi), **topee** *n.* (*pl.* **topis**, **topees**) a sunhat, a pith helmet.
19C. Hindi *ṭopī* hat.
• A fuller form is *sola topi*, where *sola* has no connection with English *solar* but is the name of the Indian swamp plant that yields the pith from which the helmet is made.

toque (tōk) *n.* **1** a small, brimless, close-fitting hat. **2** (*Hist.*) a cap or headdress, usu. small and close-fitting, worn at various periods by men and women.
16C. French, from Spanish *toca*, of unknown orig.
• Some sources relate the word to German *Tuch* cloth, fabric.

Torah (taw´rə) n. **1** the Pentateuch. **2** the scroll containing this, used in synagogue services. **3** the will of God, the Mosaic law.
16C. Hebrew *tōrāh* direction, instruction, doctrine, law, from *yārāh* to throw, to show, to direct, to instruct.

torc (tawk) n. (*Hist.*) a twisted necklace of gold or other metal, worn by the ancient Gauls etc.
19C. French, var. of TORQUE.

torchère (tawsheə´) n. (*pl.* **torchères** (tawsheə´)) a tall ornamental flat-topped stand for a candlestick.
early 20C. French, from *torche* torch, ult. from Latin *torqua*, var. of *torques* necklace, wreath, from *torquere* to twist, and the source of English *torch*.

torchon (taw´shən) n. **1** torchon lace. **2** a dishcloth.
19C. French duster, dishcloth, from *torcher* to wipe, from *torche* straw plaiting.
• A handful of twisted straw will serve to wipe with. It will also serve for burning or lighting. Hence related English *torch*.

tore (taw) n. a torus.
17C. French, from Latin TORUS.

toreador (toriədaw´, tor´-) n. a bullfighter, esp. one who fights on horseback.
17C. Spanish, from *torear* to fight bulls, from *toro* bull, from Latin *taurus*.

torero (toreə´rō) n. (*pl.* **toreros**) a bullfighter, esp. one who fights on foot.
18C. Spanish, from *toro* bull, from Latin *taurus*. Cp. TOREADOR.

torii (taw´riē) n. (*pl.* **torii**) a gateless gateway composed of two uprights with (usu.) three superimposed crosspieces, at the approach to a Shinto temple.
18C. Japanese, from *tori* bird + *i* to sit, to perch.

torque (tawk) n. **1** the movement of a system of forces causing rotation. **2** TORC. ~*v.t.* to apply a twisting force to, to apply torque to.
19C. French, from Latin *torquere* to twist.

Torschlusspanik (taw´shluspahnik) n. a sense of alarm or anxiety at the passing of life's opportunities.
mid-20C. German last-minute panic, from *Tor* door, gate + *Schluss* closure + *Panik* panic.

torso (taw´sō) n. (*pl.* **torsos**, (*N Am.*) **torsi** (-sē)) **1** the trunk of a statue or body without the head and limbs. **2** an unfinished or partially destroyed work of art or literature.
18C. Italian stalk, stump, trunk of a statue, from Latin THYRSUS.

torte (taw´tə, tawt) n. (*pl.* **torten**, **tortes**) a rich gateau or tart, with fruit, cream etc.
18C. German *Torte* tart, pastry, cake, from Italian *torta*, from Late Latin. Prob. rel. to English *tart*.

tortelli (tawtel´i) n. a dish of small pasta parcels filled with a meat, cheese or vegetable mixture.
mid-20C. Italian, pl. of *tortello* small cake, fritter, dim. of *torta*, from Late Latin.

tortellini (tawtelē´ni) n. tortelli rolled and formed into small rings.
mid-20C. Italian, pl. of *tortellino*, dim. of *tortello*. See TORTELLI.

tortilla (tawtē´yə) n. in Mexican cooking, a thin flat maize cake baked on an iron plate.
17C. Spanish, dim. of *torta* cake, from Late Latin. See TORTE.

torus (taw´rəs) *n.* (*pl.* **tori** (-rī), **toruses**)
1 (*Geom.*) a ring-shaped surface
generated by a circle rotated about a
line which does not intersect the circle.
2 (*Bot.*) the receptacle or thalamus of a
flower, the modified end of a stem
supporting the floral organs. **3** (*Archit.*)
a semicircular projecting moulding, esp.
in the base of a column. **4** (*Anat.*) a
rounded ridge of bone or muscle.
16C. Latin swelling, bolster, round
moulding.

tosa (tō´sə) *n.* a smooth-haired large
heavy dog bred from the mastiff, orig.
kept for dogfighting.
mid-20C. *Tosa,* a former province on the
island of Shikoku, Japan.

touché (tooshā´) *int.* used to
acknowledge a hit in fencing, or a point
scored in argument.
early 20C. French, p.p. of *toucher* to
touch.

toujours perdrix (toozhuə peədrē´)
adv. too much of a good thing.
18C. French, lit. always partridge.
● Partridge is one of the richer meats
among game birds.

toupee (too´pā), **toupet** (too´pā, -pit)
n. **1** a small wig to cover a bald spot, a
hairpiece. **2** †an artificial lock or curl of
hair.
18C. Alt. of **French** *toupet* tuft of hair,
from Old French *toup* tuft, from base
also of English *top.*

tour de force (tuə də faws´) *n.* (*pl.*
tours de force (tuə)) an outstanding
feat of performance, skill, strength etc.
19C. French, lit. turn of strength.

tour d'horizon (tuə dorizõ´) *n.*
(*pl.* **tours d'horizon** (tuə)) an extensive
tour or broad general survey.
mid-20C. French, lit. tour of (the)
horizon.

tournedos (tuə´nədō) *n.* (*pl.* **tournedos**
(dōz)) a thick round fillet steak.
19C. French, from *tourner* to turn + *dos*
back.
● The dish is said to be so called
because it was not placed directly on
the table but passed behind the back of
the guests. But this is probably folk
etymology.

tourniquet (tuə´nikā) *n.* a bandage for
compressing an artery and checking
haemorrhage.
17C. French, ? alt. of Old French
tournicle, var. of *tounicle, tunicle* coat
of mail, tunicle, by assoc. with *tourner*
to turn.

tous-les-mois (toolāmwah´) *n.* a food
starch from the roots of species of a
canna, esp. *Canna indica,* a perennial
Peruvian herb.
19C. French all the months, every
month, but prob. alt. of *toloman,* the
name in the French Antilles.

tout (too) *a.* all, whole. ~*adv.* entirely.
18C. French, from Latin *totus* all,
whole.
● The word is now usually found as
part of a phrase, as those below.

tout court (too kuə´) *adv.* simply,
without further addition.
18C. French, lit. all short.

tout de suite (too də swēt´, toot swēt´)
adv. immediately.
18C. French, lit. all following.

tout ensemble (toot āsā´blə) *n.* the
parts of a thing viewed as a whole.
18C. French, lit. all together. See TOUT,
ENSEMBLE.

tout le monde (too lə mōd´) *n.*
everybody.
18C. French, lit. all the world.

tovarish (təvah´rish, tov-), **tovarich** n. in Russia, the former Soviet Union etc., comrade.
early 20C. Russian tovarishch, from Turkic, ? from Tatar.
• A connection is made by some with Russian tovar goods, wares, commodity, with reference to a trading partner or fellow merchant.

tracasserie (trəkas´əri) n. **1** a turmoil, an annoyance. **2** a fuss, a minor dispute.
17C. French, from tracasser to bustle, to worry oneself.

traduttori traditori (trahdutawri trahditaw´ri) int. it is impossible to translate without misrepresenting the original.
early 20C. Italian, lit. translators (are) traitors.
• The phrase is also found in the singular: traduttore traditore (a) translator (is a) traitor.

tragedienne (trəjēdien´) n. an actress in tragedy.
19C. French tragédienne, fem. of tragédien tragedian.

trahison des clercs (trah·izō dā kleə´) n. the betrayal of standards by intellectuals influenced by politics.
early 20C. French, lit. treason of the clerks.
• The phrase originated in La Trahison des Clercs The Treachery of the Intellectuals (1927), by Julien Benda, in which the author denounces as moral traitors those who betray truth and justice for racial and political considerations.

trait (trāt, trā) n. **1** a distinguishing or peculiar feature, esp. of a person's character or behaviour. **2** a stroke, a touch (of).
15C. French, from Latin tractus drawing, draught, p.p. (used as n.) of trahere to drag.

tranche (trahnsh) n. a portion, esp. of a larger sum of money, block of shares etc.
15C. Old French, from trancher to divide.

transire (tranzī´ri, tranzīə´) n. a customs warrant authorizing the passage of dutiable goods.
16C. Latin to go across.

trattoria (tratərē´ə) n. (pl. **trattorias**, **trattorie** (-rē´ā)) an Italian restaurant.
19C. Italian, from trattore innkeeper.

trauma (traw´mə, trow´-) n. **1** (Psych.) a psychological shock having a lasting effect on the subconscious. **2** a distressing experience. **3** a wound or external injury. **4** physical shock produced by a wound or injury. **5** distress, anguish.
17C. Greek wound.

trecento (trāchen´tō) n. the 14th cent. as characterized by a distinctive style of Italian literature and art.
19C. Italian three hundred (i.e. the 1300s).

tref (trāf), **treif**, **trefa** (-fə) a. in Judaism, not kosher.
early 20C. Hebrew ṭĕrēpāh flesh of an animal torn or mauled, from ṭārap to tear, to rend.
• The dietary law follows the biblical ordinance: 'Neither shall ye eat any flesh that is torn of beasts in the field; ye shall cast it to the dogs' (Exod. xxii.31).

trehala (trihah´lə) n. a kind of manna formed by the substance of the cocoons of a coleopterous insect in Asia Minor.
19C. Turkish tigale, from Persian tīġāl.

treillage (trā´lij) n. **1** a light frame of posts and rails to support espaliers. **2** a trellis.
17C. French, from treille, from Latin trichila bower, arbour.

trek (trek) *v.i.* (*pres.p.* **trekking**, *past,* *p.p.* **trekked**) **1** to journey, esp. with difficulty on foot. **2** (*Hist., esp. S Afr.*) to travel by ox-wagon. **3** (*S Afr.*) (of oxen) to draw a vehicle or load. ~*n.* **1** any long, arduous journey, esp. on foot. **2** a stage or day's march. **3** a journey with a wagon.
19C. **Afrikaans and Middle Dutch** *trekken* to draw, to pull, to travel.

tremolo (trem´əlō) *n.* (*pl.* **tremolos**) (*Mus.*) **1** a tremulous or quavering effect in singing, playing etc. **2** an organ or harmonium stop producing a vibrating tone. **3** (*also* **tremolo arm**) a lever on an electric guitar used to vary the pitch of a played note.
18C. **Italian**, from Latin *tremulus* shaking.

trente-et-quarante (trătākarăt´) *n.* ROUGE-ET-NOIR.
17C. **French**, lit. thirty-and-forty.
● The reference is to the winning and losing scores in this game.

très (trā) *adv.* (*coll. or facet.*) very (esp. in reference to some fashionable or superior quality).
19C. **French**, from Latin *trans* across, beyond.

triage (trī´ij, trē´ahzh) *n.* **1** the sorting of hospital patients, casualties of war etc. according to urgency of treatment and likelihood of survival. **2** the act of sorting according to quality, prioritization. **3** refuse of coffee beans.
18C. **Old French**, from *trier* to sift, to pick out.

tricot (trē´kō) *n.* **1** a hand-knitted woollen fabric or a machine-made imitation. **2** a soft, ribbed cloth.
18C. **French**, from *tricoter* to knit.

tricoteuse (trikotœz´) *n.* (*pl.* **tricoteuses** (trikotœz´)) a woman who, during the French Revolution, sat knitting at meetings of the Convention or at executions by guillotine.
19C. **French**, from *tricoter* to knit. Cp. TRICOT.

tric-trac (trik´trak), **trick-track** *n.* a complicated form of backgammon.
17C. **French**, imit. of the clicking sound made by the pieces when being played.

triduum (trid´ūəm, trī´-) *n.* in the Roman Catholic Church, a three days' service of prayer etc.
18C. **Latin**, use as n. of a., from *tres, tria* three + *dies* day.

trio (trē´ō) *n.* (*pl.* **trios**) **1** a set of three. **2** (*Mus.*) **a** a musical composition for three voices or three instruments. **b** a set of three singers or players. **c** the second part of a minuet, march etc. **3** in piquet, three aces, kings, queens, knaves or tens.
18C. **Italian**, from Latin *tres, tria* three, based on DUO.

triptyque (triptēk´) *n.* a customs pass, made out in triplicate, for importing or exporting a motor vehicle.
early 20C. **French** triptych.

triquetra (trīkwē´trə, -kwet´-) *n.* (*pl.* **triquetrae** (-trē)) an ornament composed of three interlacing arcs.
16C. **Latin**, fem. of *triquetrus* three-cornered, triangular.

Trisagion (trisag´iən, -sā´-) *n.* a hymn with a threefold invocation of God as holy, in the liturgies of the Greek and Eastern Churches.
14–15C. **Greek**, neut. of *trisagios* thrice holy, from *tris* thrice + *hagios* holy.

triste (trist) *a.* (*poet.*) sad, gloomy.
14–15C. **Old French**, from Latin *tristis*.

tristesse (tristes´) *n.* sadness.
14–15C. **Old French** *tristesce* (Modern French *tristesse*), from Latin *tristitia*, from *tristis*. See TRISTE.

triumvir (trīŭm´viə) *n.* (*pl.* **triumvirs, triumviri** (-rī)) any one of three men united in office, esp. a member of the first or second triumvirate in ancient Rome.
14–15C. Latin, from *triumviri* (pl.), back-formation from *trium virorum*, gen. of *tres viri* three men.

trivia (triv´iə) *n.pl.* **1** trifles, inessentials. **2** inconsequential information.
early 20C. Modern Latin, pl. of Latin *trivium* place where three ways meet, from *tri-*, comb. form of *tres* three + *via* way.
● The English senses have now been influenced by *trivial*, a word ultimately from the same source.

troika (troi´kə) *n.* **1** a team of three horses harnessed abreast. **2** a vehicle drawn by this. **3** a group of three people, esp. a triumvirate.
19C. Russian *troĭka*, from *troe* set of three.

trommel (trom´əl) *n.* (*Mining*) a rotating cylindrical sieve for cleaning and sizing ore.
19C. German drum.

trompe (tromp) *n.* an apparatus worked by a descending column of water for producing a blast in a furnace.
19C. French trumpet.

trompe l'oeil (tromp lœy', trŏp) *n.* (*pl.* **trompe l'oeils** (lœy´)) (a painting etc. giving) a very deceptive appearance of reality.
19C. French, lit. deceives the eye, 3rd pers. sing. pres. of *tromper* to deceive + *l'* the + *œil* eye.

tronc (trongk) *n.* a system whereby waiters and other employees in a restaurant share in the tips.
early 20C. French collecting box, trunk.

troppo (trop´ō) *adv.* (*Mus.*) too much, excessively (esp. in the phrase *ma non*

troppo but not too much, modifying a musical direction).
early 20C. Italian too much.

troubadour (troo´bədaw) *n.* **1** any one of a class of lyric poets who flourished in Provence in the 11th cent., writing chiefly of love and chivalry. **2** a singer or poet.
18C. French, from Provençal *trobador*, from *trobar* to compose in verse, to invent, to find. Cp. TROUVÈRE.
● The idea is of someone who 'searches out' appropriate words and music. Cp. 'Such as found out musical tunes, and recited verses in writing' (Ecclus. xliv.5).

trou-de-loup (troodəloo´) *n.* (*pl.* **trous-de-loup** (troodəloo´)) a conical pit with a stake in the centre, used against enemy cavalry.
18C. French, lit. wolf-pit.

troupe (troop) *n.* a company of actors, performers etc.
19C. French troop.

trousseau (troo´sō) *n.* (*pl.* **trousseaux** (-sōz), **trousseaus**) the clothes and general outfit of a bride.
12–14C. French, dim. of *trousse* truss.

trouvaille (troo´vīy) *n.* a lucky find.
19C. French, from *trouver* to find.

trouvère (troovea´) *n.* a medieval poet of N France, composing chiefly narrative poems.
18C. Old French trovere (Modern French *trouvère, trouveur*), from *troveor*, from *trover* (Modern French *trouver* to find) to compose in verse, to invent, to find, ult. of unknown orig. Cp. TROUBADOUR.

trumeau (troomō´) *n.* (*pl.* **trumeaux** (-ōz´)) a piece of wall, a pier or pillar, between two openings or dividing a doorway.
19C. French, lit. calf of the leg.

tsar (zah), **czar**, **tzar** *n*. **1** (*Hist.*) the emperor of Russia. **2** a very powerful person.
16C. Russian *tsar'*, Old Church Slavonic *cěsarĭ*, ult. representing Latin *Caesar*, prob. through Germanic.

tsarevich (zah´revich) *n*. (*Hist.*) the son of a tsar, esp. the eldest son.
18C. Russian, from *tsar'* TSAR + patronymic *-evich*.

tsarevna (zahrev´nə) *n*. (*Hist.*) the daughter of a tsar.
19C. Russian, from *tsar'* TSAR + fem. patronymic *-evna*.

tsarina (zahrē´nə) *n*. (*Hist.*) the wife of a tsar.
18C. Italian and Spanish *tzarina*, from German *Zarin*, fem. of *Zar* TSAR.

tsaritsa (zahrit´sə) *n*. (*Hist.*) an empress of Russia.
17C. Russian, fem. of *tsar'* TSAR.

tsotsi (tsot´si) *n*. (*pl.* **tsotsis**) (*S Afr.*, *coll.*) a violent criminal operating esp. in black townships.
mid-20C. ? **Nguni** *-tsotsa* to dress in exaggerated clothing.

tsukemono (tsookimon´o, -mō´nō) *n*. a Japanese side dish of pickled vegetables.
19C. Japanese, from *tsukeru* pickle + *mono* thing.

tsunami (tsoonah´mi) *n*. (*pl.* **tsunamis**) a very large wave at sea caused by a submarine earthquake, volcanic eruption etc.
19C. Japanese, from *tsu* harbour + *nami* wave.
● A *tsunami* is sometimes wrongly thought of in English as a term for a tidal wave. It has no connection with the tide, however. Even so, the two terms are popularly used synonymously.

tuan (tooahn´) *n*. (in Malay-speaking countries) sir, lord (used as a title of respect).
18C. Malay.

tuba (tū´bə) *n*. (*pl.* **tubas**, **tubae** (-bē)) **1** a brass wind instrument of the saxhorn kind, with a low pitch. **2** a tuba player. **3** a powerful reed-stop in an organ.
14–15C. Italian, from Latin.

tuchun (toochoon´) *n*. (*Hist.*) a Chinese military governor or warlord.
early 20C. Chinese *dūjūn*, from *dū* to govern + *jūn* military.

tufa (tū´fə, too´-) *n*. **1** a soft calcareous rock deposited by springs and streams. **2** tuff.
18C. Italian, obs. local var. of *tufo*, from Late Latin *tofus*.

tugrik (too´grēk), **tughrik** *n*. the standard unit of currency in Mongolia.
mid-20C. Mongolian *dughurik*, lit. round thing, wheel.

tulle (tūl) *n*. a fine silk net, used for veils etc.
19C. *Tulle*, a town in SW France, where originally made.

tum-tum (tŭm´tŭm) *n*. **1** a West Indian dish of boiled plantain beaten soft. **2** a tom-tom.
19C. Orig. unknown.

tumulus (tū´mūləs) *n*. (*pl.* **tumuli** (-lī)) a mound of earth, sometimes combined with masonry, usu. sepulchral, a barrow.
14–15C. Latin, rel. to *tumere* to swell.

tuna (tū´nə) *n*. a prickly pear, esp. *Opuntia tuna*, or its fruit.
16C. Spanish, from Taino.

tundra (tŭn´drə) *n*. a marshy treeless plain in the Arctic and subarctic regions, with permanently frozen subsoil and covered largely with mosses and lichens.
16C. Russian, from Lappish *tundar* elevated wasteland.

tungsten (tŭng´stən) *n.* (*Chem.*) a heavy, greyish-white metallic element, at. no. 74, chem. symbol W, of unusually high melting point; also called *wolfram*.
18C. **Swedish**, from *tung* heavy + *sten* stone.
• The name was coined in 1781 by the Swedish chemist Karl Scheele, who recognized the metal in scheelite.

tunku (tung´koo) *n.* a male title of rank in some states of W Malaysia.
18C. **Malay**.
• The title approximates to English 'prince'.

Tupamaro (toopəmah´rō) *n.* (*pl.* **Tupamaros**) a member of a Marxist urban guerrilla group in Uruguay.
mid-20C. *Tupac Amaru* I, d.1571, and II, *c.*1740–81, Inca leaders.
• Tupac Amaru II, born José Gabriel Condorcanqui, was a descendant of Tupac Amaru I and was identified with him.

tupik (tū´pik), **tupek** (-pek) *n.* an Inuit animal-skin tent.
19C. **Inuit** *tupiq*.

tuque (took) *n.* a Canadian cap made by tucking in one end of a knitted cylindrical bag both ends of which are closed.
19C. **Canadian French**, from French TOQUE.

Turco (tœ´kō) *n.* (*pl.* **Turcos**) (*Hist.*) an Algerian sharpshooter in the French army.
20C. **Spanish**, **Portuguese and Italian** Turk.

tusche (tush) *n.* a substance used in lithography for drawing in the design which resists the printing medium.
19C. **German**, back-formation from *tuschen*, from French *toucher* to touch.

tussore (tŭs´aw), **tusser** (-ə), (*N Am.*) **tussah, tussur** *n.* **1** an Indian silkworm moth, *Antheraea mylitta*, feeding on the jujube tree etc. **2** a Chinese oak-feeding silkworm moth, *A. pernyi*. **3** (*also* **tussore-silk**) a strong, coarse silk obtained from these.
16C. **Hindi** *tasar, ṭasar*, appar. from Sanskrit *tasara* shuttle.
• The spelling with -*ore* was probably influenced by Indian place names such as *Mysore*.

tutenag (tū´tənag) *n.* **1** zinc or spelter from China or SE Asia. **2** a white alloy of copper.
17C. **Portuguese** *tutunaga, tutenaga*, from Tamil *tuttunākam*. Cp. Kannada *tuttu, tutte* copper sulphate, Sanskrit *nāga* tin, lead, ult. from Akkadian *anāku* tin.

tutoyer (tutwah´yā) *v.t.* **1** to address in French with the singular and more familiar pronoun *tu* you rather than the (grammatically) plural and more formal *vous*. **2** to treat or address with familiarity.
17C. **French**, from *tu* you + *toi* you.
• The usage corresponds to former English *thou* and *thee* as distinct from *ye* and *you*. Most other European languages have retained the distinction.

tutti (tut´i) *adv.* (*Mus.*) all together. ~*n.* (*pl.* **tuttis**) a composition or passage for singing or performing all together.
18C. **Italian**, pl. of *tutto* all, from Latin *totus.*

tutti-frutti (tootifroo´ti) *n.* (*pl.* **tutti-fruttis**) a confection, such as ice cream, made of or flavoured with different fruits.
19C. **Italian** all fruits. Cp. TUTTI.

tutti quanti (tuti kwan´ti) *n.* everyone, everything, all of a particular kind.
18C. **Italian**, lit. all those who (which), pl. of *tutto* all + *quanto* how much, as much.

tutu (too´too) *n.* a ballet dancer's short,
stiff skirt that spreads outwards.
early 20C. French, childish alt. of *cucu*,
dim. of *cul* buttocks, bottom.

tuyère (twēyeə´, tooyeə´), **tuyere**, **twyer**
(twī´ə) *n.* the blast-pipe or nozzle in a
furnace, forge etc.
18C. French, from *tuyau* pipe.

tycoon (tīkoon´) *n.* **1** a financial or
political magnate. **2** (*Hist.*) a title given
to the shogun of Japan, from 1857 to
1868.
19C. Japanese *taikun* great lord, great
prince, from Chinese *dà* great + *jūn*
prince.

tzatziki (tsatsē´ki) *n.* a Greek dip of yogurt
flavoured with cucumber, garlic etc.
mid-20C. Modern Greek, from Turkish
cacˇk.

tzigane (tsigahn´), **tzigany** (tsig´əni) *n.*
(*pl.* **tziganes**, **tziganies**) a Hungarian
gypsy. ~*a.* of or relating to the Hungarian
gypsies or their music.
18C. French, from obs. Hungarian
czigany (now *cigány*). Cp. ZINGARO.

tzimmes (tsim´is), **tsimmes** *n.*
(*pl.* **tzimmes**, **tsimmes**) **1** a sweetened
stew of vegetables and/or fruit. **2** (*coll.*)
a fuss, a to-do.
19C. Yiddish *tsimes*, of unknown orig.

U

Übermensch (ü'bəmensh) *n.* (*pl.*
Übermenschen (-shen)) a superman,
an idealized superior being.
19C. German, back-formation from
übermenschlich superhuman, from *über*
over + *menschlich* human, from *Mensch*
person, man. Cp. UNTERMENSCH.
• The concept of the *Übermensch* was
important in the philosophical writings
of Friedrich Nietsche (1844–1900) and
was adopted by G.B. Shaw for his
comedy *Man and Superman* (1903). It
subsequently became part of the Nazi
ideology of the 'master race'.

uhlan (oo'lən, ū'-) *n.* (*Hist.*) a cavalryman
armed with a lance, in the old German
and some other European armies.
18C. French *uhlan*, German *Ulan*,
Uhlan, from Polish *u'an*, *hu'an*, from
Turkish *oğlan* youth, servant, boy.

Uitlander (āt'landə, oit'-) *n.* (*S Afr.*) a
foreigner.
19C. Afrikaans, from Dutch *uit* out +
land land. Cp. English *outlandish*, from
Old English *ūtland* foreign country.

ujamaa (ujamah') *n.* a system of village
cooperatives set up by President
Nyerere in Tanzania in the 1960s and
designed to encourage self-reliance.
mid-20C. Kiswahili consanguinity,
brotherhood, from *jamaa* family, from
Arabic *jamā'a* group (of people),
community.

ukase (ūkāz') *n.* **1** an edict or decree of
the Imperial Russian Government. **2** any
arbitrary decree.
18C. Russian *ukaz* ordinance, edict,
from *ukazat'* to show, to order, to
decree.

ukulele (ūkəlā'li) *n.* a small,
four-stringed instrument resembling
a guitar.
19C. Hawaiian, lit. jumping flea, from
uku louse, flea + *lele* to fly, to leap.
• The instrument is said to be so called
from the Hawaiian nickname of Edward
Purvis, a British army officer noted for
his small size and agility, who
popularized it when it was brought to
Hawaii by the Portuguese in *c.*1879.

ulema (oo'limə) *n.* **1** a body of Muslim
doctors of law and interpreters of the
Koran. **2** a member of this body.
17C. Arabic *'ulamā'*, pl. of *'ālim*, *'alīm*
learned, from *'alima* to have (religious)
knowledge. Cp. ALMA.

ultimatum (ŭltimā'təm) *n.* (*pl.*
ultimatums, **ultimata** (-tə)) **1** a final
proposal or statement of conditions by
one party, the rejection of which may
involve rupture of diplomatic relations,
a declaration of war etc. **2** anything
final, essential, or fundamental.
18C. Use as n. of neut. of **Late Latin**
ultimatus in the Medieval Latin sense
final, completed.

ultimo (ŭl´timō) *a.* (*formal*) in or during last month.
16C. Latin *ultimo*, abl. sing. m. of *ultimus* last, final, in phrs. *ultimo die* on the last day, *ultimo mense* in the last month. Cp. PROXIMO.

ultra (ŭl´trə) *a.* extreme; advocating extreme view or measures. ~*n.* an extremist.
19C. Independent use of English *ultra-*, from Latin *ultra* beyond, esp. orig. as abbr. of French *ultra-royaliste*.

ultra vires (ŭltrə vīə´rēz, vē´rāz) *a., adv.* beyond one's legal power or authority.
18C. Latin beyond the powers, from *ultra* beyond + acc. pl. of VIS.

umiak (oo´miak), **oomiac**, **oomiak** *n.* an Inuit boat made of skins stretched on a framework, used by women.
18C. Inuit *umiaq*.

umlaut (um´lowt) *n.* **1** a change of the vowel in a syllable through the influence of an *i*, *r* etc. (now usu. lost or modified) in the following syllable. **2** (*Print.*) the diaeresis mark (¨) used over German vowels. ~*v.t.* to sound with or modify by an umlaut.
19C. German, from *um-* about + *Laut* sound.

una corda (oonə kaw´də) *a., adv.* (*Mus.*) using the soft pedal.
19C. Italian one string.
● The depression of a piano's soft pedal causes the hammer to strike only one of the three strings. The direction to release the pedal is thus *tre corde*, Italian three strings.

una voce (oonə voch´ā) *adv.* unanimously.
16C. Latin with one voice, from abl. sing. fem. of *unus* one and *vox* voice.

und so weiter (unt zō vī´tə) *adv.* and so on.
19C. German and so forth.

Untermensch (un´təmensh) *n.* (*pl.* **Untermenschen** (-shən)) a person who is regarded as socially or racially inferior.
mid-20C. German, from *unter* under + *Mensch* person, man. Cp. ÜBERMENSCH.
● The term was adopted in Nazi ideology to describe a racially inferior person.

Upanishad (oopan´ishad) *n.* any one of the philosophical treatises forming the third division of the Vedas.
19C. Sanskrit *upaniṣad*, from *upa* near + *ni-ṣad* to sit down.
● The treatise is so called from the notion of sitting at the foot of a teacher.

upsilon (ŭp´silon) *n.* the 20th letter in the Greek alphabet (Υ, υ).
17C. Greek *u psilon* simple u, slender u, from *psilos* slender.
● The letter is so called from the need to distinguish upsilon from the diphthong *oi* formed by omicron and iota, which was pronounced the same way.

ur- (uə) *comb. form* original, primitive, as in *Urtext*.
19C. German.

urbi et orbi (œbi et aw´bi) *adv.* (esp. of a papal proclamation) for general information, to everyone. ~*n.* (**Urbi et Orbi**) the blessing given by the pope on a major feast day in the Roman Catholic Church.
19C. Latin to the city (of Rome) and to the world.

ut (ut) *n.* (*Mus.*) the first note or keynote in Guido's musical scale, now usu. superseded by *doh*.
12–14C. Latin, the lowest of the series

ut, re, mi, fa, sol, la, the initial syllables of each half-line, and *si* the initial letters of the closing words *Sancte Iohannes* (St John), of a stanza of the Latin office hymn for the Nativity of St John the Baptist.

• The Latin hymn itself runs: *Ut queant laxis / resonare fibris / Mira gestorum / famuli tuorum / solve polluti / labii reatum / Sancte Iohannes,* That with full voices thy servants may be able to sing the wonders of thy deeds, purge the sin from their unclean lips, O Holy John.

Utopia (ūtō´piə), **utopia** *n.* a place or state of ideal perfection.

16C. Modern Latin, lit. no-place (from Greek *ou* not + *topos* place), title of a book (1516) by Sir Thomas More.

• The term is sometimes popularly interpreted as meaning good place, from Greek *eu-* good + *topos* place.

ut sup. (ut sup) *abbr. ut supra,* as mentioned above.

14–15C. Abbr. of **Latin** *ut supra,* from *ut* as + SUPRA.

Uzi (oo´zi) *n.* a type of sub-machine gun designed in Israel.

mid-20C. *Uzi*el Gal, the Israeli army officer who developed it after the Arab–Israeli war of 1948.

V

va banque (va bāk´) *int.* in baccarat, I am willing to bet against the banker's whole stake.
mid-20C. French, lit. go bank. Cp. BANCO.

vacherin (vash´rī) *n.* **1** a kind of soft French or Swiss cheese made of whole cow's milk. **2** a dessert consisting of whipped cream, ice cream, fruit etc. in a meringue shell.
mid-20C. French, from *vache* cow.

vade-mecum (vahdimā´kəm, vādimē´-) *n.* (*pl.* **vade-mecums**) a pocket companion or manual for ready reference.
17C. French, from Modern Latin use as n. of Latin *vade mecum* go with me.
● The phrase is recorded in the Modern Latin writings of the German humanist Petrus Lotichius Secundus, 1528–60.

vae victis (vī vik´tis, -tēs) *int.* woe to the conquered!, a cry for the humiliation of the vanquished by their conquerors.
17C. Latin, from *vae* woe + dat. pl. of *victus*, p.p. (used as n.) of *vincere* to conquer.
● The phrase comes from Livy's *Ab Urbe Condita* (V) (1C BC) as the words of the Gallic king, Brennus, on capturing Rome in 390 BC.

Vaishnava (vīsh´nəvə) *n.* a member of a sect that worships Vishnu as supreme among the Hindu gods.
18C. Sanskrit *vaiṣṇava* relating to Vishnu, worshipper of Vishnu.

Vaisya (vīs´yə) *n.* **1** the third of the four chief Hindu castes, the traders. **2** a member of this.
17C. Sanskrit *vaiśya* peasant, tradesman.

vale (vah´lā) *int.* farewell. ~*n.* a farewell.
16C. Latin, imper. of *valere* to be strong, to be well.

Valenciennes (valāsyen´) *n.* a fine variety of lace, the design of which is made with and of the same thread as the ground.
18C. *Valenciennes*, a town in NE France.

valet (val´it, val´ā) *n.* **1** a manservant who acts as a personal attendant to his employer, looking after his clothes, serving his meals etc. **2** a person employed in a hotel, liner etc. to perform similar functions. ~*v.t.* (*pres.p.* **valeting**, *past, p.p.* **valeted**) **1** to act as valet to. **2** to clean the interior of (a car). ~*v.i.* to act as a valet.
15C. Old French, var. of *vaslet, varlet* varlet, ult. rel. to English *vassal*.

valet de chambre (valā də shābr´, shā´brə) *n.* (*pl.* **valets de chambre** (valā)) a valet.
17C. French, lit. valet of the chamber.

Valhalla (valhal´ə) *n.* **1** in Norse mythology, the palace of immortality where the souls of heroes slain in battle were carried by the Valkyries. **2** a building used as the final resting place of the great men of a nation, esp. the Temple of Fame, near Regensburg, built by Louis I of Bavaria, 1830.
17C. Modern Latin, from Old Norse *Valh"ll*, from *valr* those slain in battle, rel. to Old English *wæl* slaughter + *h"ll* hall. Cp. VALKYRIE.

valise (vəlēz´) *n.* **1** a bag or case, usu. of leather, for holding a traveller's clothes etc., esp. one for carrying in the hand, a travelling bag. **2** a kitbag.
17C. French, from Italian *valigia*, corr. to Medieval Latin *valesia*, of unknown orig.
• The word is not related to VALET, despite the association of sense.

Valium® (val´iəm) *n.* the tranquilizer diazepam.
mid-20C. Orig. unknown. ? From Latin *valere* to be well.

Valkyrie (val´kiri, -kiə´ri) *n.* in Norse mythology, each of twelve maidens of Valhalla who were sent by Odin to select those destined to be slain in battle and to conduct their souls to Valhalla.
18C. Old Norse *Valkyrja*, lit. chooser of the slain, from *valr* those slain in battle (see VALHALLA) + *-kyrja* chooser, ult. from *kjósa* to choose.

vallum (val´əm) *n.* (*pl.* **vallums**) an ancient Roman rampart, an agger.
17C. Latin collect. n., from *vallus* stake, palisade.

valse (vals) *n.* a waltz.
18C. French, from German *Walzer* WALTZ.

valuta (vəloo´tə, -lū´-) *n.* **1** the value of one currency in terms of another. **2** a currency considered in respect of its exchange value.
19C. Italian value.

vamoose (vəmoos´) *v.i.* (*N Am., sl.*) to decamp, to be gone, to be off.
19C. Spanish *vamos* let's go, 1st pers. pl. pres. indic. (used as imper.) of *ir* to go.

vaporetto (vapəret´ō) *n.* (*pl.* **vaporetti** (-tē)) a small motor vessel (orig. a steamship) used for public transport on the canals of Venice.
early 20C. Italian small steamboat, dim. of *vapore*, from Latin *vapor* steam.

vaquero (vəkeə´rō) *n.* (*pl.* **vaqueros**) in Mexico and Spanish-speaking parts of America, a herdsman, a cowherd.
19C. Spanish, from *vaca* cow.
• The Spanish word also gave *buckaroo* as a now dated US colloquialism for a cowboy.

vara (vah´rə) *n.* a Spanish–American measure of length, varying from 33–43 inches (84–110 centimetres).
17C. Spanish and Portuguese rod, yardstick, from Latin forked pole, trestle, from *varus* bent.

varec (var´ik) *n.* kelp or the ash obtained from kelp.
17C. French, from Middle Low German and Dutch *wrak* wrack.

variorum (veəriaw´rəm) *a.* **1** (of an edition of a work) with notes of various commentators inserted. **2** including variant readings. ~*n.* a variorum edition.
18C. Latin, lit. of various (people), gen. pl. of *varius* various.
• The usual full phrase was *editio cum notis variorum* edition with the notes of various (commentators).

varna (vah´nə) *n.* any of the four great Hindu castes.
19C. Sanskrit *varṇa*, lit. appearance, aspect, colour.

Vaterland (fahˊtəlant) *n.* Germany as the fatherland.
19C. German, from *Vater* father + *Land* land.

vatu (vahˊtoo) *n.* (*pl.* **vatus**, **vatu**) the standard monetary unit of Vanuatu.
late 20C. Bislama, shortening of *Vanuatu*.

vaudeville (vawˊdəvil, vō´-) *n.* **1** (*N Am.*) a miscellaneous series of sketches, songs etc., a variety entertainment. **2** a slight dramatic sketch or pantomime interspersed with songs and dances. **3** a topical or satirical song with a refrain.
18C. French, earlier *vau de ville, vau de vire*, from *chanson du Vau de Vire* song of the valley of the Vire (in NW France), influ. by *ville* town.
● The title is said to have been originally applied to the songs composed by Olivier Basselin, a 15C fuller who lived in the *Vire* valley. French etymologists, however, generally prefer an origin in dialect *vauder* to go round and *virer* to turn, referring to the 'circulating' nature of the songs and sketches.

Veadar (vēˊədah) *n.* a supplementary or intercalary month inserted into the Jewish calendar every third year after the month Adar.
14–15C. Hebrew *wĕ-'ăḏār*, lit. and Adar (i.e. the second Adar). See ADAR.

Veda (vāˊdə) *n.* the ancient Hindu scriptures, divided into four portions or books (the *Rig-, Yajur-, Sāma-,* and *Artharva-Veda*).
18C. Sanskrit (sacred) knowledge, sacred book, ult. from Indo-European base meaning to know, represented also in English *wit*.

vedette (videtˊ), **vidette** *n.* **1** a sentinel (usu. mounted) stationed in advance of an outpost. **2** a small vessel used for scouting purposes etc.
17C. French, from Latin *vedetta*, alt. (based on *vedere* to see) of S Italian *veletta*, ? from Spanish *vela* watch, from *velar* to keep watch, from Latin *vigilare*.

veduta (vedooˊtə) *n.* (*pl.* **vedute** (vedooˊtā)) an accurate landscape or esp. townscape in Italian art.
early 20C. Italian view, from *vedere* to see.

vega (vāˊgə) *n.* an extensive and fertile plain in Spain or Spanish America.
17C. Spain.

veilleuse (vāyœzˊ) *n.* a night lamp, shaded and usu. artistically decorated.
19C. French, fem. of *veilleur*, from *veiller* to stay awake, to keep watch.

veld (velt, felt), **veldt** *n.* (*S Afr.*) open country suitable for pasturage, esp. the high treeless plains in N Transvaal and NW Natal.
18C. Afrikaans, from Dutch field.

veldskoen (veltˊskoon, feltˊ-) *n.* an ankle-length boot, orig. made of raw hide, now usu. of soft suede or leather.
19C. Afrikaans field shoe, alt. (by assim. to VELD) of earlier *velschoen*, from *fel* skin + *schoen* shoe.

veleta (vəlēˊtə), **valeta** *n.* a dance or dance tune in slow waltz time.
early 20C. Spanish weathervane.
● The dance is so named from its revolving movements.

veloce (vilōˊchā) *adv.* (*Mus.*) with great quickness.
19C. Italian rapid, from Latin *velox, velocis* swift.

velour (viluəˊ), **velours**, **velure** (-ūəˊ) *n.* **1** velvet, velveteen or other fabric resembling velvet. **2** a pad of velvet or silk for smoothing a silk hat. **3** †a hat made of velour.

18C. French *velours* velvet, from Old French *velour*, *velous*, from Latin *villosus* hairy, from *villus* hair.
● The French phrase *velours croché* hooked velvet gave the proprietary name *Velcro* for a form of fastening for fabrics.

vendange (vădăzh´) *n.* (*pl.* **vendanges** (vădăzh´)) the grape harvest in France.
18C. French, from Latin *vindemia*, from *vinum* wine + *demere* to harvest.

Vendémiaire (vădāmyeə´) *n.* the first month of the French revolutionary calendar (22 September–21 October).
18C. French, from Latin *vindemia* grape harvest, from *vinum* wine + *demere* to take away.

vendetta (vendet´ə) *n.* **1** a blood feud, often carried on for generations, in which the family of a murdered or injured man seeks vengeance on the offender or any member of his family, prevalent esp. in Corsica, Sardinia and Sicily. **2** this practice. **3** a feud, private warfare or animosity.
19C. Italian, from Latin *vindicta* vengeance.

vendeuse (vădœz´, von-) *n.* a saleswoman, esp. in a fashionable dress shop.
early 20C. French, fem. of *vendeur*, from *vendre* to sell.

Venite (vinī´tē) *n.* **1** the 95th psalm, 'O come let us sing', used as a canticle. **2** a musical setting of this.
12–14C. Latin, 2nd pers. pl. imper. of *venire* to come, first word of Vulgate (Latin) version of Ps. xcv.
● The first full phrase of the psalm is *Venite, exultemus Domino* O come, let us sing unto the Lord.

veni, vidi, vici (vā´ni vē´di vē´ki) *int.*
I came, I saw, I conquered, used in reference to any swift success or crushing victory, e.g. in sport.

16C. Latin, from 1st pers. sing. perf. of *venire* to come, *videre* to see and *vincere* to conquer.
● The words were recorded by Plutarch as those spoken by Caesar in reference to his victory over Pharnaces II, King of Pontus, at Zela in 47 BC.

Ventôse (vă´tōz) *n.* the sixth month of the French revolutionary year (19 February–20 March).
19C. French, from Latin *ventosus*, from *ventus* wind.

ventre à terre (văntr a teə´) *adv.* flat out, at full speed.
19C. French, lit. belly to the ground.
● The reference is to a painting of a horse running at full speed with its legs stretched out in line with its belly.

venue (ven´ū) *n.* **1** a place chosen as the site of an organized event or meeting. **2** a meeting place. **3** (*Law*) the place or country where a crime is alleged to have been committed and where the jury must be empanelled and the trial held.
12–14C. Old French, use as n. of fem. p.p. of *venir* to come, from Latin *venire*.
● The original sense was sally, attack, then (16C) location where a cause must be tried and a jury gathered. The current sense dates from the 19C.

veranda (viran´də), **verandah** *n.* **1** a light external gallery or portico with a roof on pillars, along the front or side of a house. **2** (*Austral., New Zeal.*) a roof or canopy over the pavement in front of a shop.
18C. Hindi *varaṇḍā*, from Portuguese *varanda* railing, balustrade, balcony, of unknown orig.

verbatim (vœbā´tim) *adv., a.* word for word.
15C. Medieval Latin, from Latin *verbum* word + adv. suf. *-im*. Cp. LITERATIM.

verboten (vœbō´tən, fœ-) *a.* forbidden by authority.
early 20C. German forbidden, p.p. of *verbieten* to forbid.

verb. sap. (vœb sap´), **verb. sat.** (sat´) *int.* used to indicate that there is no need for a more explicit statement, warning etc.
19C. Abbr. of **Latin** *verbum sapienti sat est* a word is sufficient for a wise person.
● The proverb echoes a line from Plautus: *Dictum sapienti sat est*, A sentence is enough for a sensible man (*Persa*, 2C BC).

verd-antique (vœdantēk´) *n.* **1** an ornamental stone composed chiefly of serpentine, usu. green and mottled or veined. **2** a green incrustation on ancient bronze. **3** green porphyry.
18C. Obsolete French *verd* (now *vert*) *antique* ancient green.

Verfremdungseffekt
(feəfrem´dungzefekt) *n.* a theatrical technique whereby familiar aspects of reality are given the appearance of being unfamiliar in order to arouse the critical judgement of the audience.
mid-20C. German *Verfremdung* alienation, distancing + *Effekt* effect.
● The term was coined by the German dramatist and theatrical producer Bertolt Brecht (1898–1956) for his theory of theatrical alienation.

verglas (veə´glah) *n.* a film of ice on rock.
19C. French, from *verre* glass + obs. *glas* (now *glace*) ice.

verismo (veriz´mō) *n.* realism, esp. in late 19th-cent. Italian opera.
early 20C. Italian, from *vero* true.

verkrampte (fəkramp´tə) *a.* (*S Afr.*) opposed to liberalization, esp. in matters of racial segregation. ~*n.* a person holding such views.
mid-20C. Afrikaans narrow, cramped.
● The term is explicitly or implicitly contrasted with VERLIGTE.

verligte (fəlikh´tə) *n., a.* (*S Afr.*) (a person) of more liberal outlook, esp. in matters of racial segregation.
mid-20C. Afrikaans enlightened.
● The term is essentially the converse of VERKRAMPTE.

vermicelli (vœmichel´i, -sel´i) *n.* **1** pasta in the form of long slender tubes or threads like macaroni. **2** chocolate vermicelli.
17C. Italian, pl. of *vermicello*, dim. of *verme* worm, from Latin *vermis*.

vernissage (veənēsahzh´) *n.* (*pl.* **vernissages** (veənēsahzh´)) a private viewing of an art exhibition before it opens to the public.
early 20C. French, lit. varnishing.
● The term originally denoted the day before an exhibition set aside for the artist to varnish his paintings.

veronique (verənēk´) *a.* (*used after n.*) served with white grapes, as in *sole veronique*.
early 20C. French *Véronique* Veronica.
● The dish *sole véronique* was invented in 1903 by the French chef Auguste Escoffier, who named it after André Messager's light opera *Véronique* (1898), then still popular.

vers (veə) *n.* verse.
18C. French verse.

vers de société (veə də sosyātā´) *n.* light, witty and polished verse.
18C. French, lit. verse of society.

vers libre (veə lēbr´, lē´brə) *n.* unrhymed verse that disregards the traditional rules of prosody.
early 20C. French, lit. free verse.

verso (vœ´sō) *n.* (*pl.* **versos**) **1** a left-hand page of a book lying open. **2** the back of a sheet of printed or manuscript paper. **3** the other side of a coin or medal to that on which the head appears.
19C. Latin (*folio*) *verso* (the leaf) being turned, abl. neut. sing. of *versus*, p.p. of *vertere* to turn.

verst (vœst) *n.* a Russian measure of length, 3500.64 feet, nearly two thirds of a mile (about one kilometre).
16C. Russian *versta*, rel. to *vertet'* to turn, itself rel. to Latin *vertere* to turn.
● The original literal sense was a turn of the plough.

versus (vœ´səs) *prep.* against.
14–15C. Medieval Latin use of Latin *versus* towards, in sense of *adversus* against.
● The Latin word gave the familiar abbreviation *v.* in sporting and legal contexts, e.g. *New Zealand v. France*, *Reynolds v. Times Newspapers*.

vertex (vœ´teks) *n.* (*pl.* **vertices** (-tisēz), **vertexes**) **1** the highest point, the top, summit, or apex. **2** (*Geom.*) **a** the meeting point of the lines of an angle. **b** each angular point of a polygon, polyhedron etc. **c** the point of intersection of a curve with its axis. **3** (*Anat.*) the top of the arch of the skull.
14–15C. Latin whirl, vortex, crown of the head, highest point, from *vertere* to turn.

vertigo (vœ´tigō) *n.* giddiness, dizziness, a feeling as if one were whirling round.
14–15C. Latin whirling about, giddiness, from *vertere* to turn.

veto (vē´tō) *n.* (*pl.* **vetoes**) **1** the power or right of a sovereign, president or branch of a legislature to negate the enactments of another branch. **2** the act of exercising such right. **3** a document or message conveying a rejection. **4** any authoritative prohibition, refusal, negative, or interdict. ~*v.t.* (*3rd pers. sing. pres.* **vetoes**, *pres.p.* **vetoing**, *past, p.p.* **vetoed**) **1** to refuse approval to (a bill etc.). **2** to prohibit, to forbid.
17C. Latin I forbid, 1st pers. sing. pres. ind. of *vetare* to forbid.
● The word was used by Roman tribunes of the people to oppose measures of the Senate or actions of the magistrates.

vexillum (veksil´əm) *n.* (*pl.* **vexilla** (-sil´ə)) **1** in ancient Rome, a square flag carried by a vexillary, forming the standard of a maniple. **2** a maniple or other body of troops under a separate vexillum. **3** the large upper petal of a papilionaceous flower. **4** the vane of a feather. **5** the flag or pennon on a bishop's staff, usu. wound round it. **6** a processional banner or cross.
18C. Latin flag, banner, from *vehere*, *vex-*, *vect-* to carry, to convey.

via (vī´ə, vē´ə) *adv.* by way of, through.
18C. Latin, abl. sing. of *via* way, road.

Via Crucis (vēə kroo´chis) *n.* any extremely painful experience or ordeal.
19C. Latin way of the cross. Cp. VIA DOLOROSA.
● The term properly relates to the route followed by Christ to Calvary, represented in the Roman Catholic Church by the stations of the cross.

Via Dolorosa (vēə dolərō´sə) *n.* a painful series of experiences or prolonged ordeal.
19C. Latin, lit. sorrowful way.
● The term properly relates to the original stations of the cross in Jerusalem, tracing the route taken by Christ to Calvary. Cp. VIA CRUCIS.

via media (vīə mē´diə, vēə mä´diə) *n.* a
middle way, a mean between extremes.
19C. Latin.
● The term was adopted by John Henry
Newman (1801–90) to denote a middle
way between 'Popery' (Roman
Catholicism) and 'Dissent'
(Protestantism).

viaticum (vīat´ikəm) *n.* (*pl.* **viatica** (-kə),
viaticums) **1** the Eucharist as given to
a person at the point of death. **2** in
ancient Rome, a supply of provisions or
an allowance of money for a journey
granted to a magistrate, envoy etc.
16C. Latin, use as n. of neut. of *viaticus*
pertaining to a journey, from *via* way,
road.

vibrato (vibrah´tō) *n.* (*Mus.*) a pulsating
effect, esp. in singing or string-playing,
produced by the rapid variation of
emphasis on the same tone.
19C. Italian, p.p. of *vibrare* to vibrate.

vice (vīs) *prep.* in place of.
18C. Latin, abl. of *vic-* change, from
*vix (found only in oblique cases).

vice anglais (vēs āglā´) *n.* any vice
supposedly characteristic of the English,
esp. the use of corporal punishment for
sexual stimulation.
mid-20C. French, lit. English vice.

vice versa (vīsi vœ´sə, vīs) *adv.* the order
or relation being inverted, the other way
round.
17C. Latin, lit. the position being
reversed, from VICE + *versa*, abl. fem.
sing. of *versus*, p.p. of *vertere* to turn.

vichyssoise (vēshiswahz´) *n.* a cream
soup usu. served chilled, with
ingredients such as leeks and potatoes.
mid-20C. French, short form of *crême
vichyssoise glacée*, lit. iced cream soup
of Vichy (a town in central France).
● The soup was created in New York in
the early 20C by the French chef Louis

Diat, who came from the Bourbonnais,
not far from Vichy. He did not use the
name *vichyssoise* in his own recipes,
however.

victor ludorum (viktə loodaw´rəm)
n. the overall champion in a sports
competition, esp. at a school.
early 20C. Latin victor of the games.

vicuña (vikoon´yə), **vicuna** (vikū´nə) *n.*
1 a South American animal, *Vicugna
vicugna*, allied to the camel, a native
of the Andean regions of Bolivia and
N Chile. **2** a fine cloth made from its
wool or an imitation made of worsted
yarn.
17C. Spanish, from Quechua *wikúña*.

vide (vid´ā, vē´-, vī´di) *int.* (as an
instruction in a book) see, consult.
16C. Latin, imper. sing. of *videre* to see.

videlicet (vidē´liset, -dā´liket) *adv.*
namely, that is to say, to wit (usu.
abbreviated to *viz.*).
14–15C. Latin, from *vide*, stem of
videre to see + *licet* it is permissible.
Cp. SCILICET.
● The word is almost always
abbreviated to *viz.*, the z representing
the Medieval Latin contraction for *-et.*

vidimus (vī´diməs) *n.* (*pl.* **vidimuses**) an
examination or inspection of accounts
etc.
14–15C. Latin we have seen, 1st pers. pl.
perf. of *videre* to see.

vie en rose (vē ã roz´) *n.* life seen
through rose-coloured spectacles.
mid-20C. French, lit. life in pink.
● The phrase was popularized by the
song *La Vie en rose* (1945), made famous
by the singer Edith Piaf.

vielle (viel´) *n.* a hurdy-gurdy.
18C. French, from an imit. source rel.
to VIOLA and English *violin*.

vieux jeu (vjœ zhœ´) *a.* old-fashioned, hackneyed.
19C. French, lit. old game.

vigia (vijē´ə) *n.* a warning of a suspected rock, shoal etc., whose existence is unconfirmed, on a hydrographical chart.
19C. Portuguese lookout, from *vigiar*, from Latin *vigilia* wakefulness, from *vigil* awake, alert.

vigilante (vijilan´ti) *n.* **1** a self-appointed upholder of law and order or administerer of justice. **2** (*N Am.*) a member of a vigilance committee.
19C. Spanish, from Latin *vigilans*, *vigilantis*, pres.p. of *vigilare* to keep awake.

vigneron (vēn´yərō) *n.* a wine-grower.
14–15C. French, from *vigne* vine.

vignette (vinyet´) *n.* **1** a short descriptive essay or sketch. **2** a similar descriptive or evocative scene in a film or play. **3** an engraving not enclosed within a definite border, esp. on the title page of a book. **4** a photograph, drawing or other portrait showing the head and shoulders with a background shading off gradually. **5** (*Archit.*) an ornament of tendrils and vine leaves. ~*v.t.* **1** to shade off (a portrait, drawing etc.) gradually. **2** to make a photograph or portrait of in this style.
14–15C. Old French, dim. of *vigne* vine.
● A vignette was originally a running ornament of vine leaves, tendrils and grapes on the title page of a book or at the beginning or end of a chapter.

vigoroso (vigərō´sō) *adv.* (*Mus.*) with energy.
19C. Italian *vigorous*.

vihara (vihah´rə) *n.* a Buddhist or Jain temple or monastery.
17C. Sanskrit *vihāra*.

vilayet (vilah´yit) *n.* an administrative division of Turkey.

19C. Turkish *vilâyet*, from Arabic *wilāyat* government, rule, administrative district.

villa (vil´ə) *n.* **1** in ancient Rome, a country house or farmhouse with subsidiary buildings on an estate. **2** a large detached or semi-detached suburban house. **3** a large house in the country. **4** a sizeable property, usu. in a holiday resort, for rent as a holiday home.
17C. Partly from **Latin** *villa* country house, farm, partly from **Italian** *villa*, from Latin.

villanelle (vilənel´) *n.* a poem in five tercets and a final quatrain on two rhymes.
16C. French, from Latin *villanella*, fem. of *villanello* rural, rustic, from *villano* peasant, rustic, from Medieval Latin *villanus* villager, from Latin VILLA.

villeggiatura (vilejətoo´rə) *n.* retirement to or a stay in the country.
18C. Italian, from *villeggiare* to live at a villa, from VILLA.

ville lumière (vēl lümyeə´) *n.* a brightly lit city or town, esp. one with modern attractions.
early 20C. French city (of) light.
● The name *La Ville Lumière* is specifically associated with Paris.

vim (vim) *n.* (*coll.*) energy, vigour.
19C. Prob. from **Latin** *vim*, acc. sing. of *vis* strength, energy. Cp. VIS.

vin (vĩ) *n.* (*pl.* **vins** (vĩ)) (a) wine.
17C. French. Cp. VINHO VERDE, VINO.

vina (vē´nə) *n.* an Indian stringed instrument with a fretted fingerboard over two gourds.
18C. Sanskrit and Hindi *vīṇā*.

vinaigrette (vinigret´) *n.* **1** (*also* **vinaigrette sauce**) a salad dressing

consisting of oil, vinegar and seasoning.
2 (*also* **vinegarette**) an ornamental
bottle or perforated case of gold or other
metal etc. for holding aromatic vinegar
etc., a smelling bottle.
14–15C. French, dim. of *vinaigre*
vinegar, from *vin* wine + *aigre* sour.

vinasse (vinas´) *n.* a residual product
containing potassium salts left after
distilling spirits, esp. brandy, or
obtained from beets from which sugar
has been extracted.
19C. French, from Latin *vinacea*, fem.
of *vinaceus* relating to wine.

vin blanc (vī blã) *n.* white wine.
18C. French.

vindaloo (vindəloo´) *n.* a type of hot
Indian curry.
19C. Prob. from **Portuguese** *vin d'alho*
wine and garlic sauce, from *vinho* wine
+ *alho* garlic.

vin de table (vī də tah´blə) *n.* ordinary
wine suitable for drinking with a meal.
mid-20C. French table wine. Cp.
TAFELWEIN.
• The term usually implies distinction
from a fortified wine.

vin du pays (vī dü pāē´) **vin de pays**
(də) *n.* local wine; wine of the third
highest category in France meeting
certain requirements as to area of origin,
strength etc.
18C. French, lit. wine of the country.

vingt-et-un (vantãœ´) *n.* a card game in
which the object is to make the
aggregate number of the pips on the
cards as near as possible to 21 without
exceeding this; pontoon.
18C. French twenty-one.

vinho verde (vēnyō veə´di) *n.* any of a
number of light, immature, sharp-tasting
Portuguese wines.
19C. Portuguese, lit. green wine.

vino (vē´nō) *n.* (*pl.* **vinos**) (*coll.*) wine,
esp. cheap wine.
17C. Spanish and Italian wine. Cp. VIN,
VINHO VERDE.

vin ordinaire (vī awdineə´) *n.*
inexpensive usu. red table wine for
everyday use.
19C. French, lit. ordinary wine.

vint (vint) *n.* a Russian card game similar
to auction bridge.
19C. Russian, of uncertain orig. ? From
German *Gewinde* thread.

viola (viō´lə) *n.* **1** an instrument like a
large violin, the alto instrument in the
violin family tuned an octave above the
cello. **2** a viola player. **3** a viol.
18C. Spanish and Italian, prob. from
Provençal, from a source of imit. orig.
? Rel. to English *fiddle*.

viola da gamba (viōlə də gam´bə) *n.* a
viol held between the player's legs, esp.
the tenor viol from which the modern
cello was developed.
16C. Italian, lit. leg viol.

viola d'amore (viōlə damaw´rā) *n.* an
instrument of the viol family with
sympathetic strings under the
fingerboard and a particularly sweet
tone.
18C. Italian, lit. viol of love.

violoncello (vīəlonchel´ō) *n.* (*pl.*
violoncellos) (*formal*) a cello.
18C. Italian, dim. of VIOLONE.

violon d'Ingres (violō dī´grə) *n.* an
activity or pastime for which a person
is not primarily known.
mid-20C. French, lit. Ingres' violin.
• The French painter Ingres
(1780–1867) was said to have been more
proud of his violin playing than of the
paintings by which he made his name.

violone (viəlō´ni) *n.* a medieval double-bass viol.
18C. Italian, from *viola* viola. See VIOLA.

virage (virahzh´) *n.* a hairpin bend.
mid-20C. French, from *virer* to burn.

virago (virah´gō, -ā´-) *n.* (*pl.* **viragoes**, **viragos**) 1 a bad-tempered, violent or scolding woman, a termagant, a shrew. 2 †a woman of masculine strength and courage.
pre-1200. Latin, from *vir* man.
• The original sense (to the 16C) was woman, with specific reference to the name given by Adam to Eve in Gen. ii.23, 'This schal be clepid virago, for she is takun of man' (Wyclif's translation, 1388), 'she shall be called Woman, because she was taken out of Man' (AV, 1611).

virement (vīə´mənt) *n.* a transfer of funds from one account to another.
early 20C. French, from Old French *virer* to turn.

virginibus puerisque (viəginibəs puərēs´kwi) *a.* of literary works, suitable for the young.
19C. Latin for girls and boys, from dat. pl. of *virgo* girl and *puer* boy + *-que* and.
• The phrase comes from Horace's *Odes* (III) (1C BC): *Virginibus puerisque cano* I sing to virgin girls and boys. The words were popularized by the title of R.L. Stevenson's *Virginibus Puerisque* (1881), the first of a series of collected essays.

virgo intacta (vœgō intak´tə) *n.* (*esp. Law*) a girl or woman who has never had sexual intercourse.
18C. Latin, lit. untouched virgin.

virgule (vœ´gūl) *n.* a slanting line used as a division within or between words, a solidus or slash.
19C. French comma, from Latin *virgula*, dim. of *virga* rod.

virtu (vœtoo´), **vertu** *n.* 1 a taste for or knowledge of the fine arts. 2 rare, old or beautiful objects collectively. 3 the quality of rareness or beauty. 4 intrinsic goodness or worth.
18C. Italian *virtù* virtue.

virtuoso (vœtūō´sō, -zō) *n.* (*pl.* **virtuosos**, **virtuosi** (-sē, -zē)) 1 a skilled performer in some fine art, esp. music. 2 a connoisseur of articles of virtu. ~*a.* showing great skill.
17C. Italian learned, skilful, from Late Latin *virtuosus* virtuous, good.

vis (vis) *n.* (*pl.* **vires** (vī´rēz)) force, energy, potency.
17C. Latin. Cp. ULTRA VIRES.

visa (vē´zə) *n.* an official endorsement on a passport showing that it has been examined and found correct, esp. one enabling the holder to travel to or through a particular country. ~*v.t.* (*3rd pers. sing. pres.* **visas**, *pres.p.* **visaing**, *past, p.p.* **visaed**, **visa'd**) to certify or put a visa on.
19C. French, from Latin things seen, neut. pl. of p.p. of *videre* to see.

visagiste (vēzəzhēst´) *n.* a person who specializes in facial make-up.
mid-20C. French, from *visage* face.

vis-à-vis (vēzahvē´) *prep.* 1 in relation to. 2 opposite to; face to face with. ~*adv.* face to face. ~*n.* (*pl.* **vis-à-vis**) 1 a person facing another as in certain dances, e.g. a quadrille. 2 one's counterpart or opposite number. 3 (*N Am.*) a date or escort at a social event. 4 a carriage or couch for two persons sitting vis-à-vis.
18C. French, lit. face to face, from Old French *vis* face (Modern French *visage*) + *à* to.

Vishnu (vish´noo) *n.* the preserver god of the Hindu sacred triad, appearing in many incarnations and worshipped by some as the saviour.
17C. Sanskrit *Viṣṇu*.

vista (vis´tə) *n.* **1** a long view shut in at the sides, as between rows of trees. **2** a mental view far into the past or future.
17C. Italian view, ult. from Latin *videre* to see.

vita nuova (vētə nwō´və) *n.* a fresh start or new direction in life.
mid-20C. Italian new life.
● The words come from the title of Dante's *La vita nuova* (*c.*1293), a celebration of his love for Beatrice in verse and prose.

vitrine (vit´rēn, -rin) *n.* a glass showcase.
19C. French, from *vitre* glass, from Latin *vitrum*.

viva (vē´və) *n.* an exclamation of joy or applause. ~*int.* long live.
17C. Italian live!, 3rd pers. sing. pres. subj. of *vivere* to live, from Latin. Cp. VIVAT, VIVE.

vivace (vivah´chā) *adv.* (*Mus.*) in a brisk, lively manner.
17C. Italian brisk, lively, from Latin *vivax*, *vivacis*.

vivandière (vēvãdyeə´) *n.* (*Hist.*) a female sutler attached to a Continental, esp. French, regiment.
16C. French, fem. of *vivandier*, from *viande* food, (now) meat, ult. from Latin *vivere* to live.

vivarium (vīveə´riəm) *n.* (*pl.* **vivariums**, **vivaria** (-riə)) a park, enclosure or other place artificially prepared in which animals etc. are kept alive as nearly as possible in their natural state.
17C. Latin warren, fish pond, use as n. of neut. of *vivarius*, from *vivus* alive, from *vivere* to live.

vivat (vī´vat, vē´-) *n.*, *int.* (a shout of) long live.
16C. Latin may he live, 3rd. pers. sing. pres. subj. of *vivere*. Cp. VIVE.

viva voce (vīvə vō´chi, -chā) *adv.* by word of mouth, orally. ~*a.* oral. ~*n.* an oral examination.
16C. Medieval Latin, lit. by the living voice, abl. of *viva vox* living voice.
● The phrase is often abbreviated to *viva* in the noun sense.

vive (vēv) *int.* long live, up with.
16C. French may he live, 3rd pers. sing. pres. subj. of *vivre* to live, from Latin *vivere*. Cp. QUI VIVE.

vive la différence (vēv la diferãs´) *int.* (*facet.*) long live the difference!, a jocular expression of approval of the difference between the sexes.
mid-20C. French.

vivo (vē´vō) *adv.* (*Mus.*) with life and animation, vivace.
18C. Italian alive, lively, from Latin *vivus*. Cp. VIVACE.

vizsla (vizh´lə) *n.* a Hungarian breed of hunting dog with a smooth red or rust-coloured coat.
mid-20C. *Vizsla*, a town in Hungary.

vlei (vlī, flī) *n.* (*S Afr.*) a swampy tract, a place where water lies in rainy seasons.
18C. Afrikaans, from Dutch *vallei* valley.

vodka (vod´kə) *n.* a strong alcoholic liquor distilled from rye, orig. from Russia.
19C. Russian, dim. of *voda* water.

voetsek (fut´sek) *int.* (*S Afr., offensive*) go away.
19C. Afrikaans, from Dutch *voort zeg ik* be off I say.

vogue (vōg) *n.* **1** a fashion prevalent at any particular time. **2** currency, popular acceptance or usage.
16C. French, from Italian *voga* rowing, fashion, from *vogare* to row, to be going well.

vogue la galère (vog la galeə´) *int.* let's give it a go.
  18C. French, lit. let the galley be rowed.
  ● The phrase was used by Rabelais (*c.*1494–1593) but was probably already current.

voilà (vwahla´) *int.* there you are! that's it!
  18C. French, lit. see there, from *vois*, 2nd pers. sing. imper. of *voir* to see + *là* there.

voile (voil, vwahl) *n.* a thin, semi-transparent dress material.
  19C. French veil.

voir dire (vwah diə´) *n.* (*Law*) the preliminary examination of a witness by a judge; an oath administered to such a witness.
  17C. Law French, from Old French *voir* true, truth + *dire* to say.

voix céleste (vwah sālest´) *n.* (*pl.* **voix célestes** (sālest´)) a soft organ stop with a distinctive tremulous sound.
  19C. French, lit. heavenly voice.
  ● The stop is so called as its undulating tone was held to be reminiscent of celestial voices.

volante (volan´ti) *n.* a two-wheeled covered horse-drawn vehicle with very long shafts and a body slung in front of the axle.
  18C. Spanish, from pres.p. of *volar* to fly, from Latin *volare*.

vol-au-vent (vol´ōvā) *n.* a small, round puff pastry case with a filling, often savoury.
  19C. French, lit. flight in the wind.
  ● The pie is so called because it is light and delicate.

vole (vōl) *n.* the act of winning all the tricks in a deal.
  17C. French, appar. from *voler*, from Latin *volare* to fly.

volet (vol´ā) *n.* a wing or panel of a triptych.
  19C. French, lit. shutter, from *voler*, from Latin *volare* to fly.

volk (folk) *n.* (*S Afr.*) the people or nation, esp. that of the Afrikaners.
  19C. Afrikaans (from Dutch) **and German** nation, people.

Völkerwanderung (fœlkəvan´dərung) *n.* a migration of peoples, esp. that of the Germanic and Slav peoples into S and W Europe in the 2nd–11th cents.
  mid-20C. German, from *Völker* nations (VOLK) + *Wanderung* migration.

volplane (vol´plān) *v.i.* to glide down to earth in an aircraft with the engine shut off. ~*n.* such a descending flight.
  early 20C. French *vol plané*, from *vol* flight + *plané*, p.p. of *planer* to soar.

volt (volt) *n.* **1** (*also* **volte**) a circular tread, the gait of a horse going sideways round a centre. **2** a sudden leap to avoid a thrust in fencing. ~*v.i.* to make a volt in fencing.
  16C. French *volte*, from Italian *volta* turn, use as n. of fem. p.p. of *volgere* to turn, from Latin *volvere* to roll.

volta (vol´tə) *n.* (*pl.* **volte** (-tā)) a lively Italian dance of the 16th and 17th cents.; a piece of music to accompany this.
  16C. Italian turn. Cp. LAVOLTA.

volte-face (voltfas´) *n.* **1** a complete change of opinion, attitude etc. **2** a turn round.
  19C. French, from Italian *voltafaccia*, from *voltare* to turn (ult. from freq. of Latin *volvere* to roll) + *faccia* (ult. from Latin *facies*) face. Cp. English 'about-face'.

voodoo (voo´doo) *n.* **1** a cult involving animistic deities, witchcraft and communication in trances practised by

Creoles and blacks in Haiti and other parts of the West Indies and in the S US. **2** a sorcerer or conjurer skilled in this. **3** a charm, spell or fetish used in this. ~*v.t.* (*3rd pers. sing. pres.* **voodoos**, *pres.p.* **voodooing**, *past, p.p.* **voodooed**) to put a spell on or bewitch with voodoo.
19C. Louisiana French *voudou*, from Fon *vodū* tutelary deity, fetish.

voortrekker (vuə´trekə, fuə´-, -trek´ə) *n.* **1** (**Voortrekker**) any of the Dutch farmers from Cape Colony who took part in the Great Trek into the Transvaal in 1836 and following years. **2** a pioneer.
19C. Afrikaans, from *voor-* before + *trekken* TREK.

vortex (vaw´teks) *n.* (*pl.* **vortices** (-tisēz)) **1** a whirling or rotating mass of fluid, esp. a whirlpool. **2** any whirling motion or mass. **3** a situation, activity, way of life etc. which seems likely to engulf anyone who becomes involved in it. **4** (*Physics*) a portion of fluid the particles of which have a rotary motion.
17C. Latin (var. of VERTEX) eddy of water, whirlwind, from *vortere, vertere* to turn.

voulu (voolü´) *a.* lacking in spontaneity, contrived.
19C. French, p.p. of *vouloir* to wish.

voussoir (vooswah´) *n.* any of the wedge-shaped stones forming an arch.
12–14C. Old French *vausoir, vaussoir* (Modern French *voussoir*), from Popular Latin *volsorium*, ult. from Latin *volsus*, p.p. of *volvere* to roll, to turn.

vox pop (voks pop´) *n.* (*coll.*) public attitudes or opinion as represented by comments by ordinary people; radio or TV interviews to elicit these.
mid-20C. Abbr. of **Latin** *vox populi* voice of the people.
● The Latin phrase is taken from the adage *vox populi, vox Dei* 'the voice of the people (is) the voice of God', current in English from the 15C.

voyeur (vwahyœ´) *n.* **1** a person who derives sexual gratification from watching sexual acts, people undressing etc. **2** an obsessive observer of the sordid or unpleasant.
early 20C. French, from *voir* to see.

vraisemblance (vrāsāblās´) *n.* an appearance of truth, verisimilitude.
19C. French, from *vrai* true + *semblance*, from *sembler* to seem.

wacke (wak´ə) *n.* (*Geol.*) an earthy or clayey rock produced by the decomposition of igneous rocks.
19C. German, from Middle High German large stone, from Old High German *wacko* pebble.

wadi (wod´i), **wady** *n.* (*pl.* **wadis**, **wadies**) the valley or channel of a stream that is dry except in the rainy season.
17C. Arabic *wādī* valley, river bed.
● The Arabic word forms the first element of the Spanish river name *Guadalquivir*, literally great river. The French form of the word is *oued*, found in N African place names such as *Oued-Zem*, Morocco, and *El Oued*, Algeria.

wagon-lit (vagōlē´) *n.* (*pl.* **wagons-lits** (vagōlē´), **wagon-lits** (-lēz´)) a sleeping car on a Continental train.
19C. French, from *wagon* railway coach + *lit* bed.

Wahabi (wəhah´bi), **Wahhabi** *n.* (*pl.* **Wahabis**, **Wahhabis**) a member of a sect founded about the middle of the 18th cent. cultivating a strict form of Islam.
19C. Arabic *wahhābī*, from Muḥammad ibn 'Abd-al-*Wahhāb*, 1703–92, founder of the sect.

wahine (wah·hē´ni) *n.* a Maori or Polynesian woman.

18C. Maori woman, wife.
● The variant form *vahine* is familiar from the titles of paintings by the French artist Paul Gauguin (1848–1903), e.g. *Vahine no te tiare* Woman with a Flower (1891).

wallah (wol´ə), **walla** *n.* (*coll.*) **1** (*often in comb.*) an agent, worker or any person concerned with a usu. specified thing. **2** (*sometimes derog.*) a person, a fellow.
18C. Hindi *-vālā*, suf. expressing relation, from Sanskrit *pālaka* keeper.
● The Hindi suffix is conventionally understood by Europeans as a noun meaning man, fellow.

Walpurgisnacht (valpuə´gisnahkht) *n.* the eve of 1 May, when witches are supposed to hold revels and dance with the Devil, esp. on the Brocken mountain in Germany.
19C. German, from *Walpurgis*, gen. of *Walpurga* Walburga, d.779, Anglo-Saxon saint, abbess of Heidenheim, Germany + *Nacht* night.
● Walpurga's feast day, 1 May, coincided with a pagan feast for the beginning of summer and the revel of witches. The German word is sometimes partially translated as English *Walpurgis night*.

waltz (wawlts, wawls, wols) *n.* **1** a dance in triple time in which the partners pass round each other smoothly as they progress. **2** the music for such a dance. ~*v.i.* **1** to dance a waltz. **2** (*coll.*) to move quickly, confidently or casually. ~*v.t.* to move (a person) in or as in a waltz. **18C.** German *Walzer*, from *walzen* to roll, to revolve, to waltz. Cp. VALSE. Rel. to English *welter*.

wampum (wom´pəm) *n.* small beads made of shells, used by North American Indians formerly as money, or for decorating belts, bracelets etc. **17C.** Abbr. of **obsolete Algonquian** *wampumpeag* (mistakenly analysed as *wampum* + *peag*), from *wap* white + *umpe* string + pl. suf. *-ag*.
● The Algonquian word refers to a string of shells used as money.

Wanderjahr (van´dəyah) *n.* a year of roaming or travel, esp. when undertaken by a young person. **19C.** German, from *wandern* to wander + *Jahr* year.
● The term was formerly used of a period of travel by an apprentice to gain experience. It is now the equivalent of English 'gap year'.

wanderlust (won´dəlust) *n.* the desire to travel. **early 20C.** German.

wat (waht) *n.* a Thai Buddhist temple or monastery. **19C.** Thai, from Sanskrit *vāṭa* enclosure.
● The word is familiar from the name of the medieval temple *Angkor Wat* in NW Cambodia.

Wehrmacht (veə´mahkht) *n.* (*Hist.*) the armed forces of Germany from 1921–45. **mid-20C.** German, lit. defence force.

Weimaraner (vīmərah´nə, wī-) *n.* a type of gun dog with a very short, usu. grey coat. **mid-20C.** *Weimar*, a city in E Germany + *-aner* of (the place named).
● The breed was developed by German nobles of the court of Weimar.

Wein, Weib und Gesang (vīn vīb unt gəzang´) *n.* wine, women and song, the hedonistic pursuits of the young male. **19C.** German.
● The expression is attributed to Martin Luther (1489–1546) in a couplet running: *Wer nicht liebt Wein, Weib und Gesang, / Der bleibt ein Narr sein Leben lang* 'Who loves not wine, women and song / Remains a fool his whole life long'.

Weltanschauung (velt´anshow·ung) *n.* (*pl.* **Weltanschauungen** (-ən)) (*Philos.*) a view of the world as an entity, a personal philosophy of life etc. **19C.** German, from *Welt* world + *Anschauung* perception.

Weltpolitik (velt´politik) *n.* a policy aiming at the participation or predominance of a country, specifically Germany, in the affairs of the whole world. **early 20C.** German, from *Welt* world + *Politik* politics.

Weltschmerz (velt´shmeəts) *n.* a melancholic or pessimistic outlook on life. **19C.** German, from *Welt* world + *Schmerz* pain.

Westpolitik (vest´politēk) *n.* (*Hist.*) the foreign policy of establishing normal relations with Western nations on the part of the Communist states. **late 20C.** German, from *West* west + *Politik* politics. Cp. OSTPOLITIK.

whangee (wang·gē´) *n.* a flexible bamboo cane. **18C.** Chinese *huáng* old bamboo shoots, hard white-skinned bamboo.

whare (wor´i) *n.* a Maori hut or other simple dwelling place.
19C. Maori.

wie geht's? (vē gāts´) *int.* how are things? how's it going?
early 20C. German, lit. how goes it? Cp. French *comment ça va?* See ÇA VA.

wiener (wē´nə), (*coll.*) **weenie** (wē´ni), **wienie** *n.* **1** (*N Am.*) a type of frankfurter. **2** (*taboo sl.*) the penis. **3** (*derog.*) a man.
19C. German, abbr. of *Wienerwurst* Vienna sausage, from *Wien* Vienna + WURST.

Wiener schnitzel (vēnə shnit´səl) *n.* a cutlet of veal or pork, coated with a breadcrumb mixture and fried.
19C. German. See WIENER, SCHNITZEL.

wili (vil´i), **willi** *n.* a spirit of a betrothed girl in Slavic legend who has died from grief after being abandoned by her lover.
mid-20C. German or French, from Serbo-Croat *víla* nymph, fairy.
• The term is particularly associated with the plot of the ballet *Giselle* (1841), subtitled *Les Wilis*.

wok (wok) *n.* a large metal bowl with curved sides and handles used in Chinese cooking.
mid-20C. Chinese.

won (won) *n.* the standard unit of currency in North and South Korea.
mid-20C. Korean *wån.*

wonton (wonton´) *n.* a small Chinese dumpling with a savoury filling, usu. served in soup or deep-fried.
mid-20C. Chinese (Cantonese dial.) *wăn t´ān.*

wunderkind (vun´dəkint) *n.* (*pl.* **wunderkinds**, **wunderkinder** (-kində)) (*coll.*) **1** a child prodigy. **2** a person who is outstandingly successful or clever at a relatively young age.
19C. German, from *Wunder* wonder + *Kind* child.

wurst (vœst, vuəst, w-) *n.* a type of large German or Austrian sausage.
19C. German, of unknown orig.

wushu (wooshoo´) *n.* the Chinese martial arts.
late 20C. Chinese *wŭshù*, from *wŭ* military + *shù* technique, art.

X Y Z

xi (zī, ksī, sī, ksē) *n.* the 14th letter of the Greek alphabet (Ξ, ξ).
14–15C. Greek.

xu (soo) *n.* (*pl.* **xu**) a unit of currency in Vietnam, equal to one hundredth of a dong.
mid-20C. Vietnamese, from French *sou*. See SOU.

Yahweh (yah´wā), **Yahveh** (-vā), **Jahveh** *n.* the Hebrew name for God in the Old Testament, Jehovah.
19C. Hebrew YHVH, with added vowels.

yakitori (yakitaw´ri) *n.* a Japanese dish of boneless chicken pieces, grilled on skewers and served with a thick sweet sauce.
mid-20C. Japanese, from *yaki* toasting, grilling + *tori* bird. Cp. TORII.

yakuza (yəkoo´zə) *n.* a Japanese gangster or racketeer.
mid-20C. Japanese, from *ya* eight + *ku* nine + *za* three.
● The term derives from the worst kind of hand in a gambling game.

yam (yam) *n.* **1** the fleshy edible tuber of various species of the genus *Dioscorea*, tropical climbers orig. from India. **2** the plant yielding this. **3** (*N Am.*) the sweet potato.
16C. Portuguese *inhame*, or from obs.

Spanish *iñhame* (Modern Spanish *ñame*), prob. of W African orig. Cp. Fulani *nyami* to eat.

yamen (yah´men) *n.* (*Hist.*) the office or official residence of a Chinese mandarin.
18C. Chinese *yámen*.

yang (yang) *n.* the masculine, positive, bright principle in nature, according to Chinese philosophy, which interacts with its complement, *yin*.
17C. Chinese *yáng* sun, positive, male genitals.

yarmulke (yah´mulkə), **yarmulka** *n.* a skullcap worn all the time by Orthodox Jewish men, and during prayer by others.
early 20C. Yiddish *yarmolke*, from Polish *jarmu'ka* cap, prob. from Turkish *yağmurluk* raincoat, cape, from *yağmur* rain.

yashmak (yash´mak) *n.* the veil worn by many Muslim women in public.
19C. Turkish *yaşmak*, use as n. of *yaşmak* to hide oneself.

yataghan (yat´əgan) *n.* a Turkish sword or scimitar with a double-curved blade and without a guard or crosspiece.
19C. Turkish *yatağan*.

yen (yen) *n.* (*pl.* **yen**) the standard unit of currency of Japan.
19C. Japanese *en* round. Cp. YUAN.

yenta (yen´tə) *n.* a gossip or busybody.
early 20C. Yiddish.
● The Yiddish word represents the female personal name Yenta, from Italian *gentile* gentle.

yerba (yœ´bə), **yerba maté** (mat´ā) *n.*
Paraguay tea, maté.
19C. Spanish herb. See also MATÉ.

yeshiva (yəshē´və), **yeshivah** *n.* (*pl.*
yeshivas, **yeshivahs**, **yeshivoth** (-vōt))
1 a Jewish school devoted to the study of the Talmud. **2** an Orthodox Jewish day school providing religious and secular instruction.
19C. Hebrew *yĕšīḇāh*, from *yāshaḇ* to sit.

yeti (yet´i) *n.* (*pl.* **yetis**) a hypothetical manlike, apelike or bearlike creature, whose tracks are alleged to have been found in the snows of the Himalayas, also called *Abominable Snowman*.
mid-20C. Tibetan *yeh-teh* little manlike animal.

Yggdrasill (ig´drəsil) *n.* in Scandinavian mythology, an ash tree binding together heaven, earth and hell with its roots and branches.
18C. Old Norse, appar. from *Yggr*, a name of Odin + *drasill* horse.

YHVH *n.* the Tetragrammaton, a four-letter symbol representing Yahweh, Jehovah.
19C. Hebrew. See YAHWEH.

yin (yin) *n.* the feminine, passive, dark principle in nature, according to Chinese philosophy, which interacts with its complement and opposite, *yang*.
17C. Chinese *yīn* shade, feminine, the moon.

yod (yod) *n.* **1** the tenth letter of the Hebrew alphabet. **2** its sound, a palatal semivowel.

18C. Hebrew *yōḏ*. Cp. IOTA.
● The letter is the smallest of the Hebrew alphabet.

yoga (yō´gə) *n.* **1** a Hindu system of abstract meditation and rigid asceticism by which the soul is supposed to become united with the eternal spirit of the universe. **2** certain exercises and practices assisting this, HATHA YOGA.
18C. Sanskrit, lit. union.

yogi (yō´gi) *n.* (*pl.* **yogis**) a devotee or adept of yoga.
17C. Sanskrit *yogin*, nom. pl. *yogī*, from YOGA.

yogurt (yog´ət, yō´-), **yoghurt**, **yoghourt**, **yogourt** *n.* a custard-like food made from milk fermented in a special way.
17C. Turkish *yoğurt*.

yojan (yō´jən) *n.* a measure of distance in the Indian subcontinent, usu. about five miles (eight kilometres).
18C. Sanskrit *yojana* yoking, distance travelled without unyoking. Cp. YOGA.

Yom Kippur (yom kip´ə, -puə´) *n.* the Day of Atonement, a Jewish day of fasting.
19C. Hebrew *Yōm Kippūr*, from *yōm* day + *kippūr* atonement.

yoni (yō´ni) *n.* the Hindu symbol of the fertility of nature under which the consort of a male deity is worshipped, represented by an oval figure (the female genitalia).
18C. Sanskrit source, womb, female genitals.

yuan (yuahn´) *n.* (*pl.* **yuan**) the standard unit of currency of China.
early 20C. Chinese *yuán*, lit. round. Cp. YEN.

yuga (yoo´gə) *n.* any of the Hindu ages or cycles of the world.
18C. Sanskrit yoke, an age of the world.

yukata (yukat´a) *n.* a type of light cotton kimono, frequently worn after a bath.
19C. Japanese, from *yu* hot water, bath + *kata*(*bira*) light kimono.

yurt (yuət, yœt) *n.* **1** a circular, collapsible tent made of skins and used by nomads in central Asia. **2** a hut built partially underground and covered with turf or earth.
18C. Russian *yurta*, from Turkic *jurt.*

zabaglione (zabalyō´ni) *n.* a warm whipped dessert of egg yolks, sugar and marsala.
19C. Italian, ? ult. from Late Latin *sabaia*, an Illyrian drink.

zaffre (zaf´ə), (*N Am.*) **zaffer** *n.* impure cobalt oxide used for enamelling and as a blue pigment for painting on glass, porcelain etc.
17C. Italian *zaffera*, or from Old French *safre*, ? rel. to English *sapphire.*

zakuska (zəkus´kə) *n.* (*pl.* **zakuski** (-ki)) a snack, an hors d'oeuvre.
19C. Russian (usu. as pl. *zakuski*), from *kusat'* to bite.

zamindar (zamindah´), **zemindar** (zem-) *n.* (*Hist.*) **1** a member of a class of Bengali landowners formerly paying a certain land tax to the British government. **2** a local governor and farmer of the revenue under the Mughal empire paying a fixed sum for his district.
17C. Urdu, from Persian *zamīndar*, from *zamīn* land + *dār* holder.

zapateado (zapatiah´dō) *n.* (*pl.* **zapateados**) **1** a flamenco dance characterized by much clicking of the heels, and stamping and tapping of the feet. **2** the foot movements in such a dance.
19C. Spanish, from *zapato* shoe.

zarf (zahf) *n.* an ornamental cup-shaped holder for a hot coffee cup.
19C. Arabic *ẓarf* vessel.

zariba (zərē´bə), **zareeba**, **zareba** *n.* **1** a stockade, hedge or other enclosure for a camp or village in Sudan. **2** anything which encloses or confines.
19C. Arabic *zarība* pen for cattle.

zarzuela (zahzwā´lə) *n.* **1** a traditional Spanish form of musical comedy or comic opera. **2** a Spanish seafood stew.
19C. Spanish, prob. from *La Zarzuela*, royal residence near Madrid where it was first performed 17C.
• The name of the palace comes from Spanish *zarza* bramble.

zecchino (zekē´nō) *n.* (*pl.* **zecchini** (-nē)) (*Hist.*) a Venetian gold coin, the sequin.
16C. Italian sequin.

Zeitgeist (tsīt´gīst) *n.* the spirit, or moral and intellectual tendency, of the times.
19C. German, from *Zeit* time + *Geist* spirit.

zeloso (zelō´sō) *adv.* (*Mus.*) with energy.
19C. Italian, from *zelo* zeal.

zemstvo (zemst´vō) *n.* (*pl.* **zemstvos**, **zemstva** (-və)) (*Hist.*) a Russian elective local assembly dealing with economic affairs in the decades preceding the Russian Revolution.
19C. Russian, from obs. *zem'* (now *zemlya*) land.

Zen (zen) *n.* a form of Mahayana Buddhism, teaching that truth is in one's heart and can be learned only by meditation and self-mastery.
18C. Japanese, from Chinese *chán* quietude, from Sanskrit *dhyāna* meditation.

zenana (zinah´nə) *n.* in the East (esp. India or Iran), the portion of the house in a Hindu or Muslim household which is reserved for the women.
18C. Persian and Urdu *zanānah*, from *zan* woman, rel. to Greek *gunē*.

Zend (zend) *n.* **1** a section of commentary on the Avesta. **2** †Avestan.
18C. French, abstracted from Persian *Awastā wa Zand*, lit. Avesta and interpretation. See AVESTA.

zeta (zē´tə) *n.* the sixth letter of the Greek alphabet (Z, ζ).
14–15C. Greek *zēta*.

zeugma (zūg´mə) *n.* (*Gram.*) a figure in which a verb or adjective governs or modifies two nouns to only one of which it is logically applicable.
14–15C. Latin, from Greek, lit. yoking, from *zeugnunai* to yoke, rel. to *zugon* yoke.

Zigeuner (tsigoi´nə), (*fem.*) **Zigeunerin** (-nərin) *n.* (*pl.* **Zigeuner, Zigeunerinnen** (-nərinən)) a gypsy.
19C. German, from Old Bulgarian *atsiganin*, from Byzantine Greek *tsiganos*, shortened form of *atsinganos*, pop. var. of *athinganos* not touching, from *a-* not + *thinganō* I touch. Cp. French *tsigane*, Russian *tsygan*.
● The Greek word was originally the name of a sect of Manichaeans who came from Phrygia to Byzantium and who were regarded as magicians.

ziggurat (zig´ərat) *n.* an ancient Mesopotamian temple tower of a rectangular or tiered design.
19C. Akkadian *ziqquratu* height, pinnacle.

zillah (zil´ə), **zila** *n.* an administrative district in India or Bangladesh.
19C. Persian and Urdu *ẓila*, from Arabic *ḍila'* division.

Zingaro (zing´gərō, ts-) *n.* (*pl.* **Zingari** (-rē)) a gypsy.
17C. Italian gypsy, from source of ZIGEUNER.

zloty (zlot´i) *n.* (*pl.* **zloty, zlotys, zloties**) a coin and monetary unit of Poland.
early 20C. Polish *z'oty*, from *z'oto* gold.

zollverein (tsol´fərīn) *n.* **1** a customs union among states maintaining a tariff against imports and usu. having free trade with each other. **2** (*Hist.*) a customs union among German states in the early 1830s led by Prussia.
19C. German, from *Zoll* toll + *Verein* union.

zonda (zon´də) *n.* a hot dry W wind blowing from the Andes, usu. during July and August, in Argentina.
19C. American Spanish.

zori (zaw´ri, zor´i) *n.* a Japanese flat sandal of straw or rubber, similar to a flip-flop.
19C. Japanese *zōri*, from *sō* grass, straw + *ri* footwear, sole.

Zouave (zooahv´) *n.* **1** a soldier belonging to a French light infantry corps, orig. composed of Algerian recruits and still wearing an Oriental uniform. **2** (*pl.*) trousers with wide tops tapering to a narrow ankle, worn by women.
19C. French, from Kabyle *Zouaoua*, name of a tribe.

zouk (zook) *n.* a kind of lively music combining Latin American, African and Western influences, originating in the French Caribbean.
late 20C. French, appar. from Guadeloupian Creole, lit. to party.
● The French word may have been influenced by US slang *juke* to have a good time (the source of *jukebox*). *Zouk* was popularized in France in the 1980s by the group Kassav and then spread to the British and American music scene.

zucchetto (tsuket´ō) *n.* (*pl.* **zucchettos**)
the skullcap of a Roman Catholic
ecclesiastic, black for a priest, purple
for a bishop, red for a cardinal, white
for a pope.
19C. Italian *zucchetta*, dim. of *zucca*
gourd, head.

zucchini (zukē´ni) *n.* (*pl.* **zucchini**,
zucchinis) a courgette.
early 20C. Italian, pl. of *zucchino* small
marrow, courgette, dim. of *zucca* gourd.

zugzwang (tsook´tsvang, zŭg´zwang) *n.*
a blocking position in chess making any
move by an opponent disadvantageous.
~*v.t.* to place (an opponent) in this
position,
early 20C. German, from *Zug* move
+ *Zwang* compulsion, obligation.

zwieback (zwē´bak, tsvē´-) *n.* a type of
biscuit or rusk.
19C. German, lit. twice-bake. Cp.
English *biscuit*, from Old French, from
Latin *bis* twice + *coctus* cooked.
● In both the German and the English
words the reference is to a twofold
cooking process, first baking then
drying out in a slow oven.